Encouraging Transnational Learning Through Virtual Exchange in Global Teacher Education

Alina Slapac
University of Missouri-St. Louis, USA

Cristina A. Huertas-Abril
University of Córdoba, Spain

IGI Global
PUBLISHER of TIMELY KNOWLEDGE

A volume in the Advances in Educational Technologies and Instructional Design (AETID) Book Series

Published in the United States of America by
IGI Global
Information Science Reference (an imprint of IGI Global)
701 E. Chocolate Avenue
Hershey PA, USA 17033
Tel: 717-533-8845
Fax: 717-533-8661
E-mail: cust@igi-global.com
Web site: http://www.igi-global.com

Library of Congress Cataloging-in-Publication Data

Names: Slapac, Alina, 1973- editor. | Huertas-Abril, Cristina A., 1987- editor.
Title: Encouraging transnational learning through virtual exchange in global teacher education / edited by Alina Slapac, Cristina A. Huertas-Abril.
Description: Hershey, PA : Information Science Reference, 2024. | Includes bibliographical references and index. | Summary: "The focus of this co-edited book is to provide teachers, faculty and educational leaders with an opportunity to share theoretical, conceptual and practical approaches to the internalization of curriculum in higher education, specifically, in teacher training programs for pre-service and in-service teachers. By internationalization, we mean the process of adding global, intercultural, or international elements into the content of the curriculum of a course through online international collaborations. Teachers, instructors, administrators and instructional designers need to acquire, practice and model essential skills of using new pedagogies of teaching and online technology communication in order to successfully teach their students to work in their own global classrooms"-- Provided by publisher.
Identifiers: LCCN 2023029656 (print) | LCCN 2023029657 (ebook) | ISBN 9781668478134 (hardcover) | ISBN 9781668478172 (paperback) | ISBN 9781668478141 (ebook)
Subjects: LCSH: Teachers--Training of. | Teachers--Professional relationships. | Transnational education. | Globalization and education.
Classification: LCC LB1707 .E634 2023 (print) | LCC LB1707 (ebook) | DDC 370.71/1--dc23/eng/20230814
LC record available at https://lccn.loc.gov/2023029656
LC ebook record available at https://lccn.loc.gov/2023029657

This book is published in the IGI Global book series Advances in Educational Technologies and Instructional Design (AE-TID) (ISSN: 2326-8905; eISSN: 2326-8913)

British Cataloguing in Publication Data
A Cataloguing in Publication record for this book is available from the British Library.
All work contributed to this book is new, previously-unpublished material. The views expressed in this book are those of the authors, but not necessarily of the publisher.
For electronic access to this publication, please contact: eresources@igi-global.com.

Dedication

Dedicated to my beloved family:

To my daughter, Adelle and my son, Oliver, whose love, cuddles, and laughter have brightened my days.

To my husband, Richard, whose love, unwavering support and encouragement sustained me through every step of this project.

And, to my mother, Stela, whose love, pride and belief in me never wavered.

With deepest gratitude and love,

Alina

Dedicated to my beloved family:

To my son, David, who has completely changed my life.

To my husband, Jose, who has been extraordinarily supportive during all this long process.

I do hope I make you both proud.

With all my love,

Cristina

Table of Contents

Detailed Table of Contents

Internationalisation is a key factor both for professional development in the 21st century and international university rankings, and it is indeed at the very core of the European Higher Education Area (EHEA). This chapter analyses policies of internationalisation for higher education both in Spain and the international arena, such as the dimensions of major university rankings, together with tools for the concept known as internationalisation at home, such as the offer of English friendly courses and degrees offered in English as a medium of instruction (EMI), together as the use of COIL (collaborative online international learning) and eTwinning. Its main goal is to indicate successful strategies for the internationalisation of higher education programmes and means of effective collaborative instruction through digital technologies.

Formal aspects, such as contents, methodologies, objectives, or resources, are key elements in the teaching-learning process, and necessary to ensure its quality. However, well-being and socio-emotional competencies are also crucial. If teachers experience good levels of well-being and feel socially, emotionally, and morally competent, they will be able to achieve a high-quality professional performance. This is fundamental in the training of teachers, given the demands of their position. Different approaches are advocating for the inclusion of well-being and socio-emotional and moral competencies in the educational curriculum to foster educational contexts aiming the optimal development and functioning of students. After conceptualizing the constructs of well-being and socio-emotional and moral competencies, this chapter aims to review related educational practices, thus underlining the complex process of their inclusion in the curriculum. The relevance and usefulness that virtual learning environments have acquired in the

In implementing virtual exchange programs such as COIL, faculty could also be impacted by issues of inequity related to their academic-professional development. More positive experiences could influence decision-making in embarking on internalization opportunities such as COIL programs. When faculty internationalization efforts are recognized, motivation and engagement positively impact involvement in programs such as COIL. In this study, authors explore the accounts of experiences and perceptions of US-based faculty who taught COIL (collaborative online international learning) courses in collaboration with Latin America institutions. The findings suggest that faculty is motivated but not supported properly.

The sudden onset of the COVID-19 pandemic ushered in immense shifts in several sectors of society, including education. Social distancing was recommended as one of the measures to reduce the transmission of the Coronavirus, which resulted in many countries introducing lockdowns and the closure of schools. This chapter reports on the challenges experienced and transnational 'learning through crisis' by two teacher educators based in South Africa and San Francisco (USA). A qualitative methodological approach was used to highlight two case studies of how teaching strategies and curriculum delivery to postgraduate students were redesigned. Findings from critical reflections and personal narrative accounts highlighted the tensions or challenges of social inequalities and lack of resources, technological and emotional challenges, school closures, and isolation. Curriculum innovation and redesign and mapping as a pedagogical tool were captured as opportunities. Teachers 'learning through crisis' involved engaging in culturally relevant pedagogy and living the curriculum.

Educators need to offer students a curriculum that reflects their funds of knowledge (mirrors), exposes them to the cultures and experiences of others (windows), and develops in them an understanding and empathy for those who are different from them (sliding glass doors). In this chapter, the authors describe a six-week-long scholarship of teaching and learning (SoTL) project, which included 63 pre-service teachers (PST) in the US and 36 in-service teachers (IST) in Israel. The authors describe how they used Flip and Facebook to provide PST and IST who are racially, linguistically, and culturally different with an opportunity to engage in asynchronous dialogue. Analysis of survey and extant data confirmed that these transnational learning experiences provided participants with "windows" and "mirrors" for digital, global, and cultural literacy. Readers can use the authors' description of the two asynchronous assignments, the results of the SoTL study, and lessons learned to guide, design, and implement similar

Global competence development is part of the process of internationalization of the curriculum and pedagogical tools, like virtual exchange (VE), to create internationalization opportunities. This chapter focuses on an interdisciplinary VE project between two higher education institutions of the Global North. After the semester-long collaboration, students enrolled in a teacher training program and students from a foreign language classroom evaluated the importance of certain global competence skills and reflected on their own development thereof. The authors present the organizational setup and analyze the self-assessment in light of global citizenship skills and their relevance in teacher training or foreign language learning.

The purpose of this study was twofold. First, the study developed two survey instruments that measured students' metacognitive practice and social and emotional engagement in online collaborative discussions. Both instruments were developed by modifying from existing scales and empirical studies. An exploratory factor analysis (EFA) was employed to extract the underlying factors revealed by both instruments. The results of the study demonstrated that metacognitive practice in online collaborative discussions (MP-OCD) could be separated into four factors, while social and emotional engagement in online collaborative discussions (SEE-OCD) could be extracted into two factors. Second, the study used validated survey instruments to characterize college students' online collaborative discussion profiles. The results showed that four clusters of online collaborative discussion profiles were identified. This study has significant implications for educators who wish to improve students' metacognitive regulation and social and emotional engagement in online collaborative discussions.

The pedagogical practice implemented enabled the students, through dialogue and intercultural exchange, to acquire a global perspective of the different situations and problems encountered in each of their contexts. The work through the COIL methodology and the Design Thinking tool stimulated the development of skills focused on creativity and problem solving. This type of pedagogical practice enriches learning through the exchange of experiences, ideas, and knowledge from each of the disciplines involved in the process, contributing to professional and personal strengthening and development.

This chapter describes a service-learning (SL) project designed through telecollaboration aiming to improve the linguistic competence in English as a foreign language (EFL) and the intercultural awareness of children at risk of social exclusion studying in a local association in Málaga (Spain). Due to the restrictions posed by COVID-19 in spring of 2020, the project was based on telecollaborative service-learning (TSL) and carried out through several online workshops designed by a pre-service EFL teacher and held by international students doing an exchange program in the city of Málaga. This case study shows that this TSL project provided children at risk of social exclusion with the opportunity of being in contact with international students, other cultures, and using the English language in a real, meaningful context, while initial teacher training also improved by facing real-world situations.

This chapter explores the theoretical foundation as well as the practice of one model of virtual global engagement for preservice teachers, IGlobal. A virtual, global, teacher-training laboratory centered on the United Nations Sustainable Development Goals (UNSDGs), IGlobal provides online global fieldwork for preservice teachers and professional development for inservice teachers, both domestic and international. Designed specifically for preservice and inservice teachers, IGlobal reimagines virtual learning to create an online international teaching and learning laboratory where all participants gain global awareness, cross-cultural collaboration experience, as well as practice in globally collaborative online teaching and learning.

In this chapter, a project to globalize an online asynchronous instructional technology course will be detailed. While participating in the Longview Foundation's Global Teacher Education (GTE) Fellows Program, the author internationalized her course through the use of the Global Read Aloud. The Global Read Aloud is a project created by a teacher in 2010 to bring together classrooms across the globe through the shared experience of a read aloud on a global topic. To participate in the Global Read Aloud, teachers self-organize using a variety of instructional technologies. The author arranged for her class to participate in a Canadian 5th grade teacher's slow chat on Twitter. Planning, development, and assessment of the globalized elements of the course will be shared.

Foreword

I have often wondered how I developed a global mindset. I did not study abroad as part of my secondary or post-secondary education—I did not even spend more than a couple of weeks in another country until as recently as 2021. Neither my bachelor's nor master's degree programs were explicitly global or international in nature, and much of my doctoral study focused on domestic educational leadership and administration. Language study? I have merely a conversational mastery of Spanish and basic familiarity with French. What's more, my heritage is not diverse; according to 23 & Me, my DNA is 100% Ashkenazi Jewish, my grandparents and great grandparents having emigrated to the United States over 100 years ago. Nothing in my biography contains the traditional ingredients thought to develop a person's global perspective on the world's diversity, complexity, and interconnectivity. Nothing, except for one thing: Many of my teachers in the early 1980s participated in Florida International University's (FIU) Global Awareness Program (GAP), a pre- and in-service teacher education program conceived and directed by Jan L. Tucker until his death in 1997. I am convinced that my global mindset was shaped by the way my secondary school teachers designed and facilitated my classroom learning experience.

The GAP was a multi-faceted intervention that prepared K-12 teachers to embed global learning into the education of all Miami-Dade County Public School (MDCPS) students. I was one of those students, having received my entire primary and secondary education in MDCPS schools between 1972 and 1984. The GAP exposed my teachers to a spectrum of cultural perspectives, beliefs, and values systems. It guided them to explore theories of conflict, social change, intercultural communication, and complexity. The program was a laboratory in which teachers developed new global educational content, teaching strategies, and community engagement projects for me and my peers in Miami's increasingly diverse public schools. The GAP provided global teacher preparation through multiple approaches: new FIU undergraduate and graduate teacher education courses and programs; in-service workshops; local, state, and national conferences; visiting scholar programs; international travel and study grants; school library development; and, professional development workshops for teacher educators. No stone was left unturned in the GAP's efforts to influence the ways in which MDCPS teachers taught and their students learned. In Tucker's words (1982), the GAP was a "broad and long-term change process" to empower teachers to "marshal the resources of the community and the schools in support of global education" (p. 213).

How do I know that the GAP had an impact on me and my mindset? Just take a look at FIU's university-wide *Global Learning for Global Citizenship* undergraduate curriculum internationalization initiative. Believe it or not, I was unaware of the GAP and my connection to it until I began writing a book about the initiative, *Making Global Learning Universal: Promoting Inclusion and Success for All Students* (Landorf et al., 2018). While researching FIU's global education history, I discovered a Special Collection on the GAP containing in-service teacher education folders with agendas from workshops delivered in the schools I attended, enrollment rosters with my teachers' names, and lesson plans outlining workshop readings and activities. I had long grappled with the question, "How did a person like me grow up to help lead a global learning initiative like this?" I finally found the answer: global teacher education.

My teachers equipped me with the knowledge, skills, and attitudes I needed to help shape a comprehensive curriculum internationalization program—a program that I later discovered reflected many of the same concepts embedded in the GAP. When I was asked to lead a program that would promote global citizenship, I recognized this concept as familiar and real, not a vague theoretical abstraction. My secondary school teachers shaped my understanding of the world's complexity and diversity and the ways in which these factors influence people's beliefs, behaviors, and well-being. My mindset enabled me to help FIU faculty design classroom learning experiences that would develop students' global awareness, perspective, and engagement—just as my teachers had once developed those attributes in me.

I am still on a quest to fully understand how teachers mold their student's global mindset. In his Pulitzer Prize winning novel *The Overstory,* Richard Powers writes, "You can't see what you don't understand. But what you think you already understand, you'll fail to notice" (p. 439). I am elated to have this text in hand because it helps me re-think what I thought I already knew about global education and see a new range of possibilities for reaching students through global teacher preparation. *Encouraging Transnational Learning Through Virtual Exchange in Global Teacher Education* is full of actionable insights related to telecollaboration, a methodology that was only in its infancy during the GAP's implementation. Like the GAP, this text provides multiple avenues for reaching teachers and preparing them to reach their students. The chapters take deep dives into the ways in which virtual exchange can advance pre-service teacher competencies, serve as an incubator for global learning lesson planning, support in-service communities of practice, and promote community engagement and equitable access to global education. Editors Alina Slapac and Cristina A. Huertas-Abril have assembled a diverse community of scholar-practitioners who make compelling connections between sociocultural and discipline-based approaches to professional development and who draw conclusions based on intertwined analyses of theory and research. The rich mix of concepts treated in each chapter provokes a clearer, more nuanced understanding of the intricacies underlying the process of global teacher preparation. Oh, how I wish this book had been available to me while developing *Global Learning for Global Citizenship*!

I feel a deep personal connection to the editors and authors of this book. We share an understanding that student learning is predicated on teacher learning, and we have committed ourselves to promoting all students' global learning through teacher education. I invite you to join us in this work. I challenge every reader not just to consume the ideas in this book, but also to apply and amplify them in the courses you teach, conferences you attend, publications you write, and workshops you facilitate. Let us use our learning from this text to develop countless more globally minded teachers and students for many years to come.

Stephanie Doscher
University of Minnesota, USA

Stephanie Doscher *is the contributing editor and co-author of The Guide to COIL Virtual Exchange (Routledge 2022) and co-author of Making Global Learning Universal: Promoting Inclusion and Success for All Students (Routledge 2018)*

REFERENCES

Landorf, H., Doscher, S., & Hardrick, J. (2018). *Making global learning universal: Promoting inclusion and success for all students*. Routledge.

Powers, R. (2018). *The overstory: A novel* (1st ed.). Norton & Company.

Tucker, J. L. (1982). Developing a global dimension in teacher education: The Florida international university experience. *Theory into Practice*, *21*(3), 212–217. doi:10.1080/00405848209543008

Preface

In the ever-evolving landscape of higher education, globalization and internationalization stand as paramount concerns, permeating discussions on competencies, mobility, policies, and knowledge transfer across borders. These dynamics have gained further momentum in recent years, spurred by the global COVID-19 pandemic and the rapid advancement of educational technology. As universities adapt to these changes, the imperative to foster transnational connections and embrace innovative pedagogies becomes increasingly evident.

It is within this context that this co-edited book, *Encouraging Transnational Learning Through Virtual Exchange in Global Teacher Education*, emerges. Our collaboration seeks to address the pressing need for educators, faculty, and leaders to navigate the complexities of internationalization in teacher education programs. By integrating global elements into curriculum through online collaborations, we aim to equip educators with the tools and insights necessary to cultivate global citizenship within their classrooms.

At its core, this book serves as a platform for sharing theoretical frameworks, scholarly research studies, practical strategies, critical issues and impactful examples of transnational teaching and learning through virtual exchanges, Collaborative Online International Learning (COIL) or telecollaboration. Through contributions from educators and researchers around the globe, we explore the intersections of technology, pedagogy, and intercultural competence. By bridging theory and practice, we illuminate the transformative potential of international online collaborations in shaping the next generation of teachers.

Key objectives of this volume include showcasing research-informed practices and effective pedagogies fostering cross-cultural understanding, and providing actionable recommendations for internationalizing curriculum. From discussions on virtual exchanges and collaborative online learning to examinations of social justice issues and global communication technologies, each chapter offers valuable insights for educators seeking to expand their international reach and provide their students with transformative learning experiences.

Furthermore, this book serves as a resource for institutions looking to cultivate meaningful, transnational partnerships and enhance their global footprint in teacher development and beyond. By fostering dialogue and collaboration, we aim to contribute to the ongoing discourse on international education and its role in fostering equitable and inclusive learning environments.

We extend our gratitude to the contributors whose expertise and dedication have enriched this volume. This book features international authors representing 16 different countries, diverse perspectives and experiences through practical tools and scholarly research, including resources and recommendations from experienced (teacher) educators, practitioners and researchers from Canada, Chile, Colombia, Germany, Israel, Nepal, Peru, Spain, South Africa, Switzerland, Ukraine, United States of America, Taiwan, Thailand, Türkiye and Zambia. It is our hope that *Encouraging Transnational Learning Through*

Virtual Exchange in Global Teacher Education will serve as a catalyst for innovation and collaboration in the field of teacher education and in other fields, inspiring educators to embrace the possibilities of global connectivity.

TARGET AUDIENCE

This book is ideal for pre-service and in-service teachers, teacher educators, practitioners (instructors, staff and administrators) and researchers within teacher education programs in particular, interested or engaged in administration, teaching and/or research related to global education through Virtual Exchanges, Collaborative International Online Learning (COIL), Tellecollaboration and/or Globally Networked Learning (GNL) projects and partnerships. Moreover, this co-edited book could be used as a supplemental text in undergraduate or graduate courses within the curriculum of colleges and university classrooms in teacher education programs with a transnational and intercultural focus. However, other educators and stakeholders (i.e. administrators, program coordinators, practitioners or researchers from other fields) who are involved in such international partnerships could also benefit from using this book, as it provides very useful examples of empirical research and practices related to the internationalization of the curriculum and the process involved in the implementation of such projects and collaborations.

ORGANIZATION OF THE BOOK

The book has 16 chapters that went through a rigorous double-blind review and editors' final detailed review. Due to the nature of the chapters, the editors organized the book by theoretical pieces, scholarly research and reflective analyses or case studies. A brief description of each chapter in this book is provided below:

Chapter 1, "Recommendations and Tools to Promote Internationalisation at Home in Higher Education," by Raquel Sánchez Ruiz and Isabel López Cirugeda, provides an insightful analysis of internationalization policies in higher education, focusing on Spain and international dimensions. The chapter explores strategies for implementing internationalization at home, including English-friendly courses, COIL and eTwinning, offering practical guidance for enhancing collaborative instruction through digital technologies.

Chapter 2, "Socio-Emotional Competencies and Well-Being in Online Educational Settings," by Rocío Luque-González, Inmaculada Marín-López, and Mercedes Gómez-López, delves into the importance of well-being and socio-emotional and moral competencies in the teaching-learning process. The authors examine the inclusion of these elements in educational practices, particularly in virtual learning environments, highlighting their significance for fostering optimal student development.

Chapter 3, "Exploring International Educators' Learning About Local and Global Social Justice in a Virtual Community of Practice," by Bima Sapkota, Xuwei Luo, Muna Sapkota, Murat Akarsu, Emmanuel Deogratias, Daphne Fauber, Rose Mbewe, Fidelis Mumba, Ram Panthi, Jill Newton, and JoAnn Phillion, examines the reflections of educators involved in a virtual international community of practice focused on social justice. The chapter highlights themes related to social justice in local and global contexts, offering valuable insights for advancing educators' understanding and collaboration.

Chapter 4, "Towards a 'Response-Able Pedagogy' in Teacher Development Through Collaborative Online International Learning (COIL): An American-South African Partnership," by Karen Collett, Alina Slapac, Sarah Coppersmith, and Jingxin Cheng, explores the implementation of a COIL course through Flip and the critical issues guided by a "Response-able Pedagogy" framework. The chapter discusses the research study with focus on the development of global awareness/citizenship and intercultural competencies through a South African-American online collaboration. The authors highlight challenges and offer solutions and recommendations for future COIL courses based on the research findings.

Chapter 5, "Mapping Experiences of USA-Based Faculty COILing With LATAM: Un-Fueling Inequities," by Maria Marino, Stephanie Tadal, and Nurhayat Bilge, investigates the experiences of US-based faculty teaching COIL courses in collaboration with Latin American institutions. The chapter examines the impact of faculty internationalization efforts on participation and engagement in COIL programs, shedding light on existing challenges and motivations.

Chapter 6, "Tensions and Opportunities of Teachers 'Learning Through Crisis': A Tale of Two Cities," by Jaqueline Naidoo and Noah Borrero, explores the experiences of teacher educators in South Africa and San Francisco during the COVID-19 pandemic. Through case studies, the chapter examines the challenges and opportunities of curriculum redesign and innovation in response to crisis situations, offering insights into culturally relevant pedagogy and curriculum development.

Chapter 7, "Using Flip and Facebook to Create Windows and Mirrors for Transnational Learning: A United States-Israel Scholarship of Teaching and Learning Project," by Crystal Machado and Tami Seifert, describes a Scholarship of Teaching and Learning project designed to provide transnational learning experiences for pre-service and in-service teachers in two contexts: United States and Israel. The chapter examines the use of Flip and Facebook to facilitate asynchronous dialogue, promoting digital literacy and cultural understanding among participants.

Chapter 8, "Designing and Implementing a Globally Focused Interdisciplinary STEM Program: A Model for Preservice Teacher Preparation Programs," by Moe Greene, Yaoying Xu, and Jill Blondin, describes a STEM program designed to prepare preservice teachers for global challenges. The authors outline the development and implementation of a service-learning project, highlighting its effectiveness in promoting global awareness and interdisciplinary collaboration. The chapter concludes with a model for establishing program goals and objectives and leveraging the affordances of technology to enhance student learning.

Chapter 9, "Virtual Collaboration for English Language Teacher Education: Professional Negotiations With Ukraine and Türkiye," by Banu Cicek Basaran Uysal, Oksana Andriivna Chernysh, Ilknur Yüksel, Ümit Özkanal, Emine Eren Gezen, and Natalia Andriichuk, investigates the role of telecollaboration in fostering professional development for future English language teachers. Through participant perceptions, the chapter highlights the significance of telecollaboration in enhancing global competence skills and professional growth. The chapter concludes with insights into areas where improvements can be made to optimize the telecollaboration experience for teacher development.

Chapter 10, "Virtual Exchange in Teacher Training and the Foreign Language Classroom: Global Competence Skills and Development in an Interdisciplinary Pilot," by Sandra McGury and Robert Klosinski, examines an interdisciplinary virtual exchange project between higher education institutions in the global north. The chapter assesses student self-assessment data to evaluate the development of global citizenship skills and their relevance in teacher training and foreign language learning contexts.

Chapter 11, "Self- and Socially Shared Metacognitive Regulation and Engagement in Online Collaborative Discussions: Constructs and Students' Characteristics," by Theerapong Binali and Yossiri

Yossatorn, investigates students' metacognitive practice and social engagement in online discussions. The chapter explores different profiles of online collaborative discussion participation, offering insights for educators seeking to enhance students' engagement and regulation.

Chapter 12, "Collaborative International Online Learning (COIL): An Opportunity for Comprehensive and Intercultural Learning," by Yorladis Alzate Gallego and Sonia Stevens Bruzzese, explores pedagogical practices that promote global perspectives and problem-solving skills through COIL methodology and Design Thinking. The chapter emphasizes the value of interdisciplinary collaboration in enriching learning experiences and fostering personal and professional development.

Chapter 13, "International Telecollaboration on Teaching English to Children at Risk: A Case Study," by Cristina Villegas-Troya, Francisco Javier Palacios-Hidalgo, and Cristina A. Huertas-Abril, examines a Telecollaboration Service-Learning (TSL) project designed to improve English language proficiency and intercultural awareness among children at risk of social exclusion in Spain. This case study shows how this TSL project provided the participants with the opportunity of being in contact with international students, other cultures, and using the English language in a real, meaningful context, while initial teacher training also improved by facing real-world situations.

Chapter 14, "Creating Boundary Spaces Through Virtual Global Engagement: Training Preservice Teachers in Virtual Collaboration," by Allison Witt, Lu Xu, Aigul Rakisheva, and Sadia Mazid, presents the IGlobal model, a virtual teacher-training laboratory centered on the United Nations Sustainable Development Goals (UNSDGs). This chapter explores how IGlobal fosters global awareness and cross-cultural collaboration among preservice and inservice teachers through online learning experiences.

Chapter 15, "The Global Read Aloud for Global Collaboration in an Instructional Technology Course," by Lauren Angelone, discusses the integration of the Global Read Aloud project into an instructional technology course, enhancing global collaboration among participants. Through detailed planning and assessment, the chapter illustrates how this project enriches the online learning experience and promotes global literacy.

Chapter 16, "Envisioning a Sustainable and Equitable Transnational Engagement: Cross-Disciplinary Collaborative Online International Learning," by Delane Bender-Slack, Lauren DeVeau, Ruth Espinoza Pure, and Ray McAdams, explores COIL experiences between two Jesuit universities. Focusing on global citizenship and access to international education, the chapter highlights best practices for fostering collaboration and intercultural competence.

CONCLUSION

Encouraging Transnational Learning Through Virtual Exchange in Global Teacher Education represents a comprehensive exploration of the intersection between internationalization and teacher education in higher education. Throughout this volume, contributors have offered valuable insights, practical strategies, and impactful examples to guide educators in navigating the complexities of transnational education.

From recommendations for promoting internationalization at home to case studies of virtual global engagement, each chapter underscores the transformative potential of online collaborations in fostering global citizenship and intercultural competence among teachers and students alike. Through theoretical frameworks, empirical studies, and reflective analyses, this book provides a rich resource for educators seeking to enhance their international reach and cultivate inclusive learning environments.

Moreover, this volume serves as a catalyst for dialogue and collaboration among institutions, policymakers, and educators invested in advancing transnational learning opportunities. By showcasing effective pedagogies, fostering cross-cultural understanding, and providing actionable recommendations, we aim to contribute to the ongoing discourse on international education and its role in shaping the future of teacher preparation.

We want to again thank those whose expertise and dedication have enriched this volume. It is our hope that *Encouraging Transnational Learning Through Virtual Exchange in Global Teacher Education* will inspire educators to embrace the possibilities of global connectivity and contribute to the cultivation of inclusive, equitable, and globally-minded learning communities.

Alina Slapac
University of Missouri-St. Louis, USA

Cristina A. Huertas-Abril
University of Córdoba, Spain

Acknowledgement

This co-edited book would not have come to fruition without the wonderful contributions of our diverse authors representing 16 countries (Canada, Chile, Colombia, Germany, Israel, Nepal, Peru, Spain, South Africa, Switzerland, Ukraine, United States of America, Taiwan, Thailand, Türkiye and Zambia). Despite the challenges encountered along their journeys, their work and their students' towards valuable international virtual partnerships through virtual exchanges, Collaborative Online International Learning (COIL) and/or telecollaboration, and towards the internationalization of their respective curricula and/or programs within their higher institutions in teacher education is remarkable.

We would like to thank and acknowledge everyone whose expertise and dedication have enriched this co-edited book. We are very grateful to all our chapter reviewers and for their attention to detail and quality reviews. Moreover, we extend our gratitude to Fatemeh Ashrafabadi, doctoral candidate in College of Education at the University of Missouri-St. Louis (USA) who has supported us in the final chapter reviews with the APA 7th formatting and style.

We are deeply touched by the Foreword written by Stephanie Doscher (author, co-editor, and Assistant Vice Provost for Internationalizing Curriculum and Campus at the University of Minnesota) and her continued support and dedication to global education endeavors.

Many thanks to the IGI Global staff, in particular to Kaylee Renfrew (Assistant Development Editor), Nina Eddinger (Assistant Development Editor) and the Development and Marketing Team for their support with this project.

Finally, yet importantly, we would also like to thank our families and friends for their love, kindness and constant support throughout this meaningful and laborious project.

Alina Slapac
University of Missouri-St. Louis, USA

Cristina A. Huertas-Abril
University of Córdoba, Spain

Chapter 1
Recommendations and Tools to Promote Internationalisation at Home in Higher Education

Raquel Sánchez Ruiz
https://orcid.org/0000-0003-0022-7734
Universidad de Castilla-La Mancha, Spain

Isabel López Cirugeda
https://orcid.org/0000-0003-0000-5437
Universidad de Castilla-La Mancha, Spain

ABSTRACT

Internationalisation is a key factor both for professional development in the 21st century and international university rankings, and it is indeed at the very core of the European Higher Education Area (EHEA). This chapter analyses policies of internationalisation for higher education both in Spain and the international arena, such as the dimensions of major university rankings, together with tools for the concept known as internationalisation at home, such as the offer of English friendly courses and degrees offered in English as a medium of instruction (EMI), together as the use of COIL (collaborative online international learning) and eTwinning. Its main goal is to indicate successful strategies for the internationalisation of higher education programmes and means of effective collaborative instruction through digital technologies.

INTRODUCTION

The main aim of this chapter is to share different resources and recommendations that contribute to the internationalization of the curriculum, especially at home, by means of transnational learning through telecollaboration in global teacher education with the idea to promote such international virtual exchange in initial teacher training not only addressed to teacher trainers, but also to researchers, pre-service, and in-service teachers with a rationale followed by specific indications for the case of eTwinning. For that,

DOI: 10.4018/978-1-6684-7813-4.ch001

the background section offers a review of the concept of internationalization, including the so-called 'internationalization at home', related to that of 'transnationalization', as well as how programs like Erasmus+, particularly Key Action 2 (KA2), or the measures of this European initiative supporting cooperation among organizations and institutions, commit to it and their impact on foreign language policies, especially at a European level that later is translated to national and regional legal documents.

Then, a section of policies on internationalization at university levels starts by reviewing different strategic plans which focus on internationalization as a key axis like *EU Strategic Plan 2020-2024* and *Spanish Strategy for Science, Technology, and Innovation 2021-2027 EECTI 2021-2027*. This section continues with a review of the three main university rankings worldwide, QS, THE, ARWU (Quacquarelli Symonds, Times Higher Education, and Academic Ranking of World Universities, respectively), and the position of Spanish universities in them. Later, a particular case of a university that is included in such three rankings is presented, and also the internationalization policies at the regional level in which this university is contextualized are explored. This section comes to an end with the impact of such policies on higher education communities as well as some opportunities the abovementioned offer. Afterwards, the authors focus on those specific resources and recommendations, starting by redefining the concept of 'internationalization at home' and Collaborative Online International Learning (COIL) to explain their potential. Then, the contribution of eTwinning, now within the European School Education Platform (ESEP), to these two concepts is explained. Before the conclusions, the authors finish with recommendations and examples of good practices and experiences from already implemented eTwinning projects that permit internationalization at home and somehow lead to the success of both issues.

Therefore, the specific objectives of this paper are: (i) to review and define the concept of internationalization, including the one called 'at home'; (ii) to share the contribution of some programs policies to such concept; (iii) to review different internationalization strategies at global, European (including in European Higher Education Area or EHEA, Eurydice and European Education Area 2025), Spanish new Act of Education and the already mentioned EECTI 2021-2027 Strategy for Science), and regional level, and the position of Spanish universities in the three main rankings worldwide; (iv) to examine the impact of internationalization at home on students, academic and administrative staff; (v) to explore the opportunities and potential of internationalization at home through COIL experiences (especially dealing with the case of eTwinning); and (vi) to share recommendations and provide examples of good practices based on the authors' experiences that fostered internationalization at home through eTwinning, and the success of such kind of projects.

BACKGROUND

Technology and transport revolutions, which have led to the acceleration of economic, social, political, and cultural globalization, have also permitted an increasingly connected global net of higher education institutions. Universities must then adapt to a new, changing scenario requiring updated, knowledgeable, and prepared work forces ready for efficient exchange in international contexts (see Jahanian, 2020). As a result of that, internationalization has become indeed a mainstream factor of higher education in the 21st century. Thereupon, former cooperation and overseas exchange have evolved into major guidelines for university policies with strong impact on institutional governance. Internationalization unfolds multidimensional by means of action plans mainly concerning: 1) academic mobility, 2) the promotion of international relationships, and 3) foreign language learning. Such actions are oriented to seek talent attraction, and generation of knowledge, and its appliance to the productive system by virtue of international synergies.

Erasmus+, the European program in the fields of education, training, youth and sport, encompasses a diversified offer of calls for applications, out of which Key Action 1, implying individual physical mobility, has been the reference for international academic exchange for over 35 years. This constitutes one of the main goals of the European Higher Education Area (EHEA), and includes student mobilities for both studies and internships, together with professor and administrative staff lifelong learning. By means of such program, which regularly obtains a degree of satisfaction of over 90% of both practitioners and learners, students have been found to improve their employability better than 70% of all students (European Commission, 2017). The program Erasmus+ has been consistently reported as a tool for expanding students' knowledge, improving their skills in foreign languages, and boosting their professional and personal skills, such as those related with productivity, curiosity, and resilience (Gardel Vicente, 2022). This type of mobility has increased every single year ever from its foundation in 1987 (with 7.1 million participants) to 2021 (with 12.5 million), and not even the COVID-19 pandemic stopped the growing figures. The new program 2021-2027 has doubled its Erasmus+ budget under the expectation of this rise to be maintained in the following years (European Commission, 2022).

Despite this unprecedented success in terms of academic mobility, not every higher education student or staff member has the motivation or enjoys personal circumstances leading to applying for a scholarship. This situation has generated university policies under the purpose of expanding strategies aimed at producing comparable benefits inside the institution. Such measures are grouped under the term *internationalization at home*.

The action plans concerning both the policies related to the promotion of international relationships, and foreign language learning, even though they may also imply student and staff mobility, remain usually inside this concept. International relationships represent a strategic goal for higher education competitiveness relying on international agreements. One line of action consists of the design and implementation of joint and double Bachelor's and Master's degrees and doctoral programs, apart from establishing a common frame that eases mutual recognition of degrees. Erasmus+ is also oriented towards that kind of synergies: this way, while, as already mentioned, Key Action 2 supplies cooperation projects, Key Action 3 is devoted to policy development activities (European Commission, 2022). This implies a reinforcement of the dimension of the European construction. A reminder here that Erasmus+ has four main actions: Key Action 1 or Learning Mobility of Individuals; Key Action 2 or Cooperation among organizations and institutions; Key Action 3 or Support to policy development and cooperation; and Jean Monnet Actions (for more information, see https://erasmus-plus.ec.europa.eu/programme-guide/part-b/part-b-information-about-the-actions-covered-by-this-guide).

Besides, foreign language training not only is crucial for employability, but also an official requirement to complete a degree in any European tertiary institution. The Bologna process (see Eurydice, 2003) and its call for cultural diversity urged universities to develop their own language policies, understood as "the body of decisions made by interested authorities concerning the desirable form and use of languages by a speech group" (Cooper, 1989, p. 160), which affect vehicular language of classes to increasingly widen the international angle.

POLICIES ON INTERNATIONALIZATION AT UNIVERSITY LEVEL

As Rubin puts it, "[o]ver the past half-century, internationalization has become a stated goal of many higher education institutions around the world and in many cases is an element of the university's strategic plan" (2017, p. 28). In the European Union context, the *Strategic plan 2020-2024* covers six main goals as stated on its official webpage: 1. Environment and climate with the aim of being the first climate-neutral continent; 2. A digital strategy in line with high-quality science, knowledge and innovation which brings the Union closer to achieving Sustainable Development Goals (SDGs); 3. Adjusting jobs and economy to the concept of Industry 5.0, which acknowledges the role of industry in the achievement of societal goals in search of resilience and prosperity and, in the production sector, respects the boundaries of the Earth and takes care of workers' wellbeing; 4. Protecting citizens and their health and defending European values, as well as to tackle emerging threats and improve crisis preparedness; 5. Strengthening the EU as a global leader, championing multilateralism and a rules-based global order to make Europe attractive especially for business and in which international cooperation is a strategic priority, assisted by a revamped association policy for Horizon Europe; and 6. Democracy and rights to face the challenges of rising extremism, election interference to spread of manipulative information and threats against journalists, both online and offline and not to take democracy for granted.

A key example for internationalization is the European Higher Education Area (EHEA), which was born as "a unique international collaboration on higher education" (http://www.ehea.info/). It appeared indeed at the turn of the century with the aim to merge in a common project of university, focusing on professional development and employability, and stands on three pillars: 1) the creation of a shared university district for the mobility of students, professors, and professionals in the labor market; 2) transparency and mutual international recognition of university degrees; and 3) the fostering of lifelong learning (Eurydice, 2003). With these opportunities for internationalization in mind, the European Education Area, which advocates for quality education and training for all, establishes five key areas contributing to such dimensions: 1) improving quality and equity in education and training; 2) teachers, trainers and school leaders towards high-quality initial education and professional development opportunities; 3) digital education; 4) green education; and 5) the European Education Area in the world, to strengthen international cooperation with countries and regions around the world and to promote Europe as a partner for education.

Another international association working in parallel with the EHEA, and with a considerably longer tradition, is the Association of Commonwealth Universities (ACU). It consists of a historical net founded in 1913 as the Universities Bureau of the British Empire, which nowadays comprise more than 500 higher education institutions in 50 countries of the British Commonwealth. Its purpose is to exchange scholarships, research, and projects in order to strengthen ties among members.

Spanish policies follow this line. The incoming law for the regulation of the university system, *Ley Orgánica 2/2023, de 22 de marzo, del Sistema Universitario*, best known as LOSU, reinforces the existing European dimension of Spanish university, and boosts its connection with the Ibero-American Space of Higher Education and Knowledge, comprising about 600 million people under the same language, and its deriving measures in terms of mutual degree recognition, academic offer, and institutional cooperation. The law aims to balance the percentage of non-Spaniard professors (3%) to the approximate 15% of the population born outside the Spanish borders. The knowledge and use of foreign languages by all members of higher education institutions is promoted in all their activity, aligned with the in-force

Strategy for External Action. International alliances, joint degrees, and the creation of higher education centers abroad are prioritized in the international guidelines of Spanish university policies.

Besides, regarding research, the Spanish Science, Technology and Innovation Strategy (EECTI, for its name in Spanish *Estrategia Española de Ciencia, Tecnología e Innovación*) 2021-2027 particularly state an international strategic motivation (Spanish Ministry of Science and Innovation 2021, p. 11), in which internationalization is the 13th axis (out of 14), included in the relationships between agents. Within such internationalization, four lines are sought: promotion of participation in international programs, such as Horizon Europe and other joint initiatives; international collaboration supported by scientific diplomacy; international cooperation for sustainable development; and fostering and participating in international scientific and technological infrastructure and facilities (Spanish Ministry of Science and Innovation, 2021, p. 26). Another important mentioned aspect is the emerging technological and scientific opportunities and the potential of public/state-private collaboration (Spanish Ministry of Science and Innovation, 2021, p. 41). On the other hand, both the mentioned national strategy and the educational law consider the 17 United Nations' (UN) SDGs to transform the world. Within them and regarding the field of education, internationalization contributes to objectives 4. Quality education; objective 9. Industry, innovation and infrastructure; and objective 17. Partnerships for the goals.

Despite the controversies that may arise regarding ranking competition seen as a product of marketisation in higher education, rankings can serve as an indicator of the quality of education, since they are international acknowledged tools which allow the comparison of different universities by using a common and recognized instrument. The three main rankings worldwide (for more info, see Komotar, 2019; Moskovkin et al., 2022): 1) the British ranking Quacquarelli Symonds (QS), which ponders the International Faculty Index, the International Faculty Index, and the Inbound-Outbound Exchange of Students; 2) Times Higher Education (THE); and 3) Chinese Shanghai Ranking Consultancy (the Academic Ranking of World Universities; ARWU). First of all, Figure 1 shows the methodology these rankings use to classify the different institutions.

Figure 1. Indicators considered in the methodology in the three main rankings worldwide
Source: Own elaboration

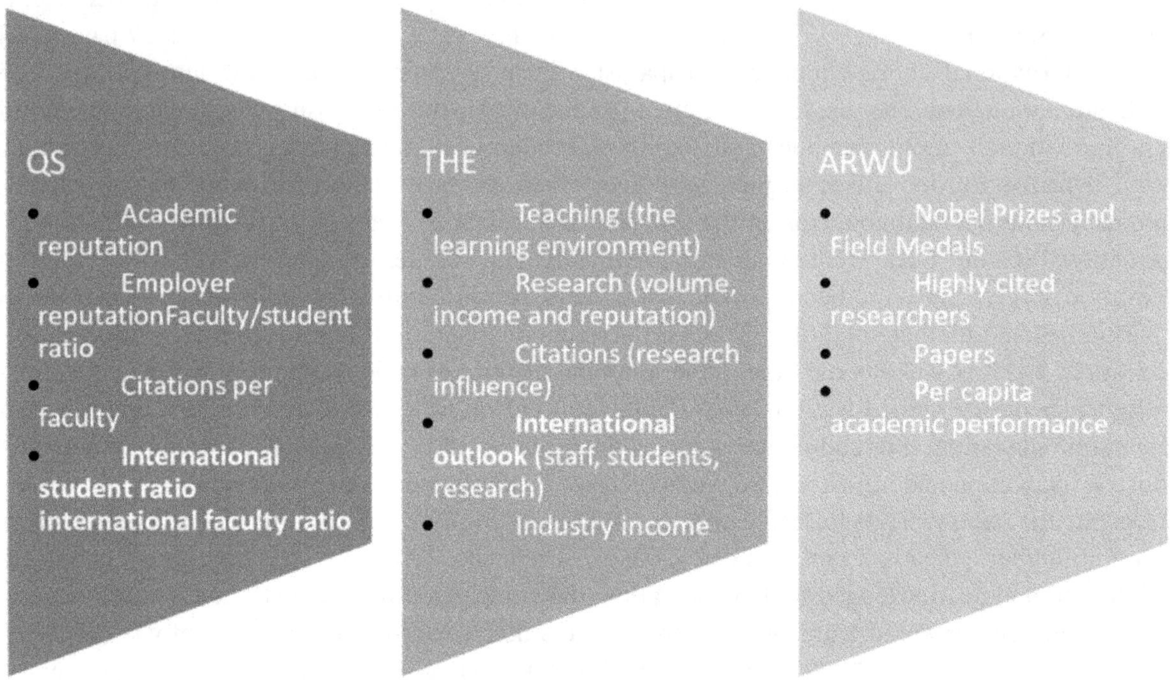

At this point, the position of Spanish universities in such three prestigious indexes is reviewed. If filtered by the region of Spain, QS indexes 31 results for Spanish Universities in 2023. THE, which also offers the numbers for number of FTE (full-time equivalent), number of students per staff, the percentage corresponding to international students and female: male ratio and refers to all universities by the translation of their proper names in English, includes 59 results. It is also interesting to note that THE also offers the detailed score for each measured indicator; that is, the categories of teaching, research, citations, industry income and international outlook. And, finally, ARWU includes 40 institutions, which are ranked both at a global and national level. All such mentioned results, alphabetically ordered by university, are shown in Table 1.

Table 1. Spanish universities' position in the three main rankings worldwide

University	QS		THE		ARWU	
	Rank	Overall score	Rank	Overall score	World rank	National rank
CEU Universities	1001-1200	-	X	X	X	X
Complutense University of Madrid	=226	41.2	401-500	42.1-44.9	201-300	2-5
ESIC	X	X	Reporter	n/a	X	X
European University of Madrid	X	X	1001-1200	24.4-29.7	X	X
European University of Valencia	X	X	Reporter	n/a	X	X
IE University	=347	31.1	X	X	X	X
Jaume I University	X	X	1001-1200	24.4-29.7	601-700	16-21
Miguel Hernández University of Elche	X	X	1001-1200	24.4-29.7	801-900	31-34
MIOTI Tech and Business School	X	X	Reporter	n/a	X	X
National University of Distance Education (UNED)	X	X	1201-1500	18.4-24.3	X	X
Open University of Catalonia	X	X	501-600	39.3-42.0	X	X
Pablo de Olavide University	X	X	801-1000	29.8-33.9	601-700	16-21
Public University of Navarre	X	X	1001-1200	24.4-29.7	X	X
Technical University of Cartagena	X	X	1001-1200	24.4-29.7	X	X
UNIR – International University of La Rioja	X	X	1201-1500	18.4-24.3	X	X
Universidad Autónoma de Madrid	=215	42.2	301-350	47.0-48.7	301-400	6-8
Universidad Carlos III de Madrid (UC3M)	=320	33.7	1001-1200	24.4-29.7	901-100	35-40
Universidad de Alcalá	511-520	-	801-1000	29.8-33.9	801-900	31-34
Universidad de Castilla-La Mancha	1001-1200	-	1001-1200	24.4-29.7	701-800	22-30
Universidad de Oviedo	1001-1200	-	1001-1200	24.4-29.7	701-800	22-30
Universidad de Sevilla	561-570	-	1001-1200	24.4-29.7	401-500	9-11
Universidad de Valladolid	1001-1200	-	1201-1500	18.4-24.3	901-100	35-40
Universidad de Zaragoza	551-560	-	1001-1200	24.4-29.7	501-600	12-15
Universidade da Coruña	1001-1200	-	1001-1200	24.4-29.7	X	X
Universidade de Santiago de Compostela	751-800	-	601-800	34.0-39.2	401-500	9-11
Universidade de Vigo	1001-1200		1001-1200	24.4-29.7	501-600	12-15
Universidad Loyola	X	X	Reporter	n/a	X	X
Universidad Politécnica de Madrid (UPM)	=488	24.6	1001-1200	24.4-29.7	601-700	16-21
Universidad Pontificia Comillas	601-650	-	1501+	10.4-18.3	X	X
Universidad Rey Juan Carlos	1001-1200	-	1001-1200	24.4-29.7	901-100	35-40

Continued on following page

Table 1. Continued

University	QS		THE		ARWU	
	Rank	Overall score	Rank	Overall score	World rank	National rank
Universitat Autònoma de Barcelona	178	45.8	=183	55.6	201-300	2-5
Universitat de Barcelona	184	45.5	182	55.7	151-200	1
Universitat de Valencia	571-580	-	501-600	39.3-42.0	201-300	2-5
Universitat Internacional de Catalunya	X	X	801-1000	29.8-33.9	X	X
Universitat Pompeu Fabra (Barcelona)	=233	39.9	186	55.4	301-400	6-8
Universitat Politècnica de Catalunya · BarcelonaTech (UPC)	=343	31.4	801-1000	29.8-33.9	701-800	22-30
Universitat Politècnica de Valencia	=400	28.4	X	X	401-500	9-11
Universitat Ramon Llull	651-700	-	501-600	39.3-42.0	X	X
Universitat Rovira i Virgili	751-800	-	601-800	34.0-39.2	601-700	16-21
University of Alicante	801-1000	-	1201-1500	18.4-24.3	601-700	16-21
University of Almería	X	X	1001-1200	24.4-29.7	X	X
University of Burgos	X	X	1001-1200	24.4-29.7	X	X
University of Cádiz	X	X	1201-1500	18.4-24.3	901-100	35-40
University of Cantabria			X	X	901-100	35-40
University of Córdoba	X	X	601-900	34.0-39.2	801-900	31-34
University of Deusto	X	X	801-1000	29.8-33.9	X	X
University of Extremadura	X	X	1001-1200	24.4-29.7	601-700	16-21
University of Girona	X	X	801-1000	29.8-33.9	801-900	31-34
University of Granada	=494	24.4	601-800	34.0-39.2	201-300	2-5
University of Jaén	X	X	801-1000	29.8-33.9	701-800	22-30
University of La Laguna	X	X	801-1000	29.8-33.9	701-800	22-30
University of Las Palmas de Gran Canaria	X	X	1001-1200	24.4-29.7	901-100	35-40
University of León	X	X	1001-1200	24.4-29.7	X	X
University of Lleida	X	X	801-1000	29.8-33.9	701-800	22-30
University of Málaga	X	X	1201-1500	18.4-24.3	701-800	22-30
University of Murcia	801-1000	-	1001-1200	24.4-29.7	701-800	22-30
University of Navarra	=253	38.3	251-300	48.9-51.1	501-600	12-15
University of Salamanca	601-650	-	801-1000	29.8-33.9	501-600	12-15
University of the Balearic Islands	X	X	801-1000	29.8-33.9	701-800	22-30
University of the Basque Country	701-750	-	801-1000	29.8-33.9	301-400	6-8
University of Vic – Central University of Catalonia	X	X	501-600	39.3-42.0	X	X

Source: Own elaboration

One university included in the three aforementioned rankings is Universidad of Castilla-La Mancha

(UCLM), which is presented here in depth an example of the regional level, as it is also the context of the authors and so the one they know best. Regarding policies at such level, the Council of Education, Culture and Sports in Castilla-La Mancha establishes its Smart Specialisation Strategies (RIS3) for 2021-2027 around six specialization sectors and four cross-cutting areas: 1) digital transformation, 2) circular economy and sustainability, 3) talent and entrepreneurship, and 4) internationalization – they all essential in the field of education. UCLM's *Strategy 2020* aligns with such objectives and includes internationalization as one of its two academic values so as to adopt a proactive and cross-cutting approach towards the internationalization of university (Vice-Rectorate for Economy and Planning, UCLM, 2018, p. 7). Moreover, such term does not only cover the widely known role of research in the different fields of knowledge, but also other areas like training and innovation, or employment and teaching, which situates this university in the top 15 best Spanish universities and one of the 500 best in the world. Precisely, the UCLM is indexed in six out of the seven most influential international rankings and in one of the two most relevant national rankings. The first ones include ARWU (Academic Ranking of World Universities), CWUR (Center for World University Rankings), GreemMetric World University Ranking on Sustainability; QS World University Rankings, (THE) Times Higher Education, U-Multirank and Webometrics. And the second ones are Ranking CYD and U-Ranking. The following table illustrates the position of UCLM (in 2022, last update according to the institutional *Observatorio de Rankings –Observatory of University Rankings–*), both in the world and in Spain, and the status of internationalization in such rankings.

Table 2. UCLM's position in international and national rankings

International level			
Ranking	**World Position**	**Position in Spain**	**Indicators**
ARWU (see Illustration 1)	701-800 out of >2500	22-30	Nobel Prizes and Field Medals, highly cited researchers, papers, and per capita academic performance
CWUR	746 out of 2000	23	Education, employability, faculty, research
GreenMetric	449	18	Settings and infrastructure, energy and climate change, waste, water, transportation and education and research
QS (see Illustration 1)	1001-1200	25-31	Academic reputation, employer reputation, faculty/student ratio, citations per faculty, and **international student ratio** & **international faculty ratio**
THE Young (see Illustration 1)	1001-1200 301-350	28-48 19-24	Teaching (the learning environment), research (volume, income and reputation), citations (research influence), **international outlook** (staff, students, research) and industry income (knowledge transfer)
U-Multirank	-	-	Research and research linkages, economic engagement, teaching and learning, **international orientation** and applied knowledge partnerships
Webometrics	509	15	Presence (public knowledge shared), visibility (web contents impact), transparency or openness (top cited researchers) and excellence or scholar (top cited papers)
National level			
Ranking CYD	-	-	Teaching & learning, research, knowledge transfer, **international orientation,** contribution to regional development, employability
U-Ranking	-	7	Teaching (including **mobility programs**) and innovation & research (including **international** funding and publications)

Source: Own elaboration

Thus, as seen in Table 2, internationalization, which has become a major dimension for professional development, has a direct projection on the most influential global university rankings, which have set their focus on indicators seizing its impact. In fact, as QS World University Rankings put it on their official webpage, a university advocating for expanding internationalization yields in several benefits, including their ability to attract both quality students and staff from across the world and providing global professional environments.

UCLM defined internationalization as an essential factor both to improve the quality and efficiency of Spanish universities. Moreover, this concept is not limited to student mobility and international agreements, but comprises a series of initiatives and projects to gather valuable human capital and attract talent according to the new requirements of a global, ever more competitive, market influenced by globalization and need for knowledge; considering at the same time all the benefits that internationalization brings to improve education, research, innovation and regional socio-economic development (Lucas Borja, 2020). In this line, the *Guidelines for Internationalisation* (Vice-Rectorate for Internationalization, UCLM, 2022, p. 21) acknowledge the following initiatives and programs: Language Centre or *Centro de Lenguas* (CEL) in Spanish, Confucius Institute at UCLM, ADRIT (Attraction, Development and International Retention of Talent of the UCLM) program, Study Abroad at UCLM and Spanish courses. It must be noted that UCLM has been accredited by Instituto Cervantes and offers training on Spanish language and culture, business courses, the Spanish health system, new perspectives and technology for sustainability and the environment, quality of agricultural products and sustainable management of irrigation water. Apart from those, other actions to promote internationalization include coexistence activities for the university community, Erasmus+ actions (including KA131 grants, KA220 and KA171 actions, welcome and orientation seminars for international students, celebration of International Students' Day and Erasmus Staff Week), strengthening of relationships with Latin America (through postgraduate courses, grants to study a degree in Ibero-America, for research Santander and for Fundación Carolina, and cooperation actions for development and solidarity (Vice-Rectorate for Internationalization, UCLM, 2022, pp. 22-23). The UCLM also offers official studies, both BA degrees and Master's Degrees, with courses taught in English and English-friendly courses, which can be consulted in the official webpage (https://bit.ly/3SJXn72).

Moreover, higher education students must have global perspectives so as to be able to think and act in a current world where various cultures, backgrounds, perspectives, values and beliefs coexist and must be addressed properly in different contexts, such as work, leisure, etc. (Braskamp et al., 2009).

Furthermore, on one side, the COVID-19 pandemic posed a big challenge for educational systems worldwide and showed that teachers, institutions and officials need to have a protocol both to address the crisis but also to reassure students and parents. On the other side, the pandemic showed the education community some of the advantages of remote teaching and how asynchronous learning, especially in digital formats, can be beneficial (Daniel, 2020). In fact, some authors advocated for the migration of courses, alignment of the curriculum competencies and scaling up of teachers' training for online learning instruction during the pandemic, some features of which may remain due to students' convenience and the opportunities technologies offer to surmount educational challenges, ranging from planning to implementation and assessment (Toquero, 2020).

One means to address the abovementioned spheres of asynchronous learning and internationalization is COIL or Collaborative Online International Learning, whose potential and contribution to such two fields are explained below.

DEFINING 'INTERNATIONALIZATION AT HOME'

As Prieto Martínez et al. (2014, p. 159) claim, 'internationalization at home' is a broad term, whose understanding depends on academic tradition and different approaches to it suggest the inclusion of various elements. However, after reviewing the origin of the concept and the evolution of internationalization at home in the last 15 years, by reviewing the trends in Europe, the United States, Australia and Colombia, these same authors conclude that some manifestations of internationalization at home are: interculturality, bilingualism and learning of foreign languages, the internationalization of the curriculum, international accreditation, international forums and chairs and collaborative degrees (dual degrees and joint degrees). An international curriculum has multiple benefits, as Rodríguez Pinto et al. (2007) pinpoint in their final report: increase of knowledge of international aspects of the areas of study; understanding and skills to communicate with professionals from other countries; access to internationalization opportunities for students and teaching staff from areas with a traditional low degree of exposure to the world; improvement of skills in other languages; strengthening of competitiveness in the national and international labor market; improvement of competitiveness in internationalized occupations; introduction of new experiences and methods through the interaction of international students and professors; social and cultural integration in mixed-nationalities student groups; strengthening of students' social skills, promotion of interdisciplinary cooperation and multidisciplinary and multinational perspectives (which leads to a deeper development, for instance, regarding international research networks, among others).

Another important concept here is COIL, that is, "a voluntary partnership between professors in different countries collaborating on jointly constructed learning experiences to enhance international and intercultural understanding" (Harris et al., 2021, p. 1351). These authors also highlight that these experiences do not follow the path of other bureaucratic processes, which involve legal texts and application filling, but rely on the willingness of "likeminded faculty colleagues worldwide who are eager to bring classrooms, projects, and performances together through technology" (p. 1352). Other authors, like Rubin (2017) display the value of internationalization and the limits of physical mobility, to which COIL can contribute. Rubin (2017) also lists a series of necessary pre-conditions that COIL experiences must have to be successful, such as: the development of social networks and collaborative online tools, measures and actions to overcome threats to security, the potential that COIL means to bridge the mitigation of students' fears regarding internationalization, and the contribution of COIL to compensate low student mobility rates.

COIL TO PROMOTE INTERNATIONALIZATION: THE CASE OF ETWINNING

Considering the importance of internationalization at global, European, national, and regional levels, as well as the possible drawbacks that COVID-19 or financial crisis could pose for such purposes, the aim of this section is to explore the potential of different resources and provide with recommendations to promote internationalization at home at university, especially exploiting the chances offered by COIL and focusing on eTwinning.

In this line, one of the most powerful tools, which can be considered within COIL experiences and promotes internationalization, is eTwinning. eTwinning is the biggest education, community for learners and teaching staff in Europe. Two of its best features are that it is completely safe, as all the members are verified individually, and it is completely free. eTwinning is now part of the European Program

Erasmus+ 2021-2027, concerning education, training, youth and sports. However, it was born in 2005 as an eLearning program and later integrated into Lifelong Learning Program2007-2013 and Erasmus+ 2014-2020. Its main aim is to promote and facilitate connecting opportunities, ideas exchanges and collaborative learning between students and teaching staff of the participating countries through information and communication technology, better known as ICT (Huertas-Abril et al., 2023, Palacios-Hidalgo & Huertas-Abril, 2023). To coordinate this action around Europe, eTwinning is supported by a Central Support Service in Brussels and a National Support Service (NSS) in each country. In the case of Spain, this NSS belongs to the National Institute of Education Technology and Teacher Training (INTEF), which at the same time depends on the Ministry of Education and Professional Training. Moreover, each of region has an eTwinning representative, who are also assisted by the role of eTwinning ambassadors, that is, representing teachers with experience in the program and who have participated in numerous eTwinning projects, have been recognized with the National or European Quality Label one or several times or have been awarded with the National or European eTwinning Award.

Precisely, this year 2023, eTwinning has been migrated into a new platform, since both this and School Education Gateway have merged into European School Education Platform (ESEP). This latter platform, powered by the European Commission, offers seven different sections:

1. Home, in which they define what the platform is, count how many people are registered, offer updates –including news, teaching materials and publications– about the eTwinning community, feed the monthly topic, and publicize events, like MOOC, webinars and info sheets.
2. More information, about ESEP and which deals with governance, eTwinning and NSO (National Support Organizations), supportive partners, Initial Teacher Education, National Agencies, contact and newsletter.
3. Insights, which include expert viewpoints and surveys on school education, publications –reports and studies regarding school education policies from both European and national levels, research, practices or inspiring projects, schools and classrooms across Europe; teaching materials, including lesson plans; tutorials, with practical ideas and guidelines for teachers and schools; and news and events on European school policy and action.
4. Development, which focuses both on school and system development and on professional development, in which free courses and webinars on different topics (for instance, building collaborative culture, Erasmus+ funding or mobility, among others) are offered and events and conferences are publicized.
5. Recognition, which covers the 5 labels of eTwinning National Quality Label, eTwinning European Quality Label, eTwinning School Label, European Language Label and Erasmus Accreditation Excellence Label; and awards, including both the eTwinning European Prizes and the European Innovative Teaching Awards.
6. Networking, with the aim of providing a space to find people, organizations and schools to collaborate with, as well as to participate in projects and professional development opportunities or discover European education trends through eTwinning; this is where partner-finding fairs are located. This precise subsection is also conceived as a way to find opportunities for school staff to undertake teaching assignments and job shadowing in host schools abroad.
7. The last section is devoted to eTwinning. Once a teacher registers, the NSS verifies by sending an email to the headmaster and head of studies that such person works in the center they have filled in. After confirming, the CSS verifies and gives access to the teacher. This guarantees a

safe environment, which is essential when working with minors. Moreover, eTwinning is mainly addressed at non-university studies. However, since 2015, three Faculties from three Universities in Spain and others around Europe and neighboring countries were included in a Pilot Project to train their university teaching staff in the platform, so that they could introduce it in the corresponding studies to become a teacher and so in initial teacher training. Then such project became the Teacher Training Initiative, which is still in force. eTwinning, now inside ESEP, still offers the same applications as in the previous platform: notifications, a dashboard, TwinSpaces, groups and profile; and a quick menu with four sections: overview, groups, projects and support. Within eTwinning, TwinSpaces are an essential part of the platform, since it is where the project is actually developed. Once the project is founded, the teaching staff or the NSS can invite students, so that they can start collaborating and exchanging information to create their projects following their teachers' instructions. This TwinSpace is individual per project and includes the sections of home, pages, materials, forums, online meetings, members and support. Despite having maintained many of the previous functions, both colleagues and students have complained this 2023 about the fact that some of them do not work properly; for example, uploading videos and embedding them on groups' pages or disappearing institutions that are actually registered.

RECOMMENDATIONS FOR ETWINNING

The authors of this chapter work at one out of the three faculties in Spain which were initially included in the above-mentioned pilot project of Teacher Training Institutions (TTI), aimed to provide eTwinning instruction to pre-service teachers. Thus, the educational platform has been promoted and integrated by creating and founding different eTwinning projects, about diverse topics and with varied timings, in each and every course of the Degrees and Master's Degrees they teach, with the corresponding reflection in their electronic guides and evaluation criteria, ever since (see López-Cirugeda, 2017 or López-Cirugeda & Sánchez-Ruiz, 2023). Their efforts were acknowledged in 2022 through a nomination for the first eTwinning Teacher Awards.

From the authors' extended experience, eTwinning offers the perfect scenario for:

- Promoting internationalization both at university and faculty level; something crucial for bilingual studies or degrees taught in English as a medium of instruction (EMI). This is also applicable to that offer of courses catalogued as English-friendly to precisely welcome foreign students into the classroom, even when such course is not taught in English. English-friendly courses are born "with the intention to facilitate the international students the class materials in English." Moreover, it does not only include the possibility of having some of the instruction in English but also the chance for students to do their progress tests and examinations in English if they choose so (Vice-Rectorate for Internationalization, UCLM, 2022-2023, p. 5).
- Integrating students with different backgrounds and cultures, but also coming from different mobility programs, such as Erasmus+, or speaking foreign languages.
- Exchanging good practices, both for the teaching staff and students.
- Using the real language in a genuine context, which also gives meaning for students and motivates them as they are learning the language by using the language for obtaining a tangible result.

- Having real cultural exchanges, within a social group usually composed by heterogeneous and mixed-nationality groups, which advocates for the promotion and understanding of the intercultural communicative competence.
- Integrating foreign culture and language in the classroom, and so putting into practice Coyle's (2006) model of the 4Cs (content, communication, cognition and culture), to which the fifth C of competence can also be added. This model is applied to CLIL or content and language integrated learning (Coyle et al., 2010); that is, in the so-called bilingual education in which content is taught through a foreign language. In such model, the following four dimensions interrelate when teaching and learning both the mother and the foreign language: a) content or knowledge belonging to a genuine sociocultural context; b) communication or the use of the language for such purposes; c) cognition or thinking skills involved in the instructional process; and d) culture or intercultural skills to understand one's and other cultures (Chaya & Inpin, 2020). Project- and task-based learning and work and application of lower-order and higher-order thinking skills (LOTS and HOTS), as well as soft skills. Anderson and Krathwohl (2001) revised Bloom's Taxonomy and updated his theory by establishing the following hierarchy driving human learning, integrating the different types and levels of knowledge, such as factual, conceptual, procedural and metacognitive; therefore, LOTS start with 'remember', follow with 'understand' and finish with 'apply', whereas HOTS are 'analyze', 'evaluate' and 'create' in ascending order. Furthermore, eTwinning projects also allow students to compare and contrast the education systems of their countries, finding strengths –which could be considered for the exchange of good practices, as a role model or as a starting point for job shadowing even in the initial training period– and weaknesses as things to improve or potential gaps for education innovation and research.
- Enhancing group and cooperative work, promoting students' autonomy. In short, acquiring and developing 21st-century skills, which is based on another 4Cs model –comprising critical thinking, communication, collaboration, and creativity– for learning and innovation skills, plus life and career skills and information media and technology skills. This covers four cross-cutting essential domains of education; that is, standards and assessment, curriculum and instruction, professional development and learning environments (Battelle for Kids, 2023).
- Fostering students' entrepreneurial and management skills through the platform at the same time they use and undergo the process of digital tools, especially for evaluation. Likewise, eTwinning projects usually entail the creation, edition and, in short, management of videos. Thus, digital skills and digitalization, considering privacy, data protection and copyright or Creative Commons protection, among others are also worked on.
- Supporting education innovation and technology, which usually entails motivation and where the participation of every member of each group is sought. In fact, eTwinning projects allowed both students and teaching staff to continue and stay connected, relieving some of the stress from being in lockdown; thus, making education during the pandemic possible.
- Training for teachers' future career finding the application of this platform in their real teaching practice. In fact, eTwinning is directly connected to initial teacher training; moreover, it can be included as curriculum making in the European Education Area.
- Developing curricular design and teaching planning. The platform also allows the connection between disciplines and the teaching of such disciplines.
- Connecting different methods and approaches, and active methodologies, such as digital storytelling, school radio and video-making. eTwinning projects also can make use of different types of

evaluation and assessment. As they usually include the assessment of the students –which can also comprise co-evaluation, peer-peer evaluation and feedback–, the evaluation of the project –both by the teaching staff and students–, and the evaluation of the teacher, again both by the students and through self-evaluation.

- Integrating projects in real schools as service-learning, and so make knowledge transfer possible as well.
- Increasing sources or lines of research for academic papers, not only written by the teaching staff, but also as initiation research and innovation papers, like final degree projects and master's dissertations.
- Establishing networking, both in the fields of teaching and research, but also in innovation and knowledge transfer.
- Facilitating other opportunities powered by such relationships and contacts, such as the possibility of opening Erasmus agreements, research opportunities in publications or projects, among others.
- Opening up opportunities within the own faculty to be trained in eTwinning or now ESEP, both at student and staff level.

After having implemented numerous eTwinning projects, some examples, recommendations and good practices derived from such participation that foster internationalization at home and contribute to the success of said projects are:

- Initial projects, those which are done for the first time or with a new partner, must be simple and last a feasible period of time. One- or two-month projects have been proved to be successful. Moreover, instructions –including expected tasks and detailed wordings and deadlines–for teaching staff and students are key to ensuring everyone's expectations and meeting goals. Interculturality, including expectations and cultural-based or related conceptions must also be borne in mind. More information on practices regarding eTwinning and COIL can be found in Guth et al. (2014), or Guerola et al. (2021), just to cite two examples.
- Teachers' and university lecturers' overloading is a reality, which must not be passed on to children and students either. Thus, integrating the eTwinning project in the corresponding school and university syllabi and the evaluation of the subject and course is also a good idea. In the case of Spanish universities, this is reflected in courses such as eGuides, in which teaching staff can explain how they will do a project they already did before through eTwinning and how it will impact the evaluation.
- Flexibility is also a strength in eTwinning projects; not only in the design of the project but also in order to meet the needs and requirements of both countries involved, but also along the project. Unexpected events may happen –for example, when students do not participate as much as expected or even drop the course, or even one of the participants involved is on a leave, etc.–, especially in 2022, when the migration of data led to technical problems or usual features not working properly. In these cases, both parties must be patient and enforce, if necessary, the back-up plan.
- Beginnings are always difficult, and practice makes better. Therefore, despite the initial difficulties or drawbacks, it is recommended to continue. Once you understand your partners, the following years will be easier, and the projects can be polished to increase the satisfaction and engagement of participants, especially to potentially reduce the dropout rate, to accommodate lecturers' ex-

pectations and to cater to each part's needs and so projects will improve at all levels. Moreover, fruitful innovation is supposed to show its effectiveness in the long term.

- On the whole, the aim is to cultivate good contacts, demonstrate flexibility and patience, especially considering the advantages of this format in times of uncertainty; and above all, celebrate (cultures, diversity, interculturality, languages, among others) and enjoy the potential of partnerships.

Moreover, training and implementing real eTwinning projects at the stage of initial teacher training is crucial for its (pervasive) presence when these teachers are incorporated to the labor market. Thus, the European Commission's Teacher Training Initiative is key for such purposes, as well for internationalization at home at practically zero cost in a totally safe platform, assisted by European and national official bodies. Another unique feature of eTwinning is that it is an official European platform with no publicity at all and no commercial interests. However, the main benefits derive from the implementation of the projects themselves, which naturally imply the use of digital competencies in the framework of real teaching practice, and the application of soft skills, so often forgotten in formal education, in an international context (Cinganotto, 2017; Gülbay, 2018).

FUTURE RESEARCH DIRECTIONS

Despite its introduction at university level a decade ago and its extended use at non-university levels (especially Primary and Secondary Education), eTwinning is not widely known in higher education. Considering that it is very likely that real schools work with this platform, it is important that teacher training programs include this content from a theoretical perspective, but also implement practical examples and projects. This way future teachers do not only will gain experience on the platform, but also will take advantage of it to learn through COIL. Moreover, this official European platform contributes to internationalization at zero cost, so universities should foster their use. eTwinning also aids in the construction of "robust social learning networks" with the aim of fostering and promoting "the creation and development of awareness for respect, tolerance, and understanding by ensuring the integration of young people from different countries and cultures through dialogue" (Izgí Onbaşil et al., 2022, p. 293). Therefore, eTwinning is a powerful tool to implement COIL to develop intercultural communicative competence, especially relevant in bilingual education programs.

Apart from the abovementioned usefulness of eTwinning for teachers and internationalization, the platform has proved to have multiple benefits, like "networking across Europe, acquiring new or improved ICT skills and pedagogical innovation, particularly through the introduction of team work and project-based approaches" (Guth et al., 2014, p. 11) and increasing teachers' leadership skills, social skills, pedagogical knowledge, cooperation and motivation (Gülbay, 2018). However, according to authors, like Acar and Peker (2021), there are very few studies on eTwinning and the following issues should be addressed: students' opinions on the platform, benefits of the platform from students' perspectives, potential threats or disadvantages and opinions of both parties of the teaching-learning process on the platform.

CONCLUSION

Internationalization constitutes a key factor in every mission of higher education in a process of continuous growth due to the increasingly globalized nature of societal demands. The labor market is in demand of working forces equipped with multicultural skills, such as proficiency in foreign languages and intercultural competence. These abilities conform relevant dimensions of the initial training and lifelong learning not only for those fields related to international trade, but also for each of them, including education, which must adapt to diversity in the classroom and prepare pupils in terms of citizenship. Universities have taken measures to address these needs and consequently international rankings, the main instrument to reflect academic reputation, have added significant indicators related to internationalization.

Due to obvious limitations for students, professors and researchers throughout their studies and careers, higher education institutions have developed different policies to replicate the beneficial effects of Erasmus+ Action Key 1 mobilities by means of the concept of *internationalization at home*, which creates and reinforces affinity and cooperation bonds, especially within territories with previous shared cultural tradition, such as the European Union, the Commonwealth, or the Latin American countries. For instance, bilingual or foreign language instructed courses, dual degrees, or international forum participation are acknowledged indicators of such dimension.

In this vein, COIL implies a new concept to understand higher education from an international perspective. From the experience of almost ten years of participation in the eTwinning Teacher Training Initiative, this chapter elicits a list of recommendations to successfully design projects and overcome frequent difficulties, and connect theory to practice in global teacher training from the perspective of networking as a working engine for every mission of the European Higher Education Area.

ACKNOWLEDGMENT

This paper is framed within the authors' participation in the European Commission's project *Teacher Training Initiative*, to introduce eTwinning in Higher Education, particularly in Initial Teacher Training.

REFERENCES

Acar, S., & Peker, B. (2021). What are the purposes of teachers for using the eTwinning platform and the effects of the platform on teachers? *Acta Didactica Napocensia*, *14*(1), 91–103. doi:10.24193/adn.14.1.7

Anderson, L. W., & Krathwohl, D. R. (Eds.). (2001). *A taxonomy for learning, teaching and assessing. A revision of Bloom's taxonomy of educational objectives*. Longman.

Battelle for Kids. (2023, March 29). *21st-century learning*. https://bit.ly/4829a51

Braskamp, L. A., Braskamp, D. C., & Merrill, K. C. (2009). Assessing progress in global learning and development of students with education abroad experiences. *Frontiers: The Interdisciplinary Journal of Study Abroad*, *18*(Fall), 101–118. doi:10.36366/frontiers.v18i1.256

Chaya, P., & Inpin, B. (2020). Effects of integrating movie-based mobile learning instruction for enhancing Thai university students' speaking skills and intercultural communicative competence. *English Language Teaching, 13*(7), 27–45. doi:10.5539/elt.v13n7p27

Cinganotto, L. (2017). Experiential learning for Teacher Training: A case example of language, content and technologies in a learning event by eTwinning. *Journal of eLearning and Knowledge Society: The Italian eLearning Association Journal, 13*(1), 91-111.

Cooper, R. L. (1989). *Language planning and social change*. Cambridge University Press.

Coyle, D. (2006). Developing CLIL: Towards a theory of practice. In A. d. Catalunya (Ed.), CLIL in Catalonia: From theory to practice (pp. 5-29). APAC.

Coyle, D., Hood, P., & Marsh, D. (2010). *CLIL – Content and language integrated learning*. Cambridge University Press. doi:10.1017/9781009024549

Daniel, J. (2020). Education and the COVID-19 pandemic. *Prospects, 49*(1-2), 91–96. https://bit.ly/49oK55z. doi:10.1007/s11125-020-09464-3 PMID:32313309

European Commission. (2017). *Combined evaluation of Erasmus+ and predecessor programmes*. https://bit.ly/3SIzZ9X

European Commission. (2020). *Strategic plan 2020-2024. DG Research and Innovation*. https://bit.ly/49hO5EQ

European Commission. (2022). *Erasmus annual 2021*. https://bit.ly/3SJ9Qry

Eurydice (2003). *Focus on the Structure of Higher Education in Europe (2003-2004). National Trends in the Bologna Process*. https://bit.ly/3SIxODr

Gardel Vicente, A. (2022). *Skills gained through mobility: A literature review. ErasmusJobs project consortium*. https://bit.ly/3SKUUsU

Gobierno de España. (2015). *Estrategia de Acción Exterior 2021-2024 [Strategies for External Action 2021-2024]*. https://bit.ly/48ZdnI9

Guerola, I. S., Tordera, N., & Pérez-Nebra, A. (2021). El desarrollo de competencias interculturales a través de la Colaboración International en Línea [The development of intercultural competences through Collaborative Online International Learning]. *Revista del Congrés Internacional de Docència Universitària i Innovació, 5*, 1–6.

Gülbay, E. (2018). eTwinning collaborative learning environment in initial teacher education. *International Journal of Advanced Research in Science, Engineering and Technology, 5*(1), 5234–5242.

Guth, S., Helm, F., & O'Dowd, R. (2014). Telecollaborative foreign language networks in European universities: A report on current attitudes and practices. *Bellaterra Journal of Teaching & Learning Language & Literature, 7*(14), 1–14. doi:10.5565/rev/jtl3.609

Harris, J. M., Seo, M., & McKeown, J. S. (2021). *Global competency through Collaborative Online International Learning (COIL). 7th International Conference on Higher Education Advances (HEAd'21)*. 10.4995/HEAd21.2021.13080

Huertas-Abril, C. A., Palacios-Hidalgo, F. J., & Guardeño-Carrasquilla, M. A. (2023). Telecolaboración universidad-escuela para la concienciación sobre los ODS a través de eTwinning [University-school telecollaboration for SDG awareness through eTwinning]. In J. J. Delgado-Peña, S. Cabrero, N. Fernández, & J. Martínez (Eds.), *Universidades y Agenda 2030 [Universities and the 2030 Agenda]* (pp. 709–719). Comares.

İzgi Onbaşil, U., Sezginsoy Şeker, B., Claeys, H., Mancel, C., Gülbay, E., & Powers, R. (2022). Experiences of qualified teachers of the future in the scope of an international eTwinning project. *International Online Journal of Primary Education*, *11*(2), 293–311. doi:10.55020/iojpe.1182120

Jahanian, F. (2020). How higher education can adapt to the future of work. *World Economic Forum, SGD 04: Quality Education*. https://bit.ly/490Fzuf

Jefatura del Estado. (2023). *Ley Orgánica 2/2023, de 22 de marzo, del Sistema Universitario* [Organic Law 2/2023, of 22 March, of the University System]. https://bit.ly/3UovOS0

Komotar, M. H. (2019). Global University Rankings and their impact on the internationalisation of higher education. *European Journal of Education*, *54*(2), 299–310. doi:10.1111/ejed.12332

López-Cirugeda, I. (2017). eTwinning en los Grados de Maestro y Máster de Formación de Profesorado de Secundaria de la UCLM [eTwinning in the Degrees and Master's Degree in Secondary Education in UCLM]. In R. Cózar-Gutiérrez & M. V. de Moya Martínez (Eds.). Entornos digitales humanizados [Humanized digital environments] (pp. 67-80) Síntesis.

López-Cirugeda, I., & Sánchez-Ruiz, R. (2023). eTwinning and ITE in Spain. A testimony by Universidad de Castilla-La Mancha. In A. Tosi (Ed.). Empowering future teachers for a sustainable intercultural and inclusive education. The impact of eTwinning on Initial Teacher Education (pp. 145-149). Carozzi.

Lucas Borja, M. E. (2020, March 2). Trabajando como coordinador de relaciones internacionales en el campus de Albacete. *UCLM* [Working as a coordinator of international relations in Albacete campus (UCLM)]. https://blog.uclm.es/manuelestebanlucas/ultimas-noticias/

Moskovkin, V. M., Zhang, H., Sadovski, M. V., & Serkina, O. V. (2022). Comprehensive quantitative analysis of TOP-100s of ARWU, QS and THE World University Rankings for 2014–2018. *Education for Information*, *38*(2), 133–169. doi:10.3233/EFI-211539

Palacios-Hidalgo, F. J., & Huertas-Abril, C. A. (2023). Creando sinergias a través de eTwinning para el desarrollo sostenible y la ciudadanía global mediante los ODS: Un estudio cualitativo [Creating synergies through eTwinning for sustainable development and global citizenship by means of SDGs]. In J. J. Delgado-Peña, S. Cabrero, N. Fernández, & J. Martínez (Eds.), *Universidades y Agenda 2030* [Universities and the 2030 Agenda] (pp. 463–474). Comares.

Prieto Martínez, L. D., Valderrama Guerra, C., & Allain-Muñoz, S. (2014). Internacionalización en casa. In C. Mauricio Nupia (Ed.), Reflexiones para la política de internacionalización de educación superior en Colombia [Reflections for international relations in higher education in Colombia] (pp. 159–191). Academic Press.

Rodríguez Pinto, C., Cardoso Arango, X., & Ramírez Leyton, D. (2007). *Informe final: Estudio estado del arte de la internacionalización de la educación superior en Colombia [Final Report: Study on the state of the arts of internationalisation of higher education in Colombia].* Asociación Colombiana de Universidades y Ministerio de Educación Nacional. https://bit.ly/3un1Wef

Rubin, J. (2017). Embedding Collaborative Online International Learning (COIL) at higher education institutions. An evolutionary overview with exemplars. *Internationalisation of Higher Education, 2*, 27–44.

Secretaría General de Investigación. (2021). *Estrategia Española de Ciencia, Tecnología e Innovación 2021-2027 [Spanish strategy for Science, Technology and Innovation 2021-2027].* https://bit.ly/3SJ62qn

Toquero, C. M. (2020). Challenges and opportunities for higher education amid the COVID-19 pandemic: The Philippine context. *Pedagogical Research, 5*(4), 1–5. doi:10.29333/pr/7947

United Nations. (2023, April 13). *The 17 goals.* Department of Economic and Social Affairs. https://sdgs.un.org/goals

Vice-Rectorate for Internationalization. UCLM. (2022-2023). *English subjects & English Friendly.* https://bit.ly/3SGWHPV

Vicerrectorado de Economía y Planificación. (2018). *Estrategia UCLM 2020 [UCLM Strategy 2020].* https://bit.ly/49hSFD0

Vicerrectorado de Internacionalización. (2022). *Guía de la UCLM* [UCLM Guide].

ADDITIONAL READING

Almeida, J., Robson, S., Morosini, M., & Baranzeli, C. (2019). Understanding internationalization at home: Perspectives from the Global North and South. *European Educational Research Journal, 18*(2), 200–217. doi:10.1177/1474904118807537

Beelen, J., & Jones, E. (2014). Europe calling: A new definition for internationalization at home. *International Higher Education, 83*, 12-13. https://ejournals.bc.edu/index.php/ihe/article/view/9080

Beelen, J., & Jones, E. (2018). Internationalisation at home. In P. Teixeira, J. C. Shin, A. Amaral, A. Bernasconi, A. Magalhaes, B. M. Kehm, B. Stensaker, E. Choi, E. Balbachevsky, F. Hunter, G. Goastellec, G. Mohamedbhai, H. de Wit, J. Valimaa, L. Rumbley, L. Unangst, M. Klemencic, P. Langa, R. Yang, & T. Nokkala (Eds.), *Encyclopedia of international higher education systems and institutions.* Springer. doi:10.1007/978-94-017-9553-1_245-1

Byram, M. (Ed.). (2003). *Intercultural competence.* Council of Europe.

Byram, M. (2021). *Teaching and assessing intercultural communicative competence. revisited.* Multilingual Matters. doi:10.21832/9781800410251

Camilleri, R.-A. (2016). Global education and intercultural awareness in eTwinning. *Cogent Education, 1*(3), 1–13. doi:10.1080/2331186X.2016.1210489

European Commission. (n. d.). *Horizon Europe*. https://research-and-innovation.ec.europa.eu/funding/funding-opportunities/funding-programmes-and-open-calls/horizon-europe_en

Huertas-Abril, C. A. (2021). *Tecnologías para la educación bilingüe* [Technologies for bilingual education]. Peter Lang. doi:10.3726/b17576

Huertas-Abril, C. A., & Palacios-Hidalgo, F. J. (2022). Learning English with technology: eTwinning for future teachers para la formación de docentes de inglés como lengua extranjera y educación bilingüe [Learning English with technology: eTwinning for future teachers for the training of preservice teachers of English as a foreign language and bilingual education]. In P. Alonso Velázquez (Coord.), Avances y desafíos para la transformación educativa [Advancements and challenges for educational transformation] (pp. 312–322). Universidad de Oviedo.

Palacios-Hidalgo, F. J., Gómez-Parra, M. E., Espejo-Mohedano, R., & Huertas-Abril, C. A. (2022). Bilingual education and training courses abroad: Key factors for linguistic success. *El Guiniguada*, *31*(31 (2022)), 16–27. doi:10.20420/ElGuiniguada.2022.502

Slapac, A. (2021). Advancing students' global competency through English language learning in Romania: An exploratory qualitative case study of four English language teachers. *Journal of Research in Childhood Education*, *35*(2), 1–17. doi:10.1080/02568543.2021.1880993

Slapac, A., Balcerzak, P., & O'Brien, K. G. (Eds.). (2021). *Handbook of research on the global empowerment of educators and student learning through action research*. IGI Global. doi:10.4018/978-1-7998-6922-1

Slapac, A., Collett, K., Wessels, F., Gamiet, G., & Knudsmoen, H. (2023). Social justice pedagogy and Collaborative Online International Learning (COIL): Across three partner higher education institutions. In P. Escudeiro, N. Escudeiro, & O. Bernardes (Eds.), *Handbook of research on implementing inclusive educational models and technologies for equity and diversity* (pp. 252–272). IGI Global. doi:10.4018/979-8-3693-0453-2.ch013

Slapac, A., & Coppersmith, S. A. (2019) (Eds.) Beyond language learning instruction: Transformative supports for emergent bilinguals and educators. IGI Global.

KEY TERMS AND DEFINITIONS

Collaborative Online International Learning (COIL): Linkages made by a team of teachers in different countries with the purpose to foster multicultural learning from their students.

European Higher Education Area (EHEA): Currently composed of 49 countries, share structural reforms and educational tools to facilitate mobility and improve employability.

European School Education Platform (ESEP): Online portal combining former eTwinning and School Gateway Education platforms.

eTwinning: Biggest educational community in Europe, born in 2005 as an initiative to ease connection among educational institution. It relies on a digital platform where teachers can contact as in a social network in order to design and implement educational project with the aim to contribute to the building of a European citizenship.

Internationalization: Action plans in universities with the purpose to strengthen relationships with other nations to increase their competitivity together with that of their students.

Internationalization at Home: Set of actions aimed at integrating international and intercultural dimensions into the curriculum for all students into tertiary educational settings.

University Ranking: Lists of higher education institutions which measure excellence by means of various factors, one of them being internationalization.

Chapter 2
Socio-Emotional Competencies and Well-Being in Online Educational Settings

Rocío Luque-González
Universidad de Córdoba, Spain

Inmaculada Marín-López
https://orcid.org/0000-0002-4312-6063
Universidad de Córdoba, Spain

Mercedes Gómez-López
https://orcid.org/0000-0002-6748-5466
Universidad de Córdoba, Spain

ABSTRACT

Formal aspects, such as contents, methodologies, objectives, or resources, are key elements in the teaching-learning process, and necessary to ensure its quality. However, well-being and socio-emotional competencies are also crucial. If teachers experience good levels of well-being and feel socially, emotionally, and morally competent, they will be able to achieve a high-quality professional performance. This is fundamental in the training of teachers, given the demands of their position. Different approaches are advocating for the inclusion of well-being and socio-emotional and moral competencies in the educational curriculum to foster educational contexts aiming the optimal development and functioning of students. After conceptualizing the constructs of well-being and socio-emotional and moral competencies, this chapter aims to review related educational practices, thus underlining the complex process of their inclusion in the curriculum. The relevance and usefulness that virtual learning environments have acquired in the wake of the COVID-19 pandemic will also be discussed.

DOI: 10.4018/978-1-6684-7813-4.ch002

INTRODUCTION

The teaching and learning process encompasses several essential aspects to ensure its quality. While formal elements such as content, methodology, objectives, and resources are widely addressed throughout the curricula (López, 2022), they are not the only factors that contribute to a successful academic experience. In the educational environment, aspects such as well-being and social, emotional, and moral competencies are particularly relevant due to their potential to promote mental health and positive functioning in children and young people (Hernández Barraza, 2017). Teachers and students with low levels of well-being or who do not feel socially, emotionally, or morally competent may compromise their effectiveness and performance, which will also imply a lower quality of education. These have been considered as protective in the face of the changes that have arisen, ranging from face-to-face contact to the revaluation of teaching-learning methodologies based on online tools (Ruiz-Sánchez, 2020). Quality is also a matter of concern for the international community, as evidenced by the United Nations 2030 Agenda through the Sustainable Development Goals, in which these issues are addressed in goals 3 (good health and well-being) and 4 (quality education) (United Nations, 2023).

Promoting socio-emotional and moral competencies is essential for teachers to meet the personal, social, and professional demands of their labour (Slapac et al., 2021). In recent years, there has been a growing trend towards the inclusion of these aspects in educational curricula due to the demands of the schools to integrate social and emotional learning into the teaching-learning process (CASEL, 2012). This requires a significant organisational change, involving the entire educational community (Bryk et al., 2010) with a particular emphasis on teacher training (López-López & Lagos San Martín, 2021). There are political initiatives to include socio-emotional competencies in the university curriculum aimed at preparing more skilled professionals who will have a positive impact on society (Llorent et al., 2020); nevertheless, this process needs to be developed carefully as teachers require adequate training to meet the needs of their students. A teacher who is well-trained in socio-emotional and moral competencies will have a broad set of competencies that will allow them to achieve high-quality professional performance, such as be able to perceive, understand, manage, and regulate not only their own well-being but also that of their students. (Llorent et al., 2020). The result will be the promotion of educational contexts that enhance a holistic development of students, going beyond the focus on content learning to the search for the optimal development and functioning.

Based on these premises, this chapter aims to conceptualise the constructs of well-being and socio-emotional and moral competencies, especially considering the increasing relevance of transnational learning of future teachers (Montejo-Ángel & Pava-Díaz, 2022). Secondly, educational practices related to the field will be reviewed, and the relevance of their promotion will be addressed, bearing in mind virtual learning environments as an educational tool. Finally, implications and future research lines will be suggested.

DEFINING WELL-BEING AND SOCIO-EMOTIONAL COMPETENCIES

Well-being is a complex construct with diverse theoretical and practical implications. From the framework of positive psychology, it has been defined as adequate psychological functioning and experience (Gómez-López, 2020; Ryan & Deci, 2001) and has been widely interpreted through two related approaches: hedonic and eudaimonic. The hedonic approach focuses on subjective well-being, which includes affect balance (high positive affect, low negative affect) and satisfaction with life (Pavot & Diener, 2008). The eudaimonic approach, on the other hand, views well-being as the process of fulfilling human potential (Ryan et al., 2008). One framework within this perspective is the model of psychological well-being developed by Carol Ryff (2014), composed of six dimensions that stand for what it means to be "healthy, well, and fully functioning" (Ryff & Singer, 2008, p. 19): self-acceptance, positive relationships with other people, personal growth, purpose in life, mastery of the environment and autonomy. These approaches are not without criticism, as different authors consider them related but distinct aspects encompassing positive psychological functioning (Disabato et al., 2016; Kashdan et al., 2008; Keyes et al., 2002).

In addition to considering well-being as essential for the healthy functioning of individuals, the way of perceiving and processing emotions is also an indicator of the quality of functional and healthy interpersonal relationships (Rey & Extremera, 2014). Mayer and Salovey (1997) defined emotional intelligence as a set of skills that gradually increase in complexity, with each skill providing relevant information to more complex ones (Fernández-Berrocal & Cabello, 2021). According to these authors, emotional intelligence is the ability to manage emotions, including skills such as perception, expression, and regulation (Mayer et al., 2016). In addition, other evidence points out the importance of considering the context in which people are embedded (Saarni, 1999), as it is a variable linked to another of the so-called socio-emotional skill: social competence. Considered a multidimensional construct, it encompasses the dimensions such as prosocial behaviour, social adjustment, normative adjustment, cognitive reappraisal, and social efficacy. This involves considering the well-being of others as well as one's own, respecting and supporting others, adhering to social norms and conventions, understanding emotions in a given situation, and perceiving one's own ability to be socially successful (Dirks et al., 2007; Romera et al., 2017; Rose-Krasnor, 1997; Vaughn et al., 2009).

These competencies defined so far can be encompassed within the concept of socio-emotional competencies. They are sets of skills and knowledge that aim to achieve efficient performance of activities with an ethical or moral criterion that promotes solidarity and prosocial behaviour (Bisquerra & Pérez, 2007; López-Goñi & Goñí, 2012; Zych & Ortega-Ruiz, 2021). This ethical component considers moral emotions as those related to the disposition to do good and avoid evil (Haidt, 2003; Kroll & Egan, 2004). Evidence suggests the need to apply this approach based on socio-emotional and moral competences to interpersonal relationships in the educational context (Caurín et al., 2019). Analysing socio-emotional and moral competencies as an integrated construct could enhance the findings in different fields of knowledge (Llorent et al., 2020). These competencies play a crucial role in developing quality professional activities and driving social change (Llorent et al., 2020; Repetto & Peña, 2010). They can also serve as a connection between the needs of organizations, performance, and professional success, which is particularly relevant in the academic field and, consequently, in teacher training (González & Wagenaar, 2003; MacClelland, 1999).

ADDRESSING THE RELEVANCE OF WELL-BEING AND SOCIO-EMOTIONAL COMPETENCIES IN EDUCATIONAL SETTINGS

Recent research indicates that socio-emotional competencies are directly related to students' academic success. Organizations such as United Nations Educational, Scientific and Cultural Organization (UNESCO) and the Organisation for Economic Co-operation and Development (OECD) support this claim, arguing that the comprehensive training of students should consider academic as well as social and emotional areas (Garrido & Gaeta, 2016; Llorent et al., 2020). The importance of socio-emotional and moral competences has been increasing since the end of the 20th century (Durlak et al., 2011). This relevance has materialized, among others, through the proposals of the European Higher Education Area (EHEA), which suggests an adaptation of teaching that facilitate the acquisition of these competencies, facilitating continuous learning (Ministerio de Educación, Cultura y Deporte, 2003; Valcárcel, 2005). This adaptation could be seen as a way of meeting the needs of students but also those of future teachers, who require a good command of socio-emotional competencies (Palomera et al., 2008). It has been shown that a low level of socio-emotional competencies can negatively affect both the teaching-learning process and the emotional life of teachers, which suggests the need to develop programs to improve the management of these competencies in teacher training (Alexis-Boyd, 1998; Garrido & Gaeta, 2016).

Palomera et al. (2008) have been advocated to provide future teachers with specific training in this area, both in their initial training and the ongoing training to which they will have access in their professional performance. In this sense, high levels of socio-emotional competencies guarantee the implementation of programs to develop these same competencies in the classroom. Since teachers themselves are the primary agents in promoting their students' competencies, the effect lasts longer than when the training is carried out by personnel external to the educational centers (Durlak et al., 2011). In this regard, different initiatives have been developed in several universities outside Europe, such as the Harvard Business School of Harvard University in the USA (Cantero et al., 2008), Griffith University in Queensland, or the University of South Australia (Nunan et al., 2000) with positive results. Nevertheless, research has mostly focused on analysing the impact of these practices on students, using the term *positive education* to describe educational interventions and strategies derived from positive psychology and related fields that promote both learning and well-being (Roffey, 2023; White & Murray, 2015). It is an educational approach focused on the development of positive skills and values in the school environment, such as resilience, empathy, gratitude, self-esteem, optimism, and the capacity for teamwork (Slapac et al., 2021). It is based on the premise that by fostering these values from an early age, students will have a greater capacity to face life's challenges and will be happier and more fruitful in the future, and that its benefits are not limited to the school environment but extend to everyday reality.

The potential applications of positive psychology in schools have gained interest in recent years due not only to the rise of this approach but also to the awareness of our world's complexity, ambiguity, and uncertainty (Burke & Giraldez-Hayes, 2023). Events such as the COVID-19 pandemic have strengthened the need to teach skills such as resilience, gratitude, strength, creativity, emotional regulation, or critical thinking (Slapac et al., 2021). As such, increasingly, schools are transforming their educational practices to include actions that consider optimal functioning and well-being as central goals in their curricula (Chodkiewicz & Boyle, 2017). In more specific terms, positive education can be defined as "the integration of the core principles of positive psychology with the evidence-informed structures, practices and programs that enhance both well-being and academic achievement" (Noble & McGrath, 2016, p. 19). Positive education, therefore, aims to promote success and flourishing throughout the educational community. However, this aim is not a recent development, but has been forged in education for decades. The late 20th and early 21st century saw a significant shift in education policy (Chodkiewicz & Boyle, 2017). The so-called Delors Report, carried out by the International Commission on Education for the Twenty-first century for UNESCO (1996), marked a turning point by considering, among others, *learning to be* and *learning to live together* as basic pillars of education. Learning to be, already addressed in the Faure Report (International Commission on the Development of Education, 1972), emphasized one of the central issues in positive psychology: the fulfilment of human potential (Tawil & Cougoureux, 2013).

Learning to live together, on the other hand, focused on the importance in the educational process of teaching non-violence, diversity, awareness of similarities and acceptance of differences (International Commission on Education for the Twenty-first Century, 1996).

The rise of positive psychology, although apparently not linked to these initiatives, has also contributed to this shift in focus and, to some extent, shares common goals with the previous perspective: to move towards a holistic view of students and education, encouraging educational practitioners and stakeholders to go beyond the mere teaching of academic skills and knowledge and contribute to the holistic development of students (Green et al., 2011; Song et al., 2023; Waters, 2011). Promoting well-being and using the positive psychology lens are also increasingly popular practices in education (Boniwell & Ryan, 2012; White, 2016), allowing the field to improve in the organization, scientific findings, and structure. This is exemplified by associations such as the International Positive Education Network (IPEN) and the Positive Education Schools Association (PESA) (Coulombe et al., 2021), as well as through the numerous interventions that have been taking place over the years. Some of these approaches within positive education are briefly outlined below. Although not intended to be an exhaustive list, they have been selected to illustrate different and varied educational procedures worldwide (see Table 1 for an overview). *Social and Emotional Learning* (SEL) can be defined as the

Process through which all young people and adults acquire and apply the knowledge, skills, and attitudes to develop healthy identities, manage emotions and achieve personal and collective goals, feel and show empathy for others, establish and maintain supportive relationships, and make responsible and caring decisions (Durlak et al., 2022, p. 765).

CASEL, the Collaborative for Academic, Social and Emotional Learning, was established in 1994 with the aim of integrating evidence-based social and emotional learning practices into schools (Green et al., 2021). Based on the broad consensus on the importance for positive development of promoting both intrapersonal (INTRA), interpersonal (INTER) and decision-making (DM) skills and attitudes, SEL programmes aim to develop these social and emotional competencies (SECs) in students through three pathways: cognitive, affective, and behavioural (Brackett et al., 2019). From this perspective, SEC is understood as "the capacity to coordinate cognition, affect and behaviour that enables individuals to flourish and achieve positive developmental outcomes" (Mahoney et al., 2020, p. 4), identifying five key elements: self-awareness and self-management (INTRA), social awareness and relationship skills (INTER), and responsible decision-making (DM) (Durlak et al., 2022; Green et al., 2021; Mahoney et al., 2020). It is an approach to positive education that requires coordinating programmes and practices that enhance students' social, emotional, and cognitive development, foster positive behaviour and quality interpersonal relationships, as well as academic achievement (Durlak et al., 2015; National Commission on Social, Emotional, and Academic Development, 2017). Recent developments have emphasised the importance of adopting a systemic or ecological approach to SEL to achieve greater effectiveness and adaptability to new educational challenges, given that programme success in both the short and long term depends on the interaction of individual, organisational, and social factors (Mahoney et al., 2020). An implementation process is proposed that coordinates four interrelated areas: a) build foundational support and plan by establishing teams, involving stakeholders and fostering awareness and shared vision; b) strengthen adult SEL competencies and capacity to embed SEL across the school in a coherent way; c) promote SEL for students through a coordinated approach involving the school, family and wider community; and d) practice continuous improvement through data collection and evidence-based outcomes (Mahoney et al., 2020).

Another approach emerging from positive psychology used in schools (e.g., Norrish, 2015; White & Murray, 2015) is the PERMA model developed by Martin Seligman (2011, 2018). It is a multidimensional approach to well-being that includes both hedonic and eudaimonic elements in its five key elements: *positive emotions* (P), or feeling joyful, cheerful and content; *engagement* (E), referring to connection and psychological engagement with different activities (e.g. feeling absorbed, interested); *positive relationships* (R), or feeling socially integrated, caring and being cared for by others, having meaningful and quality social ties; *meaning* (M), understood as the belief that one's life is meaningful, that it has meaning, and feeling connected to something bigger than oneself; and *accomplishment* (A), which implies making progress in achieving goals, feeling able to cope with the responsibilities and demands of everyday life and having a sense of achievement. This model has been proposed as a framework that could both adequately assess dimensions valued by students (e.g., positive emotions and relationships) and align with existing school structures (Kern et al., 2015), as well as enhance the well-being of the school community as a whole, by focusing on building educational programmes, policies and strategies that focus on building enabling resources (Alford & White, 2015).

The PROSPER framework integrates the main ideas of positive psychology and evidence-based positive psychological interventions to promote students' well-being and social-emotional learning (Noble & McGrath, 2016). In the authors' words, it is not so much a programme as a flexible framework designed to provide early childhood, primary or secondary education professionals with a guide for implementing a positive education approach in their schools (Noble & McGrath, 2016). The acronym refers to seven elements: *positivity* (P), which refers to fostering a positive mindset and affect in students through aspects such as gratitude, optimism, contentment, and pride. It involves students feeling confident, interested, having fun, and feeling that they belong to the educational community; *relationships* (R), which includes the development of meaningful and positive relationships with peers and teachers through the practice of prosocial values and social skills. It also includes building positive relationships between family and school; progress towards *outcomes and accomplishment* (O) through self-awareness, valuing effort, perseverance, hard work, and fostering a growth mindset. Special emphasis is placed here on the recognition of the achievements of the members of the educational community, including a wide range of outcomes; *strengths* (S) implies the identification of the capacities and abilities of each student in different contexts, with the aim of learning to develop them, improve them and know how to apply and use them in an appropriate and effective way; *purpose* (P), referring in the school context to believing that what is learned there is valuable and useful, that it has meaning. It also involves the pursuit of both one's own well-being and that of others; *engagement* (E) is described as the student's connection or bond with school (e.g. feeling absorbed, interested, engaged in the teaching-learning process and in school life); and *resilience* (R), which includes helping students develop the capacity to bounce back after setbacks, difficulties, problems or mistakes, with the teaching of coping skills and the creation of strong social support structures considered essential (Noble & McGrath, 2016). This model shares some similarities with the PERMA model and Carol Ryff's (2014) model of psychological well-being, but includes strengths and resilience as additional elements, considered especially relevant (Noble & McGrath, 2015).

The *Strengths Gym Programme* (Proctor et al., 2011) is a character strengths-based positive psychological intervention on adolescent life satisfaction that has been applied in schools as "the ideal place for initiatives aimed at increasing the happiness and well-being of children" (Proctor et al., 2011, p. 377). This approach defines character strengths as positive traits that are reflected in our thoughts, feelings, and behaviours (Park et al., 2004; Proctor et al., 2011) that are core to our being (Niemiec, 2014), and is based on the theoretical framework and classification system of virtues, the Values-In-Action-Inventory of Strengths (Peterson & Seligman, 2004; VIA-IS; Peterson, 2006). The VIA-IS establishes a total of 24 universal character strengths, which are contained in six broader areas (i.e. virtues): *humanity* (love, kindness, and social intelligence), *wisdom* (creativity, curiosity, judgment, love of learning, and perspective), *temperance* (forgiveness, self-regulation, prudence, and humility), *transcendence* (hope, humour, gratitude, spirituality, and appreciation of beauty and excellence), *justice* (leadership, fairness, and teamwork) and *courage* (zest, bravery, perseverance, and honesty). Burke (2021) suggests that the implementation of strengths-based educational programmes could become an essential component of a school's wellbeing strategy because of the many benefits they can bring. However, van Nieuwerburgh and Green (2023) emphasise the importance of giving educators the time and space to learn about the scientific foundations of this approach and put them into practice prior to implementing the intervention with students.

Finally, the SEARCH meta-framework has been developed to help researchers organise scientific findings in positive education, as well as to provide education practitioners with a tool to assist them in making evidence-based decisions (Waters & Loton, 2019). SEARCH is a "data-driven, multidimensional and actionable framework" (Waters & Loton, 2019, p. 36) that has been developed in two stages: the first one consisted of the identification of key pathways of positive functioning/well-being (Rusk & Waters, 2015) and the second one assessed the pathways identified through the implementation of an action-research project in different schools. Following this process, six general areas were established: *strengths* (S), *emotional management* (E), *attention and awareness* (A), *relationships* (R), *coping* (C), and *habits and goals* (H). In other words, the data suggest that students' well-being is influenced by how they identify and use their strengths and virtues, how their emotions shape their experiences, how they relate to others, how they perceive and react to the world, what they choose to focus their attention on, and what motivates them in life and the goals they want to achieve (Waters et al., 2017).

WHY POSITIVE EDUCATION?

Schools are ideal settings for such interventions, as the time students spend within them and the social interactions and exchanges that take place there provide numerous opportunities to foster individual, social and emotional development (Chodkiewicz & Boyle, 2017). Scientific evidence provides numerous reasons for adopting a positive education approach. Overall, evidence suggests that including educational practices that seek to improve students' well-being can help prevent symptoms of mental illness, such as depression, as well as improve life satisfaction, promote learning, creativity, self-esteem, and academic success (Proctor et al., 2011; Seligman et al., 2009; Waters, 2011). More specifically, research on SEL-focused programs has suggested that these skills are malleable, measurable, and improvable (Corcoran & Tormey, 2012). Recent reviews of SEL intervention programs (Clarke et al., 2021; Durlak et al., 2022; Mahoney et al., 2018) have highlighted that social, emotional, and behavioral skills are key determinants of young people's well-being and lead to positive outcomes in school, work and life, such as increased prosocial behavior, improved academic performance or fewer emotional and behavioral problems. They are consistently associated with several benefits for students, being proposed as "highly promotive of young people's positive, healthy development over multiple domains, in diverse cultural contexts, and over the past several decades" (Durlak et al., 2022, p. 24). In their study on the application of the PERMA model in adolescent students, Kern et al. (2015) found that it was associated with outcomes such as hope, gratitude, school engagement, physical vitality, and academic performance. PROSPER model has proven to be particularly relevant during the COVID-19 pandemic. For example, focusing on teachers, Datu et al. (2022) conducted a 2-month randomized control trial with in-service teachers in Hong Kong and reported that teachers assigned to the experimental condition significantly increased their levels of positivity, strengths, purpose, and resilience. Other research shows that promoting the different component dimensions can build protective psychological resources (see Datu et al., 2022 for a review). Evidence also suggests that recognizing one's own character strengths and knowing how to use and maximize them can decrease stress (Wood et al., 2011), increase positive emotions, improve coping strategies and resilience in times of adversity (Martínez-Martí et al., 2020) and enhance life satisfaction (Proctor et al., 2011). Finally, following the establishment of the SEARCH framework, Waters and Loton (2019) conducted a systematic review of the educational literature to examine evidence of the six pathways in students. Results revealed that positive education interventions that promote the SEARCH pathways increased optimism, positive affect, self-concept, self-acceptance (e.g., Broderick & Metz 2009; Kuyken et al. 2013; Schonert-Reichl & Lawlor 2010), hope (e.g., Marques et al., 2011) and life satisfaction (e.g., Proctor et al., 2011), among others. These interventions were also found to reduce symptoms of depression, anxiety, and stress (e.g., Kuyken et al., 2013; Ruiz-Aranda et al., 2012). In addition, evidence was found that these interventions strengthen academic achievement and other school-related outcomes, such as student satisfaction and engagement (e.g., Quinlan et al., 2015), academic expectations, academic motivation (e.g., Jaakkola & Liukkonen, 2006), and perceptions of academic ability (e.g., Stoeger & Ziegler, 2008).

Table 1. Overview of the different positive education approaches

Positive Education Approach	Description and Aims	Areas	Main Findings
Social and Emotional Learning (CASEL, 2022)	Fostering social and emotional competencies in students through three pathways: cognitive, affective, and behavioural.	Self-awareness; self-management; social awareness; relationship skills; responsible decision-making.	Increased prosocial behaviour; improved academic performance; fewer emotional and behavioural problems.
PERMA model (Seligman, 2011; 2018).	Improving hedonic and eudaimonic well-being of the school community through the development of educational programmes, policies and strategies that create the enabling resources.	Positive emotions (P); Engagement (E) Positive relationships (R); Meaning (M); Accomplishment (A)	Greater hope; gratitude; school engagement; physical vitality; and academic performance.
PROSPER Framework (Noble & McGrath, 2015; 2016)	Integrating the main principles of positive psychology and evidence-based positive psychological interventions to promote students' well-being and social-emotional learning.	Positivity (P); Relationships (R); Outcomes and accomplishment (O); Purpose (P); Engagement (E); Resilience (R)	Increased positive emotions, optimism; pro-social behaviour; feelings of connectedness and belonging; improved learning skills and academic achievement; identification of one's own goals and strengths; improved coping skills and reduced symptoms of depression, anxiety, and hopelessness; and increased life satisfaction.
Strengths Gym Programme (Proctor et al., 2011)	Increasing students' life satisfaction, happiness, and well-being through a character strengths-based positive psychological intervention.	*Humanity* (love, kindness, social intelligence); *Wisdom* (creativity, curiosity, judgment, love of learning, perspective); *Temperance* (forgiveness, self-regulation, prudence, humility); *Transcendence* (hope, humour, gratitude, spirituality, and appreciation of beauty, excellence); *Justice* (leadership, fairness, teamwork); *Courage* (zest, bravery, perseverance, honesty)	Decreased stress; increased positive emotions; increased life satisfaction; and improvement in coping strategies and resilience in times of adversity.
SEARCH meta-framework (Waters & Loton, 2019)	Organising scientific findings in positive education and facilitating evidence-based decision making through a meta-framework that identifies six pathways to improve student well-being.	Strengths (S); Emotional management (E); Attention and awareness (A); Relationships (R); Coping (C); Habits and goals (H)	Increased optimism; positive affect, self-concept, and self-acceptance; boosted academic performance, student satisfaction and engagement, academic expectations, academic motivation, and perceptions of academic competence.

Source: Own elaboration

WHAT ABOUT WELL-BEING AND THESE COMPETENCIES IN ONLINE EDUCATION?

Online education has become increasingly prevalent in recent years, and the COVID-19 pandemic has accelerated this trend. The pandemic contributed to increased opportunities to virtually interact, which generated a scenario in which global problems came with us in those places where we were investing our lives, at home and in the online classroom (Slapac et al., 2023). While online learning can provide flexibility and access to education, it also presents challenges, such as limited opportunities for social interaction, increased feelings of loneliness and disconnection, or even forgetfulness and ignorance of key dimensions such as the well-being, socio-emotional and moral competencies, offering a cold or even dehumanised online education. The nature itself of the online scenario can entail the lack of face-to-face interaction and the isolation that can result from online learning can negatively impact students' well-being and social, emotional, and moral competencies. Teaching in online education requires design, development, and assessment according to its particularities and the specific tasks involved (Major, 2010; Spector, 2007). As with offline education, online education has great potential for the development and promotion of both well-being and socio-emotional and moral competencies. On the other hand, the educational process, also in its virtual dimension, might have the capacity to support, promote and enrich progress in the socio-emotional, moral and well-being of both students and teachers. However, such potential may not be properly exploited.

There is still a knowledge gap in the educational field regarding the potential of teachers' well-being and socioemotional and moral competencies, and students' growth in online learning and education, as well as aspects related to transnational learning of future or practicing teachers Moreover, the educational strategies, programmes and actions taken to address these factors in schools often takes the form of one-off training pills, or specific psychoeducational programmes that the school or teacher chooses to carry out of its own volition, being not enough. This is because the curriculum does not advocate explicit and regulated work on these fundamental issues. Vuorikari et al. (2012) underlined the relevance of the investment aimed at ensuring that teachers and students develop the competencies required in the 21st century, in the interconnected and digital reality in which we live, considering that this must be addressed both in the initial training of teachers as well as in their continuing education. A well-adjusted teaching methodology that considers the characteristics of the students is a critical element in improving the quality of education of students is a relevant factor for improving the quality of the learning process and academic satisfaction, which in turn is related to academic performance (Salanova et al., 2005). This requires considering elements such as well-being and socio-emotional and moral competencies that are so present in daily life and that therefore form part, to a greater or lesser extent, of students' lives. The issue with the lack of research made into the well-being and social-emotional and moral competencies in teacher training in online contexts might be that, given the few studies focusing on that topic in face-to-face environments, it could result difficult to build strong research regarding online education.

A great deal of scientific research has supported the diverse enriching potential showed by well-being status and the social-emotional and moral competencies (Burke & Giraldez-Hayes, 2023; Durlak et al., 2022). Despite the advances made into such direction, and the speed at which online learning is gaining prominence, scarce evidence can be found regarding well-being, socio-emotional and moral competencies in online education; and even less in teachers involved in online learning or the training they receive. Coppola et al. (2002) analysed the evolving cognitive, affective, and managerial pedagogical roles of online teachers in asynchronous learning spaces. Cognitively, teachers perform tasks related to information storage, thinking, and mental processes. At the managerial level, they prepare the course in a structured and planned manner, considering the evolution of their students. Moreover, regarding their affective role, they need tools for emotional expression and the establishment of close relationships with their students.

In addition, Han and Johnson (2012) found that emotional intelligence was positively related to social bonds in online environments in research whose aim was studying the emotional intelligence impact on peer relationships and behaviour in online learning spaces. Integrating social-emotional learning into the curriculum could draw a positive circle between emotional intelligence and social bonds in online environments. Therefore, such circle would increase emotional intelligence's levels and improve the engagement in online learning. As consequences, adherence on virtual learning would improve, learners would feel lee isolated and would enhance their outcomes. Durlak et al. (2011)'s meta-analysis supports the enriching potential of social-emotional learning curricula on students' social behaviour, academic performance, and behavioural adjustment, regardless of whether they are in a traditional or online classroom setting. Hernández-Sánchez and Ortega-Maldonado (2015) emphasize that to personalize the teaching-learning process in distance education in online environments, contributing to teachers and students feeling more satisfied on a personal, professional, and social level in the fruitful and intercultural virtual educational communities that emerge in these educational environments, it is appropriate to use Gardner's multiple intelligences model (1987). These authors proposed a holistic model of affective e-Learning, whose dual purpose was to improve students' knowledge while promoting positive emotions that would contribute to an increase in subjective well-being. Such model offered a mapping of such affective e-learning, tracing the sensations, emotions and moods experienced in the educational training and their consequences. No evidence has been found yet regarding the effectiveness of such a model and its potential impact on both the teacher and the students' performance.

Despite such findings, reality in online education seems not to frequently integrate such social-emotional, moral and well-being competencies. Hilliker et al. (2022) carried out a study with university students who were studying for a teacher's qualification once their classes turned online. Their findings revealed that when teaching was delivered entirely online and therefore there was very little face-to-face interaction, being able to interact with a peer reported improvements in participants' positive emotions, levels of engagement, relationships, meaning and purpose, and achievement (PERMA). A study conducted with a representative Mexican university faculty professors indicated that 9 out of 10 did not display any affective skills in the development of their work in virtual contexts, since they focused on cognitive and technical skills (Quiñonez Pech et al., 2018). Recently, Geesa et al. (2022) developed a model to provide teachers with training and resources to effectively guide children and adolescents' social-emotional learning online, which they called o-SEL. This model had six online modules that provided teachers and educators with a set of skills, knowledge, and resources to support social-emotional learning for their students: Empower, Engage, Motivate, Include, Collaborate, extend for educators to foster inclusive o-SEL environments for PK-12 students which they termed the Collaborative Model for Teaching o-SEL. There is no evidence regarding this model's effectiveness yet. Moreover, no research has been found regarding the moral competencies in the teachers training and/or performance, which highlight the need for deepening into this matter. The lack of programmes carried out in the teacher training aimed to develop and foster well-being, social-emotional and moral competencies could be hindering the potential of online education. Therefore, more proposals focusing on such set of key well-being and competencies are in need to reach the maximum integral development of citizenship (including both the teacher, the students and, by extension the rest of the society).

IMPLICATIONS AND FUTURE RESEARCH DIRECTIONS

Addressing such relevant elements as well-being and socio-emotional and moral competencies in education is a necessity. Besides, for teachers and educators to have the necessary knowledge and skills to carry out such teaching among their students, they should achieve two prior goals. First, they should be socioemotionally and morally competent, as well as have an adequate level of well-being. Secondly, they should have the proper training that would allow them to effectively foster these competencies and well-being among their students, making them part of their teaching work as the enriching element that they are.

Teachers are at the forefront of the formation of young minds and their personal and academic growth. Therefore, it is essential that they possess the necessary skills to support the holistic development of their students. This challenge requires a commitment to offer teacher training programs that focus on fostering well-being and social, emotional, and moral competencies both offline and online. Steps in the direction of social-emotional, moral and well-being flourishing in the educational world must be taken in parallel in offline and online education.

The promotion of well-being and social-emotional and moral competencies in teacher training/development has a positive impact on classroom climate. Teachers who have good levels of well-being and socio-emotional and moral competencies are better able to create safe and supportive learning environments that promote student engagement and academic achievement. In addition, they will also be able to be positive role models in attitude and behaviour for their students. Another key implication of fostering the promotion of these elements in teacher education is that it will facilitate the development of strong relationships between teachers and students, but also with other teachers, the management team, and families. The strength of these relationships will help to generate a greater connection with all the agents of the educational community, to have a better understanding of the needs and motivations of others, and to offer the necessary support to promote success in others. In online educational settings, this involvement is even more relevant, since physical interaction is often limited and virtual communication tools must be used, through which the wellbeing and proficiency of the teacher will serve to ensure connection with students, generate a sense of community and provide personalized support.

Another implication is related to teacher health and job satisfaction. Teachers with such competencies and well-being will be less susceptible to burnout, will persist in the face of challenges despite their difficulty, and will feel greater satisfaction with their educational work. Consideration of well-being and these competencies as part of teacher education will serve as an incentive for educational institutions to attract and retain high-quality teachers committed to providing the best possible learning experiences for their students. Moreover, in online educational settings, where challenges can be even more pronounced, proficiency in a diverse array of tools and methodologies related to new technologies may be demanded in addition to the mentioned set of competencies. The heightened demand can be effectively managed when educators possess a sense of well-being and socio-emotional competencies that enable thoughtful planning and responsible decision-making throughout their teaching endeavors. In addition, the aforementioned implications will have a positive impact on the community as a whole, given the personal, occupational, socio-emotional and moral enrichment that the educational community, the students as future citizens and the example they will set for the rest of society will benefit from. Given the many and varied positive implications of the inclusion of well-being and socio-emotional and moral competencies in teacher training, both offline and online, it should be placed as a priority on the educational agenda of educational policies and institutions.

While the implications discussed above provide valuable insights for teacher training and practice, there is still much to be explored in the knowledge field of well-being and socio-emotional and moral competencies. Future research could address their relevance for teachers' development and reviewing educational practices in teacher training, a potential future research line is the exploration of the effectiveness of integrating well-being and socio-emotional and moral competencies into online teacher education programs. Research questions arising regarding such line are, among others, how can well-being and socio-emotional and moral competencies be effectively integrated into teacher training? and, would it imply any differences regarding offline educational environments and online ones? Another question could be which challenges and opportunities would we face regarding training teachers in well-being and these competencies both offline and online.? Awareness regarding such key points could help building holistic teacher training programmes maximizing their strengths and reinforcing those challenging parts to avoid failures. How can learning environments be designed to foster the development of well-being and such competencies in teacher in training? An adequate learning environment can make the teaching-learning process easier as well as an inadequate one can interrupt it. Designing learning environments taking advantage of their potential and trying to minimize their weaknesses would contribute to the achievement of more effective programs. What is the impact of developing well-being and socio-emotional and moral competencies on online teachers' performance and satisfaction? What is the impact of developing well-being and socio-emotional and moral competencies on performance and satisfaction on other educational agents such as the school management team, the rest of the staff, and families?

Knowing the real impact of this type of programs, as well as having evidence to support their beneficial potential, and analysing the different dimensions in which they have positive effects would promote the focus on these programs and their implementation with the necessary frequency. Lastly, although not least, it would be interesting studying how the development of well-being and these competencies could be assessed and measured in teacher training both offline and online. Building new instruments, validating them, and using them to precisely assess such development is important. Reliable results cannot be obtained without precise and rigorous instruments to measure them, and evidence is irrelevant when no reliable instruments support the results.

CONCLUSION

Research (e.g., Caurín et al., 2019; González & Wagenaar, 2003; Slapac et al., 2021) has shown that students' well-being and social and emotional development are closely linked to success, both academically and in other life domains. Education should care to support students' holistic development, but this is a challenge that requires well-equipped teachers, with good levels of well-being and socio-emotional competencies. Paying attention to teachers' mental, emotional, and social health, and providing them with tools to prosper both in their lives and in their profession, is therefore essential for promoting flourishing development in students. Teachers who are prepared and trained not only to teach academic content, but also to help their students thrive in a rapidly changing, complex offline and online world, should be recognised as one of the pillars of contemporary education.

REFERENCES

Alexis-Boyd, L. (1998). *The emotional life of teachers: A heuristic inquiry* [Doctoral dissertation, University of Cincinnati]. https://bit.ly/3UuO6kv https://www.proquest.com/openview/ff4818296d287edbe318642a5bd114c1/1?pq-origsite=gscholar&cbl=18750&diss=y

Alford, Z., & White, M. A. (2015). Positive school psychology. In M. A. White & A. S. Murray (Eds.), *Evidence-based approaches in positive education. Implementing a strategic framework for well-being in schools* (pp. 93–110). Springer. doi:10.1007/978-94-017-9667-5_5

Bisquerra, R., & Pérez, N. (2007). Las competencias emocionales [Emotional competencies] *Educación XXI, 10*(1), 61–82. doi:10.5944/educxx1.1.10.297

Boniwell, I., & Ryan, L. (2012). *Personal well-being: Lessons for secondary schools, positive psychology in action for 11 to 14 year olds.* McGraw-Hill.

Brackett, M. A., Bailey, C. S., Hoffmann, J. D., & Simmons, D. N. (2019). RULER: A theory-driven, systemic approach to social, emotional, and academic learning. *Educational Psychologist, 54*(3), 144–161. doi:10.1080/00461520.2019.1614447

Broderick, P. C., & Metz, S. (2009). Learning to BREATHE: A pilot trial of a mindfulness curriculum for adolescents. *Advances in School Mental Health Promotion, 2*(1), 35–46. doi:10.1080/1754730X.2009.9715696

Bryk, A., Bender Sebring, P., Allensworth, E., Luppescu, S., & Easton, J. (2010). *Organizing schools for improvement: Lessons from Chicago.* University of Chicago Press. doi:10.7208/chicago/9780226078014.001.0001

Burke, J. (2021). *The ultimate guide to implementing wellbeing programmes for school.* Routledge.

Burke, J., & Giraldez-Hayes, A. (2023). Positive schools: An introduction. In A. Giraldez-Hayes & J. Burke (Eds.), *Applied positive school psychology* (pp. 3–8). Routledge. doi:10.4324/9781003228158-2

Cantero, M. P., Miñano, P., & Gilar, R. (2008). Diferencias entre los perfiles de competencias socioemocionales de estudiantes en distintas titulaciones de magisterio. *International Journal of Developmental and Educational Psychology, 1*(4), 493–504. https://www.redalyc.org/articulo.oa?id=349832319053

CASEL. (2012). *Effective social and emotional learning programs-Preschool and elementary school edition. Casel guide 2013.* https://eric.ed.gov/?id=ED581699

CASEL. (2020). *CASEL's SEL framework: What are the core competence areas and where are they promoted?* https://casel.org/casel-sel-framework-11-2020/

Caurín, C., Morales, A. J., & Fontana, M. (2019). Convivencia en el ámbito educativo: Aplicación de un programa basado en la empatía, la educación emocional y la resolución de conflictos en un instituto español de enseñanza secundaria. *Cuestiones Pedagógicas, 27*(27), 97–112. doi:10.12795/CP.2018.i27.06

Chodkiewicz, A. R., & Boyle, C. (2017). Positive psychology school-based interventions: A reflection on current success and future directions. *Review of Education, 5*(1), 60–86. doi:10.1002/rev3.3080

Clarke, A., Sorgenfrei, M., Mulcahy, J., Davie, P., Friedrich, C., & McBride, T. (2021). *Adolescent mental health. A systematic review on the effectiveness of school-based interventions.* https://www.eif.org.uk/report/adolescent-mental-health-a-systematic-review-on-the-effectiveness-of-school-based-interventions

Coppola, N. W., Hiltz, S. R., & Rotter, N. G. (2002). Becoming a virtual professor: Pedagogical roles and asynchronous learning networks. *Journal of Management Information Systems, 18*(4), 169–189. doi:10.1080/07421222.2002.11045703

Corcoran, R. P., & Tormey, R. (2012). How emotionally intelligent are pre-service teachers? *Teaching and Teacher Education, 28*(5), 750–759. doi:10.1016/j.tate.2012.02.007

Coulombe, S., Hardy, K., & Goldfarb, R. (2021). Promoting wellbeing through positive education: A critical review and proposed social ecological approach. *Theory and Research in Education, 18*(3), 295–321. doi:10.1177/1477878520988432

Datu, J. A. D., Lee, A. S. Y., Fung, W. K., Cheung, R. Y. M., & Chung, K. K. H. (2022). Prospering in the midst of the COVID-19 pandemic: The effects of PROSPER-based intervention on psychological outcomes among preschool teachers. *Journal of School Psychology, 94*, 66–82. doi:10.1016/j.jsp.2022.08.003 PMID:36064216

Dirks, M. A., Treat, T. A., & Weersing, V. R. (2007). Integrating theoretical, measurement, and intervention models of youth social competence. *Clinical Psychology Review, 27*(3), 327–347. doi:10.1016/j.cpr.2006.11.002 PMID:17270330

Disabato, D. J., Goodman, F. R., Kashdan, T. B., Short, J. L., & Jarden, A. (2016). Different types of wellbeing? A cross-cultural examination of hedonic and eudaimonic well-being. *Psychological Assessment, 28*(5), 471–482. doi:10.1037/pas0000209 PMID:26348031

Durlak, J. A., Domitrovich, C. E., Weissberg, R. P., & Gullotta, T. P. (Eds.). (2015). *Handbook of social and emotional learning: Research and practice*. Guilford Press.

Durlak, J. A., Mahoney, J. L., & Boyle, A. E. (2022). What we know, and what we need to find out about universal, school-based social and emotional learning programs for children and adolescents: A review of meta-analyses and directions for future research. *Psychological Bulletin, 148*(11-12), 765–782. doi:10.1037/bul0000383

Durlak, J. A., Weissberg, R. P., Dymnicki, A. B., Taylor, R. D., & Schellinger, K. B. (2011). The impact of enhancing students' social and emotional learning: A meta-analysis of school-based universal interventions. *Child Development, 82*(1), 405–432. doi:10.1111/j.1467-8624.2010.01564.x PMID:21291449

Fernández-Berrocal, P., & Cabello, R. (2021). La inteligencia emocional como fundamento de la educación emocional [Emotional intelligence as a foundation for emotional education]. *Revista Internacional de Educación Emocional y Bienestar [International Journal of Emotional Education and Well-Being], 1*(1), 31–46. doi:10.48102/rieeb.2021.1.1.5

Gardner, H. (1987). The theory of multiple intelligences. *Annals of Dyslexia, 37*(1), 19–35. doi:10.1007/BF02648057 PMID:24234985

Garrido, P., & Gaeta, M. L. (2016). La competencia socioemocional docente en el logro del aprendizaje de las competencias genéricas del perfil de egreso de educación media superior. *Revista de Comunicación Vivat Academia, 137*, 108–123. doi:10.15178/va.2016.137.108-123

Geesa, R. L., Robbins, K., & Shively, K. (2022). The collaborative model for teaching o-SEL: Preparing educators to design online environments for social-emotional learning. *Journal of Online Learning Research, 8*(1), 67–100. https://eric.ed.gov/?id=EJ1342754

Gómez-López, M. (2020). *Bienestar y relaciones sentimentales en adolescentes de Andalucía* [Doctoral dissertation, University of Cordoba]. https://helvia.uco.es/xmlui/handle/10396/19671

González, J., & Wagenaar, R. (2003). Quality and European programme design in higher education. *European Journal of Education, 38*(3), 241–251. doi:10.1111/1467-3435.00144

Green, S., Leach, C., & Falecki, D. (2021). Approaches to positive education. In M. L. Kern & M. L. Wehmeyer (Eds.), *The Palgrave handbook of positive education* (pp. 21–48). Palgrave Macmillan. doi:10.1007/978-3-030-64537-3_2

Green, S., Oades, L. G., & Robinson, P. (2011). Positive education: Creating flourishing students, staff and schools. *InPsych, 33*(2), 16–17. https://psychology.org.au/publications/inpsych/2011/april/green

Haidt, J. (2003). Elevation and the positive psychology of morality. In C. L. M. Keyes & J. Haidt (Eds.), *Flourishing: Positive psychology and the life well-lived* (pp. 275–289). American Psychological Association. doi:10.1037/10594-012

Han, H., & Johnson, S. D. (2012). Relationship between students' emotional intelligence, social bond, and interactions in online learning. *Journal of Educational Technology & Society, 15*(1), 78–89. https://www.jstor.org/stable/jeductechsoci.15.1.78

Hernández Barraza, V. (2017). Las competencias emocionales del docente y su desempeño profesional [Teachers' emotional competencies and their professional performance]. *Alternativas en Psicología [Alternatives in Psychology], 37*, 79–92. https://www.alternativas.me/26-numero-37-febrero-julio-2017/147-las-competencias-emocionales-del-docente-y-su-desempeno-profesional

Hernández-Sánchez, A. M., & Ortega-Maldonado, A. (2015). Hacia la personalización del e-Learning: La afectividad y su repercusión en el bienestar subjetivo [Towards the personalization of e-learning: Affectivity and its impact on subjective well-being]. *Revista Lasallista de Investigacion [Lasallian Research Journal]. 12*(2), 194–203. doi:10.22507/rli.v12n2a20

Hilliker, S. M., Loranc, B., & Samarakkody, D. (2022). Uplifting the well-being of teacher candidates through virtual exchange during COVID-19. *Journal of Virtual Exchange, 5*, 176–192. doi:10.21827/jve.5.38320

International Commission on Education for the Twenty-first Century. (1996). *Learning: the treasure within*. UNESCO. https://unesdoc.unesco.org/ark:/48223/pf0000109590

International Commission on the Development of Education. (1972). *Learning to be. The world of education today and tomorrow*. UNESCO. https://unesdoc.unesco.org/ark:/48223/pf0000223222

Jaakkola, T., & Liukkonen, J. (2006). Changes in students' self-determined motivation and goal orientation as a result of motivational climate intervention within high school physical education classes. *International Journal of Sport and Exercise Psychology, 4*(3), 302–324. doi:10.1080/1612197X.2006.9671800

Kashdan, T. B., Biswas-Diener, R., & King, L. A. (2008). Reconsidering happiness: The costs of distinguishing between hedonics and eudaimonia. *The Journal of Positive Psychology*, *3*(4), 219–233. doi:10.1080/17439760802303044

Kern, M. L., Waters, L. E., Adler, A., & White, M. A. (2015). A multidimensional approach to measuring well-being in students: Application of the PERMA framework. *The Journal of Positive Psychology*, *10*(3), 262–271. doi:10.1080/17439760.2014.936962 PMID:25745508

Keyes, C. L. M., Shmotkin, D., & Ryff, C. D. (2002). Optimizing well-being: The empirical encounter of two traditions. *Journal of Personality and Social Psychology*, *82*(6), 1007–1022. doi:10.1037/0022-3514.82.6.1007 PMID:12051575

Kroll, J., & Egan, E. (2004). Psychiatry, moral worry, and the moral emotions. *Journal of Psychiatric Practice*, *10*(6), 352–360. https://doi.org/cnsstq. doi:10.1097/00131746-200411000-00003 PMID:15583516

Kuyken, W., Weare, K., Ukoumunne, O. C., Vicary, R., Motton, N., Burnett, R., Cullen, C., Hennelly, S., & Huppert, F. (2013). Effectiveness of the mindfulness in schools programme: Non-randomised controlled feasibility study. *The British Journal of Psychiatry*, *203*(2), 126–131. doi:10.1192/bjp.bp.113.126649 PMID:23787061

Llorent, V. J., Zych, I., & Varo-Millán, J. C. (2020). Competencias socioemocionales autopercibidas en el profesorado universitario en España. *Educación XX1, 23*(1), 297-318. doi:10.5944/educxx1.23687

López, A. I. A. (2022). Elementos curriculares para la formación y actualización del docente. *Revista Docencia Universitaria*, *3*(1), 57–66. doi:10.46954/revistadusac.v3i1.40

López-Goñi, I., & Goñi, J. M. (2012). La competencia emocional en los currículos de formación inicial de los docentes. Un estudio comparativo. *Review of Education*, *357*, 467–489. https://dialnet.unirioja.es/servlet/articulo?codigo=3811857

López-López, V., & Lagos San Martín, N. (2021). Repensar la formación inicial docente desde una dimensión socioemocional. *Review of Education*, *45*(1), 609–619. doi:10.15517/revedu.v45i1.41464

MacClelland. (1999). *A guide to job competency assessment*. McBer.

Mahoney, J. L., Durlak, J. A., & Weissberg, R. P. (2018). An update on social and emotional learning outcome research. *Phi Delta Kappan*, *100*(4), 18–23. doi:10.1177/0031721718815668

Mahoney, J. L., Weissberg, R. P., Greenberg, M. T., Dusenbury, L., Jagers, R. J., Niemi, K., Schlinger, M., Schlund, J., Shriver, T. P., VanAusdal, K., & Yoder, N. (2020). Systemic Social and Emotional Learning: Promoting educational success for all preschool to high school students. *The American Psychologist*, *76*(7), 1128–1142. doi:10.1037/amp0000701 PMID:33030926

Major, C. (2010). Do virtual professors dream of electric students? College faculty experiences with online distance education. *Teachers College Record*, *112*(8), 2154–2208. doi:10.1177/016146811011200802

Marques, S. C., Lopez, S. J., & Pais-Ribeiro, J. L. (2011). "Building hope for the future": A program to foster strengths in middle-school students. *Journal of Happiness Studies*, *12*(1), 139–152. doi:10.1007/s10902-009-9180-3

Martínez-Martí, M. L., Theirs, C. I., Pascual, D., & Corradi, G. (2020). Character strengths predict an increase in mental health and subjective well-being over a one-month period during the COVID-19 pandemic lockdown. *Frontiers in Psychology, 11*, 584567. Advance online publication. doi:10.3389/fpsyg.2020.584567 PMID:33192913

Mayer, J. D., Caruso, D. R., & Salovey, P. (2016). The ability model of emotional intelligence: Principles and updates. *Emotion Review*, *8*(4), 290–300. doi:10.1177/1754073916639667

Mayer, J. D., & Salovey, P. (1997). What is emotional intelligence? In P. Salovey & D. J. Sluyter (Eds.), *Emotional development and emotional intelligence: Educational implications* (pp. 3–31). Basic Books.

Ministerio de Educación. Cultura y Deporte. (2003). *La integración del sistema universitario español en el Espacio Europeo de Enseñanza Superior*. http://www.fce.udl.cat/EEES/eees/Documento_Marco.pdf

Montejo-Ángel, F., & Pava-Díaz, G. (2022). Competencias socioemocionales y selección de candidatos para cargos de docencia universitaria: Socio-emotional competencies and selection of candidates for university teaching positions. *Educación y Humanismo*, *24*(42). Advance online publication. doi:10.17081/eduhum.24.42.5337

National Commission on Social, Emotional, and Academic Development. (2017). *The evidence base for how we learn: Supporting students' social, emotional, and academic development*. The Aspen Institute. https://bit.ly/49r96gp https://www.aspeninstitute.org/wp-content/uploads/2017/09/SEAD-Research-Brief-9.12_updated-web.pdf

Niemiec, R. M. (2014). *Mindfulness and character strengths: A practical guide to flourishing*. Hogrefe. doi:10.1027/00376-000

Noble, T., & McGrath, H. (2015). PROSPER: A new framework for positive education. *Psychology of Well-Being*, *5*(2), 2. Advance online publication. doi:10.1186/s13612-015-0030-2

Noble, T., & McGrath, H. (2016). *The PROSPER school pathways for student wellbeing. Policy and practices*. Springer., doi:10.1007/978-3-319-21795-6

Norrish, J. M. (2015). *Positive education: The Geelong Grammar School journey*. Oxford University Press. doi:10.1093/acprof:oso/9780198702580.001.0001

Nunan, T., George, R., & McCausland, H. (2000). Implementing graduate skill at an Australian university. In S. Fallows & C. Steven (Eds.), *Integrating key skills in higher education: employability, transferable skills and learning for life* (pp. 57–66). Kogan Page.

Palomera, R., Fernández-Berrocal, P., & Brackett, M. A. (2008). La inteligencia emocional como una competencia básica en la formación inicial de los docentes: Algunas evidencias. *Electronic Journal of Research in Educational Psychology*, *15*(6), 437–454. doi:10.25115/ejrep.v6i15.1292

Park, N., Peterson, C., & Seligman, M. E. P. (2004). Strengths of character and well-being: A closer look at hope and modesty. *Journal of Social and Clinical Psychology*, *23*(5), 628–634. doi:10.1521/jscp.23.5.628.50749

Pavot, W., & Diener, E. (2008). The satisfaction with life scale and the emerging construct of life satisfaction. *The Journal of Positive Psychology*, *3*(2), 137–152. doi:10.1080/17439760701756946

Peterson, C. (2006). *A primer in positive psychology*. Oxford University Press.

Peterson, C., & Seligman, M. E. P. (2004). *Character strengths and virtues: A handbook and classification*. Oxford University Press.

Proctor, C., Tsukayama, E., Wood, A. M., Maltby, J., Eades, J. F., & Linley, A. (2011). Strengths gym: The impact of a character strengths-based intervention on the life satisfaction and well-being of adolescents. *The Journal of Positive Psychology*, *6*(5), 377–388. doi:10.1080/17439760.2011.594079

Quinlan, D. M., Swain, N., Cameron, C., & Vella-Brodrick, D. A. (2015). How 'other people matter' in a classroom-based strengths intervention: Exploring interpersonal strategies and classroom outcomes. *The Journal of Positive Psychology*, *10*(1), 77–89. doi:10.1080/17439760.2014.920407

Quiñonez Pech, S. H., Zapata González, A., & Canto Herrera, P. J. (2018). Percepción de profesores sobre la afectividad en los entornos virtuales en una universidad pública del sureste de México. *RIDE Revista Iberoamericana para la Investigación y el Desarrollo Educativo*, *9*(17), 195–224. doi:10.23913/ride.v9i17.378

Repetto, E., & Peña, M. (2010). Las competencias socioemocionales como factor de calidad en la educación. *Revista Electrónica Iberoamericana sobre Calidad, Eficacia y Cambio en Educación*, *8*(5), 82–95. https://dialnet.unirioja.es/servlet/articulo?codigo=3921000

Rey, L., & Extremera, N. (2014). Positive psychological characteristics and interpersonal forgiveness: Identifying the unique contribution of emotional intelligence abilities, Big Five traits, gratitude and optimism. *Personality and Individual Differences*, *68*, 199–204. doi:10.1016/j.paid.2014.04.030

Roffey, S. (2023). Applying positive psychology in primary schools. In A. Giraldez-Hayes & J. Burke (Eds.), *Applied positive school psychology* (pp. 9–20). Routledge. doi:10.4324/9781003228158-3

Romera, E. M., Herrera-López, M. H., Casas, J. A., Ortega-Ruiz, R., & Gómez-Ortiz, O. (2017). Multidimensional social competence, motivation, and cyberbullying: A cultural approach with Colombian and Spanish adolescents. *Journal of Cross-Cultural Psychology*, *48*(8), 1183–1197. doi:10.1177/0022022116687854

Rose-Krasnor, L. (1997). The nature of social competence: A theoretical review. *Social Development*, *6*(1), 111–135. doi:10.1111/j.1467-9507.1997.tb00097.x

Ruiz-Aranda, D., Salguero, J. M., Cabello, R., Palomera, R., & Berrocal, P. (2012). Can an emotional intelligence program improve adolescents' psychosocial adjustment? Results from the INTEMO project. *Social Behavior and Personality*, *40*(8), 1373–1379. doi:10.2224/sbp.2012.40.8.1373

Ruiz-Sánchez, S. (2020, October). *Las habilidades socioemocionales docentes en tiempos de pandemia* [Conference session]. V Congreso de investigación en habilidades socioemocionales, coaching y talento (CIGETH-2020). Cuernavaca, México.

Rusk, R. D., & Waters, L. (2015). A psycho-social system approach to wellbeing: Empirically deriving the five pathways of positive functioning. *The Journal of Positive Psychology*, *10*(2), 141–152. doi:10.1080/17439760.2014.920409

Ryan, R. M., & Deci, E. L. (2001). On happiness and human potentials: A review of research on hedonic and eudaimonic well-being. *Annual Review of Psychology*, *52*(1), 141–166. doi:10.1146/annurev.psych.52.1.141 PMID:11148302

Ryan, R. M., Huta, V., & Deci, E. L. (2008). Living well: A self-determination theory perspective on eudaimonia. *Journal of Happiness Studies*, *9*(1), 139–170. doi:10.1007/s10902-006-9023-4

Ryff, C. D. (2014). Psychological well-being revisited: Advances in the science and practice of eudaimonia. *Psychotherapy and Psychosomatics*, *83*(1), 10–28. doi:10.1159/000353263 PMID:24281296

Ryff, C. D., & Singer, B. H. (2008). Know thyself and become what you are: A eudaimonic approach to psychological well-being. *Journal of Happiness Studies*, *9*(1), 13–39. doi:10.1007/s10902-006-9019-0

Saarni, C. (1999). *The development of emotional competence*. Guilford Press.

Salanova, M., Martínez, I., Bresó, E., Llorens, S., & Grau, R. (2005). Bienestar psicológico en estudiantes universitarios: Facilitadores y obstaculizadores del desempeño académico. *Anales de Psicología*, *21*(1), 170–180. https://www.redalyc.org/articulo.oa?id=16721116

Schonert-Reichl, K. A., & Lawlor, M. S. (2010). The effects of a mindfulness-based education program on pre-and early adolescents' wellbeing and social and emotional competence. *Mindfulness*, *1*(3), 137–151. doi:10.1007/s12671-010-0011-8

Seligman, M. E. P. (2011). *Flourish: A visionary new understanding of happiness and well-being*. Free Press.

Seligman, M. E. P. (2018). PERMA and the building blocks of well-being. *The Journal of Positive Psychology*, *13*(4), 333–335. doi:10.1080/17439760.2018.1437466

Seligman, M. E. P., Ernst, R. M., Gillham, J., Reivich, K., & Linkins, M. (2009). Positive education: Positive psychology and classroom interventions. *Oxford Review of Education*, *35*(3), 293–311. doi:10.1080/03054980902934563

Slapac, A., Collett, K., Wessels, F., Gamiet, G., & Knudsmoen, H. (2023). Social justice pedagogy and Collaborative Online International Learning (COIL): Across three partner higher education institutions. In P. Escudeiro, N. Escudeiro, & O. Bernardes (Eds.), *Handbook of research on implementing inclusive educational models and technologies for equity and diversity* (pp. 252–272). IGI Global. doi:10.4018/979-8-3693-0453-2.ch013

Slapac, A., Coppersmith, S. A., O'Brien, K., & Balcerzak, P. (2021). Resilience in crisis: Developing community through Action Research. In A. Slapac, P. Balcerzak, & K. O'Brien (Eds.), *Handbook of research on the global empowerment of educators and student learning through action research* (pp. 23–48). IGI Global. doi:10.4018/978-1-7998-6922-1.ch002

Song, K. H., Kerkhoff, S. N., & Slapac, A. (2023). Educating racially, culturally, and linguistically diverse children in the global era: The world at home and at home in the world. In J. Chitiyo & Z. Pietrantoni (Eds.), *Social justice and culturally-affirming education in K-12 settings* (pp. 1–22). IGI Global. doi:10.4018/978-1-6684-6386-4.ch001

Spector, J. M. (Ed.). (2007). *Finding your online voice: Stories told by experienced online educators*. Routledge. doi:10.4324/9780203825167

Stoeger, H., & Ziegler, A. (2008). Evaluation of a classroom based training to improve self-regulation in time management tasks during homework activities with fourth graders. *Metacognition and Learning*, *3*(3), 207–230. doi:10.1007/s11409-008-9027-z

Tawil, S., & Cougoureux, M. (2013). Una mirada actual a la *Educación encierra un tesoro*. Evaluar la influencia del informe Delors de 1996. *Investigación y Prospectiva en Educación/UNESCO*, 4. https://unesdoc.unesco.org/ark:/48223/pf0000220050_spa

United Nations. (2023, March). *Sustainable development goals*. https://www.un.org/sustainabledevelopment/

Valcárcel, M. (2005). La preparación del profesorado universitario español para la convergencia europea en educación superior. *Educatio Siglo XXI, 23*, 209-213. https://revistas.um.es/educatio/article/view/130

van Nieuwerburgh, C., & Green, A. (2023). Strengths-based interventions for students and staff. In A. Giraldez-Hayes & J. Burke (Eds.), *Applied positive school psychology* (pp. 115–124). Routledge., doi:10.4324/9781003228158-14

Vaughn, B. E., Shin, N., Kim, M., Coppola, G., Krzysik, L., Santos, A. J., Inês Peceguina, I., Daniel, J. R., Veríssimo, M., DeVries, A., Elphick, E., Ballentina, X., Bost, K. K., Newell, W. Y., Miller, E. B., Snider, J. B., & Korth, B. (2009). Hierarchical models of social competence in preschool children: A multisite, multinational study. *Child Development*, *80*(6), 1775–1796. doi:10.1111/j.1467-8624.2009.01367.x PMID:19930351

Vuorikari, R., Garoia, V., Punie, Y., Cachia, R., Cao, Y., Klamma, R., Rajagopal, K., Cuong, M., Fetter, S., Sloep, P., & Scimeca, S. (2012). *Teacher networks: Today's and tomorrow's challenges and opportunities for teaching profession*. European Schoolnet (JRC75795). https://publications.jrc.ec.europa.eu/repository/handle/JRC75795

Waters, L. (2011). A review of school-based positive psychology interventions. *The Australian Educational and Developmental Psychologist*, *28*(2), 75–90. doi:10.1375/aedp.28.2.75

Waters, L., & Loton, D. (2019). SEARCH: A meta-framework and review of the field of positive education. *International Journal of Applied Positive Psychology*, *4*(1-2), 1–46. doi:10.1007/s41042-019-00017-4

Waters, L., Sun, J., Rusk, R., Cotton, A., & Arch, A. (2017). Positive education. In M. Slade, L. Oades, & A. Jarden (Eds.), *Wellbeing, recovery and mental health* (pp. 245–264). Cambridge University Press. doi:10.1017/9781316339275.021

White, M. A. (2016). Why won't it stick? Positive psychology and positive education. *Psychology of Well-Being*, *6*(2), 2. Advance online publication. doi:10.1186/s13612-016-0039-1 PMID:26900547

White, M. A., & Murray, A. S. (Eds.). (2015). *Evidence-based approaches in positive education. Implementing a strategic framework for well-being in schools*. Springer. doi:10.1007/978-94-017-9667-5

Wood, A. M., Linley, P. A., Maltby, J., Kashdan, T. B., & Hurling, R. (2011). Using personal and psychological strengths leads to increases in well-being over time: A longitudinal study and the development of the strengths use questionnaire. *Personality and Individual Differences*, *50*(1), 15–19. doi:10.1016/j.paid.2010.08.004

Zych, I., & Ortega-Ruiz, R. (2021). Promoción de las competencias socioemocionales y prevención de la violencia escolar y juvenil. *Revista Internacional de Educación Emocional y Bienestar*, *1*(1), 63–84. doi:10.48102/rieeb.2021.1.1.7

KEY TERMS AND DEFINITIONS

Educational Curricula: Set of contents available to teachers that includes curricula, criteria, fundamentals, methodology and programs to provide students with a comprehensive academic education.

European Higher Education Area (EHEA): Group of countries cooperating to achieve comparable and compatible higher education systems throughout Europe.

Positive Education: Evidence-based educational structures, practices and programs that aim to enhance, well-being, academic achievement, success and flourishing throughout the educational community.

Positive Psychology: Scientific and applied approach to identifying people's strengths and promoting their positive functioning, to determine which paths lead to a better life.

Social and Emotional Competencies: Sets of knowledge, skills and attitudes whose purpose is to achieve the performance of activities with the best level of efficiency and with an ethical moral criterion that tends to solidarity and prosocial behaviour.

Social and Emotional Learning (SEL): Process through which acquire and apply the knowledge, skills, and attitudes to develop healthy identities, manage emotions and achieve personal and collective goals, feel, and show empathy for others, establish, and maintain supportive relationships, and make responsible and caring decisions.

Well-Being: Construct referred to optimal psychological functioning and experience.

Chapter 3

Exploring International Educators' Learning About Local and Global Social Justice in a Virtual Community of Practice

Bima Sapkota
University of Texas Rio Grande Valley, USA

Xuwei Luo
Purdue University, USA

Muna Sapkota
Purdue University, USA

Murat Akarsu
Ağrı İbrahim Çeçen University, Turkey

Emmanuel Deogratias
Sokoine University of Agriculture, Tanzania

Daphne Fauber
Purdue University, USA

Rose Mbewe
https://orcid.org/0000-0003-3894-2186
Purdue University, USA

Fidelis Mumba
David Livingstone College of Education, Zambia

Ram Krishna Panthi
Kathmandu University, Nepal

Jill Newton
Purdue University, USA

JoAnn Phillion
Purdue University, USA

ABSTRACT

In this chapter, the authors report themes that emerged when a cross-cultural team of researchers involved in a virtual international community of practice (Global Social Justice in Education-GSJE) investigated reflections on activities focused on social justice in local and global contexts. The findings suggested that the activities elicited GSJE community members' understandings of the complexities of social justice associated with naming practices, privilege, and the arts within their own and across contexts. The authors discuss implications of the activities to advance diverse educators' understanding of social justice in global and local contexts. They also unpack the opportunities and challenges that resulted from the collaborative research process and the writing of this chapter completed by the international author team comprised of 11 education scholars from seven countries.

DOI: 10.4018/978-1-6684-7813-4.ch003

INTRODUCTION

Many U.S. universities are expanding opportunities for graduate and undergraduate students, including those in teacher education programs, to develop their understanding about the complexities of diversity, intercultural competence, and social justice (DeJaeghere & Cao, 2009; Krajewski, 2011). For example, universities internationalize their curricular activities to foster students' global understanding and intercultural competencies through study abroad programs (Soria & Troisi, 2014). However, study abroad programs are not accessible to all students because of economic constraints, health issues, and family commitments. Thus, creating opportunities for students to engage in intercultural interactions through virtual platforms has become increasingly prevalent (Krajewski, 2011). Studies have demonstrated that U.S. graduate and undergraduate students' interactions with international and intercultural educators is a way to develop their intercultural competencies and awareness of social justice issues (e.g., Sapkota et al., 2022; Slapac et al., 2023; Soria & Troisi, 2014).

Research has also suggested that cross-cultural collaboration involving educators from different countries is beneficial in challenging educators' preconceived conceptions about minority populations (e.g., Ference & Bell, 2004; Wormnæs, 2008). For example, Wormnæs (2008) found that collaboration between teacher educators (i.e., faculty who taught teacher education courses) and pre-service teachers (PSTs) from Norway and Egypt challenged their preconceived beliefs and perspectives about disability and education. International communities of practice with ethnically, linguistically, and racially diverse learners have also been found to be beneficial in advancing U.S. educators' and students' understandings of social justice, equity, and inclusivity globally (Jie & Pearlman, 2018; Sapkota et al., 2022).

In this chapter, the authors report how a virtual, international, intercultural community of practice, Global Social Justice in Education (GSJE), provided graduate and undergraduate students and international educators, many of whom were instructors and students in teacher education programs, from China, Kenya, Nepal, Tanzania, Türkiye, U.S., and Zambia with opportunities to unpack and advance their understandings of social justice. The following research question guided our study: What themes emerged when a cross-cultural team of researchers involved in a virtual international community of practice investigated reflections on activities focused on social justice in local and global contexts?

LITERATURE REVIEW AND THEORETICAL FRAMEWORK

The authors conceptualized GSJE around four frameworks: (a) United Nations 2030 Agenda for Sustainable Development (hereafter referred to as "UN 2030 Agenda") (UN, 2015), (b) Social justice in education (Cazden, 2012; Fraser, 2005), (c) Intercultural competence (Deardorff, 2006, 2011), and (d) Communities of practice (Lave & Wenger, 1991). In the following sections, the authors briefly describe these frameworks and how they guided GSJE and our study. In particular, they present examples on how each framework guided the development of GSJE activities.

United Nations 2030 Agenda for Sustainable Development

The overarching framework guiding the design and implementation of GSJE was the UN 2030 Agenda (UN, 2015), in which the UN proposed an action plan with sustainable goals for eliminating extreme poverty and inequality and securing the planet. The 2023 Agenda consists of the following five areas:

people, planet, prosperity, peace, and partnership; GSJE activities were developed in alignment with these areas. For example, the authors established partnership (the fifth area) with the educators in seven countries when developing and implementing GSJE.

The authors grounded GSJE activities in the UN 2030 Agenda Sustainable Development Goal (SDG) 4 which aims to "ensure inclusive and equitable quality education and promote lifelong learning opportunities for all" (p. 14). The authors developed GSJE as an inclusive learning space for culturally, linguistically, and geographically diverse educators from around the globe to reflect on and advance their understandings of local and global educational social justice issues. GSJE participants represented educators and graduate and undergraduate students from Asia (China, Nepal), Africa (Kenya, Tanzania, Zambia), Europe (Türkiye), and North America (Canada, United States). Thus, the participants had opportunities to discuss social justice and equity issues faced in their local contexts and to discuss similar challenges globally.

Through GSJE activities, the authors explored, discussed, and reflected on gender, racial, linguistic, and social equity. For example, GSJE community members investigated how a person's names highlighted aspects of context and culture. The authors also reflected on the educational implications of these issues. In another activity, they reflected on how our privileges could depend on identities and contexts. Overall, GSJE community members reflected on inclusivity and equity by drawing on examples from local contexts, including reflecting on how our conceptions changed after having opportunities to learn about social justice issues in the global context. Thus, in GSJE the authors worked towards UN 2030 SDG-4, promoting "global citizenship and appreciation of cultural diversity and of culture's contribution to sustainable development" (UN, 2015, p. 17).

Social Justice in Education

The authors grounded their understandings of social justice in education in Cazden's (2012) educational adaptation of Fraser's (2000, 2005) theory in which she proposed three dimensions (i.e., redistribution, recognition, representation) of social justice. Applying these dimensions to an educational context. This author focused on distributing educational resources, identifying cultural heritages, and representing minoritizing groups in decision-making processes. She also described potential ways to create equitable educational opportunities for marginalized populations.

Cazden's (2012) economic dimension (*redistribution*) encompasses the unfair distribution of educational resources and the lack of equal opportunities for all students to access an intellectually rich curriculum designed to cultivate critical and creative thinking in students, extending beyond the imparting of fundamental skills and knowledge. She argues that students who have been historically disadvantaged and had limited access to quality education should be provided with the resources and support necessary to receive equitable educational opportunities. The cultural dimension (*recognition*) addresses the importance of recognizing and valuing the diversity of students' cultural knowledge, history, and heritage within the educational system. In this dimension, she emphasizes the need to incorporate indigenous knowledges, histories, and cultural practices in curricular activities to ensure that all students are represented and valued in educational spaces. Finally, the political dimension (*representation*) is concerned with ensuring that the voices of underrepresented groups are heard and included in educational decision-making processes. Through this dimension, Cazden challenged educational stakeholders to address the issue of power imbalances by ensuring minority groups' representations in decisions that affect their educational experiences.

Several researchers (e.g., Klenowski, 2014; Meaney et al., 2016; Slapac et al., 2023) have utilized Cazden's (2012) or directly, Fraser's (2008, 2009)'s dimensions of social justice to investigate educational opportunities for students. As a result of an analysis of assessment strategies through the lenses of redistribution, recognition, and representation, Klenowski (2014) proposed collaboration with community members in the design of alternative student assessment practices to enhance learning outcomes for Indigenous students in Australia. Similarly, multiple mathematics education teams used Cazden's social justice framework to synthesize research conducted in Australasia between 2012 and 2015. For example, Meaney and colleagues (2016) evaluated the research focused on Indigenous students, noting the disproportionate attention to the redistribution dimension and calling for greater Indigenous community representation in mathematics education research.

In GSJE, all activities, experiences, and discussions were grounded in social justice, with purposeful attention to the economic, cultural, and political dimensions of Cazden's (2012) social justice framework, recognizing their interconnections in educational contexts. As advocated for by Klenowski (2014) and Meaney et al. (2016), the authors intentionally promoted GSJE community members' involvement in and contributions to all aspects of the GSJE experience.

Intercultural Competence

GSJE development and research were also guided by Deardorff's (2006) model of intercultural competence. The model includes the following five components: intercultural knowledge, skills, and attitudes, as well as internal and external outcomes. Intercultural knowledge consists of knowledge of one's identity, culture, and others' world views. A person's abilities to observe, listen to, analyze, communicate, and relate to their own and others' culture indicate their intercultural skills. Intercultural attitudes include a person's openness and curiosity about diverse cultures. She also maintained that intercultural knowledge, skills, and attitudes should be demonstrated in the form of internal outcomes (e.g., being non-judgmental and empathetic towards others' cultural practices) and external outcomes (e.g., demonstrating intercultural knowledge, skills, attitudes, and internal outcomes that are visible to others).

Educators and researchers have used Deardorff's intercultural competence framework in their program development and research. For example, Syahrin et al. (2023) explored how PSTs viewed their ability to communicate and interact with people from different cultures. The researchers used a questionnaire to investigate the participants' intercultural knowledge, skills, and attitudes before and after participation in a virtual exchange program. The findings suggested that the virtual exchange program contributed to increase PSTs' awareness of self, suggesting that such programs have the potential to develop their intercultural competence even without travelling abroad. Krishnan et al. (2022) reported findings from a study that involved a virtual intercultural partnership with an Indian university that enhanced U.S. students' intercultural competence; many participants reported a marked increase in their cultural self-awareness, with heightened recognition of their own cultural norms and biases. Slapac et al. (2023) found that collaborations in global partnership enhanced graduate and undergraduate students' awareness of one another's educational contexts while engaging graduate students (in-service teachers) in self-reflections on global competencies enhanced their global awareness.

Building on these suggestions about the benefits of virtual collaborations between diverse participants, the authors designed GSJE to involve educators from seven different countries, providing a wide range of opportunities to understand cultural differences. In addition, our participants experienced GSJE as an intercultural community of practice in which cultural differences were embraced as opportunities to develop intercultural knowledge. GSJE community members also practiced listening to, observing, and communicating with the diverse community members, which contributed to the development of their intercultural skills. Through several activities, the authors also provided GSJE community members with opportunities to reflect on their empathy and openness toward others' cultural practices, enhancing their intercultural attitudes.

Communities of Practice

When designing GSJE, the authors also incorporated Lave and Wenger's (1991) concept of communities of practice into our virtual, intercultural experience in which participants from the around the globe learned from each other and developed intercultural knowledge, skills, and attitudes. Participants were brought together in the GSJE community of practice with the common purpose of interrogating and reconceptualizing their prior understandings of local and global social justice and aspects of intercultural competence, with attention to meaning, practice, community, and identity (Wenger, 1998). Making meaning is a way of individually and collectively experiencing our professional and personal lives; practice is sharing historical and social resources, frameworks, and perspectives that sustain mutual engagement in action; community includes social configurations in which a common value is shared; identity changes and transforms in the context of the community. GSJE participants had opportunities to reflect on their identities and meaning-making processes through social justice activities.

In a community of practice, the role of the instructor is decentralized (Lave & Wegner, 1991). The relationships among learners in GSJE were built through mutual conversations where power dynamics were intentionally acknowledged and confronted (Patten & Parket, 2017). To achieve this, participants in GSJE were provided with opportunities to share their experiences and reflections, facilitate small and large group discussions, and design and lead activities. The community shared a common purpose of exploring social injustices in local and global contexts; the virtual platform provided a means for the development of this community of practice.

Studies have documented benefits of developing communities of practice for multiple purposes in many contexts. For example, Goncalves et al. (2022) reported that Brazilian physical education teachers developed a community of practice to empower them to confront challenges experienced in their educational environment and to provide professional development to improve their teaching practices. Similarly, Breen (2015) reported that English language teachers used communities of practice as a platform for discussion, sharing resources, and fostering student-teacher interactions. These studies demonstrate the benefits of communities of practice in cultivating supportive relationships, improving professional practices, and working toward common goals. Aligning with these benefits of communities of practice, the authors aimed to provide international educators and students with opportunities to develop relationships with colleagues around the world with the common purpose of exploring educational inequities.

Overall, the UN 2030 Agenda, Cazden's (2012) social justice framework, Deardorff's (2006) theory of intercultural competence, and Lave and Wenger's (1991) communities of practice guided the development and implementation of GSJE. The authors created a virtual community of practice in which members had opportunities to develop and enhance their intercultural competence (i.e., knowledge, skills, and attitudes) and awareness of educational social justice. In the study reported in this chapter, the authors explored the themes that emerged when an international team of researchers involved in the GSJE community investigated reflections on activities focused on social justice in local and global contexts.

METHODS

In Fall 2020, a team of faculty and graduate students at a U.S. university created Global Social Justice in Education (GSJE), a virtual, international, intercultural community of practice through a course offered in the university's teacher education program. GSJE provided U.S.-based graduate and undergraduate students and international educators from China, Kenya, Nepal, Tanzania, Türkiye, and Zambia, many of whom were instructors and students in teacher education programs (e.g., mathematics education, rural education, elementary education), with opportunities to advance their understandings of social justice in educational contexts (Zhou et al., 2022). Many of the educators were faculty members at different universities in those countries while some of them were graduate assistants and PSTs. These educators represented different ethnic and racial backgrounds, including Asian, African, and White. The graduate and undergraduate students enrolled in GSJE as a one-credit course while the international educators received a certificate of participation from the U.S. university. The primary goals of GSJE, grounded in SDG-4 of the UN 2030 Agenda, were to provide opportunities for community members to: (a) develop their intercultural knowledge and cross-cultural communication skills, and (b) understand social justice educational issues in local and global contexts.

GSJE Development and Implementation

In the wake of COVID-19 and postponement of many study-abroad programs, a faculty-student team developed GSJE to continue to provide cross-cultural experiences for students. The authors each contacted colleagues across the globe, most of whom were teacher educators who were faculty in teacher education programs, to invite them to participate in a virtual collaborative exploration of global social justice in education; partners from six countries (China, Kenya, Nepal, Tanzania, Türkiye, Zambia) engaged with us in this experience. The authors established a set of five objectives for the GSJE community: (a) Recognize and navigate personal and professional positions and perspectives, (b) Foster intercultural relationships with educators in other countries, (c) Develop intercultural communication skills, (d) Identify global (non-U.S.) sources of knowledge with attention to the value of South to North knowledge flow, and (e) Understand multiple world views related to social justice issues in education. Throughout the four semester-long iterations of GSJE in 2020-21, these objectives remained consistent. The authors searched for activities to address the objectives, modifying them as needed to serve our audience, and often designed our own activities (see Zhou et al., 2022, for a detailed description of the GSJE curriculum).

The GSJE community met bi-weekly for one-hour online meetings. Prior to each meeting, individuals completed an activity which included a task, along with a set of related questions. The meetings were structured into three sections: (a) whole-group team-building introduction, (b) small-group sharing of activity responses, and (c) whole-group debrief of small-group discussions and summary of cross-cultural learning. In the first section, several community members shared answers to given icebreaker questions to better understand each other's identities and cultures (e.g., what languages have you used or studied? How would you greet someone in one of your languages?) and were reminded about community norms related to inclusivity, mutual respect, and equitable participation. In the second section, community members were assigned to breakout rooms of three to six participants to share their responses to the activity with one another; the authors intentionally created groups that consisted of participants from different countries. In the final section, the groups were brought back together, and a representative from each group summarized highlights from their discussion. The authors concluded with closing thoughts about what was learned across the groups.

After each activity, community members were asked to write an individual reflection guided by the following questions: (1) What did you learn about yourself and/or your culture while doing this activity? (2) What did you learn from other participants and/or their cultures while sharing and discussing this activity? (3) What have you learned about social justice from this activity that you might use in your future work, particularly in educational contexts? (4) What else did you find interesting and/or important that you would like to share? In the final meeting of each semester, the authors looked back on our learning experiences together and looked forward to discussions about the upcoming semester, including community members volunteering to lead activities.

In the Summer 2021 iteration of GSJE, the authors implemented six activities: (1) What's in a Name? (2) Exploring Privilege in International Contexts, (3) Examining Social Justice Through Poetry, (4) Exploring the Role of the Arts in Social Justice in Global Contexts, (5) Investigating Diversity in our Communities, and (6) Spheres of Influence. The authors used the four frameworks to develop these activities (please check the Literature Review and Framework section). In this chapter, the authors report on the analysis of three of these activities which the authors call the Name Activity, the Privilege Activity, and the Arts Activity (see Table 1 for brief activity descriptions and sample questions, and Appendices A-C for complete activities).

Table 1. Summer 2021 GSJE activities

Activity	Activity Description	Sample Activity Questions
Name	Investigate naming practices in families, cultures, and countries with attention to social justice issues.	1. What, if any, is the meaning of your name(s)? In your family? In your country/culture? 2. Is your name gendered or gender neutral? Are most names in your country/culture gendered? 3. What potential social justice issues in education may be related to names?
Privilege	Examine individual and collectives meanings of privilege in personal, professional, and societal contexts.	1. Describe two privileges you have that you consider to be important. 2. Describe two privileges you DO NOT have that you consider to be important or not important. 3. What forms of privilege are most valued in your culture/country?
Arts	Explore the role of the arts (e.g., poetry, music) in expressing and addressing social (in)justices in local and global contexts.	1. Why did you choose to share this particular piece of art? 2. What thoughts did you have when reflecting on the piece? 3. What potential social justice issues are expressed in the piece?

Study Participants, Data Collection, and Analytic Processes

Thirty-five community members attended GSJE meetings in Summer 2021, including faculty representing Canada, U.S., Nepal, China, and Zambia, graduate and undergraduate students, and international educators; the vast majority of GSJE community members were faculty in a teacher education program. Sixteen GSJE members (graduate and undergraduate students and faculty) submitted written responses to the activity questions and/or reflection prompts for at least one of the three activities, and were therefore, participants of the study. This included participants from China (Rui, Yan), Nepal (Barsha, Mamata), Türkiye (Kadri, Musa), the United States (Delaney, Kit, Margot, Monique, Sadie, Sophie, Valerie, Vanessa), and Zambia (Franklin, Gabriel); these pseudonyms were used for reporting findings. The author team engaged as both researchers and participants; the authors attended GSJE meetings and completed activities and reflections. The activities were mandatory for the U.S. students who were enrolled as a course while these were optional for the other community members. The authors utilized the participants' activity responses and reflections from the three activities as our data set. For the description of how the authors structured meetings and activities, see GSJE development and implementation section.

The authors framed their study using interpretive qualitative approaches (e.g., Merriam & Tisdell, 2016). Qualitative research methods were necessary in order to answer the key research question as it allowed the authors to capture the contextual and unique examples, which aligned with the goal of investigating the participants' understanding local and global social justice issues (Ames et al., 2011). The authors used top-down and bottom-up interactive analysis methods (e.g., Chi, 1997) to analyze our data in a three-round process of meaning making (e.g., Smith & Osborn, 2008). In all rounds, the authors followed the iterative process of understanding the context of self and others. In the first round, community members (i.e., participants) independently completed the activity and associated questions (See Table 1 for the questions) in Week 1. In Week 2 GSJE meeting, they shared their activity experience and learned about others' experiences using the breakout room feature of Zoom before coming together as a whole group. In Week 3, they submitted individual reflections on their learning from both their individual and collective experiences. In the process of doing this, they each made sense of their own cultural norms and values and explored how they represented social justice in local and global contexts. Because the participants in this round explored social justice issues in their local context without using any frameworks, this was a bottom-up nature of data analysis.

In the second round, the authors worked in three author teams. Each team used a descriptive coding method (Saldaña, 2016) to identify issues of social justice and aspects of intercultural competence in one of the three activities (i.e., Name, Privilege, Arts). This method also followed a bottom-up approach because the authors identified social justice issues from the participants' reflections, without using any specific frameworks. For example, the authors identified patriarchy, racial discrimination, influence of western culture in the participants' reflections on naming. Afterward, each team met to discuss how community members described social justice in their activity questions and reflections; their findings were recorded in a common template (see Appendix D). Overall, the teams sought to answer: What did the activity elicit from community members about social justice? In this round, the author teams made sense of the community members' experiences and interpretations of cultural self-awareness and worldviews as they related to social justice.

In the third round, a subset of the authors (i.e., B. Sapkota, Luo, M. Sapkota, Newton, and Phillion) reviewed the findings from each author team, noted significant and overarching themes, and synthesized results across the analyses (Peel, 2020). Using the top-down approach, the authors categorized the codes identified from the second round into several overarching themes that were connected with Social Justice in Education (Cazden, 2012) and Intercultural Competence (Deardorff, 2006). For example, using the definition of Cazden's (2012) recognition (i.e., cultural dimension), the authors identify the following theme: Privilege as a complex dynamic context. As such the definition of the cultural dimension of the framework allowed us to identify how our participants' description of cultural aspects were associated with their privilege. The authors then developed parallel structures to report the findings from each activity. In this final round, the authors' meaning making focused on the overall experiences of the community members, including the author team, as they individually and collectively engaged in the development of intercultural competence through the interrogation of social justice in local and global contexts. Whenever possible in reporting the findings, the authors opted to use GSJE community members' own voices rather than feature the voices of the research team; this included attention to the representation of voices of diverse geographic, linguistic, and cultural identities of community members.

FINDINGS

In the following sections, the authors use voices of GSJE community members to illustrate the themes identified by the research team during an exploration of their responses to three activities: (1) what's in a Name? (2) exploring privilege in international contexts, and (3) exploring the role of the arts in social justice in global contexts. The authors describe insights evoked by particular activities, the members' individual experiences and learning as well as their collective learning through small- and whole-group discussions, and local and global aspects of social justice.

What's in a Name?

In the Name Activity (Appendix A), the community members were asked to reflect on their name, its meaning, if either of their parents are represented in their name, who named them, the prevalence of the name in their context, gender inferences of their name, and potential implications for social justice and educational practices. As the research team reviewed GSJE community members' Name Activity and reflections, the authors noted themes related to social justice for naming in various contexts, including: (a) several aspects of patriarchy and gender, and (b) names which may signal other social identities (e.g., race, religion).

Patriarchal and Gender Implications of Naming

Most community members (92%, 12 of 13) who completed the activity reported that they shared their father's last name. One U.S. participant said, "*And of course* I have the same last name as my father." Vanessa, a Latinx U.S. graduate student who was born in the Dominican Republic, shared that her mother's name is also included as part of her last name. The one member whose father's name is not represented noted that she has her mother's last name; however, this name also ultimately represents her patriarchal lineage as it is her grandfather's last name. Several community members mentioned that their matriarchal lineage is represented in their first or middle names (e.g., Monique's middle name is her mother's sister's name).

In addition, community members shared how first names are often gendered, particularly in some contexts; this sometimes leads to social justice issues. For example, Sadie, a White U.S. undergraduate student wrote:

One thing that I learned while discussing this activity [with GSJE community members], is that social justices are not necessarily the same throughout the world. I brought up how assuming someone's gender based on their name could be a social justice issue. And then one of my group members from

Africa [Zambia] brought up that that is not really an issue in Africa. Usually, their names are unisex so assuming someone's gender based on their name is not really an issue.

Two members of the community alluded to trends in naming which address issues related to gender. Barsha, a Nepali graduate student who was also teaching PSTs in the U.S., mentioned this when naming her daughter:

I thought about how my daughter's names can represent our (me and my husband's) identities. My husband and I also had a discussion about her surname. Traditionally, children's surnames represent only their dad's names in Nepal. But I wanted to have my surnames as well in her name. So, we decided to put both of our surnames in her name.

Delaney, a White U.S. PST, described a rationale for using gender-neutral names:

There are a lot of names that are gendered and not gendered in the United States. I think there is a trend among progressive parents to give their children gender neutral names or a first name that is associated with their biological sex and a middle name that is associated with a different biological sex, so that their child can use either name as they get older and figure out their gender identity.

These discussions about the relationships between gender and naming resulted from the activity and reflection prompts and the GSJE small and large group discussions. In addition to gender, several other social identities were highlighted by community members.

Names Signaling Other Social Identities

Beyond names signaling gender, they also often signaled other social identities and potential social inequities. For example, Musa, a Turkish faculty, mentioned that in his context, names can signal both a person's "region and religion." Rui, a Chinese-born independent scholar living in the U.S., also noted that, in China, a name may indicate whether a person is from "the city or the countryside," which has potential social justice implications in terms of opportunities available to them.

Community members most often mentioned social justice issues related to naming associated with race and ethnicity (77%, 10 of 13). These accounts represented multiple perspectives, including personal first-hand experiences, observations of others in their communities, and insights shared in GSJE discussions. Monique, a Black U.S. graduate student and teacher educator, shared her experience:

I believe that names can be strongly connected to culture and can be celebrated. However, we live in a society where discrimination is prevalent. Incidences of hiring and housing discrimination are possible. For example, recently, my friends and I booked an Airbnb location for a friend's wedding in Kentucky. The location was booked but we were recently notified that it was canceled. The hosts mentioned that the location was unavailable during our selection. However, we would have never been able to select the location if this were true. I can sometimes be an optimistic person and believe there could be multiple reasons why this lodging was canceled (i.e., hosts personal affairs or the host mistakenly made the housing available). However, Airbnb now requires you to include an Airbnb profile and list the names of all the expected guests. Therefore, one may question if the hosts just preferred not to have those that appeared to be Black guests. Of course, that is an assumption without credible evidence.

Delaney recounted her observations related to discriminatory practices in her high school:

Within the United States, the idea of 'white-washing' or 'assimilating' names is fairly common, especially within school settings. The idea is that someone with a name that does not sound 'white' has a less likely chance of receiving jobs, scholarships, or other opportunities. Additionally, they are more likely to not be taken seriously within their line of work. To combat this, many people with 'non-white' names choose alternative names to go by in order to fit the expected mold better. For example, at my high school we had many Chinese and Korean students. Most of these students had names that fit their heritage but went by a different 'English' name at school to fit in better. Students were expected to conform to the majority white student population by taking on a name and identity that more closely matched the rest of the student body.

Finally, Kit, a White U.S. PST, described what she learned through conversations with GSJE members as they discussed naming in their contexts:

While sharing this activity, I learned that names convey a sense of privilege among some and are used to discriminate against others. Essentially, an individual's name is his or her identifier. It can convey religion, ethnicity, and otherness. If an individual's name does not conform to cultural norms, he or she may be looked down upon by others. As a result, he or she may have trouble accessing resources such as loans, safe housing, and prime educational opportunities.

As Delaney alluded to in her statement, individuals with non-Western or non-White names often use a different name, either voluntarily or involuntarily. In fact, Barsha reported that she considered the challenges that Americans might have with pronunciation when selecting her daughter's Sanskrit name. In addition, Yan, a Chinese-born graduate student in the U.S., who also goes by "Julia," shared:

Many immigrant students cannot use their own names in class, or are forced to choose an English name. The original intention can be very simple: it is difficult to pronounce their names, which will affect them to make friends, or for the teachers' convenience of calling names. When some students need to give up their original names in order to be fully accepted by the school environment, we can hardly say that the school environment is fair to everyone.

Vanessa described power dynamics related to these decisions about which name to use:

We may marginalize students by not calling someone by their chosen name and asking if they go by something else. This forces students to have to let go of a piece of themselves to accommodate others, sometimes with more power, for example a professor.

Also noting the resulting devaluation of a person's worth, Margot, a White U.S. PST, added that:

The involuntary replacement of someone's name if it is deemed 'too complicated to pronounce' is an erasure of someone's culture and identity. Students' names could continuously be mispronounced resulting in an inequitable educational experience since respect is not upheld for that student. This also does not allow students to feel accepted within the school community.

While recognizing these naming dilemmas, several community members discussed pedagogical strategies for ensuring that all students feel valued in their classroom. Sophie, a White U.S. graduate student, emphasized the importance of getting to know students as individuals to demonstrate respect for social identities. Both Monique and Vanessa stated that they are purposeful in their efforts to look up and write down "phonological pronunciations" and asking students "to say it for me or spell it out… which is incredibly important because names have meaning."

Overall, GSJE community members considered and reported the social justice implications of naming, highlighting how something as seemingly innocuous as a name, can have serious consequences for individuals and groups. Kadri, a Turkish graduate student, summed this up, saying that particular names can even lead to "exclusion from society, interference with the right to life, and restriction of freedoms."

Exploring Privilege in International Contexts

In the Privilege Activity (Appendix B), GSJE community members were asked to reflect on what privilege means to them, privileges that they have or do not have and the importance of those privileges in their context/culture/country, social justice issues related to these privileges, and potential implications for educational practices. The research team identified several themes related to privilege in GSJE community members' activities and reflections, including: (a) describing privilege as a complex, dynamic construct; (b) recognizing privilege as context-specific, based on norms of society and dominant attributes/perspectives; and (c) highlighting the importance of access to education as a significant privilege. In addition, community members proposed strategies to address privilege in educational contexts.

Privilege as a Complex, Dynamic Construct

The definition of privilege that was provided by Vanessa was representative of the GSJE community members' conceptualizations: "To me, privilege is about unearned advantages that are awarded to us by society based on our dominant identities. It means getting ahead simply because you are a member of a particular group (racial, ethnic, gender, etc.)." Yan expanded on Vanessa's definition, providing a metaphor related to fish and water to describe privilege:

Ask a fish what water is, and you'll get no answer. Water simply is. Fish take it for granted. The fish in the water can't actually feel the importance of water or even the existence of water. People who really care about privilege are those fish without water.

Kadri, Delaney, and Valerie further extended the conceptualization by highlighting the complex, evolving nature of privilege. Kadri emphasized the various contexts in which privilege can be present:

Privilege does not come only with birth but can also be gained later; it is a kind of opportunity or advantage that makes one think that he/she has it and that no one else has it. These privileges can occur in different areas of life, education, work, family, and social life.

Delaney pointed out the potential of an individual's privilege to change across time:

To me, the word privilege means an advantage someone has that impacts the person's ability to navigate through life. It can be something that someone is born with (race, gender, sex, sexual orientation) but I think it can also be earned or happen by chance (scholarships, industry connections, disability status).

Valerie reported that, as she reflected on her "multiple identities through intersectionality," she realized that she often experiences discrimination based on her race and gender, stating, "Being Black in America brings its hardships. The authors often experience racism and discrimination. Being a woman also can be challenging in America. Women encounter misogyny in the workplace and less pay. As a Black woman, I experience both." However, she described privileges in other areas:

By being Christian, I do not have to worry about being harassed due to my religion. Christianity is deemed the religion of America by many. Similarly, being a heterosexual, cis-gendered person shields me from experiencing the injustices the LGBTQ+ community experiences. I'm not judged for being in a relationship with a man because heterosexual, cis-gendered relationships are considered the norm in society.

The collection of these community member quotes highlights the complex, dynamic nature of privilege, including its nuanced connections to locality, temporality, and intersectionality, and how an individual's level of awareness is dependent upon their status. This illustrates how discussions related to complex constructs such as privilege are enriched in communities of practice in which diverse global perspectives are present.

Privilege as Context-Specific, Based on Norms of Society and Dominant Attributes and Perspectives

All 14 community members who completed the activity discussed the contextual nature of privilege. Gabriel, for example, described various aspects of privilege specific to his home country of Zambia:

[The] privilege to have a green National Registration Card [NRC]. This is an important privilege for Zambians as it allows the Zambians access to national natural resources like the mighty Victoria Falls and other restricted places….The Green NRC is an identity for Zambians which grants us such chances as voting to select our leaders, and also vote in a referendum to alter our Constitution….Free movement – this is another valuable privilege, especially that back in the day during colonial rule, one was required to carry a pass known as "Chitupa" whenever they traveled even within the country.

However, he credited Zambian society for its value of entrepreneurship in which individuals are encouraged to make their "own business plans without restriction." In addition, he discussed areas in which many Zambians are lacking privilege, including access to unrestricted international travel and freedom of speech. Similarly, Rui noted limited freedom of speech as a social justice issue related to privilege in China.

Mamata discussed several aspects of privilege in Nepal, asserting that "privilege is not only the state of being provided with special rights; it is equally the preference that people get on the basis of social constructions such as gender, caste, and class." She and Monique also noted certain privileges associated with skin color and tone in their countries. Monique shared:

In the United States, Whites and those of lighter complexions are viewed as more privileged. Historically, Whites have had more access to opportunities and resources (i.e., bank loans, quality education, respect) than persons of color.…I also believe persons of color of lighter complexions have a privilege. They may be viewed to be more White passing and more attractive than darker skinned minoritized people groups. This aspect was notable during slavery since lighter individuals were typically house servants. However, we must consider how this is shown subtly throughout our society. In recent decades, our society has noted the subtleties of the preference for White or close to White color tones. Some examples include but are not limited to pantyhose, crayons, make-up, lead singers in female groups, and lead actors.

Acknowledging some progress, she added that "Recently, due to the documented social injustice of George Floyd, more Whites are recognizing their privilege." Vanessa highlighted additional forms of privilege in the United States, including gender ("men are still making decisions about women's bodies and men are paid more than women"), socio-economic status ("the USA is built on capitalism"), and professional discipline:

I learned that the notion that some fields (e.g., STEM) carry more privilege than others transcends national borders…I had always considered that a very U.S centric issue but it is not limited to this country. In reflecting on my experience this is evident in the majors that our international students from specific countries tend to be drawn to predominantly STEM careers. As an educator and someone who holds a liberal arts degree, I wish to live in a world in which the arts are deemed as important as the sciences.

Building on Vanessa's observations, Kit noted that privilege also operates at the intersection of gender and professional careers in the U.S.; this is particularly true in STEM fields which are still primarily dominated by men.

In this activity, community members shared specific aspects of privilege within their own context and society; although some of these were particular to the context (e.g., National Registration Card in Zambia), many forms of injustice related to privilege were entrenched in multiple countries (e.g., freedom of speech, skin color). In addition, group discussions revealed intersectional privileges affiliated with dominant attributes (e.g., men in STEM careers).

Access to Education as Privilege

GSJE community members from multiple countries highlighted access to educational opportunities as a significant privilege. Conceptualizing privilege as complex and context specific as described in the two previous sections, Barsha shared her experiences with language as a key component of educational privilege:

To me, privilege is always relative - you are more privileged than some people and less privileged than other groups. Back home [in Nepal], I felt I was one of the privileged kids because I could afford a good education. Also, my first language was a medium of communication in most educational institutions. But after coming to the U.S., I began thinking I was less privileged than most of my colleagues because I could not speak in English as fluently as they, which limited many of my opportunities.

Two GSJE community members from China highlighted other aspects of educational privilege that they experienced, contrasting urban/suburban and public/private schooling. Yan expressed:

As a student who grew up in a capital city, I have gained more educational resources and opportunities than those who grew up in the suburbs. At the same time, because our province is an advanced educational province, the number of research universities is far more than in other provinces.

She questioned the equity issues inherent in discrepancies related to disproportionate levels of government funding, asking why "suburban students do not have the same educational opportunities as those living in urban contexts." She also mentioned the unfair advantage that these privileges afford students in terms of high-stakes national examinations, resulting in over-representation of urban students in universities. In addition to urban/suburban inequities in China, Rui highlighted the socio-economic aspects of educational privilege, saying that "the children or the parents can choose public or private school depending on their financial situation."

Several other GSJE community members reported that, in their countries, educational privilege often leads to other privileges, including vital educational opportunities that impact the quality and quantity of life experiences and ultimately leads to financial stability. Two Turkish educators mentioned educational access as a privilege. For example, Kadri explained:

It is important to receive scholarships to go to university. Nowadays, many students cannot continue their education [in Türkiye] because of financial difficulties of his/her family. Thanks to my full scholarship, I had a very different opportunity and achieved a successful life and hope to continue my education.

Gabriel addressed educational privilege in his context, highlighting a challenge in accessing professional opportunities, saying:

In Zambia, for one to hold an official position in government, one must have a Grade 12 (GCE) Certificate or equivalent. This of late has become a social injustice because other people have other qualifications higher than the GCE Certificate such as a bachelor's degree or even a PhD, but all these qualifications are worth nothing without the GCE certificate and holders of such are sidelined as they cannot be parliamentarians or ministers.

Vanessa, whose family immigrated from the Dominican Republic to the United States, highlighted multiple aspects of educational privilege:

Through the privilege activity, I developed more self-awareness about my own privileged identities. Specifically, I learned that I am hyper aware of my educational privilege due to the fact that I hold two degrees and am currently in pursuit of a terminal degree, as well as my privilege that comes with being a United States citizen. As an immigrant to this country, I often reflect on how grateful I am to have had the opportunity to pursue education in a manner that my home country of the Dominican Republic would not have been able to offer me....I am now in the 15% of Latinos in the United States that hold a Master's Degree, and that privilege is something I hold proudly because I could have had a very different life had my parents not decided to immigrate to this country and put all their finances towards my siblings' and my education.

However, Vanessa, along with several others, also pointed out the discrepancies in educational quality and opportunities in different contexts in the U.S., saying:

Based on the economic status of an area, some schools in the country [U.S.] have no access to good learning materials and this inequality and inequity in the basic education of learners in disadvantaged schools is distorted, which has a lifelong impact on their academic life.

U.S.-born citizens Monique, Sadie, and Sophie echoed Vanessa's concerns emphasizing that all children should have access to high-quality education. For example, Sadie noted, "I think the big thing is that only certain groups have the privilege to quality education [in the U.S.]. Everyone has the privilege to be educated. But not everyone will have a quality education." Sophie highlighted particular aspects of quality education that she had access to (i.e., "terrific teachers," "fully funded schools"), noting that not all children have these privileges.

Given the focus of GSJE and the professional roles of the community members, it is not surprising that educational privilege was mentioned by all members, including multiple aspects of educational opportunities related to their specific contexts. Language, geographic location, lasting impacts of colonial systems, citizenship, socio-economic status represent some factors that were described in the activities, discussions, and reflections of community members.

Strategies to Address Privilege in Educational Contexts

In the Privilege Activity reflection, the authors asked the GSJE community members, "How might you use what you learned from this activity in your future work, particularly in educational contexts?" They responded in a variety of ways, including both awareness and action strategies. For example, Kit explained:

As a future educator, I plan on implementing what I have learned in the classroom. I now understand that individuals from different backgrounds experience different forms of privilege. I also understand that some individuals are clearly more privileged than others. This understanding will help me to avoid making snap judgments about my students and colleagues. In other words, it will help me to treat others with a greater sense of empathy because I will be able to recognize that not all individuals have experienced the same type of advantages that I have throughout my life.

In her response, she mentioned both privilege *awareness* and *action* strategies. First, she cautioned that educators should "avoid making snap judgments" about their students and colleagues, as individuals from "different backgrounds experience different forms of privilege." She also suggested use of an action strategy; that is, "treat others with a greater sense of empathy." Other community members also proposed awareness and action strategies.

Privilege Awareness Strategies

Several community members highlighted the importance of privilege awareness, including the range of privileges across students. For example, Delaney warned teachers to "make sure not to make assumptions about the privileges that students have. On the surface, students can look like they have a good, privileged life but assuming that without any evidence results in students being left behind." Sadie supported this notion, stating:

It [Privilege Activity] is also a great reminder for me as a teacher to continue to understand that not every student has the same privileges at home as other students. For example, access to WIFI, not every household may have WIFI. So that needs to be taken into consideration.

Monique offers additional insights into privilege awareness particularly in the context of COVID-19:

Specifically, as educators, we should be more cognizant of our privilege and the diversity of privilege in our learning environments. Some learners may be more privileged in their prior education background, knowledge, and skillsets. Recently, we observed privilege during the pandemic for K-12 students. Some students were able to be placed in daycare or have parents work from home. Others might have experienced their parents laid off from their jobs, working extended hours as essential workers, or parents taking on alternative work such as becoming a Door Dash delivery driver to make ends meet. We saw schools being expected to provide more resources for students without home internet resources...So, privilege is not something I think we can escape. It must be considered because there will always be someone that does not have the same privilege as another.

Teachers can only know how privilege impacts students' lives in the ways mentioned by Sadie and Monique by heeding advice offered by Sophie: "It is important to listen, and it is equally important to let each and every student feel that you consider them important." Sophie's privilege awareness leads her to the privilege action of listening to students.

Privilege Action Strategies

GSJE community members from several countries emphasized the importance of acknowledgement of and attention to students' identities when implementing privilege actions. Valerie committed to:

Using the privileges that I do have to be an ally with those who do not have the same privileges I do. Within an educational context, I will use my voice to speak up for students who may encounter difficulties due to their religion, sexual identity, and native language.

Mamata (Nepal) and Yan (China) echoed this need for advocacy for particular populations of students. Mamata stated that she tries to "figure out the privileged group in the classroom setting" and "encourage ethnic minority students" so that all students receive a high-quality educational experience. Focusing on advocacy related to the gender of her students, Yan said: "As a woman, I can set a good example and let more girls in the class cherish learning opportunities." Sophie proposed three privilege actions that address the needs of learners based on their individual identities:

First, I should look at each student as a unique individual and try not to label the student in any manner or form. Second, I should give each student the opportunity to express themselves and question me. Third, I should impart my enthusiasm for teaching to all the students by attempting to find the best learning path for each one.

Also, appreciating the importance of students' uniqueness, Sadie and Vanessa suggested using modified versions of the Privilege Activity with their own students. For example, Vanessa stated:

I really liked this activity and have done something similar with my own students. I use a social identity privilege chart that asks students to identify their own identities that they are most aware of, the ones they are not (don't think about often), and the ones that do and do not afford them advantages. Oftentimes my students have not been asked to think about themselves in this way before and by the end of the activity can see how regardless of who they are they all hold privileged identities AND marginalized identities. This activity [Privilege Activity] provided a set of debrief questions that can expand on the discussion of my activity, particularly in how it connects privilege to their cultural group. I enjoyed bridging those two things because culture can strongly dictate what a person sees as a privilege and what they may not. Additionally, this activity takes things one step further and asks us to reflect on social justice issues related to privilege which in my opinion is just as important as cultural connections.

In our analysis, the authors noted that privilege awareness strategies and privilege action strategies, although distinct in some ways, were often overlapping and interconnected as awareness seemed a necessary precursor to action. As an ally, awareness is only the beginning and impact arises only as that awareness leads to action.

Exploring the Role of the Arts in Social Justice in Global Contexts

In the Arts Activity (Appendix C), GSJE community members were asked to share a piece of art (e.g., literature, poetry, music, dance, painting) associated with social justice. They were asked to describe why they chose this artifact, the related social justice issues, and potential implications for educational practices. Twelve GSJE community members submitted the activity and/or reflection; six members shared poetry, two shared songs, two shared visual arts, and two discussed the arts generally without reference to a particular form. Many social justice issues were represented in these artifacts, including racial disparity and gender inequities; issues related to equity vs. equality, and agency of community members were also discussed. Several themes emerged from an examination of members' responses, including: (a) utilizing the powerful nature and reach of art to influence social justice; (b) interrogating social identities through reflection on the arts; and (c) providing artistic experiences in schools to cultivate belonging, agency, and hope.

Utilizing the Powerful Nature and Reach of Art to Influence Social Justice

Several GSJE community members highlighted the power of art to reach and inspire a broad audience. For example, Barsha described the impact of art on social activism and change in Nepal:

I feel art is a powerful part of social movements. In Nepal, people use many songs, poems, and dramas during political and social movements. People who were not initially interested in those movements often participated because of several forms of art that they enjoyed including songs and dramas.

Another Nepali community member, Mamata, echoed these ideas, adding: "While doing the activity, I learned how art carries the issue of equality through its representations….as art draws the attention of the masses, it has the potential to promote social justice." In the U.S. context, Kit selected the song "This Is America" by Donald Glover (https://www.youtube.com/watch?v=VYOjWnS4cMY) because it "starkly highlights the social consequences of race in society; specifically, the disparities between Black and White Americans regarding socioeconomic status and discrimination," adding that "social justice issues can be, and often are, addressed in modern pop culture." Gabriel, a PST in Zambia, highlighted gender as an important social justice issue presented in a poem written by his niece:

Girl Child by Chibuye Kuheza

Girl Child Girl Child, You Educate One You Educate the World.
Now Girl Child Go Forward
You Are Released from The Terrors of The Night
Yours Is a Life of Brightness
The Darkness Has Turned to Dawn
The Dreams You Hold Within Your Heart
Allow Them to Come Forward
They Have Been Nourished with The Water Of Life.

He shared his reflection on her poem:

I thought and felt that the education of the female gender is something which is of paramount importance to the development of any country, especially considering my country, Zambia, and art is one of those tools that can be used to deliver this dream to the masses….Secondly, the use of this piece of art also shows that poetry has become one of the tools that is used in conjunction with dances and songs as well as drama to disseminate information to the masses about basically any crosscutting issue in Zambia.

As illustrated by Chibuye's poem, the arts can elicit imagination and emotions, and nurture intimate connections. Also demonstrating the emotional power of the arts, Vanessa shared several poems by Rupi Kaur from her 2017 book, "The Sun and her Flowers," that highlighted experiences of immigrant women:

Last week's class reminded me of these specific poems on the immigrant experience as well as the experience of many women when it comes to fighting for equality and social justice. This author is one of my personal favorites because she speaks truth to power and writes from the heart, letting her audience experience her thoughts very intimately.

Valerie more broadly summarized the power of art, stating: "Art is a form of expression. It allows one to show others who they are, what they think, and how they see the world." In addition to its power to evoke emotional reactions and actions, art also has the ability to deliver impactful social justice messages to the masses in nuanced ways, often implicitly rather than explicitly. For example, Yan, selected a Chinese painting:

The following painting won many national awards in China because of its advanced idea: integration. After glancing over hundreds of images about fairness and justice, I felt heavy because many works reflect the sad reality. However, the picture I chose and posted is like a dream. Rather than revealing the current situation, the painter provides us with an image of an ideal future. The different races of people dancing together implies a harmonious life.

Yan shared the painting's implicit message related to a dream of diversity and integration. Similarly, Franklin highlighted the use of arts as "powerful tools in addressing social injustices through the use of satire" in Zambia, adding that: "Direct criticism is not effective. Satire can be used in poems, songs, plays, and short stories."

Using music, poetry, and visual arts, GSJE community members reflected on the power of art to impact a broad and diverse audience through the elicitation of human emotions (e.g., empathy, outrage, sadness) to inspire people to demand and enact change. They also expressed the value of diversity and called for equitable treatment of all people regardless of race, gender, and/or immigrant status.

Interrogating Social Identities Through Reflection on the Arts

GSJE community members also used poetry and songs to draw attention to social justice related to particular identities (e.g., gender, race, immigrant status, socio-economic status [SES]). Vanessa reflected on her experiences as an immigrant woman of color:

In this activity, I was able to reflect on my own preferences in art and poetry. I tend to gravitate towards authors who speak to injustice and experiences of minoritized individuals. Rupi Kaur, for me, despite her being Indian American, I am able to relate to her on a deep level. She is an immigrant as well and has a broad understanding of what it feels like to be at the intersection of being a woman and an immigrant...I thought a lot about my own immigrant experience as a woman of color... The issues expressed relate to women's equality and immigration. They demonstrate the need for society to develop empathy for immigrants and see them from an asset-minded place instead of from a deficit-minded one and highlight issues of gender equality.

Two Zambian scholars also highlighted women's experiences in their country and described the need for empathy. Franklin shared a Swahili song "Isambo Lyamfwa (Meeting after Burial)" by Glorious Band (https://youtu.be/3lfYtXn8MQE) that described the need for support for widows as they navigate cultural traditions after the death of their husbands. Gabriel explained his rationale for selecting the poem written by his niece (see above) as he empathized with the plight of his female students:

Firstly, Gender equality is the main issue presented by the poem... I chose to share this piece as it taps into the sad old scenario where the girl child was not perceived as an educable being but simply a future housewife and highlights the use of art in education.

Delaney's selected poem echoed concerns about girls in U.S. schools, suggesting that money spent on girls' education is a "huge waste," whereas investment in the education of boys is a wiser use of funds given their "potential." In addition to gender issues in education, Delaney and Kit highlighted other school funding inequities related to race and SES:

I think within the piece, there is a lot of talk about money and its relation to education. This is related to social justice because students in poor areas have less funding than those living in rich areas. This can result in overcrowding, not enough teachers, and a low selection of extracurriculars and other types of opportunities… That mindset further entrenches the inequalities that the poor students face in their access to a quality education. (Delaney)

I chose the song "This Is America" by Donald Glover. In schools across the nation, African American, American Indian, Latino and Southeast Asian groups frequently underperform academically compared to Caucasian and other Asian-American students. Often, minority students face unequal access to educational resources and face bias from their peers and educators alike. As the song implies, minority citizens must contend against institutional discrimination daily and are therefore disadvantaged compared to others. (Kit)

The use of art to facilitate reflection on social identities (e.g., gender, race, SES) was emphasized by many GSJE community members. They intentionally selected artifacts that brought attention to inequities and injustices experienced by members of particular social groups. Although these poems and songs broadly address these issues, each community member brought their own perspective to bear on particular injustices. These revelations inspired them to utilize artistic experiences with students in their future teaching.

Providing Artistic Experiences in Schools to Cultivate Belonging, Agency, and Hope

Given that GSJE community members were all educators, many of them related artistic experiences to opportunities for students in schools. Most members suggested curricular initiatives and pedagogical approaches to integrating arts in educational settings. Reflecting on Native American poetry that she shared with the community, Sophie stated: "Writings from Native Americans ought to be included in K-12 curriculum as well as the writings of recent/past immigrants, African Americans, and Latinos such that children can all learn from and about everyone." Vanessa also shared poetry and underscored its curricular potential:

I think these poems [from Rupi Kaur] demonstrate that how the authors teach our students about the immigrant experience matters tremendously. It can help create more understanding and open-minded citizens. I also believe that using art in the classroom can bring about meaningful discussions about social justice and the messages our society sends us. I love the concept of the hidden curriculum - what's not always intended to be taught, but still is. I think there's a lot of that happening in art too…Students pick up on important issues in our society through various forms of art. Art can represent not only mainstream perspectives and it's important for all students to see themselves and feel represented not just as individuals but their experiences as well.

Kit and Valerie also embraced the use of art in school curriculum in their future teaching, emphasizing its ability to nurture students' sense of belonging and attention to social justice:

I believe that incorporating art activities will enable me to more effectively address social justice issues revolving around race and discrimination in my future classroom. As a Caucasian and privileged individual, I recognize that I cannot fully understand nor relate to the experiences of my students who face entrenched prejudice on a daily basis. It is important to openly discuss these issues in the classroom to create a safe and productive learning environment. I now understand that modern art and media are fantastic ways to introduce and capture the experiences of those who face social injustice. (Kit)

As an educator, I want my students to feel comfortable and safe enough to freely express themselves. I think art is a great activity that allows them to do so. I would like to incorporate art into my classroom, whether that be drawing, painting, or poetry. This will allow my students and I to get to know each other better. Giving students the opportunity to show their authentic selves can produce a healthy academic environment. (Valerie)

Gabriel highlighted the promise of art to enhance curricular experiences for students, saying:

Art has been used to educate the masses and hence it is worth noting that it is one effective mode of teaching in some countries if not all, especially where learning is boring for the pupils, and a spice has to be added for them to learn. Art is the all-in-one spice as it can be used to express various ideas and feelings like happiness, sorrow, appreciation, and grief... I learnt that art can be used in many ways to teach learners as it reaches out to the soul rather than just the mind.

Sadie also acknowledged the promise of art to inspire and empower children:

As I was looking through different poems, one stood out to me the most. Children are so important in this world, and as a teacher it is important to reassure kids that they can make a change and that they can do their share in making this world a better place.

GSJE community members discussed the curricular and pedagogical potential of art to expose students to diverse messages and voices and create spaces for students to see themselves and others. These strategies are important to nurture a safe and productive learning environment that broadens perspectives, inspires change, and builds community. Art, in touching the soul, creates a sense of belonging and the agency to impact change.

As GSJE members discussed social justice across cultures through artistic perspectives, they shared what they learned through a personal exploration of their own artifact, and what they learned from others about the power of art in different countries. Social justice issues revealed in artistic forms (e.g., gender, wealth inequality) were often context-specific in their particularities and yet transcended contexts as they were present in multiple countries. In the Arts Activity, community members recognized the power of poetry, music, and visual arts to inspire a dream for a more just world.

CONCLUSION AND IMPLICATIONS

In this study, the authors identified themes that emerged when a cross-cultural team of researchers involved in a virtual international community of practice investigated reflections on activities focused on social justice in local and global contexts. The authors reported how three activities (i.e., Name, Privilege, and Arts) provided opportunities for Chinese, Nepali, Tanzanian, Turkish, U.S, and Zambian educators to reflect on and share their personal and professional educational experiences, relating them to experiences of other community members. The activities elicited members' understandings of the complexities of social justice revealed in examinations of naming practices, privilege, and the arts, within their own and across contexts. In the following sections, the authors first discuss the use of multiple frameworks that enhanced the GSJE experience (i.e., UN 2030 Agenda [UN, 2015], Social Justice in Education [Cazden, 2012], Intercultural Competence [Deardorff, 2006], and Communities of Practice [Lave &Wenger, 1991]). The authors then describe the unanticipated potential of relatively simple activities to elicit rich cross-cultural interactions and deeper understandings of country-specific social justice issues in relation to the broader global contexts. The authors also highlight the implications of these activities for educational and instructional purposes. Finally, the authors conclude by reporting the implication of our study by focusing on the opportunities and challenges experienced by our international research group's collaboration to design and disseminate the study.

Throughout this section of the chapter, the authors identify and discuss the uniqueness of GSJE and the theoretical frameworks, and the potential of cross-cultural collaborations to enhance the literature on telecollaboration in global teacher education. Voices of participants engaged in these kinds of projects are seldom featured in the current literature in the ways that the authors described from design of the course and project to conceptualizing the research, analyzing findings, and developing themes and implications. The authors argue that this is a much-needed contribution to advance global social justice in education broadly and in teacher education specifically.

Realizing the Potential of Multiple Frameworks to Enhance Virtual Communities

The multiple frameworks used in GSJE set the stage for the community experience. The overarching framework, the UN 2030 Agenda (UN, 2015), inspired us to develop a virtual community of practice with the goal of understanding social justice and equity in the global context. The authors aligned the three activities investigated in this study with the UN 2030 SDG-4, which advocates for inclusivity and equitable quality education for all. As reported in the findings, GSJE community members reflected on and discussed how racial, gender, and ethnic identities are perceived in educational spaces. In addition, they developed a global perspective about equity and social justice, which aligns with the UN 2030 goal of promoting global citizenship and broad goals for the preparation of future teachers around the world. For example, community members identified patriarchy as a global social justice issue embedded in naming practices.

The Social Justice in Education (Cazden, 2012; Fraser, 2008, 2009) framework also guided GSJE development and study. Through the prompts in all activities, community members reflected on local and global social justice issues, resulting in enhanced understandings of the three dimensions of social justice in education (i.e., redistribution, recognition, representation). For example, the Privilege Activity elicited community members' understandings of the educational implications of the redistribution dimension. As such, they identified access to quality education as one of their privileges and acknowledged that these privileges often resulted from unfair distribution of economic resources. In the Naming Activity, they also increased knowledge related to the recognition dimension as they reflected on how naming practices are rooted in gender inequity and patriarchy in many cultures. Several community members highlighted recent changes in naming practices that are beginning to address this issue. The Art Activity elicited community members' conceptions of the representation dimension. For example, they discussed how providing artistic experiences in schools has the potential to cultivate students' agency as they recognize their power to make changes in their world.

Deardorff's (2006, 2011) intercultural competence model also guided our activities and research. Through our activity and reflection prompts, the authors invited community members to explore their own identities and cultures. Our activities elicited community members' understandings of cultural worldviews and resulted in external outcomes that were observable in their communications during meetings and reflections. In the Name Activity, they recognized that names and naming practices signal social and cultural identities, including location, religion, race, and gender. The Privilege Activity contributed to develop the community members' cultural worldview as they reflected on the dynamic and complex nature of privilege that is based on norms of society and culture. In the Art Activity, community members selected and shared personally meaningful poetry, songs, and paintings, thus promoting openness and curiosity about others' cultures. In one example, Gerald shared a poem written by his young niece about the barriers faced by girls in Zambia; this intimate cross-cultural bonding experience resulted in member's reflections on girls' challenges in their own contexts.

The authors developed GSJE as an intercultural community of practice (Lave & Wenger, 1991). The community members experienced different levels of participation ranging from attending meetings to creating and facilitating GSJE activities; these participation levels evolved over time as members who all began as outsiders became more comfortable and developed an enhanced sense of belonging within the community. GSJE gradually became a shared safe space, with collectively established norms, to interrogate ideas and personal and professional experiences. The consistent common purpose of developing complex and nuanced understandings of local and global social justice in education and the explicit acknowledgement of power dynamics contributed to the flourishing of the GSJE community.

Overall, the use of multiple frameworks in GSJE provided community members with opportunities to reflect on the multifaceted relationships between identities, culture, and social justice in local and global educational contexts. The four frameworks described above collectively guided us to establish partnerships with diverse educators, develop a community in which the authors strived for everyone to feel welcomed, respected, and valued, and enhance diverse participants' understandings of local and global social justice. In addition, the frameworks collectively lead to the formulation of the guiding research question for this study. Overall, in the GSJE community and this study, the authors worked toward increasing global understanding and promoting a more just world. This set of frameworks provide lenses for PSTs to develop vocabulary to describe their experiences and position them in relation to the experiences of others.

Implications of Harnessing Powerful Impacts From Seemingly Simple Activities

One of the most surprising aspects of the GSJE experience for the leaders was how the questions asked in a relatively simple activity (e.g., Name Activity, see Appendix A) could lead to such rich, nuanced, complex discussions that revealed unique aspects of contexts and yet, at the same time, revealed universal and global aspects of culture, equity, and social justice.

The authors were purposeful in maintaining the simplicity of the GSJE activities to ensure that they were relevant and relatable to each community member's context and culture. The simplicity of the activities allowed for in-depth small and large group discussions because every member could share examples and experiences from their own countries. For example, every member could reflect on the meaning of their names, naming practices, and social justice issues associated with naming practices. They acknowledged that the activities provided them with opportunities to reflect on and analyze issues of equity and social justice that they had not explored prior to their participation in GSJE.

Because each community member could share examples from their local context, the GSJE activities provided participants with opportunities to expand their conceptions of equity from a local to a shared global perspective. For example, many members shared their privileges related to racial identities. However, they had different experiences with and understandings of race; U.S. participants reflected on privileges given to White versus Black populations while Nepali educators reflected on privileges given to populations from different castes. In addition, our prompts in the Privilege Activity elicited discussions about different types of social norms that determined privileges of the participants, ranging from privileges associated with a national identity card in Zambia to privileges related to geography (e.g., suburban vs. urban) in China. In the Art Activity, members from several countries (Nepal, U.S., Zambia) highlighted how the emotional, personal, and inspiring characteristics of art empower those who create it and those who experience it to recognize inequities and injustices and challenge them to contribute to positive changes. They also reflected on the educational implications of arts in both K-12 and university levels to develop student agency and voice. These examples illustrate how the simplicity of the activities often generated collective understandings of social justice that enabled GSJE members to move beyond their previous locally focused conceptions. These social justice-focused activities have the potential to provide opportunities for PSTs to reflect on, share their own experiences and relate them to the experiences of others from backgrounds different than their own in their teacher education programs.

GSJE Community Opportunities and Challenges

Given the GSJE team's extensive international experience, the authors were not surprised to encounter challenges in facilitating a virtual, cross-cultural community of practice across seven countries. In fact, the authors anticipated a messy experience but knew that, in the end, in spite of the complexity, the learning of the community members would be worth it. In this section, the authors briefly summarize the challenges and our efforts to mitigate them and end with the rich opportunities experienced by GSJE community members. In addition, the authors unpack the opportunities and challenges that resulted from the collaborative research process and the writing of this chapter completed by our international author team comprised of 11 education scholars from seven countries.

Here, the authors discuss two major categories of challenges, those associated with GSJE community meetings and those related to the research process, recognizing that several of them occur in both contexts. In the GSJE community meetings, the authors faced challenges due to multiple time zones, unstable internet connections, and cultural and linguistic differences. Similar challenges were also identified by other researchers such as, Slapac et al. (2023). First, finding an appropriate time for meetings proved to be an almost insurmountable problem. China and the U.S. have a 12-hour difference, so accommodating these two countries limited the participation of some geographic regions. Our community members' willingness and flexibility to participate in GSJE meetings mitigated the challenges due to time differences. For example, Chinese community members attended meetings in the evening whereas U.S. participants attended at 6, 7, or 8 am, depending on their time zone.

Second, the authors faced technological challenges related to internet connectivity during the meetings. Members from several different countries had inconsistent internet connections which limited their ability to participate actively in small- and large-group discussions. To overcome these challenges, the authors video recorded our meeting sessions and shared accessible links with the community. Indeed, some members missed our meetings but later watched the recordings and shared their written reflections. The authors also offered small stipends to international community members to improve, when possible, their internet reliability.

The third challenge related to GSJE meetings involved cultural and linguistic differences. As English was the only shared language among GSJE community members, it served as our medium of communication. This decision benefitted some community members, especially monolingual English speakers, and created potential barriers for others, often bilingual and trilingual members whose native language was not English, in fully participating in discussions. The authors addressed these challenges by explicitly discussing and collectively establishing community norms. At the beginning of each meeting, the authors reminded community members to be aware of potential cultural differences and linguistic challenges as they were interacting with one another, to encourage all community members to contribute to the conversations, and to be respectful and empathetic in their discussions. Collective efforts to mitigate these anticipated and unexpected communication challenges served to unite the community as the authors strived to value and include all GSJE community members.

The second category of challenges was associated with the complexities of the research process. First, the research team (i.e., authors of this chapter) came from different disciplinary backgrounds, and therefore, had different conceptions about what research is and what is entailed in doing it. Second, the research team members had different levels of experience, ranging from students with no formal research experience to professors with many years of experience. This diversity of research backgrounds gave less-experienced members an opportunity to learn. At the same time, the perspectives of those less entrenched in the conventions of research often brought creative insights for consideration. These challenges led us to purposefully organize research teams with members with diverse backgrounds and varying levels of research experience.

Although the authors experienced many challenges while engaging in the GSJE community and research, opportunities far outweighed challenges. In fact, even the process of collectively confronting the challenges described above resulted in intercultural problem-solving opportunities. When reflecting on the myriad additional opportunities, the authors were drawn back to the original GSJE goals and inspired by how our findings provided evidence of movement toward these goals during the community meetings and research. Therefore, the authors claim that GSJE community members actively engaged in recognizing and navigating personal and professional positions and perspectives, fostering intercultural relationships with educators in other countries, developing intercultural communication skills, identifying global sources of knowledge, and understanding multiple world views related to social justice issues in education. The educators from around the globe collectively faced the challenges inherent in the GSJE multicultural virtual community of practice and learned from one another as they actively engaged in finding solutions to these challenges. These experiences also proved particularly beneficial for future teachers as they will likely navigate linguistic, cultural, logistical, and technological challenges in their future classrooms. The PSTs, as GSJE community members, participated in confronting and solving these problems in real time during the meetings.

Our findings also indicate that international participants' collaborative explorations led to recognition of the complexity of social justice issues and their educational implications, extending the conversation about how a virtual community of practice has the potential to enhance educators' understandings of social justice issues from multiple perspectives. The authors argue that educators' increased understandings of global social justice enable them to negotiate their personal and professional identities and enhance their empathy toward marginalized populations, ultimately preparing them to create more humanizing educational experiences for all learners.

Future Research Directions

In this chapter, the authors reported possibilities of seemingly simple activities to enhance international educators' understanding of social justice in both local and global contexts. They also uncovered the opportunities and challenges of developing an international community of practice. In the future, the authors are considering extending the GSJE collaborations to educators in other countries, particularly in regions not represented in previous course iterations. Teacher educators may benefit from using the reported activities with their PSTs, offering opportunities for them to explore how this type of virtual collaboration contributes to the development of students' intercultural competence and understandings of social justice. The findings in this study were only reported from the activities conducted in one semester. Thus, the authors suggest researchers investigate the long-term impact of these activities in terms of developing educators' awareness of local and global social justice.

REFERENCES

Ames, K. E., Rennick, J. E., & Baillargeon, S. (2011). A qualitative interpretive study exploring parents' perception of the parental role in the pediatric intensive care unit. *Intensive & Critical Care Nursing*, *27*(3), 143–150. doi:10.1016/j.iccn.2011.03.004 PMID:21511474

Breen, P. (2015). Letting go and letting the angels grow: Using Etienne Wenger's community of practice theory to facilitate teacher education. *International Journal of Web-Based Learning and Teaching Technologies*, *10*(1), 14–26. doi:10.4018/ijwltt.2015010102

Cazden, C. B. (2012). A framework for social justice in education. *International Journal of Educational Psychology*, *1*(3), 178–198. doi:10.4471/ijep.2012.11

Chi, M. T. (1997). Quantifying qualitative analyses of verbal data: A practical guide. *Journal of the Learning Sciences*, *6*(3), 271–315. doi:10.1207/s15327809jls0603_1

Deardorff, D. K. (2006). Identification and assessment of intercultural competence as a student outcome of internationalization. *Journal of Studies in International Education*, *10*(3), 241–266. doi:10.1177/1028315306287002

Deardorff, D. K. (2011). Assessing intercultural competence. *New Directions for Institutional Research*, *149*(149), 65–79. doi:10.1002/ir.381

DeJaeghere, J. G., & Cao, Y. (2009). Developing US teachers' intercultural competence: Does professional development matter? *International Journal of Intercultural Relations*, *33*(5), 437–447. doi:10.1016/j.ijintrel.2009.06.004

Ference, R. A., & Bell, S. (2004). A cross-cultural immersion in the US: Changing preservice teacher attitudes toward Latino ESOL students. *Equity & Excellence in Education*, *37*(4), 343–350. doi:10.1080/10665680490518605

Fraser, N. (2008). Reframing justice in a globalizing world. In K. Olson (Ed.), *Adding insult to injury: Nancy Fraser debates her critics* (pp. 273–291). Verso.

Fraser, N. (2009). *Scales of justice: Reimagining political space in a globalizing world.* Columbia University.

Gonçalves, L. L., Parker, M., Luguetti, C., & Carbinatto, M. (2022). The facilitator's role in supporting physical education teachers' empowerment in a professional learning community. *Sport Education and Society*, *27*(3), 272–285. doi:10.1080/13573322.2020.1825371

Jie, Z., & Pearlman, A. M. G. (2018). Expanding access to international education through technology enhanced collaborative online international learning (COIL) courses. *International Journal of Technology in Teaching and Learning*, *14*(1), 1–11.

Kaur, R. (2017). *The sun and her flowers.* Andrews McMeel.

Klenowski, V. (2014). Towards fairer assessment. *Australian Educational Researcher*, *41*(4), 445–470. doi:10.1007/s13384-013-0132-x

Krajewski, S. (2011). Developing intercultural competence in multilingual and multicultural student groups. *Journal of Research in International Education*, *10*(2), 137–153. doi:10.1177/1475240911408563

Krishnan, L. A., Jin, L., Stahl, A., Sreekumar, S., Sundaram, S., Subrahmanian, M., & Davis, P. (2022). Innovative changes to study abroad: Virtual intercultural learning during the pandemic. *Teaching and Learning in Communication Sciences & Disorders*, *6*(2), 1–27. doi:10.30707/TLCSD6.2.1660595992.539519

Lave, J., & Wenger, E. (1991). *Situated learning: Legitimate peripheral participation.* Cambridge University Press. doi:10.1017/CBO9780511815355

Meaney, T., Edmonds-Wathen, C., McMurchy-Pilkington, C., & Trinick, T. (2016). Distribution, recognition, and representation: Mathematics education and Indigenous students. In K. Makar, S. Dole, J. Visnovska, M. Goos, A. Bennison, & K. Fry (Eds.), *Research in mathematics, education in Australasia: 2012–2015* (pp. 143–164). Springer. doi:10.1007/978-981-10-1419-2_8

Merriam, S. B., & Tisdell, E. J. (2016). *Qualitative Research: A guide to design and implementation* (4th ed.). Jossey-Bass.

Patton, K., & Parker, M. (2017). Teacher education communities of practice: More than a culture of collaboration. *Teaching and Teacher Education*, *67*(1), 351–360. doi:10.1016/j.tate.2017.06.013

Peel, K. L. (2020). A beginner's guide to applied educational research using thematic analysis. *Practical Assessment, Research & Evaluation*, *25*(1), 2. Advance online publication. doi:10.7275/ryr5-k983

Saldaña, J. (2016). The coding manual for qualitative researchers. *Sage (Atlanta, Ga.).*

Sapkota, B., Zhou, L., Mbewe, R., Newton, J., & Phillion, J. (2022). Fostering pre-service teachers' intercultural competencies through global cross-cultural collaborations. In C. Ullom & N. Guler (Eds.), *At school in the world: Developing globally engaged teachers* (pp. 212–237). Rowman & Littlefield.

Slapac, A., Collett, K., Wessels, F., Gamiet, G., & Knudsmoen, H. (2023). Social justice pedagogy and Collaborative Online International Learning (COIL): Across three partner higher education institutions. In P. Escudeiro, N. Escudeiro, & O. Bernardes (Eds.), *Implementing inclusive educational models and technologies for equity and diversity* (pp. 252–272). IGI Global. doi:10.4018/979-8-3693-0453-2.ch013

Slapac, A., Coppersmith, S., & Cheng, J. (2023). Global competence development through the lens of graduate students in action research courses. In C. E. Ullom & N. Guler (Eds.), *At school in the world: Developing globally engaged teachers* (pp. 98–117). Rowman & Littlefield.

Smith, J. A., & Osborn, M. (2008). Interpretative phenomenological analysis. In J. A. Smith (Ed.), *Qualitative psychology: A practical guide to research methods* (pp. 53–80). SAGE.

Soria, K. M., & Troisi, J. (2014). Internationalization at home alternatives to study abroad: Implications for students' development of global, international, and intercultural competencies. *Journal of Studies in International Education*, *18*(3), 261–280. doi:10.1177/1028315313496572

Syahrin, S., Akmal, N., Spromberg, S., & DePriest, J. (2023). Promoting intercultural competence in preservice teacher education through virtual exchange. *Studies in Media and Communication*, *11*(1), 1–11. doi:10.11114/smc.v11i1.5791

United Nations. (2015). *Transforming our world: The 2030 agenda for sustainable development.* https://undocs.org/en/A/RES/70/1

Wenger, E. (1998). Communities of practice: Learning as a social system. *The Systems Thinker*, *9*(5), 2–3.

Wormnæs, S. (2008). Cross-cultural collaboration in special teacher education: An arena for facilitating reflection? *International Journal of Disability Development and Education*, *55*(3), 205–225. doi:10.1080/10349120802268305

Zhou, L., Sapkota, B., Mbewe, R., Newton, J., & Phillion, J. (2022). Global social justice in education: Developing a virtual intercultural community of practice. In M. Suleiman & T. Huber (Eds.), *Beyond provincialism: Promoting global competencies in teacher and educator preparation* (pp. 63–101). Information Age.

ADDITIONAL READING

Chhikara, A., Oudghiri, S., Lolkus, M., Rondeau-Madrid, E., & Phillion, J. (2021). Context, curriculum, and community engagement in social justice-focused study abroad programs: A critical examination of instructor intentionality. In G. Malfatti (Ed.), *People-centered approaches toward the internationalization of higher education* (pp. 91–111). IGI Global. doi:10.4018/978-1-7998-3796-1.ch005

Dimitrov, N., & Haque, A. (2016). Intercultural teaching competence: A multi-disciplinary model for instructor reflection. *Intercultural Education*, *27*(5), 437–456. doi:10.1080/14675986.2016.1240502

Fauber, D., & Mueller, K. (2022). Investigating influences of intercultural sensitivity through undergraduate and graduate students' reflections on identities. *The Journal of Purdue Undergraduate Research*, *12*(1), 46–56. doi:10.7771/2158-4052.1540

Goodman, D. J. (2020). Cultural competence for equity and inclusion. *Understanding and Dismantling Privilege, 10*(1), 41-60. https://www.wpcjournal.com/article/view/20246

Slapac, A., Coppersmith, S.A., O'Brien, K., & Balcerzak, P. (2021). Resilience in crisis: Developing community through Action Research. In A. Slapac, P. Balcerzak, & K. O'Brien (Eds.), Handbook of research on the global empowerment of educators and student learning through action research (pp. 23-48). IGI Global.

KEY TERMS AND DEFINITIONS

Cross-Cultural Communication: Verbal and non-verbal communication (e.g., discussions and gestures) among culturally diverse educators.

Global Community of Practice: A platform in which educators from around the world come together to develop a shared understanding of an issue/topic.

Intercultural: Competence: A person's ability to understand one's and other's culture, communicate effectively with people of different cultural backgrounds; being open and empathetic towards others' cultural practices.

Patriarchy: A system or norm of society in which the father or the eldest male is considered as the superior of the family. Females and children have a legal dependency upon the eldest male members of the family.

Privilege: Special rights and advantages provided to certain groups of society.

Social Identities: Groups created by society based on the physical, social, and mental characteristics of individuals.

Virtual Intercultural International Collaboration: A collaboration between ethnically, racially, linguistically, and geographically diverse educators that requires online communication and exchanges for teaching and research purposes.

APPENDIX A

What's in a Name?

Figure 1. The most common last name in each country
https://digg.com/2019/the-most-common-last-names-in-every-country-mapped

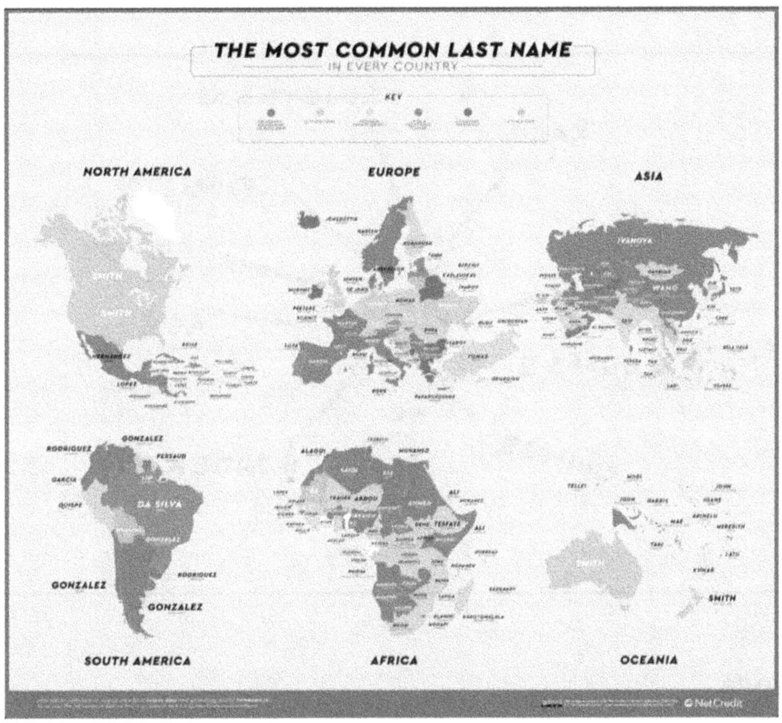

Activity Questions

1. What's your full name?
2. What, if any, is the meaning of your name(s)? In your family? In your country/culture?
3. Is your father's name or mothers' name (or both) represented in your name?
4. Who named you? Who typically names babies in your country/culture?
5. Is your name common in your culture/country?
6. Do people have trouble pronouncing your name? If so, who? How do you feel about that?
7. Is your name gendered or gender neutral? Are most names in your country/culture gendered?
8. Do you have trouble pronouncing your students' names? What do you do to prepare for this?
9. What potential social justice issues may be related to names?
10. What potential social justice issues in education may be related to names?

APPENDIX B

Exploring Privilege in International Contexts

Figure 2. Exploring privilege in international contexts
https://cecs.anu.edu.au/about/diversity-engineering-computer-science/diversity-inclusion-blogs/privilege-and-allyship

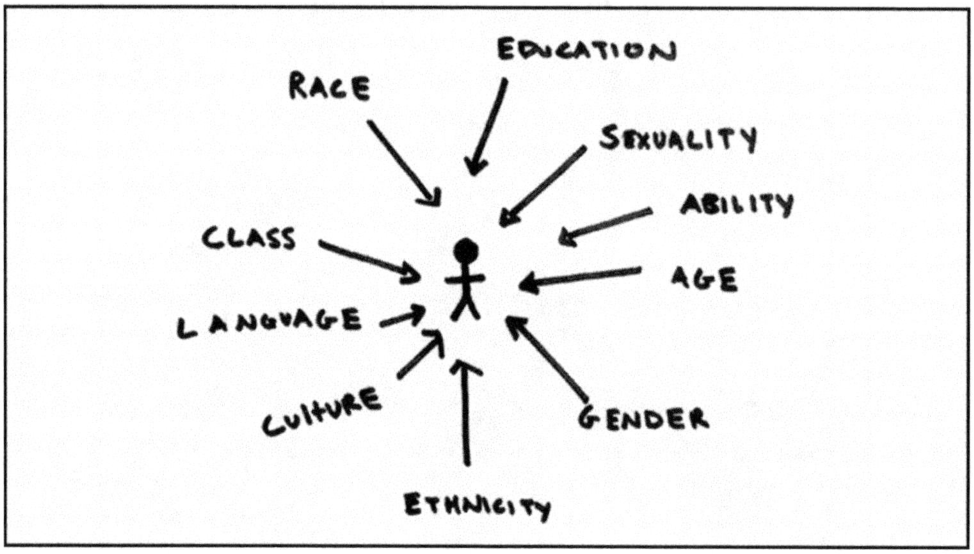

Activity Questions

1. What does the word "privilege" mean to you?
2. Describe two privileges you have that you consider to be important.
3. Describe two privileges you DO NOT have that you consider to be important or not important.
4. What forms of privilege are most valued in your culture/country?
5. What potential social justice issues may be related to privilege?
6. What potential social justice issues in education may be related to privilege?

APPENDIX C

Exploring the Role of the Arts in Social Justice in Global Contexts

Figure 3. Role of art in social justice
https://cas.wsu.edu/2017/06/15/addressing-social-justice-thr
ough-art/
https://vocal.media/poets/social-justice-poem
https://salvosocialjustice.org/tag/music/

Please select a piece of art (e.g., literature, poetry, music, dance, painting) related to social justice you wish to share and describe (i.e., something from your country, something meaningful to you and/or something you created).

Activity Questions

1. Why did you choose to share this particular piece?
2. What thoughts did you have when reflecting on the piece?
3. What potential social justice issues are expressed in the piece?
4. What social justice issues in education are related to this piece?

APPENDIX D

Initial Data Analysis Template

This template was sent to the research teams with examples as provided below; the research teams then completed the template using data from the activity they were analyzing.

1. Your name
   e.g., Bima Sapkota
2. The activity you reviewed
   e.g., What's in a Name?
3. Participants' names/country you reviewed
   e.g., Bima/Nepal, etc.,
4. Fill in the following table:

Table 2. Data analysis template

Participant Name/ Country	Activity or Reflection	Social Justice Issues	Quote	Researcher Notes
Bima/Nepal	Privilege Reflection	Gender	*Often girls do not get to go to school.*	I could relate to this gender issue. I see gender difference in- and out-of-educational contexts. Many parents in Nepal do not send their daughters to college while they invest a lot in their son's higher education

5. Social justice issues that were mentioned a lot in the reflections
   e.g., Gender, Race, etc.
6. Overarching themes you noticed from these reflections
   e.g., Gender difference is a global social justice issue as it exists in many forms in different parts of the world. For example, XXX
7. Other things you wondered about
   e.g., I wondered if it would be interesting to report Global vs Local issues associated with naming in our research paper.

Chapter 4
Towards a "Response-Able Pedagogy" in Teacher Development Through Collaborative Online International Learning (COIL): An American-South African Partnership

Karen Collett
University of the Western Cape, South Africa

Alina Slapac
https://orcid.org/0000-0002-2210-1959
University of Missouri-St. Louis, USA

Sarah A. Coppersmith
https://orcid.org/0000-0001-6275-4711
University of Missouri-St. Louis, USA

Jingxin Cheng
https://orcid.org/0000-0002-2246-7598
University of Missouri-St.Louis, USA

ABSTRACT

Using the "Response-Able Pedagogy" conceptual framework, the authors identify how their COIL course probed the enactment of the possibilities and challenges of the ethical and political practices of attentiveness, responsibility, curiosity, and rendering each other capable. In this chapter, the authors discuss how they promoted global awareness/citizenship and teacher development and strengthened their South African-American partnership through their COIL course. A total of 168 participants (120 preservice teachers from South Africa and 48 inservice teachers from the United States of America) collaborated through the online platform of Flip for 4 weeks and submitted COIL assignments used as data sources. Results will discuss the key learnings through the use of a "Response-Able Pedagogy" framework and towards strengthening the curriculum. Future pedagogical considerations to enhance COIL courses and partnership development will be addressed.

DOI: 10.4018/978-1-6684-7813-4.ch004

INTRODUCTION

The COVID-19 lockdown brought up the possibilities and challenges of online connectivity, both nationally and internationally, as faculty scrambled to keep higher education learning programs on track. While Collaborative Online International Learning (COIL) was a practice instituted between higher education institutions (HEIs) before COVID-19 as part of the internationalization of teaching and learning and teacher development, the pandemic lockdown conditions in 2020 and 2021 exacerbated the need for both faculty and students to connect online to make learning and teaching possible (Beelen, 2022; Slapac et al., 2023a). During this time, a range of Information and Communication Technologies (ICT) were used to place the global sphere into the local sphere – or globalization at home. The concept of internationalizing teaching and learning was adopted (Lilley et al., 2015), exposing students in local conditions to the potential learning and problem solving in international contexts, which promotes preservice and inservice teachers and teacher educators to experience the global context within their local context.

Researchers (Deardorff, 2019; Katre, 2020; Zhang & Pearlman, 2018) agree that the development of intercultural competencies are needed in education to prepare students towards global citizenship for the global economy and the job market. The purpose of COIL is to afford students the opportunity to develop cultural awareness and global perspectives, build intercultural communication skills, develop cultural sensitivity through collaborative synchronous and asynchronous online learning experiences, and provide accessible ways to global learning (Zhang & Pearlman, 2018). Furthermore, COIL provides opportunities for internationalization "at-home" (Beelen & Jones, 2015; Custer & Tuominen, 2017; Mundel, 2020; Slapac et al., 2023a). Virtual exchange and collaborative online international learning serve as a means to foster the development of global competencies among students by facilitating connections with people, organizations, and institutions abroad (Sierra-Huedo et al., 2024; Slapac, et al., 2021; 2023a).

Recent research studies point out the impact of COIL, specifically in students' development of intercultural competencies through collaborative multicultural experiential learning experiences, in different subject areas, diverse sociocultural contexts, and international virtual partnerships (Asojo et al., 2019; Katre, 2020; Slapac et al., 2023a). Although most partnerships encountered challenges (such as technology, time constraints, etc.), studies show that students engaged in COIL appreciate such experiences in regards to cross-cultural sensitivity learning, collaborative international learning through joint projects, and use of technology and its affordances for global connections (Katre, 2020; Quintana-Ordorika, 2024; Slapac et al., 2023a). In addition, for the teacher development arm of the COIL partnership, researchers point out that teachers need support in global competence development in order to educate and develop this in their own students (Kerkhoff et al., 2021; Slapac, 2021; Slapac et al., 2023a, 2023b; Song et al., 2023). There is an increased interest in collaborating and working together online, and "future research could describe how teachers can encourage all students in a class to share knowledge as a means of fostering values of diversity and equality" (Kerkhoff et al., 2021, p. 282). In higher education, this sharing and modeling can take place in a collaborative space through COIL, which "cannot exist on a single campus but requires integration and dialogue between institutions in different countries with varied educational mandates and structures, different academic calendars and teaching styles, and which reside in a wide range of time zones" (Rubin, 2017, p. 33).

The authors' COIL course focused on opening up the potential for the development of intercultural competence and comparative action research between students and faculty from higher education institutions in South Africa and the United States of America. This chapter uses the lenses of a "Response-able Pedagogy" (Bozalek & Zembylas, 2017) to reflect on practice. It concludes by highlighting key lessons, recommendations, and future directions to enhance a response-able pedagogy in higher education COIL courses.

BACKGROUND

Significance of COIL Collaborations

Collaborative Online International Learning (COIL) is an educational approach that fosters cross-cultural collaboration and learning among students and faculty. It involves bringing together individuals from different cultural backgrounds to participate in shared learning, discussions, and collaborative activities within the context of their academic courses. Faculty collaborate to design the COIL experience, while students work in partnerships to engage in the designed activities. By integrating COIL into courses, students gain valuable intercultural experiences that enrich their educational journey (Marcillo-Gómez & Desilus, 2016; SUNY COIL Center, n. d.). In addition to synchronous video conferencing between classes, instructors and students leveraged various online collaboration tools available on partner campuses. These platforms include but are not limited to CourseSites, Moodle, Blackboard, and Flip. Examples of online collaboration spaces are Zoom, Google Docs, Google Slides, YouTube and social media platforms such as Facebook and Twitter.

The noteworthy benefits of COIL, as revealed and supported by various studies include enhancing intercultural competence, fostering global citizenship, improving intercultural communication skills, increasing student engagement and motivation, and developing digital literacy and technological skills (e.g., Guimarães & Finardi, 2021; Jie & Pearlman, 2018; Naicker et al., 2022; Slapac et al., 2023a). In addition, the significance of COIL collaborations in higher education also lies in broadening students' perspectives and enhancing their critical thinking skills. By engaging with peers from different cultural and disciplinary backgrounds, students are exposed to diverse ideas, alternative viewpoints, and different problem-solving approaches (e.g., Guimarães et al., 2019; Vahed & Rodriguez, 2021), promoting equity and inclusion by providing access to global learning experiences for a diverse range of students. These collaborations enable students who may not have the opportunity to study abroad to engage in intercultural and international experiences (e.g., DeWinter & Klamer, 2021; Slapac et al., 2023a; Vahed, 2022; Wyman & Bellot, 2021). The COIL Center at the State University of New York (SUNY) highlights the importance of COIL collaborations in "expanding access to global learning opportunities for diverse student populations" (COIL Center, n. d.).

Transnational Learning and Global Citizenship in Teacher Education Development

Since the start of the 21st century, the higher education sector has experienced a notable increase in transnational education arrangements, specifically the establishment of joint venture universities (Che, 2023). The UNESCO/Council of Europe (COE) (2001, n.p.) states transnational education as "all types of higher education study programs, or sets of courses of study, or educational services (including those of distance education) in which the learners are located in a country different from the one where the awarding institution is based" (Section I). Transnational education has a significant impact on fostering global citizenship among students. By engaging in educational experiences that transcend national boundaries, students are exposed to diverse perspectives, cultures, and global issues, enabling them to develop a broader understanding of the world and their roles as global citizens. It also enhances cultural awareness and appreciation through which students develop a deeper understanding of cultural diversity, challenge stereotypes, and learn to respect and value different perspectives (Dyrness, 2021; Moon, 2010). Students learn to navigate linguistic and cultural differences, develop empathy, and adapt their communication styles to diverse audiences.

Transnational education helps students recognize the interconnectedness of global challenges (e.g., climate change, poverty, and inequality), and understand how these issues transcend national boundaries (Balta & Altan-Olcay, 2016; De Oliveira Andreotti, 2014). This form of education also helps with developing global perspectives of students through exposing them to diverse educational systems, teaching methods, and research findings. Students gain insights into different approaches to solving educational challenges and are better equipped to address global issues from multiple angles, bringing fresh perspectives to problem-solving (Hahn, 2015).

Building on the concept of internationalization of teaching and learning (Lilley et al., 2015) and on the increase of the number of students with diverse cultural and linguistic backgrounds, teacher education is expected to prepare prospective teachers with knowledge of Global Citizenship Education (GCE), as well as to promote students' global citizenship in the transnational era (Kim & Slapac, 2015; Song et al., 2023). Transnational teacher education supports teacher candidates in developing heightened respect for pluralism, and the tools to critically analyze the historical, economic, political, linguistic and sociocultural circumstances, and the goal of producing citizens with a pluralistic view of society (Ruiz & Baired, 2013). The growing interconnectedness of modern society allows individuals to inhabit multiple realms simultaneously, not just in a physical sense, but also virtually through the aid of ICT. COIL serves as an innovative approach to foster intercultural encounters within the context of internationalizing higher education and offers a platform to address and navigate the complexities arising from local, national, and global tensions in the internationalization process. This approach embraces a 'glonacal' perspective (Marginson, 2022) acknowledging the roles of individuals, local and national governments, and higher education institutions in promoting intercultural understanding and cooperation. COIL presents an opportunity for meaningful engagement and collaboration across borders, transcending physical limitations and facilitating virtual connections that bridge cultural divides (Guimarães & Finardi, 2021; King de Ramirez, 2021; Kopish & Marques, 2020; Slapac et al., 2023a).

The "Response-Able Pedagogy" Conceptual Framework

In this chapter, the authors engaged with the dimensions of Bozalek and Zembylas' (2017) conceptualization of a response-able pedagogy to explore faculty and student experiences of their COIL collaboration. Bozalek and Zembylas (2017) argue that engagement with the dimensions of a response-able pedagogy holds the potential to extend thinking and practices related to critical pedagogy in higher education. In fact, a response-able pedagogy represents ethical-political practices that "constitute relational processes through which social, political, and material entanglements in higher education (i.e. students, facilitators, discourses, texts, performances, drawings, face-to-face and online comings together) are rendered capable through each other to bring about social transformation" (Bozalek & Zembylas, 2017, p. 64). Like Moje (2007), they affirm that both socially just and social justice pedagogies have a role in addressing injustice in higher education environments.

Drawing from a post-humanist and feminist ontology, Bozalek and Zembylas (2017) argue for the engagement by HEI practitioners with the interrelated ethical-political practices of *attentiveness, curiosity, responsibility and rendering each other capable*. They argue that this type of pedagogical practice is deeply relational and ethical: "Response-able pedagogies are not simply examples of the type of learning that can take place when power, relations, materiality, and entanglements are acknowledged; they also constitute ethico-political practices that incorporate a relational ontology into teaching and learning activities" (p.62).

By using the dimension of a response-able pedagogy (Bozalek & Zembylas, 2017) to reflect on student and faculty experiences, the authors also looked at the ways in which their COIL courses supported both socially just and social justice pedagogy (Moje, 2007). Zembylas and Bozalek (2017) and Moje (2007) argue that socially just pedagogies, while necessary to address issues of equity, do not challenge or eradicate structural inequalities or question curriculum content and pedagogy. Moje (2007) also asserts that socially just pedagogies can run the risk of reproducing the status and dominant knowledge structures. Therefore, Zembylas and Bozalek (2017) suggest that socially just pedagogies need to "consider specifically how it is entangled with notions of justice at the societal level and whether it really creates spaces in higher education that nurture relational values such as care, compassion, respect, and solidarity" (p. 3). Their dimensions of a response-able pedagogy (see Figure 1) hold resonance with Tronto's (2013) political ethics of care as issues of social justice are fundamentally linked to an engagement with care ethics. In our reflection on our COIL collaboration, we draw on student and faculty data to highlight strengths and weaknesses in our COIL courses as they attempted to address the dimensions of attentiveness, curiosity, responsibility and rendering each other capable.

Figure 1. Dimensions of a "response-able pedagogy"
Source: Adapted from Bozalek and Zembylas (2017)

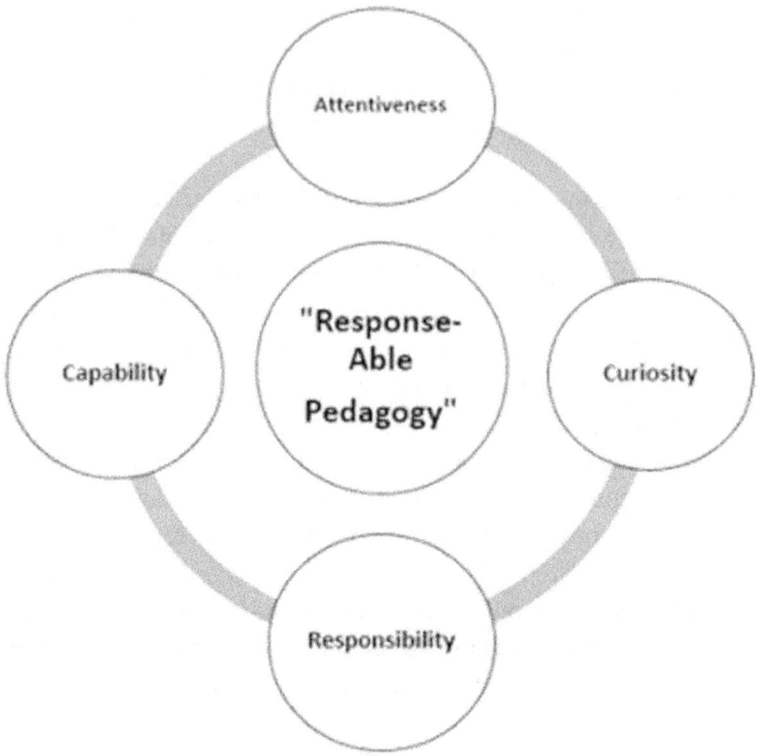

Each of these dimensions is elaborated on below:

Attentiveness is defined as the "ability to apprehend, to listen, to be open and respectful, and the ability to inhabit just practices in a collective space" (Bozalek & Zembylas, 2017, pp. 67-68). In order to be able to respond appropriately, the capacity to be attentive should be first finely attuned, including the ability to "pay due attention, to read, or listen with discernment and care to what is and what is not being expressed" (Bozalek & Zembylas, 2017, p. 67) as well as an awareness of how one is affected by another, both human and non-human. Bozalek and Zembylas (2017) affirm the need for a sensitivity and "attunement between what is done and how it is done in the classroom with an openness to multiple needs, leads to a becoming-with the other." (p. 67) As students and academics who teach and learn in both face-to-face and online learning platforms our attentiveness towards each other, and our contexts are highlighted by this dimension. Processes that negatively influence the ability for participants to engage and deepen their COIL collaboration can also limit the ability of individuals to be attentive to each other.

Curiosity is that space of learning and engagement that is opened up through our engagement. Bozalek and Zembylas (2017) highlight the importance of this process of discovery in creating surprising and unanticipated encounters in higher education either with the course content, or on an interpersonal level. They affirm that careful attention is "necessary to cultivate practices of curiosity" (Bozalek & Zembylas, 2017, p. 68). Within the COIL environment a number of technologies and online platforms as well as icebreaker activities and joint tasks can stimulate learner curiosity at a personal, interpersonal, cultural, national, and global level. Opportunities for curiosity can be stimulated by successes and challenges participants face.

Responsibility as a dimension acknowledges the inherent nature of responsibility in the teaching and learning relationship which is often multi-directional and often, asymmetrical (Barad, 2007; Bozalek & Zembylas, 2017). Responsibility (or accountability) is defined by as, "how entanglements are enacted—how and what we know, how and what we do in the context of what exists in the world of which we are part", knowing that "asymmetrical power differentials implicit in relationships need to be borne in mind when thinking about responsibility and accountability, particularly with regard to pedagogical encounters in higher education." (Bozalek & Zembylas, 2017, p. 68). These scholars acknowledge the complexity of power dynamics in the processes of taking responsibility:

The recognition that difference is embodied and entangled rather than existing in abject others is important for designing ethical curricula that bring together differently positioned disciplines, institutions and humans. Taking responsibility for dependence means a commitment to ourselves and others to avoid what has been referred to as "privileged irresponsibility" where the services of another to meet one's own needs are used but not acknowledged. (Bozalek & Zembylas, 2017, p. 69)

Collett et al. (2018) argue that for "effective learning to take place, it is imperative that students take a share of the responsibility for their learning and become self-directed learners." (p. 11). In the design of COIL courses, faculty (the authors) engaged with how they took responsibility for the planning of student learning and assessment in their curriculum design and pedagogical choices. Varying conditions in the learning and social environments influenced the extent to which students and teacher educators could take on responsibility for engagement and learning. Issues of language, levels of connectivity, and different levels of experience or access affected the extent to which students or faculty were able to take on responsibility or to respond appropriately to needs expressed. Group or individual dynamics have an influence on levels of responsibility taken.

Capability as a dimension means rendering oneself and each other capable, "enlarging the competency of all players" and "enabling the capacity to respond to what matters" (Bozalek & Zembylas, 2017, p. 69). This is a process, they argue, of "cultivating ethical (how to flourish together in a complex world of living and dying), ontological (being and becoming, making-with) and epistemological (knowing-with, enlarging each other's thinking) response-abilities." (Bozalek & Zembylas, 2017, p. 69). Thus, capability contains the larger idea and goal of a process of engagement with others. Rendering each other capable, as a fourth dimension, "does not happen through duty ethics—feeling that one has to do something—but through the capacity to respond to what matters." (Bozalek & Zembylas, 2017, p. 69). The COIL curriculum and assessment activities provided a structure to enable the development of capability. The quality of engagement in the other phases of the COIL collaboration influences the extent to which both students and faculty were rendered more capable through the COIL intervention.

In the section below, COIL experience as faculty and students are explored through the lens of response-able pedagogy in order to highlight aspects of socially just and social justice pedagogy. In their discussion, the authors draw on related COIL research to explore key learnings. Their findings aim to enhance their future COIL practices and those of other faculty who strive towards a more response-able pedagogy in COIL courses internationally.

METHODOLOGY

This COIL partnership lasted four weeks (February-March 2023) and involved three faculty and a graduate research assistant from two differently positioned higher education institutions. The authors met as a Professional Learning Community (PLC) several times via Zoom in January to discuss and plan the COIL course and continued the PLC throughout the end of the course. Planning included logistical considerations, assessment tasks, and timelines (as South African and American students had different overall dates of their respective courses and national, religious holidays or breaks), course goals, and the research design. Due to the differences in time zones and course restrictions such as numbers of students and access to technology and data, the collaborating faculty decided in this second iteration of the COIL pilot to design the COIL activities asynchronously.

The Flip Design and Experience

Although the students had different teaching experiences, the faculty agreed on common COIL learning outcomes, opportunities for COIL interactions, and transnational learning. The students used the Flip platform. The graduate research assistant developed an instructional video for students on how to develop and submit the videos at the start of the partnership. The American students were asked to avoid using jargon, abbreviations, to speak slowly and clearly, and to ask questions keeping in mind their South African partners who had limited teaching experiences. Students were encouraged to use the Comment box (as needed) within the Flip platform to continue engaging with their partners. For their assessment tasks students were required to submit two videos: in Video 1, they introduced themselves and described a local educational challenge or a problem of practice, along with a question for their COIL partner(s); and in Video 2, the students were asked to reply to the question their COIL partners posed (see Box 1). Students were also engaged in readings related to the value of COIL courses and global education. They were given a week or two between videos to create the Video 2 response and submit a reflection.

Table 1. Flip assignment description

Objectives:

- Develop an action research study related to teaching in diverse and global classrooms and multicultural learning environments.
- Explore cultural diversity through collaborative international online learning.
- Share local challenges and solutions to your educational practice with international peers through video and reflections.
- Enhance respect for local challenges and research needs in different teaching global contexts.

TASK 1: VIDEO 1: Using the Flip instructions and platform, please record a short video (3-5 minutes maximum) using Flip with the following parts by February 23rd.

1. Introduce yourself (name, what you study, main interests related to education).
2. Describe a problem /controversial issue/limitation/curiosity that you have found when teaching at school (or doing practicum, substitute teaching etc.). US students are asked to discuss their chosen action research topic (interventions, if any).
3. Pose at least one question about your topic for your colleague(s) from the other university based on the problem discussed. For example, how can you use technology to impact your students' learning in your local context? What are some possible challenges and solutions?

TASK 2: By February 23rd, write a short written reflection (1 page) explaining the topic you have presented in the video. Answer these three questions:

a) What is the topic you have presented in the video?
b) Why have you chosen this topic?
c) What question(s) have you asked your colleague(s) from the other university?

Write your (group) number, your full name, title: Reflection 1, followed by a short reflection. Submit this written Reflection assignment in Canvas (US Students) or in iKamva (S.A. students)

TASK 3: **VIDEO 2:** Watch at least two videos of your counterparts from the other university, and select the video from your COIL assigned partner (partner number) to respond to through another 3-5 min video. You will need to answer their questions using Flip. At least one of your answers must be in the form of a short video. Label your video with your number, university, First and Last name. Post your video in the Task 3 Flip folder.

TASK 4: Write a short reflective piece (1 page) describing your experience of engaging with your COIL partner. Answer these 5 questions (write the questions in the response)

1. Describe the question your COIL partner asked and the answer you provided them in the video.
2. What was the value for you in giving this feedback to your COIL partner?
3. What was the value for you in the feedback you received from your COIL partner on your question?
4. How did this COIL exchange help you think about your research topic AND your global competencies?

Do you have any suggestions / comments on how a COIL collaboration could be improved to deepen your learning and research about other contexts?

Source: Own elaboration

Research Design, Sites, and Participants

A participatory action research (PAR) design (Chambers, 2007; Kemmis & McTaggart, 2005) informed this research. This approach to research supported the collaborative ownership and understanding of change and involvement in the improved action by participants (Rudolph et al., 2008; Whitehead, 2012). The PAR process included ongoing and iterative cycles of action and research by participants in order to inform and improve practice. Although greater student involvement was anticipated, this was limited to student processes of engagement in data generation and in making recommendations for improvements to future COIL courses.

Three faculty members and their students from two higher education institutions (HEIs) participated in this research, including one graduate research assistant from the American university (the fourth author). One of the institutions was based in America and the other university was based in South Africa. Both these HEIs were involved in a research collaboration which began in 2021. All three faculty met monthly to reflect in an ongoing way as a Professional Learning Community (PLC) on their implementation of a second iteration of the COIL pilot which had begun in 2023. Faculty from both universities took responsibility for ensuring the collection of data from students throughout the pilot period. All students who participated in the research signed informed consent to participate in this research. The total of 168 student participants who directly participated in the COIL engagement were as follows: from the American university, 48 graduate students (inservice teachers) enrolled in Action Research I, an 8-week online course; and from the South African university, 120 undergraduate students (preservice teachers) enrolled in an Introduction to Educational Research course. Specifically, student participants from the American university included 48 graduate students enrolled in two sections (Section 1 with 25 students, Section 2 with 23 students) of an Action Research 1 course during their Master's of Education program. The participants were seeking majors mainly in elementary education, secondary education, special education and general education. Years of teaching experience as full-time teachers ranged from none to over 16 years. Participants' schools were rural, suburban or urban, public, charter or private, within the state and beyond at various grade levels and subject areas taught.

Student participants who gave consent to participate in the research process from the South African University included 120 students from a class of 365 students who did the COIL tasks. The 120 students from SA were group leaders who connected to the Flip site and then shared content and engagement with another 245 students from this single class who had been divided into groups. These students were fourth year teacher education students, with over 75% of them being between the ages of 18 and 25 years old. Students came from a range of socio-economic and ethnic backgrounds with the majority of students being first generation students in higher education. Students spoke a range of languages with English being the second or third language spoken by most students. All South African students attended classes in a hybrid format with face-to-face lectures and online learning platforms such as Flip. They were all enrolled in a course titled an Introduction to Educational Research. These students were required to develop a research proposal linked to an action research design.

Data Collection

The research questions for the study were as follows:

1. How were dimensions of the "respons-able pedagogy" framework represented through a COIL course by faculty and students (in-service & pre-service teachers)?
2. What were the possibilities and challenges of the COIL course as a result of the use of the "respons-able pedagogy" framework for all those involved?

A number of processes of data gathering took place between February and May 2023 through the asynchronous COIL courses. Data from faculty were generated from ongoing reflections on practice using Google Meet or Zoom platforms in a professional learning community (PLC). Overall, student data sources included students' two reflections and videos, and a survey. The survey was adapted based on the Global Learning Experience (GLE) Student Survey Questions (n. d.) developed by DePaul University, and although it gathered quantitative and qualitative data, for the purpose of this study, the authors used only the qualitative data (besides demographic data). In addition, two focus group interviews were held with students from the South African university to probe student survey responses collected. Overall, both groups had 72% of participants identified as females, and 28% identified as males and 68% of participants were of ages between 18 and 25. Fifty-two percent of participants were interested in educational topics related to secondary education. Seventy-one percent of participants stated that they have not traveled to any other countries outside their own.

From the American university, data collected included two student reflections after the first and second Flip videos gathered from 48 students and the online survey completed by 34 students (out of 48). The survey was administered to students at the end of the COIL course.

From the South African university, data collected included two student reflections after the first and second Flip videos and survey data gathered from all 120 students. In addition, data from two focus group interviews were collected. The focus group interviews were held on two separate days, and lasted an hour each, with five students in one group and two students in the other group. The interviews were recorded, transcribed for accuracy and verified by participants.

Data Analysis

At the end of the COIL course, student and faculty data were analyzed using the dimensions of "response-able pedagogy" (Bozalek & Zembylas 2017), to probe the possibilities and challenges of the COIL collaboration in enhancing the dimensions of *attentiveness, curiosity, responsibility and capability.* Thus, the data were analyzed first via an "a priori" approach where the framework for investigation is built before thematic coding occurs - "The procedure is deductive because the category system is established before coding the text" (Mayring, 2014, p. 97).

Our data analysis process was informed first by our two key research questions. Themes were identified from participant responses through grouping patterns and experiences (Braun & Clarke, 2012) using firstly closed coding related to the broad categories of the conceptual frameworks of response-able pedagogy" (Bozalek & Zembylas, 2017) and then using a process of open coding to identify any aspects that emerged from the data that were new. The "Response-able Pedagogy" framework served as a systematic framework to capture, analyze, and relate participants' ideas, questions, and statements in relation to the study's purpose and research questions.

FINDINGS

The dimensions of the response-able pedagogy were used to structure our presentation of findings. Under each of the dimensions of *attentiveness, curiosity, responsibility and rendering each other capable,* the authors draw on both student and faculty data from both institutions to highlight strengths and weaknesses in their COIL course design and delivery. Although these findings are presented under the different dimensions, it is important to note that each of these dimensions affects and is affected by the other dimensions. For example, factors affecting the ability of students to be attentive will influence their ability to take responsibility. In the section that follows, the authors discuss these findings in order to draw out key lessons and recommendations related to improving future COIL projects. Both supporting and constraining factors are identified under each four dimensions of a response-able pedagogy. Responses of students and faculty from both institutions are presented under each dimension (spelling and grammar for student responses were left verbatim).

Attentiveness

Attentiveness to each other's needs, and those conditions that support attentiveness, are key to the ability of faculty and students to respond appropriately to the needs of others within teaching and learning contexts. For example, attentiveness has been shown by students when watching the Flip videos of their assigned partners and others of their choice, and responding to the questions asked respectfully, with openness and sensitivity using a second Flip Video tool as a reply. The following key factors were identified as supporting the ability of students and faculty to be attentive in this COIL collaboration as related to knowledge construction and transnational learning and the use of the Flip online platform. These included: building international relationships; sharing perspectives; interest in sharing ideas and research finding solutions; effort put into completing tasks; and Flip affordances. For example, within the element of attentiveness, students and faculty alike found the collaboration 'exciting' while building on the intercultural communication through the Flip videos:

It was interesting to connect with educators from another country and see similarities between our experiences and teaching practices. (American student, survey)

I liked hearing from students from the other campus and learning about their experiences so far in education. It was neat realizing how similar education can be even halfway around the world. (American student, survey)

I think there's something so exciting about making those connections. You know that in a course that you would normally just have done on your own or with your peers now suddenly it's like a window opens and you opened into another whole universe and I think that experience is very powerful for students... I think students were so excited and many students spoke about wanting to get the email addresses and maintain that contact with other students beyond this. (South African Faculty, PLC)

Learning that we will be doing an international collaboration was very exciting. I think at first like before COIL, a lot of my perceptions were based off of like the Internet. Like what I've read about that certain country and that certain place. But then having spoken to our partner and having watched other Flip videos, I learned that we have a lot of similarities and that calls for a great connection between us as educators and I feel like I am not alone. (South African student Group B, P1, interview)

Students recognized that learning others' perspectives on local challenges and solutions was valuable while they reflected on this intercultural collaboration:

I really enjoyed hearing other people's perspective on encoding and decoding and the challenges their students face in early literacy. In the past year or two I have become very focused on the major gaps in encoding and decoding that are preventing American students from being successful readers. It was very interesting for me to hear that this is a challenge that other countries are facing as well. I would love to collaborate more with them in the future. It's neat to realize that there are so many caring educators all around the world and that we do share so many of the same values about children and teaching. Seeing their faces and listening to their voices made this project personal and that small connection from me to these people across the world was very unique and not something I would have experienced otherwise without this class. (American Student, reflection)

American students were interested in finding answers to their own classroom dilemmas which they were addressing through action research, being curious and attentive about their partners' thoughts:

A question I asked my colleagues was, what do you do for low readers in your classroom? This might give me helpful information that I might not have thought to do as far as reading interventions. I'm excited to hear some strategies that work for other teachers (American Student, reflection)

Seeking any help they could find, the Americans sought answers and strategies on topics for their own research, such as engaging students in reading, improving writing, building a sense of community with social skills, and inquiries into what were some methods of providing positive behavior supports or working with students with special needs: "I asked any early childhood educators what strategies they may use to foster the transfer of symbols and sounds into decoding". (American Student). Going further: *"I am curious to know about the student relationships for our partners in South Africa and methods that they use to mitigate student verbal aggression*" (American Student). One response revealed careful thought on comparing the two countries' practices regarding behavior management and a sincere desire to learn more:

I do not want to assume that students in South Africa present the same typical behavioral challenges as those in the United States, such as cussing, fighting, and work refusals. Yet, I desire to know what interventions are universally used by teachers. This will help to broaden my understanding of the topic positive behavior supports, classroom management, and teacher perspectives. (American student, reflection)

Faculty in both institutions felt that the Flip online platform worked well for the students and worked well for them in being able to connect to student responses and to be able to respond to students as well as see comments from each other. These comments from the faculty highlight their view of the value of the Flip platform used.

People could use a platform that enables them to share a whole video and then to be able to have the chances of commenting back on a video so that you won't lose that information so I think there are good affordances of that platform... (South African Faculty, PLC)

Flip is quite user friendly and we were able to sort this out. (American Faculty 2, PLC)

I think the platform worked well as well to show videos and then also be able to give feedback. I also gave feedback to some of your students like on one of two things about how I experienced it and that was that was really nice you know to see how they're presented. From a lecturer perspective it was good so see how they presented. I didn't give a lot of feedback, I was just a bit cautious but it was really nice to for me as a lecturer to see what your Masters students were involved with and just to interact with them a little bit. (South African, Faculty, PLC).

While most responses about Flip were positive, such as "I could immediately go into my and your students' posts and see what was in their heads" (South African, Faculty PLC), one posted this reply: "Some of them gave feedback to other students and some people did not respond" (South African, Faculty PLC), giving a 'negative case' (Lincoln & Guba, 1985) or a finding which doesn't align with the majority of the data. This actually can strengthen the credibility of a study as it reveals transparency in reporting. Additional negative, or contrasting factors identified by students regarding being able to be attentive in the COIL collaboration included challenges with connectivity; not all students in large classes were able to participate directly on the platform or with partners and had to be represented by a group leader; only asynchronous contact limited engagement; limited time to submit tasks; inappropriate or limited responses from COIL partners.

Curiosity

Faculty planned the exchanges to support their students' ability to be curious about their engagement with the COIL partners. Students engaged in exploring common areas of research and teaching practices with curiosity in finding solutions and in learning if similar issues or challenges are experienced globally. Some of the key factors identified as supporting their ability to be curious were: interest in exploring a common area of research and sharing ideas; learning about each other's contexts; learning from a more experienced professional (the American students being inservice teachers, most of them full-time teachers). Students chose to discuss topics that were relevant to them, in connection to their action research topics. Students engaged in exploring common areas of research and teaching practices with curiosity about how these practices are addressed in classrooms or in the others' cultural local contexts:

I really like the idea of this project because it allows teachers to learn from each other in all parts of the world. Even though where we live is different, from watching other teachers' videos, there are trends in topics in education. This project allows us to learn from each other and bring many diverse experiences to each other's research questions. (American student, survey).

U.S. teachers were eager to inquire and seek information from their partners on their particular classroom learning situations related to the research contexts for their coursework. There was an eagerness to learn partners' perceptions and discuss teaching strategies and techniques in topics such as coding and decoding in reading, behavior and self-management, reading comprehension, sensory inputs, sensory breaks, socio emotional learning, and bullying, among others. Reviewing the students' inquiries below gives a glimpse into what was important to these researchers related to their own teaching and learning… (American student, reflection)

I can go anywhere and then I can fit in as an educator because we're dealing with the same issues just in different contexts. Like the different contexts for us as South African educators because we had the apartheid system and that's what caused a lot of influence on governance and education. But then it's still not too different from the American context. Because they also had their own issues of segregation even in education. So when he's talking, when the partner was talking like I could relate. So I think it helped me to feel as though I'm part of a big community instead of like, you know, just isolated in South Africa. (South African student Group B, P1, interview)

The South African students appreciated that they had the opportunity to engage with graduate level, classroom teachers:

The other part that made me curious was the fact that our COIL partner was a Master's student. So, she had much more information to what we were researching, then what we had. (South African student Group A, P2, interview)

So, it is through our COIL partner, she did have experience. So, she is more experienced and I think that is what also helped us with our research. So that our research and our proposal wasn't shallow because we were not that informed. But because of the feedback that she gave us her response to our questions or with statements that may have helped us in our research. (South African student Group A, P1, interview)

The following key factors were identified by South African students as having a negative effect on fostering student curiosity about their COIL partner and their research were: limited time to engage; no synchronous engagement; limited or incorrect responses; and different student professional levels. For example, regarding timing of the COIL engagement, an American student commented: *The project was a bit difficult because it was being rolled out and developed during the class. I think it will be easier once the relationship with the school and the guidelines around the project are more established.* (American Student, survey). Some students mentioned their preference for also having synchronous collaborations however, due to several factors (time difference, restrictions on 100% online type-courses, students' work and family schedules) the synchronous option was a challenge to fit in.

The importance of having a form of connectivity which enabled students to clarify questions and probe for responses related to aspects they were curious about in a more direct way was highlighted by the South African students. Some students mentioned they would have liked to have Zoom meetings as well… So with the Zoom idea as much as I would have liked it was pretty hard to connect. They also said they would have linked to connect further with the students and say maybe they would continue to connect like pen pals and they wished the experience was longer (American faculty 1, PLC)

At times, students received limited or incorrect responses to their questions posted through the Flip video, such as some of the students were not happy they did not receive any responses from the students (American Faculty 1, PLC).

The COIL students just took a bit long to respond on our message, and the fact that I think the question we had, but he responded with something different and did not understand us. So we had to make another video and respond to his response. So, it was a bit confusing, but we, we made it through. (South African student Group B, P2, interview)

Another challenge was related to having differences in teaching experiences (inservice vs. preservice teachers) or socio-cultural schooling experiences:

Some of the students wished to be linked to teachers that were practicing teachers. (American faculty 1, PLC)

Responsibility

A number of factors were identified as supporting or limiting students or faculty from taking *responsibility*. Factors supporting responsibility included having a clear task brief; the challenge of the assessment task; delegation of responsibilities; making a good impression; interest in engaging with other students; wanting to connect and learn authentically; and responsibility linked to assessment grades. Factors limiting responsibility included disappointing responses from COIL partners; perceptions of a lack of clarity on

COIL expectations; poor communication; and resistance to collaborative work. In addition, the limited time to complete the tasks and the desire for some to get to know their partners a bit better were factors relating to student perceptions of when and how they should be responsible (to whom and to what).

It was the faculty's responsibility to make sure that students clearly understood the assignments, reflections, and tasks asked of them. Using the online Canvas course system for the American course and the iKamva system for the South African course helped students to understand the goals and submit the assignments for COIL and beyond for grading. The COIL asynchronous student-student connection was through the Flip videos. One student noted the importance of "*Having clear instructions on what is expected*". (South Africa student, survey). The challenge of the assessment task, working with partners, expectations, and delegation of responsibilities were described in this way:

It really motivates me to try and find out how in actual reality how they [the American inservice teachers] conduct the you know, education system and how they, they deal with things like these, like with our topic... (South African student Group A, P5, interview)

The element of engaging as a collective with an international audience was identified by one group as influencing their motivation to put effort into engaging with other students. A group member noted, *"Previously when doing group work, it was easy to pick up someone's lack but this time around, everyone had to show up. So subpar work was unacceptable because we are representing not only ourselves but this institution and country"* (South African student, survey).

Interest in engaging with other students and appreciation for receiving replies [responsibility to the task] were described: *"It was really nice to see how excited they were to hear about learning from each other and the topics"* (American faculty, PLC). Delegating responsibility and accountability in groups was identified as helping students to take responsibility and to monitor if other group members were responsible and participating. A South African student commented, *"We gave ourselves more time to do the research, we made sure that each person in the group gets to do equal work and submit the work on time"* (South African student, survey).

They were mentioning how surprised they were regarding the similarities of the local challenges so you know the educational topics they thought about knowing that somebody else in a different part of the world has a similar situation or similar challenge related to the classroom management or behavior they were also they were appreciative for learning from each other, the ones who received answers they appreciated those connections (American faculty, PLC).

In contrast, the following key factors were identified as having a negative effect on fostering a student level of responsibility in their COIL engagement and their research.

Disappointing responses by COIL partners: "*Our partner didn't give us a straight answer for our questions, so we had to assume what he meant in his answering.*" (South African student, survey). American students asked questions of their partners around their own research topic and teaching. were expectant of replies from partners and their' educational responsibilities, with expectations to reply and also to engage on these important educational topics:

At the end of my video, I asked my colleagues if they have any strategies for keeping students engaged online (if they've ever taught online) and what they were". How do you motivate students to actively engage/participate in reading activities other than saying reading is for fun, gaining knowledge, or stating that these interventions may affect their current reading comprehension skills? (American student, reflection).

These findings reflect a snapshot of the American students' thinking and perceptions regarding expectations of their COIL partners' engagement and responsibility to these same classroom challenges. In a way, the American students thought that their South African counterparts had experienced similar educational challenges and might have had similar responsibilities, thereby being hopeful for rendering possible helpful solutions.

Rendering Capable

Rendering each other capable within response-able pedagogy must naturally occur in relationships (Bozalek & Zembylas, 2017). The COIL collaboration offered and supported the process of participant engagement, giving opportunities for foregrounding capability within student learning. In general, most students and faculty felt they had benefitted through the COIL collaboration through their actions and responses. Reasons participants gave for feeling that this experience empowered and rendered them capable varied. These reasons included experience of a COIL course; changing perceptions of each other's contexts; finding solutions to current practice; building confidence to interact internationally; possibilities for ongoing contact, modeling a pedagogy for future use; and strengthening their research focus and understanding.

Changing perceptions of other contexts and learning within local contexts were evident:

You might learn more about you, the particular context you're in, so, it's not only about learning. About the international context, you know. (South African student Group B, P1, interview)

Getting to hear from people in a different part of the world was so cool! I found it incredibly reassuring and interesting that my partners had similar experiences and inquiries as I have had in my education and teaching practice. (American student, reflection). So, for me, the most valuable thing that I learned is that we, in the world, our learners - are basically the same. (South African student, Group A P3 interview). Positive perspectives included: "This type of connectivity makes the world feel smaller and more united." (American student, reflection).

We all come from different backgrounds internationally, but this made me realize that we have more in common in those very differences. And there is beauty in sharing these differences that connect us. It was eye opening and made me grateful to be a teacher in the modern age. (South African student, survey).

I think we have not thought that maybe America has the same problems as we do. For example, we're doing overcrowding, So, how can they have it? Because we have never seen that on the movie. For example, so we wouldn't think that we have the same problem. So, we have the same situations or anything but I think we can actually learn from each other and even if he didn't quite understand our question, maybe he just saw it from another perspective and answered it with another perspective. (South African student Group B, P2, interview)

To know that we're not alone. As in the South African context, we're not alone, facing all these problems. (South African student Group B, P1, interview)

But then we learn about other people and their countries and we just come to recognize that we're all dealing with, you know, many issues in different ways and some of them, they're so similar. So that made me feel like, it's not us alone like we're all tackling, you know, different issues. (South African student Group B, P1, interview).

In contrast, American students noted:

I did not get much of an enriching experience with these tasks. There was not much interaction between myself and my group. This part of the class seemed completely separate from the rest of the class. (American Student, reflection).

More clear (COIL) expectations and lines of communication would help improve students. (American student, reflection)

This revealed the challenges of students trying to incorporate the action research process with the COIL collaboration, implying that more interaction and clear assignment alignment would be beneficial. Common thoughts around engaging more with partners revealed student desires to focus on theirs and their partners' capability within the relationships:

I think once the relationship is more established it will be easier to have set guidelines and due dates for responses. It would have been great to talk to them throughout the semester and to have them involved in our literature reviews and action research projects more. (American student, reflection).

I just wish that we could have more meetings with our COIL partner...And who knows, become pen pals and friends. And collaborated in our research and moved forward. It really developed or helped in my development as a teacher and I am looking forward to research and being a lifelong learner like Jennie because whatever decisions you do, whatever you said you do. (South African student Group A, P1, interview).

This supports the theme of students desiring more time in the partner relationship and gives evidence to the response-able pedagogy element of capability – as capability began to be developed students saw in each other potential for future connections.

Evidence did show that students recognized their own thinking processes during the collaboration: The group also gave many helpful suggestions about what could be done to improve this issue including improving literacy at home. Their response really made me think... (South African student, survey). It helps me to think critically of situations (South African student, survey)

I think a one for me, is that the way that we both gather information, might not be the same but it comes out the same. So that is one thing that maybe that I've learned ... Was that the maybe we didn't do things the same way, but we thought the same things and had the same ideas, or the same conclusion. (South African student Group A, P4, interview)

It was heavy because we've never done something like this before but having a COIL part and also hearing what they have to say you know to your thoughts, your ideas about your research, takes you further than just what you were thinking. So, having a COIL partner made us or helped us think out of the box. (South African student Group A, 1 interview).

Being exposed to a different kind of pedagogy through COIL was identified by South African students interviewed as opening up ideas for them about how they could do things in the future in their own classrooms. They commented "I felt really empowered by just engaging with the student from Masters and I want, I mean, I'm at this age and I'm already empowered. What more if you started from the beginning of your schooling years?" (South African student Group A, P5, interview). Another student commented:

...it's something great to do. Especially in a classroom, maybe Google meet or Zoom with learners from overseas. You don't know what type of feeling you will create under your learners you know, ... Actually try to do the best so that they can maybe one day meet those learners and even work with them in a COIL project just like we have so it is really something great to do. (South African student Group A, P1, interview)

American students also pointed out the link between COIL and future ideas or opportunities for international partnerships in their own classrooms, per this student's statement in regards to:

I would love to be able to Zoom or video chat with a practicing teacher in another country and be able to plan a way for our classrooms to connect, like an open Q&A for our students. I think it would be such a meaningful experience. (American student, survey)

Evidence from these participants suggests that the COIL collaboration played an important role in rendering both faculty and students more capable through the sharing of resources, ideas and shifting perceptions. In addition, exposure to a COIL course provided a learning experience into the use of COIL as a pedagogical practice in enhancing teacher and researcher development. Furthermore, participation in this COIL collaboration gave faculty the opportunity to reflect on the extent to which they designed and implemented a response-able pedagogy.

SOLUTIONS AND RECOMMENDATIONS

Drawing on both student and faculty data, as well as key learnings from related literature conclude with a number of recommendations to strengthen a *response-able pedagogy* in COIL courses in higher education. The four dimensions of the response-able pedagogy were connected throughout as students paid attention to each other's videos and responses with curiosity, rendering themselves capable to engage actively through COIL while listening, advising, learning (learning from each other and learning how to use the Flip video platform) and being responsible to reply to their COIL partners on time.

The results showed that the participants had a range of perspectives from appreciation to suggesting changes for COIL and Flip leading to questions on the integration of COIL in the action research curriculum. Positive findings indicate that students engaged in COIL experience to receive advice, with an eagerness to learn and discuss teaching strategies and techniques related to topics they were researching (such as, behavior and self-management, reading, sensory inputs, sensory breaks, differentiated instruction, socio emotional learning, bullying) to other topics related to pedagogical strategies to enhance teaching and learning, student engagement or achievement or collaboration within their subject areas or grade levels. Aspects of the COIL engagement that enhanced curiosity included hearing others' perspectives and experiences and 'seeing others' faces and hearing their voices' on the videos. Experiencing videos that contained visually contextualized information were identified as deepening curiosity and providing greater insight into contextual conditions.

This COIL experience through the expanded and diverse curriculum did support engagement related to issues in other contexts that helped students and faculty to compare and widen their knowledge and shift perceptions (Oparinde et al., 2022). These are critically important components of internationalizing the curriculum (Leask, 2015; Mbaki et al. 2021; Oparinde et al., 2022) and ensuring inclusion. Findings show that students reacted to others' input with curiosity, wonder, and inquiry as this was new to them. Participants expressed reassurance in learning that partners had similar experiences and inquiries while comparing educational challenges globally outside of local encounters.

While students were connecting with each other on topics related to their action research projects and classroom practices, the faculty involved also connected through the use of their PLC within the "respons-able pedagogy framework" with attentiveness, curiosity, responsibility and capability (Figure 2). The faculty spent numerous hours planning, discussing, and reflecting on the learning of students and their own. Within the "response-able framework" pedagogy and their participatory action research, the authors also became invested, supportive of each other and their students, and respectful of each other's environments, possibilities and challenges. In a previous study, the authors discussed the powerful nature of action research, and in particular the power of community that "provides both social connection and a focus on collaborative problem solving" (Slapac, 2021, p. 43). Through participatory action research, the authors, as faculty, were able to reflect on our curriculum design, and to support student agency through engaging in their transnational learning. Factors supporting COIL by faculty were paying attention to the design of the assessment task as one strategy to support an internationalized curriculum and including this in our course outcomes. Beelen (2022) highlights the importance of integrating internationalization into course curricula and outcomes.

Figure 2. "Response-able pedagogy" in COIL using phases of participatory action research
Source: Own Elaboration

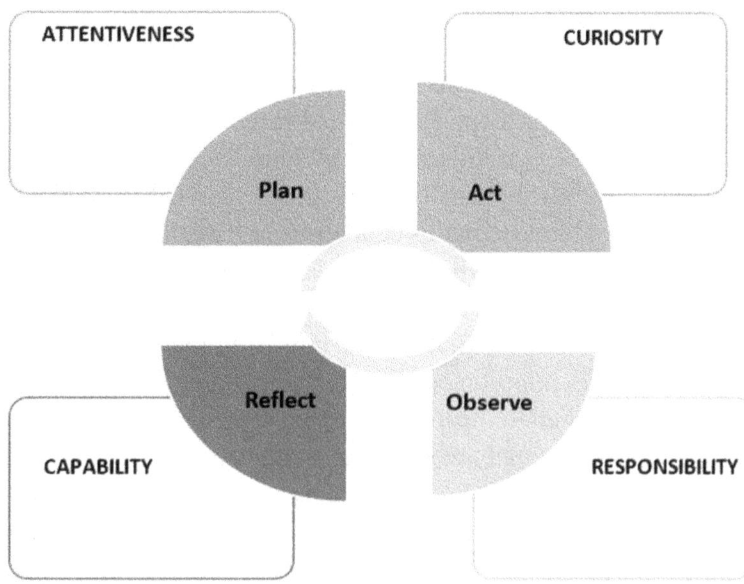

Orientation to COIL and the COIL goals, while supported through a level of class engagement at the start of the course, (with the sharing of related articles), in the long run needed a greater focus and reflection on the position of the project within the overall course curriculum. The data showed that some students found the COIL goals to be unclear at the start of the course, though the COIL experience inducted participants into a pedagogical practice they could try out in the future. A recommendation would be to allocate greater time for reflection on COIL courses in both the course orientation and conclusion to promote the value of COIL as a pedagogical practice in teacher and researcher development.

Faculty and students felt that the Flip online platform generally worked well for them. It enabled students and faculty to respond to tasks uploaded and to read comments or watch videos from all submissions. Providing an instructional video and support for a platform that most students used for the first time was very useful and appreciated. Induction to new technologies used are recommended to ensure that participants feel connected and empowered through the use of technological tools selected for the COIL course.

Reviewing the data, it was evident that participants experienced positive as well as challenging experiences with the COIL project, with limitations or constraints due to technological affordances and communication opportunities. Challenges to online inter-continental and time zone engagement via COIL courses raise the notion of all dimensions of a "response-able" pedagogy to new levels of awareness. In addition, South African students had connectivity challenges due to (power outages) or load shedding of electricity.

While most students commented on the ease of using Flip to create the videos and connect with the COIL partners, a number of students found the use of only this platform as limiting. Being able to connect synchronously for tasks would provide a level of flexibility for students to engage in their own time; however, they also experienced the limitations of the asynchronous engagement provided by Flip and the task brief. Levels of student curiosity and attentiveness were limited by students not being able to elicit immediate feedback to comments and questions or to probe responses more directly. A recommendation to improve attentiveness and curiosity would be to include both asynchronous and synchronous dimensions to the COIL contact. In addition to designing both these forms of engagement through technology, the authors would recommend including options for more flexible engagement by students to select their own engagement platforms such as WhatsApp and Zoom. Promoting these opportunities would build in opportunities for more regular and deeper engagement by more students.

The challenges of ensuring that all students in large classes of over 300 students are included in the COIL collaboration was not fully addressed in this course due to logistical and administrative challenges. Although South African students had identified group leaders who had the responsibility of linking to the Flip platform and sharing information with their peers, many students felt excluded from more direct and synchronous engagement. These findings are similar to the previous findings in Slapac et al. (2023a). Beelen (2022) stresses the importance of all students being involved in a purposeful way for courses to make claims about internationalization at home. A recommendation to enhance students in large classes to be able to participate equally would be to engage more flexibly with a range of technologies that could support both synchronous and asynchronous engagement by large classes and delegating greater responsibility to students.

COIL courses provide the opportunity for an experience of internationalization at home for both students and faculty. Using a response-able pedagogy lens to reflect on their practice helped consider in more depth how the authors' experiences of internationalization using COIL could match up to what De Wit and Beelen (2014) refer to as both high moral principles, as well as a commitment to pursue them in practice. Engaging in collaboration and research into their COIL practice has helped to strengthen what Gregersen-Hermans and Lauridsen (2021) contend is internationally informed research that can strengthen teaching and learning, as well as develop skills relevant for future national and global competence that supports inclusion.

FUTURE RESEARCH DIRECTIONS

Faculty involved in this COIL collaboration aim to deepen and extend the strengthening of their COIL course design and research in 2023 and 2024 through an inter-institutional collaboration. The authors intend to redesign their next COIL course taking into consideration the need to improve on those aspects of a "response-able" pedagogy they recommend be changed.

The study's authors have found the dimension of a response-able pedagogy (Bozalek & Zembylas, 2017) to provide a useful lens to help us reflect in a more depth and in a critical way on our COIL courses from the perspective of both students and faculty. It is recommended that other academics involved in COIL collaboration consider using the dimensions of a "response-able" pedagogy to support reflection on improvement in their research and practice from a social justice perspective. Particular areas of interest to research would be the relationship between the affordances of different technologies used to promote a response-able pedagogy in large COIL classes; researching the relationship between exposure to COIL courses and student update of COIL practices in their own future classrooms; the role of COIL in supporting collaborative action research, and strengthening COIL course curriculum design to promote internationalization and the development of global competencies in teacher and research development.

CONCLUSION

This chapter highlighted lessons learnt about the value of COIL from the authors' course in supporting a "response-able pedagogy" in higher education courses and teacher development programs. The results enhanced the positive aspects of providing students and faculty with such opportunities for interactions, transnational learning and self-reflection to promote the deepening of learning, shifting and expansion of perceptions and joint problem solving. Results show that the sharing of videos via the Flip online platform as well as the reflexive nature of the COIL task which gave students assessment credits, stimulated attentiveness and curiosity towards their action research project, to each other and their global research and teaching contexts. COIL modeled a promising pedagogical practice in teacher and researcher development. Faculty experienced Flip as a useful platform to administer and respond to students. Challenges students encountered to their attentiveness and level of responsibility included limitation of the asynchronous engagement and reduced levels of responsibility by students not directly involved on Flip in large classes. Future pedagogical considerations in strengthening a "response-able pedagogy" would include flexible opportunities for synchronous and asynchronous engagement using a range of online platforms for all students. Future research by faculty into the design and curriculum of COIL courses as a "response-able pedagogy" to support internationalization and the building of global competence is recommended.

ACKNOWLEDGMENT

The authors wish to thank all their students who participated in the COIL course in Spring 2023 and to their own higher education institutions for their continued support for global education practices. This COIL partnership was funded through the University of Missouri South African Education Program (UMSAEP).

REFERENCES

Asojo, A. O., Kartoshkina, Y., Jaiyeoba, B., & Amole, D. (2019). Multicultural learning and experiences in design through Collaborative Online International Learning (COIL) framework. *Journal of Teaching and Learning with Technology*, *8*(1), 5–16. doi:10.14434/jotlt.v8i1.26748

Balta, E., & Altan-Olcay, Ö. (2016). Strategic citizens of America: Transnational inequalities and transformation of citizenship. *Ethnic and Racial Studies*, *39*(6), 939–957. doi:10.1080/01419870.2015.1103882

Barad, K. (2007). *Meeting the universe halfway*. Duke University Press. https://www.dukeupress.edu/Meeting-the-Universe-Halfway

Beelen, J. (2022). Why we should continue to ask critical questions about internationalisation at home. *Perspectives in Education*, *40*(4), 325–327. doi:10.38140/pie.v40i4.7004

Beelen, J., & Jones, E. (2015). Redefining internationalisation at home. In A. Curai, L. Matei, R. Pricopie, J. Salmi, & P. Scott (Eds.), *The European higher education area: Between critical reflections and future policies* (pp. 67–80). Springer. doi:10.1007/978-3-319-20877-0_5

Bozalek, V., & Zembylas, M. (2017). Towards a response-able pedagogy across higher education institutions in post-apartheid South Africa: An ethico-political analysis. *Education as Change*, *21*(2), 62–85. doi:10.17159/1947-9417/2017/2017

Braun, V., & Clarke, V. (2012). Thematic analysis. In H. Cooper, P. M. Camic, D. L. Long, A. T. Panter, D. Rindskopf, & K. J. Sher (Eds), APA handbook of research methods in psychology, Vol. 2: Research designs: Quantitative, qualitative, neuropsychological, and biological (pp. 57-71). American Psychological Association. doi:10.1037/13620-004

Chambers, R. (2007). From PRA to PLA and pluralism: Practice and theory (No. 286). The University of Sussex Brighton, Institute of Development Studies.

Che, A. A. M. A. (2023). Benefits and challenges of transnational education: Reflections from a Sino-British joint venture university. *International Journal of Chinese Education, 12*(1). doi:10.1177/2212585X221144903

Collett, K., Von der Heyden, B., Pott, R. W. M., & Stander, J. (2018). A collaborative auto-ethnographic exploration of socially just practices by new academics in two South African higher education institutions. *South African Journal of Higher Education*, *32*(6), 582–603. doi:10.20853/32-6-2983

Custer, L., & Tuominen, A. (2017). Bringing "Internationalization at Home" opportunities to community colleges: Design and assessment of an online exchange activity between U.S. and Japanese students. *Teaching Sociology*, *45*(4), 347–357. doi:10.1177/0092055X16679488

De Oliveira Andreotti, V. (2014). Critical and transnational literacies in international development and global citizenship education. *Sisyphus— Journal of Education*, *2*(3), 32–50. https://www.redalyc.org/pdf/5757/575763895003.pdf

De Wit, H., & Beelen, J. (2014). *Reading between the lines: Global internationalisation survey*. University World News. https://surl.li/rfibh

Deardorff, D. K. (2019). *Manual for developing intercultural competencies: Story circles*. Routledge. doi:10.4324/9780429244612

DePaul University. (n.d.). *Global learning experience (GLE) student survey questions*. https://resources.depaul.edu/teaching-commons/programs/global-learning/Documents/GLEStudentSurveyQuestions_v.042018.pdf

DeWinter, A., & Klamer, R. (2021). Can COIL be effective in using diversity to contribute to equality? Experiences of iKudu, a European-South African consortium operating via a decolonised approach to project delivery. In M. Satar (Ed.), Virtual exchange: Towards digital equity in internationalisation (pp. 29-40). Research-publishing.net. doi:10.14705/rpnet.2021.53.1287

Dyrness, A. (2021). Rethinking global citizenship education with/for transnational youth. *Globalisation, Societies and Education*, *19*(4), 443–455. doi:10.1080/14767724.2021.1897001

Gregersen-Hermans, J., & Lauridsen, K. M. (2021). *Internationalising programmes in higher education: An educational development perspective*. Routledge. doi:10.4324/9780429344503

Guimarães, F. F., & Finardi, K. R. (2021). Global citizenship education (GCE) in internationalisation: COIL as alternative Thirdspace. *Globalisation, Societies and Education*, *19*(5), 641–657. doi:10.1080/14767724.2021.1875808

Guimarães, F. F., Mendes, A. R. M., Rodrigues, L. M., dos Santos Paiva, R. S., & Finardi, K. R. (2019). Internationalization at home, COIL and intercomprehension: For more inclusive activities in the Global South. *SFU Educational Review*, *12*(3), 90–109. doi:10.21810/sfuer.v12i3.1019

Hahn, C. L. (2015). Teachers' perceptions of education for democratic citizenship in schools with transnational youth: A comparative study in the UK and Denmark. *Research in Comparative and International Education*, *10*(1), 95–119. doi:10.1177/1745499914567821

Jie, Z., & Pearlman, A. M. G. (2018). Expanding access to international education through technology enhanced collaborative online international learning (COIL) courses. *International Journal of Technology in Teaching and Learning*, *14*(1), 1–11. https://files.eric.ed.gov/fulltext/EJ1211995.pdf

Katre, A. (2020). Creative economy teaching and Learning–A collaborative online international learning case. *International Education Studies*, *13*(7), 145–155. doi:10.5539/ies.v13n7p145

Kemmis, S., & McTaggart, R. (2005). *Participatory action research: Communicative action and the public sphere*. Sage Publications Ltd. doi:10.4135/9781473921290.n45

Kerkhoff, S. N., Mardi, F., & Rong, H. (2021). An action research study on globally competent teaching in online spaces. In A. Slapac, P. Balcerzak, & K. O'Brien (Eds.), *Handbook of research on the global empowerment of educators and student learning through action research* (pp. 264–288). IGI Global. doi:10.4018/978-1-7998-6922-1.ch012

Kim, S., & Slapac, A. (2015). Culturally responsive, transformative pedagogy in the transnational era: Critical perspectives. *Educational Studies (Ames)*, *51*(1), 17–27. doi:10.1080/00131946.2014.983639

King de Ramirez, C. (2021). Global citizenship education through collaborative online international learning in the Borderlands: A case of the Arizona–Sonora megaregion. *Journal of Studies in International Education*, *25*(1), 83–99. doi:10.1177/1028315319888886

Kopish, M., & Marques, W. (2020). Leveraging technology to promote global citizenship in teacher education in the United States and Brazil. *Research in Social Sciences and Technology*, *5*(1), 45–69. doi:10.46303/ressat.05.01.3

Leask, B. (2015). *Internationalizing the curriculum*. Routledge. doi:10.4324/9781315716954

Lilley, K., Barker, M., & Harris, N. (2015). Exploring the process of global citizen learning and the student mind-set. *Journal of Studies in International Education*, *19*(3), 225–245. doi:10.1177/1028315314547822

Lincoln, Y. S., & Guba, E. G. (1985). Naturalistic inquiry. *Sage.*

Marcillo-Gómez, M., & Desilus, B. (2016). Collaborative online international learning experience in practice opportunities and challenges. *Journal of Technology Management & Innovation*, *11*(1), 30–35. doi:10.4067/S0718-27242016000100005

Marginson, S. (2022). Space and scale in higher education: The glonacal agency heuristic revisited. *Higher Education*, *84*(6), 1365–1395. doi:10.1007/s10734-022-00955-0 PMID:36415669

Mayring, P. (2014). *Qualitative content analysis: Theoretical foundations, basic procedures and software solutions.* Philipp Mayring. https://nbn-resolving.org/urn:nbn:de:0168-ssoar-395173

Mbaki, Y., Todorova, E., & Hagan, P. (2021). Diversifying the medical curriculum as part of the wider decolonising effort: A proposed framework and self-assessment resource toolbox. *The Clinical Teacher*, *18*(5), 459–466. doi:10.1111/tct.13408 PMID:34467663

Moje, E. B. (2007). Chapter 1 Developing socially just subject-matter instruction: A review of the literature on disciplinary literacy teaching. *Review of Research in Education*, *31*(1), 1–44. doi:10.3102/0091732X07300046001

Moon, S. (2010). Multicultural and global citizenship in a transnational age: The case of South Korea. *International Journal of Multicultural Education*, *12*(1), 1–15. doi:10.18251/ijme.v12i1.261

Mundel, J. (2020). International virtual collaboration in advertising courses: Building international and intercultural skills from home. *Journal of Advertising Education*, *24*(2), 112–132. doi:10.1177/1098048220948522

Naicker, A., Singh, E., & van Genugten, T. (2022). Collaborative online international learning (COIL): Preparedness and experiences of South African students. *Innovations in Education and Teaching International*, *59*(5), 499–510. doi:10.1080/14703297.2021.1895867

Oparinde, K. M., Govender, V., & Moyo, S. (2022). Entrenching internationalisation in African Higher Education Institutions. *Perspectives in Education*, *40*(4), 104–116. doi:10.38140/pie.v40i4.6849

Quintana-Ordorika, A., Garay-Ruiz, U., Camino-Esturo, E., & Portillo-Berasaluce, J. (2024). The impact of using Collaborative Online International Learning during the design of maker educational practices by pre-service teachers. *Sustainability (Basel)*, *16*(3), 1–14. doi:10.3390/su16031222

Rubin, J. (2017). Embedding Collaborative Online International Learning (COIL) at higher education institutions: An evolutionary overview with exemplars. *Internationalisation of Higher Education, 2*, 28-44. https://bit.ly/48N6p8i

Rudolph, N., Monson, J., Collett, K., & Sonn, B. (2008). *How to build a caring school community.* Children's Institute, University of Cape Town and South African Democratic Teachers' Union. https://bit.ly/4a4gOgP

Ruiz, N. T., & Baird, P. J. (2013). Transnational teacher education: Towards theory and practice. *NABE Journal of Research and Practice*, *4*(1), 60–100. doi:10.1080/26390043.2013.12067768

Sierra-Huedo, M. L., Bruton, L., & Fernández, C. (2024). Becoming global at home: An analysis of existing cases and a proposal for the future of internationalization at home. *Journal of Education*, *204*(1), 241–254. doi:10.1177/00220574221108053

Slapac, A. (2021). Advancing students' global competency through English language learning in Romania: An exploratory qualitative case study of four English language teachers. *Journal of Research in Childhood Education*, *35*(2), 231–247. doi:10.1080/02568543.2021.1880993

Slapac, A., Collett, K., Wessels, F., Gamiet, G., & Knudsmoen, H. (2023a). Social justice pedagogy and Collaborative Online International Learning (COIL): Across three higher education institutions (American, Norwegian and South African). In P. Escudeiro, N. Escudeiro, & O. Bernardes (Eds.), Implementing inclusive educational models and technologies for equity and diversity (pp. 252-272). IGI Global. doi:10.4018/979-8-3693-0453-2.ch013

Slapac, A., Coppersmith, S., & Cheng, J. (2023b). Global competence development through the lens of graduate students in action research courses. In C. E. Ullom & N. Guler (Eds.), *At school in the world: Developing globally engaged teachers* (pp. 98–117). Rowman & Littlefield.

Slapac, A., Coppersmith, S. A., O'Brien, K., & Balcerzak, P. (2021). Resilience in crisis: Developing community through action research. In A. Slapac, P. Balcerzak, & K. O'Brien (Eds.), *Handbook of research on the global empowerment of educators and student learning through action research* (pp. 23–48). IGI Global. doi:10.4018/978-1-7998-6922-1.ch002

Song, K. H., Kerkhoff, S. N., & Slapac, A. (2023). Educating racially, culturally, and linguistically diverse children in a global era: The world at home and at home in the world. In J. Chitiyo & Z. Pietrantoni (Eds.), *Social justice and culturally-affirming education in K-12 settings* (pp. 1–22). IGI Global. doi:10.4018/978-1-6684-6386-4.ch001

Suny COIL Center. (n. d.). What is COIL? https://online.suny.edu/introtocoil/suny-coil-what-is/

Tronto, J. (2013). *Caring Democracy: Markets, Equality, and Justice*. New York University Press.

UNESCO/Council of Europe (COE). (2001). *Code of good practice in the provision of transnational education*. https://rm.coe.int/090000168097c674

Vahed, A. (2022). Factors enabling and constraining students' collaborative online international learning experiences. *Learning Environments Research*, *25*(3), 895–915. doi:10.1007/s10984-021-09390-x

Vahed, A., & Rodriguez, K. (2021). Enriching students' engaged learning experiences through the collaborative online international learning project. *Innovations in Education and Teaching International*, *58*(5), 596–605. doi:10.1080/14703297.2020.1792331

Whitehead, J. (2012). Educational research for social change with living educational theories. *Educational Research for Social Change, 1*(1), 5-21. https://bit.ly/4a95nEn

Wyman, S., & Bellot, A. (2021). Integrating sustainability education with diversity, equity & inclusion in COIL virtual exchange projects on literary studies and culture. *Proceedings of International Virtual Exchange Conference*, 104-105. https://iveconference.org/wp-content/uploads/2022/03/IVECFinal_Proceedings_2021.pdf#page=105

Zembylas, M., & Bozalek, V. (2017). Re-imagining socially just pedagogies in higher education: The contribution of contemporary theoretical perspectives. *Education as Change*, *21*(2), 1–5. doi:10.17159/1947-9417/2017/3051

Zhang, J., & Pearlman, A. M. G. (2018). Expanding access to international education through technology enhanced collaborative online international learning (COIL) courses. *International Journal of Technology in Teaching and Learning*, *14*(1), 1–11. doi:10.37120/ijttl.2018.14.1.01

ADDITIONAL READING

Baralt, M., Doscher, S., Boukerrou, L., Bogosian, B., Elmeligi, W., Hdouch, Y., Istifan, J., Nemouchi, A., Khachatryan, T., Elsakka, N., Arana, F., Cobos-Solis, J., Perez, G., Mouchane, S.-E., & Vassigh, S. (2022). Virtual tabadul: Creating language-learning community through virtual reality. *Journal of International Students*, *12*(S3), 168–188. doi:10.32674/jis.v12iS3.4638

Crawford, I., Fowler, J., Doscher, S., & Haug, E. (2021, February 9). *Enhancing global learning and intercultural competence through VE/COIL: lessons from the field* [Conference presentation]. ACENET [online]. https://www.acenet.edu/Events/Pages/Enhancing-Global-Learning-and-Intercultural-Competence-through-VECOIL-Lessons-from-the-Field.aspx

Ketteringham, M., Shiel, J., & Valavanis, A. (2022). Using the transnational setting to develop the intercultural communication skills of electronic and electrical engineering students. *Proceedings of the 8th International Symposium for Engineering Education*. 10.17868/strath.00082037

Landorf, H., Doscher, S., & Hardrick, J. (2018). *Making global learning universal: Promoting inclusion and success for all students*. Stylus Publishing, LLC.

Quintana-Ordorika, A., Camino-Esturo, E., Portillo-Berasaluce, J., & Garay-Ruiz, U. (2023). Integrating COIL in teacher training: An estimation of learners´ motivational attitudes. *Frontiers in Education*, *8*, 1–9. doi:10.3389/feduc.2023.1141620

Rubin, J., & Guth, S. (2022). The Guide to COIL virtual exchange: Implementing, growing, and sustaining collaborative online international learning. Stylus Publishing, LLC.

Rubin, J., Haug, E., Succi, O., & El Masri, A. (2020). *Webinar: Collaborative online international learning (COIL): Connecting classrooms across the globe*. International Education Week 2020, 2. https://source.sheridancollege.ca/conferences_iew_2020/2

KEY TERMS AND DEFINITIONS

Collaborative Online International Learning (COIL): Is an approach that brings students and professors together across cultures to learn, discuss and collaborate as part of their class. Professors partner to design the experience, and students partner to complete the activities designed.

Flip: (Formerly Flipgrid) is a video-based tool that allows for discussion across digital devices, but in a fun and engaging way that makes it ideal for use in education. At its most basic, Flip is a video tool that allows teachers to post "Topics" that are essentially videos with some accompanying text. This is then shared with students, who can be prompted to respond.

Global Citizenship: Is the umbrella term for social, political, environmental, and economic actions of globally minded individuals and communities on a worldwide scale. The term can refer to the belief that individuals are members of multiple, diverse, local and non-local networks rather than single actors affecting isolated societies.

Global Competence: Is a multi-dimensional construct that requires a combination of knowledge, skills, attitudes and values successfully applied to global issues or intercultural situations.

Glocal: A viewpoint that posits the world as the sum of complex, interconnected parts. A viewpoint that tries to understand the place or places of individuals, groups, cultures and societies in the world and how they relate to each other.

Glonacal: Referred to three interacting scales of activity and agency: global + national + local.

Participatory Action Research (PAR): Is an approach to action research emphasizing participation and action by members of communities affected by that research. It seeks to understand the world by trying to change it, collaboratively and following reflection.

Transnational Learning/Education: Refers to study programs or educational services in which the learners are located in a country different from the one where the awarding institution is based.

Transnational Teacher Education: Refers to the teacher education programs that seek to develop a paradigm of connectedness and solidarity with the target people, culture, and educational community.

Chapter 5
Mapping Experiences of USA-Based Faculty COILing With LATAM:
Un-Fueling Inequities

Maria Ines Marino
Florida International University, USA

Stephanie Tadal
Florida International University, USA

Nurhayat Bilge
Fashion Institute of Technology, USA

ABSTRACT

In implementing virtual exchange programs such as COIL, faculty could also be impacted by issues of inequity related to their academic-professional development. More positive experiences could influence decision-making in embarking on internalization opportunities such as COIL programs. When faculty internationalization efforts are recognized, motivation and engagement positively impact involvement in programs such as COIL. In this study, authors explore the accounts of experiences and perceptions of US-based faculty who taught COIL (collaborative online international learning) courses in collaboration with Latin America institutions. The findings suggest that faculty is motivated but not supported properly.

INTRODUCTION

Internationalization of Education and COIL Pedagogy

As per the American Council on Education (ACE), colleges and universities within the United States have expressed a commitment to internationalization of education (ACE, 2017). The internationaliza-

DOI: 10.4018/978-1-6684-7813-4.ch005

tion of education is an iterative process, mostly because of the constant shifts in global demands, post-secondary education expectations, and the continued evolution of socio-political climates throughout the world. These dynamic and ever-changing variables impact how internationalization is carried out; and specifically, how the process of globalization impacts the opportunities for implementation of strategies to support internationalization in higher education (Knight, 2003). For the purpose of this chapter, internationalization is defined "as the process of integrating an international, intercultural, or global dimension into the purpose, functions, or delivery of postsecondary education" (Knight, 2003, p.2).

There are many ways in which higher education institutions (HEIs) address internationalization, including study abroad as well as virtual study abroad programs. One particular framework used in institutions of higher education to advance the mission towards internationalization is Virtual Exchange (VE). VE is a "pedagogical approach which involves the engagement of groups of learners in extended periods of online intercultural interaction and collaboration with partners from other cultural contexts or geographical locations" (O'Dowd, 2020, p. 2). VE programs also referred to as cross-border online education programs and transnational online education programs that create the opportunity for students to interact with individuals from other geographical locations both synchronously and asynchronously.

Although facilitated virtually, campus inequities are still perpetuated in global learning programs (Duranczyk & Pishcherskaia, 2018; Mudiamu, 2020), and most studies on digital inequities fail to address how formal inequities (access and resources) in education are intertwined with durable social inequities (i.e., race, class, ethnicity, gender, and other lines of oppression). There is an urgent need to comprehensively study inequity in digital international higher education programs such as Collaborative Online International Learning or COIL (Collin & Brotcorne, 2019; Papendieck, 2018; Slapac et al., 2023).

The team of researchers did just this and findings of their study indicated that VE programs such as COIL need to be designed to include cultural practices and support a culturally sensitive environment for underrepresented participants. Students, in this case Hispanic students, were allowed to connect to their international counterparts through 'home' language and cultural commonalities (Laird, 2015; Marino & Tadal, 2022; Numanee et al., 2020). In this instance, COIL was able to provide underrepresented college students with global learning opportunities which advance social and economic mobility (Appiah-Kubi & Annan, 2020; Esche, 2018; Mudiamu, 2020; O'Dowd, 2020) by building global knowledge and skills for the 21st century workplace (Standley, 2015).

Interestingly, while implementing VE programs such as COIL, faculty could also be impacted by issues of inequity related to their academic-professional growth. Basically, faculty are expected to fulfill increased demands of expectations, responsibilities, and time, negatively impacting minorities and women faculty particularly (Witkowsky & Gibbes, 2020). Furthermore, these inequities could be exacerbated if institutions do not commit in deeper ways (Witkowsky & Gibbes, 2020). Some of the main obstacles would be lack of institutional structure that can provide a balanced load between time and academic responsibilities, and lack of monetary incentives to participate in academic development opportunities. For example, Slapac et al. (2023) emphasize the urgent need for institutional logistical and technology support to make faculty participation in internationalization training opportunities, such as COIL, possible.

The authors propose that one way to address these challenges in the implementation of VE programs, such as COIL, could be through exploring and addressing faculty experiences. This will help identify instrumental strategies in establishing expectations, regulating behaviors through intercultural and technology training and support, and facilitating interactions that allow for the creation of inclusive and supportive environments (Brighton, 2020; Ho & Lin, 2016; Kavrayici, 2021; Keshavarz et al., 2022; Pearl et al, 2023; Seufert et al., 2022).

Finally, researchers (Vatrapu & Suthers, 2007) advise VE faculty to document the intersections and relationships between learning and technology, and their socio-cultural structures to better inform the design, implementation, and delivery of VE courses such as COIL. Documenting these experiences will allow for the careful construction of VE learning spaces that prioritizes the building of mutual values between cultures (Wimpenny et al., 2022).

BACKGROUND

Learning is achieved through communication, and effective communication is crucial for participation (Hidecker, 2010; Jaldemark, 2008). The way we communicate and how we understand communication exists hand-in-hand with contextual and cultural factors (Hall, 1977, 1990; Jaldemark, 2008). In other words, our culture teaches us how to communicate with others, what to pay attention to, and how to interpret messages when we communicate. Consequently, cultural differences have an impact on participation in educational contexts, specifically in VE education (Hall, 1990). Different cultures respond to communication in ways that could not be expected in one's own culture.

Thus, effective VE programs require the implementation of participatory strategies that can generate an environment in which students and faculty can develop their intercultural skills in a structured and safe manner (Brighton, 2020). However, among the core barriers and challenges in participation when embarking in internationalization programs such as COIL VE are linked to the existence of socio-cultural differences together with differences in technical considerations, and the lack of physical presence and diverse communication modes are (Ismailov, 2021; King Ramirez, 2022; McLaughlin & Ricevuto, 2021; Voogt et al., 2015).

The use of effective communication is essential in fostering participation, through meaningful interpersonal and socio-cultural-emotional interactions and academic learning, and student-teacher relationships in which students develop a sense of belonging (Ho & Lin, 2016). On the other hand, inclusion requires communication across individuals and groups in multicultural contexts, in which dialogue and exchange between individuals and groups with different cultural identifications may occur (Meer & Modood, 2012). So, the ability to effectively communicate could have a powerful impact not only on participation behaviors and the building of inclusive educational environments, it can also impact teaching quality as well as teacher stress and job dissatisfaction. (Seufert et al., 2022; Keshavarz et al., 2022).

Participation and Collaboration in VE: The Role of Culture

Culture, communication, and participation are interconnected concepts in the building of equity in educational contexts, specifically among faculty. Culture is a construct in which we develop and understand our thoughts and behaviors. Therefore, furthering our knowledge of the different cultural perspectives helps in building meaningful relationships across contexts, such as the educational context. Hall (1977) states that "culture controls behavior in deep and persisting ways, many of which are outside of awareness and therefore beyond conscious control of the individual" (p. 25). In reference to culture and learning, Hall (1977) asserts that "how one learns is culturally determined, as is what one learns" (p. 190). There are numerous definitions of culture, but Hall's (1977) definition is the most appropriate to analyze the intimate link between culture and participation in virtual exchange programs. This definition addresses how culture affects behavior and views culture as a multi-level (personal, relational, and structural) and dynamic-learned structure and process of shared interpretations. This affects members of the cultural group by shaping how they interpret reality, their relationships, and the social structure in which they interact.

Communication is a pivotal component and goes hand in hand with participation. Seemingly, participation is an essential prerequisite for developing higher-order thinking skills (HOTS) and constructing knowledge in collaborative settings such as VE programs (So et al., 2010). Consequently, faculty experiences in COIL design and delivery need to be studied to be able to align COIL experiences with the key factors that influence decision making to participate in VE programs. In addition, broader integrative and culturally sensitive designs and cross-cultural strategies for VE programs (such as COIL) need to be devised to generate opportunities for increased participation among students and faculty.

Understanding and considering culture is necessary to assess participation behaviors effectively and successfully in Virtual Exchange programs. Participation is triggered by the sense of cultural connection and belonging and a sign of increased integration and engagement (Camarillo & Bonilla, 2001; Garcia, 2017; Jagers et al., 2019). Thus, it is essential to design effective and empowering strategies and spaces for faculty participation in the implementation of VE programs, which may facilitate the development of pedagogies that re-center the concepts of cultural diversity and effective communication towards equity in education (Kim & Bonk, 2002; Szelei et al., 2020).

In sum, equity starts with inclusivity, and inclusivity starts with open and meaningful dialogue. Understanding faculty experiences in Virtual Exchange programs would help reduce the current limitations of faculty participation (Scardamalia & Bereiter, 2010) in such programs. It will also allow us to explore and predict real causes of participation patterns, and it will generate inclusive VE opportunities by consciously integrating differences in experiences, perspectives, and needs (Huang et al., 2010; Sweeney, 2013) based on meaningful and empowering support, guidance, and exchange (Szelei et al., 2020).

US-Based Faculty Experiences COILing With Latin America

Researchers acknowledge the essential role of faculty in addressing and advancing internationalization (Witkowsky & Gibbes, 2020). The preparation of faculty to advance internationalization goals in the bringing of innovative solutions to global needs and issues and in preparing students for global citizenship should focus on "transformative and instrumental outcomes requires recognition of patterns of inequity in faculty development strategies" (Witkowsky & Gibbes, 2020, p.76).

In the USA, Hispanic students are an underrepresented population in higher education (Mukherji et al., 2017). Yet by 2065, Hispanics will comprise 24% of the US population (Gonzalez et al.; 2020; Lopez et al., 2017), and they are the fastest growing ethnic group, with college enrollment doubling since 2000 (de Brey et al., 2019). HEIs can lessen marginalization by creating opportunities for Hispanics to enact their identity through interactions and connections with their linguistic and cultural heritage (Garcia, 2017; Garcia et al., 2019). This is the case with the fast-growing practice of US-Latin America COIL partnering (Mudiamu, 2020). Such engagements may reinforce identity and belonging and lessen injustice and inequity by strengthening representation through policy making and economic support (Camarillo & Bonilla, 2001; Garcia, 2017; Jagers et al., 2019).

Internationalization rates in Latin American educational institutions are among the lowest in the world, leaving North America and Europe dominating discussions and research and therefore perspectives (ICEF Monitor, 2022; IESALC, 2019; King Ramírez, 2022; OECD, 2019). Therefore, this gap impacts the interest in initiatives as well as ability to design and implement VE programs such as COIL which are intimately linked to the economic and social structures of each region, impacting the accessibility of academic resources.

Furthermore, limited technological infrastructure, unreliable internet access, and limited faculty training, support, and adaptability to online learning pedagogies are among the main limitations to VE implementation and growth while student mobility opportunities are only 1% (Humberto, 2016; ICEF Monitor, 2022; IESALC, 2019; Ramírez, 2021, 2022; Slapac et al., 2023).

Faculty internationalization experiences, in this case through the implementation of COIL/VE practices, need to be prioritized around transformative global goals to prepare students as global citizens (Eatman, 2018; Niehaus & Williams, 2016; Slapac et al., 2023; Witkowsky, & Gibbes, 2020). This entails pedagogies that integrate different cultural perspectives, knowledge, and content, aiming at transforming students' perspectives, per Witkowsky and Gibbes (2020): "Curriculum internationalization efforts must incorporate skill building for faculty around both content (instrumental) and ethnorelative attitudes and beliefs (transformative)" (p. 74).

VE programs such as COIL could be instrumental for underrepresented populations in higher education who seek social and economic mobility through higher education (O'Dowd, 2020). Thus, these programs can be designed and implemented to generate engagement and sense of belonging and increase representation and decrease marginalization of their underrepresented cultural groups (Cronin et al., 2012; Levin et al., 2006; O'Dowd, 2020; Tropp et al., 2004, 2012). In achieving these goals, it is essential to identify the several aspects (such as careful planning and design, and the facilitation of opportunities to address local and global issues) that need to be addressed and facilitated at a course and institutional level (Slapac et al., 2023) to ensure inclusion and participation of faculty. For example, researchers (Szelei et al., 2020) highlight the role of school administrators in facilitating environments that "helps teachers in transcending the stages of feeling that they struggle" (p. 792) to support and empower students through the implementation of Virtual Exchange programs such as COIL.

In sum, when working with COIL, creating intentional approaches towards building equity (Gautier, 2016; Gleason et al., 2021; Jie et al., 2018; O'Dowd, 2020; Slapac et al., 2023; van Rooij, 2016) entails the understanding of faculty experiences in attempting to plan and apply these approaches.

METHODOLOGY

The Study: Issues and Research Questions

In a previous study (Marino & Tadal, 2022), the authors examined perceptions and experiences of US-based Hispanic students who collaboratively participated in COIL courses with Latin American institutions. The authors found that pedagogy of virtual exchange could help lessen the marginalization of US-based Hispanic students, specifically students whose cultural background is one deriving from a Spanish-speaking country from Latin America. Basically, when VE programs such as COIL are designed to include cultural practices and support a culturally sensitive environment for underrepresented students, underrepresented populations are allowed to enact their cultural identity which positively impacts students' sense of belonging, resulting in increased engagement to learning, meaningful communication with their peers, and collaboration, reinforcing presence and representation. Specifically, the study was significant in helping inform professional practices to explore and predict causes of marginalization and to create virtual exchange opportunities that inclusively support underrepresented populations (Marino & Tadal, 2022).

Due to the findings in the previous research, the authors believe it is essential to explore perceptions and experiences of US-based faculty COILing with Latin America institutions as the role of faculty in facilitating such programs is indispensable. Therefore, in the current research study, the authors explore challenges and barriers from the perspective of USA-based faculty COILing with LATAM (Latin America). The authors aim to:

1. Identify challenges and barriers to access and engagement of USA-based Faculty COILing with Latin America higher education institutions.
2. Identify the impact of COIL experiences of USA-based Faculty COILing with Latin American higher education institutions.

The study addresses the following questions:

1. What are the experiences of USA-based Faculty COILing with Latin America higher education institutions?
2. What challenges and barriers to access and engagement do USA-based faculty encounter when COILing with higher education institutions?
3. What are the faculty recommendations for un-fueling inequities in US-based COIL programs within Latin American higher education institutions?

Research Design

This project employs qualitative methods to explore the accounts of experiences and perceptions of US-based faculty who taught COIL college courses in collaboration with Latin American institutions. A qualitative methodology allows researchers to build connections between the collected data and the context in which the study was performed (Bengtsson, 2016). Therefore, it is useful for understanding voices, views, and perceptions about phenomena. In this study, the authors attempt to understand the role of faculty experiences in advancing equity among US-based faculty engaging in VE programs with Latin American institutions. As explained in the literature review, higher education is becoming more international. Programs such as COIL allow teachers to offer a globalized and cross-cultural educational setting for their students. To achieve effective teaching in these platforms, teachers and teacher educators need to understand the role of the faculty as well as challenges faced during instructions. In this study, data mainly derived from nine US-based faculty testimonies who taught COIL undergraduate classes in collaboration with Latin American higher education institutions. The authors' research focuses on teaching in collaboration with Latin American institutions, but it can and should serve as a case study helping them to create teacher education programs that are relatable and meaningful to faculty. The data allows the authors to design experiences that speak specifically to the challenges faculty face, and the gaps in preparation. The researchers of this study are also faculty in different universities across the USA and have been teaching COIL undergraduate courses between three to six years, including COIL courses in collaboration with Latin America institutions. Thus, they can offer multitude of perspectives and recommendations for teacher education programs. Although the researchers are from different Universities, the commonality is that teacher preparation programs are limited and scarce. There are not enough opportunities to fully prepare faculty to embark on COIL. The mission was to fill this void in teacher preparation programs. All three researchers of this study have also been involved in previous research studies on COIL and underrepresented student populations. Having COIL experience (in teaching and researching) brings a deeper knowledge of COIL pedagogies.

Participants

After the authors successfully attained IRB approval, the authors sent email invitations to faculty who self-identified as having taught COIL undergraduate courses in collaboration with Latin American universities. Nine faculty successfully responded to their call and the authors proceeded to conduct nine interviews through Zoom.

Data Collection

Originally, the authors had scheduled ten interviews but one interviewee dropped participation from the study. Therefore, the authors conducted nine open-ended guided approach interviews (Johnson & Christensen, 2014) via Zoom. The researchers informed the interviewees of the purpose of the study, confidentiality procedures, and provided each participant with the university consent form to sign electronically and review before starting the interview. Interviews were guided by the protocol prepared by the researchers before the interview. Semi-structured interview questions were created so questions would follow a particular order, and the wording of questions listed was modified as required for clarification purposes during the interview (Johnson & Christensen, 2014). Each interview lasted forty-five minutes approximately. For data accuracy and analysis, the three researchers were involved in transcribing the interviews and in order to ensure anonymity and confidentiality, participant names were replaced by numbers. After transcription and before proceeding to data analysis, the three researchers resolved any arising question through team discussion.

Data Analysis and Data Interpretation

The purpose of this study was to analyze experiences of US-based faculty who have taught COIL courses in collaboration with Latin America institutions for the advancement of diversity, equity, and inclusion in VE programs in higher education. The authors were guided by internationalization approaches (Bedenlier & Zawacki-Richter, 2015) to VE pedagogies.

The authors employed qualitative content analysis. Content analysis allows researchers to build connections between the collected data and the context in which the study was performed. Patton (1990) describes content analysis as “any qualitative data reduction and sense-making effort that takes a volume of qualitative material and attempts to identify core consistencies and meanings” (p.453).

The authors removed all identifiable information from the participants and later individually immersed themselves in the transcripts and let the themes emerge from raw data guided by research questions. At first, more general themes emerged, researchers searched connections between themes (Seidman, 1998) that described the content, and reviewed emerging themes to verify connections. The authors kept a record of details related to our observations in a thematic chart, organizing data in themes and sub-themes.

The emerging themes informed the study questions which examined two aspects of the participants’ testimonies: (1) impact of experiences for USA-based Faculty COILing with Latin America, (2) challenges to access and engagement of USA-based Faculty COILing with Latin America, and (3) faculty recommendations for un-fueling inequities in US-based COIL programs within Latin American higher education institutions.

Finally, to ensure reliability researchers performed member-checking of transcripts, writing memos about emerging themes and sub-themes and constantly comparing them (continuous assessment of data), allowing for cross-checking of themes (Creswell, 2013; Miles & Huberman, 1994).

FINDINGS

Table 1 shows the themes which emerged from the data guided by the research questions representing three different aspects of the study: (1) impact for faculty, (2) challenges for faculty, and (3) recommendations from faculty. The emergent themes are multi-dimensional and intertwined, exhibiting multi-faceted concepts, which the authors explore and explain in the following section.

Table 1. Themes emerged from participant testimonies about their participation in COIL courses with Latin America higher education institutions

Faculty Impacts	Faculty Challenges	Faculty Recommendations
● Professional growth and networking ● Positive student outcomes and evaluations	● Connectivity and access ● Planning and collaboration ● Socio-cultural and political understanding	● Course design, cultural awareness training, and course evaluations strategies ● Professional and academic support

Source: Own elaboration

These themes are distinct, yet intertwined. For instance, the technology challenges that the participants experienced are directly influenced by the impacts and challenges for US-based faculty COILing with LATAM. The authors will explain these themes further through our analysis in the next section.

Faculty Impacts

The positive impact of incorporating COIL pedagogies was a constant topic that arose among all interviewed participants. Unanimously, participants reported that teaching through COIL pedagogies had brought tremendous benefits not only for the students but also for their professional and personal growth. Among the most beneficial impacts were that (1) COIL generated deeper collaboration, motivation and creativity from partnering with faculty in Latin American institutions, and that (2) COIL influenced evaluations and outcomes in a positive manner.

Professional Growth and Networking

Faculty often discuss the benefits of participating in VE/COIL learning experiences. Although there are many benefits to teaching students, there are specific experiences that COIL faculty have in common. These include collaboration with another COIL-inclined faculty and greater student satisfaction.

Basically, faculty reported building positive relationships with their co-facilitating faculty in a deeper, more connected manner. Participant # 1 stated, "I worked closer with them than any of my colleagues in my department in a very long time. That's for sure." These deep connections were important to faculty and one of the main reasons why faculty said they would engage in COIL again. Participant # 3 said,

I really enjoy the collaboration with the Faculty that I worked with. He was brilliant, he was. It was really great working with someone who's more brilliant than you but coming up with something together, so I enjoy the coil experience.

Furthermore, participants agreed that preparation of COIL courses is far more intense, requiring more time and planning, but most participants expressed a feeling of motivation that resulted from their "rich" and "enjoyable" collaborations. In general, participants addressed the gratification they felt in connecting with another faculty from a different culture. Moreover, participants felt that the most prominent benefits of these COIL collaborative opportunities were cultural perspective taking, networking, and creativity. Participant # 3 expresses the sense of cultural awareness awakening as: "I now realize that my impact, my perspective, my assumptions and prejudices of this world are informed by a very localized community." On a similar note, Participant # 4 said, "it's a, you know, two way and learning is not only the students but also the Faculty we are learning how to deal with other professors, we are learning how to understand."

The intercultural exchange was also perceived as a positive challenge and opportunity to improve their awareness of other academic structures and expectations, but most importantly they expressed how positive it was to learn different ways to pedagogically run the classes. For example, Participant # 3 explains,

COIL allows you to be so creative because most coil partners are not teaching the exact course you're teaching. You need to identify a module within your particular course or subject that aligns pedagogically with another topic within another subject matter…So, I enjoy the challenge of the creativity of weaving our subject matters together.

Finally, these collaborations were seen as a great benefit for themselves (faculty) and students due to the sharing of diverse readings and academic resources.

Positive Student Outcomes and Evaluations

The faculty in the study reported that students in higher education are looking for experiences that can help them prepare for working in the 21st century. For example, Participant #3 said:

I think it's so meaningful to them because it delivers on the promise of higher education and that diverse perspectives are an Aha-mind-blowing moment and my students, fortunately, are open to it and are so blatantly confronted with it, that they can't help but stand back in their own minds, creating new connections in this realization of truth and learning and growth.

Student satisfaction in these types of learning activities benefit the faculty, especially when it comes to student-teacher feedback evaluations. These evaluations are a high-stakes assessment on teacher performance as it holds implications for future course offerings, promotion, sabbatical, and other benefits high performing faculty are eligible for. Participant # 3 made this reference in the interview, "Because of those experiences my evaluations for the last two semesters were generally good." Faculty who had positive student responses to the COIL activities, stated they were more inclined to continue doing Virtual Exchange experiences.

Faculty Challenges

US-based faculty testimonies consistently reveal the presence of challenges in three main areas in COILing with LATAM. These are in the areas of (1) connectivity and access, (2) planning and collaboration, and (3) cultural and socio-political understanding.

These three areas are interconnected, however, in general they are perceived or experienced as a positive challenge and not as an impediment or limitation to participation in future VE experiences. Participant # 1 explains the sentiment as: "I wouldn't do this if I wouldn't love it. It's a lot of work. A hell of a lot of work that I don't get anything extra." On the contrary, participants almost unanimously agree that the experiences are of utmost importance for students in advancing global citizenship and DEI (diversity, equity, inclusion) goals. Moreover, participants perceived challenges as learning experiences to improve the pedagogical goals.

Connectivity and Access

Most technological challenges were reported in the area of connectivity and access, and the lack of common online learning platforms. Unanimously, participants reported connectivity issues related to slow bandwidth, limiting access to videoconferencing applications, mainly Zoom. Connectivity correlated with how remote the location of the partner was. For example, Participant # 2 explains: "There were connectivity problems. I would say that they, with this particular group from Colombia that come from a very remote area in the jungle." Participant # 5 expands on this issue when stating: "I didn't personally experience any technical challenges. But I know that Internet connections in Brazil weren't that great. So sometimes the students had a hard time connecting with each other."

In general, connectivity issues were present and fluctuating based on the task students needed to perform and type of content to be shared. In general, videos were difficult to upload, and videoconferencing was challenging:

[Internet] was slow when you have to upload things to that platform and especially for the students in Venezuela. They have a very unreliable Internet so it was difficult for them to use because [zoom] didn't work well. Then they went through WhatsApp. Latin American people are more used to working with What's up so they will share documents and ideas through WhatsApp. (Participant # 4).

Internet connectivity was another factor faculty mentioned as being an issue when working cross-nationally. A lack of consistency in access, due to sociopolitical factors (in our study these included impoverished areas or areas without appropriate infrastructure to support Wi-Fi), proved to be a challenge when students were COILing with other countries. Faculty stated without access to consistent and stable internet, it was difficult to communicate with other faculty (in order to set up and create assignments for students) or to help facilitate and troubleshoot communication barriers.

These types of issues impacted the perception of reliability of the platform, consequently, participants mostly reported Zoom as unreliable and problematic. WhatsApp was repeatedly reported as the main mode of communication and collaboration when COILing with Latin American institutions. Thus, unanimously participants reported replacing face-to-face interactions by video conferencing applications (Zoom) to text or audio-based interactions (WhatsApp), and thus seems to impact on planning decisions about what type of activities to design: "Well, the technology hurdles are always a big issue, I think. Having spoken to other people that have done COIL, if you're going to have a synchronous activity, the Internet connectivity and different locations can be really tough" (Participant # 6).

Even though connectivity and access issues were part of most participants' testimonies, perceptions on what is good or poor connectivity seem to be different for US-based participants who seem to be more sensitive to connectivity issues. For example, Participant # 3 summarizes the experience: "we're sensitive to bandwidth issues and we're popular for this particular age group so we used Slack as basically the LM [learning mode]".

Access to content was affected not only by poor connectivity but also by access restrictions to the collaborative platforms, impacting planning and collaboration regardless of having a strong technology support:

I think the collaborative opportunities were terrific. The infrastructure in place that each of the institutions had to be able to support was excellent. The student engagement was excellent. So, just having the right tools available to be able to facilitate it are really good. The thing that makes it difficult is because of our restrictions on our systems' access. They can't access our Microsoft teams. They can't access canvas. They can't access it. So, you've got to come up with other creative ways of doing that (Participant # 6).

All participants pointed out the need and convenience for the adoption of shared online learning platforms where COILing classes (from different countries) can collaboratively work, share content, and communicate. Participants agreed that the utilization of shared online learning platforms would facilitate collaboration and engagement for students and faculty, specifically impacting workload, time and communication in a more effective manner. Additionally, the possibility of a shared online platform could be the vehicle for more flexibility in planning and equity in distribution of roles and workload. Participant # 2 summarizes these common concerns: "Having a platform where we can collaborate and we can both take the lead."

Planning and Collaboration

Challenges related to planning and collaboration were common amongst faculty who participated in the study. Faculty mentioned the separation of physical space and differences in time zones; as well as the sociopolitical factors influencing access to the internet and specific technologies impeded student performance, participation in the class discussions, and faculty motivation towards wanting to do COIL in the future. The transformation of the classroom into an online space requires a significant amount of planning and proactivity to prevent interruption of learning.

VE and COIL activities require students to be able to collaborate in a meaningful way. When faculty are unable to account for and manage the communication amongst students, learning and progress in the project can be impacted. Factors which faculty stated impacted communication included access to stable internet and the difference in time zones. For example, Participant # 5 stated:

There were two things that were challenging. It was the timing. There was a time difference...and also the fact that the students in Brazil, like most of them, were working full time...and we're going part time to school, so they could only work on things on the weekend. So, the timing then for my students was different because they were trying to work on things through, you know, throughout the week.

This participant suggested that when one group of students are able to engage in the work, and the other group is not, the momentum of the activity is compromised and students quickly lose motivation and engagement. But lack of engagement was also perceived as a positive challenge by some participants. Such is the case of Participant # 6 who experienced the challenges of engagement (due to internet and technical system restrictions) as a chance to find other creative ways to overcome the limitations to student engagement: "The thing that makes it difficult is because of our restrictions on our systems' access...So you've got to come up with other creative ways of doing that."

In general, participants agreed that planning and collaboration goes hand-in-hand with setting a clear plan of expectations before COIL experience starts. The plan should include specific ways to student interaction, emergency plan to overcome interaction and/or engagement limitations, common platform and communication goals, common grading expectations, among the most referenced. For example, participant # 3 summarized the above points as:

There needs to be a soft launch and commitment before the engagement begins... I think there needs to be at least one synchronous component, where the spirit of the assignment and the expectations of the assignment from both faculty to share.

According to participants' statements, this type of planning will also aid in understanding and clearing the socio-cultural and political as well as language differences.

Socio-Cultural and Political Understanding

Finally, participants focused on the need for political, social, and cultural awareness of the partner country, in this case Latin America, as these are significant factors in planning the types of tools and collaborative activities and thus preventing misunderstanding and frustrations. For example, being up-to-date about the political and social practices and situation of the partner country would help in setting expectations and in providing pedagogical alternatives in case of connectivity and access issues. Participant #9 exemplifies this challenge: "In Venezuela, we found out that they were going through some kind of social, you know, their government. So, they were cutting all the Internet. We had problems with the Internet."

Language limitations were also a reported consideration when searching for common tech tools and platforms as participants often expressed that they chose platforms or tools that could translate in English and Spanish: "They posted all of their collaboration in Slack and for their final videos, they uploaded their videos from Zoom and they used Wicks, which is a platform that could be translated in both English and Spanish" (Participant # 3).

As faculty discussed their experiences in Virtual Education, and working with different cultures, the notion of a language barrier continued to come up. As Participant 6 said:

We really had to give a lot of thought and effort to putting together the series of activities, so that everybody was pretty much on the same page. We had to make sure we were careful in the language issues so that when it was necessary to do a translation, we had that programmed so that it didn't catch us by surprise.

Faculty expressed how being cognizant of the language barrier encourages students to use translators and other similar techniques in order to ensure effective communication with their global peers, but those were also not always effective. For example, Participant # 9 said:

The first time I worked with Chile, the person who I worked with didn't speak English very well. So, I really didn't, couldn't connect the way I really wanted to connect. There was really no common ground. There was a disconnect, it was a disconnect, it was, but it wasn't done effectively or efficiently, because It was a big language issue, and my partner didn't communicate well.

Finally, the existence of some differences in language can be cumbersome but did not set boundaries for collaboration. The COIL experience was perceived as an opportunity for involvement in cultural perspective and intercultural engagement, in which participants (faculty and students) could apply the new knowledge about the "new" culture in the academic context. Moreover, socio-cultural and political differences and linguistic challenges increased collaboration instead of hindering communication, bridging their differences through a reported sense of motivation.

Faculty Recommendations

Faculty provided recommendations related to inequities in two main areas: (1) COIL pre-implementation strategies (course design, planning, and training), and (2) professional and academic support, development and recognition. Participants showed consensus on the need for the establishment of clearer and stronger pre-COIL collaboration meetings. These meetings should be related to (1) faculty-students on course expectations, (2) faculty-students on cultural awareness, and (3) faculty-faculty on COIL collaboration expectations.

Course Design, Cultural Awareness Training, Course Evaluation Strategies

Faculty consistently focused on the importance of allocating time to meticulously design the COIL courses before the COIL courses start. Mainly, participants recommended that the design of the courses need to be in collaboration with their partners around the world and should incorporate developing clear and systematic expectations. Aside from course assignments expectations, faculty should discuss and set course management expectations. These should include topics such as how to address and manage language differences, how to resolve technology issues and provide options to communicate, how and when to grade assignments, how to address cultural competence and awareness, etc. For example, participants recommended to plan sessions synchronously and in conjunction with the partner institution as this would help in circumventing language issues and misunderstandings. Moreover, participants who had already implemented such practices correlated this type of meetings with increased motivation and more successful student outcomes. For example, Participant # 3 explained:

I think one is you need to have a clear plan and expectations. There needs to be a soft launch and commitment before the engagement begins. And there needs to be at least one icebreaker synchronous component, where the spirit of the assignment and the expectations of the assignment from both faculty is shared. We had separate synchronous moments, where we did that, and it was very confusing, especially since there were some language barriers.

Moreover, another recommendation was the planning of informational meetings with students before the COIL class starts so students could have the opportunity to meet and informally discuss course expectations while answering questions, helping reduce the anxiety of the unknown and supporting engagement. Participant # 4 explains how their students would benefit from this type of informational meetings pre-COIL experience starts:

I think at first, the students were a bit concerned about, you know, what is this, what are we going to do, where are we going to interact with them. I think of addressing those questions from the very beginning. I think informational meetings would be useful.

Participants as well indicate that students should be informed of their participation in a COIL course when registering for the course: "It might be useful if you put in the course "This is a COIL course," so that the students will be aware of that" (Participant # 2). According to participants, this type of information also helps in the set of expectations and opens the door for students to find information COIL modality.

Secondly, cultural awareness training through synchronous meetings came up in most interviews. According to the participants, these meetings prepared students for more meaningful interactions and therefore, engagement. Participant # 6 explained how the COIL experience was strategically planned to improve cultural understanding and awareness:

There was an activity about their perceptions about those countries initially. And then there were discussions among the students progressively throughout the semester that then heightened the things that were real versus imagined. And so, they got to really understand more about the cultural differences and the perceptions that were skewed or not based on those perceptions.

Furthermore, participants repeatedly acknowledged the need for faculty training on cultural understanding that prepares them to plan accordingly, reducing anxiety of uncertainty. Many participants stated that even if they were knowledgeable of cultural differences, it could be challenging when planning and teaching with a different culture.

Another way to address possible cultural differences proposed by participants would be through meetings in which faculty jointly create shared rubrics and agree on the expectations of class assessments to reduce inconsistencies in evaluation. For example, Participant # 3 found that lack of shared consensus on assessment evaluation was a significant challenge:

And then create a rubric with someone else with what you think are important and what they think are important. I felt I was being too lenient and my partner was being a little too strict, and then there are some other ones, where I was being too strict and my partner was being too lenient. So, finding common ground for assessment was another one of the most difficult challenges.

The establishing of a matchmaking process is recommended as another possible solution to smooth differences. Participant # 3 synthesized faculty needs as:

I think there needs to be a more efficient explicit matchmaking process, we should be paired with our faculty partners or teaching or facilitator partners a whole semester before. There should be milestones where you're turning in your kind of COIL worksheet and expectations, where there's directors on each side that are holding the Faculty accountable. And I think there needs to be a message in the syllabus and even in panther soft notes or whatever registration software and university of my use communicating to students what the expectations are and that a course will be COILed.

Finally, the need for course evaluation strategies before and after COIL experience is addressed by participants as essential in the improvement of future design, delivery and planning in preparing students in global awareness. Participant # 4 talks about how evaluation was implemented:

We had the students do a survey before the COIL experience and after the COIL experience to kind of gather data and how they felt and if they change their cultural perspective or the approaches to education from the COIL experience.

Moreover, participants express the concern of how lack of feedback of students' perceptions and experiences affects faculty evaluation scores. The need for feedback influences the lack of parameters for planning activities. Participant # 2 talks about how implementing the same strategies from a regular course into a COIL (Collaborative Online International Learning) course could be detrimental: "I am very pushy and with COIL they get a little bit more stressed. So, they do the course evaluations. Mine [evaluations] are always low [with COIL]. They [students] see a little turbulence but not all of them are prepared."

Professional and Academic Support

Professional and academic support, development and recognition are addressed in all interviews. Participants unanimously talk about the fact that COIL courses require more time and preparation, imposing heavier commitments. Participants express the need for upper administrative and departmental level actions in recognizing the extra work to counterbalance the workload and motivate faculty to adopt COIL pedagogies. For example, Participant # 3 refers to the need for monetary recognition: "There is no stipend or anything like that for doing the COIL, but we do talk about it in our faculty meetings. But there's not any other significant recognition that I'm aware of." Participants also comment on the administrative and /or departmental need of taking other motivational actions to replace financial incentives when monetary incentives are not possible. For example, participant # 2 refers to tasks' distribution recognition: "It would be great if they recognize [COIL] as part of your service at the department" Participant # 7 adds: "So maybe finding a way for the COIL to be part of the service or part of the teaching evaluation process, and that may incentivize more professors to engage in COIL."

Participant # 3 presents another need which is the fact that monetary incentives are usually offered to full-time faculty: "Our university tries to secure incentives for participating, like I said, they're very few and rare and also they're probably primarily only open to full time faculty which I am not." This is important because the number of adjunct faculty joining COIL initiatives is usually high due to the time commitment these initiatives require. But, on the other hand, full-time faculty finds it challenging to join COIL initiatives due to the nature of the commitment: "The decision of doing COIL has to do more with the challenges and the projects that I am working with. You know the dynamics are always difficult because faculty have a lot of things to do, especially tenure track professors who have to publish and the rest of us to do service." Consequently, participants expressed the need for a broader COIL implementation plan that includes adjunct and full-time faculty needs.

SOLUTIONS AND RECOMMENDATIONS

Participants have unanimously reported that COIL brings mostly positive benefits to students and faculty, impacting evaluations and outcomes positively and generating collaboration, motivation and creativity. Decision-making of US-based faculty to implement Virtual Exchange pedagogies in their courses, seems to involve a balance act between (1) faculty's willingness to participate in VE opportunities, (2) the benefits to faculty engaged in VE opportunities, and (3) equity. There are three main causes that impact decision-making for US-based faculty to join COIL programs and consequently drive experiences. First, supporting King Ramírez (2022) research findings, the authors found that the differences in infrastructure between Latin American institutions and US-based institutions to support connectivity and access is a main challenge for US-based faculty. A second challenge is related to differences in planning and course design; impacting course expectations, socio-cultural understanding, and evaluations. These findings correlate with a long line of research that focuses on the need and urgency to facilitate faculty training and opportunities on pedagogies that re-center the concepts of cultural diversity and effective communication towards equity in education (Kim & Bonk, 2002; Slapac et al., 2023; Szelei et al., 2020). The third cause addresses concerns about the limited recognition of US-based faculty efforts. These concerns center around the reported lack of time (as part of faculty service) and money recognition. This finding is supported by researchers who add that these concerns impact minority faculty in stronger ways:

For women and minority faculty members to engage in development activities to contribute to internationalization efforts can further exacerbate inequalities if the work is not valued by the institution or if they are consuming a greater share of responsibility for internationalization work on campus (Witkowsky & Gibbes, 2020, p.76).

These three main causes seem to fuel the possibility of growing inequities among US-based faculty as the internationalization opportunities have been connected with faculty growth and exposure.

In order to address these causes, it is imperative to (1) explore and improve strategies helping faculty to prepare for the planning and design of VE experiences, and to address (2) the role of (upper) administrators in supporting faculty initiatives.

Faculty Inequities: COILing With Latin America

Results show that COILing with LATAM could impose further challenges to VE planning and implementation due to connectivity and access, negatively influencing experiences and perceptions of faculty when planning and implementing such COIL courses.

These challenges mainly seem to stem from the need of pre-COIL program training on designing and planning, cultural bias and competence, and faculty-to-faculty more intentional agreements on course expectations and flexibility (Brighton, 2020; Ho & Lin, 2016). Results confirm that lack of these training options and support negatively affect the decision-making of participating and implementing Virtual Exchange programs. Researchers McLaughlin and Ricevuto (2021) synthesize these needs as:

Professional development and training should not be focused on specific tools as this could prove to be a waste of time and money when tools change frequently. Faculty instead need habits of minds such as flexibility, openness to ambiguity, calculated risk taking, and the ability to play (p. 6).

Participants also agreed on the importance of participating in COIL/VE institutional opportunities for their professional and academic growth. These opportunities should also be tailored for both adjunct and full-time faculty. However, results show that unaddressed challenges by institutions could impose obstacles in further participation in such initiatives and could be one of the main factors in motivating faculty to join VE programs (O'Meara et al., 2018; King Ramírez, 2022; Slapac et al., 2023; Witkowsky & Gibbes, 2020). Thus, motivation to implement VE programs such as COIL is directly affected by institutional and administrative support.

Faculty Inequities: The Role of Administrators

Usually, the focus is on the professor, but it is essential that institutional administrators commit to finding ways to improve students' collaborative online international course efforts to fulfill larger goals of inclusivity (Jie et al., 2018). The role of the administrators and university stakeholders is fundamental and essential in balancing the workload with recognition of their efforts (McLaughlin & Ricevuto, 2021), and could have a powerful impact on teacher stress and job dissatisfaction.

Findings from this study have proven that participation in VE programs help faculty professional and academic growth, however if not addressed administratively, it could potentially generate inequalities due to extra responsibilities and time commitments VE programs require. Factors such as time, money, class size and management, and resources are main concerns for continuing internationalization programs such as VE. The researchers found that faculty experiences COILing with Latin American institutions were similar to the ones found by King Ramírez (2022). According to King Ramírez (2022), faculty commitment and participation in international efforts highly depend on faculty service and economic recognition to compensate faculty for the time and energy investment that VE programs require.

Consequently, what can the university do in order to recognize and embrace those needs? For example, some questions that faculty COILing with Latin American institutions mentioned in our research were: (1) how can COIL experiences be designed for large classes?; (2) What can the university and administrator do to recognize these types of academic work?; (3) How can these types of extra work be financially or time wise acknowledged? Thus, for these types of programs to advance, it is imperative that the university administrators provide tools, training, money, flexibility and recognition. For example, department Chairs should try to involve themselves in these types of projects and consciously generate spaces for conversations to motivate faculty to engage in these programs. Ramírez (2022)'s findings are congruent with our findings, supporting the need for increasing a sustainable integration of VE projects across the curriculum at each institution. These points also correlate with Witkowsk and Gibbes (2020) that addresses the importance of motivating faculty in engaging in internationalization efforts by addressing concerns about unequal share of work that requires more time and workload commitments.

Furthermore, findings of this study correlate with experiences of LATAM faculty participating in VE programs (Ramírez, 2022). The creation of mutual administrative agreements and initiatives could lessen obstacles and therefore help in narrowing inequity among faculty who strive to join internationalization programs.

VE/COIL programs have been proven to bring a great number of benefits for the preparation of students as global citizens and professionals; however, there is a lack of faculty and students' pedagogical, instructional, research, and financial support in higher education (Gleason et al., 2021; Jie et al., 2018; O'Dowd, 2020; van Rooij, 2016). Thus, there is an urgent need for institutional administrators and stakeholders to work together to increase support, resources, and efforts to increase internationalization opportunities to fulfill larger goals of inclusivity.

Limitations

Several limitations were noted in this study. An important limitation was the need for a more racially diverse population in the sample. Having voices from faculty who have taught COIL graduate courses through different modes (fully online or hybrid courses) would make the study more robust in representing the richness of this cultural paradigm. The second limitation is that the COIL programs of the participants were designed and approached from a Western perspective, based on the frameworks informed and constrained by the Western World understanding (Zhang & Kenny, 2010). Third limitation is related to researchers' background as two out of three researchers are from Hispanic background. Consequently, findings are likely skewed due to the influence of our own cultural background.

FUTURE RESEARCH DIRECTIONS

The authors hope to continue future research in exploring perceptions and experiences of other underrepresented student populations (for example, experiences of students with disabilities in Virtual Exchange programs) as well as faculty and administrators. The authors also believe that it is necessary to study other non-western designs of virtual exchange programs, as a way to practice what they advocate for, in this case lessening marginalization through the integration of marginalized voices.

Therefore, not involving in VE opportunities could be detrimental to narrowing equity and inclusion practices interdependently for both students and faculty. In order to address these causes, it is imperative to (1) explore and improve strategies in increasing VE participation, (2) the role of administrators in supporting and empowering faculty initiatives, and (3) interviewing faculty from Latin America would bring a stronger scope and relevance to the study.

CONCLUSION

This study is significant because it contributes to both the scholarly research and practical designs for VE, helping achieve community goals by addressing and fulfilling the diverse needs of faculty that arise from the implementation of Virtual Exchange pedagogies such as COIL. The long-term goal of this line of research is to promote inclusion and equality in faculty VE decision making and implementation.

When successfully implemented, virtual pedagogies can lead students towards deeper, more connected learning. Furthermore, it is a vehicle for providing underrepresented student populations with global learning opportunities which advance social and economic mobility (Appiah-Kubi & Annan, 2020; Esche, 2018; Mudiamu, 2020; O'Dowd, 2020; Slapac et.al., 2023)

In supporting and empowering students, studying faculty experiences of VE will allow for uncovering best practices (Szelei et al., 2020) as they encourage cognitive, emotional, and behavioral engagement where all contributions are acknowledged, appreciated, and brought together. For example, appropriate planning for virtual learning experiences, such as COIL, can lead to the development of critical thinking and higher-order thinking skills (HOTS) when students have the opportunity for reflection, collaboration, and assessments that encourage intercultural communication (Rufai et al., 2015).

Seemingly, VE programs such as COIL opportunities would allow faculty to strengthen their professional growth and could represent one less limitation for their economic and social mobility (Simm & Marvell, 2017; Bedenlier & Zawacki-Richter, 2015). Yet, without proper faculty support and recognition to implement VE programs to overcome challenges, faculty choosing to participate in these programs are left with added burdens (Witkowsky & Gibbes, 2020), increasing inequities and limitations for professional growth.

As research shows, VE programs facilitate equity for both students and faculty (Keshavarz et al., 2022; Ramírez, 2022; Seufert et al., 2022). Yet, lack of support and recognition while implementing these programs can impact motivation to participate in them. The findings suggest that faculty is motivated but not supported properly. Thus, a significant implication is the need for stronger administrational support and recognition of VE programs.

REFERENCES

Appiah-Kubi, P., & Annan, E. (2020). A review of a Collaborative Online International Learning. *International Journal of Engineering Pedagogy*, *10*(1), 109–124. doi:10.3991/ijep.v10i1.11678

Bedenlier, S., & Zawacki-Richter, O. (2015). Internationalization of higher education and the impacts on academic faculty members. *Research in Comparative and International Education*, *10*(2), 185–201. doi:10.1177/1745499915571707

Bengtsson, M. (2016). How to plan and perform a qualitative study using content analysis. *NursingPlus Open*, 2, 8–14. https://doi-org.ezproxy.fiu.edu/10.1016/j.npls.2016.01.001

Brighton, C. (2020). Training for Virtual Exchange. *Journal of Virtual Exchange, 3 (SI-IVEC2019)*, 69–79. doi:10.21827/jve.3.35810

Camarillo, A. M., & Bonilla, F. (2001). Hispanics in a multicultural society: A new American dilemma. *America becoming: Racial trends and their consequences, 1*, 103-134. https://blogs.umass.edu/cnle/files/2008/01/ab1-4.pdf

Castillo, T. I., King, L. F., & Ruíz, L. P. (2021). El intercambio virtual: experiencias desde instituciones en el Caribe colombiano [Virtual exchange: experiences from Colombian Caribbean institutions]. *Edutec. Revista Electrónica de Tecnología Educativa, 75*, 90-109. doi:10.21556/edutec.2021.75.1893

Collin, S., & Brotcorne, P. (2019). Capturing digital (in)equity in teaching and learning: A sociocritical approach. *The International Journal of Information and Learning Technology*, *36*(2), 169–180. doi:10.1108/IJILT-05-2018-0059

Creswell, J. (2013). *Qualitative inquiry and research design: Choosing among five approaches* (3rd ed.). Sage.

Cronin, T. J., Levin, S., Branscombe, N. R., van Laar, C., & Tropp, L. R. (2012). Ethnic identification in response to perceived discrimination protects well-being and promotes activism: A longitudinal study of Latino college students. *Group Processes & Intergroup Relations*, *15*(3), 393–407. doi:10.1177/1368430211427171

de Brey, C., Musu, L., McFarland, J., Wilkinson-Flicker, S., Diliberti, M., Zhang, A., ... Pishcherskaia, E. (2018). Bridging countries and cultures through accessible global collaborations. *Education Sciences*, *8*(4), 199–210. doi:10.3390/educsci8040199

Eatman, T. K. (2018). Faculty as colearners: Collaborative engagement and the power of story in faculty development. In B. Berkey, E. E. Rountree, P. M. Green, & C. Meixner (Eds.), *Reconceptualizing faculty development in service-learning/community engagement* (pp. 59–82). Routledge.

Esche, M. (2018). *Incorporating collaborative online international learning (COIL) into study abroad courses: A training design*. https://digitalcollections.sit.edu/capstones

Garcia, G. A. (2017). Defined by outcomes or culture? Constructing an organizational identity for Hispanic-serving institutions. *American Educational Research Journal*, *54*(1_suppl), 111S–134S. doi:10.3102/0002831216669779

Garcia, G. A., Núñez, A. M., & Sansone, V. A. (2019). Toward a multidimensional conceptual framework for understanding "servingness" in Hispanic-serving institutions: A synthesis of the research. *Review of Educational Research*, *89*(5), 745–784. doi:10.3102/0034654319864591

Gautier, M. C. (2016). Ethnic identity and Latino youth: The current state of the research. *Adolescent Research Review*, *1*(4), 329–340. doi:10.1007/s40894-016-0034-z

Gleason, B., & Jaramillo Cherrez, N. (2021). Design thinking approach to global collaboration and empowered learning: Virtual exchange as innovation in a teacher education course. *TechTrends*, *65*(3), 348–358. doi:10.1007/s11528-020-00573-6

Gonzalez, E., Ortega, G., Molina, M., & Lizalde, G. (2020). What does it mean to be a Hispanic-Serving Institution? Listening to the Latina/o/x voices of students. *International Journal of Qualitative Studies in Education : QSE*, *33*(8), 796–809. doi:10.1080/09518398.2020.1751896

Hall, E. T. (1977). *Beyond culture*. Doubleday.

Hall, E. T. (1990). *Understanding cultural differences*. Intercultural Press.

Hidecker, C. (2010). Communication activity and participation research. *Developmental Medicine and Child Neurology*, *52*(5), 408–409. doi:10.1111/j.1469-8749.2009.03460.x PMID:20059523

Ho, T. K., & Lin, Y. T. (2016). The effects of virtual communities on group identity in classroom management. *Journal of Educational Computing Research*, *54*(1), 3–21. doi:10.1177/0735633115611645

Huang, H. M., Rauch, U., & Liaw, S. S. (2010). Investigating learners' attitudes toward virtual reality learning environments: Based on a constructivist approach. *Computers & Education*, *55*(3), 1171–1182. doi:10.1016/j.compedu.2010.05.014

Humberto, R. L. R. (2016). Los retos que impone la educación a distancia en México [The challenges of distance education in Mexico]. *Revista Iberoamericana de producción académica y gestión educativa, 6*, 1-12. https://www.pag.org.mx/index.php/PAG/article/view/631

IESALC. (2019). *Movilidad en la educación superior: retos y oportunidades en un convenio renovado para el reconocimiento de estudios, títulos, y diplomas [Mobility in higher education: challenges and opportunities in a renewed agreement for the recognition of studies, degrees, and diplomas].* Instituto Internacional para Educación Superior en América Latina y el Caribe. https://bit.ly/3UZgxHx

Ismailov, M. (2021). Virtual exchanges in an inquiry-based learning environment: Effects on intra-cultural awareness and intercultural communicative competence. *Cogent Education*, *8*(1), 1982601. Advance online publication. doi:10.1080/2331186X.2021.1982601

Jagers, R. J., Rivas-Drake, D., & Williams, B. (2019). Transformative social and emotional learning (SEL): Toward SEL in service of educational equity and excellence. *Educational Psychologist*, *54*(3), 162–184. doi:10.1080/00461520.2019.1623032

Jaldemark, J. (2008). Participation and genres of communication in online settings of higher education. *Education and Information Technologies*, *13*(2), 129–146. doi:10.1007/s10639-008-9057-9

Jie, Z., & Pearlman, A. M. G. (2018). Expanding access to international education through technology enhanced collaborative online international learning (COIL) courses. *International Journal of Technology in Teaching and Learning*, *14*(1), 1–11. https://files.eric.ed.gov/fulltext/EJ1211995.pdf

Johnson, R., & Christensen, L. (2014). *Educational research: Quantitative, qualitative, & mixed methods* (5th ed.). Sage.

Kavrayici, C. (2021). The relationship between classroom management and sense of classroom community in graduate virtual classrooms. *Turkish Online Journal of Distance Education*, *22*(2), 112–125. doi:10.17718/tojde.906816

Keshavarz, M., Mirmoghtadaie, Z., & Nayyeri, S. (2022). Design and validation of the virtual classroom management questionnaire. *International Review of Research in Open and Distance Learning*, *23*(2), 120–135. doi:10.19173/irrodl.v23i2.5774

Kim, K., & Bonk, C. (2002). Cross-cultural comparisons of online collaboration. *Journal of Computer-Mediated Communication*, *8*(1), 0. Advance online publication. doi:10.1111/j.1083-6101.2002.tb00163.x

King Ramírez, C. (2020). Influences of academic culture in Collaborative Online International Learning (COIL): Differences in Mexican and U.S. students' reported experiences. *Foreign Language Annals*, *53*(3), 438–457. doi:10.1111/flan.12485

King Ramírez, C. (2022). Virtual exchange in Latin America: A profile of faculty and staff participants. *Journal of Virtual Exchange*, *5*, 105–132. doi:10.21827/jve.5.38284

Knight, J. (2003). Updated definition of internationalization. *Industry and Higher Education*, (33), 1–3. doi:10.6017/ihe.2003.33.7391

Laird, L. (2015). Empathy in the classroom: Can music bring us more in tune with one another? *Music Educators Journal*, *101*(4), 56–61. doi:10.1177/0027432115572230

Levin, S., Van Laar, C., & Foote, W. (2006). Ethnic segregation and perceived discrimination in college: Mutual influences and effects on social and academic life. *Journal of Applied Social Psychology*, *36*(6), 1471–1501. doi:10.1111/j.0021-9029.2006.00068.x

Marino, M. I., & Tadal, S. (2022). Matching students: Strategies for maximizing inclusion and success. In J. Rubin, S. Gut, S. Doscher, & C. Wojenski (Eds.), *The guide to COIL virtual exchange* (pp. 298–311). Stylus.

McLaughlin, L. A., & Ricevuto, J. (2021). Virtual instruction support for faculty. *Issues in Informing Science and Information Technology, 18*, 1-30. doi:10.28945/4792

Meer, N., & Modood, T. (2012). How does interculturalism contrast with multiculturalism? *Journal of Intercultural Studies (Melbourne, Vic.)*, *33*(2), 175–196. doi:10.1080/07256868.2011.618266

Miles, M., & Huberman, A. (1994). *Qualitative data analysis: A sourcebook of new methods* (2nd ed.). Sage.

Monitor, I. C. E. F. (2022). *Latin American institutions increasingly prepared to compete for international students*. https://bit.ly/48ySm69

Mudiamu, S. S. (2020). *Faculty use of collaborative online international learning (COIL) for internationalization at home* (Doctoral dissertation, Portland State University). doi:10.15760/etd.7342

Mukherji, B. R., Neuwirth, L. S., & Limonic, L. (2017). Making the case for real diversity: Redefining underrepresented minority students in public universities. *SAGE Open*, *7*(2). Advance online publication. doi:10.1177/2158244017707796

Niehaus, E. K., & Williams, L. (2016). Faculty transformation in curriculum transformation: The role of faculty development in campus internationalization. *Innovative Higher Education*, *41*(1), 59–74. doi:10.1007/s10755-015-9334-7

Numanee, I. Z., Zafar, N., Karim, A., & Ismail, S. A. M. M. (2020). Developing empathy among first-year university undergraduates through English language course: A phenomenological study. *Heliyon*, *6*(6), e04021. doi:10.1016/j.heliyon.2020.e04021 PMID:32518850

O'Dowd, R. (2020). A transnational model of virtual exchange for global citizenship education. *Language Teaching*, *53*(4), 477–490. doi:10.1017/S0261444819000077

O'Meara, K., Jaeger, A., Misra, J., Lennartz, C., & Kuvaeva, A. (2018). Undoing disparities in faculty workloads: A randomized trial experiment. *PlosOne, 13*(12), 1–15. https://doi.org/.0207316 doi:10.1371/journal.pone

OECD. (2019). Education at glance: OECD indicators. https://bit.ly/3wDG8fb

Papendieck, A. (2018). Technology for equity and social justice in education: A critical issue overview. *Texas Education Review (Austin, Tex.), 6*(1), 1–9. http://hdl.handle.net/2152/64974

Patton, M. Q. (1990). How to use qualitative methods in evaluation. *Sage.*

Pearl, M., Tzoumis, K., & Lockie, B. (2023). Unlocking the potential of global learning: The impact of virtual exchange programs on self-efficacy. *International Journal on Studies in Education, 5*(4), 585–609. doi:10.46328/ijonse.162

Rufai, M. M., Alebiosu, S. O., & Adeakin, O. A. S. (2015). A conceptual model for virtual classroom management. *International Journal of Computer Science. Engineering and Information Technology, 5*(1), 27–32. doi:10.5121/ijcseit.2015.5103 PMID:26029735

Scardamalia, M., & Bereiter, C. (2010). A brief history of knowledge building. *Canadian Journal of Learning and Technology/La revue canadienne de l'apprentissage et de la technologie, 36*(1), 1-16. doi:10.21432/T2859M

Seidman, I. E. (1998). *Interviewing as qualitative research: A guide for researchers in education and the social sciences* (2nd ed.). Teachers College Press.

Seufert, C., Oberdörfer, S., Roth, A., Grafe, S., Lugrin, J. L., & Latoschik, M. E. (2022). Classroom management competency enhancement for student teachers using a fully immersive virtual classroom. *Computers & Education, 179*, 1–17. doi:10.1016/j.compedu.2021.104410

Simm, D., & Marvell, A. (2017). Creating global students: Opportunities, challenges and experiences of internationalizing the geography curriculum in higher education. *Journal of Geography in Higher Education, 41*(4), 467–474. doi:10.1080/03098265.2017.1373332

Slapac, A., Collett, K., Wessels, F., Gamiet, G., & Knudsmoen, H. (2023). Social justice pedagogy and Collaborative Online International Learning (COIL): Across three partner higher education institutions. In P. Escudeiro, N. Escudeiro, & O. Bernardes (Eds.), *Handbook of research on implementing inclusive educational models and technologies for equity and diversity* (pp. 252–272). IGI Global. doi:10.4018/979-8-3693-0453-2.ch013

Standley, H. J. (2015). International mobility placements enable students and staff in higher education to enhance transversal and employability-related skills. *FEMS Microbiology Letters, 362*(19), 1–5. doi:10.1093/femsle/fnv157 PMID:26347299

Sweeney, K. (2013). Inclusive excellence and underrepresentation of students of color in study abroad. *Frontiers: The Interdisciplinary Journal of Study Abroad, 23*(1), 1–21. doi:10.36366/frontiers.v23i1.326

Szelei, N., Tinoca, L., & Pinho, A. S. (2020). Professional development for cultural diversity: The challenges of teacher learning in context. *Professional Development in Education, 46*(5), 780–796. doi:10.1080/19415257.2019.1642233

Tropp, L. R., Hawi, D. R., Van Laar, C., & Levin, S. (2012). Cross-ethnic friendships, perceived discrimination, and their effects on ethnic activism over time: A longitudinal investigation of three ethnic minority groups. *British Journal of Social Psychology*, *51*(2), 257–272. doi:10.1111/j.2044-8309.2011.02050.x PMID:21895704

van Rooij, S. W., & Zirkle, K. (2016). Balancing pedagogy, student readiness and accessibility: A case study in collaborative online course development. *The Internet and Higher Education*, *28*, 1–7. doi:10.1016/j.iheduc.2015.08.001

Vatrapu & Suthers, D. (2007). Culture and computers: A review of the concept of culture and implications for intercultural collaborative online learning. *Intercultural Collaboration*, 260–275. doi:10.1007/978-3-540-74000-1_20

Voogt, J., Laferrière, T., Breuleux, A., Itow, R. C., Hickey, D. T., & McKenney, S. (2015). Collaborative design as a form of professional development. *Instructional Science*, *43*(2), 259–282. doi:10.1007/s11251-014-9340-7

Wimpenny, K., Finardi, K. R., Orsini-Jones, M., & Jacobs, L. (2022). Knowing, being, relating and expressing through third space global South-North COIL: Digital inclusion and equity in international higher education. *Journal of Studies in International Education*, *26*(2), 279–296. doi:10.1177/10283153221094085

Witkowsky, P., & Gibbes, C. (2020). Preparing faculty for internationalization: Opportunities through teaching, research, and service. *New Directions for Higher Education*, *2020*(192), 73–84. doi:10.1002/he.20393

Zhang, Z., & Kenny, R. F. (2010). Learning in an online distance education course: Experiences of three international students. *International Review of Research in Open and Distance Learning*, *11*(1), 17–36. doi:10.19173/irrodl.v11i1.775

KEY TERMS AND DEFINITIONS

Collaboration: The ability to mutually build relationships with colleagues and peers to solve problems.

Collaborative Online International Learning (COIL): A Virtual Exchange framework that has emerged as a response to globalization by preparing students as global thinkers and equipping them in ways that are more relevant and useful to advance and succeed within the global society of the 21st century.

Cross-Cultural Collaboration: The ability to work productively with individuals from different cultural backgrounds.

Cross-Cultural Communication: The ability to communicate effectively with individuals who come from different cultural backgrounds.

Cultural Competence: The ability to understand, communicate and work effectively with persons from different cultural backgrounds.

Culture: A shared group of learned behavior.

Internationalization: The process of integrating global perspectives, pedagogies, or dimensions into education.

Participation: An active and complex process of taking part and which involves doing, communication, thinking, feeling, and belonging.

Virtual Exchange: A pedagogical collaborative approach that involves educational institutions, partners, and/or students from different cultures and geographical locations.

Chapter 6
Tensions and Opportunities of Teachers "Learning Through Crisis":
A Tale of Two Cities

Jaqueline Naidoo
University of KwaZulu-Natal, South Africa

Noah Borrero
University of San Francisco, USA

ABSTRACT

The sudden onset of the COVID-19 pandemic ushered in immense shifts in several sectors of society, including education. Social distancing was recommended as one of the measures to reduce the transmission of the Coronavirus, which resulted in many countries introducing lockdowns and the closure of schools. This chapter reports on the challenges experienced and transnational 'learning through crisis' by two teacher educators based in South Africa and San Francisco (USA). A qualitative methodological approach was used to highlight two case studies of how teaching strategies and curriculum delivery to postgraduate students were redesigned. Findings from critical reflections and personal narrative accounts highlighted the tensions or challenges of social inequalities and lack of resources, technological and emotional challenges, school closures, and isolation. Curriculum innovation and redesign and mapping as a pedagogical tool were captured as opportunities. Teachers 'learning through crisis' involved engaging in culturally relevant pedagogy and living the curriculum.

DOI: 10.4018/978-1-6684-7813-4.ch006

INTRODUCTION

This chapter reports on the learning experiences of two lecturers at two public higher education institutions, one in KwaZulu-Natal, South Africa, and the other in California, United States. The sudden onset of the COVID-19 pandemic in 2020 ushered in immense shifts in several sectors of society, including education. The chapter aims to reflect upon teacher learning during the crisis of the COVID-19 pandemic and how lecturers revised and redesigned their teaching.

The authors draw on Kumashiro's (2000) framework of learning through crisis and the notion of culturally relevant pedagogy (Ladson-Billings, 1995) to explore the opportunities and tensions of teaching during the COVID-19 pandemic. Reflecting on our teaching of postgraduate programs, we examine how we as lecturers continue to address the "institutional demands, disciplinary constraints and social pressures" (Kumashiro, 2015, p. 2) as we look towards a future of educational research and classroom pedagogies that reflect the changing world in which we are living. This chapter also intends to contribute to the field of teaching and learning through crisis as a way to highlight possibilities for transnational, socially transformative pedagogy (Borrero et al., 2020).

BACKGROUND

The COVID-19 Pandemic and Higher Education Institutions

In March 2020, there was global concern about reports of the rapid spread of the deadly Coronavirus (COVID-19), which was declared a pandemic by the Director-General of the WHO (Adedoyin & Soykan, 2020). Social distancing was recommended as one of the measures to reduce the transmission of the Coronavirus, which resulted in many countries introducing strict lockdowns and the closure of schools. UNESCO (2020) estimates that school closures in mid-April 2020 affected 1.3 billion students in 195 countries. Therefore, lecturers were thrust into uncertain terrain and forced to shift their teaching from traditional approaches to online approaches and remote teaching. The crisis of the COVID-19 pandemic also heightened the importance of lecturers' emotional well-being as they navigated the slippery slope toward online teaching and revising curriculum delivery.

Lecturers work alongside classroom teachers who are in the midst of all the turmoil and challenges associated with a world in crisis: COVID-19, war, climate devastation, structural racism, among others. Therefore, lecturers experience the impacts of these crises on their educational systems while trying to provide mentorship and guidance for a new generation of teachers. Perhaps, now more than ever, teachers are vital in any hope for a sustainable, peaceful future. Green and Collett (2018) highlight that professional learning communities offer a supportive environment that contributes to the personal and professional growth of teachers. Therefore, if lecturers are to provide educational spaces and support for classroom teachers, they must expand communities of practice (Wenger, 1998), reach beyond traditional approaches to teacher education, and embrace the tensions in the world around us. Globalization and policy imperatives of Higher Education Institutions emphasise the internationalisation of the curriculum and global citizenship (Jooste & Hagenmeier, 2022; Guimarães & Finardi, 2021), and the emerging trend of telecollaboration and online learning (O'Dowd, 2016). Lecturers and teachers need to be ongoing learners and create spaces for teaching and learning in order for meaningful, relevant teaching to take place (Kumashiro, 2015). Transnational research and telecollaboration as scholars must be a part of this future in education.

Ongoing Impacts of the COVID-19 Pandemic

The shockwaves of COVID-19 were felt in education systems globally (Reimers, 2022) and resulted in unprecedented disruptions to educational institutions in South Africa. On 18 March 2020, South African schools, colleges and universities were closed due to the national lockdown. This was a time of crisis characterized by uncertainty, isolation, fear, trauma and sadness. The extended period of the lockdown and school closures exacerbated the despair and anguish of lecturers and teachers, who were grappling with how to respond to COVID-19 (Hlatswayo et al., 2021). There was a rapid shift and rethink about notions of teaching and learning. While teachers and lecturers were accustomed to face-to-face teaching and social interaction with our students before COVID-19, they had to swiftly transition to remote and online teaching and learning during COVID-19. Some teachers were familiar with using online platforms such as Zoom and Microsoft Teams, however, many teachers were overwhelmed and had to learn how to use these online platforms during the crisis of COVID-19.

South Africa is a country characterized by high levels of inequality, unemployment and poverty, as a result of apartheid. The World Bank Report (World Bank, 2018) describes South Africa as one of the most unequal countries globally plagued by critical socio-economic, socio-political and socio-cultural challenges. Fataar and Badroodien (2020) and Borrero and Naidoo (2023) suggest that social exclusion and South Africa's legacy of apartheid and past inequities were intensified and exacerbated by the COVID-19 pandemic. In other words, the COVID-19 pandemic not only heightened but also entrenched the inequalities in the South African education system. Teachers and students at well-resourced schools and universities had access to the internet and laptops and were able to engage in online and remote teaching and learning. On the other hand, Dube (2020) asserts that the vast majority of teachers and students from African, rural communities did not have access to the internet and laptops, resulting in a halt in teaching and learning. Le Grange (2020) maintains that the shift to online teaching accentuated 'the digital divide' in South Africa as poor students from rural contexts encountered challenges due to limited access to laptops and internet connectivity.

In the United States, the devastation inflicted by school closures in March 2020 lingers. Not only were lives deeply shaken by the pain, sadness, and fear of COVID-19 and its toll on human lives, but, a core part of teachers' identity was taken away as the social interaction that lies at the heart of teaching was instantly gone. While lecturers tried to stay connected with their students on Zoom, it was apparent that live, in-person teaching and learning were irreplaceable (Borrero, 2023). There is no doubt that the original shock of school closures upended the realities of teachers, and at a systemic level, as the days turned into weeks and the weeks turned into months of turmoil in the spring of 2020, it became clear that COVID was disproportionately impacting working-class communities of Color in the United States (Chen et al., 2022). Through a specific focus on schooling and access to meaningful learning opportunities, public school closures played a major role in this disproportionality, and under the spotlight of COVID-19, deep, ongoing structural inequities in the educational system were showcased (Yeh et al., 2022).

As is the case in schools in South Africa, these systemic inequities-working-class students of Color having less access to quality education-existed long before the COVID-19 pandemic in the United States (Kozol, 2012) and continue to this day. The historical legacies of public education in the United States portray a colonial project rooted in racism and the forced assimilation of indigenous peoples and communities of Color (Delpit, 1988; Emdin, 2016; Flores, 2016). In the current context, the ongoing impacts of the COVID-19 pandemic exacerbate these deep-seated problems. Students of Color are disproportionately impacted by the rattling of the public education system because they attend schools with less resources, fewer qualified teachers, and inadequate facilities in comparison to white students (Chen et al., 2022; Crenshaw, 2019). While the vast majority of all public schools have returned to live, in-person teaching and learning, the structural forces working against students of Color continue to intensify. And, as societal realities (e.g., war, gun violence, hate crimes, climate catastrophe) compound the impacts of the grief and sadness of the COVID-19 pandemic, classroom teachers are on the front lines of absorbing and addressing daily challenges with their students.

Envisioning a New Future in Education

We live in a globalized world and it is imperative to network and collaborate online across transnational boundaries. O'Dowd (2015) highlights that, in literature and research, there is growing awareness of telecollaboration, which is also referred to as virtual exchange, online intercultural exchange or collaborative online international learning. In addition, he asserts telecollaboration allows individuals from different cultures to engage in intercultural exchange using online technologies. O'Dowd (2015) developed a model outlining four competences that teachers need to employ in order to promote telecollaboration, namely, organisational, pedagogical, digital and attitudes and beliefs. According to O'Dowd (2016, p.292), "intercultural dialogue is at the center of learning in telecollaboration". As lecturers, we engaged in intercultural dialogue and collaborated online via emails and WhatsApp calls to discuss our transnational learning. However, as lecturers teaching in different cities and countries with diverse socioeconomic backgrounds, we were acutely aware of the challenges, such as lack of resources, laptops and internet connectivity, that we would encounter in planning for our postgraduate students to engage in telecollaboration (Slapac et al., 2023).

CONCEPTUAL FRAMEWORK

Learning through Crisis: Kumashiro

The authors draw on the notion of learning through crisis (Kumashiro, 2000) to reflect on our teacher learning as lecturers and how we embraced the tensions and grasped opportunities to engage in meaningful dialogue through education. Kumashiro (2000) contends that it is essential for teachers to critically examine their day-to-day choices about teaching and learning and design anti-oppressive education that upholds social justice. Kumashiro's (2000) notion of learning through crisis offers a framework that attempts to connect the realities of the ongoing impacts of the COVID-19 pandemic with future possibilities for educational equity and transformation in our schools. Slapac et al. (2021) also outline resilience in crisis of teacher-researchers who designed creative strategies to conduct action research during the COVID-19 crisis.

We utilize this conceptual framework for our work together as lecturers and scholars to understand the power and potential of education as a human right. The classroom is a place and space where ideas are generated, contested, and proliferated, and education can transform the social conditions of society. The global crises discussed above continue to disrupt educational contexts around the globe, and while there is no denying the resultant harm and suffering, we also feel that there are opportunities for new and re-imagined possibilities in education as we teach and learn through these crises (Kumashiro, 2000).

The COVID-19 pandemic and its ongoing impact on teachers and learners is a catalyst to seek out something new and different because of the seismic shift that our educational system has undergone (Roy, 2020). We are in the midst of learning through crisis (Kumahsiro, 2000) as the isolation, sadness, and fear of the unknown linger in our lives. While the death toll of COVID-19 may be residing, the ongoing impacts of structural racism, war, climate change, and violence rage on. Young people are feeling these realities, they bring the stressors of these realities with them to school, and they need places to express their pain, anger, fear, hope, and dreams. As lecturers and teachers, we must attempt to embrace these challenges and think of school and schooling in new ways. We must think about our own abilities to learn through crisis, attempt to model this for students, create spaces for them to learn through their crises, and together envision a new pathway for educational equity (Slapac et al., 2023). This could offer possibilities for transnational collaboration in teaching and teacher education.

Culturally Relevant Pedagogy: Ladson-Billings

Globally, teachers are faced with teaching an increased population of culturally diverse students. Simms (2013) draws attention to the need for lecturers to engage in culturally responsive teaching and prepare preservice and in-service teachers to teach in school contexts that are ethnically diverse. Capper (2022) agrees that teachers should 'tailor' their curriculum and use teaching materials that are relevant to the racial and cultural demographics of their students. According to Ladson-Billings (1995), culturally relevant pedagogy "helps students to accept and affirm their cultural identity while developing critical perspectives that challenge inequities that schools perpetuate" (p. 469). In addition, Ladson-Billings (2014) contends that culturally relevant pedagogy is underpinned by the principles of cultural competence, academic achievement and socio-political consciousness. Gay (2018) contends that culturally relevant teaching draws on "the cultural knowledge, prior experiences, frames of reference and performance styles of ethnically diverse students to make learning encounters more relevant to and effective for them" (p. 36). Milner (2011) asserts that culturally relevant pedagogy should integrate culture in the curriculum and teaching, understand the socio-political issues around how society works and empower. Also, Hefflin (2002) suggests that teachers adjust their teaching to suit the personal, social and cultural aspects of their students' lives.

Borrero and Naidoo (2023) and Simms (2013) highlight the importance of teachers engaging in culturally relevant pedagogy and action research. Action research is viewed as an important component of teacher professional development and offers teachers opportunities to be educational change agents (Koshy et al., 2011; Slapac et al., 2021). Cohen et al. (2018) suggest that action research comprises self-reflexive, political, risk-taking, social, situated and collaborative elements.

MAIN FOCUS OF THE CHAPTER

Research Context and Methodological Procedures

This study used a comparative case study research design to report on the critical reflections of teaching and learning by two lecturers, who were also the researchers, at two universities, one in KwaZulu-Natal,

South Africa and the other in California, Unites States of America (Baxter & Jack, 2008; Creswell & Creswell, 2018). The study reports on two cases of lecturers' critical reflections on their teaching and learning during the COVID-19 pandemic, between April and November 2020 (eight months). The two cases served as a catalyst to discuss the possibilities of transnational learning through telecollaboration.

The following research questions were developed collaboratively to focus our inquiry:

1. What tensions/challenges did lecturers encounter while teaching during the COVID-19 pandemic?
2. How did lecturers address the challenges they encountered during the COVID-19 pandemic?
3. What were the main lessons lecturers learned through crisis in their transnational learning?

The lecturer in South Africa is a senior lecturer and reflects on teaching a Bachelor of Education Honors class while the lecturer in San Francisco is a professor and reflects on teaching a Master's class. In both contexts, these classes are part of university-based teacher education programs focused on developing the theoretical and pedagogical foundations and skills of practicing teachers. Students in both classes are practicing teachers who are earning their credentials and graduate degrees in the field of teacher education. The interaction and collaboration of lecturers and teachers, in both contexts, contributed to their teacher learning and developed a pedagogy of teacher education. The Community Mapping project was done by the lecturer at the university in California, United States and the artifact activities were done by the lecturer at the university in KwaZulu-Natal, South Africa. Data was generated from critical reflections of two lecturers on shifts in their teaching to online and culturally relevant pedagogy during the COVID-19 pandemic in 2020. A description of their reflections on teaching and learning in two contexts - rural South Africa and urban United States - and how social and structural inequities in education were (and continue to be) exacerbated by the COVID-19 pandemic is presented in the two cases that follow.

Case study: Master of Arts in Teaching at a University in California

As a part of the final stages of earning their Master of Arts in Teaching degree and teaching credentials at a university in California, students conducted an action research project in their classrooms. The projects described below are samples from the action research projects of a group of 18 students as they completed their coursework while teaching. For these projects, they developed a problem statement, built a theoretical framework, and designed a classroom intervention to address one aspect of the structural inequities they see facing their K-12 students. The descriptions and reflections of and on their work is presented in an attempt to display possible pedagogical innovations in the current educational context. Given the impacts of school closures initiated by COVID-19 in spring 2020 and the intensification of social and educational injustices faced by communities of Color, teachers created an innovative curriculum to highlight the collective strengths and solidarity of local communities (Borrero et al., 2020). One ongoing project involved the application of mapping activities as a way for lecturers, new teachers, and K-12 students to research, visually display, and collectively share the cultural assets in their communities (Borrero & Yeh, 2016; Futch & Fine, 2011; Marx, 2022; Slapac et al., 2021).

This community mapping project began when in-person schooling was abruptly halted and teachers needed to transform the curriculum to meet the lived experiences of life beyond the classroom. Mapping has long been a pedagogical (Borrero & Yeh, 2016) and methodological (Futch & Fine, 2014) approach in education, utilized to show relationships and connections across cultural and educational contexts

(Marx, 2022). Community asset mapping was adapted as a project in teacher education, encouraging new teachers to create projects for their K-12 students to explore the resources in their own communities. This was particularly relevant and challenging during the forced shutdowns as a part of the onset of the COVID-19 pandemic. Young students were at home instead of at school, there were significant questions about what supplies and resources were available in different communities, and lecturers and students were adjusting to a new reality in which a "shelter in place" mantra defined much of their interactions with the world around them.

Mapping provided a valuable possibility as a pedagogical tool and a curricular innovation, because while lecturers and students were adapting to the isolation of the shutdown, they were constantly exposed to visual portraits of the impacts of COVID-19. For example, news outlets and social media were continually showing maps about the spread of the virus, comparisons of spread across regions, and deaths by region, state, country, among others. In this way, the maps were arguably adding to the crises of the pandemic, and while the data from these maps were important, the images often themselves reinforced separation as opposed to connection. To combat this, asset mapping was developed as a way to encourage young people to begin the process of creating their own maps of their own communities starting with their families, neighbourhoods, and cities. They started by interviewing peers, elders, community leaders, and family members about the strengths and resources in their communities. The data from these interviews were then connected to visual representations of the area collected by the students (photos, personal descriptions, google maps overlays) to create a personalized asset map.

These asset maps were then shared with the entire class. The idea of sharing maps was first a way to compare and contrast students' experiences especially for students from the same neighbourhood. It was also a way for students to learn about different experiences within the same school, district, or city. Sharing community assets generated opportunities for students to express cultural strengths within their own communities, learn about one another, see across differences, and ultimately build connections with one another. It also revealed that the images and maps often seen in the media do not portray the multiple layers of communities. And, particularly in communities of Color with strong traditions in collectivist cultural identities, these asset maps revealed the love and care that families have for one another-even across racial and ethnic groups.

As an action-research project, community asset mapping provided lecturers, new teachers, and K-12 students opportunities to live the curriculum and together, generate meaningful, relevant, culturally-engaging content to teach and learn from one another. The fact that everyone created a map, teachers and students alike, showcases their shared experiences even across generations, racial groups, and, in the current context, living through the ongoing tumult of the COVID-19 pandemic and its toll on daily life.

Case Study: Bachelor of Education Honors in Teacher Development Studies at a University in KwaZulu-Natal

In the Teacher Development Studies Discipline at a university in KwaZulu-Natal, all Bachelor of Education Honors students, who are teachers, choose to conduct an action research project to study and improve their classroom practice. As postgraduate students, they critically reflect on their classroom practice to identify challenges or problems they face in their teaching. They adopt a critical perspective or framework and design an action research project that involves the four steps of planning, acting, observing and reflection (Macintyre, 2012; Slapac et al., 2021). As a result of the national lockdown and school closures in March 2020 due to COVID-19, teachers and their students were at home. Therefore,

BEd Honors students were unable to conduct their action research projects within the confines of their classrooms and had to re-think the design of their interventions. Fataar (2020) argues that the COVID-19 pandemic forced teachers to adapt their teaching strategies and adopt a 'pedagogy of care' to align their teaching with the new online education landscape. Teachers and students in rural, Black communities lacked resources such as the internet, laptops, tablets and reference books due to deeply entrenched social inequalities (Dube, 2020; Le Grange, 2020).

The lecturer at the South African university had to redesign the curriculum and rethink curriculum delivery and assessment in line with COVID-19 protocols of school closures. In addition, she had to attend online training sessions on how to use online platforms such as Zoom and Microsoft Teams to facilitate her teaching. This was a new learning experience and a monumental shift for her, as she had not used these online platforms in her teaching prior to the COVID-19 pandemic. The South African case study reports on a BEd Honors module titled Teacher Identities and Teacher Change. This module focuses on teachers' personal and professional identities as a foundational aspect of teacher learning and development for change. In this module, students explored the concept of teacher identity within a context of changing education policy and practice, within a range of social realities. It also provides opportunities to explore links between teachers' personal and professional identities, teachers' self-inquiry and teacher development.

After critically reflecting on the course readings and lesson activities, the facilitation of the curriculum in this module had to be redesigned. There were 19 students registered for this module. Although the lecturer had not met the students face-to-face, she was aware that they came from culturally diverse backgrounds. Reflecting on her 'learning through crisis', she decided to revise the curriculum design and re-think the lesson activities and adopt culturally relevant materials. Firstly, lectures were planned to use music to encourage students to reflect on their childhood memories and significant people who influenced the development of their identities. The music video and lyrics for the song 'Coat of many colors' by Dolly Parton were selected. The lecturer received minimal training given the time constraints and had to 'learn through crisis' how to use Zoom. Anxiety and frustration were experienced when technical glitches arose while using the Zoom platform since lecturers were isolated from their colleagues and administrative staff, who would normally assist during face-to-face lectures. Therefore, she had to fend for herself and use google to learn about the Zoom platform. Students enjoyed watching the music video and listening to the lyrics of the song. The song was relevant to them and they seemed to identify with the narrative of poverty and socio-economic challenges. This suggests that using music is a useful, culturally relevant material to capture the interest of students.

The use of artifacts is very useful when studying teacher identities and Turkle (2007) argues that artifacts have the power to evoke and trigger childhood experiences and emotions. A self-box activity was designed that required students to reflect on three or four artifacts that were significant in the development of their personal and professional identities. Students had to design a self-box that included their selected artifacts and record a short video explaining the significance of each object, and share these short videos on the WhatsApp group. Students selected artifacts that were culturally relevant such as African hats, shields, animal skins and garments. They also selected clay ornaments such as clay pots and animals, that were made by their ancestors and held a sentimental and culturally significant meaning for them.

Culturally relevant materials designed by African scholars whose backgrounds the majority of the students could identify with were selected. The 'Tree of Life' approach developed by the Zimbabwean psychologist Ncube (2006) was used. Through a metaphorical representation of a tree, students had to engage in three activities to discuss their past (the roots of the tree), their beliefs and values as a teacher (the trunk), and their hopes and agency as a teacher (the leaves and blossoms) working in a context of educational change both nationally and internationally. In addition, the TED talk by Chimamanda Ngozi Adichie "The danger of a single story" was used to get students to reflect on their lives and their multiple identities. Students had to draw on their personal experiences to explain the danger of a single story.

Braun and Clark (2012) contend that "thematic analysis is a method for systematically identifying, organising, and offering insight into, patterns of meaning (themes) across a dataset" (p. 2). An inductive or 'bottom up' approach was used to code and analyse the case studies. This means that the codes and themes were derived from the case studies. Initially, each of the two researchers analyzed their own case study using thematic analysis. The six-phase approach to thematic analysis outlined by Braun and Clark (2012) was adopted in this study: familiarising yourself with the data, generating initial codes, searching for themes, reviewing potential themes, defining and naming themes and producing the report.

Main Themes

The two researchers collaboratively reviewed initial codes and potential themes and identified the following three themes in relation to the research questions:

- Tensions/Challenges: Social inequalities and lack of resources, technological and emotional challenges, school closures, isolation
- Opportunities: Curriculum innovation and redesign, mapping as a pedagogical tool
- Learning through crisis: Culturally relevant pedagogy, living the curriculum

These themes are interlinked and highlight the dynamic nature of 'learning through crisis' during the COVID-19 pandemic. Hence, there may be overlap of themes in the discussion of the findings.

FINDINGS

Tensions/Challenges

The tensions or challenges shared by the lecturers of teaching during the COVID-19 pandemic in two different contexts were similar. The following sub-themes were identified: school closures, isolation, technological and emotional challenges and social inequalities and lack of resources. Responses from the South African lecturer are coded SA while responses from the lecturer from San Francisco are coded SF.

Social Inequalities and Lack of Resources

The most common tension or challenge encountered by both lecturers were social inequalities and lack of resources while teaching during the COVID-19 pandemic. Given the shift to online teaching and using platforms such as Zoom, Microsoft Teams or WhatsApp, this meant that teachers and students from deep rural contexts who lacked internet connectivity and teachers and students from poor socio-economic backgrounds who did not have laptops or reference books were severely compromised in terms of their learning and assessment. SF explained that through the community asset mapping project students could "compare and contrast students' experiences" which highlighted the differences "within the same school, district, or city…even across racial and ethnic groups" SF shared the following:

Intensification of social and educational injustices faced by communities of Color,[…]there were significant questions about what supplies and resources were available in different communities.

In the same vein, SA mentioned the high levels of inequality, unemployment and poverty in South Africa and that these were exacerbated by the COVID-19 pandemic. SA described the 'digital divide' between urban and rural communities and mentioned:

Teachers and students in rural, Black communities lacked resources such as the internet, laptops, tablets and reference books due to deeply entrenched social inequalities.

Isolation of Shutdown

Both lecturers also discussed how, in their respective countries, the COVID-19 pandemic forced schools and other institutions to shut down or go into lockdown. This resulted in feelings of isolation not only in teachers but also in students. SA stated:

As a result of the national lockdown and school closures in March 2020 due to COVID-19, teachers and their students were at home.

Due to the rapid shift to online teaching during the COVID-19 pandemic, teachers had to adapt from traditional face-to-face teaching and experienced difficulty adjusting to teaching online from home. SA described this feeling of isolation and stated:

Lecturers were isolated from their colleagues and administrative staff, who would normally assist during face-to-face lectures.

Teachers in San Francisco also felt isolated during the shutdown as a result of the COVID-19 pandemic. SF described how "*the social interaction that lies at the heart of teaching was instantly gone… while we were adapting to the isolation of the shutdown*".

Technological and Emotional Challenges

Teaching during the COVID-19 pandemic also resulted in teachers experiencing challenges in dealing with technology as well as their emotions. Not all teachers had been trained to use online platforms, such as Zoom, Microsoft teams, and Google docs, in their teaching. SA shared:

Teacher educators received minimal training given the time constraints and had to 'learn through crisis' how to use Zoom.

Being isolated from colleagues at school or university, also meant that teachers did not have the support to assist them with challenges they experienced using online platforms to teach. SA described how:

Anxiety and frustration were experienced when technical glitches arose while using the Zoom platform.

The crisis and death during the COVID-19 pandemic were also very emotional for teachers in South Africa and San Francisco. Teachers had to deal with feelings of anxiety, frustration, grief and sorrow. However, SF explains that the emotional challenges that teachers experienced during the COVID-19 pandemic are not over and stated that "*the sadness and uncertainty brought about by the initial months of the global health crisis linger*".

School Closures

Both lecturers mentioned school closures as a tension or challenge they encountered while teaching during the COVID-19 pandemic. This meant that lecturers were abruptly shifted out of their traditional teaching spaces and had to rapidly adapt to teaching remotely or online. For example, SA mentioned that "As a result of the national lockdown and school closures in March 2020 due to COVID-19, teachers and their students were at home." SF shared a similar response:

In-person schooling was abruptly halted... challenging during the forced shutdowns as a part of the onset of the COVID-19 pandemic.

It is important to state that the authors too-as teachers, as scholars, and as citizens-continue to be deeply affected by the ongoing impacts of the COVID-19 pandemic. The sadness and uncertainty brought about by the initial months of the global health crisis linger, and there is no doubt that their roles and goals as teacher educators continue to adapt to shifting realities in education. For example, while nearly all of their students (new teachers) were teaching in-person, some of their university courses were utilizing a hybrid schedule (some sessions in person and some sessions on Zoom). This created challenges for them as teachers, for their students, and for the future of their profession. While we do not embrace online teaching as a worthy substitute for face-to-face instruction, the authors understand that their reality demanded adaptation and flexibility. This created tension, and, as lecturers, the authors felt that they needed to sit with, reflect upon, and work alongside new teachers to learn from that tension as a way of creating new possibilities for change and sustainability in education.

Opportunities

Although lecturers mentioned the tensions and challenges they experienced as a result of the immense shift from traditional face-to-face to online teaching, this study highlighted that teaching during the COVID-19 pandemic also afforded teachers opportunities to be creative and innovative. In other words, adapting to teaching during the COVID-19 pandemic offered creative spaces for teachers to develop and grow as curriculum developers.

Curriculum Innovation and Redesign

The major opportunity mentioned by both lecturers was that teaching during the COVID-19 pandemic motivated teachers to become more creative in designing lesson topics and strategies in their online teaching. Teachers had to redesign not only the curriculum content or topics to be taught but also the delivery of the curriculum. SF shared:

Given the impacts of school closures initiated by COVID-19 in spring 2020 and the teachers created innovative curriculum to highlight the collective strengths and solidarity of local communities.

SA also explained how lecturers had to consider innovative ways to plan lesson activities and encourage and motivate students online. She elaborated how she used a music video and lyrics of the song 'Coat of many colors' by Dolly Parton and that students not only enjoyed the music video but also related to the reference to poverty and hardship in the lyrics of the song. Furthermore, she mentioned:

Lecturers had to redesign the curriculum and rethink curriculum delivery and assessment[…]the facilitation of the curriculum in this module had to be redesigned[…]decided to revise the curriculum design and re-think the lesson activities.

Mapping as a Pedagogical Tool

As a result of school closures and the shutdown in San Francisco, lecturers had to rethink the delivery of the curriculum. Linked to curriculum innovation, SF described how a community mapping project was adapted "when in-person schooling was abruptly halted and teachers needed to transform curriculum to meet the lived experiences of life beyond the classroom". This community mapping project was designed by new teachers and encouraged their students to explore and map community resources, which was pertinent during the forced shutdowns. SF shared that "mapping provided a valuable possibility as a pedagogical tool and a curricular innovation".

In addition, SF explained:

Sharing community assets generated opportunities for students to express cultural strengths within their own communities, learn about one another, see across differences, and ultimately build connections with one another.

Learning Through Crisis

Lecturers had to learn new ways of designing lesson activities and teaching during the COVID-19 pandemic. The fear and anxiety of death and illness associated with the COVID-19 pandemic resulted in education and teaching being in crisis. The uncertainty and stress of the COVID-19 pandemic was a new phenomenon or crisis that teachers had to navigate. Other examples of crises that teachers have experienced over the years include war, violence and natural disasters such as floods, earthquakes and hurricanes. In crisis situations, individuals have to learn to survive and cope with the devastation of the crisis to address social inequities and social transformation.

Culturally Relevant Pedagogy

Both lecturers described how the COVID-19 pandemic offered opportunities to learn new teaching strategies design relevant learning materials and lesson activities. SA explained how she redesigned her lessons to include culturally relevant materials. Furthermore, she described selected literature and learning materials designed by African scholars, which would be culturally relevant to her students. She shared:

Using music is a useful, culturally relevant material to capture the interest of students[...]Students selected artefacts that were culturally relevant such as African hats, shields, animal skins and garments. They also selected clay ornaments such as clay pots and animals, that were made by their ancestors and held a sentimental and culturally significant meaning for Culturally relevant materials designed by African scholars whose backgrounds the majority of the students could identify with were selected.

SF also mentioned:

Together, they were generating meaningful, relevant, culturally-engaging content adopt culturally relevant materials.

This suggests that lecturers considered the social inequalities of our students and their culturally diverse backgrounds to enhance their teaching and bridge the cultural divide.

Living the Curriculum

The COVID-19 pandemic inspired not only lecturers but also teachers to reflect on and refine the curriculum they taught. Teachers were encouraged to create meaningful curricula which suggest that they were living the curriculum. In other words, the immense shift in their teaching as they transitioned to online teaching, highlights the potential to transform the curriculum and make it relevant to the lived experiences and social realities of their students. SF mentioned that *"asset mapping provided lecturers, new teachers, and K-12 student opportunities to live the curriculum"*.

Both lecturers mentioned that they embraced the tensions or challenges of online teaching during the COVID-19 pandemic (Le Grange, 2020) and acknowledged the opportunities this offered to engage with meaningful curricula that focused on the lived experiences of their students. Lecturers learning through crisis (Kumashiro, 2000; Slapac et al. 2021) also resulted in the transformation of the curriculum.

The framework that we present above is our attempt to show that existing scholarship can help pave the way for meaningful change in the pursuit of social justice in education (Borrero, 2023). The lived experiences of students must be central to all teaching and learning, and as such, what we teach must be culturally relevant (Ladson-Billings, 2014) and applicable to students' cultural realities (Gay, 2018). In the current context, this means that we must acknowledge, learn from, and struggle together amidst the ongoing crises in our world: the COVID-19 pandemic, global racial inequity, climate devastation, war, violence, etc. Learning in and through crisis (Kumashiro, 2010) is a requirement if we are to truly model what it means to live the curriculum as a teacher today.

In accord with Kumashiro (2015), this study suggests that the COVID-19 pandemic presented a crisis that not only made teacher learning possible but also introduced educational shifts that made teacher learning difficult. Lecturers had to learn through the crisis of COVID-19, consider the social inequalities of their students (who are teachers) and draw on the knowledge of their culturally diverse backgrounds to enhance their teaching and bridge the cultural divide. Drawing on Ladson-Billings' (2014) notion that culture is fluid, lecturers had to synthesize past ideas and views to develop innovative and new teaching strategies. Moreover, lecturers had to reflect critically on race and culture and draw on their previous knowledge of teaching and learning to design and teach culturally relevant lessons (Capper, 2022; Hefflin, 2002).

PRACTICAL RECOMMENDATIONS

The case studies presented highlighted mapping community strengths and music, artifacts and culturally relevant materials as examples from the authors' own teaching. They do not showcase them as exemplars or best practices. Instead, the authors highlight them as attempts to learn through the crises brought about by the school closures and shelter-in-place mandates at the start of the COVID-19 pandemic in spring 2020. Like most classroom teaching, these projects are flawed, incomplete and adaptations of other projects. What is important, is that the authors attempted to develop these projects alongside their students with the hopes of learning with and from one another by teaching into the pandemic. That is, the authors were not trying to pursue business as usual in our classrooms. They were trying to teach and live in the moment by understanding their collective experiences with the crises around this. This, the authors believe, is a foundation for meaningful, culturally relevant teaching, and is something they hope to model in this chapter as transnational teacher education.

A noteworthy result from this study was that lecturers redesigned and created innovative curricula in an effort to address the challenges ushered in by the school closures and shift to online teaching. Therefore, it is recommended that staff development workshops should be planned for lecturers to improve their knowledge and understanding of curriculum design and innovation. It is also recommended from the data that steps should be taken to provide opportunities for lecturers to design culturally relevant materials.

FUTURE RESEARCH DIRECTIONS

Culturally relevant pedagogy is crucial to prepare teachers to teach culturally diverse students and in ethnically diverse school contexts (Simms, 2013). For example, teachers should be knowledgeable to 'tailor' the curriculum and select culturally relevant materials appropriate for their students' race and culture (Capper, 2022; Song et al., 2023). This chapter highlighted that lecturers created innovative curricula, redesigned and transformed the curriculum and generated relevant, culturally engaging content. The context of the COVID-19 pandemic also showcased the social inequalities and lack of resources and highlighted the technological and emotional challenges that lecturers encountered.

Therefore, suggestions for future research directions include examining the curricula of pre-service and in-service programs at universities as a tool to develop teachers' knowledge and skills in designing culturally relevant materials as well as designing and setting up cross-cultural international projects where possible. Professional development workshops planned by education departments should also be examined to build the capacity of teachers and support them to cope with technological and emotional challenges of crises in education. Further research that examines social inequalities and lack of resources and how teachers 'learn through crisis' would extend this study.

CONCLUSION

As lecturers, the authors continue to learn that they must step away from their own existing curricula and find new pathways toward projects that let students explore and express their lived experiences. In the past few years, these experiences have involved incredible change and uncertainty. Living through the ongoing COVID-19 pandemic and other global crises is rife with tension and the authors need to find ways to embrace this tension and find opportunities to teach into it. The authors believe that the case studies discussed in this chapter reveal their attempts to do so. They have learned about the incredible fortitude and resilience of their own students and how their students will lead them into a future that the authors cannot envision at this point. The authors have also learned that they need to find ways to step aside and let young people lead them. This is both humbling and daunting, but it is their work as lecturers. Collaboration with an international colleague offered opportunities to share teaching strategies, such as the community mapping project and use of artifacts, and deepen understanding about Kumashiro's framework of 'learning through crisis'. International collaboration can contribute to teacher and lecturer development, and internationalisation of the curriculum.

The case studies highlighted teaching during the COVID-19 pandemic as well as transnational learning and telecollaboration of two lecturers based in South Africa and San Francisco. It showcased how through transnational learning and telecollaboration, they critically examined their choices about teaching and learning and redesigned the curriculum to uphold social justice. It would be interesting to examine how lecturers in other countries addressed the tensions or challenges and opportunities generated in their transnational learning and telecollaboration. How will social inequalities and lack of resources be addressed? Will teachers be trained to address the technological and emotional challenges? What support programs could be designed to assist teachers? Future studies could research and examine these questions.

ACKNOWLEDGMENT

Many thanks to the reviewers for their feedback on the draft chapter. This research received no specific grant from any funding agency in the public, commercial, or not-for-profit sectors.

REFERENCES

Adedoyin, O. B., & Soykan, E. (2020). COVID-19 pandemic and online learning: The challenges and opportunities. *Interactive Learning Environments*, *31*(2), 863–875. doi:10.1080/10494820.2020.1813180

Baxter, P., & Jack, S. (2008). Qualitative case study methodology: Study design and implementation for novice researchers. *The Qualitative Report*, *13*(4), 544–559. doi:10.46743/2160-3715/2008.1573

Borrero, N. E. (2023). Embracing the collective: Challenges and opportunities in teaching and teacher education in the wake of COVID-19. *Social Sciences (Basel, Switzerland)*, *12*(3), 194. doi:10.3390/socsci12030194

Borrero, N. E., Camangian, P. R., Ayers, R., Martinez, S., & Flores, E. (2020). *Half an inch from the edge: Teacher education, teaching, and student learning for social transformation*. Rowman & Littlefield.

Borrero, N. E., & Naidoo, J. (2023). Teachers living the curriculum: Culturally relevant pedagogy and action research. In N. Wahlström & B. Karseth (Eds.), *International Encyclopedia of Education* (4th ed., Vol. 7, pp. 357–362). Elsevier. doi:10.1016/B978-0-12-818630-5.03063-3

Borrero, N. E., & Yeh, C. J. (2016). Ecological asset mapping as a pedagogical tool for new urban teachers. *International Journal of Multicultural Education*, *18*(3), 114–137. doi:10.18251/ijme.v18i3.1183

Braun, V., & Clarke, V. (2006). Using thematic analysis in psychology. *Qualitative Research in Psychology*, *3*(2), 77–101. doi:10.1191/1478088706qp063oa

Capper, K. (2022). Culturally relevant pedagogy in the English curriculum. *Journal of Education*, *202*(4), 397–405. doi:10.1177/0022057421991856

Chen, C. Y. C., Byrne, E., & Vélez, T. (2022). Impact of the 2020 pandemic of COVID-19 on families with school-aged children in the United States: Roles of income level and race. *Journal of Family Issues*, *43*(3), 719–740. doi:10.1177/0192513X21994153 PMID:38603084

Cohen, L., Manion, L., & Morrison, K. (2018). *Research methods in education* (8th ed.). Routledge. doi:10.4324/9781315456539

Crenshaw, K. (2019). The marginalization of Harriet's daughters: Perpetual crisis, misdirected blame, and the enduring urgency of intersectionality. *Kalfou*, *6*(1), 7–23. doi:10.15367/kf.v6i1.226

Creswell, J. W., & Creswell, J. D. (2018). Research design: Qualitative, quantitative, and mixed methods approaches. *Sage.*

Delpit, L. D. (1988). The silenced dialogue: Power and pedagogy in educating other people's children. *Harvard Educational Review*, *58*(3), 280–298. doi:10.17763/haer.58.3.c43481778r528qw4

Dube, B. (2020). Rural online learning in the context of COVID-19 in South Africa: Evoking an inclusive education approach. *Multidisciplinary Journal of Educational Research*, *10*(2), 135–157. doi:10.17583/remie.2020.5607

Emdin, C. (2016). *For white folks who teach in the hood ... and the rest of ya'll too: Reality pedagogy and urban education*. Beacon Press.

Fataar, A. (2020). *A pedagogy of care: Teachers rise to the challenge of the 'new normal'*. https://www.dailymaverick.co.za

Fataar, A., & Badroodien, A. (2020). Editorial notes. Special issue: Emergent educational imaginaries during the Covid-19 pandemic. *Southern African Review of Education*, *26*(1), 1–5.

Flores, N. (2016). A tale of two visions: Hegemonic whiteness and bilingual education. *Educational Policy*, *30*(1), 13–38. doi:10.1177/0895904815616482

Futch, V. A., & Fine, M. (2014). Mapping as a method: History and theoretical commitments. *Qualitative Research in Psychology*, *11*(1), 42–59. doi:10.1080/14780887.2012.719070

Gay, G. (2018). *Culturally responsive teaching. Theory, research, and practice*. Teachers College Press.

Green, L., & Collett, L. (2021). Teaching thinking in South African schools: Selected school leaders' perceptions. *South African Journal of Education, 41*(2), 1–13. doi:10.15700/saje.v41n2a1893

Guimarães, F. F., & Finardi, K. R. (2021). Global citizenship education (GCE) in internationalisation: COIL as alternative Thirdspace. *Globalisation, Societies and Education, 19*(5), 641–657. doi:10.1080/14767724.2021.1875808

Hefflin, B. R. (2002). Learning to develop culturally relevant pedagogy: A lesson about cornrowed lives. *The Urban Review, 34*(3), 231–250. doi:10.1023/A:1020603323594

Hlatshwayo, M. N., Khumalo, S. D., & Nzimande, N. (2021). The pandemic is our portal: Reimagining teaching and learning in the time of Covid-19. *African Perspectives of Research in Teaching and Learning, 5*(1), 59–77.

Jooste, N., & Hagenmeier, C. (2022). Policy framework for the internationalisation of higher education in South Africa: A compass for comprehensive internationalisation? *Journal of Studies in International Education, 26*(4), 415–435. doi:10.1177/10283153221105318

Koshy, E., Koshy, V., & Waterman, H. (2011). Action Research in Healthcare. *Sage.*

Kozol, J. (2012). *Savage inequalities: Children in America's schools.* Crown.

Kumashiro, K. K. (2000). Teaching and learning through desire, crisis and difference: Perverted reflections on anti-oppressive education. *The Radical Teacher, 58*, 6–11.

Kumashiro, K. K. (2015). *Against common sense: Teaching and learning toward social justice* (3rd ed.). Routledge. doi:10.4324/9781315765525

Ladson-Billings, G. (2014). Culturally relevant pedagogy 2.0: A.k.a. the remix. *Harvard Educational Review, 84*(1), 74–84. doi:10.17763/haer.84.1.p2rj131485484751

Le Grange, L. (2020). Could the COVID-19 pandemic accelerate the Uberfication of the university? *South African Journal of Higher Education, 34*(4), 1–10. doi:10.20853/34-4-4071

Macintyre, C. (2012). *The art of action research in the classroom.* David Fulton Publishers. doi:10.4324/9780203065228

Marx, S. (2022). Mapping as critical qualitative research methodology. *International Journal of Research & Method in Education.* Advance online publication. doi:10.1080/1743727X.2022.2110231

Milner, H. R. IV. (2011). Culturally relevant pedagogy in a diverse urban classroom. *The Urban Review, 43*(1), 66–89. doi:10.1007/s11256-009-0143-0

Ncube, N. (2006). The Tree of Life project: Using narrative ideas in work with vulnerable children in Southern Africa. *The International Journal of Narrative Therapy and Community Work, 1*, 3–16.

O'Dowd, R. (2015). Supporting in-service language educators in learning to telecollaborate. *Language Learning & Technology, 19*(1), 64–83. http://llt.msu.edu/issues/february2015/odowd.pdf

O'Dowd, R. (2016). Emerging trends and new directions in telecollaborative learning. *CALICO Journal, 33*(3), 291–310. doi:10.1558/cj.v33i3.30747

Reimers, F. M. (Ed.). (2022). *Primary and secondary education during COVID-19.*, doi:10.1007/978-3-030-81500-4

Roy, A. (2020). The pandemic is a portal. *Financial Times, 3*(4).

Simms, M. (2013). A teacher educator uses action research to develop culturally conscious curriculum planners. *Democracy & Education, 21*(2), 3. https://democracyeducationjournal.org/home/vol21/iss2/3

Slapac, A., Collett, K., Wessels, F., Gamiet, G., & Knudsmoen, H. (2023). Social justice pedagogy an Collaborative Online International Learning (COIL): Across three partner higher education institutions. In P. Escudeiro, N. Escudeiro, & O. Bernardes (Eds.), *Handbook of research on implementing inclusive educational models and technologies for equity and diversity* (pp. 252–272). IGI Global. doi:10.4018/979-8-3693-0453-2.ch013

Slapac, A., Coppersmith, S. A., O'Brien, K., & Balcerzak, P. (2021). Resilience in crisis: Developing community through action research. In A. Slapac, P. Balcerzak, & K. O'Brien (Eds.), *Handbook of research on the global empowerment of educators and student learning through action research* (pp. 23–48). IGI Global. doi:10.4018/978-1-7998-6922-1.ch002

Song, K. H., Kerkhoff, S. N., & Slapac, A. (2023). Educating racially, culturally, and linguistically diverse children in the global era: The world at home and at home in the world. In J. Chitiyo & Z. Pietrantoni (Eds.), *Social justice and culturally-affirming education in K-12 settings* (pp. 1–22). IGI Global. doi:10.4018/978-1-6684-6386-4.ch001

Turkle, S. (2007). The secret power of things we hold dear. *New Scientist, 194*(2607), 50–52. doi:10.1016/S0262-4079(07)61446-8

UNESCO. (2020). *Global Education Monitoring Report 2020: Inclusion and education: All means all.* UNESCO.

Wenger, E. (1998). *Communities of Practice: Learning, Meaning, and Identity*. Cambridge University Press. doi:10.1017/CBO9780511803932

World Bank. (2018). *The World Bank Annual Report*. World Bank. https://www.worldbank.org/annualreport

Yeh, C. J., Stanley, S., Ramirez, C. A., & Borrero, N. E. (2022). Navigating the "Dual Pandemics": The cumulative impact of the COVID-19 pandemic and rise in awareness of racial injustices among high school students of Color in urban schools. *Urban Education*. doi:10.1177/00420859221097884

ADDITIONAL READING

Carloni, G., & Franzé, F. (2021). A telecollaborative international exchange for foreign language learning and reflective teaching. In G. Carloni, C. Fotheringham, A. Virga, & B. Zuccala (Eds.), *Blended learning and the Global South. Virtual exchanges in higher education* (pp. 131–158). Venice University Press. doi:10.30687/978-88-6969-529-2/008

Chen, J. (2023). Mentoring international postgraduate students and early career researchers through transnational telecollaboration: A supervisor's autoethnography. *Journal of Applied Learning & Teaching*, *6*(2), 370–377.

Chun, D. M. (2015). Language and culture learning in higher education via telecollaboration. *Pedagogies*, *10*(1), 5–21. doi:10.1080/1554480X.2014.999775

Dooly, M., & O'Dowd, R. (Eds.). (2018). *In this together: Teachers' experiences with transnational, telecollaborative Language Learning projects*. Peter Lang. doi:10.3726/b14311

Dooly, M., & Vinagre, M. (2022, July). teaching and learning. *Language Teaching*, *55*(3), 392–406. doi:10.1017/S0261444821000069

Dube, B. (2020). Rural online learning in the context of COVID-19 in South Africa: Evoking an Inclusive Education approach. *Multidisciplinary Journal of Educational Research*, *10*(2), 135–157. doi:10.17583/remie.2020.5607

Godwin-Jones, R. (2019). Telecollaboration as an approach to developing intercultural communication competence. *Language Learning & Technology*, *23*(3), 8–28. http://hdl.handle.net/10125/44691

Hughes, H. E., Moulton, M., & Andrews, G. (2016). Learning through crisis and paradox in justice-oriented Teacher Education, *Middle Grades Review*, *1*(3), Article 4. https://scholarworks.uvm.edu/mgreview/vol1/iss3/4

Slapac, A., Balcerzak, P., & O'Brien, K. G. (Eds.). (2021). *Handbook of research on the global empowerment of educators and student learning through action research*. IGI Global. doi:10.4018/978-1-7998-6922-1

KEY TERMS AND DEFINITIONS

Culturally: Relevant Pedagogy: Teachers draw on the cultural knowledge and lived experiences of their students to adjust their teaching so that it is relevant to their racial and cultural contexts.

Learning Through Crisis: During crisis situations, teachers examine their teaching and learning choices critically and develop learning materials that address social inequities and anti-oppression and promote transformation and social justice.

Living the Curriculum: Teachers reflect on and refine their teaching and design meaningful learning activities to transform the curriculum so that it is relevant to lived experiences and social realities of their students.

Online Teaching: Teachers using online platforms such as Zoom, Microsoft Teams and Google docs to facilitate learning activities and discussions.

Social Inequality: Unequal distribution of and access to resources in society brought as a result of differences in race, power, gender, religion, class, and sexual orientation.

Telecollaboration: Individuals from diverse cultural backgrounds engage in intercultural dialogue through virtual exchange or online technologies.

Transnational Learning: Learning provided by higher education institutions or programmes to students in another country.

Chapter 7
Using Flip and Facebook to Create Windows and Mirrors for Transnational Learning:
A United States–Israel Scholarship of Teaching and Learning Project

Crystal Machado
Indiana University of Pennsylvania, USA

Tami Seifert
https://orcid.org/0000-0002-2703-2251
Tel Aviv University, Israel

ABSTRACT

Educators need to offer students a curriculum that reflects their funds of knowledge (mirrors), exposes them to the cultures and experiences of others (windows), and develops in them an understanding and empathy for those who are different from them (sliding glass doors). In this chapter, the authors describe a six-week-long scholarship of teaching and learning (SoTL) project, which included 63 pre-service teachers (PST) in the US and 36 in-service teachers (IST) in Israel. The authors describe how they used Flip and Facebook to provide PST and IST who are racially, linguistically, and culturally different with an opportunity to engage in asynchronous dialogue. Analysis of survey and extant data confirmed that these transnational learning experiences provided participants with "windows" and "mirrors" for digital, global, and cultural literacy. Readers can use the authors' description of the two asynchronous assignments, the results of the SoTL study, and lessons learned to guide, design, and implement similar transnational learning experiences.

DOI: 10.4018/978-1-6684-7813-4.ch007

INTRODUCTION

There is a growing awareness, prompted by globalization and COVID-19, that educators need to learn how to view concepts, issues, events, and themes from the perspective of diverse ethnic and cultural groups (Banks, 1989; Bourn & Shiel, 2009; Byram et.al., 2016; Miller, 2002). This can be accomplished by internationalizing the curriculum in higher education (Teichler, 2009, 2017), which is the process of adding global, intercultural, or international elements into a course. Over the last couple of decades, faculty have used many different approaches including, but not limited to content integration (Lehtomäki et al., 2016) and equity pedagogy (Spiteri, 2017), to foster intercultural dialogue and transnational learning. In this chapter, the authors describe how they used the ISTE Standards for Educators (2017), Banks' transformative approach (1989), and social media to further pre-service teachers (PST) in the US and in-service teachers (IST) in Israel's knowledge of communication technologies and access to professional networks for transnational learning. It is described how the two asynchronous activities, completed over six weeks, provided their students with an opportunity to reflect on the funds of knowledge they possess *(mirrors)*, and on the cultures and experiences of others *(windows)* (Bishop, 1990).

LITERATURE REVIEW

According to Stephanie (2022) the Future Skills 2030 report identifies the essential skills students in teacher education programs need, which include but are not limited to: cognitive flexibility, digital literacy and computational thinking, judgment and decision-making, emotional, and social intelligence, and a creative and innovative mindset. One of the basic requirements of 21st-century teachers is integrating interculturality into their work, and this is done most effectively using technology for global communication and transnational teaching projects (Byram et.al., 2016). This section includes a brief synthesis of the literature that guided the analysis, course design, and the related Scholarship of Teaching and Learning (SoTL) project.

TRANSNATIONAL LEARNING

The global and interdependent nature of today's world has created the demand for educators to be prepared to operate in a global world and to provide a learning environment that meets those needs (Bourn & Shiel, 2009; Miller, 2002). The Collins Dictionary describes transnationalism as an experience that extends beyond the boundaries of a single nation (n.d.). The UNESCO/Council of Europe Code of Good Practice in the Provision of Transnational Education describes transnational education as:

All types of higher education study programmes, or sets of courses of study, or educational services (including those of distance education) in which the learners are located in a country different from the one where the awarding institution is based. (UNESCO, 6 June 2001)

In other words, transnational learning is the process of acquiring knowledge and skills through cross-border educational experiences and activities. It encompasses, among other opportunities, collaboration between institutions across borders.

The benefits of transnational learning are numerous. It allows individuals to broaden their perspectives, develop intercultural competencies, and gain exposure to diverse educational systems and approaches (Kulich, 2015; Williams, 2005). The core elements in the process of acquiring intercultural competence according to Gopal (2011) are attitudes to other cultures, developing culture-specific knowledge and skills that involve self-reflection, reflexivity, and the development of one's communication abilities. Transnational learning offers opportunities for personal growth and professional development and helps to foster a more connected and diverse global community (Parkhouse & Massaro, 2019). With this end in mind higher education faculty in many countries around the world are attempting to design instruction that shapes learners' future relationships within a multicultural world and how they envision and enact their relationships with diverse others (Killick & Foster, 2021).

Pre-Service Teachers' Use of Social Media for Transnational Learning

Global education initiatives, which connect students in different locations, are becoming more common and include digital tools to support collaborative intercultural learning. One of the main goals of the intercultural aspect of education is to prepare students to be able to interact in intercultural contexts effectively and appropriately (Perry & Southwell, 2011) and to acknowledge both the similarities and differences of each other's cultures (Dervin, 2017). Technology enhances educators' ability to host and facilitate learning across countries (DeMeyer, 2012; Fitzgerald, 2012; Gopal, 2011). Studies have shown that social media can be a valuable tool for PST to develop intercultural competencies (Parkhouse & Massaro, 2019), increase their exposure to diverse educational systems (Bakshy et al., 2011), and learn from their peers globally (Sawyer & Chen, 2012). PST can use social media for professional learning (Carpenter & Krutka, 2014; Robson, 2018), as a part of teaching and learning activities (Junco et al., 2013), and to engage in real-time interactions with students and teachers from different countries (Jin, 2015).

Social media platforms provide PST with opportunities to connect with educators and students in general as well as from around the world and share educational resources (Boholano, 2017). Online social media use for collaborative learning has been found to have a significant contribution to students' academic performance and satisfaction (Zhu, 2012). To effectively engage and teach generation Z students, it is important for PST or future teachers who study to become certified educators to use social media as a tool for learning and teaching and to gain new knowledge and skills (Seifert, 2016). Future educators must have professional development in utilizing social media in instruction to promote a collaborative learner-centered environment to which students will relate and respond (Boholano, 2017).

THEORETICAL FRAMEWORK

Children in many parts of the US have limited access to literature that presents diverse groups in a positive light. Larrick's (1965) analysis of 5000 picture book demographics, published over a period of three years, revealed that only 6.7% of them represented African American children. Of these, some were depicted as slaves or servants, which perpetuated stereotypes (Koss, 2015). The phrase "*mirrors and windows*" was initially introduced by Emily Style for the National SEED Project (Style, 1996). A "mirror affirms one's value and reflects identities and experiences and a window expands one's worldview" (Buchanan & Fox, 2019, p.192). Multicultural education scholar Rudine Sims Bishop (1990, 2012) furthered the concept when she added "*glass sliding doors*" to the phrase to explain how children see themselves in books.

Even though the population in the US is becoming increasingly diverse (Thomas et al., 2016) and greater attention is being paid to the production of books that feature non-stereotypically diverse populations (Koss, 2015; Thomas et al., 2016) the issues identified by Larrick (1965) and Bishop (2012) continue to be true today. Empirical evidence shows a lack of ethnicity (Naidoo, 2008), gender (Byrne, 2021), racial (Möller, 2014; Westby, 2022), and linguistic diversity (Wearden, 2018) in picture books for young children. There appears to be a similar trend in higher education. Often, textbooks are used to provide college and university students with a scholarly foundation perpetuate hegemony. Except for courses that target critical issues and issues of diversity, university course materials do not authentically encompass the experience of all individuals and social groups (Abo-Zena et al., 2019). Scholarly literature confirms that PST and IST have limited access to literature that presents people of different ethnicities (Klassen et al., 2011), religions (Clarke & Drudy, 2006), and linguistic backgrounds in a positive light (Bangura, 2018).

The authors bridged the gap between theory and practice by internationalizing the curriculum with two asynchronous activities that required PST in the US to use Flip (formerly known as Flipgrid) and Facebook with IST in Israel over a period of six weeks. The authors hoped that the asynchronous transnational learning experience would enhance PST and IST digital, cultural, and global literacy. With this end in mind, they aligned the two assignments with three of the seven ISTE Standards for Educators (2017) and the windows, mirrors, and sliding glass doors metaphor (Bishop, 1990, 2012). Figure 1 is based on Bishop's (1990, 2012) work. The International Standards for Technology Education (ISTE) standards seek to empower educators to grow as citizens (ISTE Standard 2.3), collaborators (ISTE Standard 2.4) and facilitators (ISTE Standard 2.6). The authors hoped that this transnational learning experience would enable students to reflect on their funds of knowledge *(mirrors)*, expose them to the cultures and experiences of others (*windows)*, and develop in them an understanding and empathy for those who are different from them (*sliding glass doors*). At the end of the semester, the authors used ISTE Standards 2.3, 2.4, and 2.6 (see Box 1) and the "*windows, mirrors, and glass sliding doors*" metaphor to guide deductive analysis of survey data.

Figure 1. Metaphor that guided data analysis
Source: Own Elaboration.

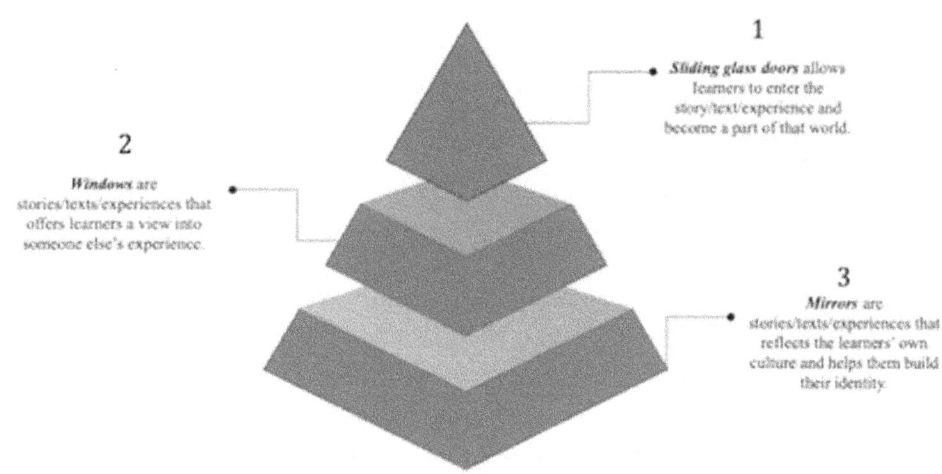

PROJECT: SCOPE, OBJECTIVES, AND ASSIGNMENT

Collaboration between and across geographic boundaries is possible when educators value the process and are willing to invest the extra time it takes to design rich learning experiences. In this section, the authors describe the rationale for our collaboration, the purpose of the project, and the project design.

Project Scope and Objectives

The authors met at the Society for Information Technology and Teacher Education Conference. They quickly discovered that they worked with similar populations and shared research interests. They both study innovative teaching pedagogy that includes collaborative teaching applications, social networks, mobile technologies, and online teaching and evaluation methods. Therefore, they decided to engage the 63 PST and 36 IST enrolled in their respective courses: *ACE103 Digital Instructional Technology* (US) and *Social Networks in Educational Settings (*Israel*),* in two mutually beneficial asynchronous transnational learning experiences that had the potential to foster digital, global, and cultural literacy. Figure 2 presents the scope of their project.

Figure 2. Scope of the six-week project
Source: Own Elaboration

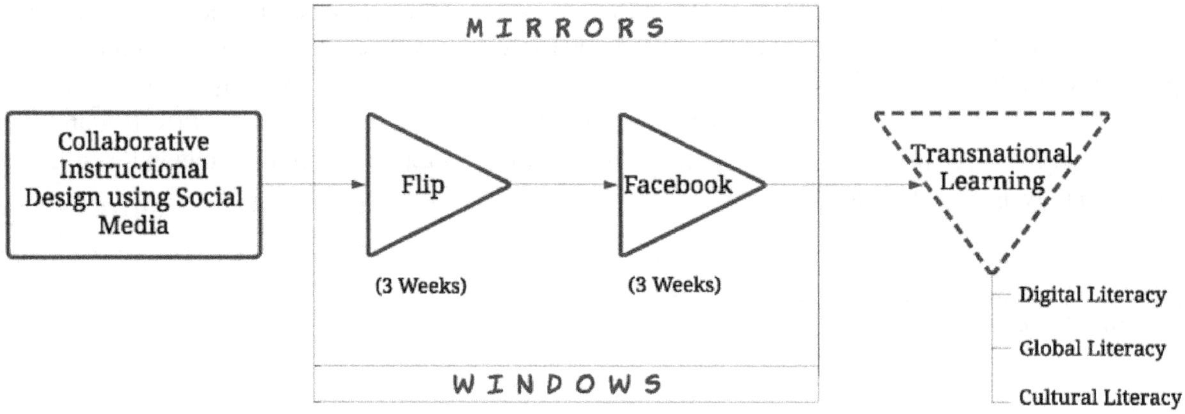

The authors met several times via Zoom to discuss the design, analysis, and implementation phases of the project. They hoped the project would provide PST in the US and IST in Israel with transnational learning experiences that:

1. Enhance their ability to communicate with people who are racially, linguistically, and culturally different from them (Banks, 1989; Bishop, 1990, 2012).
2. Challenge them to become culturally aware by viewing concepts, issues, events, and themes from the perspective of diverse ethnic and cultural groups (Banks, 1989).
3. Develop digital, global, and cultural literacy skills described by the 2017 ISTE Standards for Educators.

The authors had to align the activities very carefully because a new semester in the US and Israel begins at different times, in late August and November, respectively. Keeping this in mind, they designed the learning experience to unfold in two phases over a period of six weeks. Details about each phase are described in the sections that follow.

Design of the Flip Experience

Author 1 designed the Flip assignment and related instructional content for phase one (see Figure 1). During this phase, PST and IST used Flip, a powerful video discussion platform, which affords students accessibility, flexibility, involvement, motivation, and convenient follow-up of participation to engage with each other. In September, Author 1 sent a welcome letter to the PST enrolled in her courses in the US. The letter included a link to the prompt in Flip where they were instructed to contribute a 90-second video introduction. This introductory activity, which was completed asynchronously over a period of one week, gave the PST an opportunity to get to know each other during the first part of their 15-week semester. They learned each other's names and interests more quickly. After giving IST in Israel a week to get accustomed to their new semester which began in November, Authors 1 and 2 administered the Flip assignment to their respective students in both countries (see Box 1).

Table 1. Flip assignment description

Box 1. Flip Assignment Description Purpose: As digital citizens, 21st century teachers should inspire students to positively contribute to and responsibly participate in the digital world (ISTE Standard 2.3, 2.4). They should also facilitate learning with technology to support student achievement (ISTE Standard 2.6). Flip, a powerful video discussion platform used by tens of millions of PreK to PhD educators, students, and families in 150 countries, can be used to develop these skills. This assignment will provide you with an opportunity to use Flip to: 1. expand students' authentic, real-world learning experiences by engaging virtually with experts, teams, and students, locally and globally (ISTE 2.4.c). 2. build a relationship with an in-service and/or pre-service teacher in another country (ISTE Standard 2.3.a). 3. communicate ideas and knowledge (ISTE Standards 2.6.d) related to teaching with technology and participation in digital platforms, virtual environments, hands-on maker spaces, or in the field (ISTE 2.6b). 4. discuss how technology can be used to promote curiosity, critical examination of online resources, and foster digital literacy and media fluency (2.3.b). 5. take ownership of your learning goals and outcomes in an online setting (ISTE 2.6.a). Task (November 5-11): Each IST in Israel will choose two PST dialogue partners; one from each of the Flips listed below: 1. Podium Class (link to Flip). 2. Asynchronous Class (link to Flip). IST will begin by viewing the introductory videos posted by the PST they have chosen. They will comment on the video, with information about themselves, and initiate a dialogue that allows them to meet the standards listed above. PST will respond with video comments. Dialogue partners should interact asynchronously at least 3-4 times during the 7-day period.

As per the assignment description (Box 1), the dialogue partners kept the conversations going with video posts about their use of technology as learners and teachers. The authors extended the deadline for the activity by a week, partly because of air strikes in Gaza but also because some participants needed more time to get comfortable with Flip. In short, the duration of the Flip experience lasted three weeks, inclusive of the first week in September when PST posted their introductory videos.

Design of the Facebook Experience

Author 2 designed the Facebook assignment and created the Facebook group for phase two, which lasted three weeks (see Box 2). This time, the 36 IST took the lead by posting social media initiatives in the private Facebook group. PST and IST had the freedom to view, like, and comment on these posts.

Table 2. Facebook assignment description

Box 2. Facebook Assignment Description
Important: This task will be completed over a period of two weeks, in two phases. Phase 1: November 12-19 **Both American and Israeli students** join the closed Facebook group: SN2019 - Pennsylvania-Israel. This can be done in the following ways: 1. Use the link: (link to Facebook group) 2. Search for the Facebook group by name: Name of group anonymized. **IST** in Israel must post an existing initiative that includes social networks meant for teaching, and learning purposes, in the closed Facebook Group. An example of such an initiative is To See The World, a unique educational initiative aimed to access experts' knowledge, experience, and inspiration; and bring them into classrooms in Israel through conference calls. Each initiative presented should include: 1. A brief description of the initiative. 2. A link to the initiative and to any related information. 3. Description of the potential and contribution of the initiative to the field of education. 4. Any improvements, modifications or adjustments suggested. Israeli students are requested to read the initiatives posted in the Facebook Group and introduce one that has not yet been presented. Phase 2: November 19-December 2 **IST and PST** read, interact, and comment on multiple initiatives presented by different Israeli IST. The minimum expectation is 3-4 interactions. **PST** (US) can comment on the initiatives presented by Israeli students by following the instructions below: 1. Adding information about the potential of the initiative and the ways in which it is beneficial to their education as well as others. 2. Adding suggestions for the implementation of the initiative. 3. Adding information about an example initiative with which they are familiar and is like what they found in the group. 4. Writing any other comments and/or suggestions regarding the initiatives that they have analyzed.

Support Provided During the Six Weeks

For the majority, this was their first interaction with teachers from another country. It became clear during the Flip experience that PST did not know how to sustain an asynchronous dialogue with strangers. To help PST break the ice, Author 1 modeled the use of different questions. She also engaged PSTs in discussions about the best way to make accommodations for people who may not be proficient in English, how to sustain a conversation with people who are culturally different, how to be professional, and how to practice privacy literacy. She provided PST in her podium classroom with oral feedback and encouragement in class and created videos to provide her asynchronous class with similar support. During the Facebook experience, Author 1 facilitated discussions related to unexpected incidents that occurred during this time, like the conflict that erupted when an Israeli air strike killed a Jihad leader in Gaza. Similarly, Author 2 used a variety of strategies to prepare her IST for transnational learning. Recognizing that some of her IST would need assistance with English she used class time to facilitate discussions related to the project class. This helped IST who were not confident in expressing themselves in English to gain assistance from both the lecturer, Author 2, and from three English speakers' peers.

METHODOLOGY

As part of a larger mixed methods study, the authors used the Scholarship of Teaching and Learning (SoTL) approach to examine survey and extant data from Facebook and Flip, related to the following questions:

1. How did PST and IST engage on Flip? In what ways did it provide them with opportunities to reflect on their funds of knowledge (*mirrors*) and the cultures and experiences of others (*windows*), for transnational learning?
2. How did PST and IST engage on Facebook? In what ways did it provide them with opportunities to reflect on their funds of knowledge (*mirrors*), and the cultures and experiences of others (*windows*), for transnational learning?

Scholarship of Teaching Approach

The authors used the SoTL approach, which includes a systematic research-based inquiry, reflective thought, and action to bridge the divide that often exists between the scholarship of discovery and the scholarship of teaching. The SoTL has been popular with teacher-scholars since the former Carnegie Foundation President Ernest Boyer published his report *Scholarship Reconsidered* in 1990. Scholars became even more familiar with this approach after Glassick et al.'s (1997) follow-up publication *Scholarship Assessed*. Since then, there is a growing awareness that "engaged SoTL research output at the institutional level can send a powerful signal to prospective students and other stakeholders that the university takes teaching and learning seriously" (Asarta et al., 2018, p. 737). In addition to using the findings for individual and collective learning regarding PST and IST's learning experience and their own teaching practice (Dyck, 2017; Hanc, 2016) the authors shared the findings of this study with teacher-scholars at several conferences (Hutchings et al., 2011).

Participants

PSTs enrolled in Author 1's podium and asynchronous course in the US and Author 2's blended course in Israel participated in this six-week experience (see Table 1). The participants included many more PST as compared to IST. Proportionately more PST were enrolled in the asynchronous class (n =38) compared to the podium class (n = 25).

Table 3. Participants' country, class standing, course, and course delivery model

Country	Student Status	Course Title	Course Delivery	Participants
US	PST taught by Author 1	Digital Instructional Technology (001)	Podium Course	25
		Digital Instructional Technology (801)	Asynchronous Course	38
Israel	IST taught by Author 2	Social Networks in Educational Context	Blended Course	39
	Total			102

Source: Own Elaboration

Table 2 shows that the majority taught and/or were interested in teaching middle and high school students (n = 74). Others were either teaching or planning to teach young children (n = 21) or students in the vocational field (n = 4).

Table 4. Course delivery model chosen by participants of different majors

Majors	PST Podium Course	PST Asynchronous Course	IST Blended Course
Early Childhood, Early Childhood/ Special Education and Disability Services	8	7	6
Health and Physical Education, Respiratory	6	7	
Middle and High School (English, Art, Theater and Spanish Education)	7	7	19
Middle/High School (Math, Chemistry, Biology, Social Studies, Family and Consumer Science; Undecided)	5	13	14
Vocational Education		4	

Source: Own Elaboration

Data Sources, Data Quality, and Analysis

The authors used the following three sources of data to answer the research questions:

1. A survey with six demographic items, two scaled items, and two open-ended items.
2. Analytics provided by Flip which includes number and timestamp of posts, views, likes, and comments per user.
3. Analytics provided by Facebook which includes number and timestamp of views, likes, and comments per user.

The authors used the Likert-style items and open-ended questions in the survey, administered at the end of the semester, to gain insight into participants' experiences with the two asynchronous activities. They triangulated this data with the extant data obtained through Flip and Facebook to evaluate the number of times participants viewed, liked, and commented on posts on Flip and Facebook.

Given that the authors played dual roles as course instructors and researchers, they employed several steps to enhance the validity and reliability of the survey and the trustworthiness of qualitative data nested in the survey. Author 1 developed the first survey draft. Author 2, who has 23 years of experience with instructional technology, reviewed this draft to establish face validity (Marshall & Rossman, 2016). The validated version of the survey included six demographic items, two scaled items, and two open-ended items. Once the survey was finalized Author 2 translated the survey into Hebrew to enhance Israeli ISTs' comfort level (Squires, 2009). Following data collection, Author 2 used Google Translate to translate the open-ended responses from Hebrew to English. Next, she closely read the data in both languages to verify accuracy. After cleaning the numeric data, Author 1 used SPSS, a quantitative research software, to run descriptive statistics. She manually coded the qualitative data generated through open-ended questions. Next, she used NVivo, a qualitative research software, for typological and interpretive coding

(Hatch, 2002). Finally, to enhance the trustworthiness of the data, Author 1 engaged in memoing and peer debriefing with Author 2. These procedures help minimize misinterpretation and author bias; and eliminate the over or under-emphasis of ideas (Edmonson & Irby, 2008).

RESULTS

The authors used SPSS and NVivo to analyze the three sources of data. The results are presented below, organized by the two research questions.

Using Flip as a Mirror (Reflection of Self) and Window (View of Others)

Research question one explores how participants engaged in the asynchronous Flip experience and the ways in which it provided PST and IST with an opportunity to reflect on themselves *(mirrors)* and others *(windows)* after viewing, liking, and commenting on their dialogue partners' videos. Author 1 used SPSS to analyze Flip analytics of the two grids where engagement occurred (see Table 3). Table 3 shows that both PST and IST spent many hours on Flip (33.8 hours of engagement). There was variability in the number of posts; on average they posted two or more videos (n = 251). It also shows that participants viewed each other's videos numerous times (n = 1495).

Table 5. Participants' views, comments, and hours of engagement

PST/IST	Videos	Views	Hours of Engagement
Flip 1 (interaction between Podium course PST and IST)	104	632	14.2
Flip 2 (interaction between Asynchronous course PST/ IST)	147	863	19.6
Total	251	1495	33.8

Source: Own Elaboration

Additionally, Author 1 used Nvivo, a qualitative research software, to quantize the qualitative data generated by open-ended questions nested in the survey to answer research question one. She found that the Flip experience served as a "*mirror*" by providing PST and IST with an opportunity to reflect on their view of themselves. Some PST and IST acknowledged that they had difficulty interpreting the assignment (n = 3 and n = 8, respectively). The Flip experience made PST and IST more aware of their technology challenges (n = 10 and n = 8, respectively) and perfectionism (n = 4 and n = 7, respectively). Even though several IST reported that they experienced linguistic difficulty (n = 11) many IST reported that the Flip experience helped them develop a sense of agency (n =10) and gain confidence (n = 10).

The Flip experience also served as a "*window*" through which they could view and interact with participants who were different racially, ethnically, linguistically, and culturally different from them. Both PST and IST appreciated being able to meet people across the globe (n = 11 and n = 12, respectively). Proportionately more PST, as compared to IST, reported that the experience enhanced their global literacy (n = 19 and 5, respectively). An IST said that the experience "… allows for a "peek" into the personal environment of the student from the other country" (IST, Israel). Another said, "It is amazing to be geographically distant and to feel closeness and accessibility" (IST, Israel). Their comments reflect the insights they gained:

When talking with my partner I found the experience very beneficial as I had never interacted with someone from another country over the internet before. Doing this has made me more interested in interacting with individuals from other countries to learn more about life in other countries. (PST)

I think it was super cool to be able to talk to someone from another country. It was super neat hearing their dialogue, and I have more of an appreciation for people who must translate from one language to one that I could understand. (PST)

Several PSTs (n = 12) and a couple of ISTs (n = 2) referenced an appreciation of cultural similarities and differences. PST also described the insight they gained into teaching practices abroad (n = 7).

Using Facebook as a Mirror (Reflection of Self) and Window (View of Others)

Research question two explores how participants engaged in the asynchronous Facebook experience and the ways in which it provided PST and IST with an opportunity to reflect on themselves (*mirrors*) and others (*windows*) after reading, liking, and commenting on IST' posts in the Facebook group. Author 2 used SPSS to analyze the analytics provided by Facebook. Figure 3 presents a summary of participants' level of engagement in the group.

Figure 3. Participants' level of engagement with posts

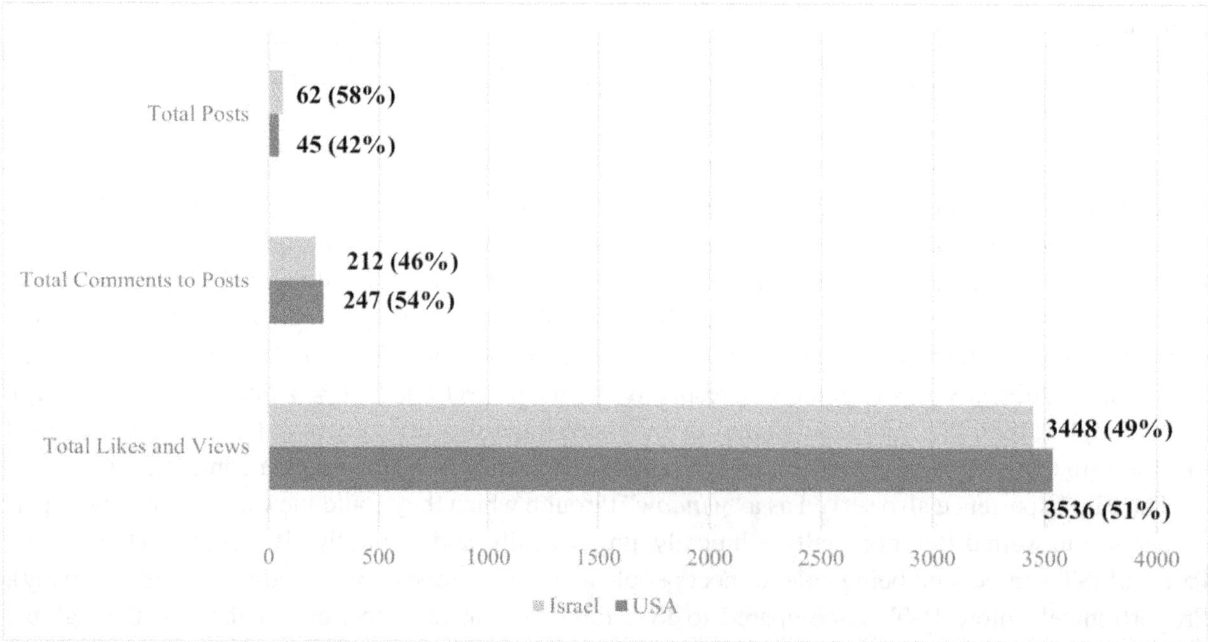

The authors expected IST to submit many more posts (n = 62, 58%) than PST because they were responsible for taking the lead. It was encouraging to see that a fair number of PST posted some original content (n = 45, 42%). As evident from Figure 3, both PST and IST actively engaged in liking and viewing the posts (n = 3536 and 3448, respectively). Fewer PST and IST commented on the posts (n = 247 and 212, respectively).

Author 2 used thematic analysis to gain insight into the ways in which the Facebook experience provided PST and IST with "*mirrors*" to reflect on themselves. Figure 4 shows a quantized summary of the qualitative responses to the open-ended questions embedded in the survey that overlapped, and those that were different.

Figure 4. The Facebook experience: Reflection on self (mirrors)
Source: Own Elaboration

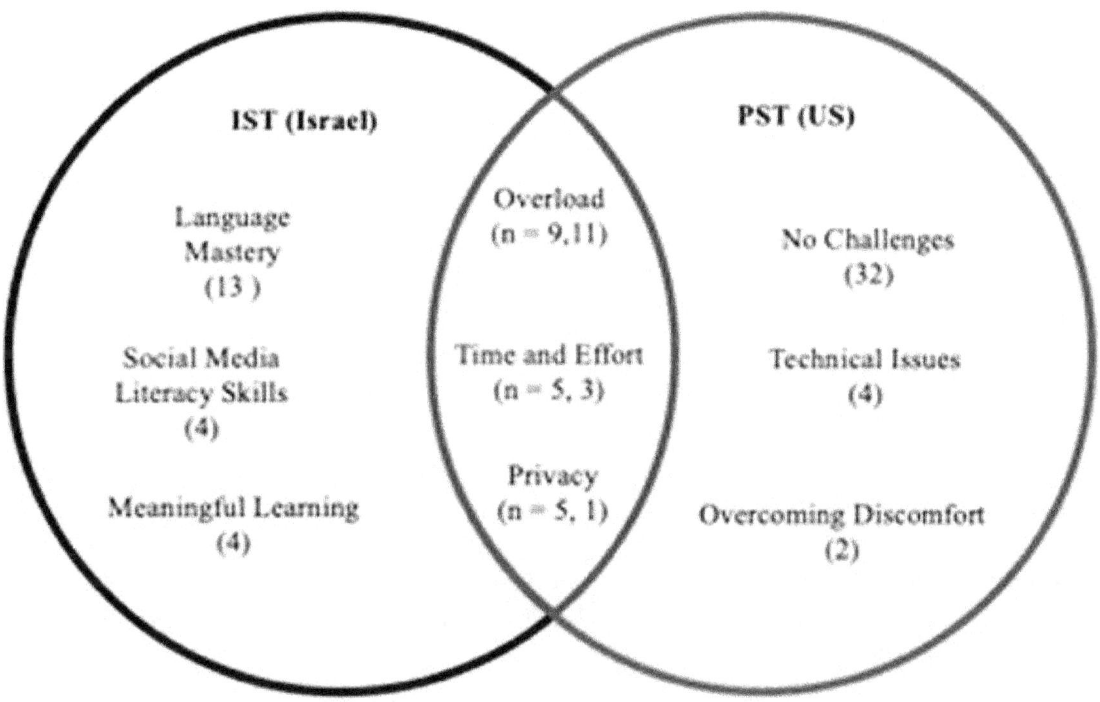

Both IST and PST were unaccustomed to using Facebook for transnational learning. Some PST reported that they experienced technical issues (n = 4). Both IST and PST reported that they felt overwhelmed with the volume of posts (n = 9 and n = 11, respectively). IST and PST reported that they had to invest more time and effort than they anticipated (n = 5 and n = 3, respectively). Their responses to the survey illustrate how they handled these challenges.

So much was posted that I couldn't keep up with all or had time to read the very long posts. To overcome this, I chose a handful that interested me and read and commented on those. (PST 12).

Sometimes I had trouble understanding the language used by the teachers in Israel. I overcame this challenge by simply trying to read between the lines. (PST 51).

Several IST reported that they found Facebook meaningful (n = 4). They also reported that it greatly enhanced their social media skills (n = 4). For example, several IST were self-conscious about their limited proficiency in English (n = 13). The experience made them conscious of areas that need improvement, and they identified ways to overcome these challenges. For example, one IST said, "English was very difficult for me, but I used a dictionary every time I had to read it write" (IST 39). Another IST said, "with the help of good friends, I formulate the initiative in English. It was very important to me to have no mistakes. I was very happy that I was able to meet the challenge that required so much mental strength" (IST 27). Over time, they noticed they gained confidence. One said, "suddenly I found myself reading English fluently and even answering… At the same time, it really improved my English and my confidence (IST 8). Another said, I overcame anxiety and wanted to impress by redoing it multiple times till I was comfortable with the whole process (IST 11).

The Facebook Group experience also served as a "*window*" through which PST and IST could view and interact with teachers who were racially, ethnically, linguistically, and culturally different from them. The experience made them more aware of the benefits of using social media to enhance digital literacy. One student said, "Learning how to use Facebook in general, and how to use it as an educational tool changed the way I see social media in certain aspects" (PST 3). Another said I like how fast people responded to one another and interacted towards the global learning network. (PST 9). A third pointed out that "In my opinion, the principle in which teaching and learning is conducted through a social network in the future of education (IST 20).

As evident from the comments below, the Facebook experience gave PST and IST a chance to gain information about a range of innovations and programs offered in another country.

Interacting and collaborating with a multitude of other educators as they promoted their innovative project that incorporated learning and technology for their students was very informative. (PST 52)

I gained insight into many other activities that are provided to help and support many different cultures and different ways to learn. It was fascinating to see that there are programs in Israel that are meant to help students accept different cultures. (PST 25)

The experience also affected them personally. One said, "I gained a perspective that people have more in common than differences. Speaking to people from a different country and finding out that we had similar interests was very humbling" (PST 16).

Several PSTs described how the Facebook experience enhanced their global awareness. One IST said, "It is very interesting to me to learn about their culture and customs. In my opinion when you share the culture and customs the ties and conditions become stronger" (IST 5). Another IST said "It is exciting to see how it is possible to communicate even with unfamiliar people not from our culture and who are overseas and still produce significant learning "(IST 14). A PST said, "I gained more cultural insight and became more sensitive" (PST 29). It gratifying to see how some PST tried to "I struggled with appropriate comments on what to post. I wanted them to be professional but complement them very well" (PST 40).

Participants even started thinking of ways they could modify their curriculum to include social media.

I have a student in my class who is going on a mission next year with his family and he is afraid. Since I am continuing with the class next year, I am thinking about using technology to connect the child with the class. (IST 31)

Limitations

This study is subject to the limitations inherent in SoTL studies that draw on survey and extant data. The first limitation is related to the uniqueness of the learning environment, which included participants' classrooms, the LMS they used, Flip, and Facebook; hence the results may be difficult to duplicate. Second, the PST and IST who participated in this study might not be representative of those enrolled in other teacher preparation programs; as such, implications should be transferred with caution. A third limitation stems from the type of data collected. Participants' views, reflected in the closed and opened ended survey items could have been influenced by preconceived ideas, a desire to present themselves in a favorable manner, lack of memory on the subject, or even boredom. The authors minimized some of these limitations by using the analytics provided by Facebook and Flip, ongoing memoing, and peer-debriefing.

LESSONS LEARNED AND IMPLICATIONS FOR FUTURE PRACTICE

Faculty often start SoTL projects to address a teaching problem (Felten, 2013). This project was no different - it started with a complex, wicked problem that is not easily solvable - the need to enhance PST' and IST' digital, global, and cultural literacy. It allowed the authors to explore the messy world of student learning by focusing on "what works" and "what is" happening in terms of student learning. The authors cannot claim that that the two asynchronous experiences, that lasted six weeks, resulted in significant learning that includes acquisition of knowledge, new ways of thinking, and attitudinal change. Nevertheless, the two assignments did provide PST and IST with "*windows*" and "*mirrors*" for transnational learning. This SoTL study was not sophisticated enough to gauge participants' experience with "*glass sliding doors*" which provides opportunities for development, understanding and empathy for others. Nevertheless, it deepened their understanding of the ways in which Flip and Facebook can be used to promote global awareness and transnational learning.

Although some participants had used Facebook for personal purposes, they had not used it for teaching or learning. Conversely, Flip was new to all students. Flip and Facebook analytics show that PST and IST were more willing to view and like comments, rather than post original content. Consistent with the work of Bower et al. (2010) this study confirmed an interrelationship between cognitive, behavioral, and affective dimensions of communication. Some of these issues can be addressed by reminding PST and IST about the purpose of the project – to facilitate dialogue and global awareness. Moving forward, the authors plan on engaging students in a discussion about how communication norms vary in different countries. Some participants were inhibited by communication anxiety, perfectionism, and the desire to impress. Some reported that they were not comfortable recording themselves. Additionally, the response time of IST was slower than expected due to a variety of reasons related to limited proficiency in English. As a result, some PST became impatient and started to lose interest. Even though Flip intimidated some participants, it eventually had a positive influence on them. Several PST reported the Flip experience helped them overcome their anxiety with video presentations and gain confidence. The authors plan to design and implement a follow-up SoTL study geared towards reducing communication anxiety with video presentations in the future. They will make a conscious effort to reduce communication anxiety and increase students' confidence by providing them with many more opportunities to see themselves on camera prior to cross-cultural communication. This could include the use of technologies like Zoom, screencasts, etc.

Survey data showed that PST and IST grew as learners (ISTE Standard 1). While some PST and IST struggled with the technology, the majority appreciated that Flip and Facebook could be used to connect with people in other countries for global awareness and transnational learning. Many reported an improvement in their digital literacy skills in general, and their technology skills (troubleshooting, practice, and visiting the sites frequently) in particular. The authors also noted an improvement in computational thinking and cognitive flexibility. Many PST and IST grew as digital citizens (ISTE Standard 3). In their response to the open-ended items of the survey, they described the choices they made especially when it came to their choice of words, being patient, and overcoming the challenges they faced when their international partners were slow to respond or unresponsive. PST reported that they grew as facilitators (ISTE Standard 6); their creative and innovative mindset was reflected in the videos on Flip and comments on Facebook. They reported that they made a conscious effort to present themselves professionally (appearance, tone, pace, choice of words etc.). Analysis of the videos that PST and IST posted on Flip is currently underway. Author 1 will share the nature of the video dialogue between PST and IST in a forthcoming publication.

PST and IST often associate "learning" with the completion of assignments, designing lesson and unit plans, taking tests, and implementing lesson plans. Accepting that "transnational learning" was a valuable endeavor was difficult for some, especially because many PST were not accustomed to communicating with strangers. The authors plan on investing more time in preparing PST and IST for experiences like this. This preparation will include discussions related to the null curriculum, primarily because transnational learning may not be part of curriculum offered by PST and IST preparation programs. They will also discuss the limitations of the explicit curriculum which often erases or misrepresents people who may be racially, ethnically, linguistically, and culturally different. The authors plan on using the "*windows, mirrors, and glass sliding door metaphor*" (Bishop, 1990, 2012) to help PST and IST understand the benefits of transnational learning. Moving forward, they intend to modify other assignments to include activities that promote interdependence across countries, and social identities. This could potentially increase engagement and facilitate a higher level of dialogue. The authors will describe the learning outcomes, based on these pedagogical changes, in subsequent SoTL publications.

CONCLUSION

Historically, scholarship related to children's literature (Bishop,1990, 2012) and scholarship on human development confirm that books provide inadequate and inaccurate representations of the lived experiences of diverse youth (Abo-Zena et al., 2019). Colonizing influences, which permeate ideologies and research practices, prevent individuals from seeing themselves in research (Patel, 2016) used to educate professionals. Additionally, many P-20 learners in rural Pennsylvania, other rural states in the US, and some parts of Israel have had limited exposure to people who are racially, ethnically, culturally, and linguistically diverse. These gaps in knowledge need to be addressed. Adichie (2009), in her powerful TED Talk, Danger of a Single Story, invites learners to take responsibility for their own learning by expanding their horizons and finding their authentic cultural voice to avoid critical misunderstandings. Teacher educators can help learners achieve this goal by modeling an openness to transnational learning and internationalizing the curricula they offer PST and IST. This can begin by including diverse perspectives in book collections, textbook selection, assignment design, and choice of instructional technologies to support transnational learning. Teacher educators can select titles with racially diverse characters and books that present intersectionality in a positive light. Many of the PST and IST who participated in the two transnational learning experiences, completed over a period of six weeks, were initially very intimidated about interacting with teachers from another country who were different in terms of cultural, religious, and linguistic backgrounds. These fears were alleviated, to some extent, by using Flip and Facebook to connect with teachers in another country. The two assignments created mirrors and windows "wide enough to include all individuals it encompasses and a perspective dynamic enough to account for all the variations in context and interactions" (Aabo-Zena et al., 2019, p. 179). Additionally, this SoTL study helped the authors identify curriculum and pedagogical changes they can make as they continue to design instruction for PST and IST. In short, this study illustrates how the metaphor of "*windows, mirrors and glass sliding doors*" (Bishop,1990, 2012) can serve as a tangible instructional practice model for decision-making related to instructional technology selection. Educators do not have to confine themselves to Flip, Facebook; they can use other types of social media like Twitter, Threads, and Instagram to design similar transnational learning experiences to enhance PST's and IST's digital, global, and cultural literacy.

ACKNOWLEDGMENT

The authors appreciate the PST and IST enrolled in their respective courses who allowed them to analyze the data they collected, for research purposes. Author 1 is grateful to Farheen Mahmood for inspiring her to use the "*windows, mirrors and glass sliding doors*" metaphor to analyze the data and for creating the figures included in this chapter.

REFERENCES

Abo-Zena, M., Brittian Loyd, A., & Cunningham, M. (2019). Introduction to mentored scholarship: Mirrors, windows, and doors to understanding and supporting research in human development. *Research in Human Development, 16*(3-4), 175–184. doi:10.1080/15427609.2020.1727821

Adichie, C. N. (2009). *The danger of a single story* [Video]. TED Global. https://www.ted.com/talks/chimamanda_ngozi_adichie_the_danger_of_a_single_story/c

Asarta, C. J., Bento, R., Fornaciari, C. J., Lund Dean, K., Arbaugh, J. B., & Hwang, A. (2018). The scholarship of teaching and learning: Changing the dominant narrative about (and in) research institutions. *Journal of Management Education, 42*(6), 731–748. doi:10.1177/1052562918777271

Bakshy, E., Hofman, J. M., Mason, W. A., & Watts, D. J. (2011, February). *Everyone is an influencer: Quantifying influence on twitter.* ACM Digital Library. doi:10.1145/1935826.1935845

Bangura, Y. (2018). *Multicultural education: The relationship between preservice teachers multicultural self-efficacy and cultural awareness when teaching in multicultural classrooms* [Doctoral dissertation, Bowling Green State University]. ProQuest Dissertations Publishing. https://rave.ohiolink.edu/etdc/view?acc_num=bgsu1522682134643678

Banks, J. A. (1989). Approaches to multicultural curriculum reform. *Trotter Review*, *3*(3), 17–19.

Bishop, R. S. (1990). Mirrors, windows, and sliding glass doors. *Perspectives: Choosing and using books for the classroom, 6*(3), 9–11.

Bishop, R. S. (2012). Reflections on the development of African American children & literature. *Journal of Children's Literature*, *38*(2), 5–13. https://www.proquest.com/docview/1266034800?pq-origsite=gscholar&fromopenview=true

Boholano, H. (2017). Smart social networking: 21st century teaching and learning skills. *Research in Pedagogy, 7*(1), 21-29. https://www.ceeol.com/search/article-detail?id=546738

Bourn, D., & Shiel, C. (2009). Global perspectives: Aligning agendas? *Environmental Education Research, 15*(6), 661–677. doi:10.1080/13504620903244167

Bower, M., Cavanagh, M., Moloney, R., & Dao, M. (2011). Developing communication competence using an online video reflection system: Pre-service teachers' experiences. *Asia-Pacific Journal of Teacher Education, 39*(4), 311–326. doi:10.1080/1359866X.2011.614685

Boyer, E. L. (1990). *Scholarship reconsidered: Priorities of the professoriate*. Princeton University Press.

Buchanan, L. B., & Fox, S. G. (2019). On windows and mirrors in teacher education program materials: A content analysis of human demographics in one picture book collection. *Multicultural Perspectives, 21*(4), 189–201. doi:10.1080/15210960.2019.1686385

Byram, M., Golubeva, I., Hui, H., & Wagner, M. (2016). *From principles to practice in education for intercultural citizenship*. Multilingual Matters. doi:10.21832/9781783096565

Byrne, C. (2021). Mirrors, windows and sliding glass doors: LGBTQIA+ perspectives. *Idiom, 57*(2), 36-38. https://slav.vic.edu.au/index.php/Synergy/article/view/530/523

Carpenter, J. P., & Krutka, D. G. (2014). How and why educators use Twitter: A survey of the field. *Journal of Research on Technology in Education, 46*(4), 414–434. doi:10.1080/15391523.2014.925701

Clarke, M., & Drudy, S. (2006). Teaching for diversity, social justice and global awareness. *European Journal of Teacher Education, 29*(3), 371–386. doi:10.1080/02619760600795239

Collins English Dictionary. (n.d.). *Definition of 'transnational.'* https://www.collinsdictionary.com/dictionary/english/transnational Council of Europe/

De Meyer, A. (2012). Reflections on the globalization of management education. *Journal of Management Development, 31*(4), 336–345. doi:10.1108/02621711211218988

Dervin, F. (2017). "I find it odd that people have to highlight other people's differences – even when there are none": Experiential learning and interculturality in teacher education. *International Review of Education, 63*(1), 87–102. doi:10.1007/s11159-017-9620-y

Dyck, B. (2017). Reflecting on 25 years of teaching, researching, and textbook writing for introduction to management: An essay with some lessons learned. *Journal of Management Education*, *41*(6), 817–834. doi:10.1177/1052562917693381

Edmonson, S., & Irby, B. (2008). *Ten tips for producing a top qualitative study*. Pearson.

Felten, P. (2013). Principles of good practice in SoTL. *Teaching & Learning Inquiry*, *1*(1), 121–125. doi:10.20343/teachlearninqu.1.1.121

Fitzgerald, E. (2012). Creating user-generated content for location-based learning: An authoring framework. *Journal of Computer Assisted Learning*, *28*(3), 195–207. doi:10.1111/j.1365-2729.2012.00481.x

Glassick, C. E., Huber, M. T., & Maeroff, G. I. (1997). *Scholarship assessed: Evaluation of the professoriate*. John Wiley & Sons.

Gopal, A. (2011). Internationalization of higher education: Preparing faculty to teach cross-culturally. *International Journal on Teaching and Learning in Higher Education*, *23*(3), 373–381. https://files.eric.ed.gov/fulltext/EJ946163.pdf

Hanc, J. (2016, June 22). Professors as teachers. *The New York Times*. https://www.nytimes.com/2016/06/23/education/teaching-professors-to-become-better-teachers.html

HarperCollins. (2000). Transnationalism. *Collins English dictionary*. https://www.collinsdictionary.com/us/

Hatch, J. A. (2002). *Doing qualitative research in education settings*. State University of New York Press.

Hutchings, P., Huber, M. T., & Ciccone, A. (2011). *The scholarship of teaching and learning reconsidered: Institutional integration and impact*. John Wiley & Sons.

Jin, S. (2015). Using Facebook to promote Korean EFL learners' intercultural competence. *Language Learning & Technology*, *19*(3), 38–51. http://llt.msu.edu/issues/october2015/action2

Junco, R., Elavsky, C. M., & Heiberger, G. (2013). Putting Twitter to the test: Assessing outcomes for student collaboration, engagement and success. *British Journal of Educational Technology*, *44*(2), 273–287. doi:10.1111/j.1467-8535.2012.01284.x

Killick, D., & Foster, M. (2021). *Learner relationships in global higher education: A critical pedagogy for a multicultural world*. Routledge. doi:10.4324/9780429294877

Klassen, R. M., Al-Dhafri, S., Hannok, W., & Betts, S. M. (2011). Investigating pre-service teacher motivation across cultures using the teachers' ten statements test. *Teaching and Teacher Education*, *27*(3), 579–588. doi:10.1016/j.tate.2010.10.012

Koss, M. D. (2015). Diversity in contemporary picture books: A content analysis. *Journal of Children's Literature*, *41*(1), 32–42. https://eric.ed.gov/?id=EJ1062015

Kulich, S. J. (2015). Does context count? Developing and assessing intercultural competence through an interview-and model-based domestic course design in China. *International Journal of Intercultural Relations*, *48*, 38–57. doi:10.1016/j.ijintrel.2015.03.013

Larrick, N. (1965). The all-white world of children's books. *Saturday Review*, *48*(11), 63–65.

Lawrence-Lightfoot, S. (2005). Reflections on portraiture: A dialogue between art and science. *Qualitative Inquiry*, *11*(1), 3–15. doi:10.1177/1077800404270955

Lehtomäki, E., Moate, J., & Posti-Ahokas, H. (2016). Global connectedness in higher education: Student voices on the value of cross-cultural learning dialogue. *Studies in Higher Education*, *41*(11), 2011–2027. doi:10.1080/03075079.2015.1007943

Marshall, C., & Rossman, G. B. (2016). *Designing qualitative research* (4th ed.). Sage.

Miller, M. A. (2002). American higher education goes global. *Change*, *34*(3), 4. doi:10.1080/00091380209601846

Möller, K. J. (2014). Mirrors and windows through literature featuring Arabs, Arab Americans, and people of Islamic faith. *Journal of Children's Literature*, *40*(2), 65–72. https://www.proquest.com/docview/1657566318?pq-origsite=gscholar&fromopenview=true

Naidoo, J. C. (2008). Opening doors. *Children & Libraries*, *6*(2), 27. https://www.proquest.com/docview/212174372?pq-origsite=gscholar&fromopenview=true

Parkhouse, H., Lu, C. Y., & Massaro, V. R. (2019). Multicultural education professional development: A review of the literature. *Review of Educational Research*, *89*(3), 416–458. doi:10.3102/0034654319840359

Patel, L. (2016). *Decolonizing educational research: From ownership to answerability*. Routledge.

Perry, L. B., & Southwell, L. (2011). Developing intercultural understanding and skills: Models and approaches. *Intercultural Education*, *22*(6), 453–466. doi:10.1080/14675986.2011.644948

Robson, J. (2018). Performance, structure and ideal identity: Reconceptualising teachers' engagement in online social spaces. *British Journal of Educational Technology*, *49*(3), 439–450. doi:10.1111/bjet.12551

Sawyer, R., & Chen, G. M. (2012). The impact of social media on intercultural adaptation. *Intercultural Communication Studies*, *21*(2), 151–169. https://digitalcommons.uri.edu/com_facpubs/15/

Seifert, T. (2016). Involvement, collaboration and engagement: Social networks through a pedagogical lens. *Journal of Learning Design*, *9*(2), 31–45. https://eric.ed.gov/?id=EJ1117665. doi:10.5204/jld.v9i2.272

Spiteri, D. (2017). Meeting people where they are in many different locations. In D. Spiteri (Ed.), Multiculturalism, higher education and intercultural communication: Developing strengths-based narratives for teaching and learning (pp. 193–219). Springer. doi:10.1057/978-1-137-51367-0_8

Squires, A. (2009). Methodological challenges in cross-language qualitative research: A research review. *International Journal of Nursing Studies*, *46*(2), 277–287. doi:10.1016/j.ijnurstu.2008.08.006 PMID:18789799

Stephanie, L. (2022, July 20). *Future skills you'll need in your career by 2030*. http://tinyurl.com/mr372ywz

Style, E. (1996). Curriculum as window and mirror. *Social Science Record*, *33*(2), 21–28.

Teichler, U. (2009). Internationalisation of higher education: European experiences. *Asia Pacific Education Review*, *10*(1), 93–106. doi:10.1007/s12564-009-9002-7

Teichler, U. (2017). Internationalisation trends in higher education and the changing role of international student mobility. *Journal of International Mobility*, (4), 177-216. http://tinyurl.com/2par2cfy

The ISTE Standards. (2017). *The ISTE Standards.* https://www.iste.org/standards/for-educators

Thomas, E. E., Reese, D., & Horning, K. T. (2016). Much ado about a fine dessert: The cultural politics of representing slavery in children's literature. *Journal of Children's Literature*, *42*(2), 6–17. https://eric.ed.gov/?id=EJ1119087

Wearden, G. (2018). Mirrors & windows: Why diversity must be better represented in children's fiction. *Wheaton Writing: A Journal of Academic Essays, 3*, 47-51. https://journals.wheaton.edu/index.php/wheaton_writing/article/view/527

Westby, C. (2022). Using books as mirrors, windows, sliding glass doors. *Word of Mouth, 33*(5), 4-6. https://journals.sagepub.com/doi/pdf/10.1177/10483950221086338a

Williams, T. R. (2005). Exploring the impact of study abroad on students' intercultural communication skills: Adaptability and sensitivity. *Journal of Studies in International Education*, *9*(4), 356–371. doi:10.1177/1028315305277681

Zhu, C. (2012). Student satisfaction, performance, and knowledge construction in online collaborative learning. *Journal of Educational Technology & Society*, *15*(1), 127–136. https://www.jstor.org/stable/10.2307/jeductechsoci.15.1.127

KEY TERMS AND DEFINITIONS

Asynchronous Course: An online class taught via a Learning Management System. The instructor provides students with the course material. Students engage with course content, the instructor, and other students and meet deadlines at their own pace.

Blended Course: A class that combines web-enhanced instruction and placed-based instruction. Web-enhanced instruction may be delivered asynchronously or synchronously.

Communication Anxiety: The feeling of fear that some people experience at the thought of being observed and evaluated by others.

Funds of Knowledge: The knowledge and life experience that a person brings with them.

Global Awareness: The ability to understand, respect, and interact with people from diverse cultures.

Perfectionism: The desire to appear flawless to avoid failure or harsh judgement.

Podium Class: A class that is taught in person as opposed to being taught online.

Scholarship of Teaching and Learning: A systematic, scholarly investigation of teaching/learning issues that results in dissemination of findings.

Screencast: A video recording of one's computer screen for tutorials or presentations.

Chapter 8
Designing and Implementing a Globally Focused Interdisciplinary STEM Program:
A Model for Preservice Teacher Preparation Programs

Moe D. Greene
https://orcid.org/0000-0001-6304-8632
Virginia Commonwealth University, USA

Yaoying Xu
Virginia Commonwealth University, USA

Jill E. Blondin
https://orcid.org/0009-0003-2433-3969
Virginia Commonwealth University, USA

ABSTRACT

This chapter presents a model for designing and developing a globally-focused interdisciplinary STEM program in preservice teacher education. It provides an overview of a STEM program model that was developed to further strengthen the participants' skills and knowledge in STEM in a collaborative and experiential learning context. The model leverages the affordances of instructional technology while drawing on the learning to teach in community conceptual framework which facilitates learning through five core components: vision, understanding, disposition, practice, and tool. The program components align well with this framework as it emphasizes the competencies of the participants in developing a vision of empowerment in culturally relevant contexts. The opportunities and challenges of developing such a program are discussed. The chapter concludes with a model for establishing program goals and objectives and leveraging the affordances of technology to enhance student learning.

DOI: 10.4018/978-1-6684-7813-4.ch008

INTRODUCTION

The authors of this chapter take an interdisciplinary approach to examining STEM education in teacher education within a global context. They aim to address critical issues, challenges and opportunities that pertain to science, technology, engineering, and math (STEM) and STEM education. There is an increasing, yet unmet, demand for workers with expertise in STEM disciplines and this increasing demand aligns with the increasing trend of shortage in STEM education (Love & Love, 2023). The increasing demand for talented workers in STEM fields troubles higher education, particularly STEM teacher education programs (Bransberger et al., 2020). Research shows that STEM preparation programs are experiencing reduced enrollment and a shortage of STEM students, especially among underrepresented minority students (Jehangir et al., 2022; Nealy & Orgill, 2019). According to the National Center for Educational Statistics (2022), only 15% or fewer minorities such as African Americans, Hispanics, Native Americans, and women earn degrees in STEM. African Americans and Hispanics constitute only 12% of students pursuing undergraduate STEM degrees even though they represent around 30% of the U.S. population. Data also indicate that 48% of students who enter college with STEM majors leave before graduation. African American students are the most likely ethnic group to drop out (29%) or change to non-STEM majors (36%).

In addition to the existence of significant underrepresentation of large demographic groups in the STEM workforce, there is considerable growing concern about achievement gaps and lack of appropriate skill development among STEM graduates (Madden et al., 2013; Patrick & Sturgis, 2013). Research (Kwok, 2018; Madden et al., 2013) indicates that colleges train and educate scientists in a traditional manner while new challenges place different demands on science. There has been broad agreement that there is a need for new curricula to engage students in meaningful and empowering ways. Madden et al. (2013) explain that although traditional science training provides a solid foundation of facts and basic science techniques, it rarely examines how to foster inter and transdisciplinary problem identification and solving skills. Along the same line of thought, Kwok (2018) argues that the traditional disciplines of science have been broken down into numerous research fields. A focus of science teaching has been on presumed inquiry procedures.

According to Kwok (2018), today researching, teaching and learning in the sciences is viewed more as a problem-solving process rather than hypothesis or theory based. Science is becoming cross- or transdisciplinary, connecting the natural and social sciences. To be relevant to the current context and age, science courses are required to be organized in terms of problems, projects, investigations, and experiments in applied settings. STEM education transcends traditionally defined STEM fields such as sciences or engineering. Fundamental knowledge and skills related to STEM can affect individuals' daily functioning as well as professional success. It takes interdisciplinary or transdisciplinary training to incorporate STEM into different fields such as education or teacher education. Research (e.g., Coiro et al., 2016; Pfeiffer et al., 2019) documented the need for individuals who are well-prepared in their professions yet who are also uniquely prepared to engage diverse knowledge, skills, and dispositions of professionals through an interdisciplinary lens.

In the field of special education, for example, individuals who are educated using an interdisciplinary framework are more likely to incorporate multiple perspectives when developing, implementing, and evaluating the effects of intervention or instruction (Coiro et al., 2016; Pfeiffer et al., 2019). Several studies established empirical support for the role of collaborative teamwork in promoting exemplary schools, increased student inclusion and mental health support, and improved student learning outcomes

(Frauenholtz et al., 2017; Hunt et al., 2004; Sandall et al., 2009; Shannon & Bylsma, 2004). Inter- and/or transdisciplinary collaboration for preparing STEM teachers of students from culturally and linguistically diverse backgrounds is especially needed because of the complexity of culturally relevant learning contexts that require professionals to be prepared between and across disciplines. Pfeiffer et al. (2019) demonstrated that interprofessional education leads to interprofessional practice. In the post-COVID-19 pandemic era, it is especially critical to explore innovative approaches to preparing future professionals equipped with the necessary knowledge and skills within and beyond the STEM profession in the global context. Highly interconnected worlds call for more globally competent citizens across disciplines and areas of study.

Madden et al. (2013) argue that in a world with greater global interconnections and large-scale challenges than ever before in human history, complex problems require sophisticated problem-solving skills and innovative, complicated solutions. Hudzik (2011) emphasizes the need for institutions of higher education to view the goal of graduating globally and interculturally competent students as not only a desired outcome but as an institutional imperative. Global and intercultural competency across disciplines can be viewed as a force that binds groups together and facilitates long-lasting knowledge, skills, and relationships. It takes coordinated and collaborative efforts from all aspects of society to meet the needs of rapidly changing technologies and the ever-growing development of individuals. An innovative curriculum should be designed to engage students, both alone and as a team member in applied science in a local community and globally-based contexts.

The purpose of this chapter is to showcase an innovative STEM program model that was developed by three universities across three countries in preservice teacher education programs to advance transnational learning in a global context. First, the authors discuss the background and context, followed by an illustration of the Learning to Teach in Community (Hammerness et al., 2005) conceptual framework that was developed to guide program design. Second, the authors describe the features of the globally focused STEM teacher education program model highlighting its unique combination of online learning and in-person field experiences. Culturally responsive approaches that informed instruction and language support in STEM content areas are also discussed. Finally, the authors present challenges and opportunities for future research and curriculum development of globally focused teacher education programs across subject areas and cultures.

BACKGROUND AND CONTEXT

The globally focused interdisciplinary STEM program model showcased in this paper was developed by three universities as international partners: one public university from the U.S., one public university from Mexico, and one private university from Colombia. The program was developed and launched as a collaborative STEM exchange program in 2021-2022. Sponsored by the 100,000 Strong in the Americas Innovation Funds, the program's goal was to develop and implement a STEM exchange program to increase the retention and mobility of minority preservice teachers and postgraduate students in STEM education, childhood education (ECE), and early childhood special education (ECSE), addressing current challenges in STEM education for inclusive settings. The program facilitated student engagement in various activities and initiatives that address STEM education pedagogy, language training, cultural competency, innovation, and best practices in STEM education. The participants were offered hands-on and collaborative opportunities to apply the knowledge and techniques they learned in cross-cultural settings through virtual and in-person study-abroad programming.

The program embedded a two-way study abroad component within a long-term partnership between universities. It involved reciprocal information sharing and increased opportunities for further partnerships. It had two phases. Phase I of the program consisted of an eight-week online course in STEM education from spring to early summer for a total of twenty-four hours. The course was scheduled to meet three hours a week. Through course activities and follow-up projects, the participants developed a deep understanding of STEM foundations including critical concepts, principles, and intercultural competency related to their STEM fields. The competencies that were emphasized in designing and implementing a globally focused interdisciplinary STEM program include intercultural communication, cultural agility, global awareness, critical thinking, and collaboration across cultures. These competencies are crucial in developing skills to navigate cultural differences and cultivate collaboration among individuals from different backgrounds. The aim was for the participants to explore different worldviews through collaborative projects and team-based activities to gain a broader understanding of the application of STEM concepts across global contexts.

Students had various opportunities to build confidence and a sense of belonging while engaging in critical reflections on pedagogies in STEM education. Phase II consisted of one week of in-person instruction at each university for selected students in Summer 2022 for 12 hours. The one-week exchange program allowed students to apply and advance their STEM skills, intercultural competency, and pedagogical knowledge in culturally relevant contexts. Ancillary English and Spanish language courses that were pedagogically aligned with online and in-person programs were developed to provide language support and mentorship to the students. These language support courses were offered concurrently with the STEM component of the program. In addition to the STEM content knowledge, Phase I of the ancillary eight-week online language courses consisted of eight weeks of online instruction, for a total of 24 hours. Phase II added 12 hours of on-campus language instruction during the summer onsite campus visit for one week. Students earned college credit from their home institutions for participation in the program.

A total of twenty-four participants, including graduate and undergraduate preservice students, from three universities participated in Phases I and Phase II of the program. To fulfill the award requirements, twelve students were selected from the United States, six from Mexico, and six from Colombia. Most of the students (about 79%) were female. The recruitment, application process, registration, orientation, and awarding of financial assistance occurred during the grant period. A recruitment plan was developed in collaboration with all stakeholders involved in program design. Student recruitment included identifying underrepresented- minority students from racial, ethnic minorities, women in STEM, and individuals from low-income backgrounds. Various university channels of communication, such as social media and emails, were leveraged to promote the program and invite underrepresented minority students to participate. The design and development of the application materials highlighted the eligibility criteria and financial support for program participation. The established selection criteria were used to screen the applications based on their academic majors and standing, interest in STEM, demonstrated knowledge of Spanish, and demonstrated fluency in English since the program was taught primarily in English. Spanish and English language support was provided concurrently throughout Phases I and II of the program. Other factors such as diversity of backgrounds and individual motivation for participating and completing the program were also taken into consideration in the selection process.

Offering online instruction allowed the participants to maximize the learning opportunities of various teaching methods and STEM educational resources. Combining Phase I online instruction with Phase

II in-person experience further strengthened their knowledge and skills through first-hand experiences within culturally relevant contexts. Cross-cultural activities which encompassed a wide range of collaborative projects, joint presentations, visits to STEM facilities, courses in different countries, resource exchanges, and international engagement played a crucial role in fostering cultural understanding and global connections. The interdisciplinary STEM curriculum structure of the program was developed because of collaboration by a team of faculty members from the three universities. These faculty members represented diverse disciplines including engineering, childhood education, special education, English language teaching and learning, and STEM education. They combined their expertise and each contributed their unique perspectives to the design and development of the STEM program curriculum. The program was well received by participating students and faculty with a reasonable cost and impactful outcome.

The program curriculum structure was developed empirically, through both an examination of the literature in the field and through an exploration of models in STEM education. The existing literature suggests that education abroad has the potential to foster student engagement and, hence, college completion (Bhatt et al., 2022; Ecker-Lyster & Kardash, 2022). Bhatt et al. (2022) stated that there is evidence that participation in education abroad is associated with increased GPA at graduation and student retention. Oseguera et al. (2022) found that STEM Intervention Programs (SIP) are likely to contribute to an increase of the representation of underrepresented students in STEM fields. Moreover, they provided an example of a STEM Intervention Program (SIP) where the students have access to academic advisors and faculty mentors. The faculty mentors provide scholars with opportunities to participate in research and help them obtain summer internships and study abroad opportunities.

The process of curriculum development began with a discussion of the overarching goals and objectives of the program. Regular meetings facilitated the exploration of key curricular themes and concepts. To create a cohesive and interdisciplinary curriculum, faculty researched and identified concepts, theories, and pedagogical approaches to discuss during their collaborative meetings. Every participating faculty member from each of the three universities had an equal opportunity to contribute their insights and recommendations, which created a sense of collective responsibility among faculty members. The development of relevant learning experiences was based on program goals that were thoroughly examined. Feedback on program design, activities, and student mobility was provided throughout the collaborative process during the monthly general body meetings to ensure that the curriculum addressed the needs of the participants. The team-maintained meeting minutes and a record of discussions in a shared folder.

Phase I and Phase II of the program facilitated a global connection of a STEM project through collaborative online courses and a study abroad program for each group of students, resulting in the signing of institutional agreements to enhance student mobility in STEM education. The program demonstrated a commitment to internationalization and learning opportunities through experiential learning in global contexts. It provided opportunities for the participants to fulfill their individual goals and career aspirations while forging global and intellectual connections. The participants were introduced to the value of teacher social networks in providing support, promoting expertise development and fostering global partnerships. As such, the program represented an essential bridge between teacher learning in university settings and teacher learning in a globally infused context. It applied a practice-based approach rooted in the key 21st-century knowledge and skills domains articulated by the National Research Council: cognitive (e.g., critical thinking, reasoning, innovation), intrapersonal (e.g., flexibility, initiative, appreciation for diversity, metacognition), and interpersonal (e.g., communication, collaboration, responsibility) (De Arment et al., 2013). The participants were given opportunities to build a foundational knowledge base in a community of learners that transcended their geographical boundaries.

CONCEPTUAL FRAMEWORK

The Learning to Teach in Community conceptual framework (Feiman-Nemser, 2001; Hammerness et al., 2005) guided the development of the globally focused interdisciplinary STEM program (Figure 1). It provided a structure for organizing program components as a learning community that is centered around reflective practice.

Figure 1. Learning to teach in STEM community
Source: Feiman-Nemser (2001)

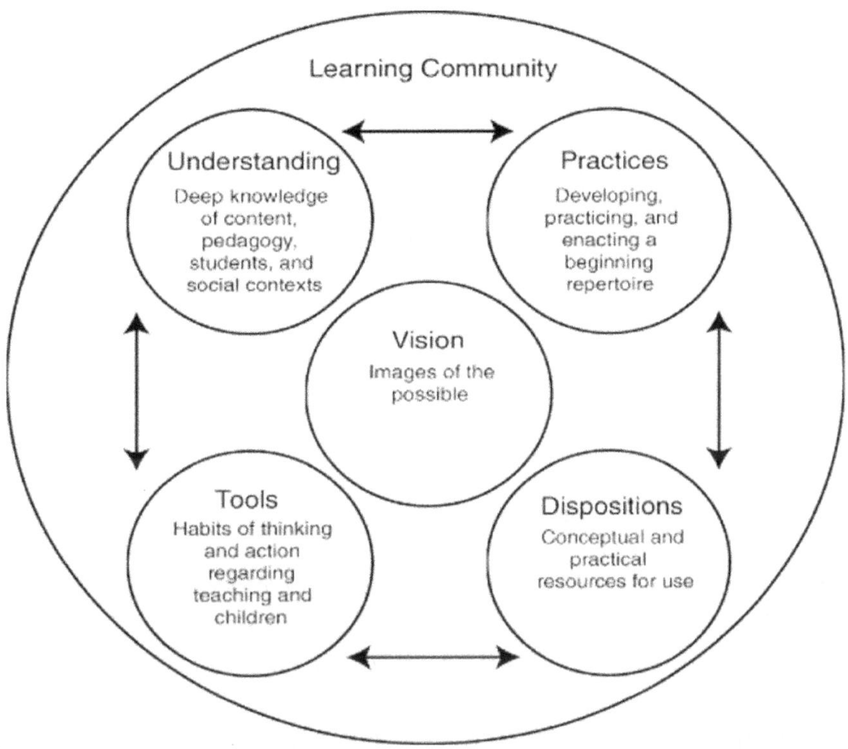

The program conceptual framework builds on professional standards that describe competencies for novice teachers by connecting research on cognitive science with effective teacher education. It draws on the teacher development literature within a learning community of educators through five core components that interact with one another: vision, understanding, disposition, practice, and tools (Darling-Hammond & Berry, 2006; Feille, 2021; Feiman-Nemser, 2001; NRC, 2001). These components are intended to support the development of effective teaching practices in a community of learners. The vision component provides a guiding framework for teachers' practice.

Hammerness et al. (2005) argue that the practice component refers to the actual teaching strategies teachers use in the classroom to meet the changing needs of the students. The understanding of the subject matter includes knowledge and expertise in designing and implementing appropriate methods and assessments. Dispositions refer to teachers' attitudes, beliefs, and values about teaching and learning. They also suggest a commitment to ongoing professional development and a willingness for continuous professional growth. Teachers are expected to use the tools and resources available to them including curriculum materials and technology tools to achieve their instructional goals. Through this conceptual framework, the authors highlight authentic diverse field experiences in culturally relevant contexts to help participants reflect on learning opportunities that are meaningful and relevant (Amador & Carter, 2016; Gonzalez et al., 2023; Incikabi & Kacar, 2017).

The following table adapted from Hammerness et al. (2005) and De Arment et al. (2013) show the relevance of the Learning to Teach in Community Framework for the STEM program.

Table 1. Relevance of learning to teach in community framework for the STEM program

<table>
<tr><th>Framework Component</th><th>STEM Program Learning Communities</th><th>STEM Program Connections</th></tr>
<tr><td>Vision</td><td>Preparation program's images of what makes high-quality teaching</td><td rowspan="5">STEM knowledge and skills of teachers
Preparation program goals are clear across program phases and components
Student reflections are aligned to a central vision throughout the program and beyond
Ongoing reflection is ensured across each program component based on engagement with others
STEM program promotes teacher development across time through sustainable relationships and innovations.</td></tr>
<tr><td>Understanding</td><td>Knowing what it means to teach</td></tr>
<tr><td>Tools</td><td>Conceptual and practical theories and strategies teachers use to act on their understandings of teaching practice</td></tr>
<tr><td>Practices</td><td>Approaches to instruction</td></tr>
<tr><td>Dispositions</td><td>Teacher candidates' understandings of their roles as a teacher with a focus on being reflective and dedicated to student learning</td></tr>
</table>

Source: Adapted from Hammerness et al., 2005 and De Arment et al., 2013.

This model guides new teachers' learning to teach in a community

[It] enables them to develop a vision for their practice; a set of understandings about teaching, learning, and children; dispositions about how to use this knowledge; practices that allow them to act on their intentions and beliefs; and tools that support their efforts. (Hammerness et al., 2005, p. 385)

Vision functions as the overarching guideline. A vision in the context of STEM education suggests that teachers have a clear sense of the approaches STEM teachers apply in teaching. It guides their expectations for the academic and social outcomes of STEM education. While learning communities develop across various phases of the teacher preparation programs, the STEM exchange program aimed to encourage the participants to embrace the vision of quality teaching in STEM education across cultural contexts and to develop the tools, understandings, practices, and dispositions necessary for effective teaching practice with adaptive expertise (De Arment et al., 2013).

The framework supported the development of adaptive and cognitive dispositions along with metacognitive skills that address the fundamental problems of learning to teach, contribute to lifelong learning, and promote sustained professional commitment (De Arment et al., 2013; Feille, 2021; Xu et al., 2021) through interdisciplinary collaborations and culturally relevant learning. Being learner-centered, the STEM exchange program established an optimal learning-community environment that stimulated dialogue and promotion of new ideas, learning, and thinking (Ehiyazaryan-White, 2012; Ring & Ramirez, 2012). It requires the participants to think about and understand teaching differently from their past experiences and exposures. It also shapes their roles and responsibilities as teachers in culturally relevant communities. This model prepares future educators with tools to bridge the gap between understanding and practicing STEM education. In the Learning to Teach in Community framework (Hammerness et al., 2005), understandings and tools are integrated into a set of practices and pedagogical strategies with the goal of impacting teacher dispositions and their belief system.

Figure 2, which was adapted from Feiman-Nemser (2001), presents a Learning to Teach in Community model that includes cultural, linguistic and interdisciplinary elements incorporated into the STEM program. As illustrated in Figure 2 and highlighted in the program components, STEM education takes place in culturally meaningful communities that involve diverse cultures, languages, and professions beyond traditionally defined science or engineering disciplines. Through ongoing and interactive reflections on their practices, participants are offered a variety of culturally relevant opportunities to share knowledge and skills across disciplines (contents) and cultures (contexts) which leads to strong dispositions with the goal to promote the quality of life for their future students.

Figure 2. Learning to teach in STEM community
Source: Feiman-Nemser (2001)

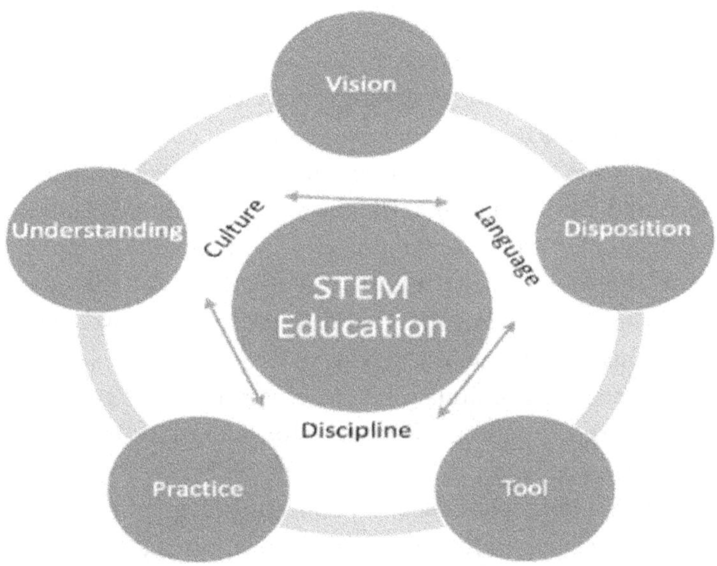

The Learning to Teach in Community framework connects theories to practice through interactions, reflections, and engagement. Theoretical foundations of interdisciplinary STEM education such as constructivism, inquiry-based learning, project-based learning, community-based learning experiences, collaboration, and reflection (Adams, et al., 2015; Gibbons, 2003; Kara, 2019) informed the program development. These theoretical foundations promote active learning and encourage the construction of knowledge through exploration and discovery. They have implications for the use and application of technological tools, content and pedagogy. Collaborative learning activities combine technology, pedagogy and content and encourage discovery learning as they incorporate the co-construction of knowledge supporting Vygotsky's social constructivist orientation (Gibbons, 2003), which maintains that interactions with peers are important to learning.

The underlying assumption of constructivism is that people draw upon available cultural resources to construct meaning and create mental representations or accounts of the world to carry on actions (Vygotsky & Cole, 2018). They emphasize the way the forms of knowledge available to people channel what people think and do. Learning communities are believed to help students network and create bonds beyond the boundaries of the program. The adoption of a social constructivist approach to teaching and learning with technology in STEM program development resulted in learning scenarios where students were involved in their own learning. Program activities incorporated included community engagement through digital networking and group assignments. The STEM model emphasized that learning to teach occurs within communities online and in person.

PROGRAM DESIGN

The STEM program aimed to foster student learning in STEM in the context of intercultural and global engagement through online and in-person collaboration. In this program, students, faculty, administrators, and staff worked collaboratively and creatively to promote the transfer of learning across disciplines and globally situated learning contexts in alignment with the mission of the participating institutions. The program curriculum was designed in consideration of emerging pedagogy and student learning outcomes across disciplines including science, technology, engineering, mathematics, education, English, and foreign languages. The goal was to assist students in making connections between their courses in STEM and other disciplines while developing intercultural and global competency. As such, applying the Learning to Teach in Community conceptual framework, the program design reflects teamwork and adaptive expertise that includes elements of communication, collaboration, application, and experiential learning taking into consideration the socio-cultural global context of formal and informal learning. Curricular features involved applied learning that engaged students in transdisciplinary work to promote deep engagement and intercultural competency in STEM.

Designing a globally focused interdisciplinary STEM program required careful planning and collaboration among faculty at the three institutions. Some key considerations in the design process included researching global competencies relevant to STEM education and teacher development, identifying approaches to integrate STEM and global education concepts, leveraging new technology to enhance student learning, and developing a culturally responsive curriculum and assessments in alignment with the Learning to Teach in Community conceptual framework. The program design phase started with a vision for the program goals and learning outcomes, which provided a structure from which the content, schedules, assignments, resources, and support mechanisms eventually emerged. The framework addressed global challenges in applying STEM knowledge to real-world situations through interdisciplinary collaboration. The design of the structure of the program was informed by learning outcomes rooted in professional standards for developing global and intercultural competencies as well as in the Learning to Teach in Community conceptual framework.

The development of global and intercultural competencies in STEM fields through inter- or transdisciplinary collaboration requires alignment around different key elements including the application of explicit, measurable and transferable learning objectives, student professional growth, timely and differentiated support, knowledge creation, and the implementation of meaningful assessments that advance student learning (Patrick & Sturgis, 2013). Global competencies aim to promote intercultural communication skills, global awareness, and cross-disciplinary knowledge (MacFarlane, 2021). There is a need for the institutions of higher education to recognize that graduating students who possess global and intercultural competency is an essential responsibility. (Guillén-Yparrea & Ramírez-Montoya, 2023; Hudzik, 2011; Smith-Isabell & Rubaii, 2020). Global and intercultural competency across disciplines can be viewed as a force that binds groups together and facilitates long-lasting knowledge, skills, and relationships in a globally connected world.

Advances in Information Communications Technologies (ICT) have broken down geographical barriers, brought the world closer together, and created opportunities for innovation and economic growth. Virtual mobility has long been proposed and developed as an efficient way of educational mobility. Yet, the success rate of students participating in virtual mobility is not ideal, despite its advantages by breaking through the constraints of space and time (Poulová et al., 2009; Yang et al., 2021). Teaching and learning relying on the internet completely also face challenges such as meaningful engagement and interaction. Therefore, in this program, the authors combined virtual learning followed by in-person on-campus visits to maximize learning through various interactions. Colleges and universities are as much a physical place as they are a nexus of interconnected and interdependent remote and local social networks. Students in higher education encounter people from a wider range of professions, education levels, and backgrounds including peers from across the globe and world-renowned professors (Hudzik, 2011). The STEM program was designed to equip students at the university with a knowledge base and a set of competencies to support lifelong learning and the attainment of their academic and career goals. It contributes to the practical aspects of designing learning trajectories to propagate the deep learning of key STEM concepts in connected experiential learning contexts. The following table presents program objectives along with expected results.

Table 2. STEM program objectives and expected results

Program Objectives	Expected Results
● Objective # 1: Enhance the knowledge, skills, attitudes, linguistic and intercultural competency of the participants	● Demonstrated ability to apply knowledge and skills in STEM education ● Development of intercultural competencies through collaboration and engagement with diverse STEM professionals ● Development of pedagogical understanding specific to STEM ● Collaboration with peers to develop a presentation for joint virtual symposium ● Completion of a practicum in STEM ● Increased language proficiency and vocabulary in STEM
● Objective # 2: Increase collaboration, innovation and information-sharing in STEM education	● Development of a collaborative shared resource ● Development of long-term collaborative teams
● Objective # 3: Facilitate the mobility of underrepresented STEM students between the participating institutions	● Increased capacity for student mobility in STEM education ● Removal of barriers to study abroad
● Objective # 4: Establish a sustainable partnership between the participating institutions	● Establishment of a study abroad program in STEM education ● Implemented system of credit transfer

Source: Own elaboration

Program objectives laid the ground for future collaboration, innovation, and information-sharing opportunities in STEM education, leveraged technology and student mobility to advance virtual and in-person exchange programs. The element of distance and its impact on learning remained central to program design. The creation of a project map for the whole program with dates and activities made it possible to show connections between all the virtuous components of the program as they emerged during the design phase. Technology facilitated communication and collaboration among the faculty at the three universities. Three types of presence were considered in detail: teaching, social and cognitive (Guo et al., 2021). The teaching presence was designed intentionally to help participants avoid a sense of isolation, especially in the virtual context. The social presence connected participants as a cohesive community of learners. Program instruction provided the participants with opportunities for collaboration and community learning that included reflection on the learning process required for cognitive presence. The integration of video conferencing and learning management systems tools facilitated the program's emphasis on community and inquiry-based learning as well as interdisciplinary collaboration.

The program design addressed several of the challenging areas in STEM education. First, it targeted and supported students in different STEM programs. Second, the students developed skills and knowledge in STEM education in a global context, which enhanced their life-long learning skills. The program allowed for a global infusion across activities to ensure student learning from a wide variety of perspectives and contexts. Third, the program facilitated the global expansion of the project through joint online programming and study abroad, laying the ground for exchange agreements, articulating credit transfer, and creating a joint study abroad program in STEM education. Finally, it strengthened the university's commitment to internalization and global learning opportunities in and out of the classroom. The mobility of underrepresented STEM students between participating institutions was achieved through these measures that addressed study abroad barriers and facilitated student mobility. The collaboration that was developed because of this program facilitated study-abroad opportunities for students from underrepresented backgrounds. It ensures that these students receive adequate support as well as personal and academic advising specific to their needs.

PROGRAM DEVELOPMENT

Guided by the Learning to Teach in Community conceptual framework, teams from the participating institutions utilized program objectives as the first step in the initial alignment activity to associate the complement of the conceptual framework with targeted outcomes. They also identified intercultural and global experiences to integrate with program activities. In addition to STEM content, the program curriculum included elements of written and oral communication skill development in Spanish and English as well as experiential learning projects. The features of the program curriculum involved projects and applied learning that engaged students in STEM applications that promoted deep engagement and intercultural competency. A summary of program activities in alignment with the Learning to Teach in Community conceptual framework is presented in the following table (Table 3).

Table 3. STEM program activities and anticipated results

Program Objectives	Key Activities
● **Objective # 1:** Enhance the knowledge, skills, attitudes, linguistic and intercultural competency of the participants	● 8-week online course in STEM education ● 1-week in-person exchange program at the three institutions for selected students. ● Hands-on exploration as well as problem- and project-based learning ● Ancillary English and Spanish language courses
● **Objective # 2:** Increase collaboration, innovation and information-sharing in STEM education	● Collaborative team STEM project by students ● Exchange of resources and experience related to STEM education (e.g., the Science Museum education programs)
● **Objective # 3:** Facilitate the mobility of underrepresented STEM students between the participating institutions	● Institutional approvals, collaboration and coordination
● **Objective # 4:** Establish a sustainable partnership between the participating institutions	● Development of and signing of Memorandum of Understanding (MOU)

Source: Own elaboration

The Learning to Teach in Community conceptual framework supported the goals and objectives of the program by providing the participants with engagement opportunities in community-based learning experiences, collaboration with diverse learners, and reflection on their learning and teaching practices. It emphasized the importance of community-based learning experiences that provided the participants with the opportunity to engage with diverse communities and develop a deeper understanding of global issues. For example, the participants engaged in learning projects that addressed global challenges in STEM education. STEM concepts were introduced and applied to specific cultural contexts and through cross-cultural dialogues. The participants shared their cultural experiences and reflected on their own cultural biases to increase awareness of diverse cultures from different communities. Collaboration between the participants and community members in different countries was also important in community-based learning experiences.

Phase I of the program consisted of an online course in STEM education. Through course activities, the participants developed a deep understanding of STEM foundations. The course was intended to examine topics, issues, and problems related to teaching and learning within the STEM context. Course sections were designed as study abroad activities, within cross-cultural learning components. Examples of course sections include:

- The pedagogy of STEM / learning about each of our countries
- Exploring STEM by grade bands (early childhood/elementary, middle/high school)
- Planning and assessing for STEM and STEAM lessons - across ages and abilities
- Managing STEM lessons, classroom talk/discourse in STEM, nature in STEM / STEAM
- Using problem and project-based learning to teach STEM
- Sociocultural issues as a lens for engagement

Students engaged in in-depth discussion and exploration of STEM concepts within early childhood, elementary, and secondary contexts across three institutions- United States, Mexico, and Colombia. Overall course objectives focused on the following:

- Apply pedagogical understanding specific to STEM
- Increase intercultural and global competencies through collaboration
- Deliver a presentation with their peer partner at a joint virtual symposium
- Prepare for a practicum in STEM
- Reflect on the learning process and the identification of resources that enhance practice in STEM teaching.

Phase I program course requirements included active weekly synchronous and asynchronous participation as well as the development of ePortfolios and shared lesson planning on STEM concepts. Adaptive expertise was introduced and practiced through learning activities and reflections. De Arment et al. (2013) suggested adaptive expertise indicators in alignment with performance outcomes to enhance practice through ePortfolios. The following table presents a model that connects a shared vision for adaptive expertise and ePortfolio reflections.

Table 4. ePortfolio reflection activity

ePortfolio Artifact	Target Exemplar	Adaptive Expertise Indicators
● Individualized Education Plan	● Reflects on learning goals	● Using causal and hypothesis-based reasoning; selecting routine or adaptive approaches based on data and hypotheses
● Cultural Diversity Research Project	● Actively seeks out other perspectives; appreciates their point of view; may adjust own view upon reflection	● Willing to ask questions; willing to replace prior assumptions and understandings; accounting for multiple perspectives
● Learning Environment Analysis	● Reflects on time management effectiveness, adjusts routines, adopts new plans to maximize student engagement	● Inventing new procedures and balancing efficient and innovative approaches; using data and hypotheses to drive problem-solving.
● Tutoring in Reading Notebook	● Uses varied materials to build on students' prior knowledge, interests, needs; reflects and makes changes based on research and students' needs.	● Having the inclination to learn rather than simply apply knowledge; responding to variability in the classroom.

Source: Adapted from De Arment et al., 2013.

Prompted by these artifacts (identified in Table 4), students could discuss their own teaching, describing their challenges and problem-solving approaches. Students could also focus on the portfolio artifacts of relevance to their practice and the challenges of learning to teach (De Arment et al., 2013). Literature on the effectiveness of ePortfolios for promoting and assessing reflection informs the development of learning communities that promote adaptive expertise. De Arment et al. (2013) stated that a common theme across ePortfolio literature is the importance of feedback and scaffolding student reflection for promoting students' meaningful reflection. Specific prompts and feedback from faculty and peers are associated with reflective practice. Reflections in global contexts emphasize deeper learning and the development of adaptive expertise. Phase I of the STEM program provided opportunities for practicing the skills and dispositions for adaptive expertise through ongoing reflections.

Phase II of the program consisted of one week of in-person onsite instruction at each university for selected students. The one-week exchange program provided culture specific contexts for students to advance their STEM skills, intercultural competency, and pedagogical knowledge in addition to language immersion. The students engaged in experiential learning where they applied their language skills in authentic settings and learned about the culture. The students explored local cultural and historical sites of note while actively participating in workshops and program sessions that focused on STEM learning. The students concluded their participation in the program by participating in a virtual symposium. Each student collaborated with classmates representing different countries and considered the important sociocultural issues as applied to STEM and Education in their presentation.

The developed program presents a model for educators who seek to create a globally-focused interdisciplinary STEM program to advance STEM education through a focused strategy that brings the academic enterprise of the different institutions to form multi-faceted, sustainable partnerships, and robust, high-impact learning opportunities for students. Increasing student engagement in global learning environments provides opportunities for deep, cross-cultural learning and fosters student success. The STEM exchange program was committed to proactively and intentionally engaging and supporting students in meaningful international activities. Participating students were provided with opportunities for global and community-based learning experiences and innovative pedagogy to develop and apply STEM concepts in a global context.

EVALUATING STEM PROGRAMS

This section further illustrates the conceptual framework presented earlier to link the general goal, objectives, indicators, and data collection to assess the impact of an interdisciplinary STEM program. Factors that influence evaluation designs and data collection methods appropriate for a particular STEM program must be considered. The literature indicates that several initiatives, which span across different levels of education, are underway to improve the quality of STEM learning and teaching through effective measurements (Maric et al., 2023). These initiatives aim to measure the effectiveness and impact of educational interventions and experiences in STEM through qualitative and quantitative assessments. To offer guidance for teaching and learning within the STEM disciplines, the National Academies recently released the Indicators for Monitoring Undergraduate STEM Education (Carlisle & Weaver, 2018). Current National Academies' indicators, which draw on organizational theory and research, encompass progress toward three overarching goals: increasing student mastery of STEM concepts and skills, striving for equity, diversity, and inclusion, and ensuring the completion of STEM credentials (Rosenberg et al., 2018). According to Rosenberg et al. (2018) these goals present education as a complex and dynamic system of four interconnected components: inputs, processes, outcomes, and environment.

Although indicators can provide a discrete marker of quality, a conceptual framework demonstrates relationships across indicators and identified goals. Institutions should consider the status of their STEM programs and what would be required to improve them. The conceptual framework presented earlier is further illustrated below with project specific components to demonstrate the conceptual connections. It defines STEM educational quality at the intersection of STEM content, collaboration, pedagogy and diversity and it considers inputs, processes, outcomes and environment. In our case, each institution had primary responsibility for monitoring program progress and implementation. The purpose of collecting diverse data was to evaluate the impact of the program on the targeted overall goal. No identifying information was collected as part of the evaluation, and online survey responses were anonymous.

General Goal: Develop a collaborative, innovative STEM and language training exchange program that increases the intercultural awareness and sensitivity of minority preservice early childhood education

(ECE)/ early childhood special education (ECSE) teacher candidates in STEM education by expanding their educational experiences and intentionally incorporating culturally relevant and research-based strategies.

Objective #1: Enhance the knowledge, skills, attitudes, linguistic and intercultural competency of the participating underrepresented minority ECE/ECSE students in STEM education through study abroad programs.

Table 5. Performance indicators and data collection tools for Objective # 1

Performance Indicators	Data Collection Source/Tools
● Initiate project communication with the institutions ● Draft and approve a process for recruitment and selection of the participants ● Develop an eight-week online course in STEM education ● Develop a one-week in-person exchange program for selected students ● Create ancillary English language and culture courses ● Measure the participants' intercultural competency	● Faculty, staff, and administration; Student online survey ● Student performance indicators ● Student completion of program requirements ● Student enrollment data

Source: Own elaboration

Objective # 2: Increase collaboration, innovation, and information-sharing in STEM education to promote enthusiasm, self-confidence, and retention among underrepresented minority ECE/ECSE students.

Table 6. Performance indicators and data collection tools for Objective #2

Performance Indicators	Data Collection Source/Tools
● Develop collaborative team STEM projects ● Identify and share relevant resources and experience related to STEM education ● Discuss STEM education standards and STEM curriculum of different countries ● Identify criteria for student matching ● Plan a virtual symposium	● Faculty, staff, and administration; Student online survey ● Student performance indicators ● Student participation

Source: Own elaboration

Objective #3: Facilitate the mobility of underrepresented STEM students between the participating institutions by providing financial support and through targeted recruitment

Table 7. Performance indicators and data collection tools for Objective #3

Performance Indicators	Data Collection Source/Tools
● Coordinate phone and virtual meetings with leadership ● Identify and resolve barriers to student mobility ● Identify financial support resources	● Travel reports ● Assessment report of institutional capacity

Source: Own elaboration

Objective #4: Establish a sustainable partnership between the participating institutions to leverage and enhance the cost savings of credit transfer for the students through multiple institutional agreements and targeted recruitment.

Table 8. Performance indicators and data collection tools for Objective #4

Performance Indicators	Data Collection Source/Tools
● Coordinate phone and virtual meetings with leadership ● Gather institutional approvals and signatures ● Develop and sign agreements to support student mobility	● Travel reports ● Assessment report of institutional capacity

Source: Own elaboration

CHALLENGES AND OPPORTUNITIES

There are several challenges to developing and implementing a globally focused interdisciplinary STEM program. These challenges include language barriers, cultural differences, curriculum alignment, scheduling difficulties, and limited institutional and external funds to support student mobility, especially given the disproportionately higher costs in almost any destination. The cost of developing and implementing a STEM program can vary significantly depending on the size and scope of the program. Perspectives on how discipline integration can be achieved are varied from country to country and program to program. References to multidisciplinary, interdisciplinary, and transdisciplinary approaches can be difficult to grasp as these approaches are used interchangeably at times (English, 2016). Additionally, English (2016) explained different interpretations of STEM education and STEM integration is one of the problematic issues for researchers and curriculum developers.

Different countries may have unique perspectives on how STEM subjects should be taught and learned. Tytler (2020) notes there is imprecision in the disciplinary makeup of STEM across countries. The term sometimes includes the health sciences and medicine, and sometimes agriculture. In Germany, the acronym is MINT (Mathematik, Informatik, Naturwissenschaft und Technik) which makes apparent the inclusion of information technologies. In the U.S.A, the STEM acronym has largely focused on mathematics and science, these being the major high-status disciplinary subjects. Moreover, the T in STEM is increasingly associated with digital technologies as the fourth industrial revolution built on artificial intelligence, machine learning and big data processes is becoming pervasive.

In addition to the institutional and disciplinary challenges, student mobility and education abroad pose safety and health concerns. The safety of students can be jeopardized in areas with a high level of crime or political instability. Brux and Fry (2010) found that the most significant constraints in studying abroad, in rank order, were finances, family disapproval, safety concern, work responsibilities, family responsibilities, the program being too lengthy, no desired program, and academic scheduling difficulties. Parental concerns of underrepresented minority students include questions about racism (Cole, 1991). Thus, for the parents and families of minority students, several issues exist.

Implementing a globally focused STEM program requires addressing these challenges in an innovative way. It also requires considering the funding structure of several institutions. Ecker-Lyster and Kardash (2022) argued that socioeconomic status (SES) is one of the most pronounced factors that influence participation in a study abroad program. Funding makes it difficult to absorb the expense of credits or courses that may not directly contribute to the completion of study. Brux and Fry (2010) argue that because many of the constraints on minority student participation in study abroad are imposed at the institutional level, it is recommended that institutions recognize the benefits of study abroad for all students; develop special outreach programs for minority students, their families, and their instructors and advisors; allocate scholarships and financial assistance for education abroad; and consider allying their institutions with other diverse institutions. The argument for increasing focus on assisting minority students in STEM is based on the centrality of STEM knowledge and skills as well as STEM-based experience to student success.

A globally focused interdisciplinary STEM program is poised to significantly impact participating institutions by leveraging study-abroad experiences to create new partnerships. It addresses several of the challenging areas of study abroad programs. The STEM program model proposed in this chapter undertook the following:

- Provided a variety of opportunities for underrepresented minority students to expand their global and intercultural competency, which has implications for future research and practice
- Addressed language barriers by making second language instruction a vital part of the program
- Produced an affordable study abroad program for underrepresented minority STEM students at three institutions consistent with their curricular and co-curricular requirements
- Contributed to the mobility of minority student population with the goal of making a more significant impact long term
- Provided a structure and a commitment to financially support a study abroad program in STEM education to contribute to an increase in student mobility.
- Provided opportunities for underrepresented minority STEM students to build confidence and a sense of belonging while engaging in critical reflections on pedagogies for STEM activities.

These outcomes are consistent with the participating institutions' priorities. Collaborative efforts between these institutions increased legitimacy, ownership, and accountability for the challenges as well as for the solution options. The program was committed to creating opportunities to engage the participants in unique learning community-based experiences in a global context and improve STEM pedagogy to enhance the participants' development of adaptive expertise. Developing the global and intercultural competencies of students through transdisciplinary studies was a priority. Specifically, the intentional adaptation of the Learning to Teach in Community to meet with the participants in a global context provided an interactive community framework for the participating institutions to model a shared vision about teacher development.

As the three institutions collaboratively explore ways to continue to offer interdisciplinary and globally focused STEM program models, the proposed conceptual framework will be employed in program evaluation to examine effects of the STEM program and similar programs. The data collected and the findings will be analyzed for future publications. Future research should also examine common learning themes and goals of globally focused STEM programs and how they differ by program level of education, if any. In general, the literature shows that students who study abroad are more likely to develop a high level of intercultural and global competence (Bhatt et al., 2022; Giedt et al., 2015). Future research should examine the mediating and moderating factors that could contribute to increasing participation in globally focused STEM programs. Program models that could attract STEM students, including underrepresented minority groups, should be promoted to maximize student enrollment in globally focused

STEM programs. A related question could investigate the potential to further expand student experiences in globally focused STEM programs through research and education 4.0 technologies including artificial intelligence, virtual reality, and big data.

CONCLUSION

This chapter showcased an interdisciplinary and globally focused STEM teacher education model that was led by a major U.S. public university in partnership and collaboration with a private university in Colombia and a public university in Mexico. Sponsored by the U.S. Department of State, this project embedded study abroad programs and integrated transnational global education into the 100K Strong in the Americas grant projects. The purpose of the grant projects was to develop and implement a STEM exchange program to increase the retention and mobility of minority preservice teachers and postgraduate students in STEM education, early childhood education (ECE), and early childhood special education (ECSE), addressing current challenges in STEM education. The outcome was to expand the educational experiences of preservice teachers, intentionally incorporating culturally relevant, transdisciplinary, and research-based strategies in the design and implementation of the program.

The chapter examined how the program emerged through collaboration and discussed the implications of online and in-person activities that involved three different universities. The developed program presents exemplary practice in intercultural and globally oriented STEM education that aims to help educators envisage the role of global STEM programs in advancing the educational goals of preservice teachers' preparation programs and to better envision the added value these programs can offer in educating and training preservice teachers. Future directions for globally focused interdisciplinary STEM programs in teacher preparation programs should consider the importance of establishing clear goals and objectives for program development as well as an appropriate conceptual framework aligned with program goals and philosophy. Moreover, the challenges and opportunities of developing a globally-focused program across different subject areas and cultures should be considered.

ACKNOWLEDGMENT

The development of the globally focused STEM (Science, Technology, Engineering, and Mathematics) program highlighted in this paper was supported by the 100,000 Strong in the Americas (100K) Innovation Fund at Partners of the Americas and the U.S. Department of State. This initiative would not have been possible without their sponsorship and support. The authors would like to extend our heartfelt gratitude and appreciation to all faculty, staff members, and leadership at our partner universities in Colombia and in Mexico and to everyone who has contributed to the success of the STEM program.

REFERENCES

Adams, S., Bernal, E., Cole-Jackson, M., & Martin-Hansen, L. (2015). Training teachers to use educational technologies in STEM using field experience at a community-based organization. In *Society for Information Technology & Teacher Education International Conference Proceedings* (pp. 3021-3025). Association for the Advancement of Computing in Education (AACE). https://www.learntechlib.org/p/150425/

Amador, J. M., & Carter, I. S. (2018). Audible conversational affordances and constraints of verbalizing professional noticing during prospective teacher lesson study. *Journal of Mathematics Teacher Education, 21*(1), 5–34. doi:10.1007/s10857-016-9347-x

Bhatt, R., Bell, A., Rubin, D. L., Shiflet, C., & Hodges, L. (2022). Education abroad and college completion. *Research in Higher Education, 63*(6), 987–1014. doi:10.1007/s11162-022-09673-z PMID:35043032

Bransberger, P., Falkenstern, C., & Lane, P. (2020). *Knocking at the college door: Projections of high school graduates* (10th ed.). Western Interstate Commission for Higher Education. https://knocking.wiche.edu/wp-content/uploads/sites/10/2020/12/Knocking-pdf-for-website.pdf

Brux, M., & Fry, B. (2010). Multicultural students in study abroad: Their interests, their issues, and their constraints. *Journal of Studies in International Education, 14*(5), 508–527. doi:10.1177/1028315309342486

Carlisle, D. L., & Weaver, G. C. (2018). STEM education centers: Catalyzing the improvement of undergraduate STEM education. *International Journal of STEM Education, 5*(1), 1–21. doi:10.1186/s40594-018-0143-2 PMID:30631737

Coiro, M. J., Kotchick, B. A., & Preis, J. (2016). Youth social skills groups: A training platform for promoting graduate clinician interprofessional competence. *Journal of Interprofessional Education & Practice, 4*, 89–92. doi:10.1016/j.xjep.2016.04.004

Cole, J. B. (1991). Opening address of the 43rd International Conference on Educational Exchange. In L. Darling-Hammond (Ed.), *Black students and overseas programs: Broadening the base of participation* (pp. 1-8). Council on International Education Exchange.

Darling-Hammond, L., & Berry, B. (2006). Highly qualified teachers for all. *Educational Leadership, 64*(3), 14–20.

De Arment, S., Reed, E., & Wetzel, A. (2013). Promoting adaptive expertise: A conceptual framework for special educator preparation. *Teacher Education and Special Education, 36*(1), 217–230. doi:10.1177/0888406413489578

De Arment, S. T., Wetzel, A. P., & Reed, E. (2013). ePortfolios: Promoting special educator adaptive expertise through reflection in a web-based learning community. *International Journal of ePortfolio, 3*(2), 149-160. doi:10.1177/0888406413489578

Ecker-Lyster, M., & Kardash, N. (2022). Study abroad: Perspectives from historically underrepresented student populations. *Journal of College Access, 7*(1), 99–115. https://scholarworks.wmich.edu/jca/vol7/iss1/8/

Ehiyazaryan-White, E. (2012). The dialogic potential of ePortfolios: Formative feedback and communities of learning within a personal learning environment. *International Journal of ePortfolio, 2*(2), 173-185. https://eric.ed.gov/?id=EJ1107620

English, L. D. (2016). STEM education K-12: Perspectives on integration. *International Journal of STEM Education*, *3*(1), 1–8. doi:10.1186/s40594-016-0036-1

Feille, K. (2021). A framework for the development of schoolyard pedagogy. *Research in Science Education*, *51*(6), 1687–1704. doi:10.1007/s11165-019-9860-x

Feiman-Nemser, S. (2001). From preparation to practice: Designing a continuum to strengthen and sustain teaching. *Teachers College Record*, *103*(6), 1013–1055. doi:10.1111/0161-4681.00141

Frauenholtz, S., Mendenhall, A. N., & Moon, J. (2017). Role of school employees' mental health knowledge in interdisciplinary collaborations to support the academic success of students experiencing mental distress. *Children & Schools*, *39*(2), 71–79. doi:10.1093/cs/cdx004

Gibbons, P. (2003). Mediating Language Learning: Teacher interactions with ESL students in a content-based classroom. *TESOL Quarterly*, *37*(2), 247–274. doi:10.2307/3588504

Giedt, T., Gokcek, G., & Ghosh, J. (2015). International education in the 21st century: The importance of faculty in developing study abroad research opportunities. *Frontiers: The Interdisciplinary Journal of Study Abroad*, *26*(1), 167–186. doi:10.36366/frontiers.v26i1.365

Gonzalez, G., Villafañe-Cepeda, W., & Rodríguez, O. H. (2023). Leveraging prospective teachers' knowledge through their participation in lesson study. *Journal of Mathematics Teacher Education*, *26*(1), 79–102. doi:10.1007/s10857-021-09521-4

Guillén-Yparrea, N., & Ramírez-Montoya, M. S. (2023). Intercultural competencies in higher education: A systematic review from 2016 to 2021. *Cogent Education*, *10*(1), 1–14. doi:10.1080/2331186X.2023.2167360

Guo, P., Saab, N., Wu, L., & Admiraal, W. (2021). The Community of Inquiry perspective on students' social presence, cognitive presence, and academic performance in online project based learning. *Journal of Computer Assisted Learning*, *37*(5), 1479–1493. doi:10.1111/jcal.12586

Hammerness, K., Darling-Hammond, L., Bransford, J., Berliner, D., Cochran-Smith, M., McDonald, M., & Zeichner, K. (2005). How teachers learn and develop. In L. Darling Hammond & J. Bransford (Eds.), *Preparing teachers for a changing world: What teachers should learn and be able to do* (pp. 358–389). Jossey-Bass.

Hudzik, J. K. (2011). *Comprehensive internationalization: From concept to action. National Association of International Educators*. NAFSA.

Hunt, P., Soto, G., Maier, J., Liboiron, N., & Bae, S. (2004). Collaborative teaming to support preschoolers with severe disabilities who are placed in general education early childhood programs. *Topics in Early Childhood Special Education*, *24*(3), 123–142. doi:10.1177/02711214040240030101

Incikabi, L., & Kacar, A. (2017). Analyzing prospective mathematics teachers' development of teaching practices in mathematics: A lesson study approach. In J. Keengwe & G. Onchwari (Eds.), *Handbook of research on learner-centered pedagogy in teacher education and professional development* (pp. 206–225). IGI Global. doi:10.4018/978-1-5225-0892-2.ch011

Jehangir, R. R., Stebleton, M. J., & Collins, K. (2022). STEM stories: Fostering STEM persistence for underrepresented minority students attending predominantly White institutions. *Journal of Career Development*, 1–17. doi:10.1177/08948453211073706

Kara, M. (2019). A systematic literature review: Constructivism in multidisciplinary learning environments. *International Journal of Academic Research in Education*, *4*(1-2), 19–26. doi:10.17985/ijare.520666

Kwok, S. (2018). Science education in the 21st century. *Nature Astronomy*, *2*(7), 530–533. doi:10.1038/s41550-018-0510-4

Love, T. S., & Love, Z. J. (2023). The teacher recruitment crisis: Examining influential recruitment factors from a United States technology and engineering teacher preparation program. *International Journal of Technology and Design Education*, *33*(1), 105–121. doi:10.1007/s10798-022-09727-4

MacFarlane, B. (2021). *STEM education for high-ability learners: Designing and implementing programming*. Routledge. doi:10.4324/9781003238218

Madden, M. E., Baxter, M., Beauchamp, H., Bouchard, K., Habermas, D., Huff, M., Ladd, B., Pearon, J., & Plague, G. (2013). Rethinking STEM education: An interdisciplinary STEAM curriculum. *Procedia Computer Science*, *20*, 541–546. doi:10.1016/j.procs.2013.09.316

Maric, D., Fore, G. A., Nyarko, S. C., & Varma-Nelson, P. (2023). Measurement in STEM education research: A systematic literature review of trends in the psychometric evidence of scales. *International Journal of STEM Education*, *10*(1), 39. doi:10.1186/s40594-023-00430-x

National Center for Educational Statistics. (2022). *Integrated postsecondary education data system*. https://nces.ed.gov/ipeds/use-the-data/survey-components

National Research Council. (2001). *Eager to learn: Educating our preschoolers*. National Academies Press.

Nealy, S., & Orgill, M. (2019). Postsecondary underrepresented minority STEM students' perceptions of their science identity. *The Journal of Negro Education, 88*(3), 249-268. doi:10.7709/jnegroeducation.88.3.0249

Oseguera, L., Rios, J. D. L., Park, H. J., Aparicio, E. M., & Rao, S. (2022). Understanding who stays in a STEM scholar program for underrepresented students: High-achieving scholars and short-term program retention. *Journal of College Student Retention*, *24*(3), 773–809. doi:10.1177/1521025120950693

Patrick, S., & Sturgis, C. (2013). Necessary for success: Building mastery of world-class skills--a state policymakers guide to competency education. CompetencyWorks Issue Brief. *International Association for K-12 Online Learning*. https://eric.ed.gov/?id=ED561282

Pfeiffer, D. L., Pavelko, S. L., Hahs-Vaughn, D. L., & Dudding, C. C. (2019). A national survey of speech-language pathologists' engagement in interprofessional collaborative practice in schools: Identifying predictive factors and barriers to implementation. *Language, Speech, and Hearing Services in Schools*, *50*(4), 639–655. doi:10.1044/2019_LSHSS-18-0100 PMID:31411947

Poulová, P., Čern, M., & Svobodov, L. (2009). University network? Efficiency of virtual mobility. In *Proceedings of the 5th WSEAS/IASME International Conference on Educational Technologies*, 87–92.

Ring, G., & Ramirez, B. (2012). Implementing ePortfolios for the Assessment of General Education Competencies. *International Journal of ePortfolio, 2*(1), 87-97. https://eric.ed.gov/?id=EJ1107591

Rosenberg, M. B., Hilton, M. L., & Dibner, K. A. (2018). *Indicators for monitoring undergraduate STEM education*. National Academies Press., doi:10.17226/24943

Sandall, S., Hemmeter, M. L., Smith, B. J., & McLean, M. (2009). *DEC Recommended Practices: A Comprehensive Guide for Practical Application in Early Intervention/Early Childhood Special Education*. Division for Early Childhood of the Council for Exceptional Children. Sopris West.

Shannon, G. S., & Bylsma, P. (2004). *Characteristics of improved school districts: Themes from research.* Washington State Department of Education.

Smith-Isabell, N., & Rubaii, N. (2020). Considerations for improving higher education's assessment of global, international, and intercultural competencies. *Research in Comparative and International Education*, *15*(1), 3–6. doi:10.1177/1745499920901950

Tytler, R. (2020). STEM education for the twenty-first century. In J. Anderson & Y. Li (Eds.), Integrated approaches to STEM education. Advances in STEM education (pp.21-43). Springer. doi:10.1007/978-3-030-52229-2_3

Vygotsky, L., & Cole, M. (2018). Lev Vygotsky: learning and social constructivism. In S. Macblain (Ed.), *Learning theories for early years practice* (pp. 58–66). Sage Publication Ltd.

Xu, Y., Chen, C., Spence, C., Washington-Nortey, M., Zhang, F., & Brown Ruiz, A. (2021). Supporting young Spanish speaking English learners through teacher scaffolding and reciprocal peer tutoring. *Early Child Development and Care*. Advance online publication. doi:10.1080/03004430.2021.1874944

Yang, Q., Shen, J., & Xu, Y. (2021). Changes in international student mobility amid the COVID19 pandemic and response in the China context. *Fudan Journal of the Humanities and Social Sciences*, *15*(1), 23–40. doi:10.1007/s40647-021-00333-7

KEY TERMS AND DEFINITIONS

Community: Refers to both physical and virtual environments, as well as local and global settings, that provide a foundation for peer support, collaboration, and a sense of collective identity. Community-based learning experiences in a global context encourage reflection on teaching and learning practices beyond local boundaries.

Cultural Responsiveness: Deep understanding of a culture that is different from an individual's home culture. Cultural responsiveness in this chapter also includes reflections on different cultures and engagement in diverse activities, including different language activities.

Interdisciplinary: Refers to the approach of a model across disciplines through collaborations and partnerships. Interdisciplinary is approach-based.

Online Learning: Refers to both synchronous and asynchronous learning modules, activities, and projects, primarily through Canvas learning modules and Zoom meetings.

STEM Education: Goes beyond traditionally defined science, technology, engineering, and mathematics (STEM) disciplines as competence-based, student-centered, and culturally relevant STEM-related teaching and learning in global contexts.

Study Abroad: Was embedded within online learning and in-person on-campus visits in this program. Participants had opportunities to engage with others from three countries.

Transdisciplinary: Emphasizes knowledge, skills, and dispositions that are shared and valued by all team members across disciplines. Transdisciplinary is knowledge/skills-based.

Chapter 9
Virtual Collaboration for English Language Teacher Education:
Professional Negotiations With Ukraine and Türkiye

Banu Cicek Basaran Uysal
https://orcid.org/0000-0002-4978-0891
Eskisehir Osmangazi University, Turkey

Emine Eren Gezen
https://orcid.org/0000-0002-1623-3023
Eskisehir Osmangazi University, Turkey

İlknur Yüksel
Eskisehir Osmangazi University, Turkey

Oksana Andriivna Chernysh
Zhytomyr Polytechnic State University, Ukraine

Ümit Özkanal
https://orcid.org/0000-0003-2027-1337
Eskisehir Osmangazi University, Turkey

Natalia Andriichuk
Zhytomyr Polytechnic State University, Ukraine

ABSTRACT

This chapter studies the role of telecollaboration in facilitating teacher professional development, specifically focusing on the perceptions of future English language teachers. By examining how telecollaboration serves as a tool for professional growth, this study aims to shed light on the significance of this approach in teacher education. In this study, pre-service teachers from Ukraine and Türkiye participated in bi-monthly telecollaboration exchanges as part of their practicum course. Through an analysis of the data collected from an online questionnaire, the chapter shows that the participants recognized the telecollaboration exchanges as meaningful opportunities for their professional growth. The results offer valuable implications for incorporating telecollaboration into teacher professional development programs and enhancing professional experiences within the teaching community. The chapter concludes with insights into areas where improvements can be made to optimize the telecollaboration experience for teacher development.

DOI: 10.4018/978-1-6684-7813-4.ch009

INTRODUCTION

In recent years, telecollaboration has gained increasing attention as a means of enhancing English language teacher education through international and intercultural communication and collaboration (O'Dowd, 2018). Telecollaboration refers to online communication and collaboration between learners and/or teachers from different cultures and/or locations, often using digital tools such as videoconferencing, chat, and forums (Guth & Helm, 2010). As English language teaching and learning become increasingly globalized and digitalized, telecollaboration offers a promising way of developing learners' intercultural competence, communicative skills, and critical thinking abilities, as well as promoting teacher professional development (Eren, 2021; Üzüm et al., 2020). According to Wu et al. (2020), telecollaboration refers to "virtual exchanges occur among learners across cultures and distances to interact and collaborate on different online communication platforms" (p. 310). Telecollaboration allows teachers and learners to connect with their peers from different countries and engage in shared learning activities that foster cross-cultural understanding and language development (O'Dowd, 2018).

BACKGROUND

Thanks to the advancements in technology, collaboration evolved into virtual exchanges (O'Dowd, 2018) where the participants are freed from the boundaries of time and setting (Barbosa & Ferreira-Lopes, 2021). Students and teachers can create and maintain international partnerships through telecollaboration (Akiyama & Cunningham, 2018; Lawrence & Spector-Cohen, 2018). With the start of telecollaboration, students and teachers can now connect with colleagues from around the world without leaving their classrooms or homes (Akiyama & Cunningham, 2018; Lawrence & Spector-Cohen, 2018). This has opened new opportunities for international collaboration in teacher education, particularly in the wake of the COVID-19 pandemic when virtual meetings have become the norm (Wu, 2021).The significance of telecollaboration grows more vibrant in the post-COVID-19 world, where daily social exchanges have become increasingly online (Wu, 2021). Following the breakout of the pandemic, not only school walls turned into virtual classrooms, but also professional development practices emerged as online meetings. This transformation was especially imperative for teacher education settings where the practice teaching component was conducted in face-to-face mode (Kidd & Murray, 2020). The COVID-19 pandemic has emphasized the importance of technology in teacher education, as online platforms became essential for delivering courses and facilitating communication among teachers and students. Thus, the integration of technology in language teacher education has become a necessity, and telecollaboration has emerged as a promising tool in this regard.

Several studies have investigated the potential of telecollaboration for language teacher education, highlighting its benefits. For instance, O'Dowd (2012) and Schenker (2012) argue that telecollaboration can foster intercultural competence among language teachers and provide them with opportunities to learn about different cultures and pedagogical practices. Similarly, Eren (2021) and Üzüm et al. (2020) suggest that telecollaboration can enhance language teacher education by presenting a platform for critical reflection and discussion about language and identity. In the context of English language teacher education, telecollaboration has gained attention to provide pre-service and in-service teachers with opportunities to interact with native and non-native English speakers and improve their language skills and cultural awareness (O'Dowd, 2015). Furthermore, telecollaboration can provide a platform for language teachers to share their experiences, exchange ideas, and collaborate on curriculum development and material design (O'Dowd, 2018). Telecollaboration, as a specific form of professional development may enhance teachers' adaptability to different online settings. With the rapid advancement of technology and the growing prevalence of remote and hybrid learning environments, it is crucial for teachers to be proficient in using various digital tools and platforms (Başaran, 2020). Through professional development initiatives, teachers can gain exposure to and hands-on experience with these technologies, enabling them to navigate virtual environments confidently and utilize online resources effectively. Additionally, by engaging in telecollaborative projects, teachers can develop a deeper understanding of the benefits and challenges associated with intercultural exchanges in virtual environments. They can explore effective strategies for facilitating authentic language use and intercultural learning, design meaningful activities that promote communication and collaboration among students from different backgrounds and assess the impact of telecollaboration on students' language development and intercultural competence. Such adaptability is essential for teachers working with English language learners or diverse student populations, as it allows them to engage students in meaningful and interactive virtual learning experiences (Slapac et al., 2019).

Along the same lines, the research underlines the importance of international telecollaboration for teacher education since it is beneficial for both the learners and teachers (Tanghe & Park, 2016). Telecollaboration enables intercultural exchanges by bringing different learners and teacher groups together to work or study for a common goal (White, 2017). By contributing to such meetings, the participants can improve their adaptability for different online settings and improve their interactive skills in virtual environments. Research studies on telecollaboration and English language teacher education also examined other topics and issues, such as the benefits and challenges of telecollaboration, the role of intercultural competence in telecollaborative exchanges, the impact of telecollaboration on learners' language and intercultural learning, and the design and implementation of telecollaborative projects (Garcia-Esteban et al., 2019; Guth & Helm, 2010; Kukulska-Hulme & Traxler, 2019; Liu et al., 2023; O'Dowd, 2021; Ware & Kessler, 2014). Many of these studies have demonstrated that telecollaboration can provide learners with opportunities to practice authentic language use, develop intercultural competence, and engage in meaningful communication and collaboration with peers from diverse backgrounds (Belz & Thorne, 2006).

Overall, the literature suggests that international telecollaboration can play a vital role in improving teacher education practices and can provide a range of benefits for both pre-service teachers and faculty members. Although the literature explores the potential benefits of telecollaboration in language teacher education, there is still a need for further research to investigate its effectiveness and implications for teacher development. The present study aims to examine the perceived effectiveness of telecollaboration as a tool for professional development and explore the pedagogical and practical implications of telecollaboration for English language teacher education. In view of that, the goal of the current study is to investigate the beliefs of prospective Turkish and Ukrainian English as a foreign language (EFL) teachers regarding international telecollaboration by focusing on the following research question:

How do prospective EFL teachers from Ukraine and Türkiye evaluate the effectiveness of telecollaboration for their professional development?

METHODOLOGY

Study Context

The present study was done with two state universities from Ukraine and Türkiye, both of which are settings where English is taught as a foreign language. Voluntary faculty members (n=8) and the participating prospective EFL teachers attended bi-monthly live webinar sessions regarding the profession. The participants of the study were senior-year college students who were training to become English language teachers. The student-teachers both in Ukraine (n=26) and Türkiye (n=21) were taking the first of the two-term practice teaching course. For pre-service teacher education programs, practice teaching has great value since it helps future teachers to bridge the gap between theory and practice (Allen & Wright, 2014; Martins et al., 2014). Accordingly, it is central to enrich this experience through the international collaboration for improving initial teacher education.

The Turkish Setting

In the Turkish context, EFL teacher education programs are a fundamental component of preparing future English language teachers. These programs, typically offered at universities, entail a rigorous admission process that involves passing a national university entrance exam as well as an English proficiency exam. Candidates who meet the eligibility criteria are granted enrollment in the EFL teacher education programs, marking the beginning of their academic journey towards becoming proficient and qualified educators in the field.

The undergraduate EFL teacher education program in Türkiye extends over four years, encompassing a diverse range of subjects that aim to provide students with a comprehensive understanding of language teaching and related disciplines. These subjects include advanced English language courses, which focus on enhancing students' target language proficiency and ensuring their competence in both spoken and written English. Moreover, the program covers courses on English language teaching approaches and methods, which equip prospective teachers with pedagogical strategies and instructional techniques relevant to the EFL context. Another crucial area of study within the EFL teacher education program is second language acquisition. Through this course, students gain insights into the theoretical foundations and practical implications of how individuals acquire a second language. This knowledge empowers pre-service teachers to tailor their instructional practices to facilitate effective language learning experiences for their future students.

Language skills teaching is another vital component of the curriculum, which focuses on developing the competence of pre-service teachers in teaching various language skills, including reading, writing, listening, and speaking. Emphasizing both theoretical underpinnings and practical applications, this course equips aspiring teachers with the necessary tools to effectively foster language development and proficiency among their students. Considering the diverse range of learners in the EFL context, teaching English to young learners is a specialized area that receives significant attention within the program. By delving into the unique characteristics, needs, and learning styles of young learners, pre-service teachers gain the knowledge and skills to design and implement age-appropriate and engaging instructional activities tailored to the specific needs of young language learners.

In addition to these language-focused courses, the program includes foundational courses in linguistics, English literature, and educational sciences. Linguistics courses provide students with a deeper understanding of the structure, rules, and functions of the English language. English literature courses enhance their literary analysis skills and foster an appreciation for the cultural and historical dimensions of the English language. Educational sciences courses offer insights into educational psychology, curriculum development, and instructional methodologies, ensuring that pre-service teachers have a solid grounding in educational theory and practice.

The culmination of the EFL teacher education program is the practice teaching courses conducted during the final year. These courses serve as a bridge between theoretical knowledge and practical application, enabling pre-service teachers to refine their teaching skills in real classroom settings. To be eligible to participate in the practice teaching courses, students must have completed three years of coursework, ensuring they have acquired the necessary foundational knowledge and pedagogical competence. The Turkish EFL teacher education program, participating in the present study, emphasizes the completion of all methodology-related courses as a prerequisite for qualifying for the practicum courses in the final year.

These practicum courses are meticulously organized through a collaborative effort between the Ministry of National Education and universities. Annually, practicum schools are designated and announced to universities, initiating the crucial partnership between faculty coordinators and the schools for the successful implementation of the practicum activities. The practice teaching courses involve the active participation of various stakeholders, including supervisors (university-based teacher educators), mentor teachers (in-service English language teachers), and pre-service teachers (undergraduate students in the final year of the program). The duration of each practice teaching course spans 12 weeks per term, during which pre-service teachers are expected to complete a range of weekly observational tasks that focus on areas such as classroom management, error correction, assessment and evaluation procedures, language teaching techniques, and material design.

Furthermore, pre-service teachers are expected to actively engage in in-class teaching tasks, applying the theoretical knowledge they have acquired in real classroom settings. To ensure a well-rounded experience, pre-service teachers are required to teach a minimum of 10-lesson hours during their placement at assigned schools. This hands-on component of the practicum allows them to gain practical teaching experience, develop their instructional skills, and refine their pedagogical approaches. By merging theoretical knowledge with practical application, pre-service teachers are better equipped to meet the diverse needs of their future students and navigate the complexities of the EFL classroom.

The Ukrainian Setting

The language teacher education program in Ukraine holds significant importance in preparing future educators for the complex task of teaching English as a second language. Spanning an academic year composed of two semesters, the program offers a comprehensive curriculum that covers various essential courses. These courses, including Basics of Pedagogics, Innovation Technologies in ESL, Teaching English for Specific Purposes, Teaching English to primary, secondary, and high school children, and Teaching Bilingual Students, provide aspiring teachers with a solid foundation in both theoretical knowledge and practical skills.

In recognition of the diverse needs of language learners, the program also incorporates optional courses that focus on European approaches in English for specific purposes (ESP). These courses aim to broaden the horizons of prospective teachers by introducing them to different methodologies used in ESP instruction. By comparing these methodologies, students gain a deeper understanding of the pedagogical strategies employed to meet the specific language needs of learners in various professional contexts.

The selection process for admission to the language teacher education program includes the National Multisubject Test, a rigorous examination lasting three hours. This assessment evaluates students' aptitude in multiple subjects and encompasses tasks of varying difficulty levels. The comprehensive nature of the test allows for the identification of exceptionally talented students who possess a keen sense of language and a strong foundation in pedagogy. Through this rigorous selection process, the program ensures that it attracts candidates who are well-suited for the demanding nature of the teaching profession.

To successfully complete the teacher education program, students must fulfill all program requirements, which include theoretical courses, teaching practice, scientific work, and the compilation of their teachers' portfolios. The program places great emphasis on practical experience, providing students with the opportunity to engage in both passive and active teaching practice.

During the passive practice component, aspiring teachers observe classes conducted by experienced Ukrainian educators. This observation can take place in both online and offline settings, allowing students to gain insights into different teaching styles and instructional techniques. A minimum requirement of observing 20 lessons is set, providing students with ample exposure to various teaching methodologies and strategies. Additionally, students are expected to prepare detailed reviews of these observed lessons, further enhancing their critical analysis and reflective skills.

Active practice forms a vital component of the teacher education program, allowing students to apply their knowledge and skills in a hands-on teaching environment. Under the guidance and supervision of experienced mentors, students engage in practical sessions where they take an active role in delivering lessons and managing classroom dynamics. This practical experience not only helps students develop their instructional and classroom management abilities but also provides an opportunity for self-reflection and growth as future educators.

Telecollaboration

The primary objective of this study was to enhance the professional knowledge of student-teachers by revisiting key topics through online collaboration. In pursuit of this goal, participating universities cooperated to design and implement a telecollaboration series specifically tailored for prospective teachers. The researchers held two online meetings at the beginning of the term to work on the telecollaboration series. The first meeting was about determining a tentative schedule and forming the list of topics to be covered during the semester. The second meeting was held to settle the online meeting schedule and determine the instructors for each of the decided webinar topics. The topics were announced to the faculty members of both universities, and the voluntary professors selected the topic they wanted to talk about. The sessions were led by the researchers themselves in collaboration with two professors from Ukraine. In other words, there were four professors from Ukraine and four from Türkiye contributing their expertise.

The selection of session topics was informed by the relevant literature (Başaran Uysal & Savaş, 2021; Yin, 2019) and decided by the participating professors. This approach ensured that the topics addressed the most problematic aspects of English language teaching (ELT) as perceived by future teachers. The identified topics encompassed a range of crucial areas: (1) 21st-century skills, (2) native language and target language use in English classes, (3) course book adaptation, 4) overview of free ELT internet resources, 5) English for specific purposes (ESP) teaching methods, 6) corrective feedback, 7) technology use in ELT, and 8) material design in ELT. These topics were carefully chosen to address significant challenges and emerging trends within the field of ELT, allowing student-teachers to gain a deeper understanding and proficiency in these areas.

The webinar series consisted of bi-monthly meetings held over one academic semester, spanning 16 weeks. The prospective EFL teachers and the collaborating professors were informed about the meetings through instant messaging apps, and platforms such as Zoom or Google Meet were utilized for the synchronous online sessions. Each session was designed to last for approximately one hour, during which student-teachers were actively encouraged to engage in the learning process. They were given opportunities to pose questions, provide answers, and actively participate in online discussions related to the topic at hand. The online collaboration format employed in this study provided a dynamic and interactive learning environment for student-teachers. Through the utilization of modern communication technologies, such as video conferencing platforms, participants had the opportunity to connect and engage with both researchers and collaborating professors from different cultural and educational backgrounds. By revisiting important topics and facilitating online collaboration, this study aimed to offer student-teachers a platform to deepen their professional knowledge, exchange ideas, and explore innovative pedagogical practices. The interactive nature of the sessions fostered a sense of active participation and encouraged critical thinking among the student-teachers, thereby promoting their professional growth and competence in ELT.

Study Design and Research Procedures

To investigate the effectiveness of telecollaboration in enhancing the professional development of future EFL teachers in Ukraine and Türkiye, this study employed a case study design. The case study approach was selected for its ability to provide valuable insights into the dynamics of the participants and the nature of their relationships (Mills & Gay, 2016). By focusing on the specific context of telecollaboration between Ukraine and Türkiye, this research aimed to contribute to the understanding of the efficacy of this collaborative approach in fostering the professional growth of pre-service EFL teachers. In this study, the authors defined the case as follows: the future EFL teachers who participated in a professional development program, aiming to revisit the critical aspects of English language teaching, through telecollaboration between Ukraine and Türkiye.

To collect data for the study, the researchers designed and utilized an online open-ended questionnaire. The aim of the study was to understand the participants' beliefs about effectiveness of the telecollaboration for their professional development. For this reason, qualitative data were obtained through an online questionnaire. Before participating, the pre-service teachers (26 from Ukraine, and 21 from Türkiye) were given clear information that their involvement was voluntary, and their responses would be kept confidential and protected from disclosure to any external parties. To ensure ethical standards were upheld, the participants provided informed consent by endorsing a consent form before taking part in the study. At the conclusion of the telecollaboration series, the online questionnaire was administered to the prospective English as a Foreign Language (EFL) teachers (n=47) at the end of the academic term. The questionnaire consisted of three open-ended questions aimed at extracting valuable insights from the participants. The pre-service teachers were asked to answer the following questions:

1. How would you evaluate the effectiveness of the online meeting series for your professional development?
2. What was the most beneficial topic(s) for you and why?
3. What other topic(s) could be included in this series to help and improve the practice teaching process?

In the data analysis phase of this study, the responses provided by the participants were subjected to a systematic coding and examination process to evaluate the effectiveness of the conducted online meetings. To ensure methodological rigor and consistency, the coding procedures proposed by Creswell and Poth (2018) were adhered to, offering a structured framework for organizing and analyzing the data. The procedures were as follows:

1. Managing and organizing the data
2. Reading and memoing emergent ideas
3. Describing and classifying codes into themes
4. Developing and assessing interpretations
5. Representing the data (Creswell & Poth, 2018, p. 255)

The first step involved managing and organizing the collected data. This encompassed the careful arrangement and structuring of the participants' responses to facilitate subsequent analysis. By systematically organizing the data, the researchers were able to establish a coherent and manageable dataset, ensuring that relevant information was easily accessible for further scrutiny.

The second step revolved around reading and memoing emergent ideas. This process involved immersing oneself in the data by thoroughly reading through the participants' responses and making note of initial impressions, key concepts, and emerging themes. Memoing, as recommended by Creswell and Poth (2018), enabled the researchers to capture their thoughts, reflections, and interpretations, which would later contribute to the development of a comprehensive analysis.

Subsequently, the third step entailed describing and classifying codes into themes. Through a careful examination of the data, significant patterns, similarities, and differences within the participants' responses were identified. Codes, representing discrete units of meaning, were assigned to these patterns, effectively categorizing the data into meaningful themes. This process of coding and theme development allowed for a comprehensive and structured organization of the data, facilitating the identification of recurring patterns and central ideas within the dataset.

Moving forward, the fourth step involved developing and assessing interpretations. With the identified themes and associated codes, the researchers embarked on a process of interpretation to derive meaningful insights from the data. This interpretive phase entailed a critical examination of the relationships between the codes and themes, considering the context of the study, relevant theoretical frameworks, and the specific research objectives. Through this iterative process, the researchers were able to generate nuanced interpretations and develop a rich understanding of the effectiveness of the conducted online meetings based on the participants' responses.

Lastly, the fifth step encompassed representing the data. This stage involved transforming the coded data and interpretations into a format that effectively communicated the findings. Various strategies for data representation, such as tables, and narrative descriptions, were employed to present the analyzed data in a clear and concise manner. By representing the data effectively, the researchers aimed to provide a comprehensive and coherent account of the participants' responses and the emerging themes, thereby enhancing the overall validity and reliability of the study's findings.

To this end, two separate authors were engaged in the data analysis process. First, the researchers collated and organized the data gathered through the open-ended questionnaire. Then the authors coded 20% of the data independently and then convened to compare and discuss their respective codes and the emerging themes. Through collaborative deliberation, a coding template was prepared based on the agreed codes and themes, enabling the researchers to proceed with the coding process for the remaining data. Following the completion of the coding process, the coders reconvened to identify the emerged themes and establish interpretations of the findings. In order to ensure reliability and rigor, inter-coder reliability was established. The degree of agreement between the coders was calculated, resulting in an agreement percentage of 85.7% (Lombard et al., 2002). This high level of agreement attests to the consistency and reliability of the coding process. The systematic coding and subsequent thematic analysis of the collected data facilitated a comprehensive examination of the participants' perceptions and experiences. Through this process, valuable insights were gained into the impact of the online meetings on their professional growth. Furthermore, the findings of the analysis provided valuable feedback and recommendations for future improvements in the telecollaboration process.

RESULTS

The aim of the study was to investigate the following research question: How do prospective EFL teachers from Ukraine and Türkiye evaluate the effectiveness of telecollaboration for their professional development? After participating in eight telecollaboration series conducted for four months, the future EFL teachers from Ukraine and Türkiye were invited to evaluate the effectiveness of the series for their professional development by completing an online questionnaire. The data analysis revealed that the prospective EFL teachers had positive feelings about the telecollaboration between the two countries. Additionally, they believed that the topics of the meeting series were beneficial for them, especially the ones about Web 2.0 tools and corrective feedback. The participants also provided answers by suggesting topics to improve the series. Classroom management and ELT methodology topics were the two common themes suggested by the participants from both countries. An overview of the results of the study is provided in Table 1 below.

Table 1. Summary of the results of the study

Questions	Themes	Türkiye	Ukraine	Total
Q1: Overall effectiveness of the series	Beneficial	8	9	17
	Effective	6	7	13
	Informative	5	5	10
	Great	1	4	5
Q2: The most beneficial topic(s)	Web 2.0 tools	9	6	15
	Corrective feedback	6	1	7
	All of them	1	5	6
	Communicative skills	-	3	3
	Real-life experiences	2	1	3
	L1 use	2	1	3
	21st century skills	2	-	2
Q3: Topic suggestions	Classroom management	11	5	16
	ELT methodology	2	5	7
	Material design	2	-	2
	Practical activities	-	2	2
	No need	2	-	2
	Online teaching	-	2	2
	Distance education	-	2	2
	Assessment	-	2	2

Source: Own elaboration

The table shows (1) the questions asked in the open-ended questionnaire, (2) the themes identified for each question, (3) the frequency of each theme and (4) finally the frequency for each participant group, namely Ukraine and Türkiye. The results of the study are discussed in detail in the following sections.

Effectiveness of the Telecollaboration Series

The participants of the present study indicated their thoughts concerning the overall success of the telecollaboration series conducted within the scope of the study. Emerging themes were (1) *beneficial* (n=17), (2) *effective* (n=13), (3) *informative* (n=10), and (4) *great* (n=5). The results show that most of the prospective teachers (96%) were pleased with the project and regarded online collaboration useful for their professional development.

I found the webinars useful as there are different activities. There was fun and supportive content. For example, it was very enlightening for me to learn to what extent the use of L1 is allowed in the class. Although we know how important it is to use the target language in the classroom, in real life students lose interest in the lesson they do not understand, or it is difficult to learn some concepts in the target language. I have learned about many subjects like this, and I think that Webinars have a positive impact on both our internship and our professional life. (P5 from Türkiye)

The webinars have provided a great benefit for my teaching skills and knowledge. I definitely rediscovered the things I'd heard of earlier as well as managed to learn about new methods and techniques that I'm really looking forward to implementing in my teaching (P16 from Ukraine)

The meetings were productive. I would like to continue my professional development using such kind of meetings. (P10 from Ukraine)

The three quotations above, highlight the beneficial aspect of online meetings on language teachers' professional development. The participants emphasized the importance of engaging in meetings with informative content that is relevant to their needs and interests. They also noted the supportive nature of the meetings, which contributed to their motivation and enthusiasm for the learning experience. One important aspect that was highlighted by one of the participants is the use of L1 in the classroom. This topic is relevant to language teachers who face the challenge of balancing the use of the target language with the need for effective communication and comprehension. The participant found the information enlightening and relevant to their teaching practice. Another participant noted that webinars helped them rediscover previously learned information as well as gain new insights into teaching methods and techniques. This suggests that telecollaboration can be an effective tool for continuous professional development and can help teachers stay up to date with the latest trends and developments in their field.

In addition, the three statements below present the effectiveness of the webinar series conducted through Ukraine-Türkiye collaboration on the personal and professional development of the participants. In particular, P22 from Ukraine emphasizes the usefulness of the meeting series, indicating that it was a valuable experience that cannot be underestimated, while P23 from Türkiye emphasizes the practicality of the meeting contents, noting that the online series focused on how to use the knowledge gained in the classroom, which will be useful in the future. Finally, P25 from Ukraine expresses gratitude for the quality of the telecollaboration series, highlighting the effectiveness of the trainers and the applicability of the new information obtained.

I really enjoyed the webinar series which were conducted through Ukraine-Türkiye collaboration. The effectiveness of the webinar series for my personal development is hard to underrate. (P22 from Ukraine)

I think these webinars are effective in terms of our teaching profession because the contents of the webinars were about how to use our knowledge in the lessons. Thus, thanks to these webinars, I will know what to do in the future. (P20 from Türkiye)

I'm sincerely grateful for the webinar series! The subject matters were presented effectively, the trainers were knowledgeable, I obtained new information applicable to my work. (P25 from Ukraine)

All in all, the positive feedback from the participants indicates that the webinar series was successful in meeting the needs and expectations of the participants. They found the sessions to be well-organized and well-presented, providing a productive and engaging learning experience. As a result, the participants obtained valuable knowledge and skills that will be useful in their professional development. Additionally, the participants expressed their willingness to continue using such meetings to improve their teaching skills and knowledge. These findings suggest that webinars can be a valuable tool for language teachers who seek to enhance their teaching practice and stay current in their field.

The Topics Included in the Series

Within the scope of the study, the researchers also aimed to determine the most beneficial topics for the participants. The data analysis revealed that the pre-service teachers evaluated several of the topics to be beneficial for their professional development. Most of them believed that learning about *web 2.0 tools* and how to use them in their lessons (n=15) was highly helpful. It was followed by *how to give corrective feedback* (n=7*), improving communicative skills* (n=3), *sharing real-life experiences of in-service teachers* (n=3), *use of L1 in EFL classrooms* (n=3), and *improving 21st century skills* (n=2). Additionally, six of the participants stated that all the topics included were highly relevant and useful for them. Interestingly, only the participants from Ukraine agreed that *improving the communicative skills* was a useful topic, while for *improving 21st century* skills only the participants from Türkiye found it relevant.

Online teaching techniques, because as a teacher I must improve my online teaching skills. (P7 from Ukraine)

"Overview of free Internet resources to teach English", "Technology use in ELT". The sessions delivered the information I expected to receive. The subject matter was presented effectively. (P11 from Ukraine)

I think the free online English resources webinar was the most beneficial one because teachers need resources and websites while teaching. It is hard to find free resources on the internet. In the webinar, the instructor showed us the resources that we can benefit from and I will use them in my teaching profession. (P18 from Türkiye)

The statements above indicate the usefulness of including *web 2.0 tools* as a topic in telecollaboration by reflecting the importance of online teaching techniques and resources in the context of English language teaching. P7 from Ukraine emphasized the necessity of improving online teaching skills, while P11 praised the effective presentation of information on free internet resources and technology use in ELT. P18 from Türkiye found the online English resources webinar to be the most beneficial, as it provided access to free resources that can be utilized in their teaching profession. By looking at the comments of the participants, it can be suggested that the future EFL teachers are aware of the significance of using online resources and technology to enhance language teaching. Especially in light of the COVID-19 pandemic, which has led to an increased reliance on online teaching platforms, the teacher candidates from both countries found this topic highly beneficial. Furthermore, the remarks of the participants indicates that the online meetings have been successful in meeting the needs and expectations of the participants, providing them with beneficial information and skills that can be employed in their teaching practice.

Another topic, perceived rewarding by the participants from Ukraine and Türkiye, was *how to give corrective feedback*. As can be read from the quotation below, P12 stated that as teacher candidates, they needed detailed information about this topic, while P14 emphasized the importance of corrective feedback in providing motivation to students. Both participants also acknowledged that they gained valuable information on how to provide feedback at different stages and what types of feedback to give. These statements suggest that the online meeting provided practical and useful information for language teachers to effectively provide corrective feedback to their students, which is an important aspect of language learning and teaching.

The most beneficial topic was Corrective Feedback. Because we are now teacher candidates, and we need this information in detail. (P12 from Türkiye)

The issue of giving corrective feedback was the most important because it is of great importance in terms of providing motivation to the students. I got a lot of information about how to give feedback at what stage and what type of feedback should be. (P14 from Türkiye)

By examining the results of the present study, it can be said that the telecollaboration topics were relevant for the participants' needs and they were able to gain better understanding of the topics provided. They also noted that the significance of several topics for their professional development and future career goals and stated that the online gatherings were successful in equipping them with required knowledge and practical aspects for language teaching.

Suggestions for Improvement

The researchers also wanted to investigate what other topics can be included in order to improve the telecollaboration series by collecting the pre-service teachers' opinions. There were two main topics mentioned by the participants from both countries: *classroom management* (n=16), and *ELT methodology* (n=7). Other topics were mentioned by two participants from each country, such as: *material design*, *practical in-class activities*, *online teaching*, *distance education*, and *assessment*. The presence of topics such as *online teaching* and *distance education* indicate that there is a further need to go over *technology in ELT* topic. In other words, although the issue in question was already included as part of the telecollaboration series, the participants still wanted to learn more about the same subject.

In the following statements, the participants suggest the need for improving their classroom management skills to be better professionals in the field. Since the participants were fourth-year students, and also active partakers in the practicum process, they gave great importance to discovering and solving their problems related with classroom management.

Emergency situations in the classes, problematic situations in the class and the subjects related to these. (P2 From Türkiye)

In my opinion, other than topics that are always related with ELT, how to grasp the attention of new generation students or how to keep them controlled and such can also be included since our students are the subjects of our job. (P18 from Türkiye)

I think the subject of class control and time management should be added because we have a lot of problems with this. (P21 from Türkiye)

Variations and options of group work, technical supplies for the group work in distance learning. (P13 from Ukraine)

The participants' remarks suggest that they value topics that address practical and immediate concerns in the classroom, such as emergency situations, problematic situations, class control, and time management. They also express interest in topics that focus on seating arrangement and different in-class interaction patterns, such as variations and options of group work and technical supplies for group work in distance learning. These comments indicate that the participants are looking for relevant and up-to-date information that can enhance their teaching skills and improve the learning outcomes of their students.

Another frequently mentioned topic to be included in the series was *ELT methodology*. Several of the future teachers indicated a need for revising and remembering the key aspects of ELT methodology for their professional development.

There were topics that we used in our practicum and how to implement those methods to the teaching process. (P5 from Türkiye)

Methods of teaching English. (P9 from Ukraine)

EFL teaching methods. (P17 from Ukraine)

The statements indicate a shared interest in the topic of teaching methods for English language. The participants express a desire to improve their teaching skills and to learn how to apply different methods to the teaching process. The mention of the practicum suggests that the participants have hands-on experience with teaching and are interested in learning how to apply the methods they have learned in their training to real-life teaching situations. In other words, these quotations demonstrate a commitment to ongoing professional development and a desire to improve their teaching practice.

DISCUSSION

The study aimed to evaluate the effectiveness of telecollaboration between future EFL teachers from Ukraine and Türkiye in terms of their professional development. After conducting eight telecollaboration series for four months, the participants were asked to evaluate the effectiveness of the series, and the data analysis revealed that the participants had positive feelings about the telecollaboration between the two countries. The results of the study revealed that the telecollaboration series conducted within the scope of the study was effective in promoting the professional development of future EFL teachers from Ukraine and Türkiye. The participants found the series to be informative, effective, and beneficial to their personal and professional growth. The results of the participants' feedback on the telecollaboration series suggest that the online sessions were highly beneficial for language teachers in terms of their professional development. In addition, there were positive comments on the effectiveness of the meetings in terms of providing new knowledge and skills that can be used in language teaching. The feedback also revealed that the telecollaboration series were well-organized and engaging, providing a productive learning experience for the participants.

The second question asked the participants to identify the most beneficial topics they learned from the online meeting series. They believed that the topics of the meeting series were beneficial for them, especially the ones about *web 2.0 tools* and *corrective feedback*. Web 2.0 tools, which emerged as the most frequently mentioned topic, refers to various digital tools and platforms that are commonly used in language teaching, such as social media, podcasts, and online games. This result is in line with the growing importance of digital literacy and technology in language education. Corrective feedback, which is a key component of effective language teaching, was also mentioned by several participants as a beneficial topic. Additionally, the fact that some participants mentioned all topics as beneficial indicates that they found the entire webinar series useful for their professional development. This suggests that the topics covered in the series were relevant to the participants' needs and interests, and that they were able to gain new insights and knowledge from each session.

The final question asked the participants to suggest topics for future meeting series. The results showed that *classroom management* and *ELT methodology* topics were the two common themes suggested by the participants from both countries. The results indicate that the participants are interested in topics related to practical aspects of language teaching. Classroom management, which was the most frequently suggested topic, is a crucial aspect of language teaching that involves creating a positive and productive learning environment for students. ELT methodology, which was also mentioned by several participants, refers to the various approaches, methods, and techniques used in language teaching. These results suggest that the participants are interested in topics that can help them improve their teaching skills and strategies, and that they value practical knowledge and skills that they can apply in their future teaching careers.

Overall, findings of the study underscore the significant impact of telecollaboration on the professional development of future EFL teachers. The series effectively addressed the participants' needs, offering valuable insights and practical knowledge, particularly in the areas of web 2.0 tools, corrective feedback, classroom management, and ELT methodology. By engaging in collaborative online sessions, the participants were able to acquire new knowledge, gain practical skills, and broaden their perspectives on language teaching. Such findings provide valuable implications for designing future telecollaboration initiatives that cater to the professional growth of language teachers.

The positive attitudes of the participants towards telecollaboration can be attributed to its potential to provide a collaborative learning environment, where learners can share their experiences, develop intercultural competence, and enhance their language skills (O'Dowd, 2015). In addition, telecollaboration can offer learners the opportunity to engage in authentic communication and develop their communicative competence (Guth & Helm, 2010). This finding is particularly relevant to the field of EFL teacher education, as it suggests that telecollaboration can enhance the language and communication skills of future EFL teachers.

In the current study, the participating teachers actively participated in online professional development activities facilitated through international collaboration. The participants unanimously acknowledged the positive impact of these activities on their professional growth. The findings of this study align with prior research emphasizing the advantages of telecollaboration in language teaching. Shin et al. (2022) assert that webinars offer language teachers opportunities for training and professional development, allowing them to benefit from the expertise and insights of educators worldwide. The authors further underscore the cost-effectiveness, flexibility, and adaptability of webinars in accommodating the diverse needs and schedules of teachers. Similarly, Kukulska-Hulme and Traxler (2019) contend that webinars contribute to enhancing teachers' knowledge and skills in language teaching, particularly in areas such as mobile-assisted language learning and online instruction.

In addition, the participants' feedback on the effectiveness of the telecollaboration meetings in providing new knowledge and skills is consistent with the idea of continuous professional development in language teaching. As noted by Richards and Farrell (2005), language teachers need to engage in ongoing professional development to stay current with the latest teaching approaches and techniques. This is particularly important in the digital age, where new technologies and online platforms are constantly emerging, and language teachers need to adapt to the changing landscape of language teaching.

In conclusion, the present study provides evidence for the effectiveness of telecollaboration as a tool for professional development in the field of language teaching. The positive attitudes and feedback from the participants highlight the importance of engaging in online collaboration to gain access to informative content, practical knowledge, and new insights into teaching methods and techniques. Moreover, telecollaboration can help language teachers stay up to date with the latest trends and developments in their field, which is crucial for their professional growth. These findings are consistent with the existing literature on the benefits of telecollaboration for language learning and teaching. However, it is important to address the challenges associated with telecollaboration to ensure successful implementation in language teaching.

Implications for EFL Teacher Education

The findings of this study have important implications for EFL teacher education. First, telecollaboration can be used as a tool for promoting professional development among future EFL teachers. Telecollaboration can offer learners the opportunity to interact with peers from different cultural backgrounds, share experiences, and make practical inferences about their in-class teaching activities.

Second, the results of the study suggest that the topics covered during telecollaboration should be relevant to the needs and interests of the participants. Therefore, EFL teacher education programs should take into consideration the preferences of the participants when designing telecollaboration activities. This can be achieved by conducting needs analysis and surveys to identify the topics that are most relevant to the participants. Third, the findings of the study suggest that classroom management and ELT methodology are the most common themes recommended by the participants. Therefore, EFL teacher education programs should provide opportunities for pre-service EFL teachers to develop their classroom management and ELT methodology skills. This can be achieved by incorporating these themes into the EFL teacher education curriculum and providing opportunities for practice and feedback.

FUTURE RESEARCH DIRECTIONS

While there is a growing body of research on telecollaboration and English language teacher education, there is still much to be explored and understood about this area of practice. For example, more research is needed to investigate the impact of telecollaboration on teachers' professional development and teaching practices, as well as to explore the potential of emerging digital tools and technologies for telecollaboration in English language teacher education (Ware & Kessler, 2016). Further studies could focus on pre-service and in-service teacher development through telecollaboration to identify and overcome the challenges of international teamwork.

Despite the potential benefits of international collaboration, there are still many challenges to be addressed. For example, the literature identified technical issues, time constraints, and differences in pedagogical approaches as challenges for telecollaboration (Yang, 2020). Additionally, language barriers and differences in educational systems can make it difficult for teachers and students to collaborate effectively (DelliCarpini, 2009). To address these challenges, it is important for teacher education programs to provide students with the knowledge and skills they need to engage in effective international collaboration. This includes developing intercultural competence, as well as training in the use of technology for telecollaboration (Barbosa & Ferreira-Lopes, 2021; White, 2017). By doing so, teacher education programs can help to prepare students for the challenges and opportunities of teaching in an increasingly interconnected world.

Regardless of the valuable insights offered by the study, it is essential to acknowledge and consider its inherent limitations when interpreting the findings. One such limitation pertains to the reliance on self-reported feedback from the participants as the primary source of data. While the participants expressed positive views on the effectiveness of telecollaboration for their professional development, the study did not investigate the actual impact of these online sessions on their in-class performances. Future studies may aim to explore the correlation between participation in telecollaboration and observable improvements in teachers' instructional practices, thus providing a more comprehensive understanding of the benefits of such online initiatives.

Another limitation of the present study is related with relatively short-term evaluation of the series conducted. The data collection took place at the end of the telecollaboration series, providing insights into the immediate perceptions and experiences of the participants. However, the study did not explore the long-term impact or sustainability of the acquired knowledge and skills. Future research could benefit from longitudinal studies to examine the lasting effects of telecollaboration on the professional development of EFL teachers.

Similarly, in the current study, an online questionnaire was utilized as the primary data collection tool. While this tool proved valuable in capturing the participants' beliefs and perspectives regarding the webinar series, it is important to note that triangulation of the data was not achieved. To gain a more comprehensive understanding of the issues at hand, future research studies could benefit from incorporating additional data collection tools such as interview protocols, diaries, and/or observations. This multi-method approach would offer a richer and more nuanced exploration of the participants' experiences and provide a broader context for analyzing the effectiveness and impact of the webinar series on their professional development.

Additionally, the study focused on telecollaboration between future EFL teachers from Ukraine and Türkiye. In future studies, researchers could consider adopting a similar study to investigate the efficacy of online telecollaboration among diverse countries. Additionally, it would be valuable to explore alternative research avenues that involve various participant groups in international collaboration. For instance, incorporating pre-service teachers from different disciplines into initial teacher education programs, engaging in-service teachers for professional development initiatives, or involving faculty members and other teacher trainers to enhance teacher development. The outcomes derived from such investigations would contribute to the generalizability of the current study's findings.

Nevertheless, this study contributes to the growing body of research on the effectiveness of telecollaboration as a valuable tool for professional development in language teaching. The participants' positive attitudes and feedback emphasize the significance of engaging in online collaborative practices to access informative content, acquire practical knowledge, and gain fresh insights into teaching methods and techniques.

ACKNOWLEDGMENT

This research received no specific grant from any funding agency in the public, commercial, or not-for-profit sectors.

REFERENCES

Akiyama, Y., & Cunningham, D. J. (2018). Synthesizing the practice of SCMC-based telecollaboration: A scoping review. *CALICO Journal, 35*(1), 49–76. doi:10.1558/cj.33156

Allen, J. M., & Wright, S. E. (2014). Integrating theory and practice in the pre-service teacher education practicum. *Teachers and Teaching, 20*(2), 136–151. doi:10.1080/13540602.2013.848568

Bagarukayo, E., & Kalema, B. (2015). Evaluation of e-learning usage in South African universities: A critical review. *International Journal of Education and Development using ICT, 11*(2). https://www.learntechlib.org/p/151848/

Barbosa, M. W., & Ferreira-Lopes, L. (2021). Emerging trends in telecollaboration and virtual exchange: A bibliometric study. *Educational Review, 75*(3), 58–586. doi:10.1080/00131911.2021.1907314

Başaran, B. Ç. (2020). *Examining in-service English language teachers' professional needs: Towards an online teacher training program* (Unpublished PhD thesis). Middle East Technical University, Ankara.

Başaran Uysal, B. Ç., & Savaş, P. (2021). Overview of the challenges of practicum practices in English language teaching in Türkiye: A meta synthesis study on literature between 2004 and 2019. *Inonu University Journal of the Faculty of Education, 22*(2), 1669–1712. doi:10.17679/inuefd.886731

Belz, J. A., & Thorne, S. L. (2006). Introduction: Internet-mediated intercultural foreign language education and the intercultural speaker. In J. Belz & S. L. Thorne (Eds.), *Internet-mediated intercultural foreign language education* (pp. ix–xxv). Thomson Heinle.

Creswell, J. W., & Poth, C. N. (2018). *Qualitative inquiry & research design: Choosing among five approaches*. SAGE Publication Inc.

Eren, Ö. (2021). Raising critical cultural awareness through telecollaboration: Insights for pre-service teacher education. *Computer Assisted Language Learning, 36*(3), 1–24. doi:10.1080/09588221.2021.1916538

Garcia-Esteban, S., Villarreal, I., & Bueno-Alastuey, M. C. (2019). The effect of telecollaboration in the development of the learning to learn competence in CLIL teacher training. *Interactive Learning Environments, 29*(6), 973–986. doi:10.1080/10494820.2019.1614960

Guth, S., & Helm, F. (2010). *Telecollaboration 2.0: Language, literacies, and intercultural learning in the 21st century*. Peter Lang. doi:10.3726/978-3-0351-0013-6

Kidd, W., & Murray, J. (2020). The Covid-19 pandemic and its effects on teacher education in England: How teacher educators moved practicum learning online. *European Journal of Teacher Education, 43*(4), 542–558. doi:10.1080/02619768.2020.1820480

Kukulska-Hulme, A., & Traxler, J. (2019). Design principles for mobile learning. In H. Beetham & R. Sharpe (Eds.), *Rethinking pedagogy for a digital age: Designing for 21st century learning* (2nd ed., pp. 268–281). Routledge. doi:10.4324/9781351252805-12

Lawrence, G., & Spector-Cohen, E. (2018). Examining international telecollaboration in language teacher education. In D. Tafazoli, M. E. Gomez Parra, & C. A. Huertas-Abril (Eds.), *Cross-cultural perspectives on technology-enhanced language learning* (pp. 322–345). IGI Global. doi:10.4018/978-1-5225-5463-9.ch018

Liu, G.-Z., Fathi, J., & Rahimi, M. (2023). Enhancing EFL learners' intercultural communicative effectiveness through telecollaboration with native and non-native speakers of English. *Computer Assisted Language Learning*, 1–31. Advance online publication. doi:10.1080/09588221.2022.2164778

Lombard, M., Snyder-Duch, J., & Bracken, C. C. (2002). Content analysis in mass communication: Assessment and reporting of intercoder reliability. *Human Communication Research*, *28*(4), 587–604. doi:10.1111/j.1468-2958.2002.tb00826.x

Martins, M., Costa, J., & Onofre, M. (2015). Practicum experiences as sources of pre-service teachers' self-efficacy. *European Journal of Teacher Education*, *38*(2), 263–279. doi:10.1080/02619768.2014.968705

Mills, G. E., & Gay, L. R. (2016). *Education research: Competencies for analysis and applications*. Pearson Education.

O'Dowd, R. (2012). Intercultural communicative competence through telecollaboration. In J. Jackson (Ed.), The Routledge handbook of language and intercultural communication (pp. 340–356). Routledge.

O'Dowd, R. (2015). The competences of the telecollaborative teacher. *Language Learning Journal*, *43*(2), 194–207. doi:10.1080/09571736.2013.853374

O'Dowd, R. (2018). From telecollaboration to virtual exchange: state-of-the-art and the role of UNICollaboration in moving forward. *Journal of Virtual Exchange, 1*, 1-23. doi:10.14705/rpnet.2018.jve.1

O'Dowd, R. (2021). What do students learn in virtual exchange? A qualitative content analysis of learning outcomes across multiple exchanges. *International Journal of Educational Research*, *109*, 1–13. doi:10.1016/j.ijer.2021.101804

Richards, J. C., & Farrell, T. S. (2005). *Professional development for language teachers: Strategies for teacher learning*. Cambridge University Press. doi:10.1017/CBO9780511667237

Shin, J. K., Borup, J., Barbour, M. K., & Quiroga Velasquez, R. V. (2022). Webinars for English language teachers during the pandemic: Global perspectives on transitioning to remote online teaching. *AERA Open*, *8*, 1–15. doi:10.1177/23328584221083976

Slapac, A., Kim, S., & Coppersmith, S. A. (2019). Preparing and enriching linguistically and culturally responsive educators through professional development. In A. Slapac & S. Coppersmith (Eds.), *Beyond language learning instruction: Transformative supports for emergent bilinguals and educators* (pp. 282–304). IGI Global. doi:10.4018/978-1-7998-1962-2.ch012

Tanghe, S., & Park, G. (2016). "Build[ing] something which alone we could not have done": International Collaborative Teaching and Learning in language teacher education. *System*, *57*, 1–13. doi:10.1016/j.system.2016.01.002

Üzüm, B., Akayoglu, S., & Yazan, B. (2020). Using telecollaboration to promote intercultural competence in teacher training classrooms in Türkiye and the USA. *ReCALL*, *32*(2), 162–177. doi:10.1017/S0958344019000235

Ware, P., & Kessler, G. (2016). Telecollaboration in the secondary language classroom: Case study of adolescent interaction and pedagogical integration. *Computer Assisted Language Learning*, *29*(3), 427–450. doi:10.1080/09588221.2014.961481

White, C. J. (2017). Distance language teaching with technology. In C. A. Chapelle & S. Sauro (Eds.), *The handbook of technology and second language teaching and learning* (pp. 134–148). John Wiley & Sons. doi:10.1002/9781118914069.ch10

Wu, S. (2021). Unpacking themes of integrating telecollaboration in language teacher education: A systematic review of 36 studies from 2009 to 2019. *Computer Assisted Language Learning*, 1–23. Advance online publication. doi:10.1080/09588221.2021.1976800

Wu, S., Ware, P., & Liaw, M.-L. (2020). Promoting peer-to-peer synchronous online discussions: Case study of intercultural communication in telecollaboration. In L. Wilton & C. Brett (Eds.), Handbook of research on online discussion-based teaching methods (pp. 283–310). IGI Global.

Yang, S. J. (2020). Affordances and challenges of telecollaboration for pre-service teachers. *Language Learning & Technology*, *24*(3), 30–41. http://hdl.handle.net/10125/44733

Yin, J. (2019). Connecting theory and practice in teacher education: English-as-a-foreign language preservice teachers' perceptions of practicum experience. *Innovación Educativa (México, D.F.)*, *1*(4), 4. Advance online publication. doi:10.1186/s42862-019-0003-z

ADDITIONAL READING

de Wit, H., & Altbach, P. G. (2021). Internationalization in higher education: Global trends and recommendations for its future. *Policy Reviews in Higher Education*, *5*(1), 28–46. doi:10.1080/23322969.2020.1820898

Dooly, M., & O'Dowd, R. (Eds.). (2018). *In this together: Teachers' experiences with transnational, telecollaborative language learning projects*. Peter Lang. doi:10.3726/b14311

Dooly, M., & Vinagre, M. (2022). Research into practice: Virtual exchange in language teaching and learning. *Language Teaching*, *55*(3), 392–406. doi:10.1017/S0261444821000069

Lenkaitis, C. A. (2020). Teacher candidate reflection: Benefits of using a synchronous computer-mediated communication-based virtual exchange. *Teaching and Teacher Education*, *92*, 1–9. doi:10.1016/j.tate.2020.103041

Montaner-Villalba, S., Sarno-García, D. S., & María, G. S. A. (2023). *Telecollaboration applications in foreign language classrooms*. IGI Global., doi:10.4018/978-1-6684-7080-0

Slapac, A., Song, K. H., & Chasteen, C. C. (2017). Introspections on in-service teachers' intercultural responsiveness skills for English Language Learners. In K. Jones & J. Mixon (Eds.), *Intercultural Responsiveness in the second language learning classroom* (pp. 181–201). IGI Global., doi:10.4018/978-1-5225-2069-6.ch011

Turula, A., Kurek, M., & Lewis, T. (Eds.). (2019). Telecollaboration and virtual exchange across disciplines: In service of social inclusion and global citizenship. Research-publishing.net.

Wu, S. (2022). Methodologies and pedagogical applications of integrating telecollaboration in language teacher education: A synthesis of 56 studies from 2010-2020. *CALICO Journal*, *39*(3), 281–305. Advance online publication. doi:10.1558/cj.23991

Ziegler, N., & González-Lloret, M. (2022). *The Routledge handbook of second language acquisition and technology*. Routledge. doi:10.4324/9781351117586

KEY TERMS AND DEFINITIONS

Corrective Feedback: The reaction that language learners get when they make language related errors in the target language.

English as a Foreign Language (EFL): Settings in which English is neither spoken as the native language nor serves as the official language. To give an example, Japan, Ukraine, and Türkiye are EFL contexts.

Intercultural Competence: The set of abilities that are needed for effective and appropriate communication and collaboration between the individuals of different cultures.

Mentor: An in-service teacher who monitors, evaluates, and guides the pre-service teachers during the practicum process.

Practicum: The component of undergraduate teacher education where the participants are required to complete a series of practical and theoretical tasks in the appointed schools for obtaining teaching experience.

Supervisor: A university-based teacher trainer who is responsible from observing, evaluating, and supporting the prospective teachers during the practicum process.

Teacher Professional Development: A range of endeavors geared towards enriching teachers' competencies and expertise through engagement, training, and ongoing assistance.

Chapter 10
Virtual Exchange in Teacher Training and the Foreign Language Classroom:
Global Competence Skills and Development in an Interdisciplinary Pilot

Sandra McGury
https://orcid.org/0000-0002-2883-2568
Zurich University of Applied Sciences, Switzerland

Robert Klosinski
https://orcid.org/0009-0009-1730-8443
IGS Schöppenstedt, Germany

ABSTRACT

Global competence development is part of the process of internationalization of the curriculum and pedagogical tools, like virtual exchange (VE), to create internationalization opportunities. This chapter focuses on an interdisciplinary VE project between two higher education institutions of the Global North. After the semester-long collaboration, students enrolled in a teacher training program and students from a foreign language classroom evaluated the importance of certain global competence skills and reflected on their own development thereof. The authors present the organizational setup and analyze the self-assessment in light of global citizenship skills and their relevance in teacher training or foreign language learning.

DOI: 10.4018/978-1-6684-7813-4.ch010

INTRODUCTION

College education plays an important role in preparing students for 21st century global employability and citizenship (Barrett & Golubeva, 2022). Global competence training and development is part of the process of internationalization of the curriculum (Leask, 2015) and pedagogical tools such as virtual exchange (VE) open internationalization opportunities to all students. Amid an abundance of traditional student mobility options at American universities, 90% of U.S. students neither study nor intern abroad (United States Department of State, 2018), which highlights the need to incorporate international and cross-cultural experiences at home, for example, by means of VE initiatives.

Particularly in the fields of teacher education on the one hand and foreign language education on the other, scholars have stressed the importance of including global competence education in the curricula (e.g., Slapac, 2021; Slapac et al., 2023). Parmigiani et al. (2022) suggest that teacher training programs in Europe do not include components of global competence, notably, possibilities in which aspects and strategies related to global competence issues are topicalized and practiced.

Many universities offer global competence development as an add-on or extracurricular component by, for example, providing elective courses or independent certificates. However, in the foreign language learning context, they have played a slightly different role. The mere ability to speak a second language (L2) is already considered a global competence by many, and the importance of language skills to access other global competences have been undisputed (Baumgratz, 1995; Weenink, 2008). In fact, Semaan and Yamazaki (2015) observe a relationship between global competence and three of four components that are understood as constituting L2 learning motivation. Bringing together the main foci of Parmigiani et al. (2022) and Semaan and Yamazaki (2015), the goal of this chapter is to discuss VE as an effective tool in light of global competence development, its impact on and implications for teacher training programs, and the significance of VE in the L2 classroom.

This chapter is structured as follows. The background section contextualizes virtual exchange in the contexts of global competence development, teacher training, and foreign language learning setting. The subsequent section shares the sentiments and the procedure of designing and implementing a virtual exchange pilot between a university from the United States (US) and a Swiss (CH) university, followed by a presentation of its evaluation results. These results provide the basis for the analysis where the evaluations are discussed against the backdrop of teacher training and the foreign language classroom. The conclusion highlights the findings of the pilot and relates the discussion results to the Intercultural Competence Assessment (INCA) skills and key aspects of global competence in the teacher training and foreign language learner context.

BACKGROUND: GLOBAL COMPETENCE AND VIRTUAL EXCHANGE

Usually seen as part of a strategy towards the *internationalization of higher education (IHE)* or the *internationalization of the curriculum (IoC),* universities around the globe have been trying to follow society's call to engage in a process that prepares students to become future global citizens, i.e., to become "graduates, professionals, and citizens of the world to live and work effectively in a rapidly changing and increasingly connected global society" (Leask, 2015, p. 17). They have taken various measures to emphasize and include global competence training into their curricula, all siding with slightly different definitions about what constitutes a *global citizen* or what makes up a *connected global society.* The inevitable discussions concerning the *global skill repertoire,* that is, the *global,* or transcultural *competences* that students are expected to have obtained by the end of their undergraduate training, are countless and continuously developing (see O'Dowd, 2023 for a thorough overview of current frameworks and literature marrying the terms democratic citizenship, global citizenship education, global competence, and the like).

However, it is widely agreed upon that such skills include certain attitudes and awareness that enable an individual to be transculturally tolerant and empathetic (see, for example, Deardorff & Jones, 2012; Leask, 2015; OECD, 2019; Song et al., 2023; Van Roekel, 2010). Following the need to include global competence training in university study programs and in institutionalized steps towards the internationalization of the curriculum, virtual exchange has, in one form or another, become one of the most popular pedagogical approaches across the disciplines to include internationalization and global citizenship education at home. O'Dowd (2023) discusses the theoretical bases of virtual exchange and notes that "online contact with other cultural groups is beneficial for the reduction of stereotypes and cultural prejudice" (O'Dowd, 2023, p. 31), thus making the participants more tolerant and sensitive towards the group they interact with.

Furthermore, research and discussions revolving around *culture and communication* (for example, *intercultural or transcultural communication*) have been particularly prevalent in the field of foreign language learning. Byram's (1997) model of intercultural communicative competence (ICC) is one popular example that tried to capture intercultural skills and attitudes necessary to meaningfully and effectively communicate with people in a different language (Byram, 2020). It has provided the basis for numerous research in the field of foreign language learning, and it has continuously been developed over the past decades, serving as a tool to measure intercultural communicative learning outcomes in foreign language classrooms.

Now that the interconnection between global citizenship skills such as *transcultural communication*, the internationalization in higher education, virtual exchange as a pedagogical tool, and the communicative skills within foreign language learning has been established, this section will define VE, discuss VE within teacher training, and VE as part of the foreign language classroom.

Virtual Exchange

While the authors have established the connection between global competence development and virtual exchange, various considerations on the metalevel affect a virtual exchange's concept, namely, the definition of an exchange, as well as the institutional and overarching goals of such an exchange.

Similar to the inconsistencies related to the terminology evolving around IHE, IoC and global skills mentioned above, uncertainty and discrepancies dominate discussions pertaining to what constitutes virtual exchange. There is an abundance of related terms and definitions regarding virtual exchange (Helm & Beaven, 2020; O'Dowd, 2023). Many of them are chosen and adapted to fit or characterize a certain context, for example, to describe a specific virtual exchange project. However, one of the simplest understandings of virtual exchange can be defined as an "engagement of groups of learners in online [...] collaboration projects with partners from other [...] geographical locations" (O'Dowd et al., 2020, pp. 146-147). Irrespective of the main goals of an exchange or the institutional purpose behind the implementation of one, a virtual exchange in its purest constellation, therefore, requires at least two groups of learners from at least two different locations and brings these groups together virtually, i.e., online. Note that O'Dowd (2023) also adds that "VEs differ from informal online interactions in that these initiatives are generally integrated in some way into students' formal learning and students' participation in the project is provided with some form of academic recognition [...]" (O'Dowd, 2023, p. 11).

As mentioned above, virtual exchanges have become a practical pedagogical tool to implement global skills training towards the internationalization of higher education and/or the internationalization of the curriculum. By nature, virtual exchange furthermore provides the basis to check all the boxes towards various goals laid out by universities' digitalization strategies. While "digital technologies [were in 2014] still seen as an add-on to the learning experience, and [were] not always an integral and accepted part of the teaching and learning process" (Morris, 2014, p. 1), universities across the globe have since, at least in their strategic efforts, emphasized digital transformation as a necessary and beneficial step towards a "sustainable education management strategy" (Mohamed Hashim et al., 2022, p. 3171). Extrinsic motivation such as meeting or working towards various institutional goals may, therefore, influence virtual exchange projects, their design and implementation. The purpose of a virtual exchange could, for example, focus on replacing or substituting traditional mobility programs (such as Erasmus mobility) in order to provide students who cannot leave their home institutions for whatever reason with a similar international experience at home. The learning outcomes of a virtual exchange project with such a purpose would have to represent those outcomes that are expected from an actual physical exchange. Whether this is even possible shall not be of discussion here; rather, it serves to exemplify motivation, considerations and impacts beyond those posed by the facilitators involved in the planning of a VE.

In addition to the institutional and strategic goals on the metalevel as well as the specific course goals on the microlevel, the learner groups involved in such a project can be allocated somewhere between the meta- and microlevels. The effects of VE on specific learner groups need to be taken into consideration and are especially relevant to interdisciplinary virtual exchange projects, especially when keeping in mind that learning outcomes vary according to the type of VE implemented (O'Dowd, 2021). For the purpose of our VE, studies and theoretical findings on VE and teacher training as well as VE in the foreign language classroom are of particular importance.

Virtual Exchange in Teacher Training

Global skills development is not limited to tertiary education or vocational training. On the contrary; throughout the last decades, global citizenship education has been identified as part of all levels of education, with some competences such as empathy development being part of the core curriculum in early childhood care (Foerch, 2020). Within this context, the importance of global competence development in future and current teachers has also been a well-discussed topic. A case study conducted in Europe between 2010 and 2011 found that "working in contexts of diversity increases reflexivity and competence within the team as it fosters an attitude of openness toward the other and toward questioning one's own perspective. [...] In the cases analyzed the aspect of diversity is mostly addressed through intercultural issues, which seem to be receiving particular attention in contemporary society," (Urban et al., 2012, p. 101) hinting at the societal importance of interculturality that has been steadily increasing since. Future teachers, thus, need to be prepared to take on the role as facilitator of global competences on one hand, and be globally competent themselves in order to teach effectively in multicultural classrooms (Slapac et al., 2023).

It is apparent that, even long before Covid-19, the literature dedicated to global competence in teacher training had been on a steady rise albeit "concentrating [primarily] on practice rather than theory" (Yemini et al., 2019, p. 87). Darji and Lang-Wojtasik (2014) identify four connected fields (i.e., (1) attitude and capability; (2) content and topics; (3) development and discovery; (4) grounded world view and humanity within which globally competent teachers operate, and suggest steps towards incorporating global competences into pre-service teacher curricula, for example, by finding new ways to foster international and global exchange (Darji & Lang-Wojtasik, 2014). In a more recent study from teacher training programs across fifteen European countries, Parmigiani et al. (2022) found that all participants were aware of the importance of global competence training in teacher education, but that implementing such training is still too much dependent on the individual lecturers on one hand, and too complicated or difficult to put into practice for technical and organizational reasons on the other. Especially with respect to virtual exchange as a form of global competence training, both of these findings seem true, but the continuously increasing number of virtual exchanges around the globe as well as a continuous stream of grant initiatives to support international educational projects indicate a steady uptake in the future.

In addition to transcultural experiences and global competence training, VE contributes to the development of numerous other skills that are particularly important for future teachers, for example, encountering and using digital tools, reflecting on virtual activity design and assessment, or dealing with common difficulties in a multi-faceted and diverse, interdisciplinary, heterogenous (online) classroom (O'Dowd, 2023). This opportunity is unique in that it prepares students in ways that ordinary courses cannot offer them.

Taking into consideration the benefits of a VE in teacher training while planning our Swiss-American VE, the Swiss group of students was expected to benefit from this exchange in particular because, in addition to the transcultural interactions with their American partners, they would be exposed to didactic methods and tools as well as assessments that they otherwise do not encounter, at least, on a regular basis.

Virtual Exchange in the Foreign Language Classroom

In the foreign language learning context, virtual exchange not only contributes to the development and the training of globally competent individuals, but it has taken on a special role with respect to linguistic development. VE has developed as a response to the features of the communicative approach that has dominated foreign language teaching for over 50 years (Dooly & Vinagre, 2022). In particular, the interaction between participants of a VE as part of a foreign language course focuses on communicative competences, emphasizes authentic and meaningful language use, aims to develop autonomous language learners, assigns a less central role to the teacher, and highlights cooperative and collaborative learning (Dooly & Vinagre, 2022). In addition to aligning with these core principles of the communicative approach, it is widely agreed upon that VE can impact foreign language acquisition in numerous other positive ways. O'Dowd and Dooly (2022) summarize some aspects of VE projects that are particularly beneficial to foreign language learners: In addition to engaging in the target language and thusly practicing fluency, VE may also contribute to an enhancement in the pragmatic use of the target language and to a better understanding of intercultural pragmatics or of the dynamics underlying the term *culture* in a globalized context This is, of course, not only true for VE in foreign language classrooms, but in any VE that is carried out in a language other than the participants' native languages.

Taking into consideration the benefits of a VE in the foreign language classroom while planning our Swiss-American VE, the US group of students was expected to benefit from this exchange in different ways than the Swiss group. First and foremost, the US students were expected to improve their language skills in the most basic sense, i.e., practice and improve vocabulary, maybe pronunciation and fluency. Furthermore, since the US students' previous course work and curriculum had not emphasized the languages and cultures of Switzerland, the US students would be exposed to new cultural and political content such as learning about a new educational system.

SWISS-AMERICAN PILOT

The Swiss-American virtual exchange was designed to integrate an international project experience into a common college class. The exchange was piloted during the fall semester of 2022. The current section provides the framework for the exchange, the design of the VE, its implementation and the results of the course evaluations, with emphasis on certain transcultural skills following the INCA framework.

The Setup of the VE

In this interdisciplinary setup, each student group was enrolled in their own independent course at their home universities. The Swiss course, a pedagogy class on the methods and didactics of culture in the foreign language classroom in a *Teaching German as a Foreign/Second Language* program, was scheduled to meet once a week on Tuesdays for 90 minutes, from 4h-5:30h CET, between late September and mid-December, with two one-week long breaks throughout the semester. During the semester of the VE, 28 students were enrolled in the class. There was no attendance policy (as prescribed by the institution), and stipulations of the study program prescribe that there only be one obligatory (final) graded assignment. The final graded assignment was to produce a podcast on a cultural topic and its didactic potentials and limitations in a German as a foreign language classroom.

The US class, an intermediate German conversation course in a *German as a Foreign Language* program, had a total enrollment of ten students. It was scheduled to meet three times a week (Monday, Wednesday, Friday) for 50 minutes each, from 11:15h-12:05h EST, between late August and the beginning of December (excluding a week-long break in November). During the semester of the VE, ten students were enrolled in the class. There was an attendance policy, and the final course grade was distributed across 14 assignments (e.g., concerned with pronunciation, cultural differences, newspapers and dialectal differences) throughout the semester.

The main goal of this virtual exchange pilot was to offer the US and Swiss students an opportunity to connect with peers overseas. While some of the intended learning outcomes overlapped, there were also slightly different learning outcomes for each of the groups. The shared learning outcomes included the improvement of certain skills deemed important in the development of global citizenship, based on skills expanded on in the 'INCA' (INCA, 2004; Prechtl & Lund, 2007).

For the Swiss students, the VE and its activities were designed to help them reach the overarching class goals. In particular, the VE activities aimed at: (i) considering the term *culture,* and the ability to reflect on it against the backdrop of globalization, mobility, and migration; (ii) understanding the connection between language and culture, and the ability to analyze communicative situations in which differing cultural patterns can be identified; and (iii) reflecting on the term *cultural studies* and the ability to use appropriate methods to include *cultural knowledge* in the classroom.

The US students, on the contrary, were much more focused on the communicative aspect of their L2 German, which went beyond the VE and its inherent practical nature. For example, one class goal was (i) to familiarize the students with linguistic terminology relevant for the discussion of dialects. Another goal was (ii) to make the students understand their own linguistic background by comparing their dialectal features to those of other students in the classroom but also to their own origin and life stages with different geographical locations.

Virtual Exchange Design and Implementation

To plan the VE project, the authors decided to design activities that would contribute to the achievement of the learning outcomes on one hand, and that will align (with the graded) assignments on the other. As stated above, by the stipulations of the study program, the Swiss students could only be asked to complete one graded assignment. Hence, the activities of the VE were designed to serve as instructional scaffolding in that each activity would bring them a step closer towards completing their final project. The US course's framework allowed much more leeway. Some assignments, such as presentations and reflections, were directly related to one or several activities from the VE.

The main activities of the exchange were scheduled across approximately four weeks during the middle of the semesters and included synchronous online meetings in addition to and outside of any of the two official class times. The project groups had to schedule these meetings themselves, taking into consideration their individual schedules and the time zones. Several activities leading up to these initial, individual group meetings started earlier and were addressed in the respective sessions, for example, reaching out to partners overseas via email, or adding to the VE's digital introductory board. Thus, the VE pilot overall, and also some of the activities, consisted of three phases, visualized below, making use of activities and steps resembling all stages of Dooly's (2022) *Collaborate-o-meter*, which categorizes three stages of telecollaboration, namely *Cogwheels, Zig-zag,* and *Show & Tell.* Without diving too deeply into the specifics, *Cogwheels* describes *interdependent* work between the partners, the *Zig-zag* stage refers to partial exchanges in which one common output is the result of independent group work, and *Show & Tell* usually focuses on information exchange with minimal collaborative learning (Dooly, 2022, p. 20).

Table 1. VE design in phases following Dooly (2022)

Phase 1 - Preparation	Phase 2 - Collaboration	Phase 3 - Finalization
Show & Tell information exchange; introductions	Cogwheels active exchange between the students; online meetings in international groups	Zig-zag integrating others' work into a bigger output

Source: Own elaboration

During Phase 1, the introduction to the virtual exchange and the different activities and requirements were introduced in the respective classrooms, independently from each other. The groups were assigned randomly (two to three Swiss students were grouped with one US student). US and Swiss students started to interact through a digital whiteboard on Miro.com (RealtimeBoard Inc., 2022) prepared as the classroom whiteboard. They introduced themselves and commented on what the others had written, asking and answering questions. Furthermore, they exchanged emails with each other.

Phase 2 consisted of three to four online meetings and contained numerous activities. For example, after having been introduced to dialects of (Swiss) German, the US students utilized a dialect quiz (Brupbacher & Leemann, 2015) to determine the dialectal origin of each of their Swiss partners. They then compared the results to their actual geographical home area to illustrate the permeability of dialectal borders and created a *dialect map* of the Swiss students. This was the focus of a graded presentation in the US classroom. The US students shared their findings with the Swiss class. The *dialect maps* provided insights into Swiss plurilingualism that the Swiss students could include into their *podcast* activity. Another example of activities informing the meetings of Phase 2 of the VE was the *cultural* topic that the Swiss students' podcasts needed to discuss. Swiss students (pre-service teachers) discussed their ideas with US students (language students) to elicit their point of views and to, ultimately, decide how linguistically and culturally *appropriate* their topics would be. The input from the US students was crucial to initiate the reflective process necessary to design foreign language (FL) culture activities that are didactically appropriate and sound.

During Phase 3 of the VE, both classrooms included reflection activities. In the US, this was done through oral classroom presentations, while reflections and lessons learned were discussed in the Swiss students' podcasts. The individual groups were free to decide if they wanted to include their international partners in the podcast recordings. Some did.

Evaluations

After the conclusion of the project and the semesters had ended, the project participants filled out a class evaluation to rate the course overall as well as the VE. Responses were anonymous and participation was voluntary. The questions included in the course evaluation aimed to elicit general feedback from the participants and to get an overall impression of how successfully the VE was implemented. The results report on the self-reflections provided by the participants.

In order to better understand the students' transcultural competences and their development throughout the VE, students were asked to indicate both the importance of the use of specific skills during the VE and the students' perception of personal improvement of specific skills throughout the VE. Following the INCA assessment (INCA, 2004; Prechtl & Lund, 2007), the skills the authors included in the questionnaire were linguistic skills, communicative skills, awareness of the similarities and differences of other perspectives/worldviews, emotional resilience, relationship building, empathy, and flexibility.[1] The answers are provided in the following tables, presented according to specific skills. The results are presented to compare the answers between those students who indicated an overall satisfaction with the VE (N=21 out of 32) and those who were not satisfied (N=11/32) (see Table 2), and the answers within the satisfactions categories between the Swiss and US student groups. Note that none of the questions of the evaluation were obligatory, so some students chose not to answer all questions.[2]

As exemplified in Table 2, all students, no matter their affiliation or overall satisfaction of the VE, deem *linguistic skills* (language skills) important or very important. Additionally, reflecting on their own progression throughout the project, all of the US students, both satisfied and dissatisfied, felt that their linguistic skills had improved over the period of the collaboration. By contrast, roughly one third of the Swiss students, both satisfied and dissatisfied, indicated that their linguistic skills had not improved, while one third indicated that it did not apply to them, and another third saw at least minor improvement. These results are not surprising considering that the collaboration language was German, the field of study of the US students, and the first language (L1) of the majority of the Swiss students.

Table 2. Linguistic skills in VE - (Self-assessment of) importance and improvement

	Satisfied						Dissatisfied					
	US Students		CH Students		Overall		US Students		CH Students		Overall	
	N	Percent	N	Percent	N	Percent	N	Percent	N	Percent	N	Percent
Importance of Linguistic skills during the VE												
not important	0	0%	1	8%	1	5%	0	0%	0	0%	0	0%
less important	0	0%	1	8%	1	5%	0	0%	0	0%	0	0%
important	5	63%	6	46%	11	52%	1	100%	9	90%	10	91%
very important	3	38%	5	38%	8	38%	0	0%	1	10%	1	9%
Improvement of Linguistic skills after the VE												
does not apply	0	0%	4	31%	4	19%	0	0%	3	30%	3	27%
no improvement	0	0%	5	38%	5	24%	0	0%	4	40%	4	36%
minor improvement	1	13%	3	23%	4	19%	1	100%	3	30%	4	36%
some improvement	6	75%	1	8%	7	33%	0	0%	0	0%	0	0%
significant improvement	1	13%	0	0%	1	5%	0	0%	0	0%	0	0%

Source: Own elaboration

The results pertaining to the importance and improvement of the students' communicative skills, summarized in Table 3 below, are similar in the US student group. All of them, despite their overall satisfaction of the collaboration, deemed this skill important to succeed in the project, and rated their individual progress at least as "minor improvement". Contrasting communicative skills with linguistic skills, the Swiss students' answers are not surprising. While only a total of three out of 23 Swiss students rank communicative skills as *less important* (2nd line in Table 3) for a successful collaboration, the rest of them (N=20/23) indicate that this skill set is important for a successful VE. However, less than half of them (N=10/23) think that their communicative skills actually improved throughout the project.

Table 3. Communicative skills in VE - (Self-assessment of) importance and improvement

	Satisfied						Dissatisfied					
	US Students		CH Students		Overall		US Students		CH Students		Overall	
	N	Percent	N	Percent	N	Percent	N	Percent	N	Percent	N	Percent
Importance of Communicative skills during the VE												
not important	0	0%	0	0%	0	0%	0	0%	0	0%	0	0%
less important	0	0%	1	8%	1	5%	0	0%	2	20%	2	18%
important	3	38%	11	85%	14	67%	1	100%	6	60%	7	64%
very important	5	63%	1	8%	6	29%	0	0%	2	20%	2	18%
Improvement of Communicative skills after the VE												
does not apply	0	0%	1	8%	1	5%	0	0%	2	20%	2	18%
no improvement	0	0%	6	46%	6	29%	0	0%	4	40%	4	36%
minor improvement	2	25%	4	31%	6	29%	1	100%	3	30%	4	36%
some improvement	4	50%	2	15%	6	29%	0	0%	1	10%	1	9%
significant improvement	2	25%	0	0%	2	10%	0	0%	0	0%	0	0%

Source: Own elaboration

With respect to the skill to be aware of and consider perspectives other than one's own, the following can be observed: 95% (20/21) of all overall satisfied students deem these skills to be important or very important, while a third of all dissatisfied students think that it is less or not important. The same number of dissatisfied students indicated that they saw no improvement (or N/A) after the VE. On the other hand, none of the satisfied students said that their skills had not improved or stagnated. All of them saw at least minor improvement in their awareness of other perspectives. Note also that those students who indicated no importance or no improvement were only Swiss students, i.e., students enrolled in teacher training.

Table 4. Awareness of other perspectives: (Self-assessment of) importance and improvement

	Satisfied						Dissatisfied					
	US Students		CH Students		Overall		US Students		CH Students		Overall	
	N	Percent	N	Percent	N	Percent	N	Percent	N	Percent	N	Percent
Importance of Awareness of other perspectives during the VE												
not important	0	0%	0	0%	0	0%	0	0%	2	22%	2	20%
less important	1	13%	0	0%	1	5%	1	100%	1	11%	2	20%
important	6	75%	11	85%	17	81%	0	0%	3	33%	3	30%
very important	1	13%	2	15%	3	14%	0	0%	3	33%	3	30%
Improvement of Awareness of other perspectives after the VE												
does not apply	0	0%	0	0%	0	0%	0	0%	1	11%	1	10%
no improvement	0	0%	0	0%	0	0%	0	0%	3	33%	3	30%
minor improvement	0	0%	6	46%	6	29%	1	100%	4	44%	5	50%
some improvement	7	88%	6	46%	13	62%	0	0%	1	11%	1	10%
significant improvement	1	13%	1	8%	2	10%	0	0%	0	0%	0	0%

Source: Own elaboration

Similar to the previous skills, the great majority of Swiss students believe that emotional resilience is a skill less or not important to contribute to a virtual collaboration, as shown in Table 5. The self-assessed improvement resembles these numbers. On the other hand, most US students, regardless of satisfaction, thought it was an important skill (N=5/9), and, surprisingly, six of them felt that their emotional resilience had improved throughout the collaboration.

Table 5. Emotional resilience: (Self-assessment of) importance and improvement

	Satisfied						Dissatisfied					
	US Students		CH Students		Overall		US Students		CH Students		Overall	
	N	Percent	N	Percent	N	Percent	N	Percent	N	Percent	N	Percent
Importance of Emotional resilience during the VE												
not important	0	0%	4	31%	4	19%	0	0%	2	20%	2	18%
less important	4	50%	9	69%	13	62%	0	0%	6	60%	6	55%
important	4	50%	0	0%	4	19%	1	100%	2	20%	3	27%
very important	0	0%	0	0%	0	0%	0	0%	0	0%	0	0%
Improvement of Emotional resilience after the VE												
does not apply	1	13%	3	23%	4	19%	0	0%	3	33%	3	30%
no improvement	2	25%	8	62%	10	48%	0	0%	5	56%	5	50%
minor improvement	3	38%	2	15%	5	24%	0	0%	1	11%	1	10%
some improvement	2	25%	0	0%	2	10%	1	100%	0	0%	1	10%
significant improvement	0	0%	0	0%	0	0%	0	0%	0	0%	0	0%

Source: Own elaboration

The two countries also differ in their responses regarding relationship building, as visualized in Table 6. Sixteen out of 22 Swiss students deem it less or not important for a successful VE, while only one third of US students (3/9) share this opinion. However, looking at their self-indicated improvement, only ten Swiss students either checked the options *does not apply* or *no improvement.* Two US students fall into that same category. In this category, there is a correlation between satisfied students' judgment on the importance of *relationship building* within VE and the self-assessed improvement after collaboration. Amongst the students who were overall satisfied with the VE, the judgment on the importance of *relationship building* is almost split between less important and important, and almost 70% of these students indicated an improvement after the project collaboration. On the other end, 90% of the dissatisfied students deem this skill less or not important at all, and 70% indicate to not have seen an improvement or *not applicable*.

Table 6. Importance of relationship building: (Self-assessment of) importance and improvement

	Satisfied						**Dissatisfied**					
	US Students		**CH Students**		**Overall**		**US Students**		**CH Students**		**Overall**	
	N	**Percent**	**N**	**Percent**	**N**	**Percent**	**N**	**Percent**	**N**	**Percent**	**N**	**Percent**
Importance of Relationship building during the VE												
not important	1	13%	1	8%	2	10%	1	100%	2	22%	3	30%
less important	1	13%	7	54%	8	38%	0	0%	6	67%	6	60%
important	5	63%	5	38%	10	48%	0	0%	1	11%	1	10%
very important	1	13%	0	0%	1	5%	0	0%	0	0%	0	0%
Improvement of Relationship building after the VE												
does not apply	0	0%	1	8%	1	5%	1	100%	3	33%	4	40%
no improvement	1	13%	3	23%	4	19%	0	0%	3	33%	3	30%
minor improvement	4	50%	6	46%	10	48%	0	0%	3	33%	3	30%
some improvement	3	38%	3	23%	6	29%	0	0%	0	0%	0	0%
significant improvement	0	0%	0	0%	0	0%	0	0%	0	0%	0	0%

Source: Own elaboration

Empathy as a skill to successfully work in a VE was mostly deemed important by satisfied US and Swiss students as well by the majority of the dissatisfied Swiss students. Concerning the students' reflections on their own improvement of this skill, seven out of nine US students seem to have improved to some extent (see Table 7). Out of 22 Swiss students who answered this question, only ten indicated that they had improved this skill throughout the collaboration.

Table 7. Empathy: (Self-assessment of) importance and improvement

	Satisfied						**Dissatisfied**					
	US Students		**CH Students**		**Overall**		**US Students**		**CH Students**		**Overall**	
	N	**Percent**	**N**	**Percent**	**N**	**Percent**	**N**	**Percent**	**N**	**Percent**	**N**	**Percent**
Importance of Empathy during the VE												
not important	0	0%	0	0%	0	0%	0	0%	1	10%	1	9%
less important	1	13%	2	15%	3	14%	1	100%	2	20%	3	27%
important	5	63%	11	85%	16	76%	0	0%	6	60%	6	55%
very important	2	25%	0	0%	2	10%	0	0%	1	10%	1	9%
Improvement of Empathy after the VE												
does not apply	1	13%	3	23%	4	19%	0	0%	3	33%	3	30%
no improvement	1	13%	4	31%	5	24%	0	0%	2	22%	2	20%
minor improvement	3	38%	4	31%	7	33%	1	100%	4	44%	5	50%
some improvement	3	38%	2	15%	5	24%	0	0%	0	0%	0	0%
significant improvement	0	0%	0	0%	0	0%	0	0%	0	0%	0	0%

Source: Own elaboration

With respect to flexibility, the majority of students, regardless of their affiliation or overall satisfaction, indicated that it was an important skill for a successful VE, see Table 8. Looking at their development throughout the collaboration, fewer students saw an improvement. Amongst the US students, eight out of ten shared that they believe to be more flexible; however, only 12 out of 22 Swiss students saw an improvement in this area.

Table 8. Flexibility: (Self-assessment of) importance and improvement

	Satisfied						Dissatisfied					
	US Students		CH Students		Overall		US Students		CH Students		Overall	
	N	Percent	N	Percent	N	Percent	N	Percent	N	Percent	N	Percent
Importance of Flexibility during the VE												
not important	0	0%	1	8%	1	5%	0	0%	1	10%	1	9%
less important	1	13%	4	31%	5	24%	0	0%	2	20%	2	18%
important	6	75%	8	62%	14	67%	0	0%	6	60%	6	55%
very important	1	13%	0	0%	1	5%	1	100%	1	10%	2	18%
Improvement of Flexibility after the VE												
does not apply	0	0%	2	15%	2	10%	0	0%	2	22%	2	20%
no improvement	1	13%	3	23%	4	19%	0	0%	3	33%	3	30%
minor improvement	3	38%	5	38%	8	38%	0	0%	3	33%	3	30%
some improvement	3	38%	3	23%	6	29%	1	100%	1	11%	2	20%
Significant improvement	1	13%	0	0%	1	5%	0	0%	0	0%	0	0%

Source: Own elaboration

In addition to the identification and reflection on improvement of these skills, students were asked to answer some questions regarding the communication practices and difficulties within their project groups, to share if and to what extent certain tools facilitated communication with their peers, and to comment on the overall collaborative project.

Regarding communication practices and difficulties within their assigned groups as well as online collaboration tools, the evaluations were overall positive, but nothing seemed of particular importance or surprising. Amongst 33 answers, seven students indicated that agreeing on a time for online group meetings was difficult, but only two indicated that general communication throughout the project was rather difficult. Among all online communication tools used, video conference tools and emails were the tools that contributed to the groups' collaborative assignments and activities the most compared to, for example, social media applications and messengers such as WhatsApp or Instagram. Furthermore, several students indicated that they enjoyed the Miro (RealtimeBoard Inc., 2022).

The comment sections gave students the opportunity to share anything regarding their individual learning experiences, main takeaway points, or suggestions for changes. With respect to learning experiences, the answers mostly highlighted new, often personal knowledge students learned from each other; for example, regarding student life in the US or Switzerland. The answers pertaining to the main takeaway points show that students reflected on the VE in the context of their respective classes, and, partially also, tried to translate their experiences to their professional and personal lives beyond the classroom. For example, one student wrote "to understand different perspectives and to adapt oneself", another one shared "patience and courage to get out of your comfort zone is essential [...]", and another one commented on how motivation contributed to the success of the collaboration.

While the exchange during the meetings were evaluated positively, students also shared some criticism. Some of it was partially expected, for example, that there would be some disagreement regarding the number of online meetings between the group's members (some said they wished there had been more, others indicated they wanted less) or how to handle the time difference between the two countries. However, the main criticism was that the goals should have been clearer. This criticism was mainly expressed on the Swiss side: 5 out of 13 comments from the Swiss students asserted that the goals and steps involved in certain activities had not been clearly communicated by the instructor.

DISCUSSION

The evaluations revealed that 21 out of 32 students indicated that they were satisfied with the VE (Table 2). Furthermore, the self-indicated improvement across most skills leads us to believe that this VE was an overall successful pilot that needs some tweaking to further enhance the experience for the participants.

Students seem happy about the digital tools that were used throughout and the idea that a collaborative project with students from another country was possible. Of course, due to the nature of the project and its inaugural character, several challenges arose during the VE. Some of them were anticipated, while others were not. These challenges and issues are presented below to raise caution for future VE projects like this one.

One organizational aspect is attributed to the different structure inherent to respective semester plans in two university systems. The current American university started its fall semester approximately one month (i.e., end of August) before the Swiss university did (i.e., end of September). In a similar vein, the time difference between Switzerland and the US posed a challenge when it came to the actual implementation of the project. In contrast to synchronous meetings, asynchronous communication, e.g., via emails, does neither require dedicated time commitments nor immediate responses. Yet, both types of communication are needed, as one, the synchronous, presupposed the other, the asynchronous, in our VE. In other words, to be able to meet virtually requires the partners to agree on a set time via an asynchronous medium. Neither one of these two was free of challenges.

An additional organizational factor were discrepancies in the Swiss and American attendance policies. While the US university made attendance mandatory, the Swiss partner school was not allowed to in accordance with regulatory policies. Optional attendance of classes allows for a different mindset in the Swiss students, resulting in some students missing (the majority of) classes and, thus, lacking knowledge of important concepts and other background information regarding the VE and its integration into their assignment crucial to actively contribute to the success of this project. Hence, some of the group members were not aware of the minimum number of synchronous group meetings, nor of their respective meeting times, or even the content or activities related to the meetings. Unless there is some way of holding everyone involved in a VE accountable to ensure equal contribution to the project and its related activities, planning a VE should include a risk analysis and a flexible strategy to deal with potential issues such as these. These findings provide support for O'Dowd et al.'s (2020) findings on the facilitators' role to achieve a successful VE.

With regards to the actual synchronous online meetings that the students set up on their own following a suggested timeline, several challenges beyond the time difference and the lack of preparation were identified. One striking issue relates to the content discussed with the respective partners. It is crucial to provide the students with clear instructions and precise language. Furthermore, the instructor needs to support the students in any preparation work to ensure that they attend the meetings prepared. This issue is related to the attendance policy above in that Swiss students' optional attendance contributed to a lack of preparation of non-graded activities in some students which, in turn, caused stress on their US partners' side because the American students were often dependent on the Swiss students' input during the online meetings. Again, this reiterates the need for accountability in designing a VE.

Despite these hiccups, most students seem to have enjoyed the overall experience of the project and shared comments and ratings that allows us to conclude that the VE contributed to their academic development and training.

Pilot and Teacher Training

This project was piloted with Swiss students enrolled in a teacher training program. Having established the importance of certain *global* skills that teachers should possess to successfully deal with a culturally diverse and ever-changing student body, the results touching on attitudes towards and self-reflective improvement of certain skills are particularly meaningful.

Linguistic and communicative skills, awareness of the similarities and differences of other perspectives and worldviews as well as empathy and flexibility were deemed as important skills to have for a successful VE. Emotional resilience and relationship building are considered less important for Swiss students, which comes as a small surprise considering that these skills are crucial to dealing with individuals (Palomera et al., 2008). One would have expected that these two skills be deemed more important taking into account that the abilities to adapt to stressful situations and to build lasting personal bonds are crucial to connect with individuals, i.e., possibly their own future students (Selvi, 2010). However, maybe it is exactly this reason why the Swiss students think they are less important: because they differentiate between these abilities in in-person settings (such as when they are in a classroom with their own students) and virtual collaborations, which are temporary, short, online projects.

With respect to the individual reflection on how specific skills have improved throughout the pilot, two results stand out in particular, namely, emotional resilience and communicative skills. Out of 22 students who answered this question, only three saw minor improvement of this emotional resilience, while 13 saw no improvement and six checked that it did not apply to them. This is surprising and disappointing because the authors thought this pilot would help students build this skill by finding ways to adapt to stressful situations inherent to having to collaborate across different cultures, potential languages, and time zones. Furthermore, it is surprising that, among the ones who answered the question relating to the improvement of their communicative skills, half of them saw minor or some improvement, but another half did not notice an improvement (plus some who said it did not apply to them). This may be related to the insecurities they indicated pertaining to the content and goals of the collaboration, and how the collaborative meetings would contribute to their seminar's final assignment.

Note that, of course, there were some students who shared that the virtual collaboration contributed greatly to their final assignment or, for example, that these meetings taught them to *effectively discuss cultural aspects in German class,* emphasizing the point of view of those students who indicated their communicative skills had improved. Especially with regards to their professional development as future teachers, the comments were mostly positive. One student wrote that they enjoyed working with a German as a *foreign* language group for once because the study program's main focus is preparing them to teach German as a *second* language, or that they learned new methods to integrate 'culture' into their lessons, or how certain cultural topics come across to a German as a *foreign* language learner.

Pilot and the FL Classroom

As mentioned above, the VE was one component of a larger semester plan. Yet, it had the potential to provide some major benefits to the foreign language learners. In particular, it was expected that interaction with L1 German speakers contributes to the improvement of linguistic as well as communicative skills (cf. Lamy & Goodfellow, 1999; Van Lier, 1989). Indeed, as seen in Table 2 and 3, both of these skills improved for the US participants. However, in addition, awareness of other perspectives also improved for all participants (Table 4). Importance of relationship building, empathy as well as flexibility also improved, yet to a lesser extent (Tables 6-8). In contrast, emotional resilience did not improve according to the self-ratings (Table 5). Given the nature of the VE, it comes as no surprise to see a self-reported improvement on six of the seven INCA skills. Each of these is relevant as it pertains to the development of an L2. Work by Martin (2020) suggests that students show significant improvement in terms of linguistic abilities when additional opportunities to engage with the language outside of the classroom are provided. Another important factor relates to the hesitancy and even anxiety students have when they are in an official classroom setting (Horwitz et al., 1986), whereas it is possible that the home environment and the lack of an instructor facilitated engagement with the L2 language and VE partner. In addition, the fact that the VE provided the US students with an additional opportunity outside of the classroom to be exposed to authentic L1 (Swiss) German had a positive influence on the engagement, motivation and language learning of the US students. Thus, FL classroom environments can benefit when a VE is implemented, even if the number of synchronous meetings with the partners is limited.

CONCLUSION

The current chapter set out to provide an overview of a VE between a Swiss and a US university in light of global competence and the importance and subsequent development of the skills as defined by INCA. Each contributor of the VE had different goals in mind as mentioned in the setup of the VE. Thus, not every INCA skill is applicable to all of the students who participated in this project. For instance, the use and improvement of linguistic skills is more relevant to the students from the US university than it is for the Swiss counterpart due to the language of communication of the VE being German. Zooming in on the self-reported ratings, one side benefited more from the VE than the other - even beyond the linguistic component just discussed. The US partners indicated that their skills improved more than those of the Swiss interlocutors. In particular, with respect to the skills of *emotional resilience* and *communicative skills,* Swiss students indicated that they did not improve as much or at all. However, individual comments emphasize that the VE contributed to their pedagogical development (e.g., how to discuss culture; use of a new digital tool).

Besides the content of the VE, the authors believe that is first and foremost the organizational structure that impacted the development of the Swiss partners (e.g., due to the lack of attendance policies and *graded* assignments). Thus, accountability and commitment from the students' side seem to be one of the most crucial requirements for a successful VE. Future designers of such projects must, therefore, thoroughly consider regulatory conditions and organizational prerequisites posed by their institutions.

REFERENCES

Barrett, M., & Golubeva, I. (2022). From intercultural communicative competence to intercultural citizenship: Preparing young people for citizenship in a culturally diverse democratic world. In T. McConachy, I. Golubeva, & M. Wagner (Eds.), *Intercultural learning in language education and beyond* (pp. 60–83). Multilingual Matters. doi:10.21832/9781800412613-011

Baumgratz, G. (1995). Language, culture and global competence: An essay on ambiguity. *European Journal of Education*, *30*(4), 437–447. doi:10.2307/1503516

Brupbacher, M., & Leemann, A. (2015). Grüezi, Moin, Servus - Wie wir wo sprechen [Grüezi, Moin, Servus – How we speak where]. *Tages Anzeiger.* https://www.tagesanzeiger.ch/_external/interactive/2015/sprachatlas_v8/index.html#/questions

Byram, M. (2009). The intercultural speaker and the pedagogy of foreign language education. In D. K. Deardorff (Ed.), *The SAGE handbook of intercultural competence* (pp. 321–332). SAGE Publications, Inc. doi:10.4135/9781071872987.n18

Byram, M. (2021). *Teaching and assessing intercultural communicative competence: Revisited.* Multilingual Matters. doi:10.21832/9781800410251

Darji, B. B., & Lang-Wojtasik, G. (2014). Preparing globally competent teachers: Indo-German perspectives on teacher training. *International Journal of Development Education and Global Learning*, *6*(3), 49–62. doi:10.18546/IJDEGL.06.3.04

Deardorff, D. K., & Jones, E. (2012). Intercultural competence. In D. K. Deardorff, H. de Wit, J. D. Heyl, & T. Adams (Eds.), *The SAGE handbook of international higher education* (pp. 283–304). SAGE Publications, Inc. doi:10.4135/9781452218397.n16

Dooly, M. (2022). The evolution of virtual exchange and assessment practices. In A. Czura & M. Dooly (Eds.), Assessing virtual exchange in foreign language courses at tertiary level (pp. 13-27). Research-publishing.net. doi:10.14705/rpnet.2022.59.1407

Dooly, M., & Vinagre, M. (2022). Research into practice: Virtual exchange in language teaching and learning. *Language Teaching*, *55*(3), 392–406. doi:10.1017/S0261444821000069

Foerch, D. F. (2020). Global competence begins in preschool: An investigation of how to nurture empathy in young children. *Contrapontos*, *20*(1), 2–19. doi:10.14210/contrapontos.v20n1.p02-19

Helm, F., & Beaven, A. (2020). *Designing and implementing virtual exchange – a collection of case studies*. Research-publishing.net.

Horwitz, E. K., Horwitz, M. B., & Cope, J. (1986). Foreign language classroom anxiety. *Modern Language Journal*, *70*(2), 125–132. doi:10.1111/j.1540-4781.1986.tb05256.x

INCA. (2004). *INCA Assessee Manual.* Leonardo da Vinci VII Project. https://migrant-integration.ec.europa.eu/sites/default/files/2009-08/docl_9372_146280285.pdf

Lamy, M.-N., & Goodfellow, R. (1999). 'Reflective conversation' in the virtual language classroom. *Language Learning & Technology*, *2*(2), 43–61.

Leask, B. (2015). *Internationalizing the curriculum*. Routledge. doi:10.4324/9781315716954

Martin, I. A. (2020). Pronunciation development and instruction in distance language learning. *Language Learning & Technology*, *24*(1), 86–106. https://doi.org/https://doi.org/10125/44711

Mohamed Hashim, M. A., Tlemsani, I., & Matthews, R. (2022). Higher education strategy in digital transformation. *Education and Information Technologies*, *27*(3), 3171–3195. doi:10.1007/s10639-021-10739-1 PMID:34539217

Morris, N. (2014). *Moving higher education forward in a digital age: Realising a digital strategy*. International Conference E-Learning 2014, Lisbon, Portugal.

O'Dowd, R. (2023). *Internationalising higher education and the role of virtual exchange*. Routledge.

O'Dowd, R., & Dooly, M. (2022). Exploring teachers' professional development through participation in virtual exchange. *ReCALL*, *34*(1), 21–36. doi:10.1017/S0958344021000215

O'Dowd, R., Sauro, S., & Spector-Cohen, E. (2020). The role of pedagogical mentoring in virtual exchange. *TESOL Quarterly*, *54*(1), 146–172. doi:10.1002/tesq.543

OECD. (2019). An OECD Learning Framework 2030. In G. Bast, E. G. Carayannis, & D. F. J. Campbell (Eds.), *The future of education and labor. Arts, research, innovation and society* (pp. 23–35). Springer International Publishing. doi:10.1007/978-3-030-26068-2_3

Palomera, R., Fernández-Berrocal, P., & Brackett, M. A. (2008). Emotional intelligence as a basic competency in pre-service teacher training: Some evidence. *Electronic Journal of Research in Educational Psychology*, *6*(2), 437–454.

Parmigiani, D., Jones, S.-L., Kunnari, I., & Nicchia, E. (2022). Global competence and teacher education programmes. A European perspective. *Cogent Education*, *9*(1), 2022996. doi:10.1080/2331186X.2021.2022996

Prechtl, E., & Lund, A. D. (2007). Intercultural competence and assessment: Perspectives from the INCA Project. In K. Helga & S.-O. Helen (Eds.), *Handbook of intercultural communication* (pp. 467–490). De Gruyter Mouton. doi:10.1515/9783110198584.5.467

RealtimeBoard Inc. (2022). *Miro online whiteboard*. https://miro.com/

Selvi, K. (2010). Teachers' competencies. *Cultura (Iasi, Romania)*, *7*(1), 167–175. doi:10.5840/cultura20107133

Semaan, G., & Yamazaki, K. (2015). The relationship between global competence and language learning motivation: An empirical study in critical language classrooms. *Foreign Language Annals*, *48*(3), 511–520. doi:10.1111/flan.12146

Slapac, A. (2021). Advancing students' global competency through English language learning in Romania: An exploratory qualitative case study of four English language teachers. *Journal of Research in Childhood Education*, *35*(2), 231–247. doi:10.1080/02568543.2021.1880993

Slapac, A., Coppersmith, S. A., & Cheng, J. (2023). Global competence development through the lens of graduate students in action research courses. In C. E. Ullom & N. Guler (Eds.), *At school in the world: Developing globally engaged teachers* (pp. 98–117). Rowman & Littlefield.

Song, K. H., Kerkhoff, S. N., & Slapac, A. (2023). Educating racially, culturally, and linguistically diverse children in a global era: The world at home and at home in the world. In J. Chitiyo & Z. Pietrantoni (Eds.), *Social justice and culturally-affirming education in K-12 settings* (pp. 1–22). IGI Global. doi:10.4018/978-1-6684-6386-4.ch001

United States Department of State. (2018). *U.S. Study Abroad Continues to Increase and Diversify.* https://studyabroad.state.gov/value-study-abroad/highlights-and-activities/us-study-abroad-continues-increase-and-diversify

Urban, M., Vandenbroeck, M., Lazzari, A., Van Laere, K., & Peeters, J. (2012). Competence requirements in early childhood education and care. Final Report. *Online Submission.*

Van Lier, L. (1989). Reeling, writhing, drawling, stretching, and fainting in coils: Oral proficiency interviews as conversation. *TESOL Quarterly*, *23*(3), 489–508. doi:10.2307/3586922

Van Roekel, D. (2010). *Global competence is a 21st century imperative.* NEA Policy and Practice Department.

Weenink, D. (2008). Cosmopolitanism as a form of capital: Parents preparing their children for a globalizing world. *Sociology*, *42*(6), 1089–1106. doi:10.1177/0038038508096935

Yemini, M., Tibbitts, F., & Goren, H. (2019). Trends and caveats: Review of literature on global citizenship education in teacher training. *Teaching and Teacher Education*, *77*(1), 77–89. doi:10.1016/j.tate.2018.09.014

ADDITIONAL READING

Bennett, M. J. (2004). Becoming interculturally competent. In J. S. Wurzel (Ed.), *Toward multiculturalism: A reader in multicultural education* (pp. 62–77). Intercultural Resource Corporation.

Boix Mansilla, V., & Jackson, A. W. (2022). *Educating for global competence: Preparing our students to engage the world.* ASCD.

De Wit, H. (2011). *Internationalization of higher education in the United States of America and Europe: A historical, comparative, and conceptual analysis.* Palgrave Macmillan.

Delamare Le Deist, F., & Winterton, J. (2005). What is competence? *Human Resource Development International*, *8*(1), 27–46. doi:10.1080/1367886042000338227

Hunter, B., White, G. P., & Godbey, G. C. (2006). What does it mean to be globally competent? *Journal of Studies in International Education*, *10*(3), 267–285. doi:10.1177/1028315306286930

Jones, E., Coelen, R., Beelen, J., & de Wit, H. (2016). *Global and local internationalization.* SensePublishers-Rotterdam., doi:10.1007/978-94-6300-301-8

Jones, E., & Killick, D. (2013). Graduate attributes and the internationalized curriculum: Embedding a global outlook in disciplinary learning outcomes. *Journal of Studies in International Education*, *17*(2), 165–182. doi:10.1177/1028315312473655

Killick, D. (2020). Beyond competencies and silos: Embedding graduate capabilities for a multicultural globalizing world across the mainstream curriculum. *Research in Comparative and International Education*, *15*(1), 27–35. doi:10.1177/1745499920901946

O'Dowd, R. (2020). A transnational model of virtual exchange for global citizenship education. *Language Teaching*, *53*(4), 477–490. doi:10.1017/S0261444819000077

Winterton, J., Delamare Le Deist, F., & Stringfellow, E. (2006). *Typology of knowledge, skills and competences: Clarification of the concept and prototype*. Office for Official Publications of the European Communities.

KEY TERMS AND DEFINITIONS

Global Competence: An umbrella term that refers to a specific set of skills and attributes often used within the context of internationalization in higher education.

INCA: The Intercultural Competence Assessment (INCA) project is a framework for the assessment of intercultural competence linked to language and subject knowledge competence.

Internationalization: Internationalization refers to any efforts carried out or implemented by universities in order to meet the global demands and visions of an institution. In the teaching context, the internationalization of the curriculum includes designing syllabi and classroom activities that take into consideration global perspectives and international exposure.

Miro: An online tool (RealtimeBoard Inc., 2022) to create password-protected digital whiteboards, so that students and other participants can work together on collaborative projects.

Second: and Foreign Language Learning: Second language learning happens in the region where the learner lives, while foreign language learning is the learning of a language from a region outside of where it is learned. For the purpose of this chapter, the distinction is not necessary.

Teacher Training: Higher-education programs for future teachers.

Virtual Exchange: Purposeful, planned, educational online interactions and collaborations between groups of learners from different geographical regions, facilitated by teaching faculty.

ENDNOTES

1. Please refer to the INCA assessment guide for detailed information about the assessment and the different competence categories INCA. (2004). *INCA Assessee Manual*.
2. Note that the percentages provided in the tables are rounded automatically to avoid decimal points. Therefore, adding the percentages do not always equal 100.

Chapter 11
Self- and Socially-Shared Metacognitive Regulation and Engagement in Online Collaborative Discussions:
Constructs and Students' Characteristics

Theerapong Binali
https://orcid.org/0000-0002-8344-6985
National Taiwan Normal University, Taiwan

Yossiri Yossatorn
https://orcid.org/0000-0002-0740-2788
Navamindradhiraj University, Thailand

ABSTRACT

The purpose of this study was twofold. First, the study developed two survey instruments that measured students' metacognitive practice and social and emotional engagement in online collaborative discussions. Both instruments were developed by modifying from existing scales and empirical studies. An exploratory factor analysis (EFA) was employed to extract the underlying factors revealed by both instruments. The results of the study demonstrated that metacognitive practice in online collaborative discussions (MP-OCD) could be separated into four factors, while social and emotional engagement in online collaborative discussions (SEE-OCD) could be extracted into two factors. Second, the study used validated survey instruments to characterize college students' online collaborative discussion profiles. The results showed that four clusters of online collaborative discussion profiles were identified. This study has significant implications for educators who wish to improve students' metacognitive regulation and social and emotional engagement in online collaborative discussions.

DOI: 10.4018/978-1-6684-7813-4.ch011

INTRODUCTION

Metacognitive regulation and engagement play crucial roles in determining learners' achievements and performance in cognitive tasks in online learning environments (Martin & Bolliger, 2018; Ohtani & Hisasaka, 2018). In particular, online learning environments that emphasize collaboration and interaction among learners are often characterized by elevated levels of social and emotional engagement and the use of metacognitive strategies, which are key factors that encourage learners to remain active (Isohätälä et al., 2017, 2020; Molinillo et al., 2018; Shearer et al., 2020).

However, previous studies (e.g., Garrison & Akyol, 2015; Hadwin et al., 2018; Isohätälä et al., 2017; Ucan & Webb, 2015) have called for more emphasis on expanding the aspects of metacognitive regulation in online learning contexts to encompass social aspects of regulation as opposed to individualistic aspects (i.e., self-regulation). This is because in online learning environments learners are highly encouraged to both learn autonomously and learn by socializing, interacting, and collaborating actively with teachers, classmates, and even outsiders who may be knowledgeable about the topics in which learners are interested (Shearer et al., 2020; Slof et al., 2021).

Socially shared metacognitive regulation entails the ability to regulate an individual's and others' learning process, especially in collaborative learning situations. This social form of regulation relates closely to how individuals engage socially and emotionally in their learning, as research has indicated that shared emotion is paramount for maintaining reciprocal interactions and establishing a supportive socio-emotional atmosphere among group members (Isohätälä et al., 2020; Järvelä et al., 2016; Ucan & Webb, 2015). Moreover, socio-emotional interactions among group members during the learning process of collaborative learning activities (e.g., discussions, group roles, and task execution) can potentially shape the quality of socially regulated learning (Järvelä et al., 2016). Especially, through negotiation and co-construction of meaning learners are able to strive towards a mutual understanding of the task (e.g., Malmberg et al., 2017; Rogat & Linnenbrink-Garcia, 2011).

Consequently, in this chapter, the authors not only focused on learners' self- and socially shared metacognitive regulation, but also took into consideration the social and emotional aspects of their engagement when participating in an online collaborative learning context. More specifically, the authors directed their focus toward online collaborative discussions, as engaging in extensive conversations with peers and instructors is deemed one of the pedagogical practices that foster students' use of metacognitive regulation in the context of online collaborative learning (Akyol & Garrison, 2011; Shearer et al., 2020). Moreover, an online collaborative discussion activity provides insights into the various forms of metacognitive knowledge and skills that are developed during different phases of a collaborative project, especially when an individual contributes to group reflection (Papanikolaou & Boubouka, 2010).

Despite the acknowledged significance of both self- and socially shared metacognitive regulation and socio-emotional engagement in online collaborative learning contexts, there is still a necessity to design survey instruments for both constructs that are specifically customized for collaborative discussions. Given that online collaborative discussions are considered a form of domain-specific learning activity (Araos et al., 2023; Sjöberg & Brooks, 2022) and demands a high level of interaction, collaboration, and socialization (Rosé & Ferschke, 2016), in this study, two survey instruments were specifically developed. These instruments were designed to assess self- and socially shared metacognitive regulation and social and emotional engagement in online collaborative discussions, a pedagogical activity that can be unique compared to other individualized online learning activities. Furthermore, the authors sought to characterize significant patterns of students' metacognitive regulation and engagement in online collaborative discussions.

By using more contextualized survey instruments, educational practitioners will be able to gain a more accurate understanding of how learners actually regulate their learning processes and engage in the context of online collaborative discussions. In addition, by identifying patterns and characteristics in terms of how learners employ different metacognitive practices and engage socially and emotionally in this learning activity, this study will serve as a reference for both preservice and inservice teachers. In particular, it will enable them to find better solutions for supporting certain groups of learners with multifaceted characteristics with respect to metacognitive abilities and engagement levels. The study was guided by the following three research questions.

1. What factor structures emerged from the metacognitive practice in online collaborative discussion (MP-OCD) questionnaire? Was the questionnaire reliable and valid for measuring the preservice teachers self- and socially shared metacognitive regulation in online collaborative discussions?
2. What factor structures emerged from the socio-emotional engagement in online collaborative discussion (SEE-OCD) questionnaire? Was the questionnaire reliable and valid for measuring the preservice teachers' socio-emotional engagement in online collaborative discussions?
3. How could preservice teachers be characterized in terms of their profiles for online collaborative discussions?

BACKGROUND

Metacognitive Regulation in the Context of Online Collaborative Learning

Metacognitive regulation, an important element of metacognition, involves the regulation of an individual's cognitive process (Garrison, 2003; Schraw, 1998). Past studies (e.g., Carvalho & Santos, 2022; Cho & Shen, 2013; Wong et al., 2019) have revealed that metacognitive regulation plays an essential role in shaping students' online learning experiences, promoting favorable attitudes toward online collaboration, a consistent motivation to learn, the ability to overcome obstacles, and effective decision-making in various learning tasks. These factors can culminate in successful task completion, enhanced learning performance, and academic achievement. Especially in highly collaborative learning contexts, students are typically engaged in various transactive processes such as brainstorming, discussion, and reflection on their own and others' ideas (De Backer et al., 2015). These transactive processes may impose a relatively high cognitive load and require that students maintain interpersonal relations and communication with others to complete the project (Capdeferro & Romero, 2012; Kirschner et al., 2018). These can be challenging for students who possess insufficient collaborative learning experiences (Kirschner et al., 2018). Thus, facilitating the development of metacognitive abilities among students, which involves the cultivation of skills for regulating, evaluating, monitoring, and appraising their cognitive and learning processes more effectively (Broadbent et al., 2020), would to some degree enhance their capacity to cope with the cognitive demands and interpersonal dynamics within collaborative learning environments.

Self- and Socially-Shared Metacognitive Regulation

Previous research into students' regulation of learning has distinguished three types of metacognitive regulation observed within collaborative learning settings that involve high levels of interaction: self-regulation, co-regulation, and socially shared regulation (Hadwin et al., 2018; Järvelä et al., 2016; Rogat & Linnenbrink-Garcia, 2011). According to Järvelä et al. (2016), self-regulation is defined as the process by which individuals take responsibility for their own thoughts, actions, motivations, and emotions during collaborative tasks. Co-regulation refers to the way in which group members provide transitional support for one another's self-regulatory processes, which may be facilitated by technologies or contextual features of the environment. Socially-shared regulation, by contrast, involves a collaborative process in which group members synchronize and regulate their collective cognition, behavior, motivation, and emotions in a productive manner.

The present study prioritized the examination of self- and socially shared regulation over co-regulation, as the authors were interested in exploring how students utilized metacognitive regulation during specific collaborative learning activities, such as group discussions, in which students are strongly encouraged to engage in regulatory behaviors to achieve shared learning objectives in agreement with one another (Volet et al., 2013). According to Hadwin et al. (2018), in collaborative learning, self-regulation is highly metacognitive and influenced by personal and group-based beliefs and experiences, as well as the environment and engagement with the collaborative task. Moreover, these authors considered socially shared regulation to be influenced by various factors, such as individual perspectives, joint goals, collective monitoring and evaluation, and individual and group experiences and beliefs. These elements shape how group members engage in collaborative tasks and work toward achieving shared goals and standards (Volet et al., 2017). These characteristics of metacognitive self-regulation and socially shared regulation can be assessed in the context of online collaborative discussion (Järvelä et al., 2016).

Moreover, regardless of self- and socially shared metacognitive regulation, all forms of learning regulations encompass various facets involving students' ability to plan, monitor, organize, and evaluate their learning processes (Hadwin et al., 2018). Besides, research pertaining to online collaborative learning has revealed that metacognitive monitoring seems to play a more dominant and preceding role in this learning context than other metacognitive strategies (Malmberg et al., 2017). This may be attributed to the fact that metacognitive monitoring is a process that enables learners to become conscious of the need for regulation at various stages of learning and is often used by learners with varying levels of ability to regulate their learning, as opposed to other metacognitive strategies (Khosa & Volet, 2014; Sobocinski et al., 2022). Metacognitive monitoring involves observing an individual's learning process, assessing information about particular processes or actions that impact learning, and identifying ineffective performance (Sobocinski et al., 2022). Especially in collaborative learning, metacognitive monitoring can be shared, acting as a mechanism that encourages group members to monitor cognitive or socio-emotional learning processes at the group level in order to achieve common objectives or to seek out additional strategies for surmounting difficulties, as well as facilitating their learning processes (Malmberg et al., 2017; Sobocinski et al., 2022).

Therefore, in the current investigation, the authors broadly hypothesized that by developing a survey instrument to measure students' metacognitive practices in online collaborative discussions, which was modified from existing validated questionnaires and previous empirical studies, metacognitive monitoring would emerge as a separate factor from other metacognitive strategies.

Social-Emotional Learning in the Context of Online Collaborative Instruction

Social-emotional learning (SEL) involves a developmental process in which individuals learn how to regulate and identify their own and others' emotional states, establish and maintain interpersonal relationships, express emotions in an appropriate manner, formulate learning goals, and make decisions (Collaborative for Academic, Social, and Emotional Learning [CASEL], 2020; Denston et al., 2022; Hoffman, 2009). In other words, SEL places emphasis on promoting the fundamental development of learners' social and emotional competencies and a sense of belonging, connectedness, and emotional support within a learning environment, especially among individual learners, classmates, and instructors (Hoffman, 2009; Jones et al., 2019).

In the context of online collaborative instruction, learners' emotional presence, which is a reflection of their online learning experience and is interconnected with their social presence, can be impacted and observed within a community of inquiry, particularly when they interact with learning technology, course content, and other individuals (e.g., peers and instructors) and when they partake in cognitive or collaborative learning activities (Cleveland-Innes & Campbell, 2012). The implementation of SEL in online collaborative contexts can be challenging, but it is worth the effort. The promise of updated technology requires instructors to develop relevant skills to maintain classroom efficiency and relationships with students, while learners' online learning experiences, specifically in terms of emotional response, may also be affected by such technological change as well as by how they are trained to express emotions, collaborate, and socialize with one another in an appropriate manner (Chen & Lindon, 2018; Cleveland-Innes & Campbell, 2012; Miller et al., 2022).

Socio-Emotional Engagement

According to Astleitner (2018), socio-emotional engagement refers to the social and emotional connection that individuals develop to the learning process and the knowledge and skills being acquired. This emotional attachment can vary in degree, ranging from detached to closely connected. In accordance with the fundamental objectives of online education, course instructors bear the responsibility of not only disseminating information but also designing and implementing the course structure in a way that allows for the development of meaningful interactions and the evaluation of students' participation in the course (Becker et al., 2018). In particular, individuals engaged in online collaborative learning typically express a preference for a more personalized and adaptable learning experience, as well as opportunities to optimize social interactions with others (Shearer et al., 2020).

Empirical studies have witnessed that students' social presence, emotional engagement, and interaction with instructors are critical factors that influence their willingness to actively participate in the online learning process (Molinillo et al., 2018), which may result in a higher probability of achieving academic success. Specifically, Kwon et al. (2014) found that learners who actively collaborate in online learning environments are more inclined to participate in consistent socio-emotional interactions with their group members, monitor group processes, strive for group consensus, establish tasks and objectives, and evaluate learning strategies. Moreover, research has shown that learners' social and emotional engagement can be greatly enhanced through the implementation of collaborative, constructive, and purposeful tasks or assignments that promote mutual interactions, such as research projects, case scenarios, and problem-solving exercises (Astleitner, 2018; Becker et al., 2018; Shearer et al., 2020; Yu et al., 2020).

METHODOLOGY

Research Design

The current study utilized a quantitative, non-experimental research design based on a survey approach (Edmonds & Kennedy, 2017). This method enabled the researchers to observe the perceptions, trends, and behaviors of the target population and to explore the interrelationships among the educational, behavioral, and psychological variables. In this study, through modifications of existing validated scales, the authors developed two new instruments tailored to the context of online collaborative discussion. Reliability and validity assessments of the two instruments were initially performed and evaluated through an exploratory factor analysis (EFA), and the instruments were subsequently utilized to investigate the profiles and characteristics of college students' learning through online collaborative discussion. The study defined online collaborative discussion profiles as encompassing two principal components, namely self- and socially shared metacognitive regulation and socio-emotional engagement.

Participants and Procedures

The study involved 268 student teachers enrolled in the five-year teacher education programs at a public university in Central Thailand. Demographically, the participants were 46.6% males (n = 125) and 53.4% females (n = 143), with an average age of 19.41 years. The participants were recruited from five different teacher education programs, including educational technology (n = 42, 15.67%), early childhood education (n=33, 12.31%), elementary education (n = 60, 22.39%), language education (n = 87, 32.46%), and science education (n = 46, 17.17%). In general, a preservice education program in Thailand spans a duration of five years wherein prospective teachers dedicate four years to academic coursework and one year to practical training in schools. Upon fulfilling the specified assessment criteria, student-teachers become eligible for qualification and the attainment of a teacher professional license.

All participants had experiences carrying out various online learning activities (e.g., brainstorming, collaborative discussion, taking quizzes and assessments, watching educational video demonstrations, and reading online articles) as part of the courses requirements through both a learning management system and video conferencing platforms such as Zoom and Microsoft Teams.

Data were collected in the second semester of the academic year 2021. At the time that the data were collected, all courses at the college were offered in an online mode due to protective measures against the spread of the COVID-19 pandemic. The participants were recruited from seven sections of a basic intermediate English course in which most of the course lectures involved lessons through Zoom.

The informed consent form and survey questionnaire were developed utilizing Google Forms. The survey was disseminated electronically to the participants at the conclusion of the final class session, following the final examination. Prior to participating in the survey, the participants were required to complete and submit the informed consent form to acknowledge their understanding of the study's objectives and procedures. Access to the survey was granted upon submission of their informed consent. Given that there were no absences during the final examination, the response rate was 100%. Additionally, there were no missing data, as all participants were mandated to provide responses to all questions.

Development of the Questionnaires

To develop the questionnaires on metacognitive practice and socio-emotional engagement in online collaborative discussion, the authors adapted, modified and generated items from multiple theoretical and validation studies on self- and socially shared regulation of cognition in technology-enhanced learning environments (Garrison & Akyol, 2015; Raes et al., 2016; Ucan & Webb, 2015) and on social and emotional engagement in learning (Astleitner, 2018; Gebre et al., 2014; Maroco et al., 2016; Wang et al., 2016). More specifically, experts from various fields, including distance education and educational technology, participated in multiple panel meetings to evaluate and select appropriate items from the previously developed scales to ensure that the instruments were content- and construct-valid. The generated items in both instruments were assessed using a 5-point Likert scale (1 = strongly disagree, 2 = disagree, 3 = neither agree nor disagree, 4 = agree, and 5 = strongly agree).

In preparation for administering the survey to the target participants, the authors carried out the following steps. Firstly, both instruments used in this study were translated into the Thai language, which was the primary language of the participants. Secondly, to ensure that the translations were equivalent in meaning, two university lectures with expertise in language education were consulted. Finally, a pilot study was conducted with 12 Thai undergraduate students to verify that the translated survey instruments did not contain any double-barreled questions.

The Metacognitive Practice in Online Collaborative Discussion (MP-OCD) Questionnaire

The MP-OCD questionnaire was developed to measure students' use of both individual and collective metacognitive regulation during online collaborative discussion activities. The survey instrument was initially designed with 20 items and was intended to yield four distinct factors as shown in Table 1.

Table 1. Factor, definition, and sample item of the MP-OCD questionnaire

Factor	Definition	Sample Item
1. Self-regulated strategy use (SSU)	Students' ability to apply various strategies to assist their processes of learning during online collaborative discussion.	When I participate in synchronous online collaborative discussion, I search for new strategies when needed.
2. Socially shared monitoring (SSM)	Students' ability to monitor and observe the learning processes and thoughts of other group members during online collaborative discussion.	When I participate in synchronous online collaborative discussion, I observe how others are doing.
3. Socially shared strategy use (SSSU)	Students' ability to negotiate and apply various strategies to regulate their group-level learning during online collaborative discussion.	When I participate in synchronous online collaborative discussion, I challenge the learning strategies of others.
4. Self-monitoring (SM)	Students' ability to monitor and observe their own learning process and thoughts during online collaborative discussion.	When I participate in synchronous online collaborative discussion, I am aware of my effort.

Source: Authors' own elaboration

The Socio-Emotional Engagement in Online Collaborative Discussion (SEE-OCD) Questionnaire

The SEE-OCD questionnaire was designed to assess learners' social and emotional engagement during online collaborative discussion activities. It originally consisted of 11 items in total, divided into two distinct factors: social engagement (SE), consisting of six items, and emotional engagement (EE), consisting of five items. Details of both factors are shown in Table 2. Although social and emotional engagement are closely related factors in online collaborative environments, they are separate components with unique properties and characteristics that should be considered and evaluated independently.

Table 2. Factor, definition, and sample item of the SEE-OCD questionnaire

Factor	Definition	Sample Item
1. Social engagement (SE)	Students' interactions and collaboration among peers and instructors, as well as their desire to form and sustain relationships during online collaborative discussion.	When I participate in synchronous online collaborative discussion, I listen and try to understand other classmates' ideas.
2. Emotional engagement (EE)	Students' emotional connection to the learning process and content during online collaborative discussion, including their motivation and interest.	When I participate in synchronous online collaborative discussion, I enjoy learning new things.

Source: Authors' own elaboration

Data Analysis

In the first stage, the authors performed an EFA of the data from the MP-OCD and the SEE-OCD questionnaires. The factors extracted and validated from the EFA process were further utilized as variables included in a non-hierarchical *k*-means cluster analysis to discern the students' characteristics regarding metacognitive practice and engagement in the context of online collaborative discussion. Notably, as suggested by research on educational technology (e.g., Antonenko et al., 2012), the authors conducted separate clustering analyses with three, four, and five clusters to determine the solution that would produce the most distinct pattern and most insightful interpretation.

In this study, the authors did not perform a subsequent confirmatory factor analysis (CFA) for two reasons. First, the present study was exploratory in nature, aiming at exploring the underlying constructs of the questionnaires and the students' characteristics. Second, the number of participants in this study was quite limited for a survey validation study, and as suggested by methodological research (e.g., Knekta et al., 2019) using the same data set for both EFA and CFA analyses would not have been an appropriate practice.

RESULTS

Exploratory Factor Analysis for the Metacognitive Practice in Online Collaborative Discussion (MP-OCD) Questionnaire

The questionnaire used to assess metacognitive regulation in this study was modified from a valid scale developed for the Community of Inquiry framework (Garrison & Akyol, 2015). The Maximum Likelihood (ML) extraction method was chosen as the data was close to being normally distributed, and this method allows for evaluating the statistical significance of factor loadings and inter-factor correlations (Costello & Osborne, 2005; Fabrigar et al., 1999). Additionally, the Varimax was applied as the rotation technique, since it is the commonly suggested as a default option and reduces the variance of the loadings which provides a more distinct separation the factors (Hair et al. 2019; Tabachnick & Fidell, 2007). The Kaiser-Meyer- Olkin (KMO) measure was calculated and found to be 0.84, signifying that the data was suitable for further factor analysis (Kaiser, 1974).

In addition, in accordance with established practices (Hair et al., 2019), factors with eigenvalues exceeding 1.0 and items displaying factor loadings at least or greater than 0.50 were retained. The total variance of the scale was sufficient as it accounted for more than a minimum of 60%. The issue of problematic cross-loading items was resolved using Hair et al.' s (2019) suggestion of precisely checking the ratio of two variances and only the items with the ratio of cross-loadings greater than 2.0 were retained.

Overall, as listed in Table 3, the final version of the metacognitive regulation in online collaborative discussion questionnaire consisted of a total of 15 items (See Appendix 1). The factor loadings of these items ranged from 0.50 to 0.85. The retained items were classified into four factors, namely self-regulated strategy use (SSU), socially-shared monitoring (SSM), socially-shared strategy use (SSSU), and self-monitoring (SM). The eigenvalues of these factors were 4.97, 1.55, 1.32, and 1.27, respectively. The reliability of each factor as measured by the Cronbach's reliability coefficient (α) ranged from 0.66 to 0.84, signifying an adequate level of reliability.

Table 3. EFA results for the MP-OCD

	Factor 1	Factor 2	Factor 3	Factor 4
Factor1: Self-regulated strategy use (SSU), α = 0.84 (M = 4.02, SD = 0.63)				
SSU1	0.69			
SSU2	0.83			
SSU3	0.85			
SSU4	0.76			
Factor2: Socially-shared monitoring (SSM), α = 0.76 (M = 4.04, SD = 0.61)				
SSM1		0.54		
SSM2		0.77		
SSM3		0.83		
SSM4		0.74		
Factor3: Socially-shared strategy use (SSSU), α = 0.77 (M = 3.67, SD = 0.74)				
SSM1			0.50	
SSM2			0.90	
SSM3			0.87	
Factor4: Self-monitoring (SM), α = 0.66 (M = 4.03, SD = 0.57)				
SM1				0.79
SM2				0.83
SM3				0.58
Eigenvalue	4.97	1.55	1.32	1.27
% of variance	35.53	11.08	9.42	9.09

Note: Total variance explained: 65.12%
Source: Authors' own elaboration

Exploratory Factor Analysis for the Social-emotional Engagement in Online Collaborative Discussion (SEE-OCD) Questionnaire

The assessment of the validity and reliability of the questionnaire measuring social-emotional engagement in online collaborative discussion was conducted using similar analytical procedures, techniques, and requirements as were applied in the previous analysis of the metacognitive regulation questionnaire. The suitability of the data for factor analysis was indicated by a KMO value of 0.78. Table 4 shows that the social-emotional engagement items were extracted into two factors, namely social engagement (SE) and emotional engagement (EE) with a total of six items (See Appendix 2). The eigenvalues of these two factors were 2.85 and 1.90, respectively, with a total of 67.39% of the variance being explained. Additionally, the reliability as assessed through the Cronbach's alpha coefficient, whose value was 0.78 for the SE factor, and 0.73 for the EE factor, suggesting that the reliability was internally consistent to a satisfactory degree. In particular, it was observed that on average students demonstrated a higher level of social engagement (M = 4.01) as compared to their emotional engagement (M = 3.58) during the online collaborative discussion.

Table 4. EFA results for the SEE-OCD

	Factor 1	Factor 2
Factor1: Social engagement (SE), α = 0.78 (M = 4.01, SD = 0.68)		
SE1	0.81	
SE2	0.83	
SE3	0.80	
Factor2: Emotional engagement (EE), α = 0.73 (M = 3.58, SD = 0.83)		
EE1		0.75
EE2		0.83
EE3		0.77
Eigenvalue	2.85	1.90
% of variance	47.55	19.84

Note: Total variance explained: 67.39%
Source: Authors' own elaboration

Characterizing Students' Learning Profiles Through Online Collaborative Discussion

Apart from the assessments of the reliability and validity of the instruments, the authors conducted a cluster analysis to gain further insights into the engagement and metacognitive regulation strategies of university students during online collaborative discussion. The results of the cluster analysis, as depicted in Table 5 and Figure 1 indicated that the students' profiles for metacognition and engagement in online collaborative discussion could be categorized into the following four distinct clusters: Cluster 1 (less engaged, metacognitive observers), Cluster 2 (less engaged, non-metacognitive learners), Cluster 3 (highly engaged, metacognitive regulators), and Cluster 4 (moderately engaged, non-metacognitive learners). In the following paragraphs, the authors provide a description of the characteristics of the students in each profile.

Less engaged, metacognitive observers (Cluster 1). This cluster reflected 22.02% (n = 59) of the overall sample. Cluster 1 members demonstrated a superiority in terms of their utilization of self-regulated strategy and socially shared monitoring, as evidenced by scores that significantly exceeded the overall mean. In particular, their scores for socially shared monitoring were the second highest, surpassed only by those in Cluster 3. By contrast, the emotional engagement scores for Cluster 1 students were found to be significantly lower than the overall mean and represented the lowest among all the clusters. Their scores for social engagement were slightly below the overall average. These findings may imply that during online collaborative discussion, Cluster 1 students tended to adopt a more observant approach, paying particular attention to the metacognitive strategies employed by their peers. This observation-based learning may have led to their incorporation of such strategies in their own practice, yet without displaying a willingness to emotionally and socially engage with their classmates. Consequently, the authors designated members of Cluster 1 as 'less engaged, metacognitive observers.'

Less engaged, non-metacognitive learners (Cluster 2). This cluster represented 24.25% (n =65) of the overall sample. The participants belonging to this cluster recorded the lowest scores for all dimensions of self- and socially shared metacognition during online collaborative discussion. Additionally, their scores for social engagement were the lowest among all the clusters. While their scores for emotional engagement were slightly higher than those for Cluster 1, they still remained significantly below the average. The authors speculated that Cluster 2 students may have possessed inadequate knowledge, skills, and awareness to implement self- and socially shared metacognitive approaches in their learning processes during online collaborative discussion. Besides, they may have possessed a deficiency in terms of motivation to engage, either socially or emotionally, in online collaborative discussion. Thus, the authors considered Cluster 2 students to be 'less engaged, non-metacognitive learners.'

Highly engaged, metacognitive regulators (Cluster 3). This cluster had the smallest number of students (n = 58, 21.64% of the overall sample). Compared to the other clusters, Cluster 3 students achieved the highest scores for all dimensions of self- and socially shared metacognition and engagement. Their scores in all categories were also significantly higher than the overall average. The findings indicated that members of this cluster were cognizant of and able to apply different metacognitive approaches, both individual and collaborative, to facilitate the processes of their learning during online collaborative discussion. Moreover, they displayed high levels of emotional and social participation in online collaborative discussion. Due to these traits, Cluster 3 students were identified as 'highly engaged, metacognitive regulators.'

Moderately engaged, non-metacognitive learners (Cluster 4). Cluster 4 had the greatest number of students (n = 86), accounting for 32.09% of the entire sample. This indicated that approximately one-third of the students demonstrated moderate levels of social and emotional engagement in learning through online collaborative discussion. Their scores in these engagement dimensions were significantly higher than the overall mean but comparatively lower than those of Cluster 3. Students in Cluster 4 were also regarded as non-metacognitive learners, as their scores for the metacognitive dimensions of self-regulated strategy use and socially-shared monitoring were significantly below the average. Additionally, their scores for the remaining two metacognitive dimensions, self-monitoring and socially shared strategy use, were also lower than the overall mean, albeit without a significant difference. Furthermore, despite showing varying levels of social and emotional engagement in online collaborative discussion, the characteristics of Cluster 4 participants partially aligned with those of Cluster 2, in that they demonstrated a lower likelihood of utilizing metacognitive strategies to enhance their learning processes and experiences.

Table 5. Results for the cluster analysis

Aspects	Variables	Overall mean (n = 268) Mean (SD)	Cluster 1 (n = 59) Mean (SD), t-value	Cluster 2 (n = 65) Mean (SD), t-value	Cluster 3 (n = 58) Mean (SD), t-value	Cluster 4 (n = 86) Mean (SD), t-value
Metacognitive regulations	Self-regulated strategy use (a)	4.02 (0.63)	4.34 (0.49), 5.15***	3.40 (0.46), -10.83***	4.60 (0.38), 11.66***	3.86 (0.47), -3.00**
	Socially-shared monitoring (b)	4.04 (0.61)	4.45 (0.40), 7.80***	3.49 (0.41), -10.74***	4.54 (0.38), 10.15***	3.83 (0.50), -3.73***
	Socially-shared strategy use (c)	3.67 (0.74)	3.59 (0.84), -0.71	3.13 (0.47), -9.11***	4.46 (0.51), 11.85***	3.59 (0.51), -1.47
	Self-monitoring (d)	4.03 (0.57)	4.13 (0.57), 1.70	3.56 (0.45), -7.97***	4.53 (0.43), 9.24***	3.99 (0.42), -0.33
Student engagement	Social engagement (e)	4.01 (0.68)	3.99 (0.68), -0.16	3.30 (0.40), -14.49***	4.64 (0.42), 11.56***	4.13 (0.47), 2.34*
	Emotional engagement (f)	3.58 (0.83)	2.78 (0.68), -8.99***	3.11 (0.52), -7.33***	4.54 (0.45), 16.46***	3.83 (0.44), 5.27 ***
One sample t-test			(a) > Overall (b) > Overall (f) < Overall	(a) < Overall (b) < Overall (c) < Overall (d) < Overall (e) < Overall (f) < Overall	(a) > Overall (b) > Overall (c) > Overall (d) > Overall (e) > Overall (f) < Overall	(a) < Overall (b) < Overall (e) > Overall (f) > Overall

Note: 1. *$p < 0.05$; **$p < 0.01$; ***$p < 0.001$

2. Cluster 1: Less engaged, metacognitive observers; Cluster 2: Less engaged, non-metacognitive learners; Cluster 3: Highly engaged, metacognitive regulators; Cluster 4: Moderately engaged, non-metacognitive learners

Source: Authors 'own elaboration

Figure 1. The four cluster characteristics of learning through online collaborative discussion
Source: Authors' own elaboration

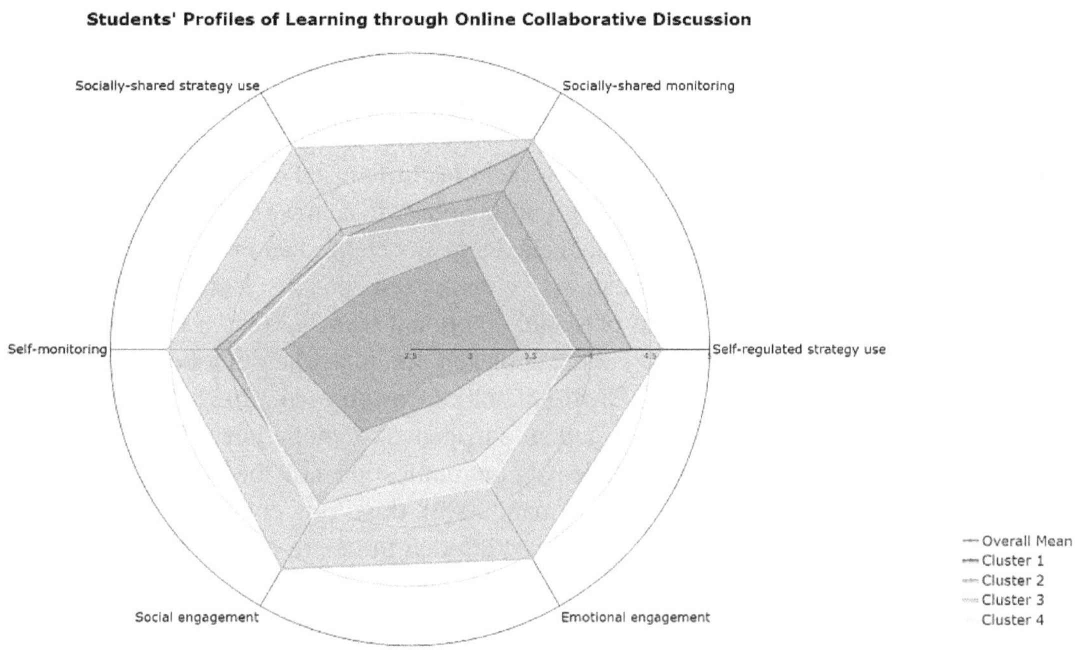

DISCUSSION AND CONCLUSION

In the realm of online collaborative learning, it is essential to provide a comprehensive analysis of the constructs of metacognitive regulation, including individual and socially shared aspects, and social and emotional engagement, particularly in the context of online collaborative discussion activities (De Backer et al., 2015; Kielstra et al., 2022). These activities emphasize the necessity of both individual and collective regulation of learning, as well as promoting high levels of interaction and collaboration between learners and instructors. In the present investigation, the authors developed survey instruments that were tailored to the specific context of online collaborative discussion and were designed to measure both students' self-regulated and socially shared metacognitive regulation and their social and emotional engagement. Subsequently, the authors utilized these newly developed and validated instruments to characterize students' learning profiles within the context of online collaborative discussion.

The first instrument, the Metacognitive Practice in Online Collaborative Discussion (MP-OCD) questionnaire, successfully generated four factors: *self-regulated strategy use*, *socially shared monitoring*, *socially shared strategy use*, and *self-monitoring*. The results aligned with the original hypothesis, given that metacognitive monitoring was identified as a separate factor from other metacognitive strategies. This seems to be consistent with previous empirical studies suggesting that metacognitive monitoring tends to have a more influential and proactive function in the learning context than other metacognitive strategies (Malmberg et al., 2017). This could be attributed to the fact that monitoring is (1) the skill that learners, irrespective of their ability to regulate learning, invariably consider as necessary during various stages of collaborative learning and (2) a mechanism that motivates individuals within a group to observe their knowledge gains and socio-emotional interactions to attain shared goals (Khosa & Volet, 2014; Malmberg et al., 2017; Sobocinski et al., 2022). Additionally, it is evident that the MP-OCD questionnaire produced distinct factors regarding self-regulation and socially shared metacognitive regulation, supporting the existence of both individual and collective regulation of learning during online collaborative discussions (Hadwin et al., 2018; Järvelä et al., 2016; Rogat & Linnenbrink-Garcia, 2011).

The second instrument, the Socio-Emotional Engagement in Online Collaborative Discussion (SEE-OCD) questionnaire, produced two different factors: *social engagement* and *emotional engagement*. The retained items that loaded onto the social engagement factor focused on how an individual learner can interact and work collaboratively with other group members to achieve the learning objectives. Meanwhile, the retained items measuring emotional engagement captured an individual's affective response to the learning environment in online collaborative discussion contexts. Both the social and emotional engagement items captured the essence of social-emotional learning (SEL) by evaluating individual learners' ability to sustain interpersonal connections and articulate their emotional states while engaging in collaborative learning activities (CASEL, 2020; Denston et al., 2022; Hoffman, 2009). Given that both social and emotional aspects of student engagement may be intricately linked, especially in online learning contexts that emphasize students' communication, collaboration, and feelings of empathy (Cleveland-Innes & Campbell, 2012; Hoffman, 2009), this study contributed to the understanding of social and emotional engagement by demonstrating that these are distinct constructs that reflected different facets of individuals' relationships with others and their personal emotional experiences in the learning process. This conclusion was drawn based on the results of the exploratory factor analysis (EFA).

Although the items designed in this study consistently loaded onto the hypothesized factors, indicating some level of content validity, future studies are still necessary to confirm convergent and discriminant validity by verifying the degree to which the factors within each instrument are correlated and whether they are distinguishable. These can be tested through a confirmatory factor analysis (CFA). Despite this limitation, the two survey instruments developed in this study can be implemented as preliminary tools to elicit learners' employment of metacognitive regulation and their social and emotional engagement. This is important since the way in which learners both apply metacognitive regulation and exhibit engagement may be challenging for instructors to observe and identify.

In addition to the two developed instruments, the results pertaining to the profiles of students' learning during online collaborative discussion demonstrated that students could be classified into four distinct categories: (1) *less engaged, metacognitive observers*; (2) *less engaged, non-metacognitive learners*; (3) *highly engaged, metacognitive regulators*; and (4) *moderately engaged, non-metacognitive learners*. The study revealed that students could be initially classified according to their levels of social and emotional engagement, which could be characterized as low, moderate, and high. Furthermore, they could be classified based on their use of metacognitive regulation, with students falling into one of three categories: regulators, observers, and general learners who were less likely to apply metacognitive strategies to their learning.

The categorization of students in Cluster 3 as highly engaged learners and metacognitive regulators was not unexpected. Previous research on self- and socially regulated learning (S-SRL) has indicated that students who utilize either self-regulated or socially regulated learning strategies possess the ability to effectively motivate themselves to attain an appropriate level of engagement (Molenaar & Järvelä, 2014). Conversely, among students who were classified as less engaged learners, such as those in Clusters 1 and 2, there appeared to be differences in their use of metacognitive regulation. While students in Cluster 1 were identified as *observers*, those in Cluster 2 were labeled as *non-metacognitive learners*. Research has indicated that students who exhibit low levels of socio-emotional engagement during collaborative learning often hold unfavorable perceptions regarding group interactions (Mänty et al., 2020). This may pose a significant challenge for them because in collaborative discussions, learners often and inevitably encounter conflicting ideas, disagreements, and discrepancies, and they may fear being judged incompetent by their peers as they seek to consider alternative perspectives on the learning content (De Backer et al., 2022; Webb, 2013).Based on these premises, the authors conjectured that students in Cluster 1, characterized by low socio-emotional engagement, may have been inclined to employ metacognitive strategies that emphasized observing how other group members learned, which they may subsequently have applied to their own individual learning strategies, rather than actively participating with others to enhance their regulation of learning. However, this conjecture needs to be verified in future research.

Moreover, it is conceivable that students who demonstrated low levels of socio-emotional engagement during collaborative online learning may have had a reduced propensity to utilize either self-regulated or socially shared metacognitive strategies to aid their learning processes in comparison to those with moderate or high levels of socio-emotional engagement (Binali et al., 2021). This may partly account for why Cluster 2 students were identified as *non-metacognitive learners.* Additionally, the authors found that the majority of students who belonged to Cluster 4 partially shared characteristics with Cluster 2 students in that they were identified as *non-metacognitive learners* but maintained moderate levels of socio-emotional engagement. The authors speculated that despite being moderately involved in collaborative discussions in terms of socialization and positive emotions, these learners may have encountered difficulties in finding a balance between maintaining sufficient motivation to participate in the activity and the highly cognitive nature of the task. This required not only high levels of cohesive and respectful interactions (Isohätälä et al., 2018) but also the use of metacognitive regulation at both the individual and group levels to effectively complete the task (Janssen et al., 2012). These rationales might aid in understanding why Cluster 4 students exhibited a lower tendency to employ metacognitive regulation while engaging in online collaborative discussion. Again, future investigations are needed to validate this speculation, particularly since the existing literature offers limited information on the relationships between students who exhibit moderate levels of engagement and other various learning-related factors.

However, it should be noted that the patterns of students' profile characteristics identified in this study can only serve as a preliminary guideline for instructors seeking to engage students in online collaborative discussions, as the generalizability of the findings to other contexts requires further investigation. This may be because learners' engagement levels and use of metacognitive regulation may vary depending on the level of expertise and familiarity required for the discussion topics as well as the role of the task type and learning environment (Molenaar & Järvelä, 2014). In addition, to gain a more comprehensive understanding of how students regulate their learning, the authors propose that future research incorporate interviews and observations as additional measures. This approach could provide further validation of the developed instruments by utilizing data from diverse sources.

Main Contributions

First, the two survey instruments developed in this study tailored to collaborative discussion activity can enable online educators to effectively assess students' utilization of metacognitive strategies and their socio-emotional engagement in online collaborative learning. These instruments can serve as assessment resources for online preservice and inservice educators and be applied in diverse online learning environments, particularly in international learning contexts that emphasize collaboration among students and educators from different countries. In particular, collaborative discussion is a transactive activity that is often integrated into coursework and is central to the collaborative online international learning (COIL) approach.

Second, it is important to acknowledge that students from diverse cultural backgrounds, linguistic abilities, and educational systems may exhibit variations in their learning styles and perceptions of instructional approaches. These variations can contribute to unsatisfactory academic performance, an unfavorable learning environment, and challenges faced by educators in optimizing the effectiveness of their classes. Consequently, the findings concerning the profile patterns of students' metacognitive characteristics and socio-emotional engagement can serve as valuable references for online international educators who integrate online collaborative discussions into their instructional practices with students of various cultural and educational backgrounds. Specifically, the different patterns exhibited by students' characteristics during online collaborative discussion, as viewed through the lens of their metacognitive regulation and levels of engagement, can assist educators in addressing students' diverse needs and preferences, creating a more inclusive and engaged learning environment, and enhancing the efficiency of students' academic performance.

REFERENCES

Akyol, Z., & Garrison, D. R. (2011). Assessing metacognition in an online community of inquiry. *The Internet and Higher Education*, *14*(3), 183–190. doi:10.1016/j.iheduc.2011.01.005

Antonenko, P. D., Toy, S., & Niederhauser, D. S. (2012). Using cluster analysis for data mining in educational technology research. *Educational Technology Research and Development*, *60*(3), 383–398. doi:10.1007/s11423-012-9235-8

Araos, A., Damşa, C., & Gašević, D. (2023). Browsing to learn: How computer and software engineering students use online platforms in learning activities. *Journal of Computer Assisted Learning*, *39*(2), 676–693. Advance online publication. doi:10.1111/jcal.12774

Astleitner, H. (2018). Multidimensional engagement in learning: An integrated instructional design approach. *Journal of Institutional Research*, *7*(1), 6–32. doi:10.9743/JIR.2018.1

Becker, M. R., McCaleb, K., & Baker, C. (2018). Paradigm shift toward student engagement in technology mediated courses. In Information Resources Management Association (IRMA) (Ed.), Student engagement and participation: Concepts, methodologies, tools, and applications (pp. 1547-1567). IGI Global. doi:10.4018/978-1-5225-2584-4.ch077

Binali, T., Tsai, C.-C., & Chang, H.-Y. (2021). University students' profiles of online learning and their relation to online learning and internet-specific epistemic justification. *Computers & Education*, *175*, 104315. Advance online publication. doi:10.1016/j.compedu.2021.104315

Broadbent, J., Panadero, E., Lodge, J. M., & de Barba, P. (2020). Technologies to enhance self-regulated learning in online and computer-mediated learning environments. In M. J. Bishop, E. Boling, J. Elen, & V. Svihla (Eds.), *Handbook of research in educational communications and technology* (5th ed., pp. 37–52). Springer. doi:10.1007/978-3-030-36119-8_3

Capdeferro, N., & Romero, M. (2012). Are online learners frustrated with collaborative learning experiences? *International Review of Research in Open and Distance Learning*, *13*(2), 26–44. doi:10.19173/irrodl.v13i2.1127

Carvalho, A. R., & Santos, C. (2022). Developing peer mentors' collaborative and metacognitive skills with a technology-enhanced peer learning program. *Computers and Education Open*, *3*, 100070. Advance online publication. doi:10.1016/j.caeo.2021.100070

Chen, S.-Y., & Lindon, N. A. (2018). Teachers can play too: Teacher-child relationships, social-emotional development, and academic engagement. In Information Resources Management Association (IRMA) (Ed.), Student engagement and participation: Concepts, methodologies, tools, and applications (pp. 288-313). IGI Global.

Cho, M.-H., & Shen, D. (2013). Self-regulation in online learning. *Distance Education*, *34*(3), 290–301. doi:10.1080/01587919.2013.835770

Cleveland-Innes, M., & Campbell, P. (2012). Emotional presence, learning, and the online learning environment. *International Review of Research in Open and Distance Learning*, *13*(4), 269–292. doi:10.19173/irrodl.v13i4.1234

Collaborative for Academic, Social, and Emotional Learning. (2020). *What is SEL?* https://www.casel.org/what-is-sel/

Costello, A. B., & Osborne, J. W. (2005). Best practices in exploratory factor analysis: Four recommendations for getting the most from your analysis. *Practical Assessment, Research & Evaluation*, *10*(7), 1–9. doi:10.7275/jyj1-4868

De Backer, L., Van Keer, H., & Valcke, M. (2015). Socially shared metacognitive regulation during reciprocal peer tutoring: Identifying its relationship with students' content processing and transactive discussion. *Instructional Science*, *43*(3), 323–344. doi:10.1007/s11251-014-9335-4

De Backer, L., Van Keer, H., & Valcke, M. (2022). The functions of shared metacognitive regulation and their differential relation with collaborative learners' understanding of the learning content. *Learning and Instruction*, *77*, 101527. Advance online publication. doi:10.1016/j.learninstruc.2021.101527

Denston, A., Martin, R., Fickel, L., & O' Toole, V. (2022). Teachers' perspectives of social-emotional learning: Informing the development of a linguistically and culturally responsive framework for social-emotional wellbeing in Aotearoa New Zealand. *Teaching and Teacher Education*, *117*(4), 103813. Advance online publication. doi:10.1016/j.tate.2022.103813

Edmonds, W. A., & Kennedy, T. D. (2017). *An applied guide to research design: Quantitative, qualitative and mixed methods* (2nd ed.). Sage. doi:10.4135/9781071802779

Fabrigar, L. R., Wegener, D. T., MacCallum, R. C., & Strahan, E. J. (1999). Evaluating the use of exploratory factor analysis in psychological research. *Psychological Methods*, *4*(3), 272–299. doi:10.1037/1082-989X.4.3.272

Garrison, D. R. (2003). Cognitive presence for effective asynchronous online learning: The role of reflective inquiry, self-direction, and metacognition. In J. Bourne & J. C. Moore (Eds.), *Elements of quality online education: Practice and direction* (pp. 47–58). The Sloan Consortium.

Garrison, D. R., & Akyol, Z. (2015). Toward the development of a metacognition construct for communities of inquiry. *The Internet and Higher Education, 24*, 66–71. doi:10.1016/j.iheduc.2014.10.001

Gebre, E., Saroyan, A., & Bracewell, R. (2014). Students' engagement in technology rich classrooms and its relationship to professors' conceptions of effective teaching. *British Journal of Educational Technology, 45*(1), 83–96. doi:10.1111/bjet.12001

Hadwin, A., Järvelä, S., & Miller, M. (2018). Self-regulation co-regulation and shared regulation in collaborative learning environments. In D. H. Schunk & J. A. Greene (Eds.), *Handbook of self-regulation of learning and performance* (2nd ed., pp. 83–106). Routledge.

Hair, J. F., Black, W. C., Babin, B. J., & Anderson, R. E. (2019). *Multivariate data analysis* (8th ed.). Cengage Learning.

Hoffman, D. M. (2009). Reflecting on social emotional learning: A critical perspective on trends in the United States. *Review of Educational Research, 79*(2), 533–556. doi:10.3102/0034654308325184

Isohätälä, J., Järvenoja, H., & Järvelä, S. (2017). Socially shared regulation of learning and participation in social interaction in collaborative learning. *International Journal of Educational Research, 81*, 11–24. doi:10.1016/j.ijer.2016.10.006

Isohätälä, J., Näykki, P., & Järvelä, S. (2020). Cognitive and socio-emotional interaction in collaborative learning: Exploring fluctuations in students' participation. *Scandinavian Journal of Educational Research, 64*(6), 831–851. doi:10.1080/00313831.2019.1623310

Isohätälä, J., Näykki, P., Järvelä, S., & Baker, M. J. (2018). Striking a balance: Socio-emotional processes during argumentation in collaborative learning interaction. *Learning, Culture and Social Interaction, 16*, 1–19. doi:10.1016/j.lcsi.2017.09.003

Janssen, J., Erkens, G., Kirschner, P. A., & Kanselaar, G. (2012). Task-related and social regulation during online collaborative learning. *Metacognition and Learning, 7*(1), 25–43. doi:10.1007/s11409-010-9061-5

Järvelä, S., Kirschner, P. A., Järvenoja, H., Malmberg, J., Miller, M., & Laru, J. (2016). Socially shared regulation of learning in CSCL: Understanding and prompting individual- and group-level shared regulatory activities. *International Journal of Computer-Supported Collaborative Learning, 11*(3), 263–280. doi:10.1007/s11412-016-9238-2

Jones, S. M., McGarrah, M. W., & Kahn, J. (2019). Social and emotional learning: A principled science of human development in context. *Educational Psychologist, 54*(3), 129–143. doi:10.1080/00461520.2019.1625776

Kaiser, H. F. (1974). An index of factorial simplicity. *Psychometrika, 39*(1), 31–36. doi:10.1007/BF02291575

Khosa, D. K., & Volet, S. E. (2014). Productive group engagement in cognitive activity and metacognitive regulation during collaborative learning: Can it explain differences in students' conceptual understanding? *Metacognition and Learning*, *9*(3), 287–307. doi:10.1007/s11409-014-9117-z

Kielstra, J., Molenaar, I., van Steensel, R., & Verhoeven, L. (2022). Supporting socially shared regulation during collaborative task-oriented reading. *International Journal of Computer-Supported Collaborative Learning*, *17*(1), 65–105. doi:10.1007/s11412-022-09365-x

Kirschner, P. A., Sweller, J., Kirschner, F., & Zambrano, J. (2018). From cognitive load theory to collaborative cognitive load theory. *International Journal of Computer-Supported Collaborative Learning*, *13*(2), 213–233. doi:10.1007/s11412-018-9277-y PMID:30996713

Knekta, E., Runyon, C., & Eddy, S. (2019). One size doesn't fit all: Using factor analysis to gather validity evidence when using surveys in your research. *CBE Life Sciences Education*, *18*(1), rm1. Advance online publication. doi:10.1187/cbe.18-04-0064 PMID:30821600

Kwon, K., Liu, Y.-H., & Johnson, L. P. (2014). Group regulation and social-emotional interactions observed in computer supported collaborative learning: Comparison between good vs. poor collaborators. *Computers & Education*, *78*, 185–200. doi:10.1016/j.compedu.2014.06.004

Malmberg, J., Järvelä, S., & Järvenoja, H. (2017). Capturing temporal and sequential patterns of self-, co-, and socially shared regulation in the context of collaborative learning. *Contemporary Educational Psychology*, *49*, 160–174. doi:10.1016/j.cedpsych.2017.01.009

Mänty, K., Järvenoja, H., & Törmänen, T. (2020). Socio-emotional interaction in collaborative learning: Combining individual emotional experiences and group-level emotion regulation. *International Journal of Educational Research*, *102*, 101589. Advance online publication. doi:10.1016/j.ijer.2020.101589

Maroco, J., Maroco, A. L., Compos, J. A. D. B., & Fredricks, J. A. (2016). University student's engagement: Development of the university student engagement inventory (USEI). *Psicologia: Reflexâo e Crítica, 29*, 1–12. doi:10.1186/s41155-016-0042-8

Martin, F., & Bolliger, D. U. (2018). Engagement matters: Student perceptions on the importance of engagement strategies in the online learning environment. *Online Learning: the Official Journal of the Online Learning Consortium*, *22*(1), 205–222. doi:10.24059/olj.v22i1.1092

Miller, K., Castañon, M., & Filiss, T. (2022). The worst we have seen: Leveraging social/emotional learning in K-12 online & blended environments amid a well-being crisis. *Journal of Online Learning Research*, *8*(1), 1–6.

Molenaar, I., & Järvelä, S. (2014). Sequential and temporal characteristics of self and socially regulated learning. *Metacognition and Learning*, *9*(2), 75–85. doi:10.1007/s11409-014-9114-2

Molinillo, S., Aguilar-Illescas, R., Anaya-Sánchez, R., & Vallespín-Arán, M. (2018). Exploring the impacts of interactions, social presence, and emotional engagement on active collaborative learning in a social web-based environment. *Computers & Education*, *123*, 41–52. doi:10.1016/j.compedu.2018.04.012

Ohtani, K., & Hisasaka, T. (2018). Beyond intelligence: A meta-analytic review of the relationship among metacognition, intelligence, and academic performance. *Metacognition and Learning, 13*(2), 179–212. doi:10.1007/s11409-018-9183-8

Papanikolaou, K., & Boubouka, M. (2010). Promoting collaboration in a project-based e-learning context. *Journal of Research on Technology in Education, 43*(2), 135–155. doi:10.1080/15391523.2010.10782566

Raes, A., Schellens, T., Wever, B., & Benoit, D. (2016). Promoting metacognitive regulation through collaborative problem solving on the web: When script does not work. *Computers in Human Behavior, 58*, 325–342. doi:10.1016/j.chb.2015.12.064

Rogat, T. K., & Linnenbrink-Garcia, L. (2011). Socially shared regulation in collaborative groups: An analysis of the interplay between quality of social regulation and group processes. *Cognition and Instruction, 29*(4), 375–415. doi:10.1080/07370008.2011.607930

Rosé, C. P., & Ferschke, O. (2016). Technology support for discussion based learning: From computer supported collaborative learning to the future of massive open online courses. *International Journal of Artificial Intelligence in Education, 26*(2), 660–678. doi:10.1007/s40593-016-0107-y

Schraw, G. (1998). Promoting general metacognitive awareness. *Instructional Science, 26*(1/2), 113–125. doi:10.1023/A:1003044231033

Shearer, R. L., Aldemir, T., Hitchcock, J., Resig, J., Driver, J., & Kohler, M. (2020). What students want: A vision of a future online learning experience grounded in distance education theory. *American Journal of Distance Education, 34*(1), 36–52. doi:10.1080/08923647.2019.1706019

Sjöberg, J., & Brooks, E. (2022). Collaborative interactions in problem-solving activities: School children's orientations while developing digital game designs using smart mobile technology. *International Journal of Child-Computer Interaction, 33*, 100456. doi:10.1016/j.ijcci.2022.100456

Slof, B., van Leeuwen, A., Janssen, J., & Kirschner, P. A. (2021). Mine, ours, and yours: Whose engagement and prior knowledge affects individual achievement from online collaborative learning. *Journal of Computer Assisted Learning, 37*(1), 39–50. doi:10.1111/jcal.12466

Sobocinski, M., Malmberg, J., & Järvelä, S. (2022). Exploring adaptation in socially-shared regulation of learning using video and heart rate data. *Technology, Knowledge, and Learning, 27*(2), 385–404. doi:10.1007/s10758-021-09526-1

Tabachnick, B. G., & Fidell, L. S. (2007). *Using multivariate statistics* (5th ed.). Pearson Education, Inc.

Ucan, S., & Webb, M. (2015). Social regulation of learning during collaborative inquiry learning in science: How does it emerge and what are its functions? *International Journal of Science Education, 37*(15), 2503–2532. doi:10.1080/09500693.2015.1083634

Volet, S., Vauras, M., Khosa, D., & Liskala, T. (2013). Metacognitive regulation in collaborative learning: Conceptual developments and methodological contextualizations. In S. Volet & M. Vauras (Eds.), *Interpersonal regulation of learning and motivation: Methodological advances* (pp. 67–101). Routledge. doi:10.4324/9780203117736-11

Volet, S., Vauras, M., Salo, A. E., & Khosa, D. (2017). Individual contributions in student-led collaborative learning environments: Insights from two analytical approaches to explain the quality of group outcome. *Learning and Individual Differences*, *53*, 79–92. doi:10.1016/j.lindif.2016.11.006

Wang, M. T., Fredricks, J. A., Ye, F., Hofkens, T. L., & Linn, J. S. (2016). The math and science engagement scales: Scale development, validation, and psychometric properties. *Learning and Instruction*, *43*, 16–26. doi:10.1016/j.learninstruc.2016.01.008

Webb, N. M. (2013). Information processing approaches to collaborative learning. In C. E. Hmelo-Silver, C. A. Chinn, C. K. K. Chan, & A. O'Donnell (Eds.), *The international handbook of collaborative learning* (pp. 30–50). Routledge.

Wong, J., Baars, M., Davis, D., Van Der Zee, T., Houben, G.-J., & Paas, F. (2019). Supporting self-regulated learning in online learning environments and MOOCs: A systematic review. *International Journal of Human-Computer Interaction*, *35*(4-5), 356–373. doi:10.1080/10447318.2018.1543084

Yu, J., Huang, C., Wang, X., & Tu, Y. (2020, August 24-27). *Exploring the relationships among interaction, emotional engagement and learning persistence in online learning environments*. Paper presented at the 2020 International Symposium on Educational Technology (ISET), Bangkok, Thailand. 10.1109/ISET49818.2020.00070

KEY TERMS AND DEFINITIONS

Emotional Engagement: Emotional investment, interest, and connection individuals have in relation to the content, instructor, peers in a particular learning community.

Metacognitive Regulation: The ability to control an individual's cognitive processes in order to enhance and optimizing learning outcomes.

Metacognitive Strategies: The conscious and deliberate techniques individuals use to regulate and control their own learning process. Specifically, these strategies involve planning, monitoring, and evaluating one's own thinking and learning, etc.

Online Collaborative Discussions: Interactive exchanges that take place in a virtual environment, where individuals engage in a shared discourse to explore and exchange ideas, perspectives, and knowledge. These discussions typically involve multiple participants who communicate and collaborate through online platforms to achieve a common understanding of solve problems collectively.

Self-Regulation of Learning: The ability of individuals to independently manage and regulate their own learning by employing metacognitive strategies such as setting goals, planning strategies, managing time and resources, and evaluating one's learning process to achieve desired learning outcomes.

Social Engagement: Active participation and interaction with others in online learning platforms, especially through conversations and group activities, to establish meaningful connections, collaborations, and a sense of belonging.

Socially Shared Regulation of Learning: The ability to engage in collaborative processes in which individuals collectively and actively manage and regulate their own learning experiences within a collaborative learning context. Such processes emphasize interactions, communication, and mutual support among learners.

APPENDIX 1

The Metacognitive Practice in Online Collaborative Discussion (MP-OCD) Questionnaire

When I participate in synchronous online collaborative discussions,….

Self-regulated strategy use (SSU)
SSU1 I change my strategy when needed.
SSU2 I search for new strategies when needed.
SSU3 I apply different strategies when needed.
SSU4 I assess my learning strategies
Socially shared monitoring (SSM)
SSM1 I pay attention to the ideas of others.
SSM2 I observe the strategies of others.
SSM3 I observe how others are doing.
SSM4 I monitor the learning of others.
Socially-shared strategy use (SSSU)
SSSU1 I look for confirmation of my understanding from others.
SSSU2 I challenge the learning strategies of others.
SSSU3 I challenge the perspectives of others.
Self-monitoring (SM)
SM1 I am aware of my effort.
SM2 I am aware of my thinking.
SM3 I know my level of motivation.

APPENDIX 2

The Social-Emotional Engagement in Online Collaborative Discussion (SEE-OCD) Questionnaire

When I participate in synchronous online collaborative discussions,….

Social engagement (SE)
SE1 I cooperate with other classmates while working on assignments.
SE2 I listen and try to understand other classmates' ideas.
SE3 I try to help others who are struggling in learning.
Emotional engagement (EE)
EE1 I feel interested in the learning atmosphere.
EE2 I feel excited about the assignments.
EE3 I enjoy learning new things

Chapter 12
Collaborative International Online Learning (COIL): An Opportunity for Comprehensive and Intercultural Learning

Yorladis Alzate Gallego
https://orcid.org/0000-0002-3427-6342
Universidad Católica de Manizales, Colombia

Sonia Elda Stevens Bruzzese
Universidad Catolica de la Santisima Concepción, Chile

ABSTRACT

The pedagogical practice implemented enabled the students, through dialogue and intercultural exchange, to acquire a global perspective of the different situations and problems encountered in each of their contexts. The work through the COIL methodology and the Design Thinking tool stimulated the development of skills focused on creativity and problem solving. This type of pedagogical practice enriches learning through the exchange of experiences, ideas, and knowledge from each of the disciplines involved in the process, contributing to professional and personal strengthening and development.

INTRODUCTION

The academic crisis stemming from COVID-19 led universities to implement student-centered teaching and learning strategies. Information and Communication Technologies (ICT) as a mediating resource for the design of new spaces for collaboration and communication, García et al. (2018) made it easier for teachers and students to continue the educational process. On the other hand, international online collaboration with peers made it possible for learning to be generated from a comprehensive and intercultural perspective, which is how alliances between universities were generated to strengthen the redesign of

DOI: 10.4018/978-1-6684-7813-4.ch012

educational processes from a perspective of internationalization of the curriculum (Castiello-Gutiérrez et al., 2022).

In this context, the Universidad Católica de Manizales, Colombia, and the Universidad Católica de la Santísima Concepción, Chile, implemented the COIL (Collaborative International Online Learning) strategy. This methodology fosters international collaboration between educational institutions for two or more countries. The pedagogical experience described in this chapter presents the COIL methodology as a space for academic collaboration between universities that promoted active learning. Teachers and students developed and recognized their own and collective skills, abilities and aptitudes that portrayed a different vision of themselves and the world around them. In the pedagogical strategy, students played a leading role that favored learning in an environment of cultural and disciplinary interaction.

Therefore, this chapter aims to share the experience of the pedagogical practice implemented by two academics from the universities mentioned above, highlighting the importance of collaborative work from an intercultural and interdisciplinary framework, in which students from different professional careers were woven under the COIL methodology.

BACKGROUND

Internationalization at Home

The focus on internationalization in higher education institutions (HEIs) has generally focused on the mobility processes of the educational community (Tangelson et al., 2014). However, this prospect of internationalization is limiting, since not all the student population have the economic resources to access these possibilities. For López (2014) "the answer must necessarily be internationalization for all as an institutional policy and for this different strategies and actions must be planned and executed to achieve the objectives of internationalization" (p. 67). From this perspective, when developing internationalization strategies, HEIs must include elements that guarantee that their processes are inclusive for the entire university community, and involve the substantive functions: research, teaching, projection, and linkage with the environment. By virtue of this, internationalization at home gains value. For Herrera (2016), this typology refers to the "set of actions carried out by educational institutions, in order to strengthen their quality management systems, and achieve recognition through Accreditation" (p. 426). On his behalf, Knight (2008) describes it as an alliance that involves cultural and ethnic groups in which they converge: "[...] study plans and programs, teaching/learning processes, extracurricular activities, and research and academic activity" (p.23).

HEIs must ensure that 100% of the student population has access to processes of interaction with other cultures from a global perspective of the discipline studied. It is important to encourage the development of skills for global citizenship in the student community, which requires the acquisition of various skills for problem solving, assertive communication, collaborative work, critical thinking, and the development and appropriation of digital skills, among others. Along these lines, Amador (2020) states that internationalization at home should include all those actions based on local teaching and research needs that are developed on and from the campus, preferably in international collaboration, in order to guarantee the institution to offer a relevant and socially relevant education, in the light of a global, dynamic and changing context to its community, made up of students, professors, administrators, and other members of the institution, to develop the knowledge, skills, abilities, attitudes, and values to perform more effectively in multicultural, international, or global contexts.

The management of internationalization at home requires interinstitutional relations, which contribute to strengthening the internationalization of both the curriculum and the management systems at the level of research and linkage with the environment. De Witt and Leask (2015) frame this question as "the process of incorporating international, intercultural and global dimensions into curriculum content, as well as learning outcomes, assessment tasks, teaching methodologies and support services in a programme study" (p.13). Consequently, the implementation of internationalization strategies in the country brings to the curriculum elements such as: national and international cooperation, cooperative and collaborative work, the development of research projects, national and international visibility, regional, national, international, and global perspectives of the discipline studied.

It is therefore relevant to understand the benefits of implementing strategies and actions for internationalization at home, with a global perspective that includes all the actors of the university community. This implementation will increase participation in cooperation networks with strategic allies, which permeate academic processes as a factor for change in society.

Collaborative Online International Learning (COIL)

Collaborative Online International Learning (COIL) is a methodology used to generate teaching and learning spaces between different countries and cultures through collaborative work around an interdisciplinary and intercultural approach that "supports curricular internationalization and allows the networking of academics and students, through the innovation of their teaching-learning processes" (Salazar, 2022, p.133)

In this methodology, "students and faculty provide meaningful opportunities for global experiences embedded in curricula" (SUNY COIL, n.d., para. 2). COIL is methodologically incorporated into an academic component, which can be developed throughout the course or in the weeks defined by the professors, who establish the interdisciplinary work modules. The development of the COIL took into account the schedules for asynchronous and synchronous work with the students, the advice to the work teams, the digital resources for the development of the strategy, the learning expected from the students and the results and conclusions obtained, among others. "This type of innovative teaching and learning methodology leverages online technologies to offer global learning and interculturality experiences through a simultaneous exchange of ways of thinking, culture, and knowledge in the classroom" (Gaytán-Oyarzun et al., 2022, p. 143).

SUNY COIL (n.d.) establishes specific phases for the effective development of collaborations. The first phase begins with an *icebreaker* activity that allows to break the tensions that may arise in the group, which provides a space for the students to get to know each other, and then the work groups are created. The second phase "includes comparative discussions and the organization of the project in which the student teams will work" (SUNY COIL, n.d., para. 6), this phase is preparatory to teamwork. As a third phase, the project focuses on the main collaborative activity, for which a joint project is created, and spaces for dialogue on a specific topic are generated. The final phase focuses on the socialization of the work developed by the students, as well as the presentation of their reflections on the lived experience. The implementation of COIL in academic programs allows to:

- **Internationalize the curriculum:** Interaction with academic peers and global perspectives, allows for updating curricula, strengthening content, and incorporating new methodologies.
- **Improve the profile of graduates:** The development of solutions provided by students to problems in the local, regional, or global context, and the interaction with various cultures and disciplines, encourage critical and reflective thinking in students.
- **Train students comprehensively:** The comprehensive training of students is promoted from an intercultural perspective, promoting research, communication processes, critical, comparative, and creative thinking, as well as problem solving. Based on soft skills, respect for cultural identity and difference is strengthened (Meza Morón, 2020).
- **Strengthen the digital competence of teachers and students:** Digital competence is understood as the "use and appropriation of technologies for the design of innovative educational environments, which favor teaching and learning with a critical, reflective and creative sense, responding to training that enhances learning" (Alzate Gallego et al., 2021, p. 47). This is how skills for the management of Information and Communication Technologies (ICT) are strengthened through COIL, as support and mediation for the execution of collaborative online activities.

Therefore, it is concluded that this methodology of internationalization as a pedagogical practice, allows academic cooperation and the creation of knowledge networks. It is a commitment to active and disruptive methodologies, in which the process of co-creation is a key factor for the development of students' skills in an increasingly globalized world.

Collaborative and Intercultural Learning

Collaborative learning is a social process in which, through joint work and the establishment of common objectives, the construction of knowledge is generated; in this collaboration there is a permanent and fluid dialogue in which various points are contrasted that generate new ideas for solutions to the issues addressed (Galindo-González et al., 2012).

The COIL methodology proposes collaborative work and an intercultural experience with a focus on the interaction that occurs between cultures and common perspectives, that is, shared values, same interests, and legitimized and accepted norms of coexistence. Interculturality is a relationship of harmony between cultures; that is, a relationship of positive exchange and social coexistence between culturally differentiated actors (Giménez et al., 2000). The COIL methodology promotes, through collaborative work between students from different cultures, a learning experience, enriched not only by the individual skills, knowledge, and abilities that each student shares with their teammates, but also by the contribution they provide from their habits, knowledge, and beliefs of their cultures, valuing and respecting cultural diversity. For intercultural collaborative learning to be achieved, the role of teachers is that of facilitators. The objectives and milestones that will be experienced when applying the methodology and integrating it into the different subjects are clearly presented to contribute to the development of the achievement of the expected learning.

Innovation and Social Technology

Since the beginning of humanity, generations have inherited their cultures, traditions, and idiosyncrasies, as well as the techniques for the construction of artifacts, with which they seek in order to improve the quality of life of human beings. The art and practical knowledge of getting things done is called "technique"; This, coupled with scientific knowledge, gives rise to the term "technology". Ochoa et al. (2007) state that technology "is the set of knowledge, skills, experiences, and scientific and empirical organization necessary to produce, distribute, market, and use goods and services" (p. 2). This indicates that technology is the body of knowledge of a scientifically valid technique.

However, scientific, and empirical knowledge based on conceptual and procedural components, when made available to society, responds to the concept of Social Technology. This category seeks to generate responses to challenges and problems to improve the quality of life and influence the design of public policies that provide benefits to communities. Technology is social when it aims to empower communities, making them autonomous and productive (Saorín & Gómez-Hernández, 2014). Social technology provides a sense of belonging, becoming a highly beneficial tool for the transformation of living conditions.

From the perspective of Science, Technology and Society (STS), technology is recognized as a mediating instrument for the advancement and development of society. On the other hand, the identification of the community, and political and economic factors that regulate science and technology, lead to the revelation of the ethical, environmental and/or cultural consequences of their development and implementation. Thus, science and technology are an "inherently social process or product where non-epistemic or technical elements (e.g., moral values, religious convictions, professional interests, economic pressures, etc.) play a decisive role in the genesis and consolidation of scientific ideas and technological artifacts" (García, et al., 2001, p. 126).

Regarding the innovation factor, Suárez (2018) defines it as "the rupture in time and space of a process, product or service, which is presented with a new incremental or radical quality, and which is accepted by the customer. Its impact may be economic, social, or environmental" (p.123). Vincent-Lancrin et al. (2019) also highlight the definition provided by the OECD, which states that innovation is: "A new or improved product or process (or combination thereof) that differs significantly from the previous products or processes of the unit and that has been made available to potential users (product) or put into use by the unit (process)" (p. 23).

Innovation, in the field of technological processes, focuses on the result of the changes that organizations manage when updating their technology or generating technological development processes. However, artifact development is not the only central issue in innovation processes, hence, it is necessary to propose practical solutions that benefit society and empower communities. (Arias, 2016). In terms of training processes, innovation "invites interdisciplinary dialogue, the disruptive transformation of pedagogical practices and the incubation of meaningful experiences for the educational communities of the region and the country" (Parra & Agudelo, 2020, p.54).

Society increasingly faces challenges typified from different perspectives: social, cultural, economic, educational, health-wise, among others. These require effective and viable responses, and timely actions, where technological innovation processes are not enough. Therefore, it is necessary that, from the field of higher education in the various disciplines, the processes of educational innovation are articulated, favoring, as indicated below, the following proposal by Parra et al, (2021) "not only the recognition of the discourses and knowledge of the different fields of knowledge, but also seeks to privilege inquiry, the critique, analysis, change and transformation of all those situations or needs specific to the contexts" (pp. 131-132).

Therefore, from the disciplinary training that students receive, it is necessary to ensure the implementation of innovation processes articulated to the social sphere, in which collective creation occurs and creativity, collaborative work, as well as problem solving expand; this favors the acquisition of cognitive and organizational skills (Howaldt, 2016).

In summary, the integration of social innovation with technology contributes to an effective and efficient response in the solution of global problems. It promotes participatory learning, in which skills are developed for collaborative work, problem solving, critical and creative thinking, respect for diversity and different thoughts, as well as multi- and interdisciplinary learning.

MAIN FOCUS OF THE CHAPTER

Research Context and Participants

The Universidad Católica de la Santísima Concepción (Chile) and the Universidad Católica de Manizales (Colombia) are members of the Organization of Catholic Universities of Latin America and the Caribbean (ODUCAL). This organization facilitates the contact and collaboration of the professors at the affiliated universities. During the pandemic, selected professors from both universities attended an online training process focused on the development of the COIL methodology, which was provided by Florida International University. ODUCAL has its own Online Collaborative Learning program for partner university organizations, which consists of a platform where COIL courses offered by partner universities are registered. When two or more professors find a COIL course for collaborative work, they register the project on the Global Experiences Portal: ODUCOIL. At the end of the process, students answer a survey, which allows them to determine the degree of satisfaction, which is also a prerequisite to opt for the certification offered by the platform to the students participating in the COIL projects.

As a result of the training, the instructors developed a work plan to implement the COIL methodology, which was executed in the first semester of 2021. This set path to the pedagogical experience presented in this chapter. Among the important features of the planning of the COIL project, the thematic areas that were articulated in the COIL course stand out. The Universidad Católica de la Santísima Concepción was linked with the Social Innovation course, and the Universidad Católica of Manizales with Technological Management. The difference in the disciplines studied became a planning challenge to adjust and articulate the learning outcomes of each of the courses to the expected learning with the implementation of the COIL project.

The "Social Innovation" course taught at the Universidad Católica de la Santísima Concepción is an elective and was supervised by the second author, in which 25 students from different faculties were enrolled; it is important to clarify that none of these students were pursuing careers related to teaching. The objective was focused on the generation of ideas and creative solutions to address the socioeconomic challenges of a given context, through collaborative and interdisciplinary work. The creation process is carried out through the Design Thinking tool. On the other hand, the first author from the Universidad Católica de Manizales was in charge of the "Technological Management" course ; this course is also elective and is part of the training of students preparing to become teachers in the area of Technology and Computer Science. Five students participated in this program. The main objective of the course is to train students to manage technological projects that respond to the needs of the socio-educational context.

In the planning of the COIL project, a period of five weeks was established for the development of each of the activities contemplated. The objective of the project presented to the students was: *To identify a social problem to design a creative solution proposal integrating technological components and us-*

ing the Design Thinking methodology. For the development of the objective, five working groups were formed, given the number of participating students. Twenty-five students from the Universidad Católica de la Santísima Concepción and five students from the Universidad Católica de Manizales participated in COIL. Thus, in each of the five working groups formed, there was a student from Colombia, the language in which the entire pedagogical experience was developed was Spanish.

The technological resources used were:

- Zoom platform for synchronous meetings.
- WhatsApp for the creation of work groups among students.
- Google Drive resources for sharing documents of interest related to the work proposal.

For the development of the project, five weeks of work were available, where the students were divided into five work teams. These were made up as follows: five students from the Social Innovation class and one from the Technology Management class. The number of members was decided according to the number of students per course. The Social Innovation students belonged to different careers, which was a challenge for the development of teamwork, given the multidisciplinary nature of each of the working groups. The COIL project proposal was called: "Social Technological Innovation, Chile – Colombia" March - May 2021. Once the teams were created, each group had the following tasks:

1- **Identify a social problem**: students were asked to talk about the problems that each member of the group empathized with and then choose one of them to address during the COIL.
2- **Obtain a prototype solution:** through the Design Thinking methodology, obtain a prototype of a creative solution, which would respond to the problems identified by them.
3- **Verification:** the proposed solution had to integrate technological elements that would facilitate social innovation and respond to the learning objectives of the COIL project.

The COIL project was carried out 100% virtually using the Zoom platform. It began with an introductory class, which included a welcome and contextualization of the project to be worked on, followed by an icebreaker activity whose purpose was the interaction and knowledge of the students. Each of the professors gave a thematic talk to familiarize the students with the concepts of Social Innovation, Social Technology and the Design Thinking process, essential elements for the development of the COIL project proposal (see Figure 1).

Figure 1. Work agenda of the Chile-Colombia COIL project
Source: Authors' own creation

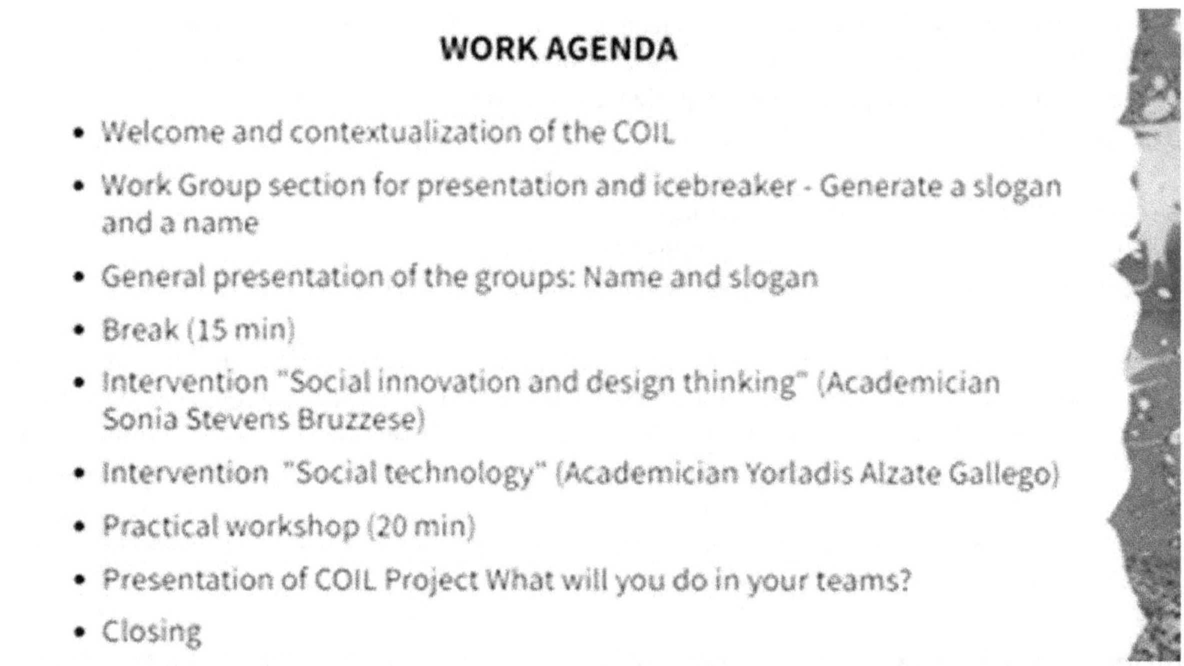

For the icebreaker activity, five groups were organized on the Zoom platform, each group made its corresponding presentation, assigned a name to the group and defined an identification slogan. Once the objective of the COIL project was socialized, a workshop was held with the following questions and elements:

- How can we work collaboratively?
    - Do we know each other?
    - Can we move forward without roles?
- How do we empathize with the external environment?
- What solutions will the Design Thinking methodology provide?
- What is a collision of ideas?
- Essential elements in the proposed solution:
    - Desirable
    - Feasible
    - Viable
    - Technology Onboarding

Finally, the points to be considered in the delivery of the COIL project were socialized, these were:

1- Present the Social Innovation proposal collaboratively, incorporating the technological component.
2- Socialize the proposal in front of classmates.
3- Individually present a reflection paper with the experience lived in the COIL project.

The methodology used for the development of the project was based on Design Thinking, which allows the construction of innovative ideas, focused on the user, the service, and the human dimension. For Brown (2008): "It is a discipline that uses the designer's sensibility and methods to match people's needs with what is technologically feasible and what a viable business strategy can turn into customer value and market opportunity" (p.4).

Neck and Corbett (2013) propose ten steps to apply a Design Thinking process, which are grouped into three important moments:

First moment: it focuses on divergent thinking, that is, contextualizing the problem or challenge to be worked on; observing and interpreting it according to the needs of the context.

Second moment: to carry out the ideation process, identifying areas of opportunity and brainstorming ideas to be modeled.

Third stage: consists of creating prototypes, experimenting, learning, and repeating the modeled ideas, and perfecting the innovative solution proposed. In this way, real solutions are created to the identified needs.

The elaboration of the project included six phases, integrated with some of the stages of Design Thinking in an abbreviated form, thus adjusting the results to the five weeks of the project (Figure 2).

Figure 2. Phases of the COIL project
Source: Authors' own creation

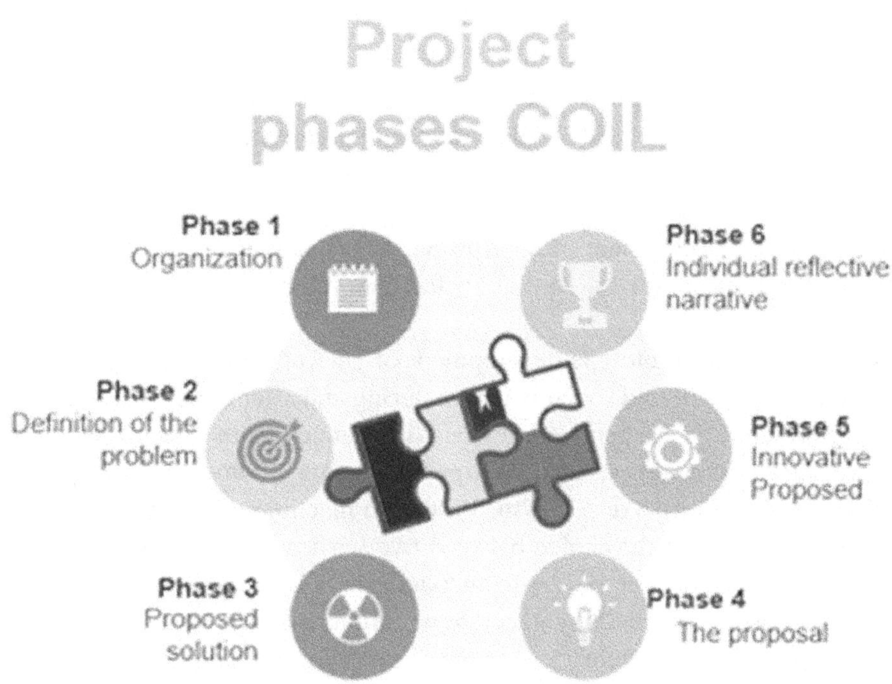

Phase 1. Organization: In this phase, the students got to know each other and talked about the way in which they were going to work collaboratively. They scheduled the days and times of the meeting and

created a WhatsApp group. They determined each participant's roles according to individual abilities and skills.

Phase 2. Problem definition: Through direct and indirect observation of the selected context, students recognized various social problems with which to empathize. Subsequently, as a team, they defined the approach to one of the problems by identifying causes and effects.

Phase 3. Solution proposal: Once the problem was defined and contextualized, a synchronous brainstorming session was held. In this process, students were invited to propose 70 ideas as possible solutions, identifying those that were achievable, moderately achievable, and unattainable. At this stage, they were urged to create space for creativity, avoiding judging and/or questioning team members' ideas. Subsequently, these ideas were grouped according to those with similar perspectives of solution. Once grouped, the students were asked to merge them, in such a way as to obtain three possible prototypes of solutions in which the technological component will be incorporated. The proposals had to be desirable (a problem really felt by a group of people), feasible (proposed solution possible to be implemented), viable (when implemented, it is possible to incorporate it in a sustainable and time-sustainable way over time), and innovative (includes surprise and/or differentiating elements from other ideas).

Phase 4. The proposal: Each work team chose one of the prototypes designed. At the time of socialization, they justified, step by step, their choice and design. The proposal was presented in a synchronous class, in which the students, the two professors and a panel of guests from the Universidad Católica de la Santísima Concepción participated. The audience asked questions about the suitability, feasibility, innovative and technological components of the chosen prototype. In this phase, the teams obtained feedback to improve the solution prototype presented.

Phase 5. Innovative proposal: Based on the feedback received in the previous phase, the work teams improved their prototype solution. A final synchronous socialization was held with the same guests from phase four. In this space, the teams argued and defended their prototypes, justifying the social innovation component. Below are some of the works done by the students:

- **AbueliTic**: prototype development of an App whose objective was to bring older adults closer to technological spaces, in such a way as to facilitate communication with their families and environment.
- **App Kays to The Brain**: prototype development of an App to provide motivational support to university students who suffered social isolation during and after the COVID-19 Pandemic. Some of the services provided by the application would be mental health issues, contact with psychologists and psychiatrists, motivational videos, tips for self-improvement.
- **Tinkerbell Wishes - Where We All Win**: Prototype machine where people deposit their mask and the machine offers them the choice between two wishes: get a discount on the purchase or a new mask. The aim of this prototype was to encourage people to dispose of masks in an authorized place and not in the street, where they generate pollution and damage to the ecosystem.
- **Card Game / App "CoviDivertete"**: prototype of a mobile application consisting of a card game, whose objective was to encourage self-care in school-age children to reduce the spread of the COVID-19 virus. The proposed game prototype had pedagogical elements to avoid the promotion of gender stereotypes, be planet-friendly, didactic and recreate quarantine protocols, confinements, and popular myths.

Phase 6. Individual Reflective Narrative: each student presented a written reflection about their work experience and the lessons learned. The questions proposed by the teachers for the construction of the reflection were: (i) What did you like most about the experience? (ii) What was the most difficult? (iii) Was the experience satisfactory? and (iv) Most importantly from the experience, what ideas do you propose that can be implemented for future experiences?

It is important to note that even though this pedagogical experience was not part of a research, the participating teachers considered it convenient to have the reflections of each student in writing in such a way that they could have feedback and co-evaluation of the process carried out. On the other hand, as mentioned in previous paragraphs, this pedagogical experience was related to the ODUCOIL platform, where each student registered for the course. Subsequently, they answered the survey offered by the platform to finally download their certificate of participation in the COIL project. The instrument designed by the ODUCOIL platform included the following criteria: motivation, communication skills and interculturality, among others.

Feedback From Students

Below are the answers given by the students through the ODUCOIL Global Experiences Portal. This portal designs the questionnaire and offers a graphical visualization of the answers obtained. Consequently, the results allow us to visualize the question and the answers given by the students, facilitating a quantitative analysis of the students' answers. According to the different dynamic axes, the following analysis is presented.

Motivation

For Carrillo et al. (2009), motivation "is that internal and positive attitude towards new learning, it is what moves the subject to learn" (p.24). Prior to the implementation of the COIL methodology, an activity was carried out in which students interacted with each other, learned about their peers: tastes, preferences, and expectations. The motivation for collaborative work became a key factor in the implementation of a pedagogical practice, that prioritized meaningful and participatory learning. For 62% of the students, motivation determined their participation in class, while for 31% it was neutral and for the remaining 8% the motivation was intermediate. (Figure 3):

Figure 3. Motivation to participate
Source: Authors' own creation

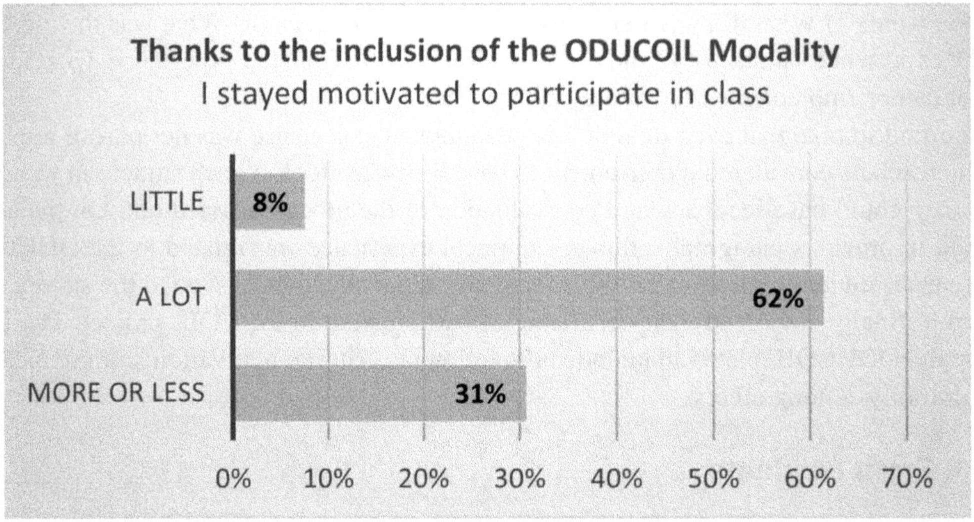

In the development of the COIL project, didactic actions were implemented that captured the attention and invited students to be an active part of the process. A total of 62 percent of students said they strongly agreed that the experience was satisfactory, and the remaining 38 percent said they disagreed. (Figure 4).

Figure 4. Learning experience
Source: Authors' own creation

Interculturality

The work carried out with the students favored openness in the development of skills for intercultural communication, understood as "the ability to express information to others about their own culture through communication with them, as well as to interpret information about the other and their culture" (UNESCO, 2017, p.15). Sixty-two percent of the students reported having practiced intercultural communication skills a lot, 31% rarely practiced them, and the remaining 8% did so little (Fig. 5)

Figure 5. Intercultural communication
Source: Authors' own creation

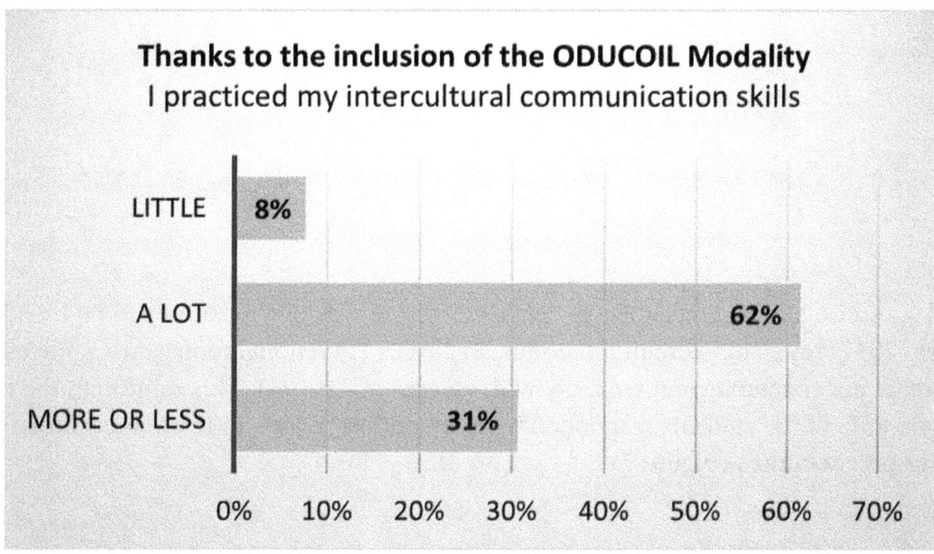

The students' motivation for the intercultural experience generated a positive evaluation. The possibility of generating learning with students of different disciplines and nationalities was highlighted, which allowed them to recognize common problems, seeking global solutions to solve problems through a creative process, which contributed to the development of critical and original thinking in students.

As for knowledge and/or understanding of another culture, for 69% of students it increased a lot, for the remaining 31% it remained average (Figure 6).

Figure 6. Knowledge/understanding of other cultures
Source: Authors' own creation

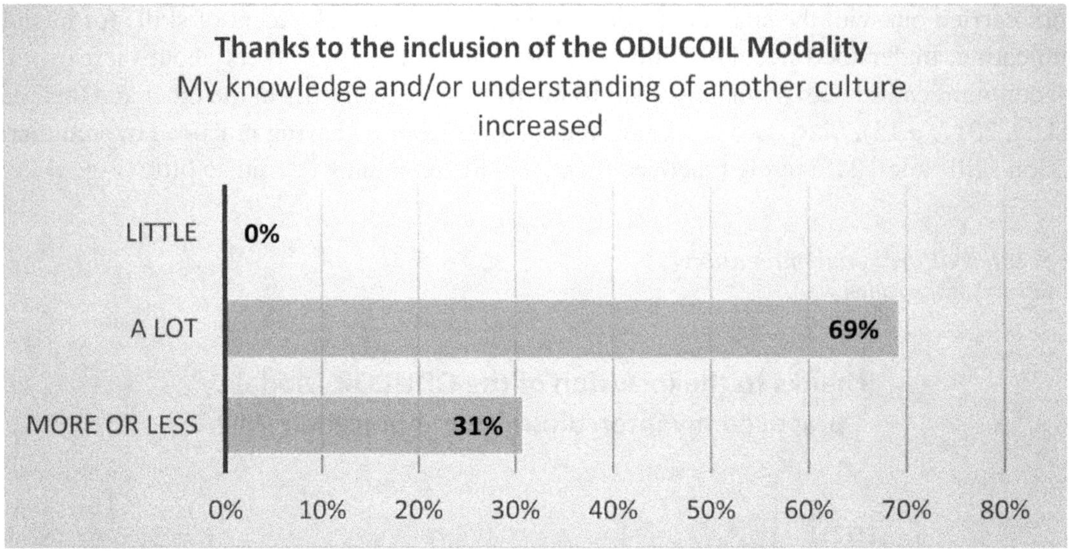

The COIL exercise allowed the students' perspective towards other cultures to be broad. In this regard, Gunther (2017) refers to intercultural competencies as "functional tools and resources to increase tolerance, mutual understanding and empathy with otherness" (p.194). This reinforces the result in this variable, where 85% of the students responded with the option "a lot", to relate their broad perspective and respect for other cultures (Figure 7).

Figure 7. Perspective and respect for other cultures
Source: Authors' own creation

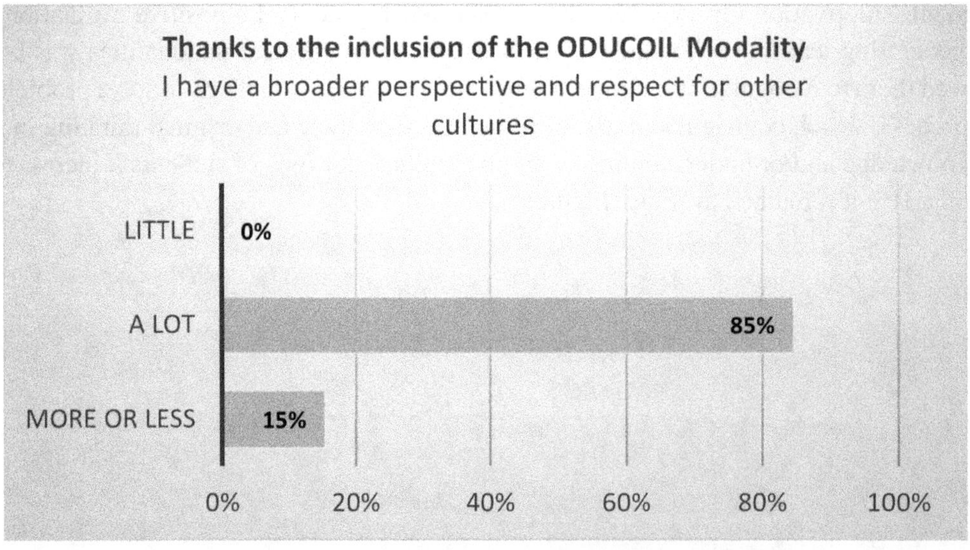

Interaction was one of the central axes in the creative process of the teams. This allowed each of the students to learn a little more about the culture of their coworkers. Sixty-two% of students stated that they felt safe interacting with people from a different culture to their own, and the remaining 38% stated that they felt safe in the COIL environment (Figure 8).

Figure 8. Interaction with other cultures
Source: Authors' own creation

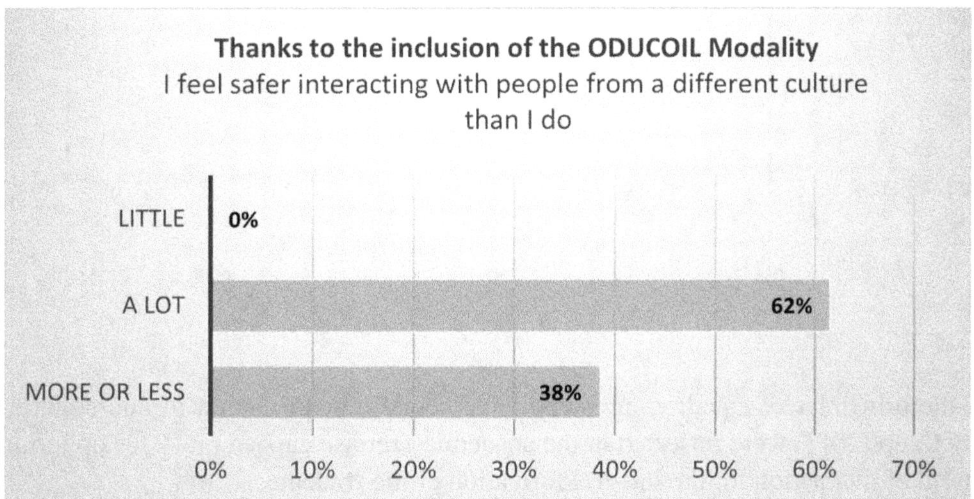

"It is necessary to teach students not only content information about a wide range of cultures, but also a general openness to difference" (UNESCO, 2017, p. 32). The approach to other cultures allowed the students to have a global vision of the world, the motivation to get to know other cultures was fostered, which considering the evidence presented, enriched not only their disciplinary knowledge, but also their personal development. Considering the above, 77% of students expressed a strong interest in studying abroad, while the remaining 23% stated an interest in it according to Figure 9.

Figure 9. Interest in studying abroad
Source: Authors' own creation

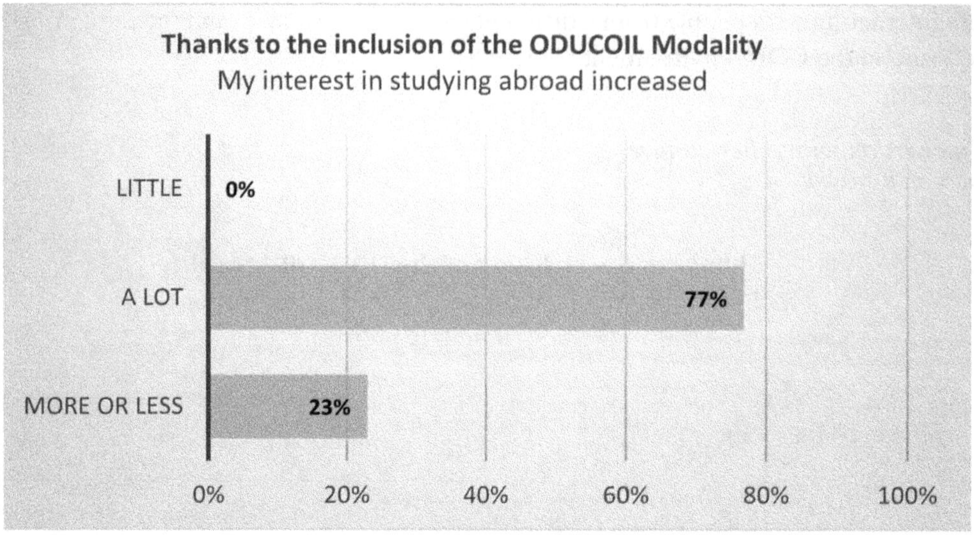

Finally, the principles of equality, interaction and social transformation in intercultural processes proposed by Cano (2013) were reflected in the academic exercise carried out. This opportunity generated a scenario of interaction for the integral formation of the students.

The biggest challenge that the students identified in the COIL experience was having to work collaboratively with students from other disciplines and countries, recognizing that this favored the exchange of opinions and the construction of knowledge, as a "process of negotiation or joint construction of meanings" (Roselli, 2016, p.224). The online interaction that was generated among the participating students evidenced the importance of dialogue and respect for different ways of thinking and self-expression. The dialogue was based on the recognition of their diversities. The mutual appreciation between students in academic settings created spaces of understanding and tolerance.

SOLUTIONS AND RECOMMENDATIONS

The execution of each of the phases of the project developed with the students consolidated and strengthened the acquisition of competencies for global performance, framed in the development of critical thinking, interdependence and collaborative work, decision-making for responsible action and collaboration in the resolution of global challenges. These competencies are part of the educational purposes of the students at the Universidad Católica de Manizales, which seek to form "a diverse, inclusive and multicultural community that contributes to a more just, supportive and fraternal society" (Universidad Católica de Manizales, 2022, p.37).

The experience of international collaboration enriched the academic curriculum of the training programs. It allowed peer-to-peer relationships, expanding to learning communities formed by students, who had the privilege of accessing training with a global perspective from each discipline in multidisciplinary and intercultural dialogue. In this sense, Marín (2020) refers to the internationalization of the curriculum as "an intentional formative process, based on the participation of educational actors and interest groups that, with institutional support, weave relationships among themselves to generate capacities through communities of practice" (p.128). In this training process, students are formed as global citizens who interact with different cultures and communities, proposing solutions to global problems from a socially responsible stance.

The development of the COIL project strengthened the relationship between the two universities, transcending into new academic collaborations. Considering that the experience was highly valued by students and professors, in the second semester of that same year, students of the Bachelor's Degree in Technology and Informatics of the Universidad Católica de Manizales, Colombia, through the subject of pedagogical and educational practice, trained a group of Chilean professors in the commune of Cañete in educational informatics; these are part of the social work carried out by the Scientific and Technological Center of the Universidad Católica de la Santísima Concepción.

FUTURE LINES OF RESEARCH

Once this pedagogical experience among the universities has been completed, the academics hope to be able to carry out research that will identify the impact of COIL projects on the development of communicative, intercultural, and digital skills of both teachers and students. The result of this study would contribute to the internationalization of the curriculum of each of the courses, contributing to a comprehensive education that responds to the changing demands of a globalized world.

CONCLUSION

The pedagogical practice implemented enabled the students, through dialogue and intercultural exchange, to acquire a global perspective of the different situations and problems encountered in each of their contexts. The work through the COIL methodology and the Design Thinking tool stimulated the development of skills focused on creativity and problem solving. For Giraldo Gómez et al. (2021) "the role of the professional must go beyond the simple image of an educated man, as he or she must become highly sensitive to the events of the country, the region and its context" (p. 84). By virtue of the above, this type of pedagogical practices enriches learning through the exchange of experiences, ideas and knowledge from each of the disciplines involved in the process, contributing to professional and personal strengthening and development.

ACKNOWLEDGMENT

The authors would like to thank their Universities and Internationalization Units, which facilitated their collaboration and training in the COIL methodology. They would also like to thank the students who actively participated in the COIL project and Professor Ada Lizarrague, collaborator of the Social Innovation course, who joined and actively cooperated.

REFERENCES

Alzate, Y., Parra, R., Canales, R., & Morales, M. (2021). Apropiación de las competencias digitales en educación superior [Appropriation of digital skills in higher education]. In R. Cabello & S. Lago (Eds.), *Ciudadanía digital, desigualdades y transformación en América Latina y el Caribe: Memorias* [Digital Citizenship, Inequalities and Transformation in Latin America and the Caribbean: Memorias] (pp. 46-58). Universidad de Sevilla (idUS). https://hdl.handle.net/11441/133942

Amador, G. (2020). Conceptual framework on internationalization in the country. In J. E. Hernández & G. Amador (Eds.), *Good internationalization practices at home. Experiences at the University of Colima* (pp. 13–20). University of Colima. http://ww.ucol.mx/content/publicacionesenlinea/adjuntos/Buenas-practicas-de-internacionalizacion-2_490.pdf

Arias, J. (2016). Social innovation, a concept linked to praxis; the case of UNIMINUTO's Social Innovation Science Park - Colombia. In D. Domanski, N. Monge, G. Quitiaquez, & D. Rocha (Eds). *Social innovation in Latin America* (pp. 255-295). Uniminuto. https://acortar.link/lI31PO

Brown, T. (2008). *Design Thinking*. Harvard Business. https://acortar.link/eC56lD

Cano, J. (2013). Intercultural competencies, curriculum and agents involved in the education system. In J. L. López (Ed.), *Cultural diversity and intercultural education* (pp. 201–224). GEEPP Ediciones. https://www.stes.es/melilla/archivos/libro_diversidad_cultural/Pdfs/Diversidad%20Cultural.pdf

Carrillo, M., Padilla, J., Rosero, T., & Villagómez, M. S. (2009). Motivation and learning. Otherness. *Journal of Education*, *4*(2), 20–32. https://www.redalyc.org/comocitar.oa?id=467746249004

Castiello-Gutiérrez, S., Pantoja Aguilar, M. P., & Gutiérrez Jurado, C. E. (2022). From crisis to opportunity: Internationalization of higher education after COVID-19. *Journal of Higher Education in Latin America*, *12*, 7–11. https://rcientificas.uninorte.edu.co/index.php/esal/article/view/14921/214421446099

De Witt, H., & Leask, B. (2015). Internationalization, curriculum and disciplines. *International Higher Education,* (83), 11-13. https://issuu.com/ceppechile/docs/higher_83

Galindo-González, L., Martínez de la Cruz, N., Ley Fuentes, M., Ruiz Aguirre, E., & Valenzuela González, E. (2012). Epistemological approach to collaborative learning. *Opening, 4*(2), 156-169. http://www.udgvirtual.udg.mx/apertura/index.php/apertura/article/view/325/290

García, E. M., González, J. C., López, J. A., Luján, J. L., Martín, M., Osorio, C., & Valdés, C. (2001). *Science, Technology and Society: A Conceptual Approach.* Organization of Ibero-American States for Education, Science and Culture https://acortar.link/7UOf0b

García, M., Reyes, J., & Godínez, G. (2018). The ICT in higher education, innovations and challenges. *RICSH Ibero-American Journal of Social Sciences and Humanities*, *6*(12), 17. doi:10.23913/ricsh.v6i12.135

Gaytán-Oyarzun, J., Cravioto-Torres, R., Mendoza-Meza, E., & Ortiz-Zarco, E. (2022). Implementation of the COIL methodology, as a strategy to enhance the teaching-learning process and academic and student mobility in the virtual modality. *Journal of Innovation and Good Practices Teachers*, *11*(1), 141–149. http://www.uco.es/ucopress/ojs/index.php/ripadoc/article/view/14142/12766

Giménez, C. (2000). Guía sobre interculturalidad [Guide on interculturality]. *Colección Cuadernos Q'anil, Proyecto. Q'anil-PNUD* [Cuadernos Q'anil Collection, Project. Q'anil-UNDP]. Editorial Serviprensa.

Giraldo Gómez, O., Zuluaga Giraldo, J. I., Jaramillo Echeverry, A., & Vargas Aguirre, J. F. (2021). Pedagogical practices that contribute to the construction of a better citizenship. *Journal of Research, 19*(34), 81–91. doi:10.22383/ri.v19i34.140

Gunther, D. (2017). Interculturality: An anthropological approach. *Educational Profiles, 39*(156), 192–207. https://acortar.link/Rtzk91

Herrera, B. L. (2016). Internationalization at home. Management processes for the internationalization of the Señor de Sipán University. *Environments, 29*(2), 423–426. https://dialnet.unirioja.es/descarga/articulo/6937140.pdf

Howaldt, J., Domanski, D., & Kaletka, C. (2016). Social innovation: Towards a new innovation paradigm. *RAM. Revista de Administração Mackenzie, 17*(6), 20–44. doi:10.1590/1678-69712016/administracao.v17n6p20-44

Knight, J. (2008). *Higher education in turmoil: The changing world of internationalization.* Brill. doi:10.1163/9789087905224

López, G. H. (2014). The internationalization of higher education and the formation of Global Citizens, Glocal Citizens. *Sophia, 10*(2), 64–69. http://www.scielo.org.co/pdf/sph/v10n2/v10n2a07.pdf

Marín, M. A. (2020). Internationalization of the curriculum from practice: Contributions from the national and international context. In G. C. Valencia González & L. E. Malagón Castro (Eds.), *Educación y región, lo dicho de lo no dicho* [Education and region, what has been said about what has not been said] (pp. 119–141). Editorial Corporación Universitaria del Meta –UNIMETA. doi:10.52043/LVDW1392

Meza Morón, O. P. (2020). The COIL Model, a transformative intercultural experience. In *Memorial of the XX Teacher Training Meeting Summer 2020* (1st ed., p. 424). Jennie Brand Barajas.

Neck, H., & Corbett, A. (2013). *Symposium for Entrepreneurship Educators2013: Material taller Design Thinking.* Banco de Chile-Babson College.

Ochoa, M. B., Valdés, M., & Quevedo, Y. (2007). Innovation, technology and technology management. *Acimed, 16*(4), 1–12. https://bit.ly/3oVtkKt

Parra, L. R., & Agudelo, A. (2020). Innovation in pedagogical practices mediated by ICTs. In R. Canales & C. Reyes (Eds.), *Access, democracy and virtual communities. Appropriation of digital technologies from the Southern Cone* (pp. 51–63). CLACSO. https://biblioteca.clacso.edu.ar/clacso/se/20201125054915/Canales-Herrera.pdf

Parra, L. R., Menjura, M. I., Pulgarín, L. E., & Gutiérrez, M. M. (2021). Pedagogical practices. An opportunity to innovate in education. *Latin American Education Studies, 17*(1), 70–94. doi:10.17151/rlee.2021.17.1.5

Roselli, N. (2016). Collaborative Learning: Theoretical bases and strategies applicable to university teaching. *Purposes and Representations, 4*(1), 219–280. doi:10.20511/pyr2016.v4n1.90

Salazar, S. (2022). The challenge of internationalization in Peruvian universities. In S. Castiello-Gutiérrez, M.P. Pantoja, & C.E. Gutiérrez (Eds.), *Internationalization of higher education after COVID-19: Reflections and new practices for different times* (pp. 124-137). Universidad Popular Autónoma del Estado de Puebla. https://acortar.link/pWOjF9

Saorín, T., & Gómez-Hernández, J. A. (2014). Literacy in social technologies for everyday life and empowerment. *ThinkEPI Yearbook, 8*, 342-348. https://acortar.link/ysRBEo

Suárez, R. P. (2018). Reflections on the concept of innovation. *Revista San Gregorio, 24*, 120-131. https://bit.ly/34OY3Sp

SUNY COIL. (n.d). *Conéctese, participe, colabore* [Connect, participate, collaborate]. https://coil.suny.edu/

Tangelson, G. (Comp.). (2014). *From the South: Views on Internationalization*. https://www.cinda.cl/wp-content/uploads/2014/09/Desde-el-sur-miradas-sobre-la-internacionalización.pdf

UNESCO. (2017). *Intercultural competences: Conceptual and operational framework*. UNESCO. https://unesdoc.unesco.org/ark:/48223/pf0000251592/PDF/251592spa.pdf.multi

Universidad Católica de Manizales. (2022). *UCM Academic Policies*. UCM Publishing Center.

Vincent-Lancrin, S., Urge, J., Kar, S., & Jacotin, G. (2019). *Measuring innovation in education 2019: What has changed in the classroom?* Educational Research and Innovation, OECD Publishing. doi:10.1787/9789264311671-en

KEY TERMS AND DEFINITIONS

COIL (Collaborative International Online Learning): An innovative online teaching and learning methodology that offers a global and intercultural classroom experience.

Critical Thinking: Ability to discern information through a process of analysis and evaluation.

Design Thinking: Methodology used in the design process, which integrates cognitive, strategic and practical processes that develop creative thinking and generate solution proposals based on the user's needs.

Empathize: Design thinking phase that allows you to identify how the user thinks and feels. Allowing you to find solutions that connect with your needs and wants.

Interculturality: Set of interrelationships that make up society, articulating cultures, ethnicities, languages, religious denomination and the various nations.

Learning: The process that enables human beings to acquire or modify skills, abilities, and behaviors through experience, reasoning, and observation.

Mirror Class: Curricular integration strategy that favors the teaching process in the field of internationalization, strengthening the bond between peers and creating learning communities.

Narrative: A literary genre that describes, orally or in writing, a real or fictitious event.

ODUCAL: Organization of Catholic Universities in Latin America and the Caribbean, through its portal offers the possibility of finding peers to create international collaborative online learning projects.

ODUCOIL: Online Collaborative Learning Program of the Organization of Catholic Universities of Latin America and the Caribbean (ODUCAL).

Prototype: A model created in the design process, to validate a solution proposal.

Chapter 13
International Telecollaboration on Teaching English to Children at Risk:
A Case Study

Cristina Villegas-Troya
https://orcid.org/0009-0001-7703-5987
Universidad de Córdoba, Spain

Francisco Javier Palacios-Hidalgo
https://orcid.org/0000-0002-4326-209X
Universidad de Córdoba, Spain

Cristina A. Huertas-Abril
https://orcid.org/0000-0002-9057-5224
Universidad de Córdoba, Spain

ABSTRACT

This chapter describes a service-learning (SL) project designed through telecollaboration aiming to improve the linguistic competence in English as a foreign language (EFL) and the intercultural awareness of children at risk of social exclusion studying in a local association in Málaga (Spain). Due to the restrictions posed by COVID-19 in spring of 2020, the project was based on telecollaborative service-learning (TSL) and carried out through several online workshops designed by a pre-service EFL teacher and held by international students doing an exchange program in the city of Málaga. This case study shows that this TSL project provided children at risk of social exclusion with the opportunity of being in contact with international students, other cultures, and using the English language in a real, meaningful context, while initial teacher training also improved by facing real-world situations.

DOI: 10.4018/978-1-6684-7813-4.ch013

INTRODUCTION

Being understood from a wide perspective, Service-Learning (SL) is an educational methodology that combines learning and community service, so that students can engage with real societal needs while learning (Erickson & Anderson, 1997; Umpleby & Rakicevik, 2008). According to Felten and Clayton (2011): "Service-learning is emerging as a central component of efforts to connect both disciplinary learning and general education with this historic and increasingly salient commitment to public purposes" (p. 75). SL is therefore accepted as a vehicle for community engagement and a high-impact pedagogy. Although SL is increasing in European universities, Spain is still far from implementing it as part of teacher training (Álvarez-Castillo et al., 2017). Furthermore, telecollaboration is nowadays seen as a powerful tool for bridging educational gaps, not only the digital gap (Lister, 2022), but also the language gap (Villegas-Paredes et al., 2022). In fact, during the COVID-19 pandemic, more telecollaboration projects were implemented to provide solutions for the impossibility of having face-to-face lessons (Huertas-Abril, 2020; Komatsu, 2023; Parsons et al., 2022).

The telecollaborative online learning project described in this chapter was developed thanks to the synergy of the SL methodology and telecollaboration. The project was carried out with the Association Altamar, which works to enhance the educational conditions of children at risk of social exclusion (i.e., "at risk of poverty, or severely materially and socially deprived or living in a household with a very low work intensity", European Commission, 2021, para. 1) in the province of Málaga (Spain), and the Erasmus Student Network (ESN) Málaga Association, an organization for international students studying in Málaga. Considering the limited literature on the connections among SL, social exclusion, language learning and telecollaboration –especially during and after the global health emergency of 2020–, this chapter aims at shedding some light on this topic. Therefore, it presents the results of a case study carried out through the use of workshops designed as part of a telecollaboration project to develop the communicative competence in English as a Foreign Language (EFL) of children at risk of exclusion.

THEORETICAL BACKGROUND

Telecollaboration for Service-Learning

Telecollaboration, also known as online or virtual collaboration, refers to the use of technology to enable communication and collaboration between people who are not in the same physical location (Huertas-Abril, 2020). It involves the use of online tools and platforms, such as video conferencing (Austin et al., 2017), messaging apps (Godwin-Jones, 2019), social media (Krajka & Gabryś-Sławińska, 2022), and cloud-based file sharing (DuFrene & Lehman, 2016), among others, to facilitate virtual communication and collaboration. Telecollaboration can help to break down geographic barriers and enable people to work together more effectively, regardless of their physical location (Clouet, 2023), and can also facilitate the exchange of ideas, knowledge, and expertise, and promote cross-cultural understanding and collaboration (Casañ-Pitarch et al., 2020; Slapac et al., 2023). Effective telecollaboration requires clear communication, strong interpersonal skills (Cleary et al., 2019), but also an understanding of the technology tools and platforms being used, as well as careful planning and coordination to ensure that everyone is working towards a common goal (Nae, 2022). Despite the potential challenges, successful telecollaboration can lead to a range of benefits (Barbosa & Ferreira-Lopes, 2023), including improved productivity, enhanced learning outcomes, and strengthened social connections.

On the other hand, SL is an educational approach that combines community service with academic learning (Umpleby & Rakicevik, 2008), involving students to participate in meaningful and relevant service activities that are integrated into their academic curriculum (Ochoa & Pérez, 2019). As a direct consequence, SL aims to promote civic engagement, social responsibility, and personal development, as well as academic achievement (Coelho & Menezes, 2021; Pulczinski, 2018). The service activities are designed to meet real community needs and provide students with opportunities to develop new skills, knowledge, and perspectives. SL often involves reflection activities, such as journaling or group discussions, which help students to connect their service experiences to their academic learning and personal growth. SL can take place in a variety of settings, including schools, universities, and community organizations, as well as at all stages of formal education, from elementary (López-Cirugeda, 2015) to higher education (Salam et al., 2019). Effective SL requires careful planning, coordination, and evaluation to ensure that learning is meaningful, sustainable, and beneficial for all stakeholders involved (Raineri, 2020). Furthermore, Telecollaborative Service-Learning (TSL), also known as eService learning (Faulconer, 2021), is a form of SL that uses technology to connect students with service opportunities and promote learning outcomes. According to Waldner et al. (2012): "Online learning is a facilitator rather than a barrier to service-learning. E-service-learning holds the potential to transform both service-learning and online learning by freeing service-learning from geographical constraints, and by equipping online learning with a tool to promote engagement" (p. 123). TSL involves students engaging in virtual service activities that are integrated into their academic curriculum, enabling them to engage in service activities from anywhere, at any time, and to connect with a diverse range of people and organizations (Marcus et al., 2020). It must be highlighted that TSL can also be more accessible and flexible than 'traditional' SL, allowing participants with different schedules or mobility challenges to participate, even in the hardest moments of the COVID-19 pandemic (Reif-Stice & Smith-Frigerio, 2021). TSL can lead to a range of benefits, including improved academic performance, enhanced digital literacy skills, and increased civic engagement (Marcus et al., 2020). TSL can be implemented considering a wide range of approaches and tasks, including:

- Online tutoring: online platforms can be used for students to connect with peers and provide academic support, so it can be used for peer tutoring, homework help, or virtual study groups.
- Virtual advocacy campaigns and virtual fundraising: students can collaborate online with organizations and associations to create and launch an advocacy campaign to raise awareness about a social issue (e.g., gender equity, or healthy habits). This way, students can work together to create social media posts, videos, infographics, and other materials to promote their cause.
- Virtual mentorship programs: Learners can partner with local community organizations and use an online platform to connect and communicate with others as mentors. The mentors can provide guidance and support to younger students, who will also help them identify SL opportunities in the community.
- Online storytelling: Learners can partner with a local organization from their context or at the international level to collect and share stories from community members, with the purpose of fostering the recovery of traditions, experiences, and historical memory. Students then can collaborate to create and share digital stories, podcasts, or videos that highlight the experiences and perspectives of community members.

- Crowdsourced research: Learners can collaborate with nonprofit organizations to conduct research on a community issue, so that they can gather and analyze data, write reports, and make recommendations for action.
- Virtual community events: The collaboration between educational institutions and sociocultural organizations and associations can lead to hosting virtual community events (i.e., online workshops, webinars, or panel discussions) to promote SL and community engagement. These fora can also help the stakeholders involved identify needs to further (T)SL projects.

As Waldner et al. (2012) state, "Service-learning can produce benefits for the students, the community partners, the participating faculty members, and the university itself" (p. 125). Therefore, TSL can also be helpful for pre-service teachers, as it may serve to overcome the lack of time and materials they find through projects where teachers in formative stages can learn how to create teaching materials, at the same time providing them with opportunities to solve real-world problems (Villegas-Troya et al., 2023).

Social Exclusion, Affective Factors, and Language Learning

As Elenbaas and Killen (2016) point out that "Persistent or prolonged experiences of exclusion in childhood are related to long term negative consequences, such as depression, social withdrawal, and anxiety" (p. 106). This condition can affect children's social interactions and social relationships, which are essential for them to achieve a healthy emotional well-being, academic success and productive work experiences in adulthood – in fact, the absence of these experiences can lead to negative long-term effects as demonstrated by numerous studies (i.e., Bradley & Corwyn, 2002; Buhs & Ladd, 2001; Prinstein & Aikins, 2004; Yoshikawa et al., 2012). Therefore, teachers need to be well aware and understand the importance of this condition and how it could affect the academic success of their students. According to Majcen and Drvodelić (2022):

The results of many relevant studies confirm that quality early childhood education and care is crucial for short-term and long-term positive outcomes in different development and learning areas, especially in the case of disadvantaged children, including children at risk of social exclusion. (Majcen & Drvodelić, 2022, p. 81)

Inclusive educational practice is a key compensating strategy for reducing children's risk of social exclusion (Balladares & Kankaraš, 2020; Frazer & Marlier, 2014; Geddes et al., 2011). A high-quality environment can ensure the correct growth and learning of children, particularly those at risk of social exclusion, contributing to their long-term well-being (Campbell-Barr et al., 2002; Vandell et al., 2010).

When examining how some factors could affect the academic performance of students at risk of social exclusion in foreign languages, Escarbajal-Frutos et al. (2015) determined that families with low socioeconomic status tend to have fewer resources to respond to their children's academic demands, and they may offer limited help in difficult times. As a consequence, these students usually have fewer opportunities to improve their academic achievement (Bornstein & Bradley, 2014; Sirin, 2005).

Moreover, affective factors are important when it comes to acquiring proficiency in a foreign language because they may enhance or hinder learning (Wang & Wu, 2020). In this line, the affective filter hypothesis developed by Krashen (1985) suggests that language acquisition can be hindered by negative emotions such as stress and anxiety, which create an 'affective filter' preventing learners from accessing language input and reducing motivation to engage in language learning. On the contrary, this author argues that a low affective filter, characterized by positive emotions such as confidence and willingness to take risks, is necessary for successful language acquisition. Consequently, creating a supportive and safe learning environment, promoting positive attitudes toward language learning, and reducing sources of stress and anxiety can all help to lower the affective filter. Similarly, some researchers defend that motivation is important within the classroom to perform the learning procedure, since without a good attitude and motivation, the learning process can be obstructed (Nayir, 2017; Pintrich, 2003). In addition, factors like anxiety can also hinder students' learning, becoming together with other affective factors as important in language learning as cognitive ones (Bao & Liu, 2021; Stern,1983; Wu, 2008; Yi, 2008; Zhang, 2011).

Social exclusion together with affective factors can then lead to the emergence of limits and barriers in children. For this reason, it is important to have good educational policies that bridge such barriers in relation to education (Gandara & Contreras, 2009; Tollefson, 2013). Furthermore, it is important that the teacher in charge of implementing the curriculum for these students adapts it according to their circumstances, abilities, and knowledge so that they can do their best. To do so, it is recommended to be aware of students' knowledge and competences, and to organize the activities and tasks according to their levels, difficulties, and interests (Flecha, 2015). Once this has been done and in order to foster inclusion in the class, the teacher must provide learners with additional support such as extending times for low achievers and assigning roles or responsibilities to every student (Boaler, 2006; Braddock & Slavin, 1992; Lotan, 2006). This would motivate learners, regardless of their social background, to improve their results and increase their academic success.

METHODOLOGY

This case study aims to develop and enhance the communicative competence in EFL of children at risk of exclusion. Several authors defend the case study as a subset of qualitative research (Denzin & Lincoln, 1994), while others argue that case studies are conducted differently and should thus be regarded as a distinct branch of research (Yin, 2011). A case study is an empirical strategy that gives a solution to a problem in a real-world setting. It is an investigation of a current phenomenon ("the case") (Yin & Davis, 2007).

In this case study, two different tools are used (see section *Study tools: Instrument and intervention*): an instrument, designed as an intervention to assess children's prior knowledge of EFL, and a series of workshops, designed as part of a TSL project that intended to serve as a real training experience for the pre-service EFL teacher and the international students involved.

To achieve the purpose of the study, the following research question is established: (RQ) Is the EFL linguistic level of children at risk of social exclusion adequate to what is expected from their age? To answer this question, a questionnaire was used; this questionnaire, which included a set of tests to evaluate the students' knowledge of vocabulary, syntax, and grammar in English, provided the authors the information to whether the EFL linguistic level of children at risk of social exclusion was adequate to what was expected for their age and to develop the workshops based on the children's English skills. In this chapter, the authors are reporting on the baseline data gathered on the children's EFL linguistic proficiency prior to the workshops.

THE LINGUISTIC IMMERSION PROJECT (2020-21)

Context and Participants

A TSL project was designed in order to develop and enhance the communicative competence in EFL of children at risk of exclusion. Three types of participants were involved: one pre-service EFL teacher who designed the project, the two entities involved (Altamar and ESN Málaga) divided into international students from Serbia, France and Portugal, local students from Málaga helping with the organization, and the pupils (n = 30) who participated in the project. As for the pupils, all were studying reinforcement lessons (i.e., lessons for students struggling with English) at Altamar Association, and all belonged to low-socio-economic-level families.

The project was based on TSL because (1) it was designed and developed through an online experience with the participants involved (telecollaboration), (2) it aimed to help children at risk of exclusion improve their knowledge of English and communicative skills (service), and (3) it served as a real training experience for the pre-service EFL teacher, and the international students involved (learning).

Description of the Project

The project was organized in collaboration with Altamar Association and ESN Málaga Association and lasted three months. The former, Altamar Association, gives school support to children from families at risk of social exclusion, either due to their intra-family situation or due to an external situation. It is located in the center of the city of Málaga (Spain). The latter, ESN Málaga, has been collaborating with Altamar for years by conducting workshops offering children opportunities to know the social and cultural reality of different countries. ESN is the biggest Erasmus student association in Europe, whose aim is to support and develop student exchange, and is present in more than 1000 Higher Education Institutions from 42 countries, with 38 of them in Spain. ESN Málaga is formed by students from the University of Málaga (Spain), and all the activities they offer are related to social inclusion, sustainability, culture, employability and abilities and health and wellness.

In times of the COVID-19 pandemic, developing online telecollaboration was essential in education (Huertas-Abril, 2020; Komatsu, 2023; Parsons et al., 2022). In this light, a project aiming at improving the exposure to English and the intercultural competence of children at risk of social exclusion through telecollaboration was designed and implemented by a pre-service EFL teacher, who was in the last year of the Degree in English Studies at the University of Málaga (Spain), as part of her final degree dissertation. This made the pre-service teacher able to learn about real-world education problems. She was volunteering in ESN Málaga (which facilitated the cooperation with Altamar Association and made the organization of the different online workshops possible). The project was organized in several online workshops that were conducted by French, Portuguese and Serbian international students from different degrees doing a mobility program in the city of Málaga (Spain) for improving both the linguistic competence in EFL and the intercultural exposure for children at risk of social exclusion through the online platform *Discord*. The project followed the TSL methodology, allowing the pre-service teacher in charge of its design to be in contact with real-world problems they would encounter in their future professional tasks. As explained before, TSL is commonly characterized as a pedagogical strategy for combining authentic community service with integrated academic results that contribute to students' learning and growth while assisting in the fulfilment of real-world community needs (Erickson & Anderson, 1997;

Umpleby & Rakicevik, 2008). In this case, this project followed a TSL methodology because, while the students were exposed to foreign language and cultures, the pre-service teacher was exposed to real situations, improving their academic and professional development.

In order to carry out this project, the ESN Spain Association financed a projector, which allowed implementing the workshops in Altamar facilities. On their part, Altamar Association got the consent of children's tutors to participate in the project.

Prior to designing and implementing the online workshops, a questionnaire to assess pupils' level of knowledge of EFL who would later participate in the workshops was administered, and then the workshops were used to reinforce students' linguistic level (that was measured before the workshops took place, as students' proficiency was not measured after the workshops due to COVID-19 restrictions). The pre-service teacher contacted ESN Málaga and created a proposal to present to Altamar. Due to COVID-19, the meetings and the creation of the proposal were carried out online through regular meetings, via *Discord* and *Google Meet* platforms. Once the project proposal was created, it was presented to Altamar, and once accepted, ESN Spain was asked for a grant through a social project to buy the projector that would facilitate the projection of the workshops' materials and the videoconferences with the international students. Then, several meetings were held online between the pre-service teacher, ESN Málaga and the international students to decide what was going to be taught within each topic of the project and for the creation of the different materials to be used. During the creation of the different materials, constant communication between all stakeholders was necessary, and feedback was provided through e-mails and the *Slack* platform.

In short, the procedure for the design of the workshops was the following: (i) the pre-service teacher created a group together with the international students and different volunteers from ESN Málaga, who were local students wanting help with the organization of the creation of the visual materials that were used in the workshops; (ii) a template was provided to the international students; (iii) the international students filled the templates with their presentations; and (iv) the pre-service teacher gave them some feedback. Once the materials used in the workshops were finished, they were sent to Altamar so that the association would have prior knowledge of the content of the presentations.

Stages and Development of the Project

The pre-service EFL teacher had to carry out several online meetings with Altamar Association and ESN Málaga in order to design and organize the TSL project. A total of four stages were followed. Firstly, the teacher created the questionnaire to analyze children's prior knowledge of English (see section *The questionnaire*). Once this was created, the teacher went to Altamar Association, administered it to the children, and analyzed the responses. Secondly, ESN Málaga and the teacher created a social media post for seeking the collaboration of international students. Once the international students contacted the association for participating in the project, several meetings were organized with them to provide information on the following steps. Thirdly, the pre-service teacher and the international students created the workshops based on the results of the questionnaire. Constant communication was essential during this whole process, although this was facilitated by frequent online meetings. Fourthly, the workshops were implemented, one per day during a total of three months (November 2020, December 2020 and February 2021). The teacher brought the projector to a big classroom at Altamar Association, and projected the international students who implemented the workshops via *Discord*. Children participated in the workshops face-to-face, while international students had to do it online. All of these stages lasted the period of five months, since the first contact with the associations, until the end of the project.

With the aim of ensuring the development of the TSL project according to appropriate health measures and social responsibility, ESN Málaga and Altamar Association checked their protocols, as well as the rooms in which they developed face-to-face activities. Regarding the protocols, the people who participated in the workshops with the children had to pass a temperature control at the entrance of the facilities and have their hands sanitized with hydroalcoholic gel; they were also equipped with a new face mask. Moreover, materials from abroad had to be authorized by Altamar Association. Regarding the space for the workshops, the Association offered several separated classrooms, with an open-air area between them, being well ventilated. To carry out the activities, a large room was used, with adequate screens to project the presentations, videos and other audiovisual material prepared.

Study tools: Instrument and Intervention

The Questionnaire

An anonymous questionnaire was designed (see Annex 1), whose purpose was to assess pupils' level of knowledge of EFL prior to implementation of the workshops. This consisted of different tests to evaluate their knowledge of vocabulary, syntax, and grammar in English (see RQ). It must be highlighted that part of the questionnaire was in Spanish, as children's level of English was not enough to fully understand the content in the foreign language. At the beginning, the questionnaire included several questions about the age, gender, place of origin and first language of the respondents (section 1). After these questions, four different tests to measure children's level of English at different linguistic levels were presented (section 2): the first two tests aimed to assess participants' vocabulary, and students just had to circle the correct spelling of some words and add the missing vowels from different animal names; in the other two tests, students had to order some words to create four full sentences and write five sentences by using the words provided.

The children who answered the questionnaire were divided into two groups depending on their age: Group 1 was formed by 16 pupils between 6 and 11 years old, while Group 2 included 14 pupils between 12 and 18 years of age. The sampling method used was not random, because the subjects were specifically children at risk of social exclusion; therefore, the project followed non-probabilistic sampling based on convenience (Taherdoost, 2016). Demographic data from the questionnaire were tabulated and analyzed using Microsoft Excel. With the data collected from the questionnaire (see Appendix 1), demographic information about pupils' gender, age, city of residence, first language, and city/country of origin were obtained. In relation to gender, in Group 1, 56.25% of the pupils (n = 9) were girls and 43.75% (n = 7) were boys, while in Group 2, 57.14% (n = 8) were girls and 42.85% (n = 6) were boys. This means that in both groups more than half of the pupils were girls. According to age, in Group 1 (primary education students aged between 6 and 11), the mean age was 8.81 years old, whereas in Group 2 (secondary education students aged between 12 and 18), the mean age was 13.57 years old. As for pupils' cities of residence, all of them (n = 30) were living at that moment in the city of Málaga, and in terms of first language, Spanish was the mother tongue of all of them (n = 30). Finally, as for their origins, 75% of the students from Group 1 (n = 12) were born in Málaga, 18.75% (n = 3) were from other Spanish cities, and 6.25% (n = 1) from Bolivia. In Group 2, all pupils (n = 14) were from Málaga.

The Workshops

Online workshops were designed by one of the researchers –a pre-service EFL teacher at that time–, and then implemented by international students in English, in which different topics related to the culture of various countries were presented together with activities to favor the learning of English among the participating pupils. The workshops allowed the direct observation of learners' performance in EFL, which were gathered by the pre-service teacher on an intervention diary.

Due to COVID-19, however, it was necessary to guarantee adequate prevention measures. Therefore, pupils from Group 1 were randomly selected to participate in the workshops; they were also randomly divided into two smaller groups of eight children each. The workshops focused on three main topics (i.e., healthy lifestyle habits and nutrition, Christmas around the world, and different cultures) and were held both in English and Spanish as the results from the questionnaire showed that children's level of English was not high enough to conduct them fully in this language. The workshops consisted of presentations developed by international students followed by different types of activities, including, among others, the following:

- Story reading: International students adapted the vocabulary from different texts to facilitate the learning process, using techniques such as repetition or question-answer dynamics.
- Singing songs: Songs were adapted to the topic of the activity; international students would work on their preparation, and compositions or motifs from their countries were included.
- Discussions: International students showed photographs that dealt with cultural issues; cultural, social or geographical differences with their own culture encouraged children to participate.
- Crafts: They imply an appreciation of different artistic manifestations and personal enrichment, when being part of different cultures, encouraging their creative capacity and promoting teamwork skills while using English vocabulary.
- Presentations of traditions and customs from different countries: By explaining customs from different cultures, international students promoted global awareness and the development of social skills among children. These also helped children learn the importance of living together, cooperating, accepting diversity, and respecting values, beliefs, and cultural differences.

Examples of these activities were carried out in the workshop "Christmas around the world", which took place in December 2020. In this workshop, children were shown a presentation about Christmas customs in different countries like Serbia and France, as international students who participated in this workshop were from these two countries (see Figures 1-4).

Figure 1. Screenshot 1 from Christmas Around the World
Source: Own elaboration.

Figure 2. Screenshot 2 from Christmas Around the World
Source: Own elaboration.

Figure 3. Screenshot 3 from Christmas Around the World
Source: Own elaboration.

Figure 4. Screenshot 4 from Christmas Around the World
Source: Own elaboration.

Children could ask questions about the meaning of the words they did not know in different pictures. Moreover, at the end of the presentations, some discussions on the content of the workshops were developed to demonstrate if they had acquired the vocabulary shown in several slides of the presentations.

With the workshops, learners were expected to improve their oral skills by means of the repetitions and the discussions on the topics after which most children were at least able to recognize most of the vocabulary that appeared in the workshops. Other activities were also held after the presentations to see if the children had acquired the expected knowledge. One of these activities was a food bingo, which carried out after the workshop on healthy lifestyle habits; in the activity, vocabulary related to the food mentioned throughout the workshop was read and children had to identify them by circling pictures in a piece of paper full of different types of food. After this activity, most pupils were able to identify and produce the vocabulary used in the workshop.

RESULTS FROM THE QUESTIONNAIRE PRIOR TO THE WORKSHOPS

The questionnaire (see Appendix 1) was useful in order to assess children's knowledge of English (see RQ) prior to the workshops, carrying out quantitative analysis of the data collected and the factors that might affect their acquisition. They were given to pupils before the development of the workshops and were completed by using paper and pencils, as the pre-service teacher went to Altamar Association before the workshops were carried out, so pupils' EFL level could be analyzed for creating the workshop presentations. These results showed that children at risk of social exclusion have not acquired the linguistic competence of EFL that is expected at their age (see Ley Orgánica 8/2013). Considering the second section of the questionnaire (Level of English), children from Group 1 (6-to-11-year-olds) were asked to respond only to the first two tests (which dealt with vocabulary), whereas learners from Group 2 (12-to-18-year-olds) were asked to answer the four tests, dealing not only with vocabulary but also with syntax and grammar. In this sense, although 63.33% of the total number of children (n = 19) were able to reach half of the correct answers in the questionnaire, all secondary school students have demonstrated that their English written skills, more specifically their syntax, did not reach their expected level according to their age and academic year prior to the implementation of the workshops.

Specifically, the results from Group 1 showed that in the first test (vocabulary – circle the words with the correct spelling), only 50% of the children in the group (n = 8) were able to respond correctly to at least half of the words provided, while in the second (vocabulary – fill in the gaps with the correct vowel), 100% of children (n = 16) were able to complete the task. Interestingly, even though 25% of the children in this group (n = 4) had no correct answers in the first test, their correct answers in the second test compensated for the overall result (in fact, 81.25% of the children in the group, n = 13, passed the questionnaire). This illustrates that these children had not acquired the expected level of English spelling for their age even though; according to the Spanish educational standards at the time of the implementation of the project, they should have known simple vocabulary and been able to write simple sentences as those presented in the questionnaire (Ley Orgánica 8/2013).

On the other hand, the results from Group 2 showed that in the first test (vocabulary – circle the words with the correct spelling), 64.29% of the children (n = 9) were able to respond correctly to at least half of the words provided, whereas in the second (vocabulary – fill in the gaps with the correct vowel), the answers of 74.57% of the learners (n = 11) were correct. Nevertheless, in the third test (syntax – order the words), only 42.86% (n = 6) were able to order the words to create correct sentences. Similarly, only 35.72% (n = 5) were able to write grammatically correct sentences using the words provided in the fourth test (grammar – sentence creation). Again, it is important to underline that even though 42.86% of children in the group (n = 6) failed the questionnaire, most of them were able to pass it thanks to their results in the first and second tests. As in the case of Group 2 and considering the Spanish educational standards (Ley Orgánica 8/2013), these results show that pupils from Group 2 had correctly acquired spelling and simple vocabulary, but their syntax and grammar skills were not enough for their age.

As already explained, only Group 1 participated in the workshops offered, as they were randomly selected for this part of the intervention considering COVID-19 prevention measures. Therefore, children in Group 1 were randomly divided into two smaller groups of eight children each. International students presented the workshops through the online platform *Discord*, and the different activities that took place to teach and reinforce the EFL vocabulary were also held through this platform.

IMPLICATIONS AND LIMITATIONS

Considering all the aforementioned, it has been demonstrated that most of the children at risk of social exclusion participating in this TSL project, did not have the knowledge of English expected for their age (see Ley Orgánica 8/2013; see RQ). This chapter has illustrated the limited efforts on the part of educational bodies to guarantee that children at risk of social exclusion were able to learn a foreign language, and in turn shows the language gap they faced due to their social and economic status (Brooks-Gunn & Duncan, 1997; Escarbajal-Frutos et al., 2015; Sirin, 2005; Trebits et al., 2022).

Furthermore, it has been possible to observe how TSL can serve as a way of implementing SL techniques within the classroom despite the complications that COVID-19 brought with it, as it was viable to compensate for the impossibility of carrying out the workshops in person (Reif-Stice & Smith-Frigerio, 2021).

Moreover, it has been discussed how (T)SL projects can improve pre-service teachers' formative stage as they help them learn how to deal with real-world problems (Umpleby & Rakicevik, 2008). Indeed, there are several initiatives that show the potential of (T)SL for future teachers. For instance, Villegas-Troya et al. (2023) developed a TSL project where, in addition to creating materials to improve the education of children in a rural school, the participating pre-service teacher was able to learn how to solve real-world problems in their formative stage despite COVID-19 restrictions. Other SL projects can also be found where the pre-service teacher developed projects during their training stage and where students improved their learning by carrying out community work. Similarly, Fernández-Jiménez (2020) developed a project to improve oral skills in a foreign language (in this case English) by raising awareness of the proper use of plastics and by collecting plastic caps to raise money to donate to the community.

It is necessary to consider the limitations of this case study. Unfortunately, only preliminary data was gathered and analyzed due to the impossibility to evaluate students' knowledge of English after the workshops. This was because COVID-19 limited the experience and the possibility of students to attend to Altamar association regularly. In this sense, if more questionnaires had been carried out, it could have been possible to determine if these telecollaboration projects were useful for teaching EFL to children at risk of social exclusion and if they helped them to improve their communicative competence in EFL. As aforementioned, effective SL requires evaluation to ensure that learning is meaningful, sustainable, and beneficial for all stakeholders involved (Raineri, 2020). In this case, the evaluation was not addressed, so it would be essential for future research to accomplish this.

In this sense, it is important to mention that it was also impossible to develop the whole project both in Group 1 and Group 2. In this regard, more available time together with an increase in facilities would have made it possible to carry out all the activities initially planned. However, the project would not have been feasible without telecollaboration, as constraints would have been encountered when getting in touch with the entities and when carrying out the workshops. In addition, only one source of information was used to analyze the EFL level of pupils, whereas other instruments would have allowed for more data that could have complemented the findings from the questionnaire. Finally, and due to time constraints, the workshops were implemented once per month, which may have meant a limited impact on pupils. In any case, this TSL project has fulfilled its three initially established objectives: (1) it has allowed the online collaboration between different educational stakeholders (telecollaboration) and (2) it has provided the pre-service EFL teacher and the international students involved with a real training experience on how to enhance the learning process of young children at risk of social exclusion (service-learning).

However, the overall experience could be considered as positive, as during the workshops the students were exposed to additional input in the foreign language and to information about new cultures, which may have enriched them. Nevertheless, it has also been seen that more teacher training regarding SL practices, language learning and social exclusion, and TSL projects are necessary.

FUTURE RESEARCH DIRECTIONS

This chapter also brings light to the lack of scientific literature on the link between social exclusion and language learning. This experience can certainly ignite future research and educational initiatives in which telecollaboration is used among pre-service and in-service teachers, local associations and international students both to create new synergies to teach and help improve the communicative competence of children at risk of social exclusion, and to enhance the training of future teachers. As it has been shown with this experience, if future teachers collaborate in more (T)SL projects with more local associations, they could learn to solve problems that occur in the real world within their training stage, while children at risk of social exclusion could benefit from new learning opportunities. Moreover, other research could be done with children from other ages, with international students from diverse countries, or using other types of topics in the workshops. Furthermore, the use of telecollaboration may be used for collaborating with students living in other countries or with different associations.

Notwithstanding these potential prospective actions, several conditions need to be met in future TSL experiences: (i) educational bodies should direct efforts to identify and bridge language gaps regarding social exclusion, (ii) teachers should be instructed for solving these problems, and (iii) researchers should be encouraged to carry out studies on language learning and social exclusion. The achievement of these conditions would lead to an improvement and solution of the problems that students at risk of social exclusion face when it comes to learning foreign languages.

AUTHOR CONTRIBUTION

All authors have contributed equally to the collection and analysis of data and writing of the chapter. Cristina Villegas-Troya, the pre-service EFL teacher at that time, was in charge of designing the workshops. Moreover, all authors are corresponding authors.

ACKNOWLEDGMENT

This case study and the experience between the international students from Serbia, France and Portugal and the children at risk of social exclusion was possible thanks to the collaboration of Altamar Association and Erasmus Student Network Málaga (Spain).

REFERENCES

Álvarez-Castillo, J. L., Martínez-Usarralde, M. J., González-González, H., & Buenestado-Fernández, M. (2017). El aprendizaje-servicio en la formación del profesorado de las universidades españolas [Service-learning in teacher training in Spanish universities]. *Revista Española de Pedagogía*, *75*(267), 199–217. doi:10.22550/REP75-2-2017-02

Austin, N., Hampel, R., & Kukulska-Hulme, A. (2017). Video conferencing and multimodal expression of voice: Children's conversations using Skype for second language development in a telecollaborative setting. *System*, *64*, 87–103. doi:10.1016/j.system.2016.12.003

Balladares, J., & Kankaraš, M. (2020). Attendance in early childhood education and care programmes and academic proficiencies at age 15. OECD Education Working Papers, No. 214. *OECD Publishing*. doi:10.1787/19939019

Bao, Y. Y., & Liu, S. Z. (2021). The influence of affective factors in second language acquisition on foreign language teaching. *Open Journal of Social Sciences*, *9*(3), 463–470. doi:10.4236/jss.2021.93030

Boaler, J. (2006). How a detracked mathematics approach promoted respect, responsibility and high achievement. *Theory into Practice*, *45*(1), 40–46. doi:10.1207/s15430421tip4501_6

Bornstein, M. H., & Bradley, R. H. (Eds.). (2014). *Socioeconomic status, parenting, and child development*. Routledge. doi:10.4324/9781410607027

Braddock, J. H., & Slavin, R. E. (1993). Why ability grouping must end: Achieving excellence and equity in American education. *Journal of Intergroup Relations*, *20*(1), 51–64. https://bit.ly/49qm1Pu

Bradley, R. H., & Corwyn, R. F. (2002). Socioeconomic status and child development. *Annual Review of Psychology*, *53*(1), 371–399. doi:10.1146/annurev.psych.53.100901.135233 PMID:11752490

Buhs, E. S., & Ladd, G. W. (2001). Peer rejection as an antecedent of young children's school adjustment: An examination of mediating processes. *Developmental Psychology*, *37*(4), 550–560. doi:10.1037/0012-1649.37.4.550 PMID:11444490

Campbell-Barr, V., & Nygård, M. (2014). Losing sight of the child? Human capital theory and its role for early childhood education and care policies in Finland and England since the mid-1990s. *Contemporary Issues in Early Childhood*, *15*(4), 346–359. doi:10.2304/ciec.2014.15.4.346

Casañ-Pitarch, R., Candel-Mora, M., Carrió-Pastor, M. L., Demydenko, O., & Tikan, I. (2020). Enhancing language and cross-cultural competence through telecollaboration. *Advanced Education*, *7*(16), 78–87. doi:10.20535/2410-8286.214539

Cleary, Y., Slattery, D. M., Flammia, M., & Minacori, P. (2019). Developing strategies for success in a cross-disciplinary global virtual team project: Collaboration among student writers and translators. *Journal of Technical Writing and Communication*, *49*(3), 309–337. doi:10.1177/0047281618775908

Clouet, R. (2023). Multicultural encounters and intercultural dialogue: Interactional experiences of international students on a short-term online language program. In S. Di Sarno-García, S. Montaner-Villalba, & A. M. Gimeno-Sanz (Eds.), *Telecollaboration applications in foreign language classrooms* (pp. 161–181). IGI Global. doi:10.4018/978-1-6684-7080-0.ch008

Coelho, M., & Menezes, I. (2021). University social responsibility, service learning, and students' personal, professional, and civic education. *Frontiers in Psychology*, *12*, 617300. doi:10.3389/fpsyg.2021.617300 PMID:33716883

Denzin, N. K., & Lincoln, Y. S. (Eds.). (2011). *The Sage handbook of qualitative research*. Sage.

DuFrene, D. D., & Lehman, C. M. (2016). *Managing virtual teams* (2nd ed.). Business Expert Press.

Erickson, J. A., & Anderson, J. B. (Eds.). (1997). *Learning with the community: Concepts and models for service-learning in teacher education*. Stylus. doi:10.4324/9781003445715

Escarbajal-Frutos, A., Sánchez, M., & Guirao, I. (2015). Factores determinantes del rendimiento académico de alumnos hijos de inmigrantes y autóctonos de origen extranjero en contextos de exclusión social [Determinants of the academic performance of immigrant and native students of foreign origin in contexts of social exclusion]. *Revista sobre la Infancia y la Adolescencia [Journal on Childhood and Adolescence]*, *9*, 31–46. doi:10.4995/reinad.2015.3772

European Commission. (2021, 11 November). *Glossary: At risk of poverty or social exclusion (AROPE)*. European Commission. https://bit.ly/41Ru9WM

Faulconer, E. (2021). eService-Learning: A decade of research in undergraduate online service–learning. *American Journal of Distance Education*, *35*(2), 100–117. doi:10.1080/08923647.2020.1849941

Felten, P., & Clayton, P. H. (2011). Service-learning. *New Directions for Teaching and Learning*, *128*(128), 75–84. doi:10.1002/tl.470

Fernández-Jiménez, E. C. (2020). *PlasticO: Una propuesta didáctica para mejorar las destrezas orales a través del aprendizaje-servicio para el aula de 4º de la ESO* [Plastico: A didactic proposal to improve oral skills through service-learning in the 4th-grade-of-secondary-education classroom] [Master's thesis, Universidad Internacional de La Rioja]. https://bit.ly/3NWTmIJ

Flecha, R. (2015). *Successful educational actions for inclusion and social cohesion in Europe*. Springer. doi:10.1007/978-3-319-11176-6

Frazer, H., & Marlier, E. (2014). *Investing in children: Breaking the cycle of disadvantage – A study of national policies assessment of what member states would need to do to implement the European Commission Recommendation, Synthesis Report*. Publications Office of the European Union., doi:10.2903/sp.efsa.2014.EN-622

Gandara, P. C., & Contreras, F. (2009). *The Latino education crisis: The consequences of failed social policies*. Harvard University Press. doi:10.4159/9780674056367

Geddes, R., Frank, J., & Haw, S. (2011). A rapid review of key strategies to improve the cognitive and social development of children in Scotland. *Health Policy (Amsterdam)*, *101*(1), 20–28. doi:10.1016/j.healthpol.2010.08.013 PMID:20822824

Godwin-Jones, R. (2019). Bridging cultural divides through telecollaboration. *Intercultural Communication Studies*, *28*(2), 113–135. https://bit.ly/3BipMYt

Huertas-Abril, C. A. (2020, December). Telecollaboration in emergency remote language learning and teaching. In *2020 Sixth International Conference on E-Learning* (pp. 87–91). IEEE. 10.1109/econf51404.2020.9385425

JumpStart Games. (2014a). *Pick and choose I for grade II, sight words.* JumpStart. http://bit.ly/3Jrm2cd

JumpStart Games. (2014b). *Put the words in place.* JumpStart. http://bit.ly/3XQjHvO

JumpStart Games. (2014c). *Spell me not, spellings worksheet for 2nd grade kids.* JumpStart. http://bit.ly/40h2duc

JumpStart Games. (2014d). *The missing vowels, free English worksheets for kids.* JumpStart. http://bit.ly/3HlWTgn

Komatsu, T. (2023). Collaborative Online International Learning (COIL) during the pandemic: The momentum for developing global competency through equitable, partnership-based intercultural learning. In A. W. Wiseman, C. Matherly, & M. Crumley-Effinger (Eds.), *Internationalization and imprints of the pandemic on higher education worldwide* (pp. 209–228). Emerald Publishing. doi:10.1108/S1479-367920230000044013

Krashen, S. D. (1985). *The input hypothesis: Issues and implications.* Longman.

Ley Orgánica 8/2013, de 9 de diciembre, para la Mejora de la Calidad Educativa [Organic Law 8/2013, of 9 December, for the Improvement of the Quality of Education]. BOE no. 295, 10 December 2013. https://bit.ly/2Nd9yHK

Lister, S. (2022). Gamifying CLIL: Unlocking the potential of game-based learning. In C. A. Huertas-Abril, E. Fernández-Ahumada, & N. Adamuz-Povedano (Eds.), *Handbook of research on international approaches and practices for gamifying mathematics* (pp. 1–20). IGI Global. doi:10.4018/978-1-7998-9660-9.ch001

López-Cirugeda, I. (2015). Radio activa: Bilingual experience in primary education. In I. Vescan (Ed.), *Spanish vs American perspectives on bilingual education* (pp. 129–138). Servicio de Publicaciones de la Universidad de Alcalá.

Lotan, R. A. (2006). Teaching teachers to build equitable classrooms. *Theory into Practice*, *45*(1), 32–39. doi:10.1207/s15430421tip4501_5

Majcen, S. A., & Drvodelić, M. (2022). Quality pedagogical practice in Early Childhood Education institutions relating to children at risk of social exclusion. *Center for Educational Policy Studies Journal*, *12*(3), 81–101. doi:10.26529/cepsj.1086

Marcus, V. B., Atan, N. A., Yusof, S. M., & Tahir, L. (2020). A systematic review of e-service learning in higher education. *International Association of Online Engineering*, *14*(6), 1–14. doi:10.3991/ijim.v14i06.13395

Nae, N. (2022). The post-pandemic "new normal" in Japanese education. *Euromentor, 13*(3), 21–31. https://bit.ly/41omfT1

Nayir, F. (2017). The relationship between student motivation and class engagement levels. *Eurasian Journal of Educational Research*, *17*(71), 59–78. doi:10.14689/ejer.2017.71.4

Ochoa, A., & Pérez, L. (2019). El aprendizaje servicio, una estrategia para impulsar la participación y mejorar la convivencia escolar [Service learning, a strategy for promoting participation and improving school coexistence]. *Psicoperspectivas*, *18*(1), 89–101. doi:10.5027/psicoperspectivas-Vol18-Issue1-fulltext-1478

Parsons, M., Garant, M., & Shikova, E. (2022). Video exchange telecollaboration: Towards developing interculturality in EFL environments. In S. M. Hilliker (Ed.), *Second language teaching and learning through virtual exchange* (pp. 145–160). De Gruyter. doi:10.1515/9783110727364-008

Pintrich, P. R. (2003). Motivation and classroom learning. In W. M. Reynolds & G. E. Miller (Eds.), Handbook of psychology: Vol. 7. *Educational psychology* (pp. 103–122). John Wiley & Sons. doi:10.1002/0471264385.wei0706

Prinstein, M. J., & Aikins, J. W. (2004). Cognitive moderators of the longitudinal association between peer rejection and adolescent depressive symptoms. *Journal of Abnormal Child Psychology*, *32*(2), 147–158. doi:10.1023/B:JACP.0000019767.55592.63 PMID:15164857

Pulczinski, J. M. (2018). *Social learning, social justice: Reading circles as fora for political friendship and civic engagement* [PhD thesis, The University of Wisconsin-Madison]. https://bit.ly/3Lg2fMu

Raineri, E. (2020). Supporting service learning with an interdisciplinary CSR marketing model. *Association of Marketing Theory and Practice Proceedings 2020*, 1–19. https://bit.ly/42pCksO

Reif-Stice, C., & Smith-Frigerio, S. (2021). Communication, flexibility, and resilience: Navigating the shift to virtual service-learning during COVID-19. *Journalism & Mass Communication Educator*, *76*(4), 477–488. doi:10.1177/10776958211022564

Salam, M., Awang-Iskandar, D. N., Ibrahim, D. H. A., & Farooq, M. S. (2019). Service learning in higher education: A systematic literature review. *Asia Pacific Education Review*, *20*(4), 573–593. doi:10.1007/s12564-019-09580-6

Sirin, S. R. (2005). Socioeconomic status and academic achievement: A meta-analytic review of research. *Review of Educational Research*, *75*(3), 417–453. doi:10.3102/00346543075003417

Slapac, A., Collett, K., Wessels, F., Gamiet, G., & Knudsmoen, H. (2023). Social justice pedagogy and Collaborative Online International Learning (COIL): Across three partner higher education institutions. In P. Escudeiro, N. Escudeiro, & O. Bernardes (Eds.), *Implementing inclusive educational models and technologies for equity and diversity* (pp. 252–272). IGI Global. doi:10.4018/979-8-3693-0453-2.ch013

Stern, H. H. (1983). *Fundamental concepts of language teaching*. Oxford University Press.

Taherdoost, H. (2016). Sampling methods in research methodology; how to choose a sampling technique for research. *SSRN*, *5*(2), 2–10. doi:10.2139/ssrn.3205035

Tollefson, J. W. (Ed.). (2013). *Language policies in education: Critical issues*. Routledge.

Trebits, A., Koch, M. J., Ponto, K., Bruhn, A. C., Adler, M., & Kersten, K. (2022). Cognitive gains and socioeconomic status in early second language acquisition in immersion and EFL learning settings. *International Journal of Bilingual Education and Bilingualism*, *25*(7), 2668–2681. doi:10.1080/13670050.2021.1943307

Umpleby, S., & Rakicevik, G. (2008). Adopting service learning in universities around the world. *The Journal of the World Universities Forum*, *1*(2), 39–48. doi:10.18848/1835-2030/CGP/v01i02/56703

Vandell, D. L., Belsky, J., Burchinal, M., Steinberg, L., & Vandergrift, N. (2010). Do effects of early child care extend to age 15 years? Results from the NICHD study of early child care and youth development. *Child Development*, *81*(3), 737–756. doi:10.1111/j.1467-8624.2010.01431.x PMID:20573102

Villegas-Paredes, G., Gutiérrez, S. C., & Moranta, I. R. (2022). Telecolaboración y competencia comunicativa intercultural en la enseñanza-aprendizaje de ELE: Un proyecto en Educación Superior [Telecollaboration and intercultural communicative competence in the teaching-learning of ELE: A project in Higher Education]. *Porta Linguarum. Monograph*, *4*, 97–118. doi:10.30827/portalin.vi.21446

Villegas-Troya, C., Palacios-Hidalgo, F. J., & Huertas-Abril, C. A. (2023). Aprendizaje-servicio y creación de materiales didácticos: Una experiencia en un centro bilingüe rural [Service-learning and teaching materials creation: An experience in a rural bilingual school]. In B. Pizà-Mir, J. G. Fernández-Fernández, M. M. Cortès-Ferrer, O. García-Taibo, & S. Baena-Morales (Eds.), *Currículum, didáctica y los Objetivos de Desarrollo Sostenible (ODS): Reflexiones, experiencias y miradas* [Curriculum, didactics and Sustainable Development Goals (SDGs): Reflections, experiences and perspectives] (pp. 851–874). Dykinson. https://bit.ly/43AuxJv

Waldner, L. S., Widener, M. C., & McGorry, S. Y. (2012). E-service learning: The evolution of service-learning to engage a growing online student population. *Journal of Higher Education Outreach & Engagement*, *16*(2), 123–150.

Wang, L., & Wu, X. (2020). Influence of affective factors on learning ability in second language acquisition. *Revista Argentina de Clínica Psicológica*, *29*(2), 1232–1240. doi:10.24205/03276716.2020.365

Wu, Q. (2008). The influence of affective factors in SLA on foreign languages teaching. *Journal of Xichang College Social Science Edition*, *20*, 147–149.

Yi, H. B. (2008). Individual affective factors in SLA and foreign language teaching. *Journal of Jixi University*, *8*, 94–95.

Yin, R. K. (2011). Applications of case study research. *Sage (Atlanta, Ga.)*.

Yin, R. K., & Davis, D. (2007). Adding new dimensions to case study evaluations: The case of evaluating comprehensive reforms. *New Directions for Evaluation*, *113*(113), 75–93. doi:10.1002/ev.216

Yoshikawa, H., Aber, J. L., & Beardslee, W. R. (2012). The effects of poverty on the mental, emotional, and behavioral health of children and youth: Implications for prevention. *The American Psychologist, 67*(4), 272–284. doi:10.1037/a0028015 PMID:22583341

Zhang, X. P. (2011). The implication of affective factors in second language acquisition on foreign language teaching. *Journal of Jinan Vocational College, 6*, 100–102. doi:10.4236/jss.2021.93030

ADDITIONAL READING

Figuccio, M. J. (2020, December). Examining the efficacy of e-service-learning. *Frontiers in Education, 5*, 606451. doi:10.3389/feduc.2020.606451

Gallegos Ibarra, I. P., & Huertas-Abril, C. A. (2022). COVID-19 pandemic's impact on English as a foreign language teaching in Spain. In W. M. El-Henawy & M. M. Suárez (Eds.), *English as a Foreign Language in a new-found post-pandemic world* (pp. 29–50). IGI Global. doi:10.4018/978-1-6684-4205-0.ch002

Huertas-Abril, C. A., & Palacios-Hidalgo, F. J. (2022). Spanish pre-service EFL teachers' perceptions of emergency remote language teaching. *Contemporary Educational Technology, 14*(4), ep390. doi:10.30935/cedtech/12525

Huertas-Abril, C. A., Palacios-Hidalgo, F. J., & Gómez-Parra, M. E. (2021). Designing materials for emergency remote language teaching contexts: A qualitative study of pre-service teachers' experiences. *TESL-EJ, 25*(2). https://bit.ly/3ktVSYg

Ngai, G., Lau, K. H., & Kwan, K. P. (2023). A large-scale study of students' e-service-learning experiences and outcomes during the pandemic. *Journal of Experiential Education*. Advance online publication. doi:10.1177/10538259231171852

Padilla-Zea, N., Burgos, D., Holloway, G., & Cullen, J. (2022). Social interaction and gamification with youth at risk of social exclusion: The technological approach of the Keystone project. *Entertainment Computing, 43*, 100502. doi:10.1016/j.entcom.2022.100502

Palacios-Hidalgo, F. J. (2023). *Enseñanza de lenguas social y culturalmente responsable. Un enfoque para la enseñanza de idiomas en el siglo XXI* [Socially and culturally responsive language teaching. An approach to language teaching in the 21st century]. Editorial Comares.

Palacios-Hidalgo, F. J., & Huertas-Abril, C. A. (2021). The potential of English for social purposes and cooperation for emergency remote language teaching: Action research based on future teachers' opinions. In A. Slapac, P. Balcerzak, & K. O'Brien (Eds.), *Handbook of research on the global empowerment of educators and student learning through action research* (pp. 68–90). IGI Global. doi:10.4018/978-1-7998-6922-1.ch004

Stefaniak, J. (2020). A systems view of supporting the transfer of learning through e-service-learning experiences in real-world contexts. *TechTrends, 64*(4), 561–569. doi:10.1007/s11528-020-00487-3

Wong, M. M. L., & Lau, K. H. (2023). E-service-learning is equally effective as traditional service-learning in enhancing student developmental outcomes. *Interactive Learning Environments*, 1–15. Advance online publication. doi:10.1080/10494820.2023.2200817

KEY TERMS AND DEFINITIONS

Discord: An instant messaging and voice chat service that allows users to communicate via voice calls, video calls, text messages, or with files and multimedia content in private conversations or as part of communities called "servers".

Linguistic Competence: The speaker's linguistic knowledge of a language. In the case of a foreign language, the knowledge that the speaker has acquired, either consciously or unconsciously, about that language in relation to grammar, vocabulary, and syntax.

Pre-Service Teacher: A person who is in training to become a teacher and is not currently working.

Primary Education: Also known as elementary education, it is typically the first formal educational stage (normally with students from 6 to 11 years old) coming after preschool/kindergarten and before secondary education.

Risk of Social Exclusion: The state of people with a low socio-economic status, which limits their opportunities with respect to the rest of society (Escarbajal-Frutos et al., 2015).

Service Learning: An educational approach that combines community service with academic learning (Umpleby & Rakicevik, 2008), involving students to participate in meaningful and relevant service activities that are integrated into their academic curriculum (Ochoa & Pérez, 2019).

Slack: An instant messaging program in which users can communicate with voice calls, video calls, text messages, media and files in private chats or as part of communities called "workspaces".

Teacher Training: Training for people who want to become teachers, whether in the form of a degree, a master's degree, or other types of training courses, and which prepares them for the working stage and the problems they may encounter when teaching.

Telecollaboration: The use of technology to create remote projects and create synergies between different people or institutions through digital resources.

Telecollaborative Service Learning: A form of service learning that uses technology to connect students with service opportunities and promote learning outcomes.

ANNEX 1. QUESTIONNAIRE

Table 1. Section 1: Demographic information

Fecha [Date]:	Sexo [Gender]: ☐ Chico [Boy] / ☐ Chica [Girl]
Fecha de Nacimiento [Date of Birth]:	Curso [Course]:
Nombre del centro: [Name of the school]	Nombre de tu pueblo o ciudad: [Town or city]
1) Nacionalidad: [Nationality] a) español/a [Spanish] b) de otro país: [Another country]	
2) Pueblo o ciudad en la que naciste: [Town or city where you were born]	
3) ¿Cuál es tu primera lengua? [What is your first language?] a) español [Spanish] b) otra: [Other/s]	

Test 1. Spell me not (JumpStart, 2014c)
Please, circle the correct spelling.

Figure 5. Spell me not

Test 2. The missing vowels (JumpStart, 2014d)
These animals need to be classified. Please, find the missing vowels.

Figure 6. The missing vowels

Test 3. Put the words in order (JumpStart, 2014b)
Please, arrange the words in the correct order and write four sentences.

Table 3. Word arrangement test

cookies	lessons	going	sleep
makes	me	beach	don't
crunchy	On	daily	I
Mom	teacher	to	lullaby
Sunday	my	like	unless
Every	music	the	sings
me	Mondays	I	mom
	teaches		a

1-
2-
3-
4-

Test 4. Pick and choose one (JumpStart, 2014a)
Please, choose any word and write five lines on it.

Figure 7. Pick and choose

1-
2-
3-
4-
5-

Chapter 14
Creating Boundary Spaces Through Virtual Global Engagement:
Training Preservice Teachers in Virtual Collaboration

Allison Witt
University of Illinois at Urbana-Champaign, USA

Lu Xu
University of Illinois at Urbana-Champaign, USA

Aigul Rakisheva
University of Illinois at Urbana-Champaign, USA

Sadia Mazid
University of Illinois at Urbana-Champaign, USA

ABSTRACT

This chapter explores the theoretical foundation as well as the practice of one model of virtual global engagement for preservice teachers, IGlobal. A virtual, global, teacher-training laboratory centered on the United Nations Sustainable Development Goals (UNSDGs), IGlobal provides online global field-work for preservice teachers and professional development for inservice teachers, both domestic and international. Designed specifically for preservice and inservice teachers, IGlobal reimagines virtual learning to create an online international teaching and learning laboratory where all participants gain global awareness, cross-cultural collaboration experience, as well as practice in globally collaborative online teaching and learning.

DOI: 10.4018/978-1-6684-7813-4.ch014

INTRODUCTION

This chapter explores the theoretical foundation as well as the practice of one model of virtual engagement for preservice teachers, IGlobal. A virtual, global teacher-training laboratory centered on the United Nations Sustainable Development Goals (UN SDGs) (United Nations, 2018), IGlobal provides online global fieldwork for preservice teachers and professional development for inservice teachers, both domestic and international. In addition, university domestic and international students gain opportunities to work together, and international students also gain connections to the campus community and their home cultures. At the same time, IGlobal creates opportunities for US and international middle school students to collaborate on real-world challenges across languages and cultures. All participants gain experience in global community engagement. Now in its third year, IGlobal has approximately 55 preservice teachers, in partnership with 12 international students, leading over 1200 middle school students from 21 countries.

IGlobal trains preservice teachers to use technology to develop collaboration in highly diverse, multicultural, multilingual and multinational environments. The virtual context creates a boundary space, a third space, where diverse views can thrive. Preservice teachers are partnered with international students and work in tandem with practicing teachers both local to campus and from around the world. Modeling cross-cultural collaboration, they virtually lead groups of multinational middle school students in extracurricular STEAM activities and projects that require cross-cultural collaboration, called here STEAM-C.

It is the multilayered, cross-cultural collaboration that distinguishes IGlobal from other models of virtual exchange, virtual internships, or collaborative online international learning (COIL). Designed specifically for preservice and inservice teachers, IGlobal reimagines virtual learning to create an online international teaching and learning laboratory where all participants gain global awareness, cross-cultural collaboration experience, as well as practice in globally collaborative online teaching and learning.

Learning Objectives for the IGlobal Program

The IGlobal model was born in the context of the pandemic. To prepare teachers for society's next generations, teacher educators must anticipate skills required in the future, what will be a globally connected yet potentially politically and socially fragmented world (Witt, 2022). The pandemic highlighted some of the skills that future generations will need (OECD, 2018). Based on the challenges faced during that crisis, the authors developed IGlobal to train teachers to teach STEAM virtually for cross-cultural collaboration toward solving global challenges, STEAM-C.

Clearly, the pandemic proved that using technology to teach was no longer an auxiliary skill for future teachers (Teo et al., 2021). Being able to seamlessly pivot to an online context must now be foundational within teacher education preparation, not only in technologically advanced countries like the US but has been proven advantageous, even in contexts where technology is less prevalent or generally not available. On the one hand, the pandemic did provide schools worldwide with practice in the virtual environment, yet that experience was often far less than exemplary (Mseleku, 2020). Current preservice teachers were students themselves during the pandemic. Anecdotally, it is known that many of them suffered learning losses during the virtual pivot of their own secondary schools and viewed online learning as at best an appropriate stopgap measure in emergencies, and at worst, an ineffective tool for teaching and learning. Now teacher education programs must help preservice teachers overcome these negative experiences in order to prepare these children of the pandemic to be teachers in a future where they will likely use online learning, at least periodically. Moreover, as discussed below, significant bodies of research from before and during the pandemic confirm that there are benefits to virtual global engagement that would not be possible in a traditional format (Dooly & Sadler, 2013; Godwin-Jones, 2019; Lawrence & Spector-Cohen, 2018). Therefore, one primary learning objective of the IGlobal project was to recruit global familiarity with online learning environments towards improved learning outcomes in a virtual context.

In addition to the need for technological training, the pandemic emphasized future society's need for STEAM skills broadly across all levels of education to counter the challenges that emerge in a globally connected, environmentally overburdened world. The pandemic demonstrated at once the triumph of science and yet, simultaneously, society's inability to keep pace with scientific advancements, as the general public lacked the knowledge, critical thinking skills, and identification with the scientific community to implement scientific advances quickly enough to save lives. Therefore, a second learning objective of the IGlobal project was a focus on STEAM to enable preservice teachers a creative space to develop and research outcomes of STEAM-based projects and activities (College of Education, University of Illinois, n.d.).

However, both the pandemic and growing environmental challenges demonstrate that STEAM skills alone will not be enough to meet future society's demands. During the pandemic, advancements made in one part of the globe did not always translate well to other regions, as cultural and political divides slowed the collaborative implementation of scientific knowledge. Clearly, no individual nation, regardless of scientific and technological strength, can solve the global challenges that current and future generations will face. The pandemic demonstrated that global challenges require quick and effective global collaboration. Coming generations must use technology and skills in collaboration, even across great cultural divides, to resolve global challenges. Siloed efforts to address the pandemic were ineffective, and surely, efforts to address similar issues on a global scale, such as climate change, require comparable levels of global, cross-cultural collaboration (Widmer et al., 2015). Future teachers, then, must learn how to enable students to use STEAM in cross-cultural collaboration, working across differences to solve shared global challenges, that is, STEAM-C. Therefore, the IGlobal team designed the curriculum to require cross-cultural collaboration, giving preservice teachers an opportunity to practice engaging students across differences to collaborate and problem-solve. Moreover, since the preservice teachers collaborate with host teachers locally and internationally, as well as international students from campus, they are afforded the opportunity to refine their own cross-cultural collaboration skills at every stage of the project.

THEORETICAL FRAMEWORK

Within teacher education, the need for teachers with strong cross-cultural communication skills is supported by a large body of research (Cushner & Brennan, 2007; Marx & Moss, 2011; Mikulec, 2019; Slapac, 2021; Slapac et al., 2023; Song et al., 2023). Among the most prevalent theories are those rooted in culturally responsive/sustaining/revitalizing pedagogies (CRP), which seek to accept and sustain pluralism on both cultural and linguistic levels (Alim & Paris, 2017; Coulter et al., 2017; Ladson-Billings, 2021; Kim & Slapac, 2015). However, much of the work in this area is drawn from a US perspective, working from contexts of US race relations, socio-cultural hierarchies, and cultural structures that may not directly translate to the global, virtual context of virtual collaboration. While the authors ascribed to the goals of CRP, they turned to a theoretical base that could ground practice in a multinational as well as a multicultural context.

The authors examined the research on virtual exchange to understand how practitioners are conceptualizing the engagement that occurs in the multinational and multicultural context. Some earlier research in virtual exchange seems to suggest that simply exposing students to those culturally different from themselves will lead to beneficial outcomes in tolerance and cultural consciousness (Godwin-Jones, 2019; Lawrence & Spector-Cohen, 2018; O'Dowd, 2019; O'Dowd & Dooly, 2020). Echoing ideas similar to contact theories (Allport, 1954), these programs work from assumptions that having contact (virtually in this case) with those different from oneself will lead to greater cross-cultural understanding (Engle & Crowne, 2014; MacNab, et al., 2012; Stough-Hunter et al., 2016). However, research within study abroad suggests this is often not the case. Without careful scaffolding, study abroad programs can devolve into academic tourism or voluntourism, reifying stereotypes and assumptions around cultural privilege. Scholars such as Ogden (2006) have found that even within the physical mobility programs, participants may metaphorically retreat to the veranda and keep the host culture at a distance. The authors believe the danger of this is actually greater in the online engagement of virtual exchange. One needs only to glance at any form of social media to see how quickly communication can break down, with differences in opinion magnified and often distorted until participants retreat into irreconcilable camps.

A growing body of research in virtual exchange is grounded in theories of the third space (Bhabha, 1990). Researchers find that the virtual classroom can function as a third space where ideas are shared and reimagined by participants, with all cultures reconstituting as a hybridized culture in which differences can be more readily accepted and discussed (Meyer, et al., 2018; Yeh & Heng, 2022). The concept of the third space has been characterized as a navigational tool, allowing researchers the opportunity to see how participants cross the boundaries of various privileged contexts, leveraging their everyday funds of knowledge and discourse. Moreover, the third space functions as a platform where everyday knowledge and discourses can be utilized to "challenge, destabilize, and expand literacy practices that are typically valued in school" (Moje et al., 2004, p. 44).

The concept of a third space is not new in teacher education and, in fact, has been used widely to explore relationships within teacher preparation structures as well as in schools themselves. For example, the third space is used to characterize relationships between university-based teacher educators and school-based mentor/supervising teachers (Bullock, 2012; Cuenca et al., 2011). Martin et al. (2011) explored the challenges faced by university-based teacher educators working in schools and conclude that working in this third space was essentially about "negotiating a web of relationships" (p. 305). In addition to school placements, the third space theory has been recruited to consider the experiences of international students who may find the classroom to be a hybrid space they must learn to navigate. More broadly, the concept of third space has also been used to research spaces in education in which dominant and marginalized communities and discourses co-exist (English, 2005; Luk-Fong, 2010; Selby, 2004). According to Moje et al. (2004), the third space has been positioned in education research as a space in which to (1) build bridges between marginalized discourses; (2) allow members to navigate across different discourse communities; and (3) create conversational spaces that bring competing discourses into dialogue with each other. This work has highlighted the way in which educators should develop third spaces to enhance "the education of youth whose experiences have not traditionally been valued in schools" (Moje et al., 2004, p. 48).

Similar to the concept of third space is the idea of boundary crossing (Akkerman & Baker, 2011), which the authors find particularly applicable to the virtual context (Witt, 2022). The authors aim to prepare teachers who can respectfully negotiate the cultural boundaries of the third space in the virtual classroom, observing and participating without trespassing or colonizing. The virtual space is not owned by one culture, and participants from all cultures are assumed to be equal citizens of the virtual third space the project creates. Of particular value here are theories of boundary crossing which place value on difference. Rather than perceiving sociocultural differences as something to be avoided or overcome, engaging across differences is viewed as necessary, with diversity recognized as a vital force for change and development. Boundaries are potential learning resources that depend on multiple perspectives from multiple parties (Akkerman & Baker, 2011).

Boundary crossing theory does not promise an easy answer to the challenges of diverse views. Rather than giving simplistic calls for agreement, boundary-crossing theory acknowledges the potential difficulty of action and interaction across systems while, at the same time, emphasizing the value of communication and collaboration. Boundary crossing does not mean imposing ideas from one side of the boundary to the other. Instead, using this framing encourages educators to accept that differences will remain. Further, boundary crossing theory argues that encountering differences is a potential catalyst for learning and growth. The difference encountered at the boundary is where and how learning occurs (Witt, 2022).

Therefore, the VGE project of IGlobal discussed here works from the assumption that encountering cultural differences is challenging and disruptive. Meeting cultural differences will not automatically result in greater understanding but instead could lead to resistance, isolationism, ethnocentrism, stereotyping, or fear. The encounter with difference must be scaffolded and treated as a learning opportunity. In fact, preliminary results of one IGlobal pilot study suggest that teachers should explicitly mentor learners to negotiate differences and, as other scholars have argued, to "grapple with differences in social, cultural, political, and religious worldviews" (Kramsch, 2014, p. 305).

Following this theoretical framing, all participants have contributions to make as well as potential knowledge to gain from each other at the boundary areas that overlap into the third space of virtual exchange. These theoretical assumptions undergird practice in IGlobal, in which the virtual space shared by multiple cultures functions as a boundary ground or third space where cultures of teaching and learning encounter each other and learn to respectfully engage in order to solve challenges through the medium of technology. The differences encountered here in this virtual space are the actual catalysts for learning.

Foundational Research

Begun during the pandemic as a virtual experience to substitute for halted study abroad programming, IGlobal was designed to capture the most impactful components of study abroad for preservice teachers. Cushner (2011) contends that a purely multicultural approach for teaching embedded in the notion of social justice is inadequate for preservice teachers. Teacher educators must also create experiences built around intercultural understanding to complement social justice education. The authors agree with his definition of intercultural competence as "the critical knowledge and skills that enable people to be successful within a wide range of culturally diverse contexts" (Cushner, 2011, p. 606). The authors designed this project to involve cross-cultural interaction within the teaching practice.

From the authors' own research on their previous study abroad programming for preservice teachers, as well as from a large body of research documenting best practices (He et al., 2017; Huang, 2023; Serbes, 2017), time spent in classrooms abroad was frequently cited by participants as the most impactful experience of their entire study abroad program (Slapac & Navarro, 2013; Witt et al., 2017; Witt & Liu, 2020). Research shows that stepping into a foreign classroom as an outsider enhanced participant awareness and empathy for challenges faced by bilingual and cross-cultural students in US classrooms. Moreover, assisting with teaching in a foreign context abroad deepened participants' awareness of cultural differences among schools and classroom practice (Slapac & Navarro, 2013; Witt & Liu, 2020). Based on this research, IGlobal was designed to place preservice participants in foreign classrooms, though in a virtual manner.

In addition to this classroom experience, the authors designed the virtual project for preservice teachers to include opportunities to engage with teachers, both locally and globally. The authors' previous research on study abroad showed that participants appreciated the experience of learning directly from host teachers, including observation and opportunities for in-class collaboration. Often, comments and suggestions from host teachers were recounted by participants as they described the impact of the study abroad experience on their own teaching practice (Witt & Liu, 2020). Moreover, scholars have shown that scaffolding this relationship is critical to creating programs that do not reify stereotypes (Santoro, 2014). Therefore, the authors developed a program that would include working in tandem with practicing teachers from global locations as a key component of the virtual exchange program.

In addition to globally based host teachers, the education study abroad programs in authors' department always include local inservice teachers as well. Modeling the education abroad programming on best practices in teacher education, it is important to recognized the critical role that cooperating teachers play in all aspects of field placement (Allen & Wright, 2014; Daza et al., 2021). The authors included local practicing teachers among the program leaders in our study abroad program in order to maintain this mentoring practice and facilitate the perspective-taking that practicing teachers are able to bring to the experience. For example, in a foreign classroom, preservice teachers may be challenged to imagine how particular practices might be adapted for a US context. Practicing teachers can help bridge this gap, providing examples from their own classrooms to help reimagine practices abroad for adaptation to a US classroom teaching context. By including practicing teachers in the VGE, the same function could be addressed.

Finally, significant bodies of research demonstrate the value of community engagement as a component of study abroad (Crawford & Berquist, 2020; Schroeder et al., 2009). While the VGE project does not directly engage NGOs or other community service providers, as an extracurricular club, it functions as a community service itself and serves various purposes within those communities. In the US context, it functions as an after-school club, an activity of the Girls and Boys Club, and an activity of 4 H (head-heart-hands-health) clubs with focus on youth development Similarly, varied community groups participate from around the world. This provides the preservice teachers a unique relationship within these communities globally, learning where and how STEAM-C education fits within different global educational contexts.

Virtual Global Engagement Model

In practice, each week, middle school student groups from around the world join for virtual synchronous club meetings to study the UN SDGs with preservice teachers partnered with international university students as club chapter leaders. Each meeting includes middle school student groups from at least five different countries, including the US, with four synchronous session times offered each week. The curriculum spans STEAM subjects and requires collaboration (STEAM-C), with students collaborating on widely ranging topics from water quality to fast fashion to food distribution networks while also sharing topics like favorite music, superheroes, and sports teams in order to build community through commonality. Synchronous meetings consist of STEAM-C projects as well as discussions in global English and multiple other languages, depending on those spoken by participants. Then, throughout the week, middle school students post reflections, photos, videos, artwork, and data collected for projects, sharing with peers globally on a university secure site. Preservice teachers encourage and monitor this ongoing communication and collaboration.

Serving as club chapter leaders, preservice teachers and international students participate in cross-cultural collaboration while learning how to teach these skills in complex virtual environments. Preservice teachers gain practice facilitating inter-cultural respect and creating spaces where multiple perspectives can be heard and addressed in proposed solutions. The preservice teachers and international students work together to make sure all participants' ideas are understood and that the multiple perspectives originating from various parts of the world are equally shared. In many of the sessions, middle school teachers join as well, adding another layer of cultural expertise and perspective as well as cross-cultural engagement to the club meetings.

In addition to synchronous club meetings with students, all preservice teachers and international student leaders meet together weekly to discuss what they learned as co-leaders in their sessions. They take turns sharing video clips that illustrate successful or challenging moments. Talking through these examples as a group allows preservice teachers and international students to both teach and learn from each other. Engaging domestic and international students is a long-standing challenge for international educators (Arkoudis et al., 2013). In this context, the communication is authentic, transcending superficial topics of holidays and foods to actually discussing aspects of cultural difference as it relates to teaching and learning, as well as the complex issues that undergird the UN SDGs. These discussions are another boundary space where ideas are exchanged, with the only goal being the development of understanding to enable collaboration. The cultural difference is a static fact, with neither group expecting the other group to alter, cover, or change these differences. As future teachers, domestic students will potentially continue to transmit what they have learned about international cultures from their international peers into their local school communities for decades to come.

Global Cooperating Teachers

Practicing teachers benefit by participating in IGlobal through professional development on using technology, teaching to the UN SDGs, as well as a connection to a global learning community of colleagues. Practicing teachers have the opportunity to continue to hone their online teaching skills, sharing ideas with the club chapter leaders, and benefiting from the weekly practice provided in the synchronous club meetings. Every other week, IGlobal hosts separate sessions just for practicing teachers and invites current university faculty, researchers, and other experts to these sessions to provide resources and training and to join discussions on current issues impacting education globally. Again, the virtual space is treated as a boundary space where all cultures of teaching and learning must be respected. All participants are invited to share resources, ensuring that the meetings are dialogic, with information flowing in all directions rather than only from the university outward, as has been one long standing criticism of both university-driven professional development and international university engagement (Witt, 2022).

Middle School Participants

While the particular impacts on middle school students are not part of the current scope of research in the IGlobal laboratory, a number of benefits for middle school participants can be observed. In addition to the positive impact on preservice and practicing teachers, IGlobal provides middle school students with an extraordinary experience of collaborating with peers worldwide around challenging and engaging real-world based material. The diversity of participants means that middle school students are introduced to world events at the human level. To take one example, currently, Ukrainian refugees are participating from their temporary home in Germany. This provides a direct connection to current events for students and their teachers, bypassing the sometimes distorting social and other media.

Moreover, middle school participants are introduced to advanced subject matter at a stage early enough in their academic career to follow interests that are ignited by this work. For example, in the US, students pursue languages, advanced math, and sciences in secondary school. Much of this coursework is not required for graduation. Participating in IGlobal exposes middle school students to exciting material related to real world problems that are outside the bounds of standard curriculum. Many students have expressed that they hope to continue in these more advanced, yet often optional, subjects in secondary school.

The Laboratory of Education Technology for Global Connection

The IGlobal project also functions as a laboratory to study potential challenges to cross-cultural uses of technology for teaching and learning. The pandemic forced unprepared teachers and schools worldwide into the virtual realm, with, at best, mixed results. In the worst cases, educators, students, and families developed an aversion to all online education, experiencing it as one more negative side-effect of the pandemic. The IGlobal laboratory recruits global familiarity with online education tools and reframes it differently from the stopgap measures of the pandemic instead towards positive global collaboration on global goals.

Though studies argue that preservice teachers would learn to implement virtual exchanges (VEs) via their own participation in such exchanges (e.g. Krengel, 2021), research has shown that teachers should be mentored, specifically in conducting VE effectively (O'Dowd, 2020). According to Grau and Turula (2019), experiential learning through participation in VE is a suitable approach to develop the necessary "telecollaborative competences" of preservice teachers (O'Dowd, 2015, p. 202). Yet, as the forced virtual education of the pandemic has shown, it is extremely challenging to conduct meaningful online education. Early preliminary data has convinced us that significant training, scaffolding, and supervised practice will dramatically improve the implementation of online teaching and learning. The IGlobal laboratory allows researchers to study this preparation, learning from it and then further refining what constitutes successful preparation. Based on the available one-year data, our findings indicate that preservice teachers have exhibited notable progress in their cultural understanding and global competence, alongside acquiring the skills necessary for impairing global competence within their classrooms. Consequently, they have gained increased confidence in effectively instructing students within a multicultural virtual environment. Concurrently, their perspective on online teaching and learning has evolved, becoming more sophisticated and nuanced as they navigate and overcome challenges encountered in their virtual teaching experiences.

Challenges to Global Virtual Engagement

Time zone alignment, project alignment, and finding suitable partners are all frequently cited issues in VE research. The IGlobal laboratory structure somewhat mitigates these challenges through its structure (Bassani & Buchem, 2019; Guth & Rubin, 2015; Patterson et al., 2012; Rubin, 2017). First, the curriculum addresses issues shared by all and strives to include multiple perspectives. While certainly there are critiques of the UN SDGs as centered on the Global North (Arora-Jonsson, 2022; Blicharska et al., 2021), the facts of climate change and other global challenges are relevant to all audiences. Differences in perspective and other ways of knowing about these challenges are given space within the dialogic borderland created in the project.

To address the challenge of time zone alignment, IGlobal has set meetings on various days and times throughout the week. Some groups of students are joining before school, some join as a part of school activities, and some join after school. Undergraduate students sign up to lead clubs at times that fit their schedules. Early Saturday morning in Central Standard Time is a popular time globally for middle school students as many are able to join during the weekend. This time is understandably less popular with undergraduate students, though many have found the project rewarding enough to get up early during the weekend to participate. Through trial and error, the meeting times are able to accommodate learners across time zones.

Within VE for language learning research and other studies on COIL (Dooly & O'Dowd, 2018; Lewis & O'Dowd, 2016; O'Dowd, 2018; Slapac et al., 2023), the dominance of English and other privileged languages is an issue that resonates within teacher education as well. Students and teachers from regions where languages are less commonly taught sometimes struggle to find partnerships based on the native language spoken. Within IGlobal, it is emphasized to use "global English" and support the translanguaging that occurs both in spoken and asynchronous writing. Chapter leaders are encouraged to use online translation to share in middle school students' native language, making the chat scroll a multilingual document that transitions between the native languages being spoken by the group. Responding to the awareness that teachers abroad are in the club in order to give their students exposure to native English, chapter leaders do predominantly speak and write in English. However, they turn on captions and often type their questions and comments in the chat box too. This allows non-English speaking middle school students to both see and hear the language and use translation tools as needed. In cases where the middle school students are less fluent, the IGlobal team recruit international students who share their native language to join the group as additional interpreters. This certainly does not eliminate the privilege of global English but attempts to work within it to create boundary spaces where knowledge can transcend limits of language.

Similar types of power imbalances, including the digital divide, are noted as well. In some locations, such as Malawi, multiple students are participating via a local teacher's phone, while in the US, each student may be participating from a home computer. Some other students join from a computer lab in their school. It is clear that access to technology remains greatly imbalanced, and preservice teachers frequently note this issue. Obviously, this project exists within this divide, and the borders to the third space are not equally accessible across the globe. At the very least, the project brings the issue to the attention of preservice teachers, inservice teachers, and students in a visceral way.

FUTURE RESEARCH DIRECTIONS

Because IGlobal functions as a laboratory in which to study the development of virtual global engagement skills in preservice teachers, multiple avenues of future research are available. Currently, all research focuses on preservice and inservice teachers. Among the topics to be considered are various frameworks of education for global learning, sustainability education, use of education technology, as well as comparisons between virtual education abroad and traditional mobility-based education abroad programming. Moreover, as the laboratory progresses, study on the middle school student participants may also be added. Other potential areas for future research include longitudinal studies on long term impacts both for the preservice and inservice teachers, as well as on the middle school participants and their later educational attainment.

CONCLUSION

This chapter provides an overview of both the theoretical foundation as well as the practice of a unique model of virtual global engagement for preservice and inservice teaching, contributing to the possibilities for online global engagement in teacher education. Though the model of IGlobal does not address all the challenges of VGE, notably the digital divide and power imbalances, it does provide a model for using VGE to create a boundary space where cultural differences can be encountered as catalysts for learning and professional growth for students and teachers alike. Built on the foundation of research on study abroad for preservice teachers and virtual exchange, the model reimagines the virtual space as a large-scale laboratory and boundary space where STEAM-C skills can develop, the skills that will be essential in our globally connected, environmentally overburdened planet.

ACKNOWLEDGMENT

The authors thank the University of Illinois College of Education, the Illinois Global Institute, and grants from the US Department of Education Title VI program, for supporting their work.

REFERENCES

Akkerman, S. F., & Bakker, A. (2011). Boundary crossing and boundary objects. *Review of Educational Research, 81*(2), 132–169. doi:10.3102/0034654311404435

Alim, H. S., & Paris, D. (2017). What is culturally sustaining pedagogy and why does it matter? In D. Paris & H.S. Alim (Eds.), Culturally sustaining pedagogies: Teaching and learning for justice in a changing world (pp. 1-24). Teachers College Press.

Allen, J. M., & Wright, S. E. (2014). Integrating theory and practice in the pre-service teacher education practicum. *Teachers and Teaching, 20*(2), 136–151. doi:10.1080/13540602.2013.848568

Allport, G. W. (1954). *The nature of prejudice*. Perseus Publishing.

Arkoudis, S., Watty, K., Baik, C., Yu, X., Borland, H., Chang, S., Lang, I., Lang, J., & Pearce, A. (2013). Finding common ground: Enhancing interaction between domestic and international students in higher education. *Teaching in Higher Education, 18*(3), 222–235. doi:10.1080/13562517.2012.719156

Arora-Jonsson, S. (2023). The sustainable development goals: A universalist promise for the future. *Futures, 146*, 103087. doi:10.1016/j.futures.2022.103087

Bassani, P., & Buchem, I. (2019). Virtual exchanges in higher education: Developing intercultural skills of students across borders through online collaboration [Interuniversity Journal of Research in Educational Technology]. *Revista Interuniversitaria de Investigación en Tecnología Educativa, 6*, 22–36. doi:10.6018/riite.377771

Bhabha, H. (1990). The third space. In J. Rutherford (Ed.), Identity: community, culture, difference (pp. 207-221). Lawrence & Wishart.

Blicharska, M., Teutschbein, C., & Smithers, R. J. (2021). SDG partnerships may perpetuate the global North–South divide. *Scientific Reports, 11*(1), 22092. doi:10.1038/s41598-021-01534-6 PMID:34824306

Bullock, S. M. (2012). Creating a space for the development of professional knowledge: A self-study of supervising teacher candidates during practicum placements. *Studying Teacher Education, 8*(2), 143–156. doi:10.1080/17425964.2012.692985

College of Education, University of Illinois. (n.d.). IGlobal. https://international.education.illinois.edu/I-global

Coulter, C., & Jimenez-Silva, M. (Eds.). (2017). *Culturally sustaining and revitalizing pedagogies: Language, culture, and power*. Emerald Group Publishing. doi:10.1108/S1479-3687201729

Crawford, P., & Berquist, B. (Eds.). (2020). *Community engagement abroad: Perspectives and practices on service, engagement, and learning overseas*. Michigan State University Press. doi:10.14321/j.ctvthhcqg

Cuenca, A., Schmeichel, M., Butler, B. M., Dinkelman, T., & Nichols, J. R. Jr. (2011). Creating a "third space" in student teaching: Implications for the university supervisor's status as outsider. *Teaching and Teacher Education, 27*(7), 1068–1077. doi:10.1016/j.tate.2011.05.003

Cushner, K. (2011). Intercultural research in teacher education: An essential intersection in the preparation of globally competent teachers. *Action in Teacher Education, 33*(5–6), 601–614. doi:10.1080/01626620.2011.627306

Cushner, K., & Brennan, S. (2007). *Intercultural student teaching: A bridge to global competence*. Rowman & Littlefield Education.

Daza, V., Gudmundsdottir, G. B., & Lund, A. (2021). Partnerships as third spaces for professional practice in initial teacher education: A scoping review. *Teaching and Teacher Education, 102*, 103338. Advance online publication. doi:10.1016/j.tate.2021.103338

Dooly, M., & O'Dowd, R. (2018). Telecollaboration in the foreign language classroom: A review of its origins and its application to language teaching practice. In M. Dooly & R. O'Dowd (Eds.), *In this together: Teachers' experiences with transnational, telecollaborative language learning projects* (pp. 11–34). Peter Lang. doi:10.3726/b14311

Dooly, M., & Sadler, R. (2013). Filling in the gaps: Linking theory and practice through telecollaboration in teacher education. *ReCALL, 25*(1), 4–29. doi:10.1017/S0958344012000237

Engle, R. L., & Crowne, K. A. (2014). The impact of international experience on cultural intelligence: An application of contact theory in a structured short-term programme. *Human Resource Development International, 17*(1), 30–46. doi:10.1080/13678868.2013.856206

English, L. M. (2005). Third-space practitioners: Women educating for justice in the Global South. *Adult Education Quarterly, 55*(2), 85–100. doi:10.1177/0741713604271851

Godwin-Jones, R. (2019). Telecollaboration as an approach to developing intercultural communication competence. *Language Learning & Technology, 23*(3), 8–28. https://hdl.handle.net/10125/44691

Grau, M. K., & Turula, A. (2019). Experiential learning of telecollaborative competences in pre-service teacher education. *Language Learning & Technology, 23*(3), 98–115. https://hdl.handle.net/10125/44698

Guth, S., & Rubin, J. (2015). Collaborative online international learning: An emerging format for internationalizing curricula. In A. S. Moore & S. Simon (Eds.), *Globally networked teaching in the humanities: Theories and practices* (pp. 27–39). Routledge.

He, Y., Lundgren, K., & Pynes, P. (2017). Impact of short-term study abroad program: Inservice teachers' development of intercultural competence and pedagogical beliefs. *Teaching and Teacher Education, 66*, 147–157. doi:10.1016/j.tate.2017.04.012

Huang, Q., Cheung, A., & Xuan, Q. (2023). The impact of study abroad on pre-service and in-service teachers' intercultural competence: A meta-analysis. *Teaching and Teacher Education, 127*, 1–14. doi:10.1016/j.tate.2023.104091

Kim, S., & Slapac, A. (2015). Culturally responsive, transformative pedagogy in the transnational era: Critical perspectives. *Educational Studies (Ames), 51*(1), 17–27. doi:10.1080/00131946.2014.983639

Kramsch, C. (2014). Language and culture. *AILA Review, 27*(1), 30–55. doi:10.1075/aila.27.02kra

Krengel, F. (2021). "Glocal Education" Through Virtual Exchange? Training Pre- Service EFL Teachers to Connect Their Local Classrooms to the World and Back. *Global Education Review, 8*(2-3), 138–153.

Ladson-Billings, G. (2021). *Culturally relevant pedagogy: Asking a different question*. Teachers College Press.

Lawrence, G., & Spector-Cohen, E. (2018). Examining international telecollaboration in language teacher education. In D. Tafazoli, M. E. Gomez-Parra, & C. A. Huertas-Abril (Eds.), *Cross-cultural perspectives on technology-enhanced language learning* (pp. 322–345). IGI Global. doi:10.4018/978-1-5225-5463-9.ch018

Lewis, T., & O'Dowd, R. (2016). Online intercultural exchange and foreign language learning: A systematic review. In R. O'Dowd & T. Lewis (Eds.), Online intercultural exchange: Policy, pedagogy, practice (pp. 21-68). Routledge.

Luk-Fong, P. Y. Y. (2010). Towards a hybrid conceptualisation of Chinese women primary school teachers' changing femininities–a case study of Hong Kong. *Gender and Education*, *22*(1), 73–86. doi:10.1080/09540250802581834

MacNab, B., Brislin, R., & Worthley, R. (2012). Experiential cultural intelligence development: Context and individual attributes. *International Journal of Human Resource Management*, *23*(7), 1320–1341. doi:10.1080/09585192.2011.581636

Martin, S. D., Snow, J. L., & Franklin Torrez, C. A. (2011). Navigating the terrain of third space: Tensions with/in relationships in school-university partnerships. *Journal of Teacher Education*, *62*(3), 299–311. doi:10.1177/0022487110396096

Marx, H., & Moss, D. M. (2011). Please mind the culture gap: Intercultural development during a teacher education study abroad program. *Journal of Teacher Education*, *62*(1), 35–47. doi:10.1177/0022487110381998

Meyer, A., Hansen, P., & Fourie, I. (2018). Assessing the potential of third space to design a creative virtual academic space based on findings from information behaviour. *Information Research*, *23*(4). https://www.informationr.net/ir/23-4/isic2018/isic1814.html

Mikulec, E. (2019). Short-term study abroad for pre-service teachers: Personal and professional growth in Brighton, England. *International Journal for the Scholarship of Teaching and Learning*, *13*(1), 1–12. doi:10.20429/ijsotl.2019.130111

Moje, E. B., Ciechanowski, K. M., Kramer, K., Ellis, L., Carrillo, R., & Collazo, T. (2004). Working toward third space in content area literacy: An examination of everyday funds of knowledge and discourse. *Reading Research Quarterly*, *39*(1), 38–70. doi:10.1598/RRQ.39.1.4

Mseleku, Z. (2020). A literature review of E-learning and E-teaching in the era of Covid-19 pandemic. *International Journal of Innovative Science and Research Technology*, *5*(10), 588–597.

O'Dowd, R. (2015). The competences of the telecollaborative teacher. *Language Learning Journal*, *43*(2), 194–207. doi:10.1080/09571736.2013.853374

O'Dowd, R. (2018). From telecollaboration to virtual exchange: State-of-the-art and the role of UNICollaboration in moving forward. *Research-publishing.net*, *1*, 1-23. doi:10.14705/rpnet.2018.jve.1

O'Dowd, R. (2019). A transnational model of virtual exchange for global citizenship education. *Language Teaching*, *53*(4), 477–490. doi:10.1017/S0261444819000077

O'Dowd, R., & Dooly, M. (2020). Intercultural communicative competence development through telecollaboration and virtual exchange. In J. Jackson (Ed.), *The Routledge handbook of language and intercultural communication* (2nd ed., pp. 361–375). Routledge. doi:10.4324/9781003036210-28

O'Dowd, R., Sauro, S., & Spector-Cohen, E. (2020). The role of pedagogical mentoring in virtual exchange. *TESOL Quarterly*, *54*(1), 146–172. doi:10.1002/tesq.543

Ogden, A. C. (2006). Ethnographic inquiry: Reframing the learning core of education abroad. *Frontiers: The Interdisciplinary Journal of Study Abroad*, *13*(1), 87–112. doi:10.36366/frontiers.v13i1.175

Organisation for Economic Co-operation and Development (OECD). (2018). The future of education and skills: Education 2030. *OECD Education Working Papers.*

Patterson, L. M., Carrillo, P. B., & Salinas, R. S. (2012). Lessons from a global learning virtual classroom. *Journal of Studies in International Education, 16*(2), 182–197. doi:10.1177/1028315311398665

Rubin, J. (2017). Embedding Collaborative Online International Learning (COIL) at higher education institutions. *Internationalization of Higher Education, 2*, 27–44.

Santoro, N. (2014). 'If I'm going to teach about the world, I need to know the world': Developing Australian pre-service teachers' intercultural competence through international trips. *Race, Ethnicity and Education, 17*(3), 429–444. doi:10.1080/13613324.2013.832938

Schroeder, K., Wood, C., Galiardi, S., & Koehn, J. (2009). First, do no harm: Ideas for mitigating negative community impacts of short-term study abroad. *The Journal of Geography, 108*(3), 141–147. doi:10.1080/00221340903120866

Selby, J. (2004). Working divides between indigenous and non-indigenous: Disruptions of identity. *International Journal of Qualitative Studies in Education : QSE, 17*(1), 143–156. doi:10.1080/0951839032000150284

Serbes, M. (2017). Teaching abroad: Why teachers prefer teaching overseas. *International Journal of Social Sciences & Educational Studies, 4*(3), 182–186. doi:10.23918/ijsses.v4i3p182

Slapac, A. (2021). Advancing students' global competency through English language learning in Romania: An exploratory qualitative case study of four English language teachers. [Special Issue on Global Education]. *Journal of Research in Childhood Education, 35*(2), 1–17. doi:10.1080/02568543.2021.1880993

Slapac, A., Collett, K., Wessels, F. J., Gamiet, G., & Knudsmoen, H. (2023). Social justice pedagogy and Collaborative Online International Learning (COIL): Across three partner higher education institutions. In P. Escudeiro, N. Escudeiro, & O. Bernardes (Eds.), *Handbook of research on implementing inclusive educational models and technologies for equity and diversity* (pp. 252–272). IGI Global. doi:10.4018/979-8-3693-0453-2.ch013

Slapac, A., Coppersmith, S., & Cheng, J. (2023). Global competence development through the lens of graduate students in action research courses. In C. E. Ullom & N. Guler (Eds.), *At school in the world: Developing globally engaged teachers* (pp. 98–117). Rowman & Littlefield.

Slapac, A., & Navarro, V. (2013). Fledgling steps to global self-awareness for preservice teachers abroad. *The Journal of Meaning-Centered Education, 1*(3), 2–20.

Song, K. H., Kerkhoff, S. N., & Slapac, A. (2023). Educating racially, culturally, and linguistically diverse children in the global era: The world at home and at home in the world. In J. Chitiyo & Z. Pietrantoni (Eds.), *Social justice and culturally-affirming education in K-12 settings* (pp. 1–22). IGI Global. doi:10.4018/978-1-6684-6386-4.ch001

Stough-Hunter, A., Guinan, J., & Hart, J. P. (2016). A comparison of teaching methods building cultural competency informed by contact theory. *Journal of Cultural Diversity, 23*(3), 91–98. https://www.ncbi.nlm.nih.gov/pubmed/29694750 PMID:29694750

Teo, T., Unwin, S., Scherer, R., & Gardiner, V. (2021). Initial teacher training for twenty-first century skills in the Fourth Industrial Revolution (IR 4.0): A scoping review. *Computers & Education, 170*, 104223. doi:10.1016/j.compedu.2021.104223

United Nations. (2018). *The 2030 Agenda and the Sustainable Development Goals: An opportunity for Latin America and the Caribbean* (LC/G. 2681-P/Rev. 3). Santiago. https://rb.gy/1abah4

Widmer, R. J., Widmer, J. M., & Lerman, A. (2015). International collaboration: Promises and challenges. *Rambam Maimonides Medical Journal*, *6*(2), e0012. doi:10.5041/RMMJ.10196 PMID:25973264

Witt, A. (2022). Postpandemic futures of Global Citizenship Education for preservice teachers: Challenges and possibilities. *Prospects*, 1–14. doi:10.1007/s11125-022-09599-5 PMID:35250097

Witt, A., & Liu, W. (2020). Transforming teacher preparation for global readiness: Scaling up education abroad. In L. Baecher (Ed.), *Study abroad for pre- and in-service teachers: Transformative learning on a global scale* (pp. 31–43). Routledge. doi:10.4324/9781003004387-3

Witt, A., Pino-Yancovic, M., & Neal, B. (2017). Study abroad for preservice teachers: Critical learning and teaching in a diverse context. In H. An (Ed.), *Handbook of research on efficacy and implementation of study abroad programs for P-12 teachers* (pp. 133–148). IGI Global. doi:10.4018/978-1-5225-1057-4.ch008

Yeh, H. C., & Heng, L. (2022). Creating a virtual "third space" in a telecollaborative project to promote English as a Foreign Language (EFL) learners' language proficiency and intercultural awareness. *Interactive Learning Environments*, 1–11. doi:10.1080/10494820.2022.2043384

KEY TERMS AND DEFINITIONS

Boundary Space: An environment or context where individuals from diverse cultures come together, creating opportunities for exchanging ideas, perspectives, and knowledge, often leading to increased understanding and collaboration.

Chapter Leader: A preservice teacher who leads a group of middle school students from one or more countries in the virtual global engagement project.

Digital Divide: A disparity between those who have access to digital technologies and information and those who do not.

Science, Technology, Engineering, Art, Math, and Collaboration (STEAM-C): An interdisciplinary approach that integrates Science, Technology, Engineering, Art, and Math with a strong emphasis on Collaboration, fostering creative problem-solving, innovation, and cooperative efforts among individuals from diverse backgrounds to address complex challenges and achieve meaningful outcomes aimed at the equitable benefit of all participants.

Third Space: The environment where participants from diverse cultures share and reinterpret ideas, leading to the emergence of a hybridized culture that fosters greater acceptance and open discussion of differences.

Virtual Exchange (VE): An educational program or classroom experience that fosters cross-cultural interactions and learning experiences among individuals from different geographic locations using online platforms and communication technologies.

Virtual Global Engagement (VGE): An educationally focused project that involves elements of virtual exchange, virtual internship, and virtual community involvement, facilitating global connections and interactions through digital means.

Chapter 15
The Global Read Aloud for Global Collaboration in an Instructional Technology Course

Lauren Angelone
Xavier University, USA

ABSTRACT

In this chapter, a project to globalize an online asynchronous instructional technology course will be detailed. While participating in the Longview Foundation's Global Teacher Education (GTE) Fellows Program, the author internationalized her course through the use of the Global Read Aloud. The Global Read Aloud is a project created by a teacher in 2010 to bring together classrooms across the globe through the shared experience of a read aloud on a global topic. To participate in the Global Read Aloud, teachers self-organize using a variety of instructional technologies. The author arranged for her class to participate in a Canadian 5th grade teacher's slow chat on Twitter. Planning, development, and assessment of the globalized elements of the course will be shared.

INTRODUCTION

Teachers graduating from teacher education programs in the United States today will serve a more diverse student body than ever before. Groups such as the Longview Foundation have called for teacher preparation program to prepare teachers for the world in which they will teach. It is imperative then, that "professional education courses teach the pedagogical skills to enable future teachers to teach the global dimensions of their subject matter" (The Longview Foundation, 2008, p.6). The Organisation for Economic Co-operation and Development (OECD) and the Asia Society provide a framework and numerous examples to support teachers in teaching for global competence (OECD/Asia Society, 2018). The framework for teaching for global competence includes four domains: investigate the world, recognize perspectives, communicate ideas, and take action.

DOI: 10.4018/978-1-6684-7813-4.ch015

It is within this context that the author became a Longview Foundation Global Teacher Education Fellow for the 2022-2023 academic year. Through the sharing of resources and guidance of experts in the field of global education, the author globalized her Instructional Technology course. Utilizing the Global Read Aloud (GRA), the author created a module and project to address the OECD/Asia Society's four domains of global competence alongside the International Society for Technology in Education's (ISTE) Standards for Educators and Students (ISTE, 2016, 2017) that call for students and teachers to participate in global networks and to collaborate globally.

Globalizing Teacher Education

Preparing globally competent teachers that can support the development of globally competent students is essential in our increasingly globalized world, one in which their future students will live and work around the world, whether in person or remotely, engaging with many and varied cultures in their lifetime (Song et al., 2023; Zhao, 2010). It is the work of teacher education then, to provide pre-service and in-service teachers with the knowledge, experiences, and pedagogies necessary to develop their own global competence and the global competence of their students. And in order to do this, teachers must develop more than a soft global citizenship, but a critical lens of global education (Andreotti, 2006; Choo, 2018; Hauerwas et al., 2023; Slapac, 2021; Slapac et al., 2023; Tichnor-Wagner et al., 2016), one that can "[e]mpower individuals to reflect critically on the legacies and processes of their cultures, to imagine different futures and to take responsibility for decisions and actions" (Andreotti, 2006, p. 48).

The work around critically globalizing teacher education has been developing over the past decade or so with many researchers providing implementation strategies, pedagogies, and reflections to support global competence in teachers. For example, Hauerwas et al. (2023) collaborated transnationally with faculty and pre-service teachers using two innovations: storytelling and social-emotional thinking routines, which allowed the teacher educator researchers to center dialogue in their critical global teaching praxis. Tichnor-Wagner et al. (2016) explored the signature pedagogies of in-service teachers who taught for global competence in several different content areas. They found that these signature pedagogies provided "visions of possibility for concrete practices teachers can adapt" (p. 2). Ramos et al. (2020) used the four domains of global competence and Global Thinking Routines (Boix Mansilla, 2016/2017; Boix Mansilla et al., 2017) as pedagogical tools to explore the lived experiences of immigration and refugees in an online asynchronous graduate education course. Slapac et al. (2023) examined the reflections of five lecturers using Collaborative Online International Learning (COIL) to strengthen social justice pedagogy. The globalizing of the Instructional Technology course outlined in this chapter will serve as a further example of globalizing teacher education.

BACKGROUND

The author is a teacher educator at a predominantly white institution in the midwestern United States. Her students, like her and the majority of teacher candidates, are mostly white and female-identifying. The university is also a mid-sized Jesuit Catholic institution in the liberal arts tradition. Though the university is historically homogenous, the newly released strategic plan has a focus on internationalization which will provide an opportunity to pursue global teacher education to support the needs of our future teachers and their future students.

An Instructional Technology course was chosen to be internationalized at this university. The course was formerly blended but became online and asynchronous to support the needs of working graduate students earning initial licensure. The course was cross-listed to serve both graduate and undergraduate students and is required for all education majors including Primary, Middle, Secondary, Special Education, and Montessori, with 30 students enrolled across two sections during the fall of 2022. The ISTE Standards for Educators and Students (ISTE, 2016, 2017) are used to organize the course. These standards include two opportunities to address global education- the Learner standard for educators, which states that educators should, "Pursue professional interests by creating and actively participating in local and global learning networks" (ISTE, 2017), and the Global Collaborator standard for students which states that students should "use digital tools to broaden their perspectives and enrich their learning by collaborating with others and working effectively in teams locally and globally" (ISTE, 2016).

Global Read Aloud

In order to globalize the course, the Global Read Aloud (GRA) became the driving force for participating in global networks to help students to collaborate globally. The Global Read Aloud was started by Pernille Ripp, a teacher in Wisconsin, who had a simple idea: one book to connect the world. Each year, Ripp selects books at each grade level for teachers to read aloud to their students, provides a timeline for pages read each week, and then encourages classrooms connecting via technology to discuss and learn together. The Global Read Aloud runs for six weeks each fall. Since its beginning in 2010, the Global Read Aloud has grown to include several books by grade level and has connected millions of students through the self-organization of teachers who follow the Global Read Aloud website and networks on Facebook and Twitter (became X in July 2023). Since the Instructional Technology course in the present study included students who will teach from preschool to high school, the middle level book was selected to have broadest application value. The 2022 selection was *Thirst* by Varsha Bajaj, a story about a young girl who experiences water scarcity in India.

The Global Read Aloud has been the focus on some research in teacher education (Carpenter et al., 2022; Kerkhoff et al., 2021) which has so far shown that the Global Read Aloud holds promise for collaboration between teachers in addition to supporting students in developing cross-cultural understanding and respect for cultural differences. This project provides further justification to support the use of GRA in a teacher education course with an aim to globalize the curriculum and support global competence of teacher candidates.

The syllabus of the Instructional Technology course was revised to include the theme of global education, which explained the inclusion of the Global Read Aloud. A module was then created to kick off the Global Read Aloud and supported student participation throughout the six weeks of GRA. Students would participate in the Global Read Aloud via a slow chat on Twitter. Using one of several online groups on Facebook to locate a collaborator, the author found a Canadian 5th grade teacher who would host the chat with weekly questions created by her students. A slow chat on Twitter is a conversation that typically takes place over a week asynchronously using a hashtag to connect the conversation. The slow chat used the hashtag #GRAThirstSlowChat and took place over the course of a week. During that time the Instructional Technology students commented on the 5th grade student questions using the Q1/A1 format, in which the moderator posts questions labeled Q1, Q2, etc. and participants label corresponding responses A1, A2, etc. along with the common hashtag. The goal of participating in GRA was for students to discuss a global text with a global audience to support global competence.

Following the six weeks of Global Read Aloud participation, students were assigned a group project in which they would create a classroom project applying and expanding the Global Read Aloud and incorporating a direct connection to the United Nation's Sustainable Development Goals (UN SDGs). In these projects, students addressed standards, collaborated with experts digitally, and created authentic experiences for their future K-12 students to further interrogate a global issue. Student projects addressed clean water and sanitation in STEM, gender equality in theater education, and quality education in special education.

PLANNING

This section will detail the planning and development of the use of the Global Read Aloud and the corresponding project within this Instructional Technology class. As a Longview Global Teacher Education Fellow, the author received a mentor aligned with her background, Dr. Shea Kerkhoff from the University of Missouri-St. Louis and former Longview Fellow, who supported the planning and development process.

Previously, in order to cover the ISTE Learner and Global Collaborator standards, students in the Instructional Technology class participated in a Personal Learning Network (PLN) project. Students were encouraged to build this network on a social media site to participate in chats throughout the semester. These chats were both internal to the class and external to other teacher groups with a social media presence. Twitter has been the primary social networking site, though Instagram has also been used.

Also previously, students in Instructional Technology were assigned a Community Collaborative Project. This project covered the ISTE Collaborator standard in which educators should be able to "dedicate planning time to collaborate with colleagues to create authentic learning experiences that leverage technology" (ISTE, 2017). The purpose of this project was to cover the ISTE standard by having students collaborate with one another to design an authentic project utilizing technology and interacting with an outside expert virtually.

Both these projects and the standards that they cover were identified by the author as areas where internationalization could occur. The author brought these ideas to her mentor and they discussed possibilities for internationalization of these courses. Two ideas came out of the discussion: one, was participating in a network via the Global Read Aloud, and the other was defining the project around the UN SDGs. Following that discussion, both ideas were then fleshed out by the author.

Additionally, a theme was added to the course in order to provide context to these two projects. The following was added to the syllabus and reviewed in the first week of the class:

The theme of this course is around global education and building your (and your future students') global competence. The reason for this is two-fold. First and foremost, one of the affordances of using technology in education is that it gives us access to a global perspective. The ISTE Standards point to global competence in two standards, the Learner standard for educators states that educators should be able to "pursue professional interests by creating and actively participating in local and global learning networks." And the Global Collaborator standard for students states that students should be able to "use digital tools to broaden their perspectives and enrich their learning by collaborating with others and working effectively in teams locally and globally." The second reason for this theme is that this year, I am a Longview Fellow for Internationalizing Teacher Preparation and am participating in educational opportunities to globalize this class.

The two main ways in which this course will be globalized is through the Global Read Aloud and a larger project focused on the United Nations' Sustainable Development Goals. As we participate in the Global Read Aloud, we will read a young adult book focused on a global issue alongside thousands of teachers and students from around the world. We will then use Twitter and other tools to participate in discussions on this book. In the larger project, which I call the Community Collaborative project, you will work with a group to create a technology-integrated unit that focuses on helping your future students take action on one of the UN's SDGs. This is exciting work! And I look forward to learning with you as we delve into global education together.

Prior to the implementation of these two modified portions of the course, students read pages 7-16 in "Teaching for Global Competence in a Rapidly Changing World" (OECD/Asia Society, 2018). This portion of the text provided background on their framework for global competence (Figure 1) alongside implications for teachers. Global competence as defined by OECD/Asia Society (2018) is:

Global competence is the capacity to examine local, global, and intercultural issues; to understand and appreciate the perspectives and world views of others; to engage in open, appropriate, and effective interactions with people from different cultures; and to act for collective well-being and sustainable development (p. 8).

The OECD/Asia society (2018) then lays out four reasons to teach for global competence. These reasons include employability in a global economy, living cooperatively in a multicultural world, communicating via old and new media, and achieving the United Nations' Sustainable Development Goals (SDGs). The ability to communicate via old and new media is particularly important in this class as students learn to use technology in the classroom with their students. Students are also afforded the opportunity to consider the ways in which new media allow for global collaboration, but can also allow for the free flow of hyper-partisan content due to algorithms that create echo chambers (Noble, 2018).

The UN SDGs were also introduced in this text and then connected to practical applications of teaching global competence in various classroom settings. Global competence is defined by the OECD/Asia Society and the PISA framework (see Figure 1).

Figure 1. Global competence framework from the Asia Society
Source: https://asiasociety.org/sites/default/files/inline-files/teaching-for-global-competence-in-a-rapidly-changing-world-edu.pdf

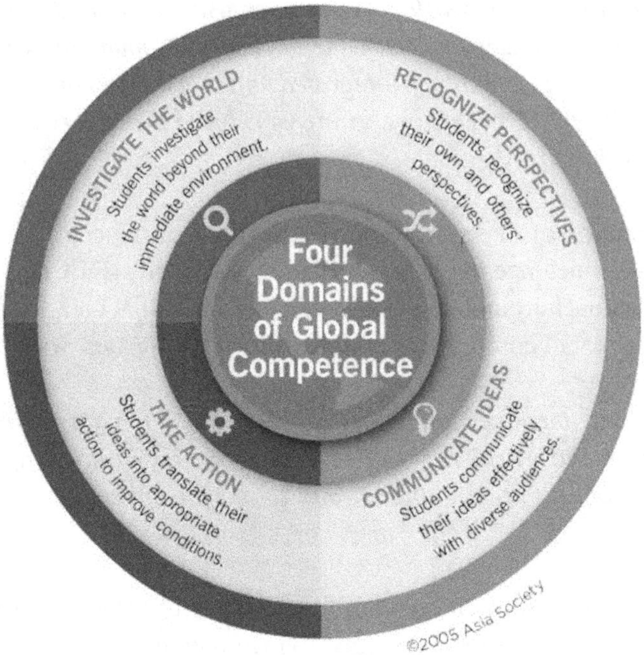

Global Read Aloud

The Global Read Aloud was added to six modules that corresponded to six weeks in the course. The author found a 5th grade teacher through a Facebook group that exists for the purpose of teacher collaboration through GRA. In the first module, the Global Read Aloud was introduced through the Global Read Aloud blog's Frequently Asked Questions page (Ripp, 2023). Students were given the reading schedule and guidelines for participating in the first Twitter slow chat posted by a 5th grade teacher in Canada who would pose questions created by her class each week. In addition to using #GRAThirstSlowChat, students were also asked to use Twitter to explore the more general hashtag #GRAThirst.

In the five weeks which followed, each module had a portion to help students continue to work through the Global Read Aloud. Students were provided the chapters to read for the week, according to Pernille Ripp's schedule, and a reminder to participate in the teacher's slow chat. The instructor planned to monitor the chat on Twitter and participate at various points. Twice, students were also asked to reflect on their experiences in relation to global competence with an assignment on the learning management system, Canvas.

Community Collaborative Project

The Community Collaborative Project was then modified from the existing assignment, to one that was focused on a UN SDG (REF) that related to the selected Global Read Aloud text, *Thirst.* The project remained similar to the first, except that the emphasis was placed on following up the Global Read Aloud by focusing on a self-selected UN SDG. Students would create a project that allowed collaboration on multiple levels for students of the class and their future students. The guidelines for the project were as follows:

Guidelines:

You and your group are going to work together (or, collaborate) to create an authentic, collaborative (in multiple ways) project to follow up the Global Read Aloud. This project should be geared toward one of the content areas that you will teach at the approximate levels that you will teach. Per the standards above, the lesson must include:

- *an authentic/real world project based on the UN Sustainable Development Goals that leverages technology;*
- *use of collaborative tools by students (Be sure students are using a tool that allows them to collaborate;*
- *virtual interaction/collaboration with an expert or a community collaborator (this could be via video, email, Twitter, etc.).*

You may use resources like OER Commons., iEarn, or #TeachSDGs to get ideas, but this project should be original. Use the rubric below (Figure 2) as a guide to be certain you get the full points. The final project should be submitted in Canvas as a link to a Google Slides presentation (be sure it is a link that we can all view). Include all links to outside resources within the Google Slides presentation. The Google Slides presentation should include:

- *Approximately 10-15 slides*
- *Title slide with the name of the project and the names of the group members*
- *Standards the project covers- Ohio, ISTE, and UN SDGs*
- *Description of the project and materials needed*
- *Timeline of the project*
- *An interactive element asking viewers to participate or showing something that you might do with students*
- *An example of how students will use collaborative tools in the project to work together*
- *Evidence of your virtual collaboration with an expert or community member*
- *A rubric for how the project will be assessed*
- *Resources (websites for background information, ideas borrowed, etc.)*

In the last week of class, you will also present your lesson to the class via video within a discussion board in Canvas. You will do this by recording a Zoom call and posting it to the discussion board. In this video, your group should share the project and include an interactive piece either by demonstrating a part of your project or asking your classmates to respond in some way within the discussion board. The presentation video should be no more than 5 minutes long.

Figure 2. Community collaborative project rubric
Source: Author's own elaboration

Community Collaborative Project

Criteria	Ratings		Pts
Authentic Project Students work together to create and authentic/real world project that could be a follow up to the Global Read Aloud and intentionally incorporates one of the 17 United Nations Sustainable Development Goals.	10 pts Full Marks	0 pts No Marks	10 pts
Collaborative Tools Within the project, students use at least one collaborative tool. The use of the tool is aligned with the project goals and TPACK. An example of the use of the collaborative tool is included.	10 pts Full Marks	0 pts No Marks	10 pts
Virtual Collaboration with Expert or Community Member Evidence of a virtual collaboration with an expert of community member is provided (video, email, social media, etc.). The individual has background or experience related to the project.	10 pts Full Marks	0 pts No Marks	10 pts
Google Slides Collaboration The group collaboratively created a Google Slides presentation that included all necessary elements. The presentation is professional and relays information about the project clearly. Elements include: Approximately 10-15 slides, Title slide with the name of the project and the names of the group members, Standards the project covers- Ohio, ISTE, and UN SDGs, Description of the project and materials needed, Timeline of the project, An interactive element asking viewers to participate or showing something that you might do with students, An example of how students will use collaborative tools in the project to work together, Evidence of your virtual collaboration with an expert or community member, A rubric for how the project will be assessed, Resources (websites for background information, ideas borrowed, etc.)	10 pts Full Marks	0 pts No Marks	10 pts
Video Presentation All students participate equally in the video presentation. The presentation is recorded in Zoom and shared to the discussion board. The presentation covers all parts of the project.	10 pts Full Marks	0 pts No Marks	10 pts
			Total Points: 50

Toward the end of the semester, students would be guided to return to "Teaching for Global Competence in a Rapidly Changing World" (OECD/The Asia Society, 2018) and read pages 20-27 as they worked on their Community Collaborative project. This portion of the text provides more information on teaching for global competence in more specific implementation terms including the point that "any teacher in any subject or grade can take steps to globalize the curriculum" (OECD/Asia Society, 2018, p. 18). There are then multiple examples of teaching for global competence shared across content and grade level. For example, a high school science teacher from North Carolina has created a project through iEarn, a non-profit organization that connects schools and teachers around the world, in which her students and peers in various countries compete to create the best solar oven.

Specific pedagogical strategies are also listed and described in order to support teaching for global competence across content and disciplines. These strategies include building a safe classroom culture through structured debates and organized discussions, particularly in ways that promote cross-cultural understanding. One strategy created by Darla Deardoff at Duke University invites students to get in small group and then take three minutes to share when they first noticed difference in skin color, religion, language, or any other characteristic (OECD/Asia Society, 2018). Students are then given 15 seconds each to share what they found memorable from the stories. Other pedagogical frameworks are also suggested to support teaching for global competence including service learning and project-based learning (OECD/Asia Society, 2018). Project-based learning in particular is highlighted as the Center for Global Education developed the SAGE framework, which includes [S]tudent choice, [A]uthentic experiences, [G]lobal significance, and [E]xhibit to a real audience (OECD/Asia Society, 2018, p. 26). An example of a teacher using project-based learning to teach for global competence is a teacher in Illinois who had his students research a religious issue in a global context, discuss the issue with someone who had direct experience with it, create an artifact to represent what they learned, and then have it critiqued by the person with whom they spoke. These examples provided practical ideas for students to consider in their in-class projects and future as classroom teachers.

Implementation

The Global Read Aloud began in mid-October. In the first week, the author posted the following module in the learning management system:

It is time to begin the Global Read Aloud! This is a great chance to practice digital citizenship! First, read over this FAQ page (https://theglobalreadaloud.com/for-participants/frequently-asked-questions/) from the creator of GRA to get a better idea of what GRA is all about.

This week, you will be reading Chapters 1-7 and participating in a slow Twitter chat over the week hosted by a middle grades teacher in Canada. She and her students will post 3-4 questions each week. Follow her @MrsHipgrave. I found her in a Facebook group dedicated to teachers connecting for the GRA. I would also like you to spend some time just exploring the larger hashtag used for this book, which is #GRAThirst. Can you find anything interesting going on?

We will be following this schedule for reading:

Week 1: Chapters 1 – 7

Week 2: Chapters 8 – 16

Week 3: Chapters 17 – 22

Week 4: Chapters 23 – 31

Week 5: Chapters 32 – 37

Week 6: Chapters 38 – end

Post screenshots of your engagement here (linked to assignment). At the very least, respond to the student's questions (there will be 3-4) posted on @MrsHipgraves Twitter account. Any other work is a bonus for this week. You will be asked some reflection questions in the End of Week Quiz.

Figure 3. Week 1 Global Read Aloud tweet
Source: https://x.com/MrsHipgrave/status/1577024309998292993?s=20

Mrs. Hipgrave then posted the questions for week 1 (Figure 3). The university students took the week to respond to each of the questions from Mrs. Hipgrave and her students using the Wk1/A1 format similar to the Q1/A1 format often used in Twitter chats. Samples of these tweets from the university students included responses such as:

Wk1 A1: I think the characteristics that best describe Minni are imaginative, and optimistic. Whatever she looks at she sees what it can be despite the circumstances. Like when she talks about how much she belives [sic] in her brothers dream even when others do not. #GRAThirst.

Wk1 A2: I loved this quote! In addition being a classic warning about how trouble breeds more trouble, his use of "chai" is extra significant because chai is a drink, and you need water to make drinks!

Wk1 Q3: I agree with the decision to send Sanjay and Amit away. At this point in the story, we don't really know how dangerous the men that saw them can be. So the safest way to avoid anything from happening to the boys would be for them to be somewhere else.

Wk1 Q4: I have a text to self connection w [sic] Faiza as I am Muslim. There's a text to world connection in that within the same city there are people in poverty w [sic] no resources & some on the opposite end. Also, that there's a stereotype between poverty & lack of education...

At the same time, Mrs. Hipgrave posted the responses from her students. She was the liaison on Twitter sharing her students' thoughts as a group. For example, in response to the week 1 post, Mrs. Hipgrave shared a Twitter thread that included three tweets sharing her students' thoughts on the first question.

Wk1 A1 (Pt 1): Many students think Minni is caring/supportive. She supports and encourages the dreams of others (e.g., Faiza's dancing, Amit's rapping, Sanjay's cooking).

Wk1 A1 (Pt 2): Other sts [shorthand for students] think Minni is intelligent/curious. She knows about desalination, is always 1st in her class, wants to learn about computers. Others think she is grateful (e.g., thankful for her painted house, the mango, that her brother wasn't hurt).

Wk1 A1 (Pt 3): Some sts think Minni is hopeful/optimistic (hopes for good jobs and access to clean water, looks on the bright side after the water mafia incident - thankful her brother is safe and well). 1 student thinks she is cautious (stays away from trouble).

Mrs. Hipgrave also shared a separate post, not in response to the chat but still using the hashtag, which showed students' drawings of scenes from the first week's readings (Figure 4). In the text of the post, she tags the author of *Thirst*, Varsha Bajaj, using her Twitter handle @varshabajaj and the author replied saying, "Please thank your students/artists!" Mrs. Hipgrave then replied to the author saying, "I sure will – thank you! They will be soooo [sic] excited to see your response! (heart emoji)" The author also retweeted this tweet, thinking that it might be interesting to the university students. The university students did not interact with the student tweets or the instructor retweet.

Figure 4. Week 1 student drawings in a Tweet
Source: https://x.com/MrsHipgrave/status/1578156285777694720?s=20

There were a few other classrooms of teachers in Canada that were also having their classes participate in the slow Twitter chat. For example, one teacher tweeted:

From a few students in my class for #GRAThirstSlowChat W1A1 Minni is kind. She's a loving sister to Sanjay and good friend to Faiza. She helps her family. Another said she was clever like using a notebook to talk to Sanjay quietly and not wake their parents. #GRA2022"

Each of the thirty students in the university class responded to Mrs. Hipgrave's tweet as four separate tweets. Minimal interaction occurred between university students and the teacher aside from liking a few posts. The author's assumption is that Mrs. Hipgrave shared the university students' responses with her students, but that might have been challenging as the number of posts were many, in addition to the fact that the university class was participating in a 5th grade Twitter chat. Mrs. Hipgrave mentions the response in the Twitter chat post the following week (See Figure 5).

Figure 5. Week 2 Global Read Aloud Tweet
Source: https://x.com/MrsHipgrave/status/1579503278102282242?s=20

In week two, the university students followed the same Wk2/A1 format to respond to each question posted by Mrs. Hipgrave. Again, they responded to each question as an individual tweet, creating 123 replies to the teacher's initial tweet. Examples of responses to these questions included:

Wk2 A1: the new pressure Minni is experiencing is that she has to take her mom's place because her mom is sick and needs to leave to get better. This pressure impacts her life because she has to put her education aside for a bit and has to grow up early.

Wk2 Q2: Minni's relationship with Faiza is a sisterly bond. They are always there for each other and trust each other. Minni even feels confident telling her where Sanjay has gone and why he had to go even though nobody is supposed to know.

Wk2 A3 My mantra is "even if you fall get back up" because if you stay down you won't ever allow yourself to heal from that fall.

Wk2 A4: I wonder what will happen that will allow for Sanjay to be able to come home. I also wonder what is making Minni's mother ill.

Mrs. Hipgrave summarized her students' responses to the week 2 questions in a series of 4 tweets as follows:

Wk2 A1: Students said, "Minni's mom is sick, brother is gone & she has a big test coming up. She is finding it difficult to focus and hard to keep up with all of her new responsibilities. She didn't realize how much her mother did in a day.

W2A2: Sts said Minni and Faiza have a sister/BFF relationship. Faiza takes notes for Minni when she misses school & goes with her to her new job (to the gate). Minni encourages Faiza's dancing and school performance. They are always there for each other.

WK2A3: Gr 5 mantras include: I can do this. Never give up. I am smart, brave, calm, and strong. I am perfect for this world. I am enough.

Wk2A4 - Gr 5 questions: Why are all these bad things happening to Minni's family? How will Minni be treated at work? Will she lose her mom's job? How will she balance school & work? Will she pass the big test? When will the boys come home? Will her mom be ok?

In separate tweets, Mrs. Hipgrave shared an interaction with the author of *Thirst* once again, who she thanked for sharing a video answering student questions. Another teacher in Canada also shared her students' responses to the slow chat questions and Mrs. Hipgrave retweeted it. Again, there was little direct interaction between the university students and Mrs. Hipgrave, though again there was an overwhelming number of responses.

Starting in week three, the author asked her students to select only one question to respond on Mrs. Hipgrave's weekly post. This would minimize the tweets from the university students in the chat to keep it to a more manageable number, perhaps increasing some interaction between Mrs. Hipgrave and her students as well as other teachers participating in the slow chat using the same hashtag. In each week that followed, there were fewer tweets from the university students, but still minimal visible interaction between them and Mrs. Hipgrave. The interaction largely took place in the in-person classroom where Mrs. Hipgrave would ostensibly share the tweets of the university students and other classes of students participating in the slow chat. She mentioned in her week four post that, "We have enjoyed reading all of the responses."

Throughout these six weeks, the university students read a global text alongside thousands of students around the world. They also engaged in discussion with, at minimum, several classrooms of middle level students in Canada through their teachers. They used Twitter to communicate with a diverse audience by answering questions around the global text which often initiated conversations around perspective taking and investigating the world outside of their immediate environment, all in line with the tenets of global competence as outlined by the OECD/Asia Society (2018). To follow up this practice of global competency, students then began the Community Collaborative project in which they would be guided to take action to improve conditions in the world via the UN SDGs.

Starting in week two of the Global Read Aloud, the Community Collaborative project was introduced. The official assignment above was reviewed with the class via a screencast and then, the groups were simply to use a group discussion board to determine how they would best communicate throughout the project. This was a strategy learned from earlier in the semester when the author had students complete a short group activity through a feature in Canvas that did not work well for the students. Most preferred to create a group chat and some preferred to meet via Zoom. This week was just a check in to establish communication methods as a foundation for the remainder of the project.

In week three, students were then provided some background readings on Project-Based Learning and asked to begin brainstorming their ideas to create a project that would follow up the Global Read Aloud in their future classrooms. In this week, students were asked to begin their shared Google Slides presentation with just three slides:

- *Title slide with the name of the project and the names of the group members*
- *Standards the project covers- Ohio, ISTE, and UN SDGs*
- *Description of the project and materials needed*

They were then to post a link that could be viewable by the entire class to a discussion board to receive feedback from the instructor and two other groups. This feedback would provide some direction before students got too far along in their planning process.

In the weeks that followed before the end of the semester, each group was reminded to check in with their group and suggestions for a portion to complete were included in the Canvas module. The Community Collaborative project was due in the second to last week of the semester, during which groups were required to create a Zoom recording of their presentation and post to a discussion board. In the final week of class, the presentations were viewed by all groups and each group was provided with feedback on their project from the instructor and their peers.

ASSESSMENT

The use of the Global Read Aloud for global collaboration in an Instructional Technology class was used for the purposes of meeting the objectives of the course while building global competence. In this section, the use of the Global Read Aloud and the subsequent Community Collaborative project will be assessed against these four domains of global competence (OECD/Asia Society, 2018), providing examples from participation in both tasks.

Investigate the World

The domain around investigating the world is further defined to include students investigating the world beyond their immediate environment (OECD/Asia Society, 2018). In the Global Read Aloud, students did this in two ways. First, students participated in reading a book by an author from India, which focused on the water crisis in India. Second, students engaged in weekly Twitter chats in which they discussed this global text with students from another context, in this case, Canada. These chats were led by a Canadian teacher and several classes of Canadian students participated in the chats through their teachers' Twitter accounts.

During these Twitter chats, students learned more about the water crisis in India through the eyes of the main character in the story, a young girl named Minni. In this story, Minni and her entire neighborhood have to wait in long lines to get water and it turns out that the water they do get makes her mother ill, calling to attention the sustainable development goal of clean water and sanitation. In addition to learning about the water crisis, Minni was also a young girl who was asked to leave school when her mother became ill, having to take on her mother's job and miss school for a period of time, calling to attention to a few more sustainable development goals including quality education and gender equality.

An example of one of the university students connecting to investigating the world domain was a tweet in response to the question from Mrs. Hipgrave, "What connections have you made to the book so far?" The university student tweeted:

A4. A connection I made was hearing about the water crisis, and knowing and being around people that have had these problems made me think of them. Some of my friends are from Michigan (connection to the water crisis in Flint).

Mrs. Hipgrave's students also shared the following in a tweet posted by Mrs. Hipgrave:

Wk1A4 (Pt 2) Text-to-World: A few students connected to the lack of clean drinking water in Indigenous communities in Canada. Last year, some students learned about a girl who had to travel long distances for water and couldn't go to school.

Recognize Perspectives

The domain around recognizing perspectives includes students recognizing their own and others' perspectives (OECD/Asia Society, 2018). Again, the Global Read Aloud supported students recognizing perspectives in two ways. First, through the reading of *Thirst*, a book written by an author from India that provides the perspective of a young girl living in Mumbai and experiencing the water crisis there. Second, as students participated in the Twitter chat, many of the questions posed by the Canadian teacher were regarding the investigation of their own perspectives alongside perspectives of different characters in the story. In addition, the Canadian students also offered their perspectives about the action of the characters in the story.

During the Twitter chats, students responded to a set of weekly questions to investigate the story in a global collaboration with students and teachers in a Canadian context. In many ways, the university students considered their own context and how it was similar and different from Minni's context through the questions posed by Mrs. Hipgrave. Students also considered the various characters in the story and their perspectives on the issues that they were dealing with, including getting caught up with the water mafia, becoming ill from the water, and having to miss school to help work and provide for the family. Finally, students were able to read the perspectives of Canadian students in grade 5 as they responded to the same questions each week.

Examples of recognizing perspectives occurred during the Twitter chat. Some examples include a university student tweet:

Wk2 A1: Minni is experiencing so many new pressures. First it is the pressure of passing the exam to remain in school longer than any other member has and then there is the pressure of assuming all the responsibilities that once belonged to her mom and brother.

The university students also struggled to recognize perspectives as evidenced by this tweet:

Wk1 Q4: Thankfully I have never had to deal with any kind of water shortages/problems or come in contact with a mafia. The only kind of connection I can make to this book so far is the knowledge of these topics from hearing stories.

Students from another Canadian classroom offered further reflection on recognizing perspectives in the Twitter chat:

W1A4: Our class had many connections. 1 student is from Mumbai, 1 has travelled there. Many have an older brother like Sanjay. Most have a best friend who has differences from them. Some practice Hinduism like Minni, some are Muslim like Faiza. Many like Chai (heart emoji).

Communicate Ideas

The domain around communicating ideas is further defined to include students communicating their ideas effectively with diverse audiences (OECD/Asia Society, 2018). During the Global Read Aloud, students composed tweets to respond to a slow Twitter chat hosted by the Canadian teacher. These tweets were viewed by the teachers and students participating in the slow chat, but also potentially by anyone else in the larger Global Read Aloud community on Twitter. Lastly, students were asked to share their Community Collaborative project within Canvas in their own classroom via a recorded Zoom presentation using Google Slides to present the information.

During the Twitter chats, students had to learn to compose a brief tweet to concisely communicate their ideas around the questions for a public audience. Students also learned to interact with tweets in the ways that teachers often participate in Twitter chats as a form of informal professional development (Carpenter & Krutka, 2015), by liking, replying to tweets, or retweeting tweets. They had to consider the varied audiences for which they were writing. Students also had to learn to collaboratively create an effective Google Slides presentation with peers, record the information via Zoom, and then interact with the presentations of others via a Canvas discussion board.

University students practiced communicating with diverse audiences throughout the Twitter chat, keeping in mind that they were participating in this chat with 5th grade students and a potentially larger worldwide community. Some further examples of tweets in this domain include:

Wk2 A2: Minni and Faiza are very close friends and support each other through the difficult things they both experience. They are almost like sisters, and can trust each other no matter what.

Wk3 Q1: Minni and Pinky have very different relationships with the material world. Minni has grown up in extreme poverty, with water and other material needs never guaranteed, but Pinky wants not for material need or desire.

Take Action

The domain around taking action includes that students translate their ideas into appropriate action to improve conditions (OECD/Asia Society, 2018). During the Global Read Aloud, students were discussing these global issues as they read a global text about the water crisis with students in Canada. These chats focused on the other domains of global competence, investigating the world, recognizing perspectives, and communicating ideas. It was the Community Collaborative project that furthered these discussions and asked students to create a project to follow up the Global Read Aloud and to address one of the United Nations' Sustainable Development goals as a way to take action in their own future classrooms and in their world.

For this project, students designed a project-based learning activity that they could use in their future classrooms in the discipline that they would teach and at the grade level that they would teach. Students also selected a UN SDG to address within the project as it relates to extending what they learned while reading *Thirst* for the Global Read Aloud. Students worked collaboratively to create these projects in an effort to make what they were learning actionable in their future classrooms and communities.

A STEM group in the class, composed of Secondary Science and Math majors designed a project in which students would "identify unsustainability, discover actionable solutions in a collaborative environment, and design a sustainable water system." This was based on the UN SDG responsible consumption and production. In this project, students would investigate water sustainability in India and southeast Asia (see Figure 6) and then work to design a water retention system for their own community. Students in their future classrooms would learn globally and then as a follow up to the Global Read Aloud, act locally.

Figure 6. Padlet used by the STEM group to gather information on water and sustainability in India
Source: Author's own elaboration

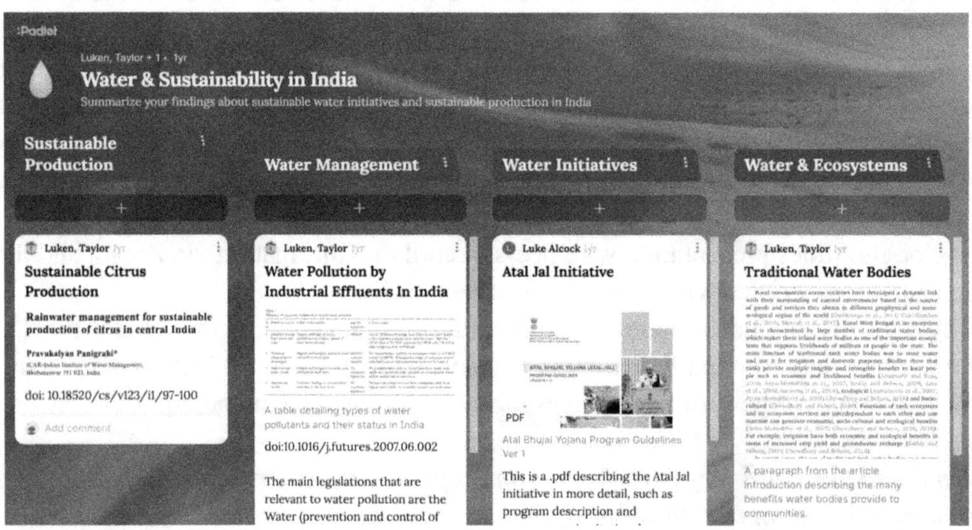

A group of Theater majors in the class, created a project to address the UN SDG Gender Equality.

We will be using the annual Kilroy list (a list of under produced plays written by women, trans women, and non-binary people of color- see Figure 7) to compare and contrast the book Thirst and the play Thirst written by C.A. Johnson. Students will then use Canva to give brief character descriptions and cast an actor to play the character.

This project built on their reading during the Global Read Aloud to address issues of gender equality in theater contexts.

Figure 7. Slide from the theater group's community collaborative project presentation
Source: Author's own elaboration

LIMITATIONS OF THE STUDY

The work shared here is a specific example of globalizing a course in teacher education. Pedagogical details, assignment language, and student work were shared in an effort to provide a model for other teacher educators undertaking the same work. This work, however, is not generalizable. The context here is a predominantly white Jesuit Catholic institution and teacher educators who plan to implement the Global Read Aloud and a follow up project should carefully consider their own contexts as they plan and implement.

FUTURE DIRECTIONS

In this chapter, the planning, development, and assessment of the globalized elements of this Instructional Technology course in a teacher education program were shared in detail including student examples. This work contributed to the nascent research on the Global Read Aloud by offering a classroom example and elucidating the ways in which the domains for global competence could be addressed through the Global

Read Aloud and a follow-up project. The work described here offers another context in which a similar promise for collaboration between teachers and supporting students in developing global competence occurred (Carpenter, et al., 2022; Kerkhoff, et al., 2021), though this was not formalized research but a detailed report on the use and effects of the Global Read Aloud in practice. More formalized research and data analysis is currently underway on a related virtual exchange in this same course.

This work also contributed to the literature around globalizing teacher education, offering another example of the ways in which teacher educators might help teachers prepare to teach global competence to a more diverse group of students living in a more connected world. Like others (Boix Mansilla, 2016/2017; Boix Mansilla et al., 2017; Hauerwas et al., 2023; Ramos et al., 2020; Slapac et al., 2023; Tichnor-Wagner et al., 2016), the author experimented with various pedagogical tools and strategies to elucidate ways in which global competence might be enacted with pre-service and in-service teachers as a model for their future and/or current work with K-12 students.

Though the use of the Global Read Aloud produced some evidence for global competence in this Instructional Technology classroom, there are a few areas for further consideration moving forward. As mentioned previously, the Global Read Aloud is designed for K-12 classroom teachers and students, so it is not a perfect fit having teacher educators and pre-service teachers participate as part of their coursework. Second, the Global Read Aloud only occurs in the fall of each year, making it difficult to participate in the Global Read Aloud on a university semester schedule. To address this need the author's mentor suggested that the author reach out to Pernille Ripp to see if a Facebook group could be started to allow teacher educators to connect and consider ways in which to use the Global Read Aloud more effectively in their courses. The Facebook group has been created and can be found here: https://www.facebook.com/groups/grateachereducators

CONCLUSION

Teaching for global competence will continue to be a need in our increasingly globalized world. Teacher educators must prepare teachers with global competence so that they can meet the varied needs of their future students and create opportunities for those students to participate for the betterment of their world. This project is one step more toward supporting teacher in experiences and planning that can translate to their future practice.

ACKNOWLEDGMENT

This work was funded by the Longview Foundation.

REFERENCES

Andreotti, V. (2006). 'Theory without practice is idle, practice without theory is blind': The potential contributions of post-colonial theory to development education. *The Development Education Journal, 12*(3), 7–10.

Boix Mansilla, V. (2016/2017). How to be a global thinker. *Educational Leadership*, *74*(4), 11–16. https://www.ascd.org/el/articles/how-to-be-a-global-thinker

Boix Mansilla, V., Perkins, K., Ritchhart, R., Tishman, S., & Chua, F. (2017). Global thinking: An ID-Global bundle to foster global thinking dispositions through global thinking routines. Project Zero, Harvard Graduate School of Education.

Carpenter, J. P., Kerkhoff, S. N., & Wang, X. (2022). Teachers using technology for co-teaching and crowdsourcing: The case of Global Read Aloud collaboration. *Teaching and Teacher Education*, *114*(June), 103719. Advance online publication. doi:10.1016/j.tate.2022.103719

Carpenter, J. P., & Krutka, D. G. (2015). Engagement through microblogging: Educator professional development via Twitter. *Professional Development in Education*, *41*(4), 707–728. doi:10.1080/19415257.2014.939294

Choo, S. S. (2018). The need for cosmopolitan literacy in a global age: Implications for teaching literature. *Journal of Adolescent & Adult Literacy*, *62*(1), 7–12. doi:10.1002/jaal.755

Hauerwas, L. B., Gomez-Barreto, I. M., Boix Mansilla, V., & Segura Fernandez, R. (2023, March). Transformative innovation in teacher education: Research toward a critical global didactica. *Teaching and Teacher Education*, *123*, 1–14. doi:10.1016/j.tate.2022.103974

International Society for Technology in Education. (2016). *ISTE Standards: Students*. https://www.iste.org/standards/iste-standards-for-students

International Society for Technology in Education. (2017). *ISTE Standards: Educators*. https://www.iste.org/standards/iste-standards-for-teachers

Kerkhoff, S., Carpenter, J., Yang, Q., & Dong, Y. (2021). Literacy education in the era of globalization: A mixed methods study of the Global Read Aloud. In T. Bastiaens (Ed.), *Proceedings of EdMedia + Innovate Learning* (pp. 850-857). Association for the Advancement of Computing in Education (AACE). https://www.learntechlib.org/primary/p/219750/

Longview Foundation. (2008). *Teacher preparation for a global age: The imperative for change*. https://longviewfdn.org/programs/internationalizing-teacher-prep/

Noble, S. U. (2018). *Algorithms of oppression: How search engines reinforce racism*. New York University Press. doi:10.18574/nyu/9781479833641.001.0001

Ramos, K., Wolf, E. J., & Hauber-Ozer, M. (2020). Teaching for global competence: A responsibility of teacher educators. *Journal of Research in Childhood Education*, *2*(35), 311–330. doi:10.1080/02568543.2021.1880998

Ripp, P. (2023) *The Global Read Aloud: Frequently asked questions*. https://theglobalreadaloud.com/for-participants/frequently-asked-questions/

Slapac, A. (2021). Advancing students' global competency through English language learning in Romania: An exploratory qualitative case study of four English language teachers. *Journal of Research in Childhood Education*, *35*(2), 1–17. doi:10.1080/02568543.2021.1880993

Slapac, A., Coppersmith, S., & Cheng, J. (2023). Global competence development through the lens of graduate students in action research courses. In C. E. Ullom & N. Guler (Eds.), *At school in the world: Developing globally engaged teachers* (pp. 98–117). Rowman & Littlefield. https://bit.ly/3UwGPRd

Song, K. H., Kerkhoff, S. N., & Slapac, A. (2023). Educating racially, culturally, and linguistically diverse children in the global era: The world at home and at home in the world. In J. Chitiyo & Z. Pietrantoni (Eds.), *Social justice and culturally-affirming education in K-12 settings* (pp. 1–22). IGI Global. doi:10.4018/978-1-6684-6386-4.ch001

Tichnor-Wagner, A., Parkhouse, H., Glazier, J., & Cain, J. M. (2016). Expanding approaches to teaching for diversity and social justice in K-12 education: Fostering global citizenship across the content areas. *Education Policy Analysis Archives*, *24*(59), 1–31. doi:10.14507/epaa.24.2138

Zhao, Y. (2010). Preparing globally competent teachers: A new imperative for teacher education. *Journal of Teacher Education*, *61*(5), 422–431. doi:10.1177/0022487110375802

KEY TERMS AND DEFINITIONS

Critically Globalizing Teacher Education: Using critical or post-colonial theory to frame globalizing teacher education with careful consideration of the dominant power structures and how those might affect the work of globalization in different contexts.

Global Competence: Global competence is defined by the OECD/Asia Society and the PISA framework (OECD/Asia Society, 2018, p. 12) through four key aspects: 1) investigate the world beyond their immediate environment by examining issues of local, global, and cultural significance; 2) recognize, understand, and appreciate the perspectives and world views of others; 3) communicate ideas effectively with diverse audiences by engaging in open, appropriate, and effective interactions across cultures; and 4) take action for collective well-being and sustainable development both locally and globally.

Global Read Aloud: A movement by teachers, started in 2010 by Pernille Ripp, to have a shared global experience reading books aloud to students and then connecting cross-culturally using various technologies.

Globalizing Teacher Education: Infusing teacher education courses and programs with a global perspective utilizing a variety of methods and strategies including global texts, virtual exchange, study abroad, etc. Also referred to as internationalizing teacher education.

ISTE Standards: International Society of Technology in Education Standards for the use of technology in the classroom.

Social Justice: Equality of treatment and equity of distribution of resources so that everyone in society is treated with fairness, humanity, and justice (Song et al., 2023).

Twitter Chat: A Twitter chat is a discussion on Twitter (now X) connected through a shared hashtag usually taking place synchronously over the course of an hour and utilized by teachers as a form of informal professional development. Slow Twitter chats typically take place over the course of a week.

Chapter 16
Envisioning a Sustainable and Equitable Transnational Engagement:
Cross-Disciplinary Collaborative Online International Learning

Delane Bender-Slack
https://orcid.org/0000-0001-7270-3870
Xavier University, USA

Lauren DeVeau
Universidad Antonio Ruiz de Montoya, Peru

Ruth Espinoza Pure
Universidad Antonio Ruiz de Montoya, Peru

Ray McAdams
Xavier University, USA

ABSTRACT

How can we individually and collectively demonstrate greater care and responsibility for what happens in our global context and in higher education? This chapter will describe Collaborative Online International Learning (COIL) experiences between two Jesuit universities, the Universidad Antonio Ruiz de Montoya in Lima, Peru and Xavier University in Cincinnati, Ohio. With a focus on global citizenship and access to international education, this teaching and learning experience will address the best practices, which included collaboration, increasing global knowledge, development of intercultural competence, and relationship-building.

DOI: 10.4018/978-1-6684-7813-4.ch016

INTRODUCTION

Internationalizing classrooms in higher education is often done with the purpose of creating globally minded students that understand their role in a global society. The authors believe that internationalizing courses and programs must be done intentionally to prepare students for negotiating the world in social and professional settings. While in the U.S. the work to globalize classrooms is often interpreted as breaking down the classroom walls to learn from and about other cultures and countries (Cushner 2012; 2018; Short, 2016), in Peru the notion of internationalization may be better described in terms of Westernization or colonization in education among other challenges of internationalization (Salazar, 2022). For this reason, the authors discuss the following Collaborative Online International Learning (COIL) project, a virtual learning experience, between Xavier University in Cincinnati, Ohio and the Universidad Antonio Ruiz de Montoya in Lima, Peru. This chapter, which can be used as a template for internationalizing teacher education, describes a 10-week virtual project between education students in a literacy course and students of various disciplines in a social justice course. Furthermore, the authors, two faculty and two university students, are interested in exploring the tension between globalizing and Westernizing higher education classrooms in this chapter while providing a model and sharing best practices.

BACKGROUND

How might one better envision a healthily sustainable and equitable transnational engagement? Impactful global teaching and learning occurs as one interrogates the concept of global citizenship while providing access to relevant international education. However, the complexity of global citizenship education cannot be captured by a single theory. In this context, Latin American scholars often work from a modernity colonial lens and an epistemic racism lens (Andreotti, 2011). For example, Argentinian scholars Dussel (1998) and Mignolo (2002) write about the paradigms of Eurocentrism and modern world systems that center Western civilization and/or constructs of modernity with colonization and capitalism. In fact, Quijano (1997), a Peruvian sociologist, conceptualizes the "coloniality of power" as a global hegemonic model of power that has been in place since the conquest and subjugation of the Americas that articulated and positioned race and labor, space and people, according to the needs of capital and how it benefited White Anglo Europeans (Escobar, 2004). Maldonado-Torres (2004) argues that the darker side of modernity is that modernity depends on coloniality for its existence and that one must challenge the racist geopolitics of knowledge that are at the root of Western discourse, thus reproducing epistemic racism. In fact, this author critiques the way multiculturalism has been operationalized – bringing diverse voices into Eurocentric sites – because it "hides in this way a deeper multiracism that only recognizes the right for difference when peoples are well domesticated by capitalism, the market economy, and liberal ideals of freedom and equality" (Maldonado-Torres, 2004, p. 49). The authors recognize, like Mignolo (2002), that it is problematic to think from the canon of Western philosophy because it reproduces "the blind epistemic ethnocentrism that makes difficult, if not impossible, any political philosophy of inclusion" (p.66).

In the light of the above, the authors would like to honor those theoretical and epistemological perspectives but take them a step further. The authors root this chapter in critical, feminist, and Ignatian pedagogies in ways that help them explore the tension between globalizing and Westernizing classrooms, which is above all political, having to do with power and social capital. A critical theoretical lens accepts and even necessitates that the pedagogical be political and vice versa. Consequently, critical theorists routinely question unequal relations between individuals and groups of people and act to offset them (Kanpol, 1994).

Examining power creates a tension with regard to the purpose and role of education. For example, Freire's (2000) notion of praxis, which involves a cycle of reflection and action upon the world - to transform it - is central. Moreover, feminist pedagogy can be defined as a political standpoint and personal practice, which seeks to transform power relations (Titus, 2000). Given the use of women's bodies to maintain and perpetuate women's oppression, the bodies that take up space in homes and classrooms are significant. If bodies are inscribed through language, then the relationship of language, identity and culture are dynamic not clear-cut and fixed (Oliver & Lalik, 2004). Finally, within Ignatian pedagogy, working and teaching for justice means practicing discernment, demonstrating an openness and generosity to anyone in need, recognizing and respecting the rights of all, especially the poor and the powerless, and working to actively secure those rights. In fact, working and teaching for social justice means using new tools to find new and more effective ways of understanding people and the earth, to communicate thought, image and feeling, and to organize action (General Congregation of the Society of Jesus, 34). Transnational engagement helps to understand others and the environment as people collaborate to resolve global issues. Justice issues are central to the tension between globalizing and Westernizing. The authors' sustainable and equitable transnational engagement is rooted here.

THE COIL PROJECT

The COVID-19 pandemic, climate change, and political tensions have highlighted the importance of global engagement and the significant role those virtual interactions will have in the future. In this light, one way to promote multiple perspectives and global awareness is through Collaborative Online International Learning (COIL) (Beelen et al., 2021). COIL is a model for fostering cross-cultural student competence (UNESCO, 2017) through the development of a multicultural learning environment that links university classes in different countries. COIL supports key goals, such as global knowledge, intercultural communication, project-based learning, and digital literacy. These virtual collaborations open spaces for dialogue and collaboration but also share challenges (Galarza et al., 2021; Slapac et al., 2023).

As previously mentioned, the participating universities, both Jesuit, Catholic, were Universidad Antonio Ruiz de Montoya (UARM) in Lima, Peru, and Xavier University (XU) in Cincinnati, Ohio in the U.S.A. The authors completed the COIL work in the fall of 2020 and 2021, a time where the U.S. students were meeting in person in masks, and the Peruvian students were meeting online due to the COVID-19 pandemic. The two courses were International Studies and Content Area Literacy. Typically done with at least two collaborators from different countries, the second year of the authors' COIL project was a bit more diverse because there were French students who were also participating in the UARM course.

The Collaborative Online International Learning (COIL) model proposes collaboration across disciplines, departments, and colleges, and sets an example for collaboration across diverse environments and circumstances. COIL connects faculty with colleagues in another/other country/countries to develop collaborative projects that students complete together across time zones, language differences, and geographical distance, using online tools as the conduit (SUNY COIL, 2023). As mentioned before, COIL was one aspect of the authors' courses, supporting student learning outcomes, giving both faculty and students the opportunity to experientially engage with course concepts and ideas, while exploring them from different cultural perspectives (SUNY COIL, 2023). Since the initial COIL project, the authors have engaged in additional COIL projects annually. COIL offers multiple intercultural interactions so that students grow to understand that boundaries are human-made and our issues are global. Moreover, COIL provides access to international education so that when students cannot travel, they are able to experience internationalization at home. The element of linguistic diversity means students have access to these transnational experiences.

The authors believe that accessibility and accompaniment (a way of "walking with" others) are key for a positive COIL experience. For many students, who often come from educational systems with limited linguistic, economic, and technological opportunities, COIL is the first step in the process of internationalization (Slapac et al., 2023). These limitations, unfortunately, make participation in international opportunities outside the scope of possibility. According to UNESCO (2023), only 0.06% of Peruvian students study abroad and only 20% of the population has a university degree. Before the pandemic, at UARM only 30 students studied abroad each year, in large part due to state funding or economic affluent classes. However, COIL has exponentially increased access to internationalization. In 2022, approximately 496 students were able to have transnational engagement due to COIL.

Limited language acquisition is a common factor in both the U.S. and Peru. In a study conducted by the US Language Bureau, 78% of Americans are only fluent in English (Batovala & Zong, 2016). Likewise, Peru consistently scores only moderately in English proficiency, 51 out of 113 countries (Education First English Proficiency Index, 2023). A benefit for students and faculty participating in COIL is that the collaboration becomes a tool for connection and communication (Beelen et al., 2021). In the authors' COIL work in 2021, there was no English or Spanish language requirement to encourage greater student participation. The course taught in Peru was bilingual (taught in English and Spanish) to incentivize English learning without making English proficiency a perquisite for taking the course. Not only was this extremely helpful for Peruvian students, but it also allowed foreign exchange students from France a supportive space to learn Spanish as their peers practice their English. COIL exchange sessions were conducted in English and Peruvian students were able to participate through the support of translation by their fellow students.

All students were provided equitable access to global experiences, which is the foundation of COIL work. International education has historically been accessible only by the privileged and wealthy. Consequently, one way to address that inequity is to provide internationalization at home through virtual teaching and learning experiences. Not only are students provided access to develop interculturally, but faculty are as well. Furthermore, critical, feminist, and Ignatian pedagogies were vital parts of preparation for COIL sessions and in classroom discussions about social justice. Offering students time to study their home context and reflect on it with their home country peers allowed for greater confidence and clarity when meeting in COIL sessions with international students. Additionally, providing the space for questions around cultural competency, history, and language provided greater understanding dialogue during COIL sessions. Much of this work, however, was complicated by the pandemic (Amador, 2022; Slazar, 2022).

The focus of the collaboration was to discuss social justice topics with the goal of developing the following global competencies from the Asia Society (Mansilla & Jacksons, 2011):

1. Students investigate the world beyond their immediate environment, framing significant problems and conducting well-crafted and age-appropriate research.

2. Students recognize perspectives, others' and their own, articulating and explaining such perspectives thoughtfully and respectfully.
3. Students communicate ideas effectively with diverse audiences, bridging geographic, linguistic, ideological, and cultural barriers.
4. Students take action to improve conditions, viewing themselves as players in the world and participating reflectively (p. 11).

In meeting these outcomes, students were encouraged to use more than one language while negotiating meeting times, talking online, and in the creation of a bilingual final project.

The COIL was planned together with students from both of the authors' courses collaborating on the activities outlined in the following table.

Table 1. Flexible timeline

Week	Social Justice (SJ) Topic	Task	Due Date
1 - September 7	Introduction	Introduction (name, course, why COIL helps students, connection to Ruiz, students share name, major, international experience, COIL overview, one hope in one word this semester) Synchronous General Meeting	September 7
2 - September 14	Identity	Share about yourselves, Discuss via Zoom weekly SJ topic	September 18
3 - September 21	Jesuit Education Men and Women for Others	Discuss weekly SJ topic Choose a SJ TOPIC for Final Project	September 25
4 - September 28	Colonialization	Discuss weekly SJ topic Create a timeline for tasks	October 2
5 – October 5	Education	Discuss weekly SJ topic Work on project	October 9
6 – October 12		No Meeting	
7 – October 19	Social Justice	Discuss weekly SJ topic Work on final group project	October 23
8 – October 26	Global Citizenship	Discuss weekly SJ topic Work on project	October 30
9 – November 2	Environment	Discuss weekly SJ topic Work on project	November 6
10 – November 9	Gender Identity	Discuss weekly SJ topic Work on project	November 13
11 – November 16	Presentations and Reflection	Final Projects Due	November 16

Source: Own elaboration

Students from each course were placed in a small group of four to six with the goal of equal representation from both Peru and the U.S. Students had the ability to choose how they would communicate, but generally, they used Zoom for synchronous sessions and used WhatsApp or Instagram to communicate asynchronously. Students met synchronously each week, recorded their group meetings, and submitted their recordings so that the instructors could observe the student interactions and discuss in class any negotiating, misunderstandings, and tensions. The weekly COIL discussion questions and activities were as presented in Table 2.

Table 2. Weekly dialogue questions and activities

Conversations Topics	Dialogue Questions and Activities
Conversation One: Identity	• What do you know about Peru? What do you know about the US? • How would you describe people from your country? Do you identify with that description? • What does your nationality mean to you? • Is there a specific social justice topic that interests you? • How does social media construct or disrupt one's identity?
Conversation Two: Jesuit Education	• Why did you choose to study at a Jesuit University? • What have you found most impactful about Jesuit education? • How can Jesuit education improve in the future? • Is spirituality a part of your life? Explain.
Conversation Three: Colonization	• How would you describe or define colonization? • What might your country look like if it had not been colonized? • What is the legacy of colonialization with regard to race in your country? And with regard to wealth and power? • Do you (your family) identify more with the colonizer or the colonized?
Conversation Four: Education	• How are schools funded/resourced? Does this funding represent the level of importance of education in your country? • How are class and race differences evident in your educational system? • In your opinion, what is the purpose of schooling? Is it to make great thinkers? Create informed, participatory citizens? Perpetuate a dominant culture? Teach conformity? • How can teaching be social activism? Should it be? • Describe the educational system in your country? How does it function? Who makes the decisions? Why?
Conversation Five: Social Justice	• What social justice topic interests you? • What is your passion? • How do you hope to link the two in your future vocation? Provide details. • What is the difference between charity and justice? • In your country is there more of a culture of justice or of charity? Explain why.
Conversation Six: Global Citizenship	• Do the people in your country vote? What is the voting process? • Do the people of your country have confidence in the validity of your elections? • What does it mean to be a global citizen? Is there a tension between being a citizen of your country and being a global citizen? • How can we make sure all voices and regions are present in our global community?
Conversation Seven: Environment:	• How does your community view environmental justice? • Is there a specific area that will most affect your community (water, food, fire, climate refugees, etc.? explain. • Is there a specific area around environmental justice that most interests you? • What policies/practices should be put in place to ensure environmental sustainability?
Conversation Eight: Gender and Identity	What are typical gender role expectations in the home? Outside of the home? How are LGBTQ people/communities treated in your country? *Do Final Project planning:* • Narrow your topic. • Choose your final project (a photo essay, an infographic, or a newsletter). If you have another idea, let us know. • Assign tasks and content • Create a timeline (Project is due November 17th) (You will have two more remote meetings – due November 3 and November 10) Group Project: • Share the content learned and tasks that have been completed • Set future content/task goals
Conversation Nine: Presentation Planning	This week was spent negotiating in various languages the design of the students' product and how the group would present it. Students could do this synchronously or asynchronously.
Conversation Ten: Reflection Written via Discussion Board	1. You had a number of intercultural conversations. How have they helped you to do any of the following? • Develop a sense of perspective and social responsibility • Overcome local thinking • Reduce your own prejudice • Appreciate difference; value and acknowledge other cultures as legitimate • Improve cultural self-awareness and understanding of one's self in the global context • Demonstrate greater appreciation of or an interest in learning about different cultures • Develop empathy and perspective awareness • Demonstrate open-mindedness and an understanding of complexity *Think about your awkward moments and misunderstandings. 2. What did you learn about the other country?

Source: Own elaboration

The written reflection was followed up by a synchronous meeting for students to present their group work. We concluded with eliciting one word from each student that summarized their experiences.

Final COIL Projects

The final COIL project options allowed student groups a choice. The goal of this assignment was to synthesize the information they had gathered from multiple sources. Following were the options.

Photo Essay

A *photo essay* is a way of storytelling, and in this case a way of sharing your topic, using photos and captions. It includes the following:

- 10-15 photos that capture the essence of your chosen social justice issue
- Visual narrative components (who, what, where, why, how)
- Visual technical components (lighting, angles, planes)
- Captions (short descriptive statements).

Infographic

An *infographic* is a visual representation of information, data, and knowledge that is intended to present information quickly and clearly. Its intent is to use imagery and charts, in addition to minimal text, to provide an easy-to-understand overview of a topic.

Create an infographic that captures, at a minimum, the following ideas and concepts:

- Your social justice topic defined
- The causes of the issue and its implications
- The consequences of the issue
- The similarities and differences in Peru and the U.S.
- An infographic that is visually appealing, neat, and creative
- An infographic that is free from spelling, punctuation, or other errors

Newsletter

A *newsletter* is a printed or electronic report containing news concerning of the activities of a business or an organization that is sent to its members, customers, employees or other subscribers. Newsletters generally contain one main topic of interest to its recipients. In this case, you will be creating a newsletter about your social justice topic both in Peru and the U.S. You may want to explore a variety of newsletter templates.

After working together weekly for over two months, each of the small groups of students were able to create a final product, demonstrating their learning. They chose to compare and contrast relevant justice issues within their own countries, and gained a transnational understanding of their justice issue by creating a text through negotiation and collaboration.

In the final projects, students chose the following topics and mediums through which to share their learning:

- A newsletter about the water crisis in Peru, France, and the U.S.
- A photo essay about the systemic inequalities of school funding
- An infographic about education and global citizenship
- A photo essay about transportation from students' home towns
- A photo essay about racial discrimination
- A newsletter about the healthcare system in the U.S. and France

Two of the groups used bilingual slides and two groups included the impact of COVID-19 on their topic, focusing on relevance. See Appendix A for student samples.

During the whole-group reflection, students were asked to share one word that reflected their participation in the collaborative international project. Some of those words included: *unity, intercultural dialogue, kindness, culture, understanding, teamwork, eye-opening, perspective, firsthand knowledge, similarities, satisfaction, empathy, open-minded, network,* and *friendship.*

LESSONS LEARNED

After building relationships and sharing a learning community (albeit a virtual one), the instructors believe students are better able to live with compassion and in solidarity with others. Key outcomes gained through COIL include the following:

- Students gained intercultural awareness and understanding.
- Students learnt about the discipline they are studying from another perspective.
- Students improved their digital literacy skills.
- Students became better prepared to work in virtual teams (a marketable skill).
- Students' communication skills were enhanced and could motivate them to explore another language, discipline, and/or study abroad.

The instructors were able to see many examples of this learning in their students' reflections.

Student Voices

In this section, two of the students who engaged in one of these COIL programs, Ruth and Ray, will share reflections of learning on the following topics: *Collaboration, Increasing Global Knowledge, Development of Intercultural Competence, and Relationship-Building.* These categories were specifically chosen because they are integral elements to successful COIL projects. These students were chosen because they were part of a group that created so much momentum in building relationships that they continued to meet the following spring semester, well after their courses were completed.

Ruth

Collaboration

The experience in collaboration with the university in the United States was extremely enriching and enjoyable. Being immersed in the context of COVID, the virtual meetings were a great support to interact with others and an opportunity to live a new experience during so much monotony. I am grateful for the opportunity because it encouraged me to practice my English, open my perspective to the point of view that my partners had of Peru and know how they conceive their country. The dialogue in a group made up of Peruvian and American students made me realize that, although the US is a powerful country, our shared concerns were similar. Surprisingly, we had more agreements than disagreements. (Ruth, Reflection)

Increasing Global Knowledge

To get to know each other better and successfully complete the activity, we organized a conversation time of one hour once a week, which could sometimes be extended. In these meetings, we talked about politics, education, our personal history, our objectives and hopes for the future. I sensed in all of us a critical judgment of the political situation that we were experiencing in both countries, the elections and social incidents that affected and moved us. We shared information through the chat in a friendly, joking way and in the meetings we shared our thoughts, indignation, and concerns regarding our countries. It is important to mention that these opinions were not always rational, as they were based on the experiences we have had with the world. What resources were you lacking? Did you have opportunities to get ahead? How much effort did it take? How many financial resources? How much did your country give these resources to you? As we talked about our experiences and our lifestyles, I realized where my opinions were coming from. (Ruth, Reflection)

Development of Intercultural Competence

Choosing the final assignment format was an easy decision as a group since we unanimously chose an artistic exhibition. Then each one shared what she was good at, what she wanted to do and naturally each one had her role. Like many assignments or art itself, we worked until the day of the presentation, concluding with a beautiful poem and colorful banner that represented what we had done in the program (see Appendix A). We found that both cultures are seeking women's equality. (Ruth, Reflection)

Relationship-Building

Personally, the program was a very rich experience on an emotional, social and cognitive level. It required forming respectful ties, often overcoming the language barrier. I also consider that this experience is like the phrase used by journalists "firsthand news." You can experience the beauty of a country when traveling as a tourist and learn about negative aspects from television or news. In conversation with the students from the USA, I got to know other, more personal aspects, which made me feel more empathetic and connected to their problems and opinions. However, this did not happen overnight; it was possible because of the constant interaction we had over time, because I got to know them and they got to know me. It was no longer just the USA, it was Ray and Ella's USA. (Ruth, Reflection)

Ray

Here are Ray's statements on the same topics:

Collaboration

For our final project, we combined the Chicha cultural art movement in Peru with our passion for women's healthcare access. One person researched both countries and how the system treats women differently. Another person took the research she had done and wrote a poem. Another person translated that poem into Spanish. Finally, another person (with some help) made a chicha protest poster. We collaborated at every turn, leaning on each other for translation help, art assistance, and cultural explanations (they had to explain to us what chicha was: it's a type of music, an art form, a corn beer, and even part of the local vernacular in some places). Internet-centric education also helps when thinking about international collaborative projects like this. Shared documents, search engines, and immediate conversational translation eliminate many faux pas and awkward ignorance that might normally plague a project like this in the past. (Ray, Reflection)

Increasing Global Knowledge

The impact of the time and location of our COIL conversations cannot be understated when discussing the global knowledge exchange I experienced while in the COIL program at Xavier University. I participated in the COIL program in the Fall of 2020 in the middle of a worldwide pandemic, just after a summer of social unrest after the murder of George Floyd, which highlighted the police brutality leveled toward African Americans in the United States. My Peruvian counterparts (Gaby and Ruth) were also impacted by the global COVID-19 pandemic while similarly dealing with political unrest due to corruption at the highest levels (the semester ended with the ousting of the President of Peru after he tried to dissolve Congress). These "nightly news" developments filled our WhatsApp messages and COIL conversations. We used the racial bias in the US and the racism against indigenous communities in Peru as a bridge to have hard (but necessary) discussions about the part we play in the continued acts of violence in the modern world while living in the shadow of colonization and chattel slavery. (Ray, Reflection).

Development of Intercultural Competence

Intercultural competence comes from listening and being open to others. This project puts students in the driver's seat, allowing them to build conversations and either stick to a strict structure (which still allows for "deep dives" and rambling) or let the train get off the rails and see what is important to others. Our group did a bit of both, allowing the structured questions to begin our conversations but never stopping a rant or an explanation that sprung from that conversation. The language barrier occasionally kept us from engaging on as deep of a level as we wished, but I felt connected to all three of the people in my group. Even as the biggest talker in the group, I still felt like I spent a lot of time listening, laughing, reflecting, and enjoying my counterparts. By focusing on them, I could better understand their culture and my ethics and philosophy. In other words, when we come to others, we also come to know ourselves. (Ray, Reflection).

Relationship-Building

While competence in the world is important, I don't think I would have been as successful without the focus this project had on relationship-building. Learning about these two students, and spending time building a friendship based in curiosity and mutual trust was paramount in creating the space to collaborate, increase knowledge, and develop intercultural competency. Everything goes back to relationships. Learning that Ruth was born into a religious family and saw how women were treated inhumanely in both countries meant trusting her and believing her when she would speak about access to abortions, rape going without punishment, women in education (especially STEM courses, where women report less engagement and encouragement from faculty in both countries), and expectations the church and the state have put on women in both countries. Learning about Gaby and her life and family in her hometown of Cusco, where she regularly gives tours to visitors, using her impeccable English to introduce both the indigenous landscape and the deep-rooted colonialism still on display was essential to understanding the colonial and post-colonial space where Peru is situated in the modern world. Cusco, her historic town, is as old as the Incan ruins in Macchu Picchu nearby. In fact, many people in the area still speak the native Quechan language. Yet, Cusco is a living relic of Peru's colonial past, rebuilt as a Spanish city in the 16th century. Understanding where these young women come from and their lived experiences helped build my intercultural competence (and an incredible global network!) but also helped me in my career and personal life. I was in this course because it is required for all educators. As an educator, understanding that my students can come from wildly different backgrounds than I have experienced or can even fathom makes my classroom stronger.

Ultimately, encouraging us to think reflectively, share openly, and communicate effectively made this project one of the highlights of my master's coursework. Of course, we learned about each other and each other's culture, but more so, we learned the importance of Others. Humans are not a monolith, and while two Peruvian women don't represent all of them, in my experience, it is a great place to start. (Ray, Reflection).

DISCUSSION

Building on the theoretical work of the aforementioned Latin American scholars (Dussel, 1998; Escobar, 2004; Maldonado-Torres, 2004; Mignolo, 2002; Quijano, 1997) and the paradigms of Eurocentrism and modern world systems that center Western civilization and/or constructs of modernity with colonization and capitalism, the authors suggest that COIL can be used to resist and even confront those paradigms. In fact, the collaborative work to increase global knowledge, develop intercultural competence, and build relationships on a personal and professional level deconstruct the paradigms of Eurocentrist modern world systems that center Western civilization by centering others and challenging the status quo. Through COIL, students discuss and unpack the ideals of freedom and equality while making room for a political philosophy of inclusion. Unlike traveling abroad, participating in COIL also challenges the market economy of internationalization, which is typically only accessed by those with wealth.

Consequently, the authors expanded the resistance to the paradigms by centering this chapter in critical, feminist, and Ignatian pedagogies to make space for exploring the tension between globalizing and Westernizing. Transformative theories of education such as critical, feminist, and Ignatian, suggest that schools are ideal sites for promoting social change; consequently, learning should focus on social critique leading to change (Freire & Macedo, 1987; Giroux, 1992; Hauck, 2023). Critical theory requires the questioning of unequal relations so that one acts to offset them (Kanpol, 1994); therefore, in order to envision a sustainable and equitable transnational engagement, this work aligned with the global competencies of the Asia Society (Mansilla & Jacksons, 2011).

Through the elements of Collaboration, Increasing Global Knowledge, Development of Intercultural Competence, and Relationship-Building discussed by the student authors above, the intersection of the competencies with the learning and the lessons learned, connecting the experience to the theoretical framework, is depicted in Table 3.

Table 3. Global competencies and learning

Global Competency	Elements for Student Reflection	Lessons Learned
1. Students investigate the world beyond their immediate environment, framing significant problems and conducting well-crafted and age-appropriate research.	Increasing global knowledge.	Students gain intercultural awareness and understanding.
2. Students recognize perspectives, others' and their own, articulating and explaining such perspectives thoughtfully and respectfully.	Development of intercultural competence.	Students can learn about the discipline they are studying from another perspective.
3. Students communicate ideas effectively with diverse audiences, bridging geographic, linguistic, ideological, and cultural barriers.	Collaboration, development of intercultural competence, relationship-building.	Students improve their digital literacy skills; Students are better prepared to work in virtual teams (marketable skill).
4. Students take action to improve conditions, viewing themselves as players in the world and participating reflectively.	Collaboration, relationship-building.	Students' communication skills are enhanced and could motivate them to explore another language and/or study abroad.

Source: Own elaboration

Cross-Disciplinary learning during COIL can be multi-layered, adding a depth and richness to learning as students make connections across their areas of study and interest. Best practices in COIL can also attend to global citizenship in that one must be collaborative, interested in developing cultural competencies and building personal relationships through acquiring global knowledge (Beelen et al.2021; Üzum et al., 2023). Global knowledge and engagement is critical to negotiating tensions between globalizing and Westernizing because attention and care are paid toward power dynamics and sensitivity to ways others may be experiencing those interactions.

Faculty and students situated in different countries and often speaking different languages are aware of differences in power as they negotiate and communicate. Regular dialogues are critical to understanding the tensions that can arise when common vocabulary such as *global citizenship* is being used. This term is contested, which provides space for further dialogue and critical analysis, in order to challenge assumptions and broaden others' understandings. Higher education institutions must create those spaces.

Worth noting is that in a final COIL classroom survey, 100 percent of UARM students recognized they were able to improve their English and were less afraid to interact in international spaces. This supports the university's effort to internationalize-at-home at UARM.

Further, the COIL teaching and learning experience described in this chapter addressed the shared Jesuit mission in education as put forth by Father Michael Garanzini, President of both the International Association of Jesuit Universities (IAJU) and the Association of Jesuit Colleges and Universities (AJCU). Garanzini has repeatedly emphasized the importance of internationalizing students, who will be influential and understanding citizens of the world (AJCU, 2023).

CONCLUSION

This chapter is intended to share the themes and content necessary to know how to apply the COIL methodology in a cross-cultural approach. There is much to consider in the intricate planning of COIL that is intentional with regard to justice issues, being open to including and fostering student voices, and as faculty, continuously reflecting individually and collaboratively in order to increase impact of growing student global knowledge through respectful and honest global engagement.

More importantly, however, this chapter intended to go beyond a simple recipe to COIL as the authors explored how to envision a healthily sustainable and equitable transnational engagement. The COIL partnership addressed the following global initiatives: sharing best practices and know-how; promoting academic collaboration; encouraging reflection; facilitating the exchange of quality knowledge; and identifying strategic colleagues in common areas and themes. Teaching is an ethical enterprise because, as educators, we must do the following:

Know and care about aspects of our shared life - our calling is to shepherd and enable the callings of others. Teachers, then, invite students to become somehow more capable, more thoughtful and powerful in their choices, more engaged in a culture and a civilization (Ayers, 2004, p. 4).

Through social justice teaching of Ignatian pedagogy, we should do the following:

Strive especially for the defense and propagation of the faith, and for the progress of souls in Christian life and doctrine, by means of public preaching, lectures, and any other ministrations, by means of the Spiritual Exercises, and the education of children (General Congregation of the Society of Jesus, 32).

COIL supports that mission through social justice teaching, as a model for preservice and practicing teachers, future journalists, psychologists, and engineers who can then impact a large number of people locally and globally.

Reconciliation, a focus of Ignatian pedagogy and Jesuit ideals, is viewed as a relational process, and COIL is one way to address the need for peace and reconciliation as the authors collaborate with other Jesuit institutions who share a similar vision. While having a shared vision, resources are not equitably shared when approximately 12 UARM students study abroad each semester while 40 XU students have a semester experience – and over 325 participate in short-term study abroad. Consequently, while 25 students a year at UARM were having international education experiences, with the implementation of

COIL and other virtual exchanges, now 300 students have access to sustainable, transnational engagement each year.

The Jesuit mission integration is evident in the transnational engagement with others, oneself, and the creation of the teaching and learning in higher education. The curricular activities incorporated into COIL offer opportunities for students to become involved in the transformative process in their own countries and abroad. The authors have been called to confront the current global justice issues.. "Our response to these new challenges will be total (involving prayer and action), corporate (collaborative), rooted in faith and experience, and multiform (different in different contexts)" (General Congregation of the Society of Jesus, 34). COIL provides a place to respond as global citizens who care about transforming the world. "Social justice involves social actors who have a sense of their own agency as well as a sense of social responsibility toward and with others, their society, and the broader world in which we live" (Bell, 1997, pp. 1-2). The authors engage globally in this critical work - with agency and a clear sense of responsibility to others.

REFERENCES

Amador, F. G. (2022). Respuesta de la education superior a los desafíos impuestos por la COVID-19: Panorama latinoamericano [Higher Education response to the challenges imposed by Covid-19: Latin American panorama]. In P. Castiello-Gutiérrez, M. P. Pantoja, & C. E. Gutiérrez (Eds.), *Internacionalizatión de la Educación Superior después de la COVID-19: Reflexiones y nuevas prácticas para tiempos distintos* [*Internationalization of Higher Education after COVID-19: Reflections and new practices for different times*] (pp. 76–103). UPAEP/AMPEI. https://tinyurl.com/34b8d99s

Andreotti, V. (2011). (Towards) decoloniality and diversality in global citizenship education. *Globalisation, Societies and Education*, *9*(3-4), 381–397. doi:10.1080/14767724.2011.605323

Association of Jesuit Colleges & Universities (AJCU). (2023). *Reverend Michael Garanzini*. https://ajcunet.edu/about/ajcu-staff/michael-garanzini/

Ayers, W. (2004). *Teaching the personal and the political: Essays on hope and justice*. Teachers College Press.

Batovala, J., & Zong, J. (2016). *Language diversity and English proficiency*. Migration Policy Institute. https://tinyurl.com/2rayfpzt

Beelen, J., Wimpenny, K., & Rubin, J. (2021). Internationalisation in the classroom and questions of alignment: Embedding COIL in an internationalised curriculum. In P. Nixon, V. Dennen, & R. Rawal (Eds.), *Reshaping international teaching and learning in higher education* (pp. 29–45). Routledge. doi:10.4324/9780429278075-2

Bell, L. A. (2023). Theoretical foundations for social justice education. In M. Adams, L. A. Bell, & P. Griffin (Eds.), *Teaching for diversity and social justice* (pp. 3–15). Routledge.

Cushner, K. (2012). Intercultural competence for teaching and learning. In B. Shaklee & S. Baily (Eds.), *Internationalizing teacher education in the United States* (pp. 41–58). Rowman & Littlefield.

Cushner, K. (2018). *Teacher as traveler*. Rowman & Littlefield.

Dussel, E. (1998). Beyond Eurocentrism: The world-system and the limits of modernity. In F. Jameson & M. Miyoshi (Eds.), *The cultures of globalization* (pp. 3–31). Duke University Press. doi:10.2307/j.ctv11cw3dt.5

Escobar, A. (2004). Beyond the third world: Imperial globality, global coloniality and anti-globalization social movements. *Third World Quarterly*, *25*(1), 207–230. doi:10.1080/0143659042000185417

Freire, P. (2000). Pedagogy of the oppressed (30th anniversary ed.). Continuum.

Freire, P., & Macedo, D. (1987). *Literacy: Reading the word and the world*. Bergin & Garvey.

Galarza, F., Arnaiz, N., & Arias, N. (2021). Retos de la enseñanza-aprendizaje virtual: Creatividad del docente, clases sincrónicas o asincrónicas, y principios didácticos [Challenges of e-learning: teacher creativity, synchronous or asynchronous classes, and didactic principles]. *Revista Conrado*, *17*(S1), 331–339.

General Congregation of the Society of Jesus, 32, Decree 4 *The Service of Faith and the Promotion of Justice*. December 2nd, 1974 - March 7th, 1975.

Giroux, H. (1992). Resisting difference: Cultural studies and the discourse of critical pedagogy. In C. Groosberg & P. Groosberg (Eds.), *Cultural studies* (pp. 199–212). Routledge.

Hauck, M. (2023). From Virtual Exchange to Critical Virtual Exchange and Critical Internationalization at Home. *The Global Impact Exchange*. https://tinyurl.com/yvw6n2rn

Kanpol, B. (1999). *Critical pedagogy: An introduction*. Bergin & Garvey.

Maldonado-Torres, N. (2004). The topology of being and the geopolitics of knowledge: Modernity, empire, coloniality. *City (London, England)*, *8*(1), 29–56. doi:10.1080/1360481042000199787

Mansilla, V. B., & Jackson, A. (2011). *Educating for global competence: Preparing our youth to engage the world*. Council of Chief State School Officers' EdSteps Initiative & Asia Society Partnership for Global Learning.

Mignolo, W. (2002). The geopolitics of knowledge and the colonial difference. *The South Atlantic Quarterly*, *101*(1), 57–94. doi:10.1215/00382876-101-1-57

Oliver, K., & Lalik, R. (2004). Critical inquiry on the body in girls' physical education classes: A critical poststructural perspective. *Journal of Teaching in Physical Education*, *23*(2), 162–195. doi:10.1123/jtpe.23.2.162

Peru (2023). *Education First English Proficiency Index (EF EPI)*. https://www.ef.com/wwen/epi/regions/latin-america/peru/

Quijano, A. (1997). Colonialidad del poder, cultural y conocimiento en América Latina [Coloniality of power, culture and knowledge in Latin America]. *Anuario Mariateguiano*, *9*, 113–122.

Salazar, S. (2022). The challenge of internationalization in Peruvian universities. In P. Castiello-Gutiérrez, P., Pantoja, M. P. & Gutiérrez, C. E. (Eds.), Internationalization of Higher Education after COVID-19: Reflections and new practices for different times (pp. 124-137). UPAEP/AMPEI, Mexico.

Short, K. (2016). A curriculum that is intercultural. In K. Short, D. Day, & J. Schroeder (Eds.), *Teaching globally: Reading the world through literature* (pp. 3–24). Stenhouse.

Slapac, A., Collett, K., Wessels, F., Gamiet, G., & Knudsmoen, H. (2023). Social justice pedagogy and Collaborative Online International Learning (COIL): Across three partner higher education institutions. In P. Escudeiro, N. Escudeiro, & O. Bernardes (Eds.), *Handbook of research on implementing inclusive educational models and technologies for equity and diversity* (pp. 252–272). IGI Global. doi:10.4018/979-8-3693-0453-2.ch013

SUNY COIL. (2023). *About COIL.* https://coil.suny.edu/about-suny-coil/

Titus, J. (2000). Engaging student resistance to feminism: 'How is this stuff going to make us better teachers?'. *Gender and Education, 12*(1), 21–37. doi:10.1080/09540250020382

UNESCO. (2017). *Intercultural competences: Conceptual and operational framework.* https://tinyurl.com/3n9vr5h5

Üzüm, B., Yazan, B., Mary, L., & Akayoglu, S. (2023). Teacher agency for social justice in telecollaboration: Locating agentive positioning in virtual language interaction. *Language Learning Journal, 51*(6), 766–782. doi:10.1080/09571736.2022.2080857

KEY TERMS AND DEFINITIONS

Eurocentric: Interpreting the world in terms of European or Anglo-American values and experiences.

Global Competencies: Knowledge, skills, and attitudes that are critical to successful intercultural engagement.

Globalization: An interconnectedness process across the world in trade, education, and technology.

Jesuits: Known as The Society of Jesus, a spiritual Catholic community with a focus on teaching the whole person and their development of many educational institutions.

Justice Issues: Obstacles that cause inequity among groups of people.

Paulo Freire: Brazilian educator and philosopher who was the father of critical pedagogy.

Reflection: Taking the time to pause and think deeply in order to evaluate thoughts, attitudes and motivations.

UNESCO: UN organization that promotes equal dignity to all cultures and focuses on equal access to education across the globe.

Virtual Exchange: The use of technology to communicate across cultures.

APPENDIX 1

COIL Group Project

For our group project, we researched abortion access in both countries, wrote a poem based on that research, translated it to Spanish, and created Chicha posters to go with the poems. First, we researched abortion and found that Peru doesn't allow abortions at all, for any reason. This adversely impacts indigenous women who can't afford contraceptives. Rural citizens are also less likely to receive sex education. Both of these things are things science has proven will reduce abortions. We also found that the same groups who speak the loudest about prohibiting abortion in all circumstances, tend to be the same groups who are against full sex education, free access to contraceptives, gun control in the US, humanitarian action at the US Southern border, and prosecution of sex crimes.

We created the poem, specifically, to elicit an emotional response to garner support for open and legal access to abortion in both countries. Currently, the US varies state-by-state, with the most recent two Supreme Court justice appointments casting some doubt into the future of legal access to abortion across the country. We imagine the poems being read while people hold the posters. Chicha culture is based in Lima and was started by Andean migrants, some of whom might have been victims of these baseless laws. It's a culture of the "common man" in Lima, popular with young people. With both of our countries being very active in protesting, we imagine this poem and the posters being used during activism like protesting, marching, or speaking engagements for activists. The basis of the poem is that 'pro-life' is a misleading term; the basis of the posters are that women deserve a choice in what happens to their body. As we communicated in our poem, we believe this group should be called "pro-birth." Through this poem and our poster, we aimed to show the hypocrisy of the values that pro-birth groups hold. Pro-birth activists and anti-abortion lobbyists focus on the birth of a child, while not addressing the issues of childhood poverty, foster care, childhood suicide rates, gun violence, the crisis at the border, and many other issues that take people's lives in our countries. This entire presentation is a conversation against that "pro-life" mindset.

Pro-Life

A young girl, pregnant, trying her best
To live her life with some respect
A man, who had no bodily authority
Forced her into submissive inferiority
As "Murderer!" insults pierce the air
She tries to avoid the hate out there
Into the clinic; she goes to escape
Didn't they know she didn't *choose* to be raped?
Her choice instead was to control her story
She didn't fit so tight into their category
Does "pro-life" include her? Does her heart beat?
Or is the fetus the extent of how we compete?

Our foster homes fill; our children go hungry
Is this Firm and Happy? In the Land of the Free?
Children die in our schools. They die in our streets.
They die in our arms when we can't find them eats
His heart beats while tears stream down his eyes
As he texts his parents his last goodbye
The gunshots ring while the rockets' red glare
His heart was beating. He died alone and scared.
Hearts beat at the border behind those bars
Hiding too many national sins and scars
Hearts beat in the country, in the Land of the Incas
Where the lawmakers don't think they need to think of us
If you know the right person or have the right connection
You can take a pill and make a correction
And risk two years in a far off prison
For one forced night, does that stand to reason?
Until our women are free from this plight
Then let the Sun renounce its light
Pro-birth is a better term. It makes more sense
But that might put the wrong team on defense.
Pro-life doesn't have to mean the heart is beating
It could mean that we want our children to keep breathing.
Traducción:

Pro Vida

Una joven embarazada, intentando lo mejor Por una vida con algo de respeto
Un hombre sin una autoridad física
la forzó a una inferioridad sumisa
Mientras la palabra "asesina" atraviesa el aire
Intenta avanzar tratando de evadir el odio en la calle
Se acerca a la clínica para escapar
¿Acaso no sabían que ella no eligió ser violada?
Sin embargo eligió controlar su historia.
Es que ella no encaja con esa categoría
¿La incluyen a ella los "pro-vida"?
¿Acaso su corazón no late?
¿O es el feto la forma de competir ahora?
Nuestras hogares llenos, nuestros niños con hambre
¿Acaso es esta la seguridad y la felicidad? ¿es esta la tierra de la libertad?
Los niños mueren en nuestras escuelas y en las calles también
Mueren en nuestros brazos, cuando no podemos alimentarlos.

Su corazón aún late mientras caen lágrimas de sus ojos
Les escribe a un último adiós a sus padres
Disparos se escuchan mientras los cohetes arden
Su corazón estuvo latiendo. Se murió solo y con miedo
Los corazones laten al borde detrás de esos barrotes
Escondiendo muchos pecados y heridas nacionales
Los corazones laten en el país, en la tierra de las incas
Donde los legisladores creen que no deben pensar en nosotros
Porque si conoces a la persona correcta o tienes contactos
Puedes tomar una pastilla y hacer una corrección
Y arriesgar dos años de prisión lejana
Por una noche forzada, ¿acaso es eso lógica?
Hasta que nuestras mujeres estén libres de esta situación
Dejarán que el sol renuncie a alumbrar
Ser provida es un mejor término. Tiene más sentido
Pero ello podría poner al equipo equivocado a la defensiva
Ser provida no significa que su corazón esté latiendo
Podría tan sólo significar que queremos que nuestros niños sigan respirando.

Figure 1. Moodboard

Figure 2. "Let Her Choose" posters
Sources:
About the children. (n.d.). About the children. https://www.adoptuskids.org/meet-the-children/children-in-foster-care/about-the-children
Broman, B. (2018, September 27). National Center on Family Homelessness. https://www.air.org/center/national-center-family-homelessness
Suicide Statistics and Facts. (n.d.). Suicide Statistics and Facts. https://save.org/about-suicide/suicide-facts/
Walker, C. (n.d.). 10 years. 180 school shootings. 356 victims. https://www.cnn.com/interactive/2019/07/us/ten-years-of-school-shootings-trnd/

Compilation of References

Abo-Zena, M., Brittian Loyd, A., & Cunningham, M. (2019). Introduction to mentored scholarship: Mirrors, windows, and doors to understanding and supporting research in human development. *Research in Human Development*, *16*(3-4), 175–184. doi:10.1080/15427609.2020.1727821

Acar, S., & Peker, B. (2021). What are the purposes of teachers for using the eTwinning platform and the effects of the platform on teachers? *Acta Didactica Napocensia*, *14*(1), 91–103. doi:10.24193/adn.14.1.7

Adams, S., Bernal, E., Cole-Jackson, M., & Martin-Hansen, L. (2015). Training teachers to use educational technologies in STEM using field experience at a community-based organization. In *Society for Information Technology & Teacher Education International Conference Proceedings* (pp. 3021-3025). Association for the Advancement of Computing in Education (AACE). https://www.learntechlib.org/p/150425/

Adedoyin, O. B., & Soykan, E. (2020). COVID-19 pandemic and online learning: The challenges and opportunities. *Interactive Learning Environments*, *31*(2), 863–875. doi:10.1080/10494820.2020.1813180

Adichie, C. N. (2009). *The danger of a single story* [Video]. TED Global. https://www.ted.com/talks/chimamanda_ngozi_adichie_the_danger_of_a_single_story/c

Akiyama, Y., & Cunningham, D. J. (2018). Synthesizing the practice of SCMC-based telecollaboration: A scoping review. *CALICO Journal*, *35*(1), 49–76. doi:10.1558/cj.33156

Akkerman, S. F., & Bakker, A. (2011). Boundary crossing and boundary objects. *Review of Educational Research*, *81*(2), 132–169. doi:10.3102/0034654311404435

Akyol, Z., & Garrison, D. R. (2011). Assessing metacognition in an online community of inquiry. *The Internet and Higher Education*, *14*(3), 183–190. doi:10.1016/j.iheduc.2011.01.005

Alexis-Boyd, L. (1998). *The emotional life of teachers: A heuristic inquiry* [Doctoral dissertation, University of Cincinnati]. https://bit.ly/3UuO6kv https://www.proquest.com/openview/ff4818296d287edbe318642a5bd114c1/1?pq-origsite=gscholar&cbl=18750&diss=y

Alford, Z., & White, M. A. (2015). Positive school psychology. In M. A. White & A. S. Murray (Eds.), *Evidence-based approaches in positive education. Implementing a strategic framework for well-being in schools* (pp. 93–110). Springer. doi:10.1007/978-94-017-9667-5_5

Alim, H. S., & Paris, D. (2017). What is culturally sustaining pedagogy and why does it matter? In D. Paris & H.S. Alim (Eds.), Culturally sustaining pedagogies: Teaching and learning for justice in a changing world (pp. 1-24). Teachers College Press.

Allen, J. M., & Wright, S. E. (2014). Integrating theory and practice in the pre-service teacher education practicum. *Teachers and Teaching*, *20*(2), 136–151. doi:10.1080/13540602.2013.848568

Allport, G. W. (1954). *The nature of prejudice*. Perseus Publishing.

Álvarez-Castillo, J. L., Martínez-Usarralde, M. J., González-González, H., & Buenestado-Fernández, M. (2017). El aprendizaje-servicio en la formación del profesorado de las universidades españolas [Service-learning in teacher training in Spanish universities]. *Revista Española de Pedagogía, 75*(267), 199–217. doi:10.22550/REP75-2-2017-02

Alzate, Y., Parra, R., Canales, R., & Morales, M. (2021). Apropiación de las competencias digitales en educación superior [Appropriation of digital skills in higher education]. In R. Cabello & S. Lago (Eds.), *Ciudadanía digital, desigualdades y transformación en América Latina y el Caribe: Memorias* [Digital Citizenship, Inequalities and Transformation in Latin America and the Caribbean: Memorias] (pp. 46-58). Universidad de Sevilla (idUS). https://hdl.handle.net/11441/133942

Amador, F. G. (2022). Respuesta de la education superior a los desafíos impuestos por la COVID-19: Panorama latinoamericano [Higher Education response to the challenges imposed by Covid-19: Latin American panorama]. In P. Castiello-Gutiérrez, M. P. Pantoja, & C. E. Gutiérrez (Eds.), *Internacionalizatión de la Educación Superior después de la COVID-19: Reflexiones y nuevas prácticas para tiempos distintos* [*Internationalization of Higher Education after COVID-19: Reflections and new practices for different times*] (pp. 76–103). UPAEP/AMPEI. https://tinyurl.com/34b8d99s

Amador, G. (2020). Conceptual framework on internationalization in the country. In J. E. Hernández & G. Amador (Eds.), *Good internationalization practices at home. Experiences at the University of Colima* (pp. 13–20). University of Colima. http://ww.ucol.mx/content/publicacionesenlinea/adjuntos/Buenas-practicas-de-internacionalizacion-2_490.pdf

Amador, J. M., & Carter, I. S. (2018). Audible conversational affordances and constraints of verbalizing professional noticing during prospective teacher lesson study. *Journal of Mathematics Teacher Education, 21*(1), 5–34. doi:10.1007/s10857-016-9347-x

Ames, K. E., Rennick, J. E., & Baillargeon, S. (2011). A qualitative interpretive study exploring parents' perception of the parental role in the pediatric intensive care unit. *Intensive & Critical Care Nursing, 27*(3), 143–150. doi:10.1016/j.iccn.2011.03.004 PMID:21511474

Anderson, L. W., & Krathwohl, D. R. (Eds.). (2001). *A taxonomy for learning, teaching and assessing. A revision of Bloom's taxonomy of educational objectives*. Longman.

Andreotti, V. (2006). 'Theory without practice is idle, practice without theory is blind': The potential contributions of post-colonial theory to development education. *The Development Education Journal, 12*(3), 7–10.

Andreotti, V. (2011). (Towards) decoloniality and diversality in global citizenship education. *Globalisation, Societies and Education, 9*(3-4), 381–397. doi:10.1080/14767724.2011.605323

Antonenko, P. D., Toy, S., & Niederhauser, D. S. (2012). Using cluster analysis for data mining in educational technology research. *Educational Technology Research and Development, 60*(3), 383–398. doi:10.1007/s11423-012-9235-8

Appiah-Kubi, P., & Annan, E. (2020). A review of a Collaborative Online International Learning. *International Journal of Engineering Pedagogy, 10*(1), 109–124. doi:10.3991/ijep.v10i1.11678

Araos, A., Damşa, C., & Gašević, D. (2023). Browsing to learn: How computer and software engineering students use online platforms in learning activities. *Journal of Computer Assisted Learning, 39*(2), 676–693. Advance online publication. doi:10.1111/jcal.12774

Arias, J. (2016). Social innovation, a concept linked to praxis; the case of UNIMINUTO's Social Innovation Science Park - Colombia. In D. Domanski, N. Monge, G. Quitiaquez, & D. Rocha (Eds). *Social innovation in Latin America* (pp. 255-295). Uniminuto. https://acortar.link/lI31PO

Arkoudis, S., Watty, K., Baik, C., Yu, X., Borland, H., Chang, S., Lang, I., Lang, J., & Pearce, A. (2013). Finding common ground: Enhancing interaction between domestic and international students in higher education. *Teaching in Higher Education*, *18*(3), 222–235. doi:10.1080/13562517.2012.719156

Arora-Jonsson, S. (2023). The sustainable development goals: A universalist promise for the future. *Futures*, *146*, 103087. doi:10.1016/j.futures.2022.103087

Asarta, C. J., Bento, R., Fornaciari, C. J., Lund Dean, K., Arbaugh, J. B., & Hwang, A. (2018). The scholarship of teaching and learning: Changing the dominant narrative about (and in) research institutions. *Journal of Management Education*, *42*(6), 731–748. doi:10.1177/1052562918777271

Asojo, A. O., Kartoshkina, Y., Jaiyeoba, B., & Amole, D. (2019). Multicultural learning and experiences in design through Collaborative Online International Learning (COIL) framework. *Journal of Teaching and Learning with Technology*, *8*(1), 5–16. doi:10.14434/jotlt.v8i1.26748

Association of Jesuit Colleges & Universities (AJCU). (2023). *Reverend Michael Garanzini*. https://ajcunet.edu/about/ajcu-staff/michael-garanzini/

Astleitner, H. (2018). Multidimensional engagement in learning: An integrated instructional design approach. *Journal of Institutional Research*, *7*(1), 6–32. doi:10.9743/JIR.2018.1

Austin, N., Hampel, R., & Kukulska-Hulme, A. (2017). Video conferencing and multimodal expression of voice: Children's conversations using Skype for second language development in a telecollaborative setting. *System*, *64*, 87–103. doi:10.1016/j.system.2016.12.003

Ayers, W. (2004). *Teaching the personal and the political: Essays on hope and justice*. Teachers College Press.

Bagarukayo, E., & Kalema, B. (2015). Evaluation of e-learning usage in South African universities: A critical review. *International Journal of Education and Development using ICT*, *11*(2). https://www.learntechlib.org/p/151848/

Bakshy, E., Hofman, J. M., Mason, W. A., & Watts, D. J. (2011, February). *Everyone is an influencer: Quantifying influence on twitter*. ACM Digital Library. doi:10.1145/1935826.1935845

Balladares, J., & Kankaraš, M. (2020). Attendance in early childhood education and care programmes and academic proficiencies at age 15. OECD Education Working Papers, No. 214. *OECD Publishing*. doi:10.1787/19939019

Balta, E., & Altan-Olcay, Ö. (2016). Strategic citizens of America: Transnational inequalities and transformation of citizenship. *Ethnic and Racial Studies*, *39*(6), 939–957. doi:10.1080/01419870.2015.1103882

Bangura, Y. (2018). *Multicultural education: The relationship between preservice teachers multicultural self-efficacy and cultural awareness when teaching in multicultural classrooms* [Doctoral dissertation, Bowling Green State University]. ProQuest Dissertations Publishing. https://rave.ohiolink.edu/etdc/view?acc_num=bgsu1522682134643678

Banks, J. A. (1989). Approaches to multicultural curriculum reform. *Trotter Review*, *3*(3), 17–19.

Bao, Y. Y., & Liu, S. Z. (2021). The influence of affective factors in second language acquisition on foreign language teaching. *Open Journal of Social Sciences*, *9*(3), 463–470. doi:10.4236/jss.2021.93030

Barad, K. (2007). *Meeting the universe halfway*. Duke University Press. https://www.dukeupress.edu/Meeting-the-Universe-Halfway

Barbosa, M. W., & Ferreira-Lopes, L. (2021). Emerging trends in telecollaboration and virtual exchange: A bibliometric study. *Educational Review*, *75*(3), 58–586. doi:10.1080/00131911.2021.1907314

Barrett, M., & Golubeva, I. (2022). From intercultural communicative competence to intercultural citizenship: Preparing young people for citizenship in a culturally diverse democratic world. In T. McConachy, I. Golubeva, & M. Wagner (Eds.), *Intercultural learning in language education and beyond* (pp. 60–83). Multilingual Matters. doi:10.21832/9781800412613-011

Başaran Uysal, B. Ç., & Savaş, P. (2021). Overview of the challenges of practicum practices in English language teaching in Türkiye: A meta synthesis study on literature between 2004 and 2019. *Inonu University Journal of the Faculty of Education, 22*(2), 1669–1712. doi:10.17679/inuefd.886731

Başaran, B. Ç. (2020). *Examining in-service English language teachers' professional needs: Towards an online teacher training program* (Unpublished PhD thesis). Middle East Technical University, Ankara.

Bassani, P., & Buchem, I. (2019). Virtual exchanges in higher education: Developing intercultural skills of students across borders through online collaboration [Interuniversity Journal of Research in Educational Technology]. *Revista Interuniversitaria de Investigación en Tecnología Educativa, 6*, 22–36. doi:10.6018/riite.377771

Batovala, J., & Zong, J. (2016). *Language diversity and English proficiency*. Migration Policy Institute. https://tinyurl.com/2rayfpzt

Battelle for Kids. (2023, March 29). *21st-century learning*. https://bit.ly/4829a51

Baumgratz, G. (1995). Language, culture and global competence: An essay on ambiguity. *European Journal of Education, 30*(4), 437–447. doi:10.2307/1503516

Baxter, P., & Jack, S. (2008). Qualitative case study methodology: Study design and implementation for novice researchers. *The Qualitative Report, 13*(4), 544–559. doi:10.46743/2160-3715/2008.1573

Becker, M. R., McCaleb, K., & Baker, C. (2018). Paradigm shift toward student engagement in technology mediated courses. In Information Resources Management Association (IRMA) (Ed.), Student engagement and participation: Concepts, methodologies, tools, and applications (pp. 1547-1567). IGI Global. doi:10.4018/978-1-5225-2584-4.ch077

Bedenlier, S., & Zawacki-Richter, O. (2015). Internationalization of higher education and the impacts on academic faculty members. *Research in Comparative and International Education, 10*(2), 185–201. doi:10.1177/1745499915571707

Beelen, J. (2022). Why we should continue to ask critical questions about internationalisation at home. *Perspectives in Education, 40*(4), 325–327. doi:10.38140/pie.v40i4.7004

Beelen, J., & Jones, E. (2015). Redefining internationalisation at home. In A. Curai, L. Matei, R. Pricopie, J. Salmi, & P. Scott (Eds.), *The European higher education area: Between critical reflections and future policies* (pp. 67–80). Springer. doi:10.1007/978-3-319-20877-0_5

Beelen, J., Wimpenny, K., & Rubin, J. (2021). Internationalisation in the classroom and questions of alignment: Embedding COIL in an internationalised curriculum. In P. Nixon, V. Dennen, & R. Rawal (Eds.), *Reshaping international teaching and learning in higher education* (pp. 29–45). Routledge. doi:10.4324/9780429278075-2

Bell, L. A. (2023). Theoretical foundations for social justice education. In M. Adams, L. A. Bell, & P. Griffin (Eds.), *Teaching for diversity and social justice* (pp. 3–15). Routledge.

Belz, J. A., & Thorne, S. L. (2006). Introduction: Internet-mediated intercultural foreign language education and the intercultural speaker. In J. Belz & S. L. Thorne (Eds.), *Internet-mediated intercultural foreign language education* (pp. ix–xxv). Thomson Heinle.

Bengtsson, M. (2016). How to plan and perform a qualitative study using content analysis. *NursingPlus Open*, 2, 8–14. https://doi-org.ezproxy.fiu.edu/10.1016/j.npls.2016.01.001

Bhabha, H. (1990). The third space. In J. Rutherford (Ed.), Identity: community, culture, difference (pp. 207-221). Lawrence & Wishart.

Bhatt, R., Bell, A., Rubin, D. L., Shiflet, C., & Hodges, L. (2022). Education abroad and college completion. *Research in Higher Education, 63*(6), 987–1014. doi:10.1007/s11162-022-09673-z PMID:35043032

Binali, T., Tsai, C.-C., & Chang, H.-Y. (2021). University students' profiles of online learning and their relation to online learning and internet-specific epistemic justification. *Computers & Education, 175*, 104315. Advance online publication. doi:10.1016/j.compedu.2021.104315

Bishop, R. S. (1990). Mirrors, windows, and sliding glass doors. *Perspectives: Choosing and using books for the classroom, 6*(3), 9–11.

Bishop, R. S. (2012). Reflections on the development of African American children & literature. *Journal of Children's Literature, 38*(2), 5–13. https://www.proquest.com/docview/1266034800?pq-origsite=gscholar&fromopenview=true

Bisquerra, R., & Pérez, N. (2007). Las competencias emocionales [Emotional competencies] *Educación XXI, 10*(1), 61–82. doi:10.5944/educxx1.1.10.297

Blicharska, M., Teutschbein, C., & Smithers, R. J. (2021). SDG partnerships may perpetuate the global North–South divide. *Scientific Reports, 11*(1), 22092. doi:10.1038/s41598-021-01534-6 PMID:34824306

Boaler, J. (2006). How a detracked mathematics approach promoted respect, responsibility and high achievement. *Theory into Practice, 45*(1), 40–46. doi:10.1207/s15430421tip4501_6

Boholano, H. (2017). Smart social networking: 21st century teaching and learning skills. *Research in Pedagogy, 7*(1), 21-29. https://www.ceeol.com/search/article-detail?id=546738

Boix Mansilla, V., Perkins, K., Ritchhart, R., Tishman, S., & Chua, F. (2017). Global thinking: An ID-Global bundle to foster global thinking dispositions through global thinking routines. Project Zero, Harvard Graduate School of Education.

Boix Mansilla, V. (2016/2017). How to be a global thinker. *Educational Leadership, 74*(4), 11–16. https://www.ascd.org/el/articles/how-to-be-a-global-thinker

Boniwell, I., & Ryan, L. (2012). *Personal well-being: Lessons for secondary schools, positive psychology in action for 11 to 14 year olds*. McGraw-Hill.

Bornstein, M. H., & Bradley, R. H. (Eds.). (2014). *Socioeconomic status, parenting, and child development*. Routledge. doi:10.4324/9781410607027

Borrero, N. E. (2023). Embracing the collective: Challenges and opportunities in teaching and teacher education in the wake of COVID-19. *Social Sciences (Basel, Switzerland), 12*(3), 194. doi:10.3390/socsci12030194

Borrero, N. E., Camangian, P. R., Ayers, R., Martinez, S., & Flores, E. (2020). *Half an inch from the edge: Teacher education, teaching, and student learning for social transformation*. Rowman & Littlefield.

Borrero, N. E., & Naidoo, J. (2023). Teachers living the curriculum: Culturally relevant pedagogy and action research. In N. Wahlström & B. Karseth (Eds.), *International Encyclopedia of Education* (4th ed., Vol. 7, pp. 357–362). Elsevier. doi:10.1016/B978-0-12-818630-5.03063-3

Borrero, N. E., & Yeh, C. J. (2016). Ecological asset mapping as a pedagogical tool for new urban teachers. *International Journal of Multicultural Education, 18*(3), 114–137. doi:10.18251/ijme.v18i3.1183

Bourn, D., & Shiel, C. (2009). Global perspectives: Aligning agendas? *Environmental Education Research, 15*(6), 661–677. doi:10.1080/13504620903244167

Bower, M., Cavanagh, M., Moloney, R., & Dao, M. (2011). Developing communication competence using an online video reflection system: Pre-service teachers' experiences. *Asia-Pacific Journal of Teacher Education, 39*(4), 311–326. doi:10.1080/1359866X.2011.614685

Boyer, E. L. (1990). *Scholarship reconsidered: Priorities of the professoriate.* Princeton University Press.

Bozalek, V., & Zembylas, M. (2017). Towards a response-able pedagogy across higher education institutions in post-apartheid South Africa: An ethico-political analysis. *Education as Change, 21*(2), 62–85. doi:10.17159/1947-9417/2017/2017

Brackett, M. A., Bailey, C. S., Hoffmann, J. D., & Simmons, D. N. (2019). RULER: A theory-driven, systemic approach to social, emotional, and academic learning. *Educational Psychologist, 54*(3), 144–161. doi:10.1080/00461520.2019.1614447

Braddock, J. H., & Slavin, R. E. (1993). Why ability grouping must end: Achieving excellence and equity in American education. *Journal of Intergroup Relations, 20*(1), 51–64. https://bit.ly/49qm1Pu

Bradley, R. H., & Corwyn, R. F. (2002). Socioeconomic status and child development. *Annual Review of Psychology, 53*(1), 371–399. doi:10.1146/annurev.psych.53.100901.135233 PMID:11752490

Bransberger, P., Falkenstern, C., & Lane, P. (2020). *Knocking at the college door: Projections of high school graduates* (10th ed.). Western Interstate Commission for Higher Education. https://knocking.wiche.edu/wp-content/uploads/sites/10/2020/12/Knocking-pdf-for-website.pdf

Braskamp, L. A., Braskamp, D. C., & Merrill, K. C. (2009). Assessing progress in global learning and development of students with education abroad experiences. *Frontiers: The Interdisciplinary Journal of Study Abroad, 18*(Fall), 101–118. doi:10.36366/frontiers.v18i1.256

Braun, V., & Clarke, V. (2012). Thematic analysis. In H. Cooper, P. M. Camic, D. L. Long, A. T. Panter, D. Rindskopf, & K. J. Sher (Eds), APA handbook of research methods in psychology, Vol. 2: Research designs: Quantitative, qualitative, neuropsychological, and biological (pp. 57-71). American Psychological Association. doi:10.1037/13620-004

Braun, V., & Clarke, V. (2006). Using thematic analysis in psychology. *Qualitative Research in Psychology, 3*(2), 77–101. doi:10.1191/1478088706qp063oa

Breen, P. (2015). Letting go and letting the angels grow: Using Etienne Wenger's community of practice theory to facilitate teacher education. *International Journal of Web-Based Learning and Teaching Technologies, 10*(1), 14–26. doi:10.4018/ijwltt.2015010102

Brighton, C. (2020). Training for Virtual Exchange. *Journal of Virtual Exchange, 3 (SI-IVEC2019)*, 69–79. doi:10.21827/jve.3.35810

Broadbent, J., Panadero, E., Lodge, J. M., & de Barba, P. (2020). Technologies to enhance self-regulated learning in online and computer-mediated learning environments. In M. J. Bishop, E. Boling, J. Elen, & V. Svihla (Eds.), *Handbook of research in educational communications and technology* (5th ed., pp. 37–52). Springer. doi:10.1007/978-3-030-36119-8_3

Broderick, P. C., & Metz, S. (2009). Learning to BREATHE: A pilot trial of a mindfulness curriculum for adolescents. *Advances in School Mental Health Promotion, 2*(1), 35–46. doi:10.1080/1754730X.2009.9715696

Brown, T. (2008). *Design Thinking.* Harvard Business. https://acortar.link/eC56lD

Brupbacher, M., & Leemann, A. (2015). Grüezi, Moin, Servus - Wie wir wo sprechen [Grüezi, Moin, Servus – How we speak where]. *Tages Anzeiger.* https://www.tagesanzeiger.ch/_external/interactive/2015/sprachatlas_v8/index.html#/questions

Brux, M., & Fry, B. (2010). Multicultural students in study abroad: Their interests, their issues, and their constraints. *Journal of Studies in International Education, 14*(5), 508–527. doi:10.1177/1028315309342486

Bryk, A., Bender Sebring, P., Allensworth, E., Luppescu, S., & Easton, J. (2010). *Organizing schools for improvement: Lessons from Chicago*. University of Chicago Press. doi:10.7208/chicago/9780226078014.001.0001

Buchanan, L. B., & Fox, S. G. (2019). On windows and mirrors in teacher education program materials: A content analysis of human demographics in one picture book collection. *Multicultural Perspectives, 21*(4), 189–201. doi:10.1080/15210960.2019.1686385

Buhs, E. S., & Ladd, G. W. (2001). Peer rejection as an antecedent of young children's school adjustment: An examination of mediating processes. *Developmental Psychology, 37*(4), 550–560. doi:10.1037/0012-1649.37.4.550 PMID:11444490

Bullock, S. M. (2012). Creating a space for the development of professional knowledge: A self-study of supervising teacher candidates during practicum placements. *Studying Teacher Education, 8*(2), 143–156. doi:10.1080/17425964.2012.692985

Burke, J. (2021). *The ultimate guide to implementing wellbeing programmes for school*. Routledge.

Burke, J., & Giraldez-Hayes, A. (2023). Positive schools: An introduction. In A. Giraldez-Hayes & J. Burke (Eds.), *Applied positive school psychology* (pp. 3–8). Routledge. doi:10.4324/9781003228158-2

Byram, M. (2009). The intercultural speaker and the pedagogy of foreign language education. In D. K. Deardorff (Ed.), *The SAGE handbook of intercultural competence* (pp. 321–332). SAGE Publications, Inc. doi:10.4135/9781071872987.n18

Byram, M. (2021). *Teaching and assessing intercultural communicative competence: Revisited*. Multilingual Matters. doi:10.21832/9781800410251

Byram, M., Golubeva, I., Hui, H., & Wagner, M. (2016). *From principles to practice in education for intercultural citizenship*. Multilingual Matters. doi:10.21832/9781783096565

Byrne, C. (2021). Mirrors, windows and sliding glass doors: LGBTQIA+ perspectives. *Idiom, 57*(2), 36-38. https://slav.vic.edu.au/index.php/Synergy/article/view/530/523

Camarillo, A. M., & Bonilla, F. (2001). Hispanics in a multicultural society: A new American dilemma. *America becoming: Racial trends and their consequences, 1*, 103-134. https://blogs.umass.edu/cnle/files/2008/01/ab1-4.pdf

Campbell-Barr, V., & Nygård, M. (2014). Losing sight of the child? Human capital theory and its role for early childhood education and care policies in Finland and England since the mid-1990s. *Contemporary Issues in Early Childhood, 15*(4), 346–359. doi:10.2304/ciec.2014.15.4.346

Cano, J. (2013). Intercultural competencies, curriculum and agents involved in the education system. In J. L. López (Ed.), *Cultural diversity and intercultural education* (pp. 201–224). GEEPP Ediciones. https://www.stes.es/melilla/archivos/libro_diversidad_cultural/Pdfs/Diversidad%20Cultural.pdf

Cantero, M. P., Miñano, P., & Gilar, R. (2008). Diferencias entre los perfiles de competencias socioemocionales de estudiantes en distintas titulaciones de magisterio. *International Journal of Developmental and Educational Psychology, 1*(4), 493–504. https://www.redalyc.org/articulo.oa?id=349832319053

Capdeferro, N., & Romero, M. (2012). Are online learners frustrated with collaborative learning experiences? *International Review of Research in Open and Distance Learning, 13*(2), 26–44. doi:10.19173/irrodl.v13i2.1127

Capper, K. (2022). Culturally relevant pedagogy in the English curriculum. *Journal of Education, 202*(4), 397–405. doi:10.1177/0022057421991856

Carlisle, D. L., & Weaver, G. C. (2018). STEM education centers: Catalyzing the improvement of undergraduate STEM education. *International Journal of STEM Education*, *5*(1), 1–21. doi:10.1186/s40594-018-0143-2 PMID:30631737

Carpenter, J. P., Kerkhoff, S. N., & Wang, X. (2022). Teachers using technology for co-teaching and crowdsourcing: The case of Global Read Aloud collaboration. *Teaching and Teacher Education*, *114*(June), 103719. Advance online publication. doi:10.1016/j.tate.2022.103719

Carpenter, J. P., & Krutka, D. G. (2014). How and why educators use Twitter: A survey of the field. *Journal of Research on Technology in Education*, *46*(4), 414–434. doi:10.1080/15391523.2014.925701

Carpenter, J. P., & Krutka, D. G. (2015). Engagement through microblogging: Educator professional development via Twitter. *Professional Development in Education*, *41*(4), 707–728. doi:10.1080/19415257.2014.939294

Carrillo, M., Padilla, J., Rosero, T., & Villagómez, M. S. (2009). Motivation and learning. Otherness. *Journal of Education*, *4*(2), 20–32. https://www.redalyc.org/comocitar.oa?id=467746249004

Carvalho, A. R., & Santos, C. (2022). Developing peer mentors' collaborative and metacognitive skills with a technology-enhanced peer learning program. *Computers and Education Open*, *3*, 100070. Advance online publication. doi:10.1016/j.caeo.2021.100070

Casañ-Pitarch, R., Candel-Mora, M., Carrió-Pastor, M. L., Demydenko, O., & Tikan, I. (2020). Enhancing language and cross-cultural competence through telecollaboration. *Advanced Education*, *7*(16), 78–87. doi:10.20535/2410-8286.214539

CASEL. (2012). *Effective social and emotional learning programs-Preschool and elementary school edition. Casel guide 2013.* https://eric.ed.gov/?id=ED581699

CASEL. (2020). *CASEL's SEL framework: What are the core competence areas and where are they promoted?* https://casel.org/casel-sel-framework-11-2020/

Castiello-Gutiérrez, S., Pantoja Aguilar, M. P., & Gutiérrez Jurado, C. E. (2022). From crisis to opportunity: Internationalization of higher education after COVID-19. *Journal of Higher Education in Latin America*, *12*, 7–11. https://rcientificas.uninorte.edu.co/index.php/esal/article/view/14921/214421446099

Castillo, T. I., King, L. F., & Ruíz, L. P. (2021). El intercambio virtual: experiencias desde instituciones en el Caribe colombiano [Virtual exchange: experiences from Colombian Caribbean institutions]. *Edutec. Revista Electrónica de Tecnología Educativa, 75*, 90-109. doi:10.21556/edutec.2021.75.1893

Caurín, C., Morales, A. J., & Fontana, M. (2019). Convivencia en el ámbito educativo: Aplicación de un programa basado en la empatía, la educación emocional y la resolución de conflictos en un instituto español de enseñanza secundaria. *Cuestiones Pedagógicas*, *27*(27), 97–112. doi:10.12795/CP.2018.i27.06

Cazden, C. B. (2012). A framework for social justice in education. *International Journal of Educational Psychology*, *1*(3), 178–198. doi:10.4471/ijep.2012.11

Chambers, R. (2007). From PRA to PLA and pluralism: Practice and theory (No. 286). The University of Sussex Brighton, Institute of Development Studies.

Chaya, P., & Inpin, B. (2020). Effects of integrating movie-based mobile learning instruction for enhancing Thai university students' speaking skills and intercultural communicative competence. *English Language Teaching*, *13*(7), 27–45. doi:10.5539/elt.v13n7p27

Che, A. A. M. A. (2023). Benefits and challenges of transnational education: Reflections from a Sino-British joint venture university. *International Journal of Chinese Education, 12*(1). doi:10.1177/2212585X221144903

Chen, S.-Y., & Lindon, N. A. (2018). Teachers can play too: Teacher-child relationships, social-emotional development, and academic engagement. In Information Resources Management Association (IRMA) (Ed.), Student engagement and participation: Concepts, methodologies, tools, and applications (pp. 288-313). IGI Global.

Chen, C. Y. C., Byrne, E., & Vélez, T. (2022). Impact of the 2020 pandemic of COVID-19 on families with school-aged children in the United States: Roles of income level and race. *Journal of Family Issues*, *43*(3), 719–740. doi:10.1177/0192513X21994153 PMID:38603084

Chi, M. T. (1997). Quantifying qualitative analyses of verbal data: A practical guide. *Journal of the Learning Sciences*, *6*(3), 271–315. doi:10.1207/s15327809jls0603_1

Chodkiewicz, A. R., & Boyle, C. (2017). Positive psychology school-based interventions: A reflection on current success and future directions. *Review of Education*, *5*(1), 60–86. doi:10.1002/rev3.3080

Cho, M.-H., & Shen, D. (2013). Self-regulation in online learning. *Distance Education*, *34*(3), 290–301. doi:10.1080/01587919.2013.835770

Choo, S. S. (2018). The need for cosmopolitan literacy in a global age: Implications for teaching literature. *Journal of Adolescent & Adult Literacy*, *62*(1), 7–12. doi:10.1002/jaal.755

Cinganotto, L. (2017). Experiential learning for Teacher Training: A case example of language, content and technologies in a learning event by eTwinning. *Journal of eLearning and Knowledge Society: The Italian eLearning Association Journal, 13*(1), 91-111.

Clarke, A., Sorgenfrei, M., Mulcahy, J., Davie, P., Friedrich, C., & McBride, T. (2021). *Adolescent mental health. A systematic review on the effectiveness of school-based interventions*. https://www.eif.org.uk/report/adolescent-mental-health-a-systematic-review-on-the-effectiveness-of-school-based-interventions

Clarke, M., & Drudy, S. (2006). Teaching for diversity, social justice and global awareness. *European Journal of Teacher Education*, *29*(3), 371–386. doi:10.1080/02619760600795239

Cleary, Y., Slattery, D. M., Flammia, M., & Minacori, P. (2019). Developing strategies for success in a cross-disciplinary global virtual team project: Collaboration among student writers and translators. *Journal of Technical Writing and Communication*, *49*(3), 309–337. doi:10.1177/0047281618775908

Cleveland-Innes, M., & Campbell, P. (2012). Emotional presence, learning, and the online learning environment. *International Review of Research in Open and Distance Learning*, *13*(4), 269–292. doi:10.19173/irrodl.v13i4.1234

Clouet, R. (2023). Multicultural encounters and intercultural dialogue: Interactional experiences of international students on a short-term online language program. In S. Di Sarno-García, S. Montaner-Villalba, & A. M. Gimeno-Sanz (Eds.), *Telecollaboration applications in foreign language classrooms* (pp. 161–181). IGI Global. doi:10.4018/978-1-6684-7080-0.ch008

Coelho, M., & Menezes, I. (2021). University social responsibility, service learning, and students' personal, professional, and civic education. *Frontiers in Psychology*, *12*, 617300. doi:10.3389/fpsyg.2021.617300 PMID:33716883

Cohen, L., Manion, L., & Morrison, K. (2018). *Research methods in education* (8th ed.). Routledge. doi:10.4324/9781315456539

Coiro, M. J., Kotchick, B. A., & Preis, J. (2016). Youth social skills groups: A training platform for promoting graduate clinician interprofessional competence. *Journal of Interprofessional Education & Practice*, *4*, 89–92. doi:10.1016/j.xjep.2016.04.004

Cole, J. B. (1991). Opening address of the 43rd International Conference on Educational Exchange. In L. Darling-Hammond (Ed.), *Black students and overseas programs: Broadening the base of participation* (pp. 1-8). Council on International Education Exchange.

Collaborative for Academic, Social, and Emotional Learning. (2020). *What is SEL?* https://www.casel.org/what-is-sel/

College of Education, University of Illinois. (n.d.). IGlobal. https://international.education.illinois.edu/I-global

Collett, K., Von der Heyden, B., Pott, R. W. M., & Stander, J. (2018). A collaborative auto-ethnographic exploration of socially just practices by new academics in two South African higher education institutions. *South African Journal of Higher Education, 32*(6), 582–603. doi:10.20853/32-6-2983

Collins English Dictionary. (n.d.). *Definition of 'transnational.'* https://www.collinsdictionary.com/dictionary/english/transnational Council of Europe/

Collin, S., & Brotcorne, P. (2019). Capturing digital (in)equity in teaching and learning: A sociocritical approach. *The International Journal of Information and Learning Technology, 36*(2), 169–180. doi:10.1108/IJILT-05-2018-0059

Cooper, R. L. (1989). *Language planning and social change.* Cambridge University Press.

Coppola, N. W., Hiltz, S. R., & Rotter, N. G. (2002). Becoming a virtual professor: Pedagogical roles and asynchronous learning networks. *Journal of Management Information Systems, 18*(4), 169–189. doi:10.1080/07421222.2002.11045703

Corcoran, R. P., & Tormey, R. (2012). How emotionally intelligent are pre-service teachers? *Teaching and Teacher Education, 28*(5), 750–759. doi:10.1016/j.tate.2012.02.007

Costello, A. B., & Osborne, J. W. (2005). Best practices in exploratory factor analysis: Four recommendations for getting the most from your analysis. *Practical Assessment, Research & Evaluation, 10*(7), 1–9. doi:10.7275/jyj1-4868

Coulombe, S., Hardy, K., & Goldfarb, R. (2021). Promoting wellbeing through positive education: A critical review and proposed social ecological approach. *Theory and Research in Education, 18*(3), 295–321. doi:10.1177/1477878520988432

Coulter, C., & Jimenez-Silva, M. (Eds.). (2017). *Culturally sustaining and revitalizing pedagogies: Language, culture, and power.* Emerald Group Publishing. doi:10.1108/S1479-3687201729

Coyle, D. (2006). Developing CLIL: Towards a theory of practice. In A. d. Catalunya (Ed.), CLIL in Catalonia: From theory to practice (pp. 5-29). APAC.

Coyle, D., Hood, P., & Marsh, D. (2010). *CLIL – Content and language integrated learning.* Cambridge University Press. doi:10.1017/9781009024549

Crawford, P., & Berquist, B. (Eds.). (2020). *Community engagement abroad: Perspectives and practices on service, engagement, and learning overseas.* Michigan State University Press. doi:10.14321/j.ctvthhcqg

Crenshaw, K. (2019). The marginalization of Harriet's daughters: Perpetual crisis, misdirected blame, and the enduring urgency of intersectionality. *Kalfou, 6*(1), 7–23. doi:10.15367/kf.v6i1.226

Creswell, J. (2013). *Qualitative inquiry and research design: Choosing among five approaches* (3rd ed.). Sage.

Creswell, J. W., & Creswell, J. D. (2018). Research design: Qualitative, quantitative, and mixed methods approaches. *Sage.*

Creswell, J. W., & Poth, C. N. (2018). *Qualitative inquiry & research design: Choosing among five approaches.* SAGE Publication Inc.

Cronin, T. J., Levin, S., Branscombe, N. R., van Laar, C., & Tropp, L. R. (2012). Ethnic identification in response to perceived discrimination protects well-being and promotes activism: A longitudinal study of Latino college students. *Group Processes & Intergroup Relations*, *15*(3), 393–407. doi:10.1177/1368430211427171

Cuenca, A., Schmeichel, M., Butler, B. M., Dinkelman, T., & Nichols, J. R. Jr. (2011). Creating a "third space" in student teaching: Implications for the university supervisor's status as outsider. *Teaching and Teacher Education*, *27*(7), 1068–1077. doi:10.1016/j.tate.2011.05.003

Cushner, K. (2011). Intercultural research in teacher education: An essential intersection in the preparation of globally competent teachers. *Action in Teacher Education*, *33*(5–6), 601–614. doi:10.1080/01626620.2011.627306

Cushner, K. (2012). Intercultural competence for teaching and learning. In B. Shaklee & S. Baily (Eds.), *Internationalizing teacher education in the United States* (pp. 41–58). Rowman & Littlefield.

Cushner, K. (2018). *Teacher as traveler*. Rowman & Littlefield.

Cushner, K., & Brennan, S. (2007). *Intercultural student teaching: A bridge to global competence*. Rowman & Littlefield Education.

Custer, L., & Tuominen, A. (2017). Bringing "Internationalization at Home" opportunities to community colleges: Design and assessment of an online exchange activity between U.S. and Japanese students. *Teaching Sociology*, *45*(4), 347–357. doi:10.1177/0092055X16679488

Daniel, J. (2020). Education and the COVID-19 pandemic. *Prospects*, *49*(1-2), 91–96. https://bit.ly/49oK55z. doi:10.1007/s11125-020-09464-3 PMID:32313309

Darji, B. B., & Lang-Wojtasik, G. (2014). Preparing globally competent teachers: Indo-German perspectives on teacher training. *International Journal of Development Education and Global Learning*, *6*(3), 49–62. doi:10.18546/IJDEGL.06.3.04

Darling-Hammond, L., & Berry, B. (2006). Highly qualified teachers for all. *Educational Leadership*, *64*(3), 14–20.

Datu, J. A. D., Lee, A. S. Y., Fung, W. K., Cheung, R. Y. M., & Chung, K. K. H. (2022). Prospering in the midst of the COVID-19 pandemic: The effects of PROSPER-based intervention on psychological outcomes among preschool teachers. *Journal of School Psychology*, *94*, 66–82. doi:10.1016/j.jsp.2022.08.003 PMID:36064216

Daza, V., Gudmundsdottir, G. B., & Lund, A. (2021). Partnerships as third spaces for professional practice in initial teacher education: A scoping review. *Teaching and Teacher Education*, *102*, 103338. Advance online publication. doi:10.1016/j.tate.2021.103338

De Arment, S., Reed, E., & Wetzel, A. (2013). Promoting adaptive expertise: A conceptual framework for special educator preparation. *Teacher Education and Special Education*, *36*(1), 217–230. doi:10.1177/0888406413489578

De Backer, L., Van Keer, H., & Valcke, M. (2015). Socially shared metacognitive regulation during reciprocal peer tutoring: Identifying its relationship with students' content processing and transactive discussion. *Instructional Science*, *43*(3), 323–344. doi:10.1007/s11251-014-9335-4

De Backer, L., Van Keer, H., & Valcke, M. (2022). The functions of shared metacognitive regulation and their differential relation with collaborative learners' understanding of the learning content. *Learning and Instruction*, *77*, 101527. Advance online publication. doi:10.1016/j.learninstruc.2021.101527

de Brey, C., Musu, L., McFarland, J., Wilkinson-Flicker, S., Diliberti, M., Zhang, A., ... Pishcherskaia, E. (2018). Bridging countries and cultures through accessible global collaborations. *Education Sciences*, *8*(4), 199–210. doi:10.3390/educsci8040199

De Meyer, A. (2012). Reflections on the globalization of management education. *Journal of Management Development, 31*(4), 336–345. doi:10.1108/02621711211218988

De Oliveira Andreotti, V. (2014). Critical and transnational literacies in international development and global citizenship education. *Sisyphus— Journal of Education, 2*(3), 32–50. https://www.redalyc.org/pdf/5757/575763895003.pdf

De Wit, H., & Beelen, J. (2014). *Reading between the lines: Global internationalisation survey.* University World News. https://surl.li/rfibh

De Witt, H., & Leask, B. (2015). Internationalization, curriculum and disciplines. *International Higher Education,* (83), 11-13. https://issuu.com/ceppechile/docs/higher_83

Deardorff, D. K. (2006). Identification and assessment of intercultural competence as a student outcome of internationalization. *Journal of Studies in International Education, 10*(3), 241–266. doi:10.1177/1028315306287002

Deardorff, D. K. (2011). Assessing intercultural competence. *New Directions for Institutional Research, 149*(149), 65–79. doi:10.1002/ir.381

Deardorff, D. K. (2019). *Manual for developing intercultural competencies: Story circles.* Routledge. doi:10.4324/9780429244612

Deardorff, D. K., & Jones, E. (2012). Intercultural competence. In D. K. Deardorff, H. de Wit, J. D. Heyl, & T. Adams (Eds.), *The SAGE handbook of international higher education* (pp. 283–304). SAGE Publications, Inc. doi:10.4135/9781452218397.n16

DeJaeghere, J. G., & Cao, Y. (2009). Developing US teachers' intercultural competence: Does professional development matter? *International Journal of Intercultural Relations, 33*(5), 437–447. doi:10.1016/j.ijintrel.2009.06.004

Delpit, L. D. (1988). The silenced dialogue: Power and pedagogy in educating other people's children. *Harvard Educational Review, 58*(3), 280–298. doi:10.17763/haer.58.3.c43481778r528qw4

Denston, A., Martin, R., Fickel, L., & O' Toole, V. (2022). Teachers' perspectives of social-emotional learning: Informing the development of a linguistically and culturally responsive framework for social-emotional wellbeing in Aotearoa New Zealand. *Teaching and Teacher Education, 117*(4), 103813. Advance online publication. doi:10.1016/j.tate.2022.103813

Denzin, N. K., & Lincoln, Y. S. (Eds.). (2011). *The Sage handbook of qualitative research.* Sage.

DePaul University. (n.d.). *Global learning experience (GLE) student survey questions.* https://resources.depaul.edu/teaching-commons/programs/global-learning/Documents/GLEStudentSurveyQuestions_v.042018.pdf

Dervin, F. (2017). "I find it odd that people have to highlight other people's differences – even when there are none": Experiential learning and interculturality in teacher education. *International Review of Education, 63*(1), 87–102. doi:10.1007/s11159-017-9620-y

DeWinter, A., & Klamer, R. (2021). Can COIL be effective in using diversity to contribute to equality? Experiences of iKudu, a European-South African consortium operating via a decolonised approach to project delivery. In M. Satar (Ed.), Virtual exchange: Towards digital equity in internationalisation (pp. 29-40). Research-publishing.net. doi:10.14705/rpnet.2021.53.1287

Dirks, M. A., Treat, T. A., & Weersing, V. R. (2007). Integrating theoretical, measurement, and intervention models of youth social competence. *Clinical Psychology Review, 27*(3), 327–347. doi:10.1016/j.cpr.2006.11.002 PMID:17270330

Disabato, D. J., Goodman, F. R., Kashdan, T. B., Short, J. L., & Jarden, A. (2016). Different types of wellbeing? A cross-cultural examination of hedonic and eudaimonic well-being. *Psychological Assessment*, *28*(5), 471–482. doi:10.1037/pas0000209 PMID:26348031

Dooly, M. (2022). The evolution of virtual exchange and assessment practices. In A. Czura & M. Dooly (Eds.), Assessing virtual exchange in foreign language courses at tertiary level (pp. 13-27). Research-publishing.net. doi:10.14705/rpnet.2022.59.1407

Dooly, M., & O'Dowd, R. (2018). Telecollaboration in the foreign language classroom: A review of its origins and its application to language teaching practice. In M. Dooly & R. O'Dowd (Eds.), *In this together: Teachers' experiences with transnational, telecollaborative language learning projects* (pp. 11–34). Peter Lang. doi:10.3726/b14311

Dooly, M., & Sadler, R. (2013). Filling in the gaps: Linking theory and practice through telecollaboration in teacher education. *ReCALL*, *25*(1), 4–29. doi:10.1017/S0958344012000237

Dooly, M., & Vinagre, M. (2022). Research into practice: Virtual exchange in language teaching and learning. *Language Teaching*, *55*(3), 392–406. doi:10.1017/S0261444821000069

Dube, B. (2020). Rural online learning in the context of COVID-19 in South Africa: Evoking an inclusive education approach. *Multidisciplinary Journal of Educational Research*, *10*(2), 135–157. doi:10.17583/remie.2020.5607

DuFrene, D. D., & Lehman, C. M. (2016). *Managing virtual teams* (2nd ed.). Business Expert Press.

Durlak, J. A., Domitrovich, C. E., Weissberg, R. P., & Gullotta, T. P. (Eds.). (2015). *Handbook of social and emotional learning: Research and practice*. Guilford Press.

Durlak, J. A., Mahoney, J. L., & Boyle, A. E. (2022). What we know, and what we need to find out about universal, school-based social and emotional learning programs for children and adolescents: A review of meta-analyses and directions for future research. *Psychological Bulletin*, *148*(11-12), 765–782. doi:10.1037/bul0000383

Durlak, J. A., Weissberg, R. P., Dymnicki, A. B., Taylor, R. D., & Schellinger, K. B. (2011). The impact of enhancing students' social and emotional learning: A meta-analysis of school-based universal interventions. *Child Development*, *82*(1), 405–432. doi:10.1111/j.1467-8624.2010.01564.x PMID:21291449

Dussel, E. (1998). Beyond Eurocentrism: The world-system and the limits of modernity. In F. Jameson & M. Miyoshi (Eds.), *The cultures of globalization* (pp. 3–31). Duke University Press. doi:10.2307/j.ctv11cw3dt.5

Dyck, B. (2017). Reflecting on 25 years of teaching, researching, and textbook writing for introduction to management: An essay with some lessons learned. *Journal of Management Education*, *41*(6), 817–834. doi:10.1177/1052562917693381

Dyrness, A. (2021). Rethinking global citizenship education with/for transnational youth. *Globalisation, Societies and Education*, *19*(4), 443–455. doi:10.1080/14767724.2021.1897001

Eatman, T. K. (2018). Faculty as colearners: Collaborative engagement and the power of story in faculty development. In B. Berkey, E. E. Rountree, P. M. Green, & C. Meixner (Eds.), *Reconceptualizing faculty development in service-learning/community engagement* (pp. 59–82). Routledge.

Ecker-Lyster, M., & Kardash, N. (2022). Study abroad: Perspectives from historically underrepresented student populations. *Journal of College Access*, *7*(1), 99–115. https://scholarworks.wmich.edu/jca/vol7/iss1/8/

Edmonds, W. A., & Kennedy, T. D. (2017). *An applied guide to research design: Quantitative, qualitative and mixed methods* (2nd ed.). Sage. doi:10.4135/9781071802779

Edmonson, S., & Irby, B. (2008). *Ten tips for producing a top qualitative study*. Pearson.

Ehiyazaryan-White, E. (2012). The dialogic potential of ePortfolios: Formative feedback and communities of learning within a personal learning environment. *International Journal of ePortfolio, 2*(2), 173-185. https://eric.ed.gov/?id=EJ1107620

Emdin, C. (2016). *For white folks who teach in the hood ... and the rest of ya'll too: Reality pedagogy and urban education.* Beacon Press.

Engle, R. L., & Crowne, K. A. (2014). The impact of international experience on cultural intelligence: An application of contact theory in a structured short-term programme. *Human Resource Development International, 17*(1), 30–46. doi:10.1080/13678868.2013.856206

English, L. D. (2016). STEM education K-12: Perspectives on integration. *International Journal of STEM Education, 3*(1), 1–8. doi:10.1186/s40594-016-0036-1

English, L. M. (2005). Third-space practitioners: Women educating for justice in the Global South. *Adult Education Quarterly, 55*(2), 85–100. doi:10.1177/0741713604271851

Eren, Ö. (2021). Raising critical cultural awareness through telecollaboration: Insights for pre-service teacher education. *Computer Assisted Language Learning, 36*(3), 1–24. doi:10.1080/09588221.2021.1916538

Erickson, J. A., & Anderson, J. B. (Eds.). (1997). *Learning with the community: Concepts and models for service-learning in teacher education.* Stylus. doi:10.4324/9781003445715

Escarbajal-Frutos, A., Sánchez, M., & Guirao, I. (2015). Factores determinantes del rendimiento académico de alumnos hijos de inmigrantes y autóctonos de origen extranjero en contextos de exclusión social [Determinants of the academic performance of immigrant and native students of foreign origin in contexts of social exclusion]. *Revista sobre la Infancia y la Adolescencia [Journal on Childhood and Adolescence], 9*, 31–46. doi:10.4995/reinad.2015.3772

Esche, M. (2018). *Incorporating collaborative online international learning (COIL) into study abroad courses: A training design.* https://digitalcollections.sit.edu/capstones

Escobar, A. (2004). Beyond the third world: Imperial globality, global coloniality and anti-globalization social movements. *Third World Quarterly, 25*(1), 207–230. doi:10.1080/0143659042000185417

European Commission. (2017). *Combined evaluation of Erasmus+ and predecessor programmes.* https://bit.ly/3SIzZ9X

European Commission. (2020). *Strategic plan 2020-2024. DG Research and Innovation.* https://bit.ly/49hO5EQ

European Commission. (2021, 11 November). *Glossary: At risk of poverty or social exclusion (AROPE).* European Commission. https://bit.ly/41Ru9WM

European Commission. (2022). *Erasmus annual 2021.* https://bit.ly/3SJ9Qry

Eurydice (2003). *Focus on the Structure of Higher Education in Europe (2003-2004). National Trends in the Bologna Process.* https://bit.ly/3SIxODr

Fabrigar, L. R., Wegener, D. T., MacCallum, R. C., & Strahan, E. J. (1999). Evaluating the use of exploratory factor analysis in psychological research. *Psychological Methods, 4*(3), 272–299. doi:10.1037/1082-989X.4.3.272

Fataar, A. (2020). *A pedagogy of care: Teachers rise to the challenge of the 'new normal'.* https://www.dailymaverick.co.za

Fataar, A., & Badroodien, A. (2020). Editorial notes. Special issue: Emergent educational imaginaries during the Covid-19 pandemic. *Southern African Review of Education, 26*(1), 1–5.

Faulconer, E. (2021). eService-Learning: A decade of research in undergraduate online service–learning. *American Journal of Distance Education, 35*(2), 100–117. doi:10.1080/08923647.2020.1849941

Feille, K. (2021). A framework for the development of schoolyard pedagogy. *Research in Science Education, 51*(6), 1687–1704. doi:10.1007/s11165-019-9860-x

Feiman-Nemser, S. (2001). From preparation to practice: Designing a continuum to strengthen and sustain teaching. *Teachers College Record, 103*(6), 1013–1055. doi:10.1111/0161-4681.00141

Felten, P. (2013). Principles of good practice in SoTL. *Teaching & Learning Inquiry, 1*(1), 121–125. doi:10.20343/teachlearninqu.1.1.121

Felten, P., & Clayton, P. H. (2011). Service-learning. *New Directions for Teaching and Learning, 128*(128), 75–84. doi:10.1002/tl.470

Ference, R. A., & Bell, S. (2004). A cross-cultural immersion in the US: Changing preservice teacher attitudes toward Latino ESOL students. *Equity & Excellence in Education, 37*(4), 343–350. doi:10.1080/10665680490518605

Fernández-Berrocal, P., & Cabello, R. (2021). La inteligencia emocional como fundamento de la educación emocional [Emotional intelligence as a foundation for emotional education]. *Revista Internacional de Educación Emocional y Bienestar [International Journal of Emotional Education and Well-Being], 1*(1), 31–46. doi:10.48102/rieeb.2021.1.1.5

Fernández-Jiménez, E. C. (2020). *PlasticO: Una propuesta didáctica para mejorar las destrezas orales a través del aprendizaje-servicio para el aula de 4º de la ESO* [Plastico: A didactic proposal to improve oral skills through service-learning in the 4th-grade-of-secondary-education classroom] [Master's thesis, Universidad Internacional de La Rioja]. https://bit.ly/3NWTmIJ

Fitzgerald, E. (2012). Creating user-generated content for location-based learning: An authoring framework. *Journal of Computer Assisted Learning, 28*(3), 195–207. doi:10.1111/j.1365-2729.2012.00481.x

Flecha, R. (2015). *Successful educational actions for inclusion and social cohesion in Europe*. Springer. doi:10.1007/978-3-319-11176-6

Flores, N. (2016). A tale of two visions: Hegemonic whiteness and bilingual education. *Educational Policy, 30*(1), 13–38. doi:10.1177/0895904815616482

Foerch, D. F. (2020). Global competence begins in preschool: An investigation of how to nurture empathy in young children. *Contrapontos, 20*(1), 2–19. doi:10.14210/contrapontos.v20n1.p02-19

Fraser, N. (2008). Reframing justice in a globalizing world. In K. Olson (Ed.), *Adding insult to injury: Nancy Fraser debates her critics* (pp. 273–291). Verso.

Fraser, N. (2009). *Scales of justice: Reimagining political space in a globalizing world.* Columbia University.

Frauenholtz, S., Mendenhall, A. N., & Moon, J. (2017). Role of school employees' mental health knowledge in interdisciplinary collaborations to support the academic success of students experiencing mental distress. *Children & Schools, 39*(2), 71–79. doi:10.1093/cs/cdx004

Frazer, H., & Marlier, E. (2014). *Investing in children: Breaking the cycle of disadvantage – A study of national policies assessment of what member states would need to do to implement the European Commission Recommendation, Synthesis Report*. Publications Office of the European Union., doi:10.2903/sp.efsa.2014.EN-622

Freire, P. (2000). Pedagogy of the oppressed (30th anniversary ed.). Continuum.

Freire, P., & Macedo, D. (1987). *Literacy: Reading the word and the world.* Bergin & Garvey.

Futch, V. A., & Fine, M. (2014). Mapping as a method: History and theoretical commitments. *Qualitative Research in Psychology, 11*(1), 42–59. doi:10.1080/14780887.2012.719070

Galarza, F., Arnaiz, N., & Arias, N. (2021). Retos de la enseñanza-aprendizaje virtual: Creatividad del docente, clases sincrónicas o asincrónicas, y principios didácticos [Challenges of e-learning: teacher creativity, synchronous or asynchronous classes, and didactic principles]. *Revista Conrado, 17*(S1), 331–339.

Galindo-González, L., Martínez de la Cruz, N., Ley Fuentes, M., Ruiz Aguirre, E., & Valenzuela González, E. (2012). Epistemological approach to collaborative learning. *Opening, 4*(2), 156-169. http://www.udgvirtual.udg.mx/apertura/index.php/apertura/article/view/325/290

Gandara, P. C., & Contreras, F. (2009). *The Latino education crisis: The consequences of failed social policies*. Harvard University Press. doi:10.4159/9780674056367

García, E. M., González, J. C., López, J. A., Luján, J. L., Martín, M., Osorio, C., & Valdés, C. (2001). *Science, Technology and Society: A Conceptual Approach.* Organization of Ibero-American States for Education, Science and Culture https://acortar.link/7UOf0b

Garcia-Esteban, S., Villarreal, I., & Bueno-Alastuey, M. C. (2019). The effect of telecollaboration in the development of the learning to learn competence in CLIL teacher training. *Interactive Learning Environments, 29*(6), 973–986. doi:10.1080/10494820.2019.1614960

Garcia, G. A. (2017). Defined by outcomes or culture? Constructing an organizational identity for Hispanic-serving institutions. *American Educational Research Journal, 54*(1_suppl), 111S–134S. doi:10.3102/0002831216669779

Garcia, G. A., Núñez, A. M., & Sansone, V. A. (2019). Toward a multidimensional conceptual framework for understanding "servingness" in Hispanic-serving institutions: A synthesis of the research. *Review of Educational Research, 89*(5), 745–784. doi:10.3102/0034654319864591

García, M., Reyes, J., & Godínez, G. (2018). The ICT in higher education, innovations and challenges. *RICSH Ibero-American Journal of Social Sciences and Humanities, 6*(12), 17. doi:10.23913/ricsh.v6i12.135

Gardel Vicente, A. (2022). *Skills gained through mobility: A literature review. ErasmusJobs project consortium.* https://bit.ly/3SKUUsU

Gardner, H. (1987). The theory of multiple intelligences. *Annals of Dyslexia, 37*(1), 19–35. doi:10.1007/BF02648057 PMID:24234985

Garrido, P., & Gaeta, M. L. (2016). La competencia socioemocional docente en el logro del aprendizaje de las competencias genéricas del perfil de egreso de educación media superior. *Revista de Comunicación Vivat Academia, 137*, 108–123. doi:10.15178/va.2016.137.108-123

Garrison, D. R. (2003). Cognitive presence for effective asynchronous online learning: The role of reflective inquiry, self-direction, and metacognition. In J. Bourne & J. C. Moore (Eds.), *Elements of quality online education: Practice and direction* (pp. 47–58). The Sloan Consortium.

Garrison, D. R., & Akyol, Z. (2015). Toward the development of a metacognition construct for communities of inquiry. *The Internet and Higher Education, 24*, 66–71. doi:10.1016/j.iheduc.2014.10.001

Gautier, M. C. (2016). Ethnic identity and Latino youth: The current state of the research. *Adolescent Research Review, 1*(4), 329–340. doi:10.1007/s40894-016-0034-z

Gay, G. (2018). *Culturally responsive teaching. Theory, research, and practice.* Teachers College Press.

Gaytán-Oyarzun, J., Cravioto-Torres, R., Mendoza-Meza, E., & Ortiz-Zarco, E. (2022). Implementation of the COIL methodology, as a strategy to enhance the teaching-learning process and academic and student mobility in the virtual modality. *Journal of Innovation and Good Practices Teachers*, *11*(1), 141–149. http://www.uco.es/ucopress/ojs/index.php/ripadoc/article/view/14142/12766

Gebre, E., Saroyan, A., & Bracewell, R. (2014). Students' engagement in technology rich classrooms and its relationship to professors' conceptions of effective teaching. *British Journal of Educational Technology*, *45*(1), 83–96. doi:10.1111/bjet.12001

Geddes, R., Frank, J., & Haw, S. (2011). A rapid review of key strategies to improve the cognitive and social development of children in Scotland. *Health Policy (Amsterdam)*, *101*(1), 20–28. doi:10.1016/j.healthpol.2010.08.013 PMID:20822824

Geesa, R. L., Robbins, K., & Shively, K. (2022). The collaborative model for teaching o-SEL: Preparing educators to design online environments for social-emotional learning. *Journal of Online Learning Research*, *8*(1), 67–100. https://eric.ed.gov/?id=EJ1342754

General Congregation of the Society of Jesus, 32, Decree 4 *The Service of Faith and the Promotion of Justice*. December 2nd, 1974 - March 7th, 1975.

Gibbons, P. (2003). Mediating Language Learning: Teacher interactions with ESL students in a content-based classroom. *TESOL Quarterly*, *37*(2), 247–274. doi:10.2307/3588504

Giedt, T., Gokcek, G., & Ghosh, J. (2015). International education in the 21st century: The importance of faculty in developing study abroad research opportunities. *Frontiers: The Interdisciplinary Journal of Study Abroad*, *26*(1), 167–186. doi:10.36366/frontiers.v26i1.365

Giménez, C. (2000). Guía sobre interculturalidad [Guide on interculturality]. *Colección Cuadernos Q'anil, Proyecto. Q'anil-PNUD* [Cuadernos Q'anil Collection, Project. Q'anil-UNDP]. Editorial Serviprensa.

Giraldo Gómez, O., Zuluaga Giraldo, J. I., Jaramillo Echeverry, A., & Vargas Aguirre, J. F. (2021). Pedagogical practices that contribute to the construction of a better citizenship. *Journal of Research*, *19*(34), 81–91. doi:10.22383/ri.v19i34.140

Giroux, H. (1992). Resisting difference: Cultural studies and the discourse of critical pedagogy. In C. Groosberg & P. Groosberg (Eds.), *Cultural studies* (pp. 199–212). Routledge.

Glassick, C. E., Huber, M. T., & Maeroff, G. I. (1997). *Scholarship assessed: Evaluation of the professoriate*. John Wiley & Sons.

Gleason, B., & Jaramillo Cherrez, N. (2021). Design thinking approach to global collaboration and empowered learning: Virtual exchange as innovation in a teacher education course. *TechTrends*, *65*(3), 348–358. doi:10.1007/s11528-020-00573-6

Gobierno de España. (2015). *Estrategia de Acción Exterior 2021-2024 [Strategies for External Action 2021-2024]*. https://bit.ly/48ZdnI9

Godwin-Jones, R. (2019). Bridging cultural divides through telecollaboration. *Intercultural Communication Studies*, *28*(2), 113–135. https://bit.ly/3BipMYt

Godwin-Jones, R. (2019). Telecollaboration as an approach to developing intercultural communication competence. *Language Learning & Technology*, *23*(3), 8–28. https://hdl.handle.net/10125/44691

Gómez-López, M. (2020). *Bienestar y relaciones sentimentales en adolescentes de Andalucía* [Doctoral dissertation, University of Cordoba]. https://helvia.uco.es/xmlui/handle/10396/19671

Gonçalves, L. L., Parker, M., Luguetti, C., & Carbinatto, M. (2022). The facilitator's role in supporting physical education teachers' empowerment in a professional learning community. *Sport Education and Society*, *27*(3), 272–285. doi:10.1080/13573322.2020.1825371

Gonzalez, E., Ortega, G., Molina, M., & Lizalde, G. (2020). What does it mean to be a Hispanic-Serving Institution? Listening to the Latina/o/x voices of students. *International Journal of Qualitative Studies in Education : QSE*, *33*(8), 796–809. doi:10.1080/09518398.2020.1751896

Gonzalez, G., Villafañe-Cepeda, W., & Rodríguez, O. H. (2023). Leveraging prospective teachers' knowledge through their participation in lesson study. *Journal of Mathematics Teacher Education*, *26*(1), 79–102. doi:10.1007/s10857-021-09521-4

González, J., & Wagenaar, R. (2003). Quality and European programme design in higher education. *European Journal of Education*, *38*(3), 241–251. doi:10.1111/1467-3435.00144

Gopal, A. (2011). Internationalization of higher education: Preparing faculty to teach cross-culturally. *International Journal on Teaching and Learning in Higher Education*, *23*(3), 373–381. https://files.eric.ed.gov/fulltext/EJ946163.pdf

Grau, M. K., & Turula, A. (2019). Experiential learning of telecollaborative competences in pre-service teacher education. *Language Learning & Technology*, *23*(3), 98–115. https://hdl.handle.net/10125/44698

Green, L., & Collett, L. (2021). Teaching thinking in South African schools: Selected school leaders' perceptions. *South African Journal of Education*, *41*(2), 1–13. doi:10.15700/saje.v41n2a1893

Green, S., Leach, C., & Falecki, D. (2021). Approaches to positive education. In M. L. Kern & M. L. Wehmeyer (Eds.), *The Palgrave handbook of positive education* (pp. 21–48). Palgrave Macmillan. doi:10.1007/978-3-030-64537-3_2

Green, S., Oades, L. G., & Robinson, P. (2011). Positive education: Creating flourishing students, staff and schools. *InPsych*, *33*(2), 16–17. https://psychology.org.au/publications/inpsych/2011/april/green

Gregersen-Hermans, J., & Lauridsen, K. M. (2021). *Internationalising programmes in higher education: An educational development perspective*. Routledge. doi:10.4324/9780429344503

Guerola, I. S., Tordera, N., & Pérez-Nebra, A. (2021). El desarrollo de competencias interculturales a través de la Colaboración International en Línea [The development of intercultural competences through Collaborative Online International Learning]. *Revista del Congrés Internacional de Docència Universitària i Innovació*, *5*, 1–6.

Guillén-Yparrea, N., & Ramírez-Montoya, M. S. (2023). Intercultural competencies in higher education: A systematic review from 2016 to 2021. *Cogent Education*, *10*(1), 1–14. doi:10.1080/2331186X.2023.2167360

Guimarães, F. F., & Finardi, K. R. (2021). Global citizenship education (GCE) in internationalisation: COIL as alternative Thirdspace. *Globalisation, Societies and Education*, *19*(5), 641–657. doi:10.1080/14767724.2021.1875808

Guimarães, F. F., Mendes, A. R. M., Rodrigues, L. M., dos Santos Paiva, R. S., & Finardi, K. R. (2019). Internationalization at home, COIL and intercomprehension: For more inclusive activities in the Global South. *SFU Educational Review*, *12*(3), 90–109. doi:10.21810/sfuer.v12i3.1019

Gülbay, E. (2018). eTwinning collaborative learning environment in initial teacher education. *International Journal of Advanced Research in Science, Engineering and Technology*, *5*(1), 5234–5242.

Gunther, D. (2017). Interculturality: An anthropological approach. *Educational Profiles*, *39*(156), 192–207. https://acortar.link/Rtzk91

Guo, P., Saab, N., Wu, L., & Admiraal, W. (2021). The Community of Inquiry perspective on students' social presence, cognitive presence, and academic performance in online project based learning. *Journal of Computer Assisted Learning*, *37*(5), 1479–1493. doi:10.1111/jcal.12586

Guth, S., & Helm, F. (2010). *Telecollaboration 2.0: Language, literacies, and intercultural learning in the 21st century*. Peter Lang. doi:10.3726/978-3-0351-0013-6

Guth, S., Helm, F., & O'Dowd, R. (2014). Telecollaborative foreign language networks in European universities: A report on current attitudes and practices. *Bellaterra Journal of Teaching & Learning Language & Literature*, *7*(14), 1–14. doi:10.5565/rev/jtl3.609

Guth, S., & Rubin, J. (2015). Collaborative online international learning: An emerging format for internationalizing curricula. In A. S. Moore & S. Simon (Eds.), *Globally networked teaching in the humanities: Theories and practices* (pp. 27–39). Routledge.

Hadwin, A., Järvelä, S., & Miller, M. (2018). Self-regulation co-regulation and shared regulation in collaborative learning environments. In D. H. Schunk & J. A. Greene (Eds.), *Handbook of self-regulation of learning and performance* (2nd ed., pp. 83–106). Routledge.

Hahn, C. L. (2015). Teachers' perceptions of education for democratic citizenship in schools with transnational youth: A comparative study in the UK and Denmark. *Research in Comparative and International Education*, *10*(1), 95–119. doi:10.1177/1745499914567821

Haidt, J. (2003). Elevation and the positive psychology of morality. In C. L. M. Keyes & J. Haidt (Eds.), *Flourishing: Positive psychology and the life well-lived* (pp. 275–289). American Psychological Association. doi:10.1037/10594-012

Hair, J. F., Black, W. C., Babin, B. J., & Anderson, R. E. (2019). *Multivariate data analysis* (8th ed.). Cengage Learning.

Hall, E. T. (1977). *Beyond culture*. Doubleday.

Hall, E. T. (1990). *Understanding cultural differences*. Intercultural Press.

Hammerness, K., Darling-Hammond, L., Bransford, J., Berliner, D., Cochran-Smith, M., McDonald, M., & Zeichner, K. (2005). How teachers learn and develop. In L. Darling Hammond & J. Bransford (Eds.), *Preparing teachers for a changing world: What teachers should learn and be able to do* (pp. 358–389). Jossey-Bass.

Hanc, J. (2016, June 22). Professors as teachers. *The New York Times*. https://www.nytimes.com/2016/06/23/education/teaching-professors-to-become-better-teachers.html

Han, H., & Johnson, S. D. (2012). Relationship between students' emotional intelligence, social bond, and interactions in online learning. *Journal of Educational Technology & Society*, *15*(1), 78–89. https://www.jstor.org/stable/jeductechsoci.15.1.78

HarperCollins. (2000). Transnationalism. *Collins English dictionary*. https://www.collinsdictionary.com/us/

Harris, J. M., Seo, M., & McKeown, J. S. (2021). *Global competency through Collaborative Online International Learning (COIL). 7th International Conference on Higher Education Advances (HEAd'21).* 10.4995/HEAd21.2021.13080

Hatch, J. A. (2002). *Doing qualitative research in education settings*. State University of New York Press.

Hauck, M. (2023). From Virtual Exchange to Critical Virtual Exchange and Critical Internationalization at Home. *The Global Impact Exchange*. https://tinyurl.com/yvw6n2rn

Hauerwas, L. B., Gomez-Barreto, I. M., Boix Mansilla, V., & Segura Fernandez, R. (2023, March). Transformative innovation in teacher education: Research toward a critical global didactica. *Teaching and Teacher Education*, *123*, 1–14. doi:10.1016/j.tate.2022.103974

Hefflin, B. R. (2002). Learning to develop culturally relevant pedagogy: A lesson about cornrowed lives. *The Urban Review*, *34*(3), 231–250. doi:10.1023/A:1020603323594

Helm, F., & Beaven, A. (2020). *Designing and implementing virtual exchange – a collection of case studies*. Research-publishing.net.

Hernández Barraza, V. (2017). Las competencias emocionales del docente y su desempeño profesional [Teachers' emotional competencies and their professional performance]. *Alternativas en Psicología [Alternatives in Psychology]*, *37*, 79–92. https://www.alternativas.me/26-numero-37-febrero-julio-2017/147-las-competencias-emocionales-del-docente-y-su-desempeno-profesional

Hernández-Sánchez, A. M., & Ortega-Maldonado, A. (2015). Hacia la personalización del e-Learning: La afectividad y su repercusión en el bienestar subjetivo [Towards the personalization of e-learning: Affectivity and its impact on subjective well-being]. *Revista Lasallista de Investigacion [Lasallian Research Journal]*. *12*(2), 194–203. doi:10.22507/rli.v12n2a20

Herrera, B. L. (2016). Internationalization at home. Management processes for the internationalization of the Señor de Sipán University. *Environments*, *29*(2), 423–426. https://dialnet.unirioja.es/descarga/articulo/6937140.pdf

He, Y., Lundgren, K., & Pynes, P. (2017). Impact of short-term study abroad program: Inservice teachers' development of intercultural competence and pedagogical beliefs. *Teaching and Teacher Education*, *66*, 147–157. doi:10.1016/j.tate.2017.04.012

Hidecker, C. (2010). Communication activity and participation research. *Developmental Medicine and Child Neurology*, *52*(5), 408–409. doi:10.1111/j.1469-8749.2009.03460.x PMID:20059523

Hilliker, S. M., Loranc, B., & Samarakkody, D. (2022). Uplifting the well-being of teacher candidates through virtual exchange during COVID-19. *Journal of Virtual Exchange*, *5*, 176–192. doi:10.21827/jve.5.38320

Hlatshwayo, M. N., Khumalo, S. D., & Nzimande, N. (2021). The pandemic is our portal: Reimagining teaching and learning in the time of Covid-19. *African Perspectives of Research in Teaching and Learning*, *5*(1), 59–77.

Hoffman, D. M. (2009). Reflecting on social emotional learning: A critical perspective on trends in the United States. *Review of Educational Research*, *79*(2), 533–556. doi:10.3102/0034654308325184

Horwitz, E. K., Horwitz, M. B., & Cope, J. (1986). Foreign language classroom anxiety. *Modern Language Journal*, *70*(2), 125–132. doi:10.1111/j.1540-4781.1986.tb05256.x

Ho, T. K., & Lin, Y. T. (2016). The effects of virtual communities on group identity in classroom management. *Journal of Educational Computing Research*, *54*(1), 3–21. doi:10.1177/0735633115611645

Howaldt, J., Domanski, D., & Kaletka, C. (2016). Social innovation: Towards a new innovation paradigm. *RAM. Revista de Administração Mackenzie*, *17*(6), 20–44. doi:10.1590/1678-69712016/administracao.v17n6p20-44

Huang, H. M., Rauch, U., & Liaw, S. S. (2010). Investigating learners' attitudes toward virtual reality learning environments: Based on a constructivist approach. *Computers & Education*, *55*(3), 1171–1182. doi:10.1016/j.compedu.2010.05.014

Huang, Q., Cheung, A., & Xuan, Q. (2023). The impact of study abroad on pre-service and in-service teachers' intercultural competence: A meta-analysis. *Teaching and Teacher Education*, *127*, 1–14. doi:10.1016/j.tate.2023.104091

Hudzik, J. K. (2011). *Comprehensive internationalization: From concept to action. National Association of International Educators*. NAFSA.

Huertas-Abril, C. A. (2020, December). Telecollaboration in emergency remote language learning and teaching. In *2020 Sixth International Conference on E-Learning* (pp. 87–91). IEEE. 10.1109/econf51404.2020.9385425

Huertas-Abril, C. A., Palacios-Hidalgo, F. J., & Guardeño-Carrasquilla, M. A. (2023). Telecolaboración universidad-escuela para la concienciación sobre los ODS a través de eTwinning [University-school telecollaboration for SDG awareness through eTwinning]. In J. J. Delgado-Peña, S. Cabrero, N. Fernández, & J. Martínez (Eds.), *Universidades y Agenda 2030 [Universities and the 2030 Agenda]* (pp. 709–719). Comares.

Humberto, R. L. R. (2016). Los retos que impone la educación a distancia en México [The challenges of distance education in Mexico]. *Revista Iberoamericana de producción académica y gestión educativa, 6*, 1-12. https://www.pag.org.mx/index.php/PAG/article/view/631

Hunt, P., Soto, G., Maier, J., Liboiron, N., & Bae, S. (2004). Collaborative teaming to support preschoolers with severe disabilities who are placed in general education early childhood programs. *Topics in Early Childhood Special Education, 24*(3), 123–142. doi:10.1177/02711214040240030101

Hutchings, P., Huber, M. T., & Ciccone, A. (2011). *The scholarship of teaching and learning reconsidered: Institutional integration and impact*. John Wiley & Sons.

IESALC. (2019). *Movilidad en la educación superior: retos y oportunidades en un convenio renovado para el reconocimiento de estudios, títulos, y diplomas [Mobility in higher education: challenges and opportunities in a renewed agreement for the recognition of studies, degrees, and diplomas]*. Instituto Internacional para Educación Superior en América Latina y el Caribe. https://bit.ly/3UZgxHx

INCA. (2004). *INCA Assessee Manual*. Leonardo da Vinci VII Project. https://migrant-integration.ec.europa.eu/sites/default/files/2009-08/docl_9372_146280285.pdf

Incikabi, L., & Kacar, A. (2017). Analyzing prospective mathematics teachers' development of teaching practices in mathematics: A lesson study approach. In J. Keengwe & G. Onchwari (Eds.), *Handbook of research on learner-centered pedagogy in teacher education and professional development* (pp. 206–225). IGI Global. doi:10.4018/978-1-5225-0892-2.ch011

International Commission on Education for the Twenty-first Century. (1996). *Learning: the treasure within*. UNESCO. https://unesdoc.unesco.org/ark:/48223/pf0000109590

International Commission on the Development of Education. (1972). *Learning to be. The world of education today and tomorrow*. UNESCO. https://unesdoc.unesco.org/ark:/48223/pf0000223222

International Society for Technology in Education. (2016). *ISTE Standards: Students*. https://www.iste.org/standards/iste-standards-for-students

International Society for Technology in Education. (2017). *ISTE Standards: Educators*. https://www.iste.org/standards/iste-standards-for-teachers

Ismailov, M. (2021). Virtual exchanges in an inquiry-based learning environment: Effects on intra-cultural awareness and intercultural communicative competence. *Cogent Education, 8*(1), 1982601. Advance online publication. doi:10.1080/2331186X.2021.1982601

Isohätälä, J., Järvenoja, H., & Järvelä, S. (2017). Socially shared regulation of learning and participation in social interaction in collaborative learning. *International Journal of Educational Research, 81*, 11–24. doi:10.1016/j.ijer.2016.10.006

Isohätälä, J., Näykki, P., & Järvelä, S. (2020). Cognitive and socio-emotional interaction in collaborative learning: Exploring fluctuations in students' participation. *Scandinavian Journal of Educational Research, 64*(6), 831–851. doi:10.1080/00313831.2019.1623310

Isohätälä, J., Näykki, P., Järvelä, S., & Baker, M. J. (2018). Striking a balance: Socio-emotional processes during argumentation in collaborative learning interaction. *Learning, Culture and Social Interaction, 16*, 1–19. doi:10.1016/j.lcsi.2017.09.003

İzgí Onbaşil, U., Sezgínsoy Şeker, B., Claeys, H., Mancel, C., Gülbay, E., & Powers, R. (2022). Experiences of qualified teachers of the future in the scope of an international eTwinning project. *International Online Journal of Primary Education, 11*(2), 293–311. doi:10.55020/iojpe.1182120

Jaakkola, T., & Liukkonen, J. (2006). Changes in students' self-determined motivation and goal orientation as a result of motivational climate intervention within high school physical education classes. *International Journal of Sport and Exercise Psychology, 4*(3), 302–324. doi:10.1080/1612197X.2006.9671800

Jagers, R. J., Rivas-Drake, D., & Williams, B. (2019). Transformative social and emotional learning (SEL): Toward SEL in service of educational equity and excellence. *Educational Psychologist, 54*(3), 162–184. doi:10.1080/00461520.2019.1623032

Jahanian, F. (2020). How higher education can adapt to the future of work. *World Economic Forum, SGD 04: Quality Education*. https://bit.ly/490Fzuf

Jaldemark, J. (2008). Participation and genres of communication in online settings of higher education. *Education and Information Technologies, 13*(2), 129–146. doi:10.1007/s10639-008-9057-9

Janssen, J., Erkens, G., Kirschner, P. A., & Kanselaar, G. (2012). Task-related and social regulation during online collaborative learning. *Metacognition and Learning, 7*(1), 25–43. doi:10.1007/s11409-010-9061-5

Järvelä, S., Kirschner, P. A., Järvenoja, H., Malmberg, J., Miller, M., & Laru, J. (2016). Socially shared regulation of learning in CSCL: Understanding and prompting individual- and group-level shared regulatory activities. *International Journal of Computer-Supported Collaborative Learning, 11*(3), 263–280. doi:10.1007/s11412-016-9238-2

Jefatura del Estado. (2023). *Ley Orgánica 2/2023, de 22 de marzo, del Sistema Universitario* [Organic Law 2/2023, of 22 March, of the University System]. https://bit.ly/3UovOS0

Jehangir, R. R., Stebleton, M. J., & Collins, K. (2022). STEM stories: Fostering STEM persistence for underrepresented minority students attending predominantly White institutions. *Journal of Career Development*, 1–17. doi:10.1177/08948453211073706

Jie, Z., & Pearlman, A. M. G. (2018). Expanding access to international education through technology enhanced collaborative online international learning (COIL) courses. *International Journal of Technology in Teaching and Learning, 14*(1), 1–11.

Jin, S. (2015). Using Facebook to promote Korean EFL learners' intercultural competence. *Language Learning & Technology, 19*(3), 38–51. http://llt.msu.edu/issues/october2015/action2

Johnson, R., & Christensen, L. (2014). *Educational research: Quantitative, qualitative, & mixed methods* (5th ed.). Sage.

Jones, S. M., McGarrah, M. W., & Kahn, J. (2019). Social and emotional learning: A principled science of human development in context. *Educational Psychologist, 54*(3), 129–143. doi:10.1080/00461520.2019.1625776

Jooste, N., & Hagenmeier, C. (2022). Policy framework for the internationalisation of higher education in South Africa: A compass for comprehensive internationalisation? *Journal of Studies in International Education*, *26*(4), 415–435. doi:10.1177/10283153221105318

JumpStart Games. (2014a). *Pick and choose I for grade II, sight words.* JumpStart. http://bit.ly/3Jrm2cd

JumpStart Games. (2014b). *Put the words in place.* JumpStart. http://bit.ly/3XQjHvO

JumpStart Games. (2014c). *Spell me not, spellings worksheet for 2nd grade kids.* JumpStart. http://bit.ly/40h2duc

JumpStart Games. (2014d). *The missing vowels, free English worksheets for kids.* JumpStart. http://bit.ly/3HlWTgn

Junco, R., Elavsky, C. M., & Heiberger, G. (2013). Putting Twitter to the test: Assessing outcomes for student collaboration, engagement and success. *British Journal of Educational Technology*, *44*(2), 273–287. doi:10.1111/j.1467-8535.2012.01284.x

Kaiser, H. F. (1974). An index of factorial simplicity. *Psychometrika*, *39*(1), 31–36. doi:10.1007/BF02291575

Kanpol, B. (1999). *Critical pedagogy: An introduction.* Bergin & Garvey.

Kara, M. (2019). A systematic literature review: Constructivism in multidisciplinary learning environments. *International Journal of Academic Research in Education*, *4*(1-2), 19–26. doi:10.17985/ijare.520666

Kashdan, T. B., Biswas-Diener, R., & King, L. A. (2008). Reconsidering happiness: The costs of distinguishing between hedonics and eudaimonia. *The Journal of Positive Psychology*, *3*(4), 219–233. doi:10.1080/17439760802303044

Katre, A. (2020). Creative economy teaching and Learning–A collaborative online international learning case. *International Education Studies*, *13*(7), 145–155. doi:10.5539/ies.v13n7p145

Kaur, R. (2017). *The sun and her flowers.* Andrews McMeel.

Kavrayici, C. (2021). The relationship between classroom management and sense of classroom community in graduate virtual classrooms. *Turkish Online Journal of Distance Education*, *22*(2), 112–125. doi:10.17718/tojde.906816

Kemmis, S., & McTaggart, R. (2005). *Participatory action research: Communicative action and the public sphere.* Sage Publications Ltd. doi:10.4135/9781473921290.n45

Kerkhoff, S., Carpenter, J., Yang, Q., & Dong, Y. (2021). Literacy education in the era of globalization: A mixed methods study of the Global Read Aloud. In T. Bastiaens (Ed.), *Proceedings of EdMedia + Innovate Learning* (pp. 850-857). Association for the Advancement of Computing in Education (AACE). https://www.learntechlib.org/primary/p/219750/

Kerkhoff, S. N., Mardi, F., & Rong, H. (2021). An action research study on globally competent teaching in online spaces. In A. Slapac, P. Balcerzak, & K. O'Brien (Eds.), *Handbook of research on the global empowerment of educators and student learning through action research* (pp. 264–288). IGI Global. doi:10.4018/978-1-7998-6922-1.ch012

Kern, M. L., Waters, L. E., Adler, A., & White, M. A. (2015). A multidimensional approach to measuring well-being in students: Application of the PERMA framework. *The Journal of Positive Psychology*, *10*(3), 262–271. doi:10.1080/17439760.2014.936962 PMID:25745508

Keshavarz, M., Mirmoghtadaie, Z., & Nayyeri, S. (2022). Design and validation of the virtual classroom management questionnaire. *International Review of Research in Open and Distance Learning*, *23*(2), 120–135. doi:10.19173/irrodl.v23i2.5774

Keyes, C. L. M., Shmotkin, D., & Ryff, C. D. (2002). Optimizing well-being: The empirical encounter of two traditions. *Journal of Personality and Social Psychology*, *82*(6), 1007–1022. doi:10.1037/0022-3514.82.6.1007 PMID:12051575

Khosa, D. K., & Volet, S. E. (2014). Productive group engagement in cognitive activity and metacognitive regulation during collaborative learning: Can it explain differences in students' conceptual understanding? *Metacognition and Learning*, *9*(3), 287–307. doi:10.1007/s11409-014-9117-z

Kidd, W., & Murray, J. (2020). The Covid-19 pandemic and its effects on teacher education in England: How teacher educators moved practicum learning online. *European Journal of Teacher Education*, *43*(4), 542–558. doi:10.1080/02619768.2020.1820480

Kielstra, J., Molenaar, I., van Steensel, R., & Verhoeven, L. (2022). Supporting socially shared regulation during collaborative task-oriented reading. *International Journal of Computer-Supported Collaborative Learning*, *17*(1), 65–105. doi:10.1007/s11412-022-09365-x

Killick, D., & Foster, M. (2021). *Learner relationships in global higher education: A critical pedagogy for a multicultural world.* Routledge. doi:10.4324/9780429294877

Kim, K., & Bonk, C. (2002). Cross-cultural comparisons of online collaboration. *Journal of Computer-Mediated Communication*, *8*(1), 0. Advance online publication. doi:10.1111/j.1083-6101.2002.tb00163.x

Kim, S., & Slapac, A. (2015). Culturally responsive, transformative pedagogy in the transnational era: Critical perspectives. *Educational Studies (Ames)*, *51*(1), 17–27. doi:10.1080/00131946.2014.983639

King de Ramirez, C. (2021). Global citizenship education through collaborative online international learning in the Borderlands: A case of the Arizona–Sonora megaregion. *Journal of Studies in International Education*, *25*(1), 83–99. doi:10.1177/1028315319888886

King Ramírez, C. (2020). Influences of academic culture in Collaborative Online International Learning (COIL): Differences in Mexican and U.S. students' reported experiences. *Foreign Language Annals*, *53*(3), 438–457. doi:10.1111/flan.12485

King Ramírez, C. (2022). Virtual exchange in Latin America: A profile of faculty and staff participants. *Journal of Virtual Exchange*, *5*, 105–132. doi:10.21827/jve.5.38284

Kirschner, P. A., Sweller, J., Kirschner, F., & Zambrano, J. (2018). From cognitive load theory to collaborative cognitive load theory. *International Journal of Computer-Supported Collaborative Learning*, *13*(2), 213–233. doi:10.1007/s11412-018-9277-y PMID:30996713

Klassen, R. M., Al-Dhafri, S., Hannok, W., & Betts, S. M. (2011). Investigating pre-service teacher motivation across cultures using the teachers' ten statements test. *Teaching and Teacher Education*, *27*(3), 579–588. doi:10.1016/j.tate.2010.10.012

Klenowski, V. (2014). Towards fairer assessment. *Australian Educational Researcher*, *41*(4), 445–470. doi:10.1007/s13384-013-0132-x

Knekta, E., Runyon, C., & Eddy, S. (2019). One size doesn't fit all: Using factor analysis to gather validity evidence when using surveys in your research. *CBE Life Sciences Education*, *18*(1), rm1. Advance online publication. doi:10.1187/cbe.18-04-0064 PMID:30821600

Knight, J. (2003). Updated definition of internationalization. *Industry and Higher Education*, (33), 1–3. doi:10.6017/ihe.2003.33.7391

Knight, J. (2008). *Higher education in turmoil: The changing world of internationalization.* Brill. doi:10.1163/9789087905224

Komatsu, T. (2023). Collaborative Online International Learning (COIL) during the pandemic: The momentum for developing global competency through equitable, partnership-based intercultural learning. In A. W. Wiseman, C. Matherly, & M. Crumley-Effinger (Eds.), *Internationalization and imprints of the pandemic on higher education worldwide* (pp. 209–228). Emerald Publishing. doi:10.1108/S1479-367920230000044013

Komotar, M. H. (2019). Global University Rankings and their impact on the internationalisation of higher education. *European Journal of Education*, *54*(2), 299–310. doi:10.1111/ejed.12332

Kopish, M., & Marques, W. (2020). Leveraging technology to promote global citizenship in teacher education in the United States and Brazil. *Research in Social Sciences and Technology*, *5*(1), 45–69. doi:10.46303/ressat.05.01.3

Koshy, E., Koshy, V., & Waterman, H. (2011). Action Research in Healthcare. *Sage.*

Koss, M. D. (2015). Diversity in contemporary picture books: A content analysis. *Journal of Children's Literature*, *41*(1), 32–42. https://eric.ed.gov/?id=EJ1062015

Kozol, J. (2012). *Savage inequalities: Children in America's schools*. Crown.

Krajewski, S. (2011). Developing intercultural competence in multilingual and multicultural student groups. *Journal of Research in International Education*, *10*(2), 137–153. doi:10.1177/1475240911408563

Kramsch, C. (2014). Language and culture. *AILA Review*, *27*(1), 30–55. doi:10.1075/aila.27.02kra

Krashen, S. D. (1985). *The input hypothesis: Issues and implications*. Longman.

Krengel, F. (2021). "Glocal Education" Through Virtual Exchange? Training Pre- Service EFL Teachers to Connect Their Local Classrooms to the World and Back. *Global Education Review*, *8*(2-3), 138–153.

Krishnan, L. A., Jin, L., Stahl, A., Sreekumar, S., Sundaram, S., Subrahmanian, M., & Davis, P. (2022). Innovative changes to study abroad: Virtual intercultural learning during the pandemic. *Teaching and Learning in Communication Sciences & Disorders*, *6*(2), 1–27. doi:10.30707/TLCSD6.2.1660595992.539519

Kroll, J., & Egan, E. (2004). Psychiatry, moral worry, and the moral emotions. *Journal of Psychiatric Practice*, *10*(6), 352–360. https://doi.org/cnsstq. doi:10.1097/00131746-200411000-00003 PMID:15583516

Kukulska-Hulme, A., & Traxler, J. (2019). Design principles for mobile learning. In H. Beetham & R. Sharpe (Eds.), *Rethinking pedagogy for a digital age: Designing for 21st century learning* (2nd ed., pp. 268–281). Routledge. doi:10.4324/9781351252805-12

Kulich, S. J. (2015). Does context count? Developing and assessing intercultural competence through an interview-and model-based domestic course design in China. *International Journal of Intercultural Relations*, *48*, 38–57. doi:10.1016/j.ijintrel.2015.03.013

Kumashiro, K. K. (2000). Teaching and learning through desire, crisis and difference: Perverted reflections on anti-oppressive education. *The Radical Teacher*, *58*, 6–11.

Kumashiro, K. K. (2015). *Against common sense: Teaching and learning toward social justice* (3rd ed.). Routledge. doi:10.4324/9781315765525

Kuyken, W., Weare, K., Ukoumunne, O. C., Vicary, R., Motton, N., Burnett, R., Cullen, C., Hennelly, S., & Huppert, F. (2013). Effectiveness of the mindfulness in schools programme: Non-randomised controlled feasibility study. *The British Journal of Psychiatry*, *203*(2), 126–131. doi:10.1192/bjp.bp.113.126649 PMID:23787061

Kwok, S. (2018). Science education in the 21st century. *Nature Astronomy*, *2*(7), 530–533. doi:10.1038/s41550-018-0510-4

Kwon, K., Liu, Y.-H., & Johnson, L. P. (2014). Group regulation and social-emotional interactions observed in computer supported collaborative learning: Comparison between good vs. poor collaborators. *Computers & Education, 78*, 185–200. doi:10.1016/j.compedu.2014.06.004

Ladson-Billings, G. (2014). Culturally relevant pedagogy 2.0: A.k.a. the remix. *Harvard Educational Review, 84*(1), 74–84. doi:10.17763/haer.84.1.p2rj131485484751

Ladson-Billings, G. (2021). *Culturally relevant pedagogy: Asking a different question*. Teachers College Press.

Laird, L. (2015). Empathy in the classroom: Can music bring us more in tune with one another? *Music Educators Journal, 101*(4), 56–61. doi:10.1177/0027432115572230

Lamy, M.-N., & Goodfellow, R. (1999). 'Reflective conversation' in the virtual language classroom. *Language Learning & Technology, 2*(2), 43–61.

Landorf, H., Doscher, S., & Hardrick, J. (2018). *Making global learning universal: Promoting inclusion and success for all students*. Routledge.

Larrick, N. (1965). The all-white world of children's books. *Saturday Review, 48*(11), 63–65.

Lave, J., & Wenger, E. (1991). *Situated learning: Legitimate peripheral participation*. Cambridge University Press. doi:10.1017/CBO9780511815355

Lawrence, G., & Spector-Cohen, E. (2018). Examining international telecollaboration in language teacher education. In D. Tafazoli, M. E. Gomez Parra, & C. A. Huertas-Abril (Eds.), *Cross-cultural perspectives on technology-enhanced language learning* (pp. 322–345). IGI Global. doi:10.4018/978-1-5225-5463-9.ch018

Lawrence-Lightfoot, S. (2005). Reflections on portraiture: A dialogue between art and science. *Qualitative Inquiry, 11*(1), 3–15. doi:10.1177/1077800404270955

Le Grange, L. (2020). Could the COVID-19 pandemic accelerate the Uberfication of the university? *South African Journal of Higher Education, 34*(4), 1–10. doi:10.20853/34-4-4071

Leask, B. (2015). *Internationalizing the curriculum*. Routledge. doi:10.4324/9781315716954

Lehtomäki, E., Moate, J., & Posti-Ahokas, H. (2016). Global connectedness in higher education: Student voices on the value of cross-cultural learning dialogue. *Studies in Higher Education, 41*(11), 2011–2027. doi:10.1080/03075079.2015.1007943

Levin, S., Van Laar, C., & Foote, W. (2006). Ethnic segregation and perceived discrimination in college: Mutual influences and effects on social and academic life. *Journal of Applied Social Psychology, 36*(6), 1471–1501. doi:10.1111/j.0021-9029.2006.00068.x

Lewis, T., & O'Dowd, R. (2016). Online intercultural exchange and foreign language learning: A systematic review. In R. O'Dowd & T. Lewis (Eds.), Online intercultural exchange: Policy, pedagogy, practice (pp. 21-68). Routledge.

Ley Orgánica 8/2013, de 9 de diciembre, para la Mejora de la Calidad Educativa [Organic Law 8/2013, of 9 December, for the Improvement of the Quality of Education]. BOE no. 295, 10 December 2013. https://bit.ly/2Nd9yHK

Lilley, K., Barker, M., & Harris, N. (2015). Exploring the process of global citizen learning and the student mind-set. *Journal of Studies in International Education, 19*(3), 225–245. doi:10.1177/1028315314547822

Lincoln, Y. S., & Guba, E. G. (1985). Naturalistic inquiry. *Sage*.

Lister, S. (2022). Gamifying CLIL: Unlocking the potential of game-based learning. In C. A. Huertas-Abril, E. Fernández-Ahumada, & N. Adamuz-Povedano (Eds.), *Handbook of research on international approaches and practices for gamifying mathematics* (pp. 1–20). IGI Global. doi:10.4018/978-1-7998-9660-9.ch001

Liu, G.-Z., Fathi, J., & Rahimi, M. (2023). Enhancing EFL learners' intercultural communicative effectiveness through telecollaboration with native and non-native speakers of English. *Computer Assisted Language Learning*, 1–31. Advance online publication. doi:10.1080/09588221.2022.2164778

Llorent, V. J., Zych, I., & Varo-Millán, J. C. (2020). Competencias socioemocionales autopercibidas en el profesorado universitario en España. *Educación XX1, 23*(1), 297-318. doi:10.5944/educxx1.23687

Lombard, M., Snyder-Duch, J., & Bracken, C. C. (2002). Content analysis in mass communication: Assessment and reporting of intercoder reliability. *Human Communication Research, 28*(4), 587–604. doi:10.1111/j.1468-2958.2002.tb00826.x

Longview Foundation. (2008). *Teacher preparation for a global age: The imperative for change.* https://longviewfdn.org/programs/internationalizing-teacher-prep/

López, A. I. A. (2022). Elementos curriculares para la formación y actualización del docente. *Revista Docencia Universitaria, 3*(1), 57–66. doi:10.46954/revistadusac.v3i1.40

López-Cirugeda, I. (2017). eTwinning en los Grados de Maestro y Máster de Formación de Profesorado de Secundaria de la UCLM [eTwinning in the Degrees and Master's Degree in Secondary Education in UCLM]. In R. Cózar-Gutiérrez & M. V. de Moya Martínez (Eds.). Entornos digitales humanizados [Humanized digital environments] (pp. 67-80) Síntesis.

López-Cirugeda, I., & Sánchez-Ruiz, R. (2023). eTwinning and ITE in Spain. A testimony by Universidad de Castilla-La Mancha. In A. Tosi (Ed.). Empowering future teachers for a sustainable intercultural and inclusive education. The impact of eTwinning on Initial Teacher Education (pp. 145-149). Carozzi.

López-Cirugeda, I. (2015). Radio activa: Bilingual experience in primary education. In I. Vescan (Ed.), *Spanish vs American perspectives on bilingual education* (pp. 129–138). Servicio de Publicaciones de la Universidad de Alcalá.

López, G. H. (2014). The internationalization of higher education and the formation of Global Citizens, Glocal Citizens. *Sophia, 10*(2), 64–69. http://www.scielo.org.co/pdf/sph/v10n2/v10n2a07.pdf

López-Goñi, I., & Goñi, J. M. (2012). La competencia emocional en los currículos de formación inicial de los docentes. Un estudio comparativo. *Review of Education, 357*, 467–489. https://dialnet.unirioja.es/servlet/articulo?codigo=3811857

López-López, V., & Lagos San Martín, N. (2021). Repensar la formación inicial docente desde una dimensión socioemocional. *Review of Education, 45*(1), 609–619. doi:10.15517/revedu.v45i1.41464

Lotan, R. A. (2006). Teaching teachers to build equitable classrooms. *Theory into Practice, 45*(1), 32–39. doi:10.1207/s15430421tip4501_5

Love, T. S., & Love, Z. J. (2023). The teacher recruitment crisis: Examining influential recruitment factors from a United States technology and engineering teacher preparation program. *International Journal of Technology and Design Education, 33*(1), 105–121. doi:10.1007/s10798-022-09727-4

Lucas Borja, M. E. (2020, March 2). Trabajando como coordinador de relaciones internacionales en el campus de Albacete. *UCLM* [Working as a coordinator of international relations in Albacete campus (UCLM)]. https://blog.uclm.es/manuelestebanlucas/ultimas-noticias/

Luk-Fong, P. Y. Y. (2010). Towards a hybrid conceptualisation of Chinese women primary school teachers' changing femininities–a case study of Hong Kong. *Gender and Education, 22*(1), 73–86. doi:10.1080/09540250802581834

MacClelland. (1999). *A guide to job competency assessment*. McBer.

MacFarlane, B. (2021). *STEM education for high-ability learners: Designing and implementing programming*. Routledge. doi:10.4324/9781003238218

Macintyre, C. (2012). *The art of action research in the classroom*. David Fulton Publishers. doi:10.4324/9780203065228

MacNab, B., Brislin, R., & Worthley, R. (2012). Experiential cultural intelligence development: Context and individual attributes. *International Journal of Human Resource Management*, *23*(7), 1320–1341. doi:10.1080/09585192.2011.581636

Madden, M. E., Baxter, M., Beauchamp, H., Bouchard, K., Habermas, D., Huff, M., Ladd, B., Pearon, J., & Plague, G. (2013). Rethinking STEM education: An interdisciplinary STEAM curriculum. *Procedia Computer Science*, *20*, 541–546. doi:10.1016/j.procs.2013.09.316

Mahoney, J. L., Durlak, J. A., & Weissberg, R. P. (2018). An update on social and emotional learning outcome research. *Phi Delta Kappan*, *100*(4), 18–23. doi:10.1177/0031721718815668

Mahoney, J. L., Weissberg, R. P., Greenberg, M. T., Dusenbury, L., Jagers, R. J., Niemi, K., Schlinger, M., Schlund, J., Shriver, T. P., VanAusdal, K., & Yoder, N. (2020). Systemic Social and Emotional Learning: Promoting educational success for all preschool to high school students. *The American Psychologist*, *76*(7), 1128–1142. doi:10.1037/amp0000701 PMID:33030926

Majcen, S. A., & Drvodelić, M. (2022). Quality pedagogical practice in Early Childhood Education institutions relating to children at risk of social exclusion. *Center for Educational Policy Studies Journal*, *12*(3), 81–101. doi:10.26529/cepsj.1086

Major, C. (2010). Do virtual professors dream of electric students? College faculty experiences with online distance education. *Teachers College Record*, *112*(8), 2154–2208. doi:10.1177/016146811011200802

Maldonado-Torres, N. (2004). The topology of being and the geopolitics of knowledge: Modernity, empire, coloniality. *City (London, England)*, *8*(1), 29–56. doi:10.1080/1360481042000199787

Malmberg, J., Järvelä, S., & Järvenoja, H. (2017). Capturing temporal and sequential patterns of self-, co-, and socially shared regulation in the context of collaborative learning. *Contemporary Educational Psychology*, *49*, 160–174. doi:10.1016/j.cedpsych.2017.01.009

Mansilla, V. B., & Jackson, A. (2011). *Educating for global competence: Preparing our youth to engage the world.* Council of Chief State School Officers' EdSteps Initiative & Asia Society Partnership for Global Learning.

Mänty, K., Järvenoja, H., & Törmänen, T. (2020). Socio-emotional interaction in collaborative learning: Combining individual emotional experiences and group-level emotion regulation. *International Journal of Educational Research*, *102*, 101589. Advance online publication. doi:10.1016/j.ijer.2020.101589

Marcillo-Gómez, M., & Desilus, B. (2016). Collaborative online international learning experience in practice opportunities and challenges. *Journal of Technology Management & Innovation*, *11*(1), 30–35. doi:10.4067/S0718-27242016000100005

Marcus, V. B., Atan, N. A., Yusof, S. M., & Tahir, L. (2020). A systematic review of e-service learning in higher education. *International Association of Online Engineering*, *14*(6), 1–14. doi:10.3991/ijim.v14i06.13395

Marginson, S. (2022). Space and scale in higher education: The glonacal agency heuristic revisited. *Higher Education*, *84*(6), 1365–1395. doi:10.1007/s10734-022-00955-0 PMID:36415669

Maric, D., Fore, G. A., Nyarko, S. C., & Varma-Nelson, P. (2023). Measurement in STEM education research: A systematic literature review of trends in the psychometric evidence of scales. *International Journal of STEM Education*, *10*(1), 39. doi:10.1186/s40594-023-00430-x

Marín, M. A. (2020). Internationalization of the curriculum from practice: Contributions from the national and international context. In G. C. Valencia González & L. E. Malagón Castro (Eds.), *Educación y región, lo dicho de lo no dicho* [Education and region, what has been said about what has not been said] (pp. 119–141). Editorial Corporación Universitaria del Meta –UNIMETA. doi:10.52043/LVDW1392

Marino, M. I., & Tadal, S. (2022). Matching students: Strategies for maximizing inclusion and success. In J. Rubin, S. Gut, S. Doscher, & C. Wojenski (Eds.), *The guide to COIL virtual exchange* (pp. 298–311). Stylus.

Maroco, J., Maroco, A. L., Compos, J. A. D. B., & Fredricks, J. A. (2016). University student's engagement: Development of the university student engagement inventory (USEI). *Psicologia: Reflexâo e Crítica, 29*, 1–12. doi:10.1186/s41155-016-0042-8

Marques, S. C., Lopez, S. J., & Pais-Ribeiro, J. L. (2011). "Building hope for the future": A program to foster strengths in middle-school students. *Journal of Happiness Studies, 12*(1), 139–152. doi:10.1007/s10902-009-9180-3

Marshall, C., & Rossman, G. B. (2016). *Designing qualitative research* (4th ed.). Sage.

Martínez-Martí, M. L., Theirs, C. I., Pascual, D., & Corradi, G. (2020). Character strengths predict an increase in mental health and subjective well-being over a one-month period during the COVID-19 pandemic lockdown. *Frontiers in Psychology, 11*, 584567. Advance online publication. doi:10.3389/fpsyg.2020.584567 PMID:33192913

Martin, F., & Bolliger, D. U. (2018). Engagement matters: Student perceptions on the importance of engagement strategies in the online learning environment. *Online Learning: the Official Journal of the Online Learning Consortium, 22*(1), 205–222. doi:10.24059/olj.v22i1.1092

Martin, I. A. (2020). Pronunciation development and instruction in distance language learning. *Language Learning & Technology, 24*(1), 86–106. https://doi.org/https://doi.org/10125/44711

Martin, S. D., Snow, J. L., & Franklin Torrez, C. A. (2011). Navigating the terrain of third space: Tensions with/in relationships in school-university partnerships. *Journal of Teacher Education, 62*(3), 299–311. doi:10.1177/0022487110396096

Martins, M., Costa, J., & Onofre, M. (2015). Practicum experiences as sources of pre-service teachers' self-efficacy. *European Journal of Teacher Education, 38*(2), 263–279. doi:10.1080/02619768.2014.968705

Marx, H., & Moss, D. M. (2011). Please mind the culture gap: Intercultural development during a teacher education study abroad program. *Journal of Teacher Education, 62*(1), 35–47. doi:10.1177/0022487110381998

Marx, S. (2022). Mapping as critical qualitative research methodology. *International Journal of Research & Method in Education.* Advance online publication. doi:10.1080/1743727X.2022.2110231

Mayer, J. D., Caruso, D. R., & Salovey, P. (2016). The ability model of emotional intelligence: Principles and updates. *Emotion Review, 8*(4), 290–300. doi:10.1177/1754073916639667

Mayer, J. D., & Salovey, P. (1997). What is emotional intelligence? In P. Salovey & D. J. Sluyter (Eds.), *Emotional development and emotional intelligence: Educational implications* (pp. 3–31). Basic Books.

Mayring, P. (2014). *Qualitative content analysis: Theoretical foundations, basic procedures and software solutions.* Philipp Mayring. https://nbn-resolving.org/urn:nbn:de:0168-ssoar-395173

Mbaki, Y., Todorova, E., & Hagan, P. (2021). Diversifying the medical curriculum as part of the wider decolonising effort: A proposed framework and self-assessment resource toolbox. *The Clinical Teacher, 18*(5), 459–466. doi:10.1111/tct.13408 PMID:34467663

McLaughlin, L. A., & Ricevuto, J. (2021). Virtual instruction support for faculty. *Issues in Informing Science and Information Technology, 18*, 1-30. doi:10.28945/4792

Meaney, T., Edmonds-Wathen, C., McMurchy-Pilkington, C., & Trinick, T. (2016). Distribution, recognition, and representation: Mathematics education and Indigenous students. In K. Makar, S. Dole, J. Visnovska, M. Goos, A. Bennison, & K. Fry (Eds.), *Research in mathematics, education in Australasia: 2012–2015* (pp. 143–164). Springer. doi:10.1007/978-981-10-1419-2_8

Meer, N., & Modood, T. (2012). How does interculturalism contrast with multiculturalism? *Journal of Intercultural Studies (Melbourne, Vic.)*, *33*(2), 175–196. doi:10.1080/07256868.2011.618266

Merriam, S. B., & Tisdell, E. J. (2016). *Qualitative Research: A guide to design and implementation* (4th ed.). Jossey-Bass.

Meyer, A., Hansen, P., & Fourie, I. (2018). Assessing the potential of third space to design a creative virtual academic space based on findings from information behaviour. *Information Research*, *23*(4). https://www.informationr.net/ir/23-4/isic2018/isic1814.html

Meza Morón, O. P. (2020). The COIL Model, a transformative intercultural experience. In *Memorial of the XX Teacher Training Meeting Summer 2020* (1st ed., p. 424). Jennie Brand Barajas.

Mignolo, W. (2002). The geopolitics of knowledge and the colonial difference. *The South Atlantic Quarterly*, *101*(1), 57–94. doi:10.1215/00382876-101-1-57

Mikulec, E. (2019). Short-term study abroad for pre-service teachers: Personal and professional growth in Brighton, England. *International Journal for the Scholarship of Teaching and Learning*, *13*(1), 1–12. doi:10.20429/ijsotl.2019.130111

Miles, M., & Huberman, A. (1994). *Qualitative data analysis: A sourcebook of new methods* (2nd ed.). Sage.

Miller, K., Castañon, M., & Filiss, T. (2022). The worst we have seen: Leveraging social/emotional learning in K-12 online & blended environments amid a well-being crisis. *Journal of Online Learning Research*, *8*(1), 1–6.

Miller, M. A. (2002). American higher education goes global. *Change*, *34*(3), 4. doi:10.1080/00091380209601846

Mills, G. E., & Gay, L. R. (2016). *Education research: Competencies for analysis and applications*. Pearson Education.

Milner, H. R. IV. (2011). Culturally relevant pedagogy in a diverse urban classroom. *The Urban Review*, *43*(1), 66–89. doi:10.1007/s11256-009-0143-0

Ministerio de Educación. Cultura y Deporte. (2003). *La integración del sistema universitario español en el Espacio Europeo de Enseñanza Superior*. http://www.fce.udl.cat/EEES/eees/Documento_Marco.pdf

Mohamed Hashim, M. A., Tlemsani, I., & Matthews, R. (2022). Higher education strategy in digital transformation. *Education and Information Technologies*, *27*(3), 3171–3195. doi:10.1007/s10639-021-10739-1 PMID:34539217

Moje, E. B. (2007). Chapter 1 Developing socially just subject-matter instruction: A review of the literature on disciplinary literacy teaching. *Review of Research in Education*, *31*(1), 1–44. doi:10.3102/0091732X07300046001

Moje, E. B., Ciechanowski, K. M., Kramer, K., Ellis, L., Carrillo, R., & Collazo, T. (2004). Working toward third space in content area literacy: An examination of everyday funds of knowledge and discourse. *Reading Research Quarterly*, *39*(1), 38–70. doi:10.1598/RRQ.39.1.4

Molenaar, I., & Järvelä, S. (2014). Sequential and temporal characteristics of self and socially regulated learning. *Metacognition and Learning*, *9*(2), 75–85. doi:10.1007/s11409-014-9114-2

Molinillo, S., Aguilar-Illescas, R., Anaya-Sánchez, R., & Vallespín-Arán, M. (2018). Exploring the impacts of interactions, social presence, and emotional engagement on active collaborative learning in a social web-based environment. *Computers & Education, 123*, 41–52. doi:10.1016/j.compedu.2018.04.012

Möller, K. J. (2014). Mirrors and windows through literature featuring Arabs, Arab Americans, and people of Islamic faith. *Journal of Children's Literature, 40*(2), 65–72. https://www.proquest.com/docview/1657566318?pq-origsite=gscholar&fromopenview=true

Monitor, I. C. E. F. (2022). *Latin American institutions increasingly prepared to compete for international students.* https://bit.ly/48ySm69

Montejo-Ángel, F., & Pava-Díaz, G. (2022). Competencias socioemocionales y selección de candidatos para cargos de docencia universitaria: Socio-emotional competencies and selection of candidates for university teaching positions. *Educación y Humanismo, 24*(42). Advance online publication. doi:10.17081/eduhum.24.42.5337

Moon, S. (2010). Multicultural and global citizenship in a transnational age: The case of South Korea. *International Journal of Multicultural Education, 12*(1), 1–15. doi:10.18251/ijme.v12i1.261

Morris, N. (2014). *Moving higher education forward in a digital age: Realising a digital strategy.* International Conference E-Learning 2014, Lisbon, Portugal.

Moskovkin, V. M., Zhang, H., Sadovski, M. V., & Serkina, O. V. (2022). Comprehensive quantitative analysis of TOP-100s of ARWU, QS and THE World University Rankings for 2014–2018. *Education for Information, 38*(2), 133–169. doi:10.3233/EFI-211539

Mseleku, Z. (2020). A literature review of E-learning and E-teaching in the era of Covid-19 pandemic. *International Journal of Innovative Science and Research Technology, 5*(10), 588–597.

Mudiamu, S. S. (2020). *Faculty use of collaborative online international learning (COIL) for internationalization at home* (Doctoral dissertation, Portland State University). doi:10.15760/etd.7342

Mukherji, B. R., Neuwirth, L. S., & Limonic, L. (2017). Making the case for real diversity: Redefining underrepresented minority students in public universities. *SAGE Open, 7*(2). Advance online publication. doi:10.1177/2158244017707796

Mundel, J. (2020). International virtual collaboration in advertising courses: Building international and intercultural skills from home. *Journal of Advertising Education, 24*(2), 112–132. doi:10.1177/1098048220948522

Nae, N. (2022). The post-pandemic "new normal" in Japanese education. *Euromentor, 13*(3), 21–31. https://bit.ly/41omfT1

Naicker, A., Singh, E., & van Genugten, T. (2022). Collaborative online international learning (COIL): Preparedness and experiences of South African students. *Innovations in Education and Teaching International, 59*(5), 499–510. doi:10.1080/14703297.2021.1895867

Naidoo, J. C. (2008). Opening doors. *Children & Libraries, 6*(2), 27. https://www.proquest.com/docview/212174372?pq-origsite=gscholar&fromopenview=true

National Center for Educational Statistics. (2022). *Integrated postsecondary education data system.* https://nces.ed.gov/ipeds/use-the-data/survey-components

National Commission on Social, Emotional, and Academic Development. (2017). *The evidence base for how we learn: Supporting students' social, emotional, and academic development.* The Aspen Institute. https://bit.ly/49r96gp https://www.aspeninstitute.org/wp-content/uploads/2017/09/SEAD-Research-Brief-9.12_updated-web.pdf

National Research Council. (2001). *Eager to learn: Educating our preschoolers.* National Academies Press.

Nayir, F. (2017). The relationship between student motivation and class engagement levels. *Eurasian Journal of Educational Research, 17*(71), 59–78. doi:10.14689/ejer.2017.71.4

Ncube, N. (2006). The Tree of Life project: Using narrative ideas in work with vulnerable children in Southern Africa. *The International Journal of Narrative Therapy and Community Work, 1*, 3–16.

Nealy, S., & Orgill, M. (2019). Postsecondary underrepresented minority STEM students' perceptions of their science identity. *The Journal of Negro Education, 88*(3), 249-268. doi:10.7709/jnegroeducation.88.3.0249

Neck, H., & Corbett, A. (2013). *Symposium for Entrepreneurship Educators2013: Material taller Design Thinking.* Banco de Chile-Babson College.

Niehaus, E. K., & Williams, L. (2016). Faculty transformation in curriculum transformation: The role of faculty development in campus internationalization. *Innovative Higher Education, 41*(1), 59–74. doi:10.1007/s10755-015-9334-7

Niemiec, R. M. (2014). *Mindfulness and character strengths: A practical guide to flourishing*. Hogrefe. doi:10.1027/00376-000

Noble, S. U. (2018). *Algorithms of oppression: How search engines reinforce racism.* New York University Press. doi:10.18574/nyu/9781479833641.001.0001

Noble, T., & McGrath, H. (2015). PROSPER: A new framework for positive education. *Psychology of Well-Being, 5*(2), 2. Advance online publication. doi:10.1186/s13612-015-0030-2

Noble, T., & McGrath, H. (2016). *The PROSPER school pathways for student wellbeing. Policy and practices*. Springer., doi:10.1007/978-3-319-21795-6

Norrish, J. M. (2015). *Positive education: The Geelong Grammar School journey*. Oxford University Press. doi:10.1093/acprof:oso/9780198702580.001.0001

Numanee, I. Z., Zafar, N., Karim, A., & Ismail, S. A. M. M. (2020). Developing empathy among first-year university undergraduates through English language course: A phenomenological study. *Heliyon, 6*(6), e04021. doi:10.1016/j.heliyon.2020.e04021 PMID:32518850

Nunan, T., George, R., & McCausland, H. (2000). Implementing graduate skill at an Australian university. In S. Fallows & C. Steven (Eds.), *Integrating key skills in higher education: employability, transferable skills and learning for life* (pp. 57–66). Kogan Page.

O'Dowd, R. (2012). Intercultural communicative competence through telecollaboration. In J. Jackson (Ed.), The Routledge handbook of language and intercultural communication (pp. 340–356). Routledge.

O'Dowd, R. (2018). From telecollaboration to virtual exchange: state-of-the-art and the role of UNICollaboration in moving forward. *Journal of Virtual Exchange, 1*, 1-23. doi:10.14705/rpnet.2018.jve.1

O'Dowd, R. (2015). Supporting in-service language educators in learning to telecollaborate. *Language Learning & Technology, 19*(1), 64–83. http://llt.msu.edu/issues/february2015/odowd.pdf

O'Dowd, R. (2015). The competences of the telecollaborative teacher. *Language Learning Journal, 43*(2), 194–207. doi:10.1080/09571736.2013.853374

O'Dowd, R. (2016). Emerging trends and new directions in telecollaborative learning. *CALICO Journal, 33*(3), 291–310. doi:10.1558/cj.v33i3.30747

O'Dowd, R. (2020). A transnational model of virtual exchange for global citizenship education. *Language Teaching, 53*(4), 477–490. doi:10.1017/S0261444819000077

O'Dowd, R. (2021). What do students learn in virtual exchange? A qualitative content analysis of learning outcomes across multiple exchanges. *International Journal of Educational Research, 109*, 1–13. doi:10.1016/j.ijer.2021.101804

O'Dowd, R. (2023). *Internationalising higher education and the role of virtual exchange*. Routledge.

O'Dowd, R., & Dooly, M. (2020). Intercultural communicative competence development through telecollaboration and virtual exchange. In J. Jackson (Ed.), *The Routledge handbook of language and intercultural communication* (2nd ed., pp. 361–375). Routledge. doi:10.4324/9781003036210-28

O'Dowd, R., & Dooly, M. (2022). Exploring teachers' professional development through participation in virtual exchange. *ReCALL, 34*(1), 21–36. doi:10.1017/S0958344021000215

O'Dowd, R., Sauro, S., & Spector-Cohen, E. (2020). The role of pedagogical mentoring in virtual exchange. *TESOL Quarterly, 54*(1), 146–172. doi:10.1002/tesq.543

O'Meara, K., Jaeger, A., Misra, J., Lennartz, C., & Kuvaeva, A. (2018). Undoing disparities in faculty workloads: A randomized trial experiment. *PlosOne, 13*(12), 1–15. https://doi.org/. 0207316 doi:10.1371/journal.pone

Ochoa, A., & Pérez, L. (2019). El aprendizaje servicio, una estrategia para impulsar la participación y mejorar la convivencia escolar [Service learning, a strategy for promoting participation and improving school coexistence]. *Psicoperspectivas, 18*(1), 89–101. doi:10.5027/psicoperspectivas-Vol18-Issue1-fulltext-1478

Ochoa, M. B., Valdés, M., & Quevedo, Y. (2007). Innovation, technology and technology management. *Acimed, 16*(4), 1–12. https://bit.ly/3oVtkKt

OECD. (2019). An OECD Learning Framework 2030. In G. Bast, E. G. Carayannis, & D. F. J. Campbell (Eds.), *The future of education and labor. Arts, research, innovation and society* (pp. 23–35). Springer International Publishing. doi:10.1007/978-3-030-26068-2_3

OECD. (2019). Education at glance: OECD indicators. https://bit.ly/3wDG8fb

Ogden, A. C. (2006). Ethnographic inquiry: Reframing the learning core of education abroad. *Frontiers: The Interdisciplinary Journal of Study Abroad, 13*(1), 87–112. doi:10.36366/frontiers.v13i1.175

Ohtani, K., & Hisasaka, T. (2018). Beyond intelligence: A meta-analytic review of the relationship among metacognition, intelligence, and academic performance. *Metacognition and Learning, 13*(2), 179–212. doi:10.1007/s11409-018-9183-8

Oliver, K., & Lalik, R. (2004). Critical inquiry on the body in girls' physical education classes: A critical poststructural perspective. *Journal of Teaching in Physical Education, 23*(2), 162–195. doi:10.1123/jtpe.23.2.162

Oparinde, K. M., Govender, V., & Moyo, S. (2022). Entrenching internationalisation in African Higher Education Institutions. *Perspectives in Education, 40*(4), 104–116. doi:10.38140/pie.v40i4.6849

Organisation for Economic Co-operation and Development (OECD). (2018). The future of education and skills: Education 2030. *OECD Education Working Papers.*

Oseguera, L., Rios, J. D. L., Park, H. J., Aparicio, E. M., & Rao, S. (2022). Understanding who stays in a STEM scholar program for underrepresented students: High-achieving scholars and short-term program retention. *Journal of College Student Retention, 24*(3), 773–809. doi:10.1177/1521025120950693

Palacios-Hidalgo, F. J., & Huertas-Abril, C. A. (2023). Creando sinergias a través de eTwinning para el desarrollo sostenible y la ciudadanía global mediante los ODS: Un estudio cualitativo [Creating synergies through eTwinning for sustainable development and global citizenship by means of SDGs]. In J. J. Delgado-Peña, S. Cabrero, N. Fernández, & J. Martínez (Eds.), *Universidades y Agenda 2030* [Universities and the 2030 Agenda] (pp. 463–474). Comares.

Palomera, R., Fernández-Berrocal, P., & Brackett, M. A. (2008). Emotional intelligence as a basic competency in pre-service teacher training: Some evidence. *Electronic Journal of Research in Educational Psychology*, *6*(2), 437–454.

Palomera, R., Fernández-Berrocal, P., & Brackett, M. A. (2008). La inteligencia emocional como una competencia básica en la formación inicial de los docentes: Algunas evidencias. *Electronic Journal of Research in Educational Psychology*, *15*(6), 437–454. doi:10.25115/ejrep.v6i15.1292

Papanikolaou, K., & Boubouka, M. (2010). Promoting collaboration in a project-based e-learning context. *Journal of Research on Technology in Education*, *43*(2), 135–155. doi:10.1080/15391523.2010.10782566

Papendieck, A. (2018). Technology for equity and social justice in education: A critical issue overview. *Texas Education Review (Austin, Tex.)*, *6*(1), 1–9. http://hdl.handle.net/2152/64974

Parkhouse, H., Lu, C. Y., & Massaro, V. R. (2019). Multicultural education professional development: A review of the literature. *Review of Educational Research*, *89*(3), 416–458. doi:10.3102/0034654319840359

Park, N., Peterson, C., & Seligman, M. E. P. (2004). Strengths of character and well-being: A closer look at hope and modesty. *Journal of Social and Clinical Psychology*, *23*(5), 628–634. doi:10.1521/jscp.23.5.628.50749

Parmigiani, D., Jones, S.-L., Kunnari, I., & Nicchia, E. (2022). Global competence and teacher education programmes. A European perspective. *Cogent Education*, *9*(1), 2022996. doi:10.1080/2331186X.2021.2022996

Parra, L. R., & Agudelo, A. (2020). Innovation in pedagogical practices mediated by ICTs. In R. Canales & C. Reyes (Eds.), *Access, democracy and virtual communities. Appropriation of digital technologies from the Southern Cone* (pp. 51–63). CLACSO. https://biblioteca.clacso.edu.ar/clacso/se/20201125054915/Canales-Herrera.pdf

Parra, L. R., Menjura, M. I., Pulgarín, L. E., & Gutiérrez, M. M. (2021). Pedagogical practices. An opportunity to innovate in education. *Latin American Education Studies*, *17*(1), 70–94. doi:10.17151/rlee.2021.17.1.5

Parsons, M., Garant, M., & Shikova, E. (2022). Video exchange telecollaboration: Towards developing interculturality in EFL environments. In S. M. Hilliker (Ed.), *Second language teaching and learning through virtual exchange* (pp. 145–160). De Gruyter. doi:10.1515/9783110727364-008

Patel, L. (2016). *Decolonizing educational research: From ownership to answerability*. Routledge.

Patrick, S., & Sturgis, C. (2013). Necessary for success: Building mastery of world-class skills--a state policymakers guide to competency education. CompetencyWorks Issue Brief. *International Association for K-12 Online Learning*. https://eric.ed.gov/?id=ED561282

Patterson, L. M., Carrillo, P. B., & Salinas, R. S. (2012). Lessons from a global learning virtual classroom. *Journal of Studies in International Education*, *16*(2), 182–197. doi:10.1177/1028315311398665

Patton, K., & Parker, M. (2017). Teacher education communities of practice: More than a culture of collaboration. *Teaching and Teacher Education*, *67*(1), 351–360. doi:10.1016/j.tate.2017.06.013

Patton, M. Q. (1990). How to use qualitative methods in evaluation. *Sage*.

Pavot, W., & Diener, E. (2008). The satisfaction with life scale and the emerging construct of life satisfaction. *The Journal of Positive Psychology*, *3*(2), 137–152. doi:10.1080/17439760701756946

Pearl, M., Tzoumis, K., & Lockie, B. (2023). Unlocking the potential of global learning: The impact of virtual exchange programs on self-efficacy. *International Journal on Studies in Education*, *5*(4), 585–609. doi:10.46328/ijonse.162

Peel, K. L. (2020). A beginner's guide to applied educational research using thematic analysis. *Practical Assessment, Research & Evaluation*, *25*(1), 2. Advance online publication. doi:10.7275/ryr5-k983

Perry, L. B., & Southwell, L. (2011). Developing intercultural understanding and skills: Models and approaches. *Intercultural Education*, *22*(6), 453–466. doi:10.1080/14675986.2011.644948

Peru (2023). *Education First English Proficiency Index (EF EPI).* https://www.ef.com/wwen/epi/regions/latin-america/peru/

Peterson, C. (2006). *A primer in positive psychology*. Oxford University Press.

Peterson, C., & Seligman, M. E. P. (2004). *Character strengths and virtues: A handbook and classification.* Oxford University Press.

Pfeiffer, D. L., Pavelko, S. L., Hahs-Vaughn, D. L., & Dudding, C. C. (2019). A national survey of speech-language pathologists' engagement in interprofessional collaborative practice in schools: Identifying predictive factors and barriers to implementation. *Language, Speech, and Hearing Services in Schools*, *50*(4), 639–655. doi:10.1044/2019_LSHSS-18-0100 PMID:31411947

Pintrich, P. R. (2003). Motivation and classroom learning. In W. M. Reynolds & G. E. Miller (Eds.), Handbook of psychology: Vol. 7. *Educational psychology* (pp. 103–122). John Wiley & Sons. doi:10.1002/0471264385.wei0706

Poulová, P., Čern, M., & Svobodov, L. (2009). University network? Efficiency of virtual mobility. In *Proceedings of the 5th WSEAS/IASME International Conference on Educational Technologies*, 87–92.

Powers, R. (2018). *The overstory: A novel* (1st ed.). Norton & Company.

Prechtl, E., & Lund, A. D. (2007). Intercultural competence and assessment: Perspectives from the INCA Project. In K. Helga & S.-O. Helen (Eds.), *Handbook of intercultural communication* (pp. 467–490). De Gruyter Mouton. doi:10.1515/9783110198584.5.467

Prieto Martínez, L. D., Valderrama Guerra, C., & Allain-Muñoz, S. (2014). Internacionalización en casa. In C. Mauricio Nupia (Ed.), Reflexiones para la política de internacionalización de educación superior en Colombia [Reflections for international relations in higher education in Colombia] (pp. 159–191). Academic Press.

Prinstein, M. J., & Aikins, J. W. (2004). Cognitive moderators of the longitudinal association between peer rejection and adolescent depressive symptoms. *Journal of Abnormal Child Psychology*, *32*(2), 147–158. doi:10.1023/B:JACP.0000019767.55592.63 PMID:15164857

Proctor, C., Tsukayama, E., Wood, A. M., Maltby, J., Eades, J. F., & Linley, A. (2011). Strengths gym: The impact of a character strengths-based intervention on the life satisfaction and well-being of adolescents. *The Journal of Positive Psychology*, *6*(5), 377–388. doi:10.1080/17439760.2011.594079

Pulczinski, J. M. (2018). *Social learning, social justice: Reading circles as fora for political friendship and civic engagement* [PhD thesis, The University of Wisconsin-Madison]. https://bit.ly/3Lg2fMu

Quijano, A. (1997). Colonialidad del poder, cultural y conocimiento en América Latina [Coloniality of power, culture and knowledge in Latin America]. *Anuario Mariateguiano*, *9*, 113–122.

Quinlan, D. M., Swain, N., Cameron, C., & Vella-Brodrick, D. A. (2015). How 'other people matter' in a classroom-based strengths intervention: Exploring interpersonal strategies and classroom outcomes. *The Journal of Positive Psychology*, *10*(1), 77–89. doi:10.1080/17439760.2014.920407

Quiñonez Pech, S. H., Zapata González, A., & Canto Herrera, P. J. (2018). Percepción de profesores sobre la afectividad en los entornos virtuales en una universidad pública del sureste de México. *RIDE Revista Iberoamericana para la Investigación y el Desarrollo Educativo*, *9*(17), 195–224. doi:10.23913/ride.v9i17.378

Quintana-Ordorika, A., Garay-Ruiz, U., Camino-Esturo, E., & Portillo-Berasaluce, J. (2024). The impact of using Collaborative Online International Learning during the design of maker educational practices by pre-service teachers. *Sustainability (Basel)*, *16*(3), 1–14. doi:10.3390/su16031222

Raes, A., Schellens, T., Wever, B., & Benoit, D. (2016). Promoting metacognitive regulation through collaborative problem solving on the web: When script does not work. *Computers in Human Behavior*, *58*, 325–342. doi:10.1016/j.chb.2015.12.064

Raineri, E. (2020). Supporting service learning with an interdisciplinary CSR marketing model. *Association of Marketing Theory and Practice Proceedings 2020*, 1–19. https://bit.ly/42pCksO

Ramos, K., Wolf, E. J., & Hauber-Ozer, M. (2020). Teaching for global competence: A responsibility of teacher educators. *Journal of Research in Childhood Education*, *2*(35), 311–330. doi:10.1080/02568543.2021.1880998

RealtimeBoard Inc. (2022). *Miro online whiteboard*. https://miro.com/

Reif-Stice, C., & Smith-Frigerio, S. (2021). Communication, flexibility, and resilience: Navigating the shift to virtual service-learning during COVID-19. *Journalism & Mass Communication Educator*, *76*(4), 477–488. doi:10.1177/10776958211022564

Reimers, F. M. (Ed.). (2022). *Primary and secondary education during COVID-19*., doi:10.1007/978-3-030-81500-4

Repetto, E., & Peña, M. (2010). Las competencias socioemocionales como factor de calidad en la educación. *Revista Electrónica Iberoamericana sobre Calidad, Eficacia y Cambio en Educación*, *8*(5), 82–95. https://dialnet.unirioja.es/servlet/articulo?codigo=3921000

Rey, L., & Extremera, N. (2014). Positive psychological characteristics and interpersonal forgiveness: Identifying the unique contribution of emotional intelligence abilities, Big Five traits, gratitude and optimism. *Personality and Individual Differences*, *68*, 199–204. doi:10.1016/j.paid.2014.04.030

Richards, J. C., & Farrell, T. S. (2005). *Professional development for language teachers: Strategies for teacher learning*. Cambridge University Press. doi:10.1017/CBO9780511667237

Ring, G., & Ramirez, B. (2012). Implementing ePortfolios for the Assessment of General Education Competencies. *International Journal of ePortfolio, 2*(1), 87-97. https://eric.ed.gov/?id=EJ1107591

Ripp, P. (2023) *The Global Read Aloud: Frequently asked questions*. https://theglobalreadaloud.com/for-participants/frequently-asked-questions/

Robson, J. (2018). Performance, structure and ideal identity: Reconceptualising teachers' engagement in online social spaces. *British Journal of Educational Technology*, *49*(3), 439–450. doi:10.1111/bjet.12551

Rodríguez Pinto, C., Cardoso Arango, X., & Ramírez Leyton, D. (2007). *Informe final: Estudio estado del arte de la internacionalización de la educación superior en Colombia [Final Report: Study on the state of the arts of internationalisation of higher education in Colombia]*. Asociación Colombiana de Universidades y Ministerio de Educación Nacional. https://bit.ly/3un1Wef

Roffey, S. (2023). Applying positive psychology in primary schools. In A. Giraldez-Hayes & J. Burke (Eds.), *Applied positive school psychology* (pp. 9–20). Routledge. doi:10.4324/9781003228158-3

Rogat, T. K., & Linnenbrink-Garcia, L. (2011). Socially shared regulation in collaborative groups: An analysis of the interplay between quality of social regulation and group processes. *Cognition and Instruction*, *29*(4), 375–415. doi:10.1080/07370008.2011.607930

Romera, E. M., Herrera-López, M. H., Casas, J. A., Ortega-Ruiz, R., & Gómez-Ortiz, O. (2017). Multidimensional social competence, motivation, and cyberbullying: A cultural approach with Colombian and Spanish adolescents. *Journal of Cross-Cultural Psychology*, *48*(8), 1183–1197. doi:10.1177/0022022116687854

Rosé, C. P., & Ferschke, O. (2016). Technology support for discussion based learning: From computer supported collaborative learning to the future of massive open online courses. *International Journal of Artificial Intelligence in Education*, *26*(2), 660–678. doi:10.1007/s40593-016-0107-y

Rose-Krasnor, L. (1997). The nature of social competence: A theoretical review. *Social Development*, *6*(1), 111–135. doi:10.1111/j.1467-9507.1997.tb00097.x

Roselli, N. (2016). Collaborative Learning: Theoretical bases and strategies applicable to university teaching. *Purposes and Representations*, *4*(1), 219–280. doi:10.20511/pyr2016.v4n1.90

Rosenberg, M. B., Hilton, M. L., & Dibner, K. A. (2018). *Indicators for monitoring undergraduate STEM education*. National Academies Press., doi:10.17226/24943

Roy, A. (2020). The pandemic is a portal. *Financial Times, 3*(4).

Rubin, J. (2017). Embedding Collaborative Online International Learning (COIL) at higher education institutions: An evolutionary overview with exemplars. *Internationalisation of Higher Education, 2*, 28-44. https://bit.ly/48N6p8i

Rubin, J. (2017). Embedding Collaborative Online International Learning (COIL) at higher education institutions. An evolutionary overview with exemplars. *Internationalisation of Higher Education*, *2*, 27–44.

Rubin, J. (2017). Embedding Collaborative Online International Learning (COIL) at higher education institutions. *Internationalization of Higher Education*, *2*, 27–44.

Rudolph, N., Monson, J., Collett, K., & Sonn, B. (2008). *How to build a caring school community.* Children's Institute, University of Cape Town and South African Democratic Teachers' Union. https://bit.ly/4a4gOgP

Rufai, M. M., Alebiosu, S. O., & Adeakin, O. A. S. (2015). A conceptual model for virtual classroom management. *International Journal of Computer Science. Engineering and Information Technology*, *5*(1), 27–32. doi:10.5121/ijcseit.2015.5103 PMID:26029735

Ruiz-Aranda, D., Salguero, J. M., Cabello, R., Palomera, R., & Berrocal, P. (2012). Can an emotional intelligence program improve adolescents' psychosocial adjustment? Results from the INTEMO project. *Social Behavior and Personality*, *40*(8), 1373–1379. doi:10.2224/sbp.2012.40.8.1373

Ruiz, N. T., & Baird, P. J. (2013). Transnational teacher education: Towards theory and practice. *NABE Journal of Research and Practice*, *4*(1), 60–100. doi:10.1080/26390043.2013.12067768

Ruiz-Sánchez, S. (2020, October). *Las habilidades socioemocionales docentes en tiempos de pandemia* [Conference session]. V Congreso de investigación en habilidades socioemocionales, coaching y talento (CIGETH-2020). Cuernavaca, México.

Rusk, R. D., & Waters, L. (2015). A psycho-social system approach to wellbeing: Empirically deriving the five pathways of positive functioning. *The Journal of Positive Psychology*, *10*(2), 141–152. doi:10.1080/17439760.2014.920409

Ryan, R. M., & Deci, E. L. (2001). On happiness and human potentials: A review of research on hedonic and eudaimonic well-being. *Annual Review of Psychology*, *52*(1), 141–166. doi:10.1146/annurev.psych.52.1.141 PMID:11148302

Ryan, R. M., Huta, V., & Deci, E. L. (2008). Living well: A self-determination theory perspective on eudaimonia. *Journal of Happiness Studies*, *9*(1), 139–170. doi:10.1007/s10902-006-9023-4

Ryff, C. D. (2014). Psychological well-being revisited: Advances in the science and practice of eudaimonia. *Psychotherapy and Psychosomatics, 83*(1), 10–28. doi:10.1159/000353263 PMID:24281296

Ryff, C. D., & Singer, B. H. (2008). Know thyself and become what you are: A eudaimonic approach to psychological well-being. *Journal of Happiness Studies, 9*(1), 13–39. doi:10.1007/s10902-006-9019-0

Saarni, C. (1999). *The development of emotional competence.* Guilford Press.

Salam, M., Awang-Iskandar, D. N., Ibrahim, D. H. A., & Farooq, M. S. (2019). Service learning in higher education: A systematic literature review. *Asia Pacific Education Review, 20*(4), 573–593. doi:10.1007/s12564-019-09580-6

Salanova, M., Martínez, I., Bresó, E., Llorens, S., & Grau, R. (2005). Bienestar psicológico en estudiantes universitarios: Facilitadores y obstaculizadores del desempeño académico. *Anales de Psicología, 21*(1), 170–180. https://www.redalyc.org/articulo.oa?id=16721116

Salazar, S. (2022). The challenge of internationalization in Peruvian universities. In P. Castiello-Gutiérrez, P., Pantoja, M. P. & Gutiérrez, C. E. (Eds.), Internationalization of Higher Education after COVID-19: Reflections and new practices for different times (pp. 124-137). UPAEP/AMPEI, Mexico.

Salazar, S. (2022). The challenge of internationalization in Peruvian universities. In S. Castiello-Gutiérrez, M.P. Pantoja, & C.E. Gutiérrez (Eds.), *Internationalization of higher education after COVID-19: Reflections and new practices for different times* (pp. 124-137). Universidad Popular Autónoma del Estado de Puebla. https://acortar.link/pWOjF9

Saldaña, J. (2016). The coding manual for qualitative researchers. *Sage (Atlanta, Ga.).*

Sandall, S., Hemmeter, M. L., Smith, B. J., & McLean, M. (2009). *DEC Recommended Practices: A Comprehensive Guide for Practical Application in Early Intervention/Early Childhood Special Education.* Division for Early Childhood of the Council for Exceptional Children. Sopris West.

Santoro, N. (2014). 'If I'm going to teach about the world, I need to know the world': Developing Australian pre-service teachers' intercultural competence through international trips. *Race, Ethnicity and Education, 17*(3), 429–444. doi:10.1080/13613324.2013.832938

Saorín, T., & Gómez-Hernández, J. A. (2014). Literacy in social technologies for everyday life and empowerment. *ThinkEPI Yearbook, 8*, 342-348. https://acortar.link/ysRBEo

Sapkota, B., Zhou, L., Mbewe, R., Newton, J., & Phillion, J. (2022). Fostering pre-service teachers' intercultural competencies through global cross-cultural collaborations. In C. Ullom & N. Guler (Eds.), *At school in the world: Developing globally engaged teachers* (pp. 212–237). Rowman & Littlefield.

Sawyer, R., & Chen, G. M. (2012). The impact of social media on intercultural adaptation. *Intercultural Communication Studies, 21*(2), 151–169. https://digitalcommons.uri.edu/com_facpubs/15/

Scardamalia, M., & Bereiter, C. (2010). A brief history of knowledge building. *Canadian Journal of Learning and Technology/La revue canadienne de l'apprentissage et de la technologie, 36*(1), 1-16. doi:10.21432/T2859M

Schonert-Reichl, K. A., & Lawlor, M. S. (2010). The effects of a mindfulness-based education program on pre-and early adolescents' wellbeing and social and emotional competence. *Mindfulness, 1*(3), 137–151. doi:10.1007/s12671-010-0011-8

Schraw, G. (1998). Promoting general metacognitive awareness. *Instructional Science, 26*(1/2), 113–125. doi:10.1023/A:1003044231033

Schroeder, K., Wood, C., Galiardi, S., & Koehn, J. (2009). First, do no harm: Ideas for mitigating negative community impacts of short-term study abroad. *The Journal of Geography, 108*(3), 141–147. doi:10.1080/00221340903120866

Secretaría General de Investigación. (2021). *Estrategia Española de Ciencia, Tecnología e Innovación 2021-2027 [Spanish strategy for Science, Technology and Innovation 2021-2027]*. https://bit.ly/3SJ62qn

Seidman, I. E. (1998). *Interviewing as qualitative research: A guide for researchers in education and the social sciences* (2nd ed.). Teachers College Press.

Seifert, T. (2016). Involvement, collaboration and engagement: Social networks through a pedagogical lens. *Journal of Learning Design*, *9*(2), 31–45. https://eric.ed.gov/?id=EJ1117665. doi:10.5204/jld.v9i2.272

Selby, J. (2004). Working divides between indigenous and non-indigenous: Disruptions of identity. *International Journal of Qualitative Studies in Education : QSE*, *17*(1), 143–156. doi:10.1080/0951839032000150284

Seligman, M. E. P. (2011). *Flourish: A visionary new understanding of happiness and well-being*. Free Press.

Seligman, M. E. P. (2018). PERMA and the building blocks of well-being. *The Journal of Positive Psychology*, *13*(4), 333–335. doi:10.1080/17439760.2018.1437466

Seligman, M. E. P., Ernst, R. M., Gillham, J., Reivich, K., & Linkins, M. (2009). Positive education: Positive psychology and classroom interventions. *Oxford Review of Education*, *35*(3), 293–311. doi:10.1080/03054980902934563

Selvi, K. (2010). Teachers' competencies. *Cultura (Iasi, Romania)*, *7*(1), 167–175. doi:10.5840/cultura20107133

Semaan, G., & Yamazaki, K. (2015). The relationship between global competence and language learning motivation: An empirical study in critical language classrooms. *Foreign Language Annals*, *48*(3), 511–520. doi:10.1111/flan.12146

Serbes, M. (2017). Teaching abroad: Why teachers prefer teaching overseas. *International Journal of Social Sciences & Educational Studies*, *4*(3), 182–186. doi:10.23918/ijsses.v4i3p182

Seufert, C., Oberdörfer, S., Roth, A., Grafe, S., Lugrin, J. L., & Latoschik, M. E. (2022). Classroom management competency enhancement for student teachers using a fully immersive virtual classroom. *Computers & Education*, *179*, 1–17. doi:10.1016/j.compedu.2021.104410

Shannon, G. S., & Bylsma, P. (2004). *Characteristics of improved school districts: Themes from research*. Washington State Department of Education.

Shearer, R. L., Aldemir, T., Hitchcock, J., Resig, J., Driver, J., & Kohler, M. (2020). What students want: A vision of a future online learning experience grounded in distance education theory. *American Journal of Distance Education*, *34*(1), 36–52. doi:10.1080/08923647.2019.1706019

Shin, J. K., Borup, J., Barbour, M. K., & Quiroga Velasquez, R. V. (2022). Webinars for English language teachers during the pandemic: Global perspectives on transitioning to remote online teaching. *AERA Open*, *8*, 1–15. doi:10.1177/23328584221083976

Short, K. (2016). A curriculum that is intercultural. In K. Short, D. Day, & J. Schroeder (Eds.), *Teaching globally: Reading the world through literature* (pp. 3–24). Stenhouse.

Sierra-Huedo, M. L., Bruton, L., & Fernández, C. (2024). Becoming global at home: An analysis of existing cases and a proposal for the future of internationalization at home. *Journal of Education*, *204*(1), 241–254. doi:10.1177/00220574221108053

Simm, D., & Marvell, A. (2017). Creating global students: Opportunities, challenges and experiences of internationalizing the geography curriculum in higher education. *Journal of Geography in Higher Education*, *41*(4), 467–474. doi:10.1080/03098265.2017.1373332

Simms, M. (2013). A teacher educator uses action research to develop culturally conscious curriculum planners. *Democracy & Education*, *21*(2), 3. https://democracyeducationjournal.org/home/vol21/iss2/3

Sirin, S. R. (2005). Socioeconomic status and academic achievement: A meta-analytic review of research. *Review of Educational Research, 75*(3), 417–453. doi:10.3102/00346543075003417

Sjöberg, J., & Brooks, E. (2022). Collaborative interactions in problem-solving activities: School children's orientations while developing digital game designs using smart mobile technology. *International Journal of Child-Computer Interaction, 33*, 100456. doi:10.1016/j.ijcci.2022.100456

Slapac, A. (2021). Advancing students' global competency through English language learning in Romania: An exploratory qualitative case study of four English language teachers. *Journal of Research in Childhood Education, 35*(2), 231–247. doi:10.1080/02568543.2021.1880993

Slapac, A., Collett, K., Wessels, F., Gamiet, G., & Knudsmoen, H. (2023). Social justice pedagogy and Collaborative Online International Learning (COIL): Across three partner higher education institutions. In P. Escudeiro, N. Escudeiro, & O. Bernardes (Eds.), *Handbook of research on implementing inclusive educational models and technologies for equity and diversity* (pp. 252–272). IGI Global. doi:10.4018/979-8-3693-0453-2.ch013

Slapac, A., Coppersmith, S. A., O'Brien, K., & Balcerzak, P. (2021). Resilience in crisis: Developing community through Action Research. In A. Slapac, P. Balcerzak, & K. O'Brien (Eds.), *Handbook of research on the global empowerment of educators and student learning through action research* (pp. 23–48). IGI Global. doi:10.4018/978-1-7998-6922-1.ch002

Slapac, A., Coppersmith, S., & Cheng, J. (2023). Global competence development through the lens of graduate students in action research courses. In C. E. Ullom & N. Guler (Eds.), *At school in the world: Developing globally engaged teachers* (pp. 98–117). Rowman & Littlefield.

Slapac, A., Kim, S., & Coppersmith, S. A. (2019). Preparing and enriching linguistically and culturally responsive educators through professional development. In A. Slapac & S. Coppersmith (Eds.), *Beyond language learning instruction: Transformative supports for emergent bilinguals and educators* (pp. 282–304). IGI Global. doi:10.4018/978-1-7998-1962-2.ch012

Slapac, A., & Navarro, V. (2013). Fledgling steps to global self-awareness for preservice teachers abroad. *The Journal of Meaning-Centered Education, 1*(3), 2–20.

Slof, B., van Leeuwen, A., Janssen, J., & Kirschner, P. A. (2021). Mine, ours, and yours: Whose engagement and prior knowledge affects individual achievement from online collaborative learning. *Journal of Computer Assisted Learning, 37*(1), 39–50. doi:10.1111/jcal.12466

Smith-Isabell, N., & Rubaii, N. (2020). Considerations for improving higher education's assessment of global, international, and intercultural competencies. *Research in Comparative and International Education, 15*(1), 3–6. doi:10.1177/1745499920901950

Smith, J. A., & Osborn, M. (2008). Interpretative phenomenological analysis. In J. A. Smith (Ed.), *Qualitative psychology: A practical guide to research methods* (pp. 53–80). SAGE.

Sobocinski, M., Malmberg, J., & Järvelä, S. (2022). Exploring adaptation in socially-shared regulation of learning using video and heart rate data. *Technology, Knowledge, and Learning, 27*(2), 385–404. doi:10.1007/s10758-021-09526-1

Song, K. H., Kerkhoff, S. N., & Slapac, A. (2023). Educating racially, culturally, and linguistically diverse children in the global era: The world at home and at home in the world. In J. Chitiyo & Z. Pietrantoni (Eds.), *Social justice and culturally-affirming education in K-12 settings* (pp. 1–22). IGI Global. doi:10.4018/978-1-6684-6386-4.ch001

Soria, K. M., & Troisi, J. (2014). Internationalization at home alternatives to study abroad: Implications for students' development of global, international, and intercultural competencies. *Journal of Studies in International Education, 18*(3), 261–280. doi:10.1177/1028315313496572

Spector, J. M. (Ed.). (2007). *Finding your online voice: Stories told by experienced online educators.* Routledge. doi:10.4324/9780203825167

Spiteri, D. (2017). Meeting people where they are in many different locations. In D. Spiteri (Ed.), Multiculturalism, higher education and intercultural communication: Developing strengths-based narratives for teaching and learning (pp. 193–219). Springer. doi:10.1057/978-1-137-51367-0_8

Squires, A. (2009). Methodological challenges in cross-language qualitative research: A research review. *International Journal of Nursing Studies*, *46*(2), 277–287. doi:10.1016/j.ijnurstu.2008.08.006 PMID:18789799

Standley, H. J. (2015). International mobility placements enable students and staff in higher education to enhance transversal and employability-related skills. *FEMS Microbiology Letters*, *362*(19), 1–5. doi:10.1093/femsle/fnv157 PMID:26347299

Stephanie, L. (2022, July 20). *Future skills you'll need in your career by 2030.* http://tinyurl.com/mr372ywz

Stern, H. H. (1983). *Fundamental concepts of language teaching*. Oxford University Press.

Stoeger, H., & Ziegler, A. (2008). Evaluation of a classroom based training to improve self-regulation in time management tasks during homework activities with fourth graders. *Metacognition and Learning*, *3*(3), 207–230. doi:10.1007/s11409-008-9027-z

Stough-Hunter, A., Guinan, J., & Hart, J. P. (2016). A comparison of teaching methods building cultural competency informed by contact theory. *Journal of Cultural Diversity*, *23*(3), 91–98. https://www.ncbi.nlm.nih.gov/pubmed/29694750 PMID:29694750

Style, E. (1996). Curriculum as window and mirror. *Social Science Record*, *33*(2), 21–28.

Suárez, R. P. (2018). Reflections on the concept of innovation. *Revista San Gregorio, 24*, 120-131. https://bit.ly/34OY3Sp

Suny COIL Center. (n. d.). What is COIL? https://online.suny.edu/introtocoil/suny-coil-what-is/

SUNY COIL. (2023). *About COIL.* https://coil.suny.edu/about-suny-coil/

SUNY COIL. (n.d). *Conéctese, participe, colabore* [Connect, participate, collaborate]. https://coil.suny.edu/

Sweeney, K. (2013). Inclusive excellence and underrepresentation of students of color in study abroad. *Frontiers: The Interdisciplinary Journal of Study Abroad*, *23*(1), 1–21. doi:10.36366/frontiers.v23i1.326

Syahrin, S., Akmal, N., Spromberg, S., & DePriest, J. (2023). Promoting intercultural competence in preservice teacher education through virtual exchange. *Studies in Media and Communication*, *11*(1), 1–11. doi:10.11114/smc.v11i1.5791

Szelei, N., Tinoca, L., & Pinho, A. S. (2020). Professional development for cultural diversity: The challenges of teacher learning in context. *Professional Development in Education*, *46*(5), 780–796. doi:10.1080/19415257.2019.1642233

Tabachnick, B. G., & Fidell, L. S. (2007). *Using multivariate statistics* (5th ed.). Pearson Education, Inc.

Taherdoost, H. (2016). Sampling methods in research methodology; how to choose a sampling technique for research. *SSRN*, *5*(2), 2–10. doi:10.2139/ssrn.3205035

Tangelson, G. (Comp.). (2014). *From the South: Views on Internationalization.* https://www.cinda.cl/wp-content/uploads/2014/09/Desde-el-sur-miradas-sobre-la-internacionalización.pdf

Tanghe, S., & Park, G. (2016). "Build[ing] something which alone we could not have done": International Collaborative Teaching and Learning in language teacher education. *System*, *57*, 1–13. doi:10.1016/j.system.2016.01.002

Tawil, S., & Cougoureux, M. (2013). Una mirada actual a la *Educación encierra un tesoro*. Evaluar la influencia del informe Delors de 1996. *Investigación y Prospectiva en Educación/UNESCO,* 4. https://unesdoc.unesco.org/ark:/48223/pf0000220050_spa

Teichler, U. (2017). Internationalisation trends in higher education and the changing role of international student mobility. *Journal of International Mobility*, (4), 177-216. http://tinyurl.com/2par2cfy

Teichler, U. (2009). Internationalisation of higher education: European experiences. *Asia Pacific Education Review, 10*(1), 93–106. doi:10.1007/s12564-009-9002-7

Teo, T., Unwin, S., Scherer, R., & Gardiner, V. (2021). Initial teacher training for twenty-first century skills in the Fourth Industrial Revolution (IR 4.0): A scoping review. *Computers & Education, 170*, 104223. doi:10.1016/j.compedu.2021.104223

The ISTE Standards. (2017). *The ISTE Standards.* https://www.iste.org/standards/for-educators

Thomas, E. E., Reese, D., & Horning, K. T. (2016). Much ado about a fine dessert: The cultural politics of representing slavery in children's literature. *Journal of Children's Literature, 42*(2), 6–17. https://eric.ed.gov/?id=EJ1119087

Tichnor-Wagner, A., Parkhouse, H., Glazier, J., & Cain, J. M. (2016). Expanding approaches to teaching for diversity and social justice in K-12 education: Fostering global citizenship across the content areas. *Education Policy Analysis Archives, 24*(59), 1–31. doi:10.14507/epaa.24.2138

Titus, J. (2000). Engaging student resistance to feminism: 'How is this stuff going to make us better teachers?'. *Gender and Education, 12*(1), 21–37. doi:10.1080/09540250020382

Tollefson, J. W. (Ed.). (2013). *Language policies in education: Critical issues*. Routledge.

Toquero, C. M. (2020). Challenges and opportunities for higher education amid the COVID-19 pandemic: The Philippine context. *Pedagogical Research, 5*(4), 1–5. doi:10.29333/pr/7947

Trebits, A., Koch, M. J., Ponto, K., Bruhn, A. C., Adler, M., & Kersten, K. (2022). Cognitive gains and socioeconomic status in early second language acquisition in immersion and EFL learning settings. *International Journal of Bilingual Education and Bilingualism, 25*(7), 2668–2681. doi:10.1080/13670050.2021.1943307

Tronto, J. (2013). *Caring Democracy: Markets, Equality, and Justice*. New York University Press.

Tropp, L. R., Hawi, D. R., Van Laar, C., & Levin, S. (2012). Cross-ethnic friendships, perceived discrimination, and their effects on ethnic activism over time: A longitudinal investigation of three ethnic minority groups. *British Journal of Social Psychology, 51*(2), 257–272. doi:10.1111/j.2044-8309.2011.02050.x PMID:21895704

Tucker, J. L. (1982). Developing a global dimension in teacher education: The Florida international university experience. *Theory into Practice, 21*(3), 212–217. doi:10.1080/00405848209543008

Turkle, S. (2007). The secret power of things we hold dear. *New Scientist, 194*(2607), 50–52. doi:10.1016/S0262-4079(07)61446-8

Tytler, R. (2020). STEM education for the twenty-first century. In J. Anderson & Y. Li (Eds.), Integrated approaches to STEM education. Advances in STEM education (pp.21-43). Springer. doi:10.1007/978-3-030-52229-2_3

Ucan, S., & Webb, M. (2015). Social regulation of learning during collaborative inquiry learning in science: How does it emerge and what are its functions? *International Journal of Science Education, 37*(15), 2503–2532. doi:10.1080/09500693.2015.1083634

Umpleby, S., & Rakicevik, G. (2008). Adopting service learning in universities around the world. *The Journal of the World Universities Forum, 1*(2), 39–48. doi:10.18848/1835-2030/CGP/v01i02/56703

UNESCO. (2017). *Intercultural competences: Conceptual and operational framework.* https://tinyurl.com/3n9vr5h5

UNESCO. (2017). *Intercultural competences: Conceptual and operational framework.* UNESCO. https://unesdoc.unesco.org/ark:/48223/pf0000251592/PDF/251592spa.pdf.multi

UNESCO. (2020). *Global Education Monitoring Report 2020: Inclusion and education: All means all.* UNESCO.

UNESCO/Council of Europe (COE). (2001). *Code of good practice in the provision of transnational education.* https://rm.coe.int/090000168097c674

United Nations. (2015). *Transforming our world: The 2030 agenda for sustainable development.* https://undocs.org/en/A/RES/70/1

United Nations. (2018). *The 2030 Agenda and the Sustainable Development Goals: An opportunity for Latin America and the Caribbean* (LC/G. 2681-P/Rev. 3). Santiago. https://rb.gy/1abah4

United Nations. (2023, April 13). *The 17 goals.* Department of Economic and Social Affairs. https://sdgs.un.org/goals

United Nations. (2023, March). *Sustainable development goals.* https://www.un.org/sustainabledevelopment/

United States Department of State. (2018). *U.S. Study Abroad Continues to Increase and Diversify.* https://studyabroad.state.gov/value-study-abroad/highlights-and-activities/us-study-abroad-continues-increase-and-diversify

Universidad Católica de Manizales. (2022). *UCM Academic Policies.* UCM Publishing Center.

Urban, M., Vandenbroeck, M., Lazzari, A., Van Laere, K., & Peeters, J. (2012). Competence requirements in early childhood education and care. Final Report. *Online Submission.*

Üzüm, B., Akayoglu, S., & Yazan, B. (2020). Using telecollaboration to promote intercultural competence in teacher training classrooms in Türkiye and the USA. *ReCALL, 32*(2), 162–177. doi:10.1017/S0958344019000235

Üzüm, B., Yazan, B., Mary, L., & Akayoglu, S. (2023). Teacher agency for social justice in telecollaboration: Locating agentive positioning in virtual language interaction. *Language Learning Journal, 51*(6), 766–782. doi:10.1080/09571736.2022.2080857

Vahed, A. (2022). Factors enabling and constraining students' collaborative online international learning experiences. *Learning Environments Research, 25*(3), 895–915. doi:10.1007/s10984-021-09390-x

Vahed, A., & Rodriguez, K. (2021). Enriching students' engaged learning experiences through the collaborative online international learning project. *Innovations in Education and Teaching International, 58*(5), 596–605. doi:10.1080/14703297.2020.1792331

Valcárcel, M. (2005). La preparación del profesorado universitario español para la convergencia europea en educación superior. *Educatio Siglo XXI, 23*, 209-213. https://revistas.um.es/educatio/article/view/130

Van Lier, L. (1989). Reeling, writhing, drawling, stretching, and fainting in coils: Oral proficiency interviews as conversation. *TESOL Quarterly, 23*(3), 489–508. doi:10.2307/3586922

van Nieuwerburgh, C., & Green, A. (2023). Strengths-based interventions for students and staff. In A. Giraldez-Hayes & J. Burke (Eds.), *Applied positive school psychology* (pp. 115–124). Routledge., doi:10.4324/9781003228158-14

Van Roekel, D. (2010). *Global competence is a 21st century imperative.* NEA Policy and Practice Department.

van Rooij, S. W., & Zirkle, K. (2016). Balancing pedagogy, student readiness and accessibility: A case study in collaborative online course development. *The Internet and Higher Education, 28*, 1–7. doi:10.1016/j.iheduc.2015.08.001

Vandell, D. L., Belsky, J., Burchinal, M., Steinberg, L., & Vandergrift, N. (2010). Do effects of early child care extend to age 15 years? Results from the NICHD study of early child care and youth development. *Child Development, 81*(3), 737–756. doi:10.1111/j.1467-8624.2010.01431.x PMID:20573102

Vatrapu & Suthers, D. (2007). Culture and computers: A review of the concept of culture and implications for intercultural collaborative online learning. *Intercultural Collaboration*, 260–275. doi:10.1007/978-3-540-74000-1_20

Vaughn, B. E., Shin, N., Kim, M., Coppola, G., Krzysik, L., Santos, A. J., Inês Peceguina, I., Daniel, J. R., Veríssimo, M., DeVries, A., Elphick, E., Ballentina, X., Bost, K. K., Newell, W. Y., Miller, E. B., Snider, J. B., & Korth, B. (2009). Hierarchical models of social competence in preschool children: A multisite, multinational study. *Child Development, 80*(6), 1775–1796. doi:10.1111/j.1467-8624.2009.01367.x PMID:19930351

Vice-Rectorate for Internationalization. UCLM. (2022-2023). *English subjects & English Friendly*. https://bit.ly/3SGWHPV

Vicerrectorado de Economía y Planificación. (2018). *Estrategia UCLM 2020 [UCLM Strategy 2020]*. https://bit.ly/49hSFD0

Vicerrectorado de Internacionalización. (2022). *Guía de la UCLM* [UCLM Guide].

Villegas-Paredes, G., Gutiérrez, S. C., & Moranta, I. R. (2022). Telecolaboración y competencia comunicativa intercultural en la enseñanza-aprendizaje de ELE: Un proyecto en Educación Superior [Telecollaboration and intercultural communicative competence in the teaching-learning of ELE: A project in Higher Education]. *Porta Linguarum. Monograph, 4*, 97–118. doi:10.30827/portalin.vi.21446

Villegas-Troya, C., Palacios-Hidalgo, F. J., & Huertas-Abril, C. A. (2023). Aprendizaje-servicio y creación de materiales didácticos: Una experiencia en un centro bilingüe rural [Service-learning and teaching materials creation: An experience in a rural bilingual school]. In B. Pizà-Mir, J. G. Fernández-Fernández, M. M. Cortès-Ferrer, O. García-Taibo, & S. Baena-Morales (Eds.), *Currículum, didáctica y los Objetivos de Desarrollo Sostenible (ODS): Reflexiones, experiencias y miradas* [Curriculum, didactics and Sustainable Development Goals (SDGs): Reflections, experiences and perspectives] (pp. 851–874). Dykinson. https://bit.ly/43AuxJv

Vincent-Lancrin, S., Urge, J., Kar, S., & Jacotin, G. (2019). *Measuring innovation in education 2019: What has changed in the classroom?* Educational Research and Innovation, OECD Publishing. doi:10.1787/9789264311671-en

Volet, S., Vauras, M., Khosa, D., & Liskala, T. (2013). Metacognitive regulation in collaborative learning: Conceptual developments and methodological contextualizations. In S. Volet & M. Vauras (Eds.), *Interpersonal regulation of learning and motivation: Methodological advances* (pp. 67–101). Routledge. doi:10.4324/9780203117736-11

Volet, S., Vauras, M., Salo, A. E., & Khosa, D. (2017). Individual contributions in student-led collaborative learning environments: Insights from two analytical approaches to explain the quality of group outcome. *Learning and Individual Differences, 53*, 79–92. doi:10.1016/j.lindif.2016.11.006

Voogt, J., Laferrière, T., Breuleux, A., Itow, R. C., Hickey, D. T., & McKenney, S. (2015). Collaborative design as a form of professional development. *Instructional Science, 43*(2), 259–282. doi:10.1007/s11251-014-9340-7

Vuorikari, R., Garoia, V., Punie, Y., Cachia, R., Cao, Y., Klamma, R., Rajagopal, K., Cuong, M., Fetter, S., Sloep, P., & Scimeca, S. (2012). *Teacher networks: Today's and tomorrow's challenges and opportunities for teaching profession.* European Schoolnet (JRC75795). https://publications.jrc.ec.europa.eu/repository/handle/JRC75795

Vygotsky, L., & Cole, M. (2018). Lev Vygotsky: learning and social constructivism. In S. Macblain (Ed.), *Learning theories for early years practice* (pp. 58–66). Sage Publication Ltd.

Waldner, L. S., Widener, M. C., & McGorry, S. Y. (2012). E-service learning: The evolution of service-learning to engage a growing online student population. *Journal of Higher Education Outreach & Engagement, 16*(2), 123–150.

Wang, L., & Wu, X. (2020). Influence of affective factors on learning ability in second language acquisition. *Revista Argentina de Clínica Psicológica, 29*(2), 1232–1240. doi:10.24205/03276716.2020.365

Wang, M. T., Fredricks, J. A., Ye, F., Hofkens, T. L., & Linn, J. S. (2016). The math and science engagement scales: Scale development, validation, and psychometric properties. *Learning and Instruction, 43*, 16–26. doi:10.1016/j.learninstruc.2016.01.008

Ware, P., & Kessler, G. (2016). Telecollaboration in the secondary language classroom: Case study of adolescent interaction and pedagogical integration. *Computer Assisted Language Learning, 29*(3), 427–450. doi:10.1080/09588221.2014.961481

Waters, L. (2011). A review of school-based positive psychology interventions. *The Australian Educational and Developmental Psychologist, 28*(2), 75–90. doi:10.1375/aedp.28.2.75

Waters, L., & Loton, D. (2019). SEARCH: A meta-framework and review of the field of positive education. *International Journal of Applied Positive Psychology, 4*(1-2), 1–46. doi:10.1007/s41042-019-00017-4

Waters, L., Sun, J., Rusk, R., Cotton, A., & Arch, A. (2017). Positive education. In M. Slade, L. Oades, & A. Jarden (Eds.), *Wellbeing, recovery and mental health* (pp. 245–264). Cambridge University Press. doi:10.1017/9781316339275.021

Wearden, G. (2018). Mirrors & windows: Why diversity must be better represented in children's fiction. *Wheaton Writing: A Journal of Academic Essays, 3*, 47-51. https://journals.wheaton.edu/index.php/wheaton_writing/article/view/527

Webb, N. M. (2013). Information processing approaches to collaborative learning. In C. E. Hmelo-Silver, C. A. Chinn, C. K. K. Chan, & A. O'Donnell (Eds.), *The international handbook of collaborative learning* (pp. 30–50). Routledge.

Weenink, D. (2008). Cosmopolitanism as a form of capital: Parents preparing their children for a globalizing world. *Sociology, 42*(6), 1089–1106. doi:10.1177/0038038508096935

Wenger, E. (1998). Communities of practice: Learning as a social system. *The Systems Thinker, 9*(5), 2–3.

Wenger, E. (1998). *Communities of Practice: Learning, Meaning, and Identity*. Cambridge University Press. doi:10.1017/CBO9780511803932

Westby, C. (2022). Using books as mirrors, windows, sliding glass doors. *Word of Mouth, 33*(5), 4-6. https://journals.sagepub.com/doi/pdf/10.1177/10483950221086338a

White, C. J. (2017). Distance language teaching with technology. In C. A. Chapelle & S. Sauro (Eds.), *The handbook of technology and second language teaching and learning* (pp. 134–148). John Wiley & Sons. doi:10.1002/9781118914069.ch10

Whitehead, J. (2012). Educational research for social change with living educational theories. *Educational Research for Social Change, 1*(1), 5-21. https://bit.ly/4a95nEn

White, M. A. (2016). Why won't it stick? Positive psychology and positive education. *Psychology of Well-Being, 6*(2), 2. Advance online publication. doi:10.1186/s13612-016-0039-1 PMID:26900547

White, M. A., & Murray, A. S. (Eds.). (2015). *Evidence-based approaches in positive education. Implementing a strategic framework for well-being in schools*. Springer. doi:10.1007/978-94-017-9667-5

Widmer, R. J., Widmer, J. M., & Lerman, A. (2015). International collaboration: Promises and challenges. *Rambam Maimonides Medical Journal, 6*(2), e0012. doi:10.5041/RMMJ.10196 PMID:25973264

Williams, T. R. (2005). Exploring the impact of study abroad on students' intercultural communication skills: Adaptability and sensitivity. *Journal of Studies in International Education, 9*(4), 356–371. doi:10.1177/1028315305277681

Wimpenny, K., Finardi, K. R., Orsini-Jones, M., & Jacobs, L. (2022). Knowing, being, relating and expressing through third space global South-North COIL: Digital inclusion and equity in international higher education. *Journal of Studies in International Education*, *26*(2), 279–296. doi:10.1177/10283153221094085

Witkowsky, P., & Gibbes, C. (2020). Preparing faculty for internationalization: Opportunities through teaching, research, and service. *New Directions for Higher Education*, *2020*(192), 73–84. doi:10.1002/he.20393

Witt, A. (2022). Postpandemic futures of Global Citizenship Education for preservice teachers: Challenges and possibilities. *Prospects*, 1–14. doi:10.1007/s11125-022-09599-5 PMID:35250097

Witt, A., & Liu, W. (2020). Transforming teacher preparation for global readiness: Scaling up education abroad. In L. Baecher (Ed.), *Study abroad for pre- and in-service teachers: Transformative learning on a global scale* (pp. 31–43). Routledge. doi:10.4324/9781003004387-3

Witt, A., Pino-Yancovic, M., & Neal, B. (2017). Study abroad for preservice teachers: Critical learning and teaching in a diverse context. In H. An (Ed.), *Handbook of research on efficacy and implementation of study abroad programs for P-12 teachers* (pp. 133–148). IGI Global. doi:10.4018/978-1-5225-1057-4.ch008

Wong, J., Baars, M., Davis, D., Van Der Zee, T., Houben, G.-J., & Paas, F. (2019). Supporting self-regulated learning in online learning environments and MOOCs: A systematic review. *International Journal of Human-Computer Interaction*, *35*(4-5), 356–373. doi:10.1080/10447318.2018.1543084

Wood, A. M., Linley, P. A., Maltby, J., Kashdan, T. B., & Hurling, R. (2011). Using personal and psychological strengths leads to increases in well-being over time: A longitudinal study and the development of the strengths use questionnaire. *Personality and Individual Differences*, *50*(1), 15–19. doi:10.1016/j.paid.2010.08.004

World Bank. (2018). *The World Bank Annual Report*. World Bank. https://www.worldbank.org/annualreport

Wormnæs, S. (2008). Cross-cultural collaboration in special teacher education: An arena for facilitating reflection? *International Journal of Disability Development and Education*, *55*(3), 205–225. doi:10.1080/10349120802268305

Wu, S., Ware, P., & Liaw, M.-L. (2020). Promoting peer-to-peer synchronous online discussions: Case study of intercultural communication in telecollaboration. In L. Wilton & C. Brett (Eds.), Handbook of research on online discussion-based teaching methods (pp. 283–310). IGI Global.

Wu, Q. (2008). The influence of affective factors in SLA on foreign languages teaching. *Journal of Xichang College Social Science Edition*, *20*, 147–149.

Wu, S. (2021). Unpacking themes of integrating telecollaboration in language teacher education: A systematic review of 36 studies from 2009 to 2019. *Computer Assisted Language Learning*, 1–23. Advance online publication. doi:10.1080/09588221.2021.1976800

Wyman, S., & Bellot, A. (2021). Integrating sustainability education with diversity, equity & inclusion in COIL virtual exchange projects on literary studies and culture. *Proceedings of International Virtual Exchange Conference*, 104-105. https://iveconference.org/wp-content/uploads/2022/03/IVECFinal_Proceedings_2021.pdf#page=105

Xu, Y., Chen, C., Spence, C., Washington-Nortey, M., Zhang, F., & Brown Ruiz, A. (2021). Supporting young Spanish speaking English learners through teacher scaffolding and reciprocal peer tutoring. *Early Child Development and Care*. Advance online publication. doi:10.1080/03004430.2021.1874944

Yang, Q., Shen, J., & Xu, Y. (2021). Changes in international student mobility amid the COVID19 pandemic and response in the China context. *Fudan Journal of the Humanities and Social Sciences*, *15*(1), 23–40. doi:10.1007/s40647-021-00333-7

Yang, S. J. (2020). Affordances and challenges of telecollaboration for pre-service teachers. *Language Learning & Technology*, *24*(3), 30–41. http://hdl.handle.net/10125/44733

Yeh, C. J., Stanley, S., Ramirez, C. A., & Borrero, N. E. (2022). Navigating the "Dual Pandemics": The cumulative impact of the COVID-19 pandemic and rise in awareness of racial injustices among high school students of Color in urban schools. *Urban Education*. doi:10.1177/00420859221097884

Yeh, H. C., & Heng, L. (2022). Creating a virtual "third space" in a telecollaborative project to promote English as a Foreign Language (EFL) learners' language proficiency and intercultural awareness. *Interactive Learning Environments*, 1–11. doi:10.1080/10494820.2022.2043384

Yemini, M., Tibbitts, F., & Goren, H. (2019). Trends and caveats: Review of literature on global citizenship education in teacher training. *Teaching and Teacher Education*, *77*(1), 77–89. doi:10.1016/j.tate.2018.09.014

Yi, H. B. (2008). Individual affective factors in SLA and foreign language teaching. *Journal of Jixi University*, *8*, 94–95.

Yin, J. (2019). Connecting theory and practice in teacher education: English-as-a-foreign language pre-service teachers' perceptions of practicum experience. *Innovación Educativa (México, D.F.)*, *1*(4), 4. Advance online publication. doi:10.1186/s42862-019-0003-z

Yin, R. K. (2011). Applications of case study research. *Sage (Atlanta, Ga.)*.

Yin, R. K., & Davis, D. (2007). Adding new dimensions to case study evaluations: The case of evaluating comprehensive reforms. *New Directions for Evaluation*, *113*(113), 75–93. doi:10.1002/ev.216

Yoshikawa, H., Aber, J. L., & Beardslee, W. R. (2012). The effects of poverty on the mental, emotional, and behavioral health of children and youth: Implications for prevention. *The American Psychologist*, *67*(4), 272–284. doi:10.1037/a0028015 PMID:22583341

Yu, J., Huang, C., Wang, X., & Tu, Y. (2020, August 24-27). *Exploring the relationships among interaction, emotional engagement and learning persistence in online learning environments.* Paper presented at the 2020 International Symposium on Educational Technology (ISET), Bangkok, Thailand. 10.1109/ISET49818.2020.00070

Zembylas, M., & Bozalek, V. (2017). Re-imagining socially just pedagogies in higher education: The contribution of contemporary theoretical perspectives. *Education as Change*, *21*(2), 1–5. doi:10.17159/1947-9417/2017/3051

Zhang, Z., & Kenny, R. F. (2010). Learning in an online distance education course: Experiences of three international students. *International Review of Research in Open and Distance Learning*, *11*(1), 17–36. doi:10.19173/irrodl.v11i1.775

Zhao, Y. (2010). Preparing globally competent teachers: A new imperative for teacher education. *Journal of Teacher Education*, *61*(5), 422–431. doi:10.1177/0022487110375802

Zhou, L., Sapkota, B., Mbewe, R., Newton, J., & Phillion, J. (2022). Global social justice in education: Developing a virtual intercultural community of practice. In M. Suleiman & T. Huber (Eds.), *Beyond provincialism: Promoting global competencies in teacher and educator preparation* (pp. 63–101). Information Age.

Zhu, C. (2012). Student satisfaction, performance, and knowledge construction in online collaborative learning. *Journal of Educational Technology & Society*, *15*(1), 127–136. https://www.jstor.org/stable/10.2307/jeductechsoci.15.1.127

Zych, I., & Ortega-Ruiz, R. (2021). Promoción de las competencias socioemocionales y prevención de la violencia escolar y juvenil. *Revista Internacional de Educación Emocional y Bienestar*, *1*(1), 63–84. doi:10.48102/rieeb.2021.1.1.7

About the Contributors

Alina Slapac is an associate professor of action research, and curriculum and instruction in the College of Education, Department of Educator Preparation & Leadership at the University of Missouri-St. Louis (UMSL), USA. Her research interests include teacher preparation and development with focus on virtual exchange (VE) contexts through the social justice lens, internationalization of teacher education and global citizenship education, (participatory) action research, culturally and linguistically responsive teaching (culture as strength), and transformative pedagogy. She has been collaborating with educators from China, Norway, Romania, Spain, South Africa, South Korea and USA on research and teaching, including Collaborative International Learning (COIL) partnerships. She has also received three prestigious university teaching awards: Governor's Award for Excellence in Teaching (UMSL, 2022), The Chancellor's Award for Excellence in Teaching (UMSL, 2020) and Emerson Excellence in Teaching Award (UMSL, 2013). Dr. Slapac has been an UMSL Global Fellow and an UMSL Inquiry Circles Fellow on global competency. Among numerous journal articles and book chapters, she also co-edited two books: Handbook of Research on the Global Empowerment of Educators and Student Learning through Action Research (Slapac, Balcerzak & O'Brien, 2021) and Beyond Language Learning Instruction: Transformative Supports for Emergent Bilinguals and Educators (Slapac & Coppersmith, 2019) (IGI Global). She currently serves as the Vice-Chair for Internationalization of Teacher Education TAG (Topic Action Group) through the American Association for Colleges of Teacher Education (ACCTE).

Cristina A. Huertas-Abril belongs to the Department of English and German Studies at the University of Córdoba, Spain. She is an interdisciplinary researcher working mainly within Second Language Acquisition, Bilingual Education, IC Studies and Translation Studies. She has participated in several interdisciplinary teaching innovation projects, and teaches at Master's level at UCO, UCA and UIMP. Moreover, she has taught both in formal and non-formal contents, and has directed and taught several specialization courses on Bilingual Education, Translation Studies and Second Language Acquisition.

* * *

Murat Akarsu is an associate professor in Mathematics Education at Ağrı İbrahim Çeçen University. He earned his master degree in the Mathematics Department at Cincinnati University in USA, and earned Ph.D. in Mathematics Education at Purdue University in USA. He was a research assistant in the School of Engineering Education within the epistemic research lab for two years, particularly the EngrTEAMS project. Implemented and published research, wrote integrated curriculums for middle school students. Dr. Murat Akarsu's work is focused on how engineering and engineering thinking promote integrated learning in K-12 mathematics and science classrooms, as well as in engineering classrooms. His professional objectives are to help all students gain a better understanding of mathematics and engineering.

Yorladis Alzate Gallego is a researcher attached to the teaching staff of the Secretary of Education of Manizales, Caldas. Her research and publications focus on the development of technologies in education and the development of digital competencies of teachers in higher education. She guides training processes in pedagogy, technology and educational informatics, and has also advised several research projects at the undergraduate level. Additionally, she has worked with Internationalization of the Curriculum for Higher Education processes. She has 22 years of experience in education. She has a master's degree in Educational Technology Management, a Specialization in Critical Pedagogy and professional training in Systems Engineering.

Lauren Angelone is an Associate Professor of Science Education and Instructional Technology. She is a former middle school science teacher with a PhD in Cultural Foundations, Technology, and Qualitative Inquiry from Ohio State University. Her teaching and research interests include the critical use of technology in teaching and teacher education, the intersection of science education and instructional technology, and current uses of technology by teachers, such as social media and AI. She was a Longview Foundation Global Teacher Education Fellow in 2022-2023, mentored by Shea Kherkoff, and has since been exploring the use of technology to globalize teacher education.

Banu Cicek Basaran Uysal works at the English Language Teaching Department at Eskisehir Osmangazi University, Türkiye. She holds a bachelor's degree in Foreign Language Education from Middle East Technical University, with a minor in psychology. She received her Ph.D. in ELT, in 2020. Currently, she teaches various EFL teacher training courses at the undergraduate level including Teaching English to Young Learners, Practice Teaching, Second Language Acquisition, and Approaches to ELT courses. Her research interests encompass several areas within the field of language education. She is particularly interested in pre-service teacher education, in-service teacher training, technology integration, online education, and corpus studies.

Delane Bender-Slack is Professor of Literacy, Co-Director of the School of Education, and the Program Director for both Reading and TESOL at Xavier University. She is a teacher educator, teaching courses in English Language Arts methods, middle childhood, adolescent, and multicultural literature, content area literacy, process writing, and reading theories. She has been published in a variety of journals and has published four books, Internationalization in the Classroom: Going Global, The Nicaraguan Literacy Campaign: The Power and Politics of Literacy, Towards Anti-Racist Educational Research: Radical Moments and Movements, and Equity-Oriented Critical Curricula: Envisioning Hope with Students. She coordinated and implemented international experiences in Peru, Nicaragua, and Costa Rica. She has been involved in planning and implementing Collaborative Online International Learning (COIL) across the campus, also collaborating with various international colleagues in Peru, Mexico, Ireland, and Ecuador. She received a Global Teacher Education Fellowship and a Fulbright-Hays Group Projects Abroad (GPA) Program Grant from the U.S. Department of Education.

Nurhayat Bilge holds a PhD in intercultural communication from Arizona State University, an MA in interpersonal and public communication from Central Michigan University, and a BA in sociology from Mimar Sinan University in Istanbul. Her research interests include intercultural communication, ethnicity and cultural identity, and gender and communication studies.

Theerapong Binali is currently working as a postdoctoral scholar at the Program of Learning Sciences, National Taiwan Normal University. He obtained his doctoral degree in Digital Learning and Education from National Taiwan University of Science and Technology in 2021. His research interests include theories and practices related to educational technology, psychology, and assessment in the fields of language education, science education, and teacher education. His research employed a combination of quantitative, qualitative, and mixed methods. He has published his research in esteemed journals such as Computers & Education, Science & Education, Behaviour & Information Technology, Research in Science & Technological Education, SAGE Open, among others.

Jill Blondin, associate vice provost for global initiatives at VCU, received her B.A. from Indiana University, and her M.A. and Ph.D. from the University of Illinois at Urbana-Champaign. Before leading GEO, Dr. Blondin served as the inaugural director of VCU Globe, a global education living-learning program devoted to building cultural agility. Under Dr. Blondin's leadership, VCU Globe received the 2015 NAFSA Senator Paul Simon Spotlight Award and the 2018 Andrew Heiskell Award from IIE. Dr. Blondin has served as a Fulbright Specialist to Brazil (2018), as a speaker with the U.S. Department of State Study Abroad Engagement Grant Program and Fulbright Portugal (2019) and as an Expert Speaker on U.S. Study Abroad with the U.S. Embassy Guyana (2022). Dr. Blondin, a 2021-2022 AIEA (Association of International Education Administrators) Presidential Fellow and serves as Chair on AIEA's Member Outreach and Awards Committee. In 2023, Dr. Blondin was named one of the PIE 50 Top Voices in North America, and IIE honored her as the Senior International Officer of the Year.

Noah Borrero is a Professor in the School of Education, San Francisco University. His research and teaching are grounded in the belief that the cultural strengths of communities provide unique opportunities for learning, teaching, and social transformation. He is a teacher, teacher educator, and scholar dedicated to the exploration of these strengths—cultural assets—as educational and pedagogical opportunities.

Jingxin Cheng has earned an Ed. D. with an emphasis on educational practice in 2021 and a Ph.D. with an emphasis on the teaching and learning process in 2024 from the University of Missouri-St. Louis. Jingxin gains and practices research experiences from both her days of academic study and teaching. Her research experiences include carrying out research projects, which require both qualitative and quantitative approaches, and publishing research articles in both Mandarin and English. Jingxin is a senior lecturer at Shenyang Normal University, China, where she teaches students in the EFL teacher education program as well as supervises student teacher educational practicum, her expertise and research focus is instruction, curriculum, and cross-cultural communication. She also holds an M.A. in Educational Studies from Katholieke Universiteit Leuven, Belgium, and a B.A. in English from Shenyang Normal University, China.

Oksana Andriivna Chernysh serves as an associate professor and as the Dean of the Faculty of Pedagogical Sciences and Lifelong Learning at Zhytomyr Polytechnic State University. She graduated from Zhytomyr Ivan Franko State University with a master's degree in pedagogical education, specializing in English language and foreign literature. With over 90 scientific works, her research spans computer lexicography, linguistics, media studies, and distance education. Her international experience includes internships across Europe and Asia. Being an E-learning specialist, she works as a coordinator for the International Distance Education Project Open Networked Learning and holds a CELTA certificate.

Karen Collett is a senior lecturer in the discipline of school leadership and management in the Educational Studies Department at the University of the Western Cape. She has worked in the areas of school/teacher development through NGEO's and higher education institutions (HEIs) in South African and Namibia. She has a particular interest in teacher well-being, school leadership development and the development of schools as thinking and learning organizations. She was the South African coordinator and co-initiator of an Erasmus Plus partnership focused on teacher well-being and language diversity in collaboration with partners in HEIs and schools in Norway, Denmark and Ireland. A new recent research interest is in the areas of Collaborative Online International Learning (COIL) and the development of student academic literacies. In the recent years, she has partnered with a professor from the United States on COIL and internationalization of the curriculum projects in teacher education.

Sarah A. Coppersmith, PhD, serves higher education in teaching, research, and grant coordination, teaching graduate research methods, teacher education courses, and world geography. She has been a University of Missouri-St. Louis Inquiry Circles Fellow on global competency, and serves the UMSL Geospatial Collaborative through the College of Education Geospatial Design Lab. Recent teaching includes Honors spatial citizenship via geospatial technology, with research examining global competencies, student agency, linguistically/culturally responsive teaching, and transformative learning and ambiguity tolerance, including new projects in international research on online learning.

Lauren De Veau is Director of Institutional Relations at the Universidad Antonio Ruiz de Montoya in Lima, Peru. Her works involve designing international and immersive community learning programs in various regions of Peru creating spaces for encounter collaboration between Amazon, Andean Communities and migrant communities. Additionally, she teaches interdisciplinary courses: Building Sustainable Communities, Global Citizenship and Social Justice. Originally from Grand Haven Michigan, Lauren has spent over 12 years in Latin America and has lived in Argentina, Ecuador and Peru. She has a Masters in Social Justice and Community Development from Loyola University Chicago and undergraduate degree in Spanish Language and Theology from the same institution. Outside the university, she works on community projects focused on education, women's empowerment, and community development.

Emmanuel Deogratias is a mathematics lecturer in the Department of Mathematics and Statistics at Sokoine University of Agriculture. He is interested in teaching, learning, researching, collaborating and consulting in mathematics education in primary and secondary schools, teachers' college and university level. He specializes in Mathematics Education and has expertise in designing and implementing engaging instructional activities in a mathematical learning context. Awarded a Doctor of Education (EdD) from the University of Alberta in Canada in 2020. Deogratias has published several articles in International Journals and proceedings. He has more than 13 teaching experiences with undergraduate mathematics student-teachers in Tanzania. He offers consulting services in mathematics education, including how to design and implement authentic activities for students in primary, secondary and university/college levels.

Emine Eren Gezen graduated from the Department of English Language Teaching at Middle East Technical University in 2011. She got her M.S. in Cognitive Science at Middle East Technical University in 2014, her M.A. in English Language Teaching at METU in 2015, and, finally, her Ph.D. in English Language Teaching at METU in 2022. She worked as a Research Assistant at the Foreign Language Education Department at Middle East Technical University for 5 years. Currently, she has been working as a Research Assistant at the Foreign Language Education Department at Eskişehir Osmangazi Üniversity since 2018. Her primary research interest is in second language acquisition, psycho-linguistics, syntax, teacher education, ICT, academic writing, technology integration in education and language learning.

Daphne Fauber is a graduate student at Purdue University in Agricultural and Biological Engineering. Her current work focuses on research education, biotechnology workforce development, computational genomics, public health, and biological Big Data. She has also conducted work aligned with LGBTQ+ advocacy with the Hack4Queer Futures project and the organization oSTEM. She is certified to teach 7-12 Biological Sciences, Computer Science, and Engineering and has a certificate in K-12 Integrated STEM Education.

Mercedes Gómez López is a Lecturer of Developmental Psychology at the University of Cordoba (Spain). She obtained her undergraduate degree in Psychology from the University of Seville and completed her postgraduate training at the University of Cordoba, where she successfully completed a Master's Degree in Psychological Research and Intervention in Justice, Health and Social Well-being. She was awarded a PhD in Psychology from the University of Cordoba in 2020, having attained the distinction of outstanding cum laude. Throughout her career, Dr Gómez-López has actively engaged in regional, national and European research projects, co-authored scientific articles and book chapters, and is a reviewer for several international impact journals. Her research focuses on the analysis of well-being and mental health during adolescence and its association with interpersonal relationships.

Moe Debbagh Greene obtained his Ph.D. in Education with a focus on Curriculum, Culture and Change/Instructional Technology and a Master's degree in Curriculum and Instruction with a concentration in Instructional Technology from Virginia Commonwealth University. Dr. Greene is a Fulbright recipient who has a record of significant and productive leadership in the areas of instructional technology, English language program management, accreditation, assessment, and curriculum development. He currently serves as the Director of VCU's English Language Program. In his current position, he works with both faculty and staff to design and develop programs that maximize the educational experiences of international and underrepresented students through access, diversity, and engagement. His research interest is in instructional technology. He examines the use of emerging technology such as makerspaces, virtual reality, and artificial intelligence (AI), in teacher education. The goal of his research is to understand how technology can support personalized learning and data-driven instructional decision-making and to explore the most effective and equitable ways to integrate technological tools into educational practices in order to enhance student learning and teacher knowledge development.

Robert Klosinski currently works as a teacher for English and German at IGS Schöppenstedt, Germany. He holds a PhD in German & Language Science from The Pennsylvania State University. For his dissertation, he focused on Swiss German as spoken in Misiones, Argentina and Ohio, USA. His research interests lie in the internationalization of the curriculum and in Germanic varieties spoken in diaspora as well as the language development across the lifespan with a particular focus on the sound system.

Isabel López Cirugeda is an associate professor in the Department of Modern Languages (area of English) of the Universidad de Castilla-La Mancha, where she teaches different courses concerning English Teacher Training (English Language, English Language Methodology for Young and Very Young Learners, Education Innovation and Research in Foreign Language Teaching) in both BA and MA studies. Her main lines of research are related to such fields and include teacher training, ELT for Very Young Learners, and CLIL. She has led an Innovation Project regarding the implementation of eTwinning in her institution. She has also been a Vice-Dean of Quality and Mobility Exchange. She has been a visiting researcher at University College Cork, and Trinity College in Dublin, Ireland; University of Northampton and Instituto Español Cañada Blanch in London, in the United Kingdom; Harvard University, in Cambridge, MA, in the United States; Instituto Franklin in Universidad de Alcalá in Alcalá de Henares, Madrid, in Spain, Pedagogical Counseling Institute - Stad Gent, in Ghent, Belgium; and in Malmö University, Sweden. She is also part of 3 Research Groups (LabinTIC, UCLM; AODIS, UCLM and IMEI, URJC). She is also a member of the Academic Committee of the Master's Degree in Bilingual Education and ICT for Early Childhood and Primary Education and UCLM's regional coordinator for Service-Learning, Educational Research and Education Innovation in State-funded educational centres in Castilla-La Mancha (Spain).

Xuwei (Sara) Luo is a Ph.D. student at Purdue University's College of Education, focusing on curriculum studies. Her academic pursuits revolve around teacher education, with a particular emphasis on pre-service teacher education, social justice, and culturally responsive teaching. In addition to her academic studies, Sara is actively involved in various projects. She currently serves as a research assistant for the LLDC Project (Literacy and Language Development Clinic) and the Purdue Freedom School Project. Sara also assists as an editor's assistant for FOSR (First Opinion, Second Reaction).

Rocío Luque-González, PhD, has a Degree in Early Childhood Education, in Psychopedagogy and Master in Psychology Applied to Education and Social Welfare at the University of Cordoba. Currently, Assistant PHD Professor of the Department of Education (Area of Theory and History of Education) at the University of Cordoba and member of the Laboratory of Studies on Coexistence and Prevention of Violence (LAECOVI). In line with the work of this team, researcher in several projects, currently in the project "Building social and emotional skills to BOOST mental health resilience in children and young people in Europe" (H2020), the project "Decision-making and moral sensitivity in the framework of peer networks and the phenomenon of bullying: a longitudinal study "(PID2020-1139RB-I00) and the project "The moral dimension as a key to understanding and prevention of bullying and cyberbullying. (PDC2021-121741-I00, continuation of project PSI2016-74871-R).

Crystal Machado is a professor in the Department of Professional Studies in Education, where she teaches pre-service and in-service teachers, faculty, and K-20 administrators. Prior to joining IUP, Crystal worked as a K-12 teacher, a middle/high school administrator, and an adjunct professor for many years in Pakistan. She holds a doctoral degree in educational leadership; two master's degrees, one in school administration and the other in primary education; and two bachelor's degrees, one in business and the other in education. Crystal's commitment to creating inclusive, technology-rich learning environments, and mentoring, is reflected in her teaching, research, and service. Crystal is a teacher-scholar. For over two decades, she has used the Scholarship of Teaching and Learning (SoTL) approach to study and improve her practice as a teacher, leader, and mentor. She also uses a qualitative and mixed-method approach to study international students' experiences, educators' use of technology in K-20 schools, equity and inclusion, and organizational learning. She has presented on these topics at international, national, and regional conferences. Her curriculum vitae documents a long history of doctoral student research mentorship.

Inmaculada Marín-López is a lecturer in the Faculty of Education at the University of Córdoba (Spain). She belongs to the Department of Education where she teaches at the undergraduate level subjects related to research methods and educational guidance for Kindergarten and Primary Teachers. She is an academic tutor for last year students of the Degree in Primary Education and for students of Master's Degree in Supervision, Evaluation and Management of Educational Centres and Programmes. She has participated in numerous national research projects and made several conference presentations and high-impact publications including journal articles and book chapters.

Maria Ines Marino has been teaching a wide range of face-to-face, online, hybrid and COIL courses for the School of Communication. Dr. Marino's research interests include emerging technologies that unite the fields of non-verbal communication and intercultural communication with a focus on diversity, equity, and inclusion (DEI). María Inés Marino earned an M.S. in Mass Communication from Florida International University and an M.A. in Educational Technology from Northwestern State University. She received her doctoral degree in Education from University of Florida.

Sadia Mazid is a doctoral candidate majoring in Human Resource Development at the College of Education, University of Illinois at Urbana-Champaign (UIUC). Her doctoral research focuses on investigating virtual members' experiences with sharing their work-related knowledge during project meetings. Her extensive background spans human resources and education leadership, enriching her academic journey with diverse perspectives and experiences. In the academic sphere, Sadia co-authored and presented her research at the American Human Resource Development (HARD) Research Conferences in 2021, 2022, and 2023 (consecutively). Those peer-reviewed manuscripts cover diverse topics- analysis of the work-life balance concept, assessment of SWOT as OD intervention in a non-profit organization, and labor history analysis- the impact of the PATCO strike 1981. Beyond academia, Sadia has made significant contributions as a practitioner and researcher in educational leadership. Her roles have involved curriculum development, instructional design for pre-service teachers in online education, and conducting training sessions.

Rose Mbewe is a Ph.D. student at Purdue University in the USA. She obtained a Master of Science in mathematics didactics from the Norwegian University of Science and Technology (NTNU) in Norway. Her bachelor's degree is from the University of Zambia. Her research interests are in global social justice in mathematics education, specifically in informal virtual professional development communities of practice. She trained as a secondary school mathematics teacher and taught mathematics before moving to teacher training as a lecturer in mathematics education. At Purdue, she has taught secondary mathematics methods and social justice in education courses.

Sandra McGury is a Senior Research Associate at the Institute of Language Competence in the Department of Applied Linguistics at Zurich University of Applied Sciences. The manager of the Swiss Global Competence Lab and the Co-Director of the Department's International Relations Office, she is interested in the link between language acquisition and assessment in the international context, within higher education, and as part of the processes in internationalization of the curriculum.

Fidelis Mumba holds a Bachelor of Arts degree with Education from the University of Zambia. His major is English while History is his minor. He has done part one (1) for Master's degree in Literacy and Applied Linguistics and is currently doing part two (2) which is research. He worked for nine years as a secondary school teacher before joining David Livingstone College of Education as a Senior Lecturer in 2000 in the Languages Department. He now heads the English section and is the International Relations Coordinator at the above mentioned college and was also once a Coordinator for the college Continuing Professional Development.

Jaqueline Naidoo is a Senior Lecturer in the School of Education, University of KwaZulu-Natal. She holds a Doctor of Philosophy from the University of KwaZulu-Natal which focuses on teacher identity and emotions in HIV and AIDS teaching. Her research interest focuses on teacher professional development, teacher identity and emotions, sexuality and HIV & AIDS education, research discourses and methodology, narrative inquiry and arts-based methods. Her research has been published widely in book chapters and journal articles, and presented at national and international Conferences.

Natalia Andriichuk is an educator specializing in language and literature. She earned her specialist degree from Zhytomyr Ivan Franko State Pedagogical University in 2001. She has held leadership roles at Zhytomyr Ivan Franko State University, focusing on foreign languages and new learning technologies. Currently, she serves as an associate professor and the Head of the Department of Pedagogical Technologies and Language Training at Zhytomyr Polytechnic State University. Her professional interests include inclusive education and the quality of higher education. She has engaged in international projects and internships, contributing to pedagogy and language teaching.

Jill Newton is a Professor of Mathematics Education at Purdue University. She began her career teaching secondary math and science and now teaches undergraduate and graduate students. She leads a study abroad program in Tanzania each year and her research focuses on the curriculum of K–12 mathematics, secondary mathematics teacher education programs, and study abroad programs.

Ümit Özkanal is the head of the Department of English Language Teaching at the Faculty of Education in Eskisehir Osmangazi University. He completed his MA in Teaching English as a Foreign Language at Bilkent University and received his doctoral degree in Curriculum Evaluation and Development at Anadolu University. After working as an EFL instructor for 18 years he continued his professional career as a language teacher educator. His research interests are curriculum evaluation, mentoring practices, written feedback, and teacher training. He offers teacher training courses including Drama and ELT, ELT Curriculum, Practicum, Translation, and Writing Skills.

Francisco Javier Palacios-Hidalgo belongs to the Department of English and German Philologies of the University of Córdoba (Spain). He is a member of the Ibero-American Network of Bilingual and Intercultural Education (IBIE) and the Research Group HUM-1006 'Research in Bilingual and Intercultural Education' (EBeI). His research focuses on the teaching of English as a foreign language, language and bilingual education teacher training, educational technologies, teacher digital literacy and queer pedagogy.

Ram Krishna Panthi is a full time faculty member of Mathematics Education from Mahendra Ratna Campus, Tahachal, Tribhuvan University, Kathmandu, Nepal. He did PhD from Graduate School of Education, Faculty of Education, Tribhuvan University, Kathmandu, Nepal. He earned his M. Phil degree in mathematics Education from Kathmandu University and M. Ed. in Tribhuvan University. He supervises preservice teachers' practicum and thesis writing in addition to teaching courses of pure mathematics and mathematics education. He has published research articles in national and international peer reviewed journals and presented his works in national and international conferences. His current research focuses assessment for learning and social justice in mathematics education.

JoAnn Phillion earned a PhD in Curriculum Studies from the Ontario Institute for Studies in Education of the University of Toronto, Canada. She is Professor of Curriculum Studies, Purdue University in the United States. Her research focuses on social justice in education nationally and globally, in particular on immigrant student education, multicultural education, teacher education and study abroad.

Aigul Rakisheva is pursuing her doctoral degree in Education Policy, Organization, and Leadership Department with Global Studies in Education concentration at the University of Illinois-Urbana Champaign (UIUC). Aigul is actively engaged in research and teaching activities as a Research and Teaching Assistant at the College of Education and Liberal Arts and Sciences at UIUC. Her research focuses on Virtual Exchange, Information and Communication Technologies, and Initial Teacher Education, contributing to various research projects in these areas.

Raquel Sánchez Ruiz wrote her PhD Dissertation on Discourse Analysis, particularly regarding political speeches, but she has three main lines of research, all of which are particularly related to technologies and digital literacy: discourse analysis; acquisition/learning of the foreign Language (English); and bilingual Education and CLIL. She has also been teaching courses in both BA and MA studies in the Department of Modern Languages (area of English) since 2008. Along these years, she has participated in different projects, including interdisciplinary work with other areas, both as an expert in CLIL and acting in the capacity of counselling, guiding and working on teaching-learning processes in English, bilingual education and CLIL. She also has experience in leading both national and international projects; as well as in research projects, as she has participated in 10 of the latter. She has also participated in 22 eTwinning projects, in 17 as a founding member. She has been a visiting researcher at Malmö University, Sweden; Roehampton University, the UK; and Instituto Español Cañada Blanch, the UK. Currently, she is the Vice-Dean of Academic Planning and Teaching Staff. She is also part of 3 Research Groups (LabinTIC, UCLM; AODIS, UCLM and IMEI, URJC). She is also a member of the Academic Committee of the Master's Degree in Bilingual Education and ICT for Early Childhood and Primary Education.

Bima Sapkota is an assistant professor at the University of Texas Rio Grande Valley. She earned her PhD in Mathematics Education from Purdue University. Her primary research focuses on practice-based teacher education, discipline-specific teaching and learning, and social justice in education. She investigates how mathematics preservice teachers develop and conceptualize discipline-specific practices when they engage in practice-based instructional activities.

Muna Sapkota is currently a second-year doctoral student in Curriculum studies at Purdue University's Department of Curriculum and Instruction. With a strong academic background, Muna's expertise lies in the field of education. Prior to her enrollment at Purdue, she spent eight years teaching secondary and undergraduate English courses in Nepal, honing her instructional skills, and gaining valuable experience. Currently, Muna serves as a course instructor for EDCI 20500: Exploring Teaching as a Career, where she imparts her knowledge and passion for education to aspiring teachers. Alongside her teaching responsibilities, she is actively involved as a graduate assistant, contributing to summer research initiatives at the Center for Intercultural Learning, Mentorship, Assessment, and Research (CILMAR). Muna's research interests primarily revolve around intercultural pedagogy and the exploration of decolonizing pedagogy, aiming to create inclusive and empowering educational environments. Her commitment to enhancing teaching practices and promoting diversity in education drives her scholarly pursuits.

Tami Seifert is a professor of education and senior researcher. Served as head of Academic ICT, head of the Department of Educational Computing, and vice-director of the Teacher Training for Graduates Program at Kibbutzim College of Ed. (2007-16). She has a Ph.D. in Urban Studies and Instructional Design and Technology from ODU, VA in 2001. Between 2003 -05 she completed a post-doctorate on the implementation of handheld computers in education. Promotes Innovative Technologies, online learning, ML, video, and Social Networks in Educational Contexts.

Sonia Stevens Bruzzese, Academic of the Faculty of Communication, History and Social Sciences of the Universidad Catolica de la Santisima Concepción Chile, is currently Director of the Social Nucleus of this University. Belonging to the Prosalud team and Creoeinnovo team, her work involves teaching in the area of health promotion, mental health, citizen participation, strengthening of social capital and in the area of social innovation,in undergraduate and postgraduate, generating links with the external environment. She has also done internships in the area of social innovation at the Universidad Catolica de Manizales Colombia and the Univerisidad EAFIT in Medellin Colombia.She obtained her degree as a social worker at University of the Oriental Republic of Uruguay, Master's in public health with emphasis on maternal and child health from San Sebastian University of Chile and University of Parma Italy, Diploma in Counseling and Family Therapy in Health from University of Concepción Chile, training in Innovation and Entrepreneurship at Babson College, Boston, United States, Diploma in Teaching Innovation for higher education lapsus. Affiliated to Harvard University.

Stephanie Tadal is responsible for leading instructional design and training innovation and facilitating the development of pedagogy leveraging modern and emerging educational technologies. She directs the identification, creation, implementation, deployment, and testing of instructional technology initiatives for the delivery of medical education, including the adoption of new instructional technologies. Tadal has conducted environmental assessments and evaluated efficacy of teaching practices in over 1,000 classrooms. As an instructor, she prepares undergraduate and graduate students for teaching in today's K-12 institutions and has served as dissertation advisor for students pursuing doctoral degrees. Tadal is a regular speaker at national and international conferences, discussing topics related to the equitable use of technology in curricular designs. And she has been consulted on educational policy both at the county and state level.

Cristina Villegas-Troya belongs to the Department English and German Philologies of the University of Córdoba, Spain. She is currently in a PhD programme in Languages and Culture, with a Degree in English Studies and a Master's degree on Advanced English Studies and Bilingual Education. She is an interdisciplinary researcher working mainly within Bilingual Education, Rural Schools, Telecollaboration, Second Language Acquisition and English as a Foreign Language.

Allison Witt is the Director of International Programs in the College of Education at the University of Illinois Urbana-Champaign where she teaches Global Studies in Education and is the Program Leader for the International Education Administration and Leadership program. Allison is a former Assistant Director of Academic Affairs at the Illinois Board of Higher Education where she contributed to state higher education policy in Illinois. She is the author of Shifting Tides in Global Higher Education (2011) published by Peter Lang. Allison earned a PhD in Education Policy Studies from the University of Illinois at Urbana-Champaign. She has worked in international education for over 20 years, now with particular interest in internationalizing teacher education.

Lu Xu is a fourth-year Ph.D. student in Education Policy, Organization and Leadership program at the College of Education, University of Illinois, with a concentration in global studies in education. With a general interest in global study and education, her research mainly focuses on global teacher education, global citizenship, and online teaching. Currently, her research aims to cultivate preservice teachers' abilities to teach in a global context, including the capacity to use technology, the development of global competence, the adaptability with different cultures, etc.

Yaoying Xu is a Professor in the department of Counseling and Special Education at Virginia Commonwealth University School of Education and Director of the School of Education International Educational Studies Center. Dr. Xu's research focuses on social interactions of children and students from culturally and linguistically diverse backgrounds and how their social interactions predict school success. Dr. Xu teaches Master's and doctoral level courses in assessment, intervention, single case research designs, and multicultural perspectives in education.

Yossiri Yossatorn is a full-time lecturer at Navamindradhiraj University, Bangkok, Thailand. His research interests lie in the area of teaching and learning education, pedagogical and educational technology, social media and information sharing, attitudes, metaphors, language and culture, and intercultural communication.

İlknur Yüksel received her MA and Ph.D. in English Language Teaching from Anadolu University. She worked as an ELT practitioner for several years before she was hired as an assistant professor in Eskişehir Osmangazi University, English Language Teaching Department. Recently she was appointed as an associate professor at the same university. She is currently the English Teacher Practicum coordinator at the same university, and she teaches several teacher training courses in the undergraduate program. She writes and presents widely on language teaching, teacher training, and vocabulary teaching. Her research interests are teacher training, second language acquisition, and instructional technologies in language teaching.

Index

Q

R

S

T

U

V

W

Y

www.ingramcontent.com/pod-product-compliance
Lightning Source LLC
LaVergne TN
LVHW062110300926
849161LV00010B/2423